The Crisis of the Seventeenth Century

HUGH TREVOR-ROPER

The Crisis of the Seventeenth Century

RELIGION, THE REFORMATION,

AND SOCIAL CHANGE

HUGH TREVOR-ROPER

LIBERTY FUND

This book is published by Liberty Fund, Inc., a foundation established to encourage study of the ideal of a society of free and responsible individuals.

The cuneiform inscription that serves as our logo and as the design motif for our endpapers is the earliest-known written appearance of the word "freedom" (*amagi*), or "liberty." It is taken from a clay document written about 2300 B.C. in the Sumerian city-state of Lagash.

01 21 22 23 24 C 5 4 3 2 1
21 22 23 24 25 P 8 7 6 5 4

Library of Congress Cataloging-in-Publication Data

Trevor-Roper, H. R. (Hugh Redwald), 1914–
   The crisis of the seventeenth century / H.R. Trevor-Roper.
      p.   cm.

   Originally published: New York: Harper & Row, 1967.
   Includes bibliographical references and index.
   ISBN 0-86597-274-5 (alk. paper)—ISBN 0-86597-278-8 (pbk.: alk. paper)
   1. Europe—History—17th century.   I. Title: Crisis of the 17th century.
   II. Title.
D246.T75   2001
940.2′52—dc21   00-025945

Liberty Fund, Inc.
11301 North Meridian Street
Carmel, Indiana 46032
libertyfund.org

CONTENTS

ILLUSTRATIONS

Louis de Geer at the age of sixty-two. From the portrait by David Beck in the collection of the de Geer family, Stockholm, Sweden   Page 31   *(Svenska Porträttarkivet, Stockholm)*

The Apocalypse of the seventeenth century. Frontispiece from *Theopolis, or the City of God* (1672) by Henry Danvers   Pages 32–33   *(Regent's Park College, Oxford)*

"A Witches' Sabbat." Engraving by Jan Ziarnko, taken from Pierre de l'Ancre's *Tableau de l'inconstance des mauvais anges et démons* (Paris, 1613)   Page 106   *(Trustees of the British Museum)*

Jean Bodin. Contemporary wood engraving, artist unknown, reproduced in the 1568 edition of *La Response de Maistre Jean Bodin . . . au paradoxe de Monsieur de Malestroit.* In the collection of the Bibliothèque Nationale   Page 136   *(Photographie Giraudon)*

Philippe Duplessis-Mornay, founder of the Protestant Academy at Saumur. Drawing attributed to Dubreuil. In the collection of the Société de l'Histoire du Protestantisme français   Page 195   *(Photographie Agraci)*

J. A. Comenius. Engraving by George Glover, 1642   Page 224   *(Trustees of the National Portrait Gallery, London)*

The Pansophic Enlightenment. Emblem by Crispin de Pass to Comenius' *Opera Didactica Omnia* (Amsterdam, 1657)   Page 225   *(Trustees of the British Museum)*

Roger Boyle, Lord Broghill, 1st Earl of Orrery. Artist unknown   Page 369   *(From a painting in the possession of Lord Cork and Orrery)*

The Union of Britain, 1641. Title-page of *The Great Happinesse of England and Scotland, by being re-united into one great Brittain*   Page 398   *(Trustees of the British Museum)*

PREFACE

These essays were written and first published on different occasions between 1956 and 1967. Most of them began as lectures or were written in tributary volumes. They were first published together, as a book bearing the title of the first essay, *Religion, the Reformation and Social Change.* The book was published by Messrs. Macmillan in London in 1967. An American edition was published in 1968 by Messrs. Harper and Row, under the present title, *The Crisis of the Seventeenth Century.* The book enjoyed a modest success. A second edition, published in London in 1972, was reprinted in 1973 and 1977 and it has been translated, in whole or in part, into German, French, Italian, Spanish, Portuguese and Japanese. Individual essays from it have appeared in Polish, Swedish, Norwegian, Danish and Icelandic: the subject of witchcraft evidently arouses particular interest among the tolerant Nordic peoples. A third and revised edition of the English text was published in London by Messrs. Secker and Warburg in 1984. I am naturally delighted that the Liberty Fund has now chosen to publish a new edition of this revised text in America.

It is customary for those who publish collected essays to claim that, however disparate in subject or appearance, they are coherent expressions of a single philosophy or a recurrent theme. That theme—if I may make the same claim—is the problem of a general crisis in the "early modern" period of history; a crisis which was not only political or economic but social and intellectual, and which was not confined to one country but was felt throughout Europe.

Many able historians have devoted themselves to the study of the Puritan Revolution in England, and some of them have ascribed to it a unique importance in modern history, as if it had been the beginning both of the Scientific and of the Industrial Revolution. I venture to think that this is too insular a view, and one which cannot survive a study of comparable developments in Europe. Therefore, in considering the problems raised by the Puritan Revolution, I have looked at them, where possible, in a European context; and for this reason I have placed together, in this book, essays both on European and on English (or rather British) subjects.

The first essay, which gave its title to the English edition of the book, arose from an examination of what has been called "the Tawney-Weber thesis": the thesis that Calvinism, in some way, created the moral and intellectual force of the "new" capitalism of the sixteenth and seventeenth centuries. This thesis has become a sociological dogma in some places and is opposed (as it seems to me) on irrelevant grounds in others. It has been called in to support the theory that English Puritanism was a forward-looking "capitalist" ideology, and also the theory that capitalism had to wait for Calvinist, or at least Puritan, inspiration before it could "conquer the world." I believe that, if the English experience is seen in its wider historical context, this view will be found to be too simple. If "sociological" historians would look at Calvinism in general—in Switzerland and Heidelberg and Scotland and Navarre and Transylvania as well as in England and Holland—and if they would look at "capitalism" in general—in medieval Italy and Flanders and Renaissance Augsburg and Liège as well as in seventeenth-century England and Holland—I think that they would be obliged to modify the exciting but simple formula which Weber based on narrow and ever-narrowing historical examples. My own modification was originally presented in a lecture delivered in 1961 in Galway, where an audience powerfully reinforced by local monks and nuns gave it an unsympathetic but, I felt, not very critical reception: but I was glad to discover, shortly afterwards, that the Swiss scholar M. Herbert Lüthy had come to conclusions very similar to mine, which he has since published in his volume *Le Passé présent*.[1] M. Lüthy and I were both unaware of each other's work until after publication. Because of its local origin my essay was first published in the proceedings of the Irish Conference of Historians at which it had been presented.[2]

The second essay, on the General Crisis of the seventeenth century, first appeared in the historical journal *Past and Present* in November 1959. It also excited some controversy, and the essay, together with some of the responses which it had elicited, was reprinted in an anthology of sixteenth- and seventeenth-century essays first published in that journal.[3] In reprinting it here—for it is directly relevant to the cen-

1. H. Lüthy, *Le Passé présent* (Monaco, 1965).

2. *Historical Studies IV. Papers read before the Fifth Irish Conference of Historians*, ed. G. A. Hayes-McCoy (1963).

3. *Crisis in Europe, 1560–1660. Essays from "Past and Present,"* ed. Trevor Aston (1965).

tral theme of this volume—I have taken the opportunity to incorporate in the essay some points which I had previously made separately, in amplification of it, in the discussion which it had provoked.

One of those who took part in that discussion was the distinguished French historian Roland Mousnier. In the course of his contribution he remarked that the general crisis of the seventeenth century was even wider than the crisis in the relation between the State and society in which I had concerned myself. It was, he suggested, "an intellectual mutation" as well as a social crisis; and he referred to the end of Aristoteleanism and the growth of belief in witchcraft as "aspects which would need to be studied if we really want to talk of the crisis of the seventeenth century." This is the justification which I would plead for the long essay on the witch-craze which was written specially for this collection. The persecution of witches is, to some, a disgusting subject, below the dignity of history. But it is also a historical fact, of European significance, and its rise and systematic organisation precisely in the years of the Renaissance and Reformation is a problem which must be faced by anyone who is tempted to overemphasize the "modernity" of that period. We can no more overlook it, in our attempts to understand the "early modern" period, than we can overlook the phenomenon of anti-semitism in "contemporary" history. Belief in witchcraft, like antipathy to Jews (and other minorities), has a long history, but the "witch-craze"—the rationalization of such beliefs and such antipathies in a persecuting ideology—is specific to certain times, and we need to relate it to the circumstances of those times.

In England the most active phase of witch-hunting coincided with times of Puritan pressure—the reign of Queen Elizabeth and the period of the civil wars—and some very fanciful theories have been built on this coincidence. But here again we must look at the whole problem before venturing general conclusions—especially since the persecution of witches in England was trivial compared with the experience of the Continent and of Scotland. Therefore in my essay I have looked at the craze as a whole, throughout Europe, and have sought to relate its rise, frequency and decline to the general intellectual and social movements of the time, from which I believe it to be inseparable. M. Mousnier, by his juxtaposition of phrases, seemed to imply—I do not know whether this was his intention—that the growth of witchcraft coincided with the decline of Aristoteleanism. It will be seen that I hold a very different view. To me, the growth of the witch-craze is a by-product, in specific social circumstances, of that hardening of Aristoteleanism (or rather, of the pseudo-Aristoteleanism of the Schoolmen) which had begun in the later Middle Ages and was intensified both by Catholics and by Protestants after the Reformation. I see it as the underside of a cosmology, a social rationalization, which went down in the general social and intellectual revolution of the mid-seventeenth century.

The witch-craze is a haunting problem and no one can claim to have solved it. My essay on the subject, like the essay on the general crisis, provoked lively discussion and was followed by other attempts to grapple with the same subject. One work in particular seems to me of the greatest interest. Christina Larner had made a particular and detailed study of the hitherto very superficially studied subject of witch-trials in Scotland. Her book *Enemies of God: The Witch-craze in Scotland* (1982) is a fascinating and stimulating sociological study. Her early death, in 1983, was a great blow to scholarship, and one that Scotland, in particular, can ill afford.

If the English Revolution of the seventeenth century cannot be isolated from a general crisis in Europe, equally, I believe, it was affected by individual European thinkers. Then as now, as in the Middle Ages, Europe was indivisible. Anyone who is tempted to see the English Puritans as "the Moderns" might do well to explore the ideological International of which they felt themselves to be a part: that cosmopolitan fraternity of the persecuted Protestants of Europe — of Germany and Bohemia, of La Rochelle and Savoy — whom the Stuarts had betrayed, whom Gustavus Adolphus had intervened to save, and whom Cromwell sought to reunite under his protection. In my essay "Three Foreigners," which is considerably enlarged since it was first published in *Encounter* in 1961, I have dealt with three men who belonged, by experience and ideas, to that European International and who, by wedding antiquated metaphysical notions to vulgarized Baconian ideas, became the philosophers of the English Puritan Revolution in its combination of intellectual reaction and utopian social novelty.

Those who see the Calvinists, or the Puritans, as "the Moderns" insensibly find themselves arguing that it was Calvinism, or Puritanism, which fathered modern science and led to the Enlightenment of the eighteenth century. The ideas of the Enlightenment, they sometimes seem to say, were the secularization of the ideas of Calvinism or "radical Protestantism." This view is commonly expressed by Marxist historians, but it also finds favour with some Scottish writers who see it realised in their own country. But the relationship of intellectual movements to religious systems is, I believe, more complex and more variable than this. Such movements are not linear, or the property of any party or sect; and parties and sects are themselves, under their apparently continuous forms, competitive and sensitive to change. In my essay on "The Religious Origins of the Enlightenment" I express a different view. Believing, as I do, that Calvinism was one form of the general intellectual reaction which accompanied the religious struggles, I have sought to look more closely at the Calvinist societies which undoubtedly contributed to the Enlightenment, and I have suggested that, here too, advance was achieved at the expense, not by the means, of Calvinism. This essay was originally written in honour of that great scholar and patron of scholarship, to whom lovers of the eighteenth century owe so much, Dr. Theodore Besterman. But its natural relation to the other essays in this volume decided me, in the end, to publish it here and to substitute another more purely eighteenth-century essay in the volume which his friends were offering to Dr. Besterman.

The remaining essays in this volume bring us back to Great Britain. All of them were first published in tributary volumes in honour of historians from whom I have learned to enjoy the study of history. The essay on "The Fast Sermons of the Long Parliament," originally published in honour of my Oxford tutor Sir Keith Feiling,[4] describes one method whereby the leaders of the Long Parliament maintained its internal cohesion and defined, from time to time, their party line. The essay on "Oliver Cromwell and His Parliaments," originally presented to that great anatomist, or rather vivisector, of English eighteenth-century parliaments, Sir Lewis Namier,[5] suggests one reason why Cromwell was so much less successful. The essay on "Scotland and the Puritan Revolution" was written for a Scottish historian of England and of Europe, David Ogg,[6] and deals with one of the many neglected episodes of Scottish history: an episode whose impact on England was, I believe, of fatal importance. All historians recognize that the split between "Presbyterians" and "Independents" was decisive in the Puritan Revolution, and many definitions of that split—political, sociological, religious—have been given. But when we look more closely and see how ragged, temporary and variable the frontier between "Presbyteri-

4. *Essays in British History, presented to Sir Keith Feiling*, ed. H. R. Trevor-Roper (1964).

5. *Essays presented to Sir Lewis Namier*, ed. Richard Pares and A. J. P. Taylor (1956).

6. *Historical Essays, 1600–1750, presented to David Ogg*, ed. H. E. Bell and R. L. Ollard (1963).

ans" and "Independents" was, I believe that we should recognize the limits of sociological or doctrinal interpretations and admit that there are times when political parties and political attitudes are not the direct expression of social or ideological theories or interests, but are polarized round political events, in this instance around the fatal Scottish intervention in the English civil war.

Fatal, in its consequences, to both countries: to England, because it saved the rebel Parliament from defeat only to sink it in revolution; to Scotland, because it led, within a few years, to the Cromwellian conquest of the country and the brief, because forced, parliamentary union; which nevertheless pointed the way—fifty years later, in a very different conjuncture—to the mutually beneficial and more lasting union of 1707.

That second union is the theme of the last essay in this book. The seventeenth century saw several attempts, by "modernising" new dynasties, to consolidate their accidental inheritances. The Count-Duke of Olivares sought to make Philip IV king not merely of Castile, Aragon and Portugal but the whole Iberian peninsula. The new Bourbon dynasty sought to unite its kingdoms of France and Navarre. James I of England aspired to "a more perfect union" with his ancestral kingdom of Scotland. In all three countries the attempts required force and led to civil war. Navarre was subjected; Portugal resisted and broke free; Catalonia was reconquered; Scotland, having resisted Charles I and survived Cromwell, settled in the end for a more limited union which saved its economy and gave England its prime need: security. My essay on this subject was written in honour of Jaime Vicens Vives, the Catalonian historian of Spain, and after his premature death was published in a memorial volume.[7]

History is a continuing and complex interaction of interests, experiments and ideas, as well as—in Gibbon's melancholy phrase—the register of the crimes, follies and misfortunes of mankind. A volume of essays cannot pretend to solve the problems of a crowded century. I shall be content if I have opened a few oblique slit-windows in the dividing wall between past and present through which some of those problems can be seen anew and provoke the thought, questions and dissent which are the life of historical study.

Hugh Trevor-Roper

7. *Homenaje a Jaime Vicens Vives* (Barcelona, 1965).

The Crisis of the Seventeenth Century

1 | Religion, the Reformation, and Social Change

If we look at the 300 years of European history from 1500 to 1800, we can describe it, in general, as a period of progress. It begins with the Renaissance and ends with the Enlightenment; and these two processes are, in many ways, continuous: the latter follows logically upon the former. On the other hand, this progress is far from smooth. It is uneven in both time and space. There are periods of sharp regression, and if the general progress is resumed after that regression, it is not necessarily resumed in the same areas. In the sixteenth century, indeed, the advance seems at first sight general. That is a century of almost universal expansion in Europe. But early in the seventeenth century there is a deep crisis which affects, in one way or other, most of Europe; and thereafter, when the general advance is resumed, after 1660, it is with a remarkable difference: a difference which, in the succeeding years, is only widened. The years 1620–60, it seems, mark the great, distorting gap in the otherwise orderly advance. If we were to summarize the whole period, we could say that the first long period, the 120 years 1500–1620, was the age of the European Renaissance, an age in which the economic and intellectual leadership of Europe is, or seems to be, in the south, in Italy and Spain; the period 1620–60 we could describe as the period of revolution; and the second long period, the period 1660–1800, would be the age of the Enlightenment, an age in which the great achievements of the Renaissance are resumed and continued to new heights, but from a new basis. Spain and Italy have become backwaters, both economically and intellectually: in both fields the leadership has fallen to the northern nations, and, in particular, to

England, Holland and France. Just as the northern nations, in the first period, looked for ideas to the Mediterranean, so the Mediterranean nations, in the second period, looked north.

Now what is the cause of this great shift? Why was the first Enlightenment, the enlightenment of the Renaissance, which spread outwards from Italy, cut short in its original home and transferred, for its continuation, to other countries? Why was the economic advance which, in the sixteenth century, seemed so general, and in which all Europe had its share, carried to completion only in certain areas: areas which, at first, had not seemed best fitted for the purpose? This is a large question and obviously no general or easy answer can be satisfactory. In this paper I wish to consider one aspect of it: an aspect which is not, of course, easily separable, and which is admittedly controversial, but whose importance no one can deny: the religious aspect.

For religion is deeply involved in this shift. We may state the case summarily by saying that the Renaissance was a Catholic, the Enlightenment a Protestant phenomenon. Both economically and intellectually, in the seventeenth century, the Protestant countries (or some of them) captured the lead from the Catholic countries of Europe. Look at Europe in 1620: the date I have chosen for the end of the Renaissance period. With the advantage of after-knowledge we are apt to say that the shift had already taken place: that Holland and England had already usurped the place of Italy and Spain. But of course this was not so. At that time the configuration of power—to a superficial observer at least—must have seemed much the same as it had been in 1520. Spain and the Empire, Italy and the Papacy, these are still the centres of power, wealth, industry, intellectual life. Spain is still the great world power; south Germany is still the industrial heart of Europe; Italy is as rich and intellectually exciting as ever; the papacy is recovering its lost provinces one by one. Now look again in 1700, and how different it is. Politically, economically, intellectually Europe is upside down. Its dynamic centre has moved from Catholic Spain, Italy, Flanders and south Germany to Protestant England, Holland, Switzerland and the cities of the Baltic. There is no escaping this great change. It is general fact; and although we may find special reasons applicable to this or that part of it, its generality is too huge and striking to be exorcised by any mere sum of particular explanations. The Inquisition may have ruined Spain, the blockade of the Scheldt Flanders, the loss of the Levant market Venice, the change of sartorial fashion Lombardy, the difficulties of transport south Germany, the opening of Swedish iron-mines Liège.

All these events may be separately true, but together they fail to convince. A wholesale coincidence of special causes is never plausible as the explanation of a general rule.

How can we explain this extraordinary rise of certain Protestant societies and the decline of Catholic societies in the seventeenth century? It is not enough to say that new discoveries or changed circumstances favoured north Europe as against south (for Catholic Flanders and Liège and Cologne are in the north, and yet shared the Catholic decline), or the Atlantic countries as against the Mediterranean (for Lisbon is better placed on the Atlantic than Hamburg). And even if opportunities did change, the question remains, why was it always Protestant, not Catholic societies which seized these opportunities? Surely we must conclude that, in some way, Protestant societies were, or had become, more forward-looking than Catholic societies, both economically and intellectually. That this was so was a commonplace in the eighteenth century; and in the nineteenth it was elevated into a dogma by those *bourgeois* propagandists — the Germanophil friend of Madame de Staël, Charles de Villers, in 1802; the Protestant statesman François Guizot in 1828; the Belgian economist, who followed his own reasoning and became a Protestant, Émile de Laveleye in 1875 — who sought to restore to their own Catholic countries the lead they had lost.[1] The success with which largely Protestant entrepreneurs industrialized France and, through France, Europe under Louis-Philippe, Napoleon III and the Third Republic is evidence that, in their own time at least, there was some truth in their theories. In the nineteenth century, if we may trust appearances, it was by becoming "Protestant" — that is, by accepting the rule of a "Protestant" *élite* and a "Protestant" ideology which convulsed the French Church, alarmed French Catholics and brought papal thunderbolts from Rome — that France caught up, industrially,

---

1. See Charles de Villers, *Essai sur l'esprit et l'influence de la réformation de Luther* (Paris, 1804); F. P.-G. Guizot, *Histoire de la civilisation en Europe* (Paris, 1828); Émile de Laveleye, "Le protestantisme et le catholicisme dans leurs rapports avec la liberté et la prospérité des peuples," in *Revue de Belgique*, 1875, and "L'Avenir des peuples civilisés," in *Revue de Belgique*, 1876. On de Villers, see Louis Wittmer, *Charles de Villers, 1765–1815* (Geneva and Paris, 1908). Both Guizot's and Laveleye's essays were widely translated and republished and had great influence: the former even provoked a Spanish reply from J. L. Balmes, *El protestantismo comparado con el catolicismo en sus relaciones con la civilisación europea* (Barcelona, 1844) — a reply considered by the too partial Menéndez y Pelayo as "obra de immenso aliento . . . es para mí el primer libro de este siglo"; the latter was introduced to the English public with a panegyric by Mr. Gladstone.

with those Protestant neighbours which, two centuries before, had out-stripped it.[2] Such empirical evidence from the nineteenth century can-not be overlooked by us, even when we are looking at the seventeenth century.

But even if we admit the obvious fact that, in some way, Protestant-ism in the seventeenth century (and evidently in the nineteenth too) was the religion of progress, the question remains, in what way? The nineteenth-century French propagandists did not argue the reason: as men of action they had not much time for reasons; they merely stated the fact and pressed the consequence. It was left to the more academic German sociologists to explain the phenomenon. They explained it in several ways. Karl Marx saw Protestantism as the ideology of capital-ism, the religious epiphenomenon of an economic phenomenon. Max Weber and Werner Sombart reversed the formula. Believing that the spirit preceded the letter, they postulated a creative spirit, "the spirit of capitalism." Both Weber and Sombart, like Marx, placed the rise of modern capitalism in the sixteenth century, and therefore both sought the origin of the new "spirit of capitalism" in the events of that cen-tury. Weber, followed by Ernst Troeltsch, found it in the Reformation: the spirit of capitalism, he said, emerged as a direct consequence of the new "Protestant ethic" as taught not by Luther but by Calvin. Som-bart rejected Weber's thesis and indeed dealt it some heavy and telling blows. But when he came to make a positive suggestion he produced a far more vulnerable thesis. He suggested that the creators of modern capitalism were the Sephardic Jews who, in the sixteenth century, fled from Lisbon and Seville to Hamburg and Amsterdam; and he traced the "spirit of capitalism" to the Jewish ethic of the Talmud.[3]

2. Propaganda in favour of Protestantism, not as being true but as being necessary to economic vitality, can be found in the works of Edgar Quinet, Ernest Renan, C. de Laboulaye, L.-A. Prévost-Paradol. See E. G. Léonard, *Le Protestant français* (Paris, 1953), pp. 220 ff., and Stuart R. Schram, *Protestantism and Politics in France* (Alençon, 1954), pp. 59–61. The alarm it caused is shown by Ernest Renauld's *Le Péril protestant* (Paris, 1899), *La Conquête protestante* (Paris, 1900). The Modernist movement in the French Church was in part a new Protestant movement and was specifically condemned as such by Pius X in the bull *Pascendi Gregis*.

3. Sombart's views are first given in *Der moderne Kapitalismus*, I (1902), i, 440, and developed in his later writings: see especially *Die Juden und das Wirtschaftsleben* (Leipzig, 1911); Weber's in *Die protestantische Ethik und der Geist des Kapitalismus* (1904–5), *Die protestantischen Sekten und der Geist des Kapitalismus* (1906), and *Wirtschafts-geschichte* (Munich, 1923); also in numerous controversial articles published in *Archiv*

Nobody, I think, would now defend Sombart's positive thesis, but much of Weber's thesis is still firm. It remains the orthodoxy of an influential school of sociologists in America. It has its defenders still in Europe. It is therefore worth while to summarize it very briefly, especially since it has often been misinterpreted. Weber did not argue that Calvin or any other Protestant teacher directly advocated capitalism or capitalist methods. He did not argue that Calvin's teaching on the subject of usury had any effect in the creation of capitalism. In fact, he explicitly repudiated such an idea. Nor did Weber deny that there had been capitalists in the Middle Ages. What he stated was that in the sixteenth century there arose a completely new form of capitalism. In the Middle Ages, as in Antiquity, men had built up great fortunes in commerce and finance; but this, said Weber, had not created even the beginnings of a capitalist system. Such men had been "Jewish adventurer-capitalists," "speculative pariah capitalists," who made money because they loved money and enjoyed making it. But the makers of modern capitalism, he said, were dedicated men who were not animated by love of money: indeed, if they made money, that was an accidental, almost an unwanted by-product of their activity. They were inspired by a moral discipline, an *innerweltliche Askese* or "worldly asceticism," which caused them to place their religion in the methodical pursuit of their "calling," and incidentally to pile up wealth which, since they eschewed all forms of luxury, extravagance and social ambition, they could only re-invest in that "calling." So, indirectly, their moral discipline created that new phenomenon, that "rational bureaucratic capitalism," that "rational organization of citizen labour," which was quite distinct from "Jewish adventurer-capitalism" and which made Europe unique in world history; and this moral discipline, according to Weber, was the Protestant, or rather the Calvinist, ethic. The Protestant ethic thus created the spirit which, when applied to economic affairs, created modern industrial capitalism. For we will not be far wrong in equating Weber's "Jewish adventurer-capitalism" with commercial capitalism and his "rational bureaucratic capitalism" with industrial capitalism.

Now, in spite of all that can be said against it, I believe that there is a solid, if elusive, core of truth in Weber's thesis. The Calvinist ethic did

---

für Sozialwissenschaft u. Sozialpolitik. Troeltsch, *Die Soziallehren der christlichen Kirchen und Gruppen* (1911); *Die Bedeutung des Protestantismus für die Entstehung der modernen Welt* (Munich, 1911), echoes Weber, of whom indeed he can hardly be considered independent (see Walther Köhler, *Ernst Troeltsch*, Tübingen, 1941, pp. 268, 358).

lead, in certain cases, to the formation of industrial capitalism. It is not enough to say that capitalism had a freer field in Protestant countries, because we have to explain why even in Catholic countries, like France or Austria, it was Protestants who throve and built up industry. And it is indisputable that extreme forms of Protestantism were popular among industrial workers, whether the miners of Bohemia and Saxony or the cloth-workers of Yorkshire and Lancashire. On the other hand, there are certain serious difficulties about Weber's thesis. Any general theory has to take account of exceptions. Since Weber himself limited the Protestant ethic to Calvinism, he had no need to explain the economic stagnation of Lutheran Germany; but what about Scotland? According to Weber's theory, Scotland, with its coal deposits and its strict Calvinist system, should have progressed faster than England, whose Anglican system was regarded by Laveleye as, economically, little better than popery. And why was it Arminian Amsterdam which created the amazing prosperity of the United Provinces, while Calvinist Gelderland remained the reserve of booby squires—that class which, according to the earliest explicit exponent of the theory, Slingsby Bethel, was always the enemy of mercantile progress?[4] Such notable exceptions suggest that even if Calvinism did create or fortify the capitalist spirit it did so in a very uncertain manner.

For these reasons I wish to consider the thesis anew—or rather, not the thesis but the historical facts to which Weber supposed it to apply. I think this is worth doing, because Weber himself merely described a theoretical connection: he never gave a single historical instance of the connection thus described; and Weber's most distinguished successor, R. H. Tawney, confined himself to English examples, thus denying himself the light which may come from a comparative method. In considering the facts, I will begin by a brief glance at Europe in the years of revolution between what I have called the period of the Renaissance and the period of the Enlightenment: i.e., in the years of the Thirty Years War.

Let us start with the Protestant powers. In the late 1620s and early 1630s the political champions of the Protestant cause were not Calvinists, they were Lutherans. They were the two kings of Scandinavia: the extravagant, catholicizing aesthete, Christian IV of Denmark and, after his defeat, the severe, mystical, crusading hero, Gustavus Adolphus of

---

4. [Slingsby Bethel] *The Present Interest of England Stated, by a Lover of his King and Country* (1671); cf. also his (also anonymous) *The Interest of Princes and States* (1680).

Sweden. In order to intervene in Europe, both these kings found them-selves obliged to mobilize new industrial and financial resources, and this meant employing great capitalists. Who were the capitalists whom they found?

Christian IV turned first to a Calvinist firm in Amsterdam, the de Willem brothers. Jan de Willem, in Copenhagen, was one of the founders of the Danish East India Company. His brothers Paul and David sat in Amsterdam and through the international money market provided credit for the purchase of arms. When the de Willem brothers ceased to serve him, Christian IV turned to another Calvinist family, of Flemish origin, the Marcelis family, who had already made a commer-cial empire in the north. At first it was a cosmopolitan empire. They sought to corner Swedish copper, handled the King of Denmark's Nor-wegian copper and the Czar of Russia's corn and armour. But in the end they plumped for Denmark. By the 1640s the brothers Gabriel and Celio Marcelis were the King of Denmark's economic advisers, con-tractors, financiers, munition merchants, timber exporters. They ad-vanced money on the Sound tolls and the copper tithes. They raised fleets. Around them, the native Lutheran aristocracy sank into mere landownership and the native Lutheran merchants became mere agents of Dutch Calvinist merchant houses. The Dutch Calvinists became, in fact, a new capitalist aristocracy in Lutheran Denmark.[5]

The King of Sweden did likewise. What the Marcelis family was for Denmark, the firm of de Geer and Trip was for Sweden. Louis de Geer, indeed, a Calvinist from Liège, settled in Amsterdam, was to be-come the seventeenth-century Fugger of the north. Driving out all his rivals (also Dutch Calvinists), he became "the indisputable master of Swedish economic life," "the Krupp of the seventeenth century." The whole copper and iron industries of Sweden were in his hands, and from them he supplied the armies and fleets not only of Sweden but also of Holland, France, Venice, Portugal, England, Scotland, Russia and the German princes. He also manufactured brass, steel, tin, wire, paper, cloth. He was a great shipper and shipbuilder: in 1645 he assembled,

5. For the Calvinists in Denmark, see Violet Barbour, *Capitalism in Amster-dam* (Baltimore, 1949), pp. 112–14; H. Kellenbenz, *Unternehmerkräfte im Hamburger Portugal- u. Spanienhandel* (Hamburg, 1954), and "Spanien, die nördlichen Niederlande u. der skandinavisch-baltische Raum," in *Vierteljahrschrift für Sozial- u. Wirtschafts-geschichte*, 1954, pp. 305–6, 311, etc.; Axel Nielsen, *Dänische Wirtschaftsgeschichte* (Jena, 1927), pp. 193–96.

chartered and equipped a naval squadron to serve Sweden against the fleet which his kinsman Gabriel Marcelis had similarly raised for Denmark. He organized and financed the Swedish African Company. In repayment of his loans to the Swedish Crown he received yet more concessions, consignments of copper, leases of Crown lands, customs dues, privileges, exemptions, titles of honour. He was the financier of Sweden's empire abroad, the founder of its extractive industry at home. To operate it, he brought to Sweden Calvinist workers from his native Liège: 300 Walloon families who never learned Swedish but whose influence was felt in Sweden for more than 300 years.

De Geer was not the only great Calvinist financier and industrialist in Sweden in those years. Willem Usselincx founded the Swedish West India Company. The brothers Abraham and Jacob Momma opened up iron- and copper-mines in Lapland and became the personal financiers of Queen Christina. The brothers Spiering controlled the Baltic corn market and farmed the Baltic tolls. It was a Dutch Calvinist from Livonia who founded the Bank of Sweden in 1658. Other Dutch Calvinists controlled the export of iron guns, the royal brass factory at Nacka, etc.[6]

If Lutheran Denmark and Sweden were modernized and financed by Calvinist entrepreneurs, what of the other supporter of European Protestantism, the Catholic monarch of France? Cardinal Richelieu, it is well known, like Henri IV before him, relied largely on Huguenot men of affairs. His bankers were French Calvinists, the Rambouillets and the Tallemants. To pay the French and Swedish armies he employed Jan Hoeufft, a Calvinist from Brabant who had been naturalized a Frenchman in 1601 and had been employed by Henri IV to drain the lakes and marshes of France. Through his brother Mattheus in Amsterdam, Hoeufft was in touch with the Calvinist international, with de Geer, and with the Baltic.[7] But in 1639 Richelieu found another Protestant financier, who was to dominate French finance for the next quarter of a century. This was Barthélemy d'Herwarth, who, in that year, brought over to the service of France the leaderless German army of his deceased employer, Bernard of Saxe-Weimar.

6. For Calvinists in Sweden, see Eli F. Heckscher, *Economic History of Sweden* (Cambridge, Mass., 1954), pp. 101–19, and "L'Histoire de fer: le monopole suédois," in *Annales d'histoire économique et sociale*, 1932. There are biographies of de Geer in Dutch by F. Breedvelt van Ven (Amsterdam, 1935), and in Swedish by E. W. Dahlgren (Uppsala, 1923); cf. also G. Edmundson, "Louis de Geer," *English Historical Review*, 1891.

7. For Hoeufft, see Barbour, *Capitalism in Amsterdam*, pp. 30 n., 105–6.

Barthélemy d'Herwarth is a famous figure in French economic history.[8] By his financial ability he kept the army of Alsace loyal to France. He financed Mazarin's German policy. "Monsieur d'Herwarth," the Cardinal once declared in the presence of the young Louis XIV, "has saved France and preserved the crown to the King. His services should never be forgotten; the King will make them immortal by the marks of honour and recognition which he will bestow on him and his family." The King duly made him *Intendant des Finances*, and relied on him more than once in moments of crisis. The *dévots* were outraged to see this Huguenot so powerful at Court, but they could do nothing: Herwarth "had rendered such service to the State by means of his credit with the German army," it was explained, "that all other considerations must yield." As *Intendant des Finances*, Herwarth filled his office with his co-religionists. Under him, wrote Élie Bénoist, the contemporary historian of the Revocation of the Edict of Nantes, "Public Finance became the refuge of the Reformed, to whom other employment was refused." Upon which a modern French historian has commented, "Herwarth after Sully, there—as far as France is concerned—is the true origin of the famous Protestant Finance; not in the intimate connection and theological reasons invoked by Max Weber and his school."[9]

"As far as France is concerned"—possibly; but possibly not. Even if the French Huguenots sought to introduce each other into financial office, does that explain their competence for these offices? And anyway, the phenomenon does not appear in France only. We have seen it in Lutheran Denmark and Lutheran Sweden. Once again, we cannot properly invoke a special reason to explain what seems to be a general rule. In order to see how general it is, let us now continue our survey of Europe. Let us go over to the other side in the Thirty Years War: the side of Catholic Austria and Catholic Spain.

For the Habsburg powers also needed industrialists and financiers to mobilize their resources and pay their armies: those armies that had to fight on so vast a theatre, from the Baltic to the Alps, from the Carpathians to the Pyrenees. That they were successful for a time was due, it is well known, to the genius of one man, Albert von Wallenstein. Wallenstein, greatest of *condottieri*, discovered the secret of keeping an army in being, paying it by contributions levied from conquered provinces and cities, feeding, clothing and arming it from his own work-

8. For Herwarth, see G. Depping, "Un Banquier protestant en France au 17ᵉ siècle, Barthélemy d'Herwarth," in *Revue historique*, vols. x and xi (1870).

9. E. G. Léonard, *Le Protestant français*, p. 52.

shops, factories and mines. But behind Wallenstein, we now know, stood another man whose presence, long hidden, has only recently been revealed: Hans de Witte, a Calvinist from Antwerp.

There is something incredible in the career of Hans de Witte, the solitary Calvinist who sat in Prague financing the army of the Catholic powers. He had come thither to serve the tolerant, eccentric Emperor Rudolf II, and had somehow stayed to finance his intolerant successors, who, however, tolerated him for his industrial and financial services. Already, by the beginning of the war, he controlled the silver and the tin of the empire. Thereafter his power never ceased to grow. It was he who advanced all the money to pay Wallenstein's armies, recouping himself with the taxes of loyal and the contributions and ransoms of conquered provinces. It was he who organized the supply of those armies with arms and armour, uniforms, gunpowder, saltpetre, lead, all drawn from Wallenstein's duchy of Friedland. Production, manufacture, transport down the Elbe—he managed it all. All the silver-mines, copper-mines, lead-mines on Wallenstein's estates were in his hands. The iron forges of Raspenau in Bohemia, the rival of the iron-mines of Arboga in Sweden, were under his control. He was the de Geer of the Catholic powers. Like de Geer he brought his co-religionists with him to work the mines, and secured guarantees that they would not be molested for their religion. It was a guarantee that only he could have secured: for as the Jesuits took control in Bohemia, the Calvinists had been remorselessly driven out. In the end only one remained: Hans de Witte, the greatest industrialist, greatest financier, richest subject of Bohemia, the banker of the Emperor and Empress, of the generalissimo, the nobility, the clergy, the Jesuits themselves. When the crash came—when Wallenstein fell and the banker's long-strained credit was finally ruined—it was still in Prague, still a Calvinist, that he met the end, drowning himself, bankrupt, in his garden well.[10]

So much for the Habsburgs of Vienna. What of the Habsburgs of Madrid? It is hardly to be expected that we should find a Calvinist entrepreneur at the ear of Philip IV; but we soon find that, to mobilize his resources, even the most Catholic king was obliged to look outside the faith. In fact, for the handling of his foreign trade and the provision of his fleets, he looked to the Lutheran merchants of Hamburg,

10. The character and history of Hans de Witte have been brought to light by Mr. Anton Ernstberger, *Hans de Witte Finanzmann Wallensteins (Vierteljahrschrift für Sozial- u. Wirtschaftsgeschichte, Beiheft,* 1954).

who, if they were heretics, were at least neutrals and nominal subjects of his cousin the Emperor. For a whole generation Lutheran Hamburg became the mercantile capital of the Spanish empire. There were centralized the sugar trade of Brazil, the spice trade of the East. Through it the King of Spain drew on the industry of Germany, the commerce of the Baltic. Through it his overseas colonies were supplied with manufactures in exchange for the precious metals which financed the war. Through it were equipped the successive armadas with which he hoped to keep his colonies and reconquer northern Europe.

But when we look more closely at Hamburg, what do we find? Numerically the Lutheran Germans are no doubt in a majority, but in quality they are eclipsed by Dutch Calvinists. It was in vain that Spain sought to avoid dependence on the hated rebels by using Hanseatic merchants: the Hanseatic merchants, on closer inspection, turn out to be Dutchmen, or Dutch agents. It was Netherlanders, not native Hamburgers, who founded the Bank of Hamburg in 1619, and formed three-quarters of its greatest depositors. In 1623, when the Spanish government pounced on the foreign ships in its harbours, no less than 160 "Hanseatic" ships were found to be really Dutch. In using the Lutheran Hanseatic cities, Spain was only concealing its real dependence on its open enemies, the Calvinist Dutch.[11]

Meanwhile, on the Rhineland front, the Spanish armies had to be maintained. The King of Spain needed a capitalist who could mobilize the salt-mines of Franche-Comté as de Geer had mobilized the copper-mines of Sweden and de Witte the iron-mines of Bohemia. He found the man he needed. François Grenus, a Swiss Calvinist from Berne, a merchant-banker in Geneva, farmed the royal salt-mines and, by his loans, sustained the Spanish forces. The other clients of this Swiss de Witte were the other enemies of European Protestantism: the Emperor, and that Duchess of Savoy, the sister of Queen Henrietta Maria, who is chiefly remembered in history for slaughtering the saints of God, the Protestants of the valleys of Piedmont.[12]

Thus in Catholic as in Protestant countries, in the mid-seventeenth century, we find that the Calvinists are indeed the great entrepreneurs.

11. See Kellenbenz, "Spanien, die nördlichen Niederlande," pp. 308, 315; E. Baasch, "Hamburg u. Holland im 17ten u. 18ten Jahrhundert," in *Hansische Geschichtsblätter*, 1910, xvi, 55–56.

12. For Grenus, see Baron de Grenus, *Notices biographiques sur les Grenus* (Geneva, 1849).

They are an international force, the economic *élite* of Europe. They alone, it seems, can mobilize commerce and industry and, by so doing, command great sums of money, either to finance armies or to reinvest in other great economic undertakings. Faced with these facts, it is easy to assume a direct connection between their religion and their economic activity; and yet, before we jump to such a conclusion, we would do well to look more closely at the picture we have sketched. We must apply the historical tests with which Weber, the sociologist, dispensed. In particular, we must ask, what was the common denominator of the actual Calvinist entrepreneurs whom we know? Was it Calvinism of the type defined by Weber? If not, what was it?

Now, certainly the men whom we have named were not all orthodox Calvinists in religion. Louis de Geer was: he indeed showed a firm, enlightened Calvinist piety from the time when, in La Rochelle, he took his vow to serve God with whatever he might gain in a life of virtuous commerce. He patronized Calvinist scholars, gave generously to dispossessed Calvinist ministers, and in all his career as an industrialist seems never to have supplied any enemy of the Calvinist cause. But in this uncompromising Calvinist piety Louis de Geer is an exception. His opposite number, Hans de Witte, though he professed Calvinism to the end, was as bad a Calvinist as it was possible to be. Not only did he serve the Jesuits and the Catholic powers against European Protestantism: he had his son baptized in the Catholic Church with Wallenstein, the terror of European Protestants, as godfather. The Swiss Calvinist François Grenus was not much better. As for Herwarth, it is not even certain that he was a Calvinist at all. As a naturalized French subject, he counted as a "Huguenot"; but he was already middle-aged when he became a Frenchman. He was born a German, of a Lutheran family, and Mazarin found him in the service of a Lutheran prince. He was probably a Lutheran.[13]

Of course, Weber himself would not admit mere doctrinal orthodoxy as a criterion. His Calvinist was not a strict believer or even practiser of his religion, but a social type, whose character, though originally formed by Calvinist teaching, could easily become detached from it. What we should look for, to confirm his theory, is not merely religious faith, but the moral deposit of faith which can be left behind even when faith has departed. To Weber this moral deposit of Calvinism was "worldly asceticism": frugality of life, refusal to buy land

---

13. Georg Herwarth, Barthélemy's great-grandfather, had headed the Lutheran party at Augsburg in the time of the Smalcaldic War.

or titles, disdain for the "feudal" way of life. Unfortunately, when we look for this moral deposit in our seventeenth-century Calvinist entrepreneurs, we are once again disappointed. In real life, all the great entrepreneurs lived magnificently. Dutch Calvinist merchants might not buy great estates in Holland, where there was so little land to buy, but abroad they let themselves go. Even Louis de Geer bought lands in Sweden "surpassing in extent the dominions of many small German princes." He acquired a title of nobility and founded one of the greatest noble houses in Sweden. So did the other Dutch capitalists in Sweden—the Momma brothers, Peter Spiering, Martin Wewitzers, Conrad van Klaenck. Hans de Witte acquired hereditary nobility and vast estates in Bohemia: at the height of his success he owned three baronies, twelve manors (*Höfe*), fifteen landed estates and fifty-nine villages. Barthélemy d'Herwarth showed even less of that Puritan asceticism which characterized Weber's ideal type. As his town house, he bought for 180,000 livres the Hôtel d'Épernon, and then, finding this palace of a duke and peer of France inadequate for his splendid tastes, he scandalized Parisian society by demolishing it and rebuilding on a yet more lavish scale. As his suburban villa he bought the maison de Gondi at St.-Cloud, where Catherine de Médicis had held her festivals and Henri III had been murdered, and sold it back to the Crown for 250,000 livres. As his country house he bought the château of Bois-le-Vicomte, once the residence of Cardinal Richelieu, of Gaston d'Orléans and of La Grande Mademoiselle. In such surroundings the Protestant financier entertained royalty and indulged, with his friends, that passion for gambling which was notorious and censured even at the indulgent Court of Louis XIV. Such were the real men whose abstract type was characterized by Weber as "rational worldly asceticism."

If the great Calvinist entrepreneurs of the mid-seventeenth century were not united by Calvinist piety, or even by its supposed social expression, what did unite them? If we look attentively at them we soon find certain obvious facts. First, whether good or bad Calvinists, the majority of them were not natives of the country in which they worked. Neither Holland nor Scotland nor Geneva nor the Palatinate—the four obvious Calvinist societies—produced their own entrepreneurs. The compulsory Calvinist teaching with which the natives of those communities were indoctrinated had no such effect. Almost all the great entrepreneurs were immigrants. Secondly, the majority of these immigrants were Netherlanders: some of them, perhaps, were Calvinists only because they were Netherlanders.

De Geer, the Momma brothers, Spiering in Sweden, the Marcelis family in Denmark, Hoeufft in France, de Witte in Bohemia, were all Netherlanders. The pseudo-Hanseates along the Baltic coast, the newly prospering merchants of the Rhineland cities, were largely Netherlanders. "We can fairly say," writes the greatest authority on the subject, "that the old system of the Hanseatic League had been interwoven with a new system, which brought all these cities into peculiar dependence on Dutch entrepreneurs." [14] Moreover, when we look closer still, we discover that these Netherlanders came generally from a particular class within the Dutch Republic. Even there they were, or their fathers had been, immigrants. Either they were "Flemings"—that is, immigrants from the southern provinces now under Spanish rule—or they were Liégeois, from the Catholic prince-bishopric of Liège.

The extent to which the new prosperity of Amsterdam, after 1600, was built up by *émigrés* from Antwerp is well known. Amsterdam, in the sixteenth century, was a fishing and shipping port: in the world of international commerce and high finance it had little significance until the reconquest of Antwerp by Alexander Farnese in 1585. The earliest form of marine insurance there dates from 1592, and it had probably been introduced by the more sophisticated southerners—the famous Isaac le Maire of Tournai and Jacob de Velaer of Antwerp—who were among its signatories. There were no bankers in Amsterdam before 1600. The Bank of Amsterdam, founded in 1609, and the Bourse of Amsterdam, founded in 1611, owed their existence to the "Flemish" immigration and were based on southern, Catholic models. The Dutch West India Company was an almost entirely Flemish company. Peter Lintgens, one of the founders of the Dutch East India Company, had brought his shipping and insurance firm, with its international connections, from Antwerp. The most famous of the great entrepreneurs of Holland in those days—Isaac de Maire, Dirck van Os, Balthasar Moucheron, Baptist Oyens, Peter Lintgens, Willem Usselincx, Isaac Coymans, Johan van der Veken—were all Flemings. It was they, far more than native Hollanders, who initiated the sudden portent of Dutch prosperity.[15]

14. Kellenbenz, "Spanien, die nördlichen Niederlande," etc., p. 308.

15. For this dependence of Amsterdam (and the Dutch Diaspora generally) on the previous expertise of Antwerp, see H. Pirenne, *Histoire de Belgique*, IV, 340; Barbour, *Capitalism in Amsterdam*, pp. 15–16, 24; Kellenbenz, "Spanien, die nördlichen Niederlande," pp. 309–10, and *Unternehmekräfte*, pp. 149, 342–43; A. E. Sayous, "Die grossen Händler u. Kapitalisten in Amsterdam," in *Weltwirtschaftliches Archiv*, XLVI and XLVII (1937–38); W. J. van Hoboken, "The Dutch West India Company: the Political Back-

If it was Flemings who built up the new prosperity of Holland, equally it was Flemings who, from Holland, formed the *élite* of the Dutch Calvinist entrepreneurs in the rest of Europe. The business life of Hamburg, we have seen, was ruled by Dutchmen; but these Dutchmen, we soon find, were largely Flemings. If thirty-two of the forty-two largest depositors in the Bank of Hamburg were Dutchmen, at least nineteen of these thirty-two were Flemings. Of the thirty-six families who controlled the Peninsular trade, which was the basis of Hamburg's spectacular fortune in the early seventeenth century, nearly two-thirds came from Antwerp, and the rest from Liège or the industrial Walloon country. In Sweden de Geer, in Bohemia de Witte might count as Dutchmen, but by birth the former was a Liégeois, the latter a Fleming from Antwerp. The most prosperous of the Netherlanders who went to Frankfurt were the Flemings. By 1600 they had a two-thirds majority in its ruling oligarchy: it was they who, in the words of its historian, made the period 1585–1603 "Frankfurt's second golden age as a Belgian colony," "the daughter town of Antwerp." [16] In Emden, trade was largely in the hands of Antwerpers. [17] Wesel was known as "Little Antwerp." All along the Rhine it was entrepreneurs from Antwerp and from Liège who, bringing their refugee workmen with them, established first the cloth, then the extractive industries and thus created, for the Catholic natives, a new prosperity. [18] Even in Calvin's Switzerland it was not Swiss Calvinists who created the new industries: for a whole century after Calvin there is not a single great Swiss entrepreneur. François Grenus, who flourished in the 1640s, was the first — if indeed he was a Swiss native and not a Walloon immigrant. [19] The in-

---

ground of its Rise and Decline," in *Britain and the Netherlands*, ed. J. S. Bromley and E. H. Kossmann (1960).

16. A. Dietz, *Frankfurter Handelgeschichte*, I (1910), 63–69, 305–6; II (1921), 1–45; G. Witzel, "Gewerbegeschichtliche Studien zur niederländischen Einwanderung in Deutschland im 16ten Jahrhundert," in *Westdeutsche Zeitschrift*, 1910.

17. Bernhard Hagedorn, *Ostfrieslands Handel u. Schiffahrt im 16ten Jahrhundert* (Berlin, 1910), I, 124–30.

18. W. Sarmenhaus, *Die Festsetzung der niederländischen Religions-Flüchtlingen im 16ten Jahrhundert in Wesel* (Wesel, 1913). Paul Koch, *Der Einfluss des Calvinismus und des Mennonitentums auf der neiderrheinischen Textilindustrie* (Krefeld, 1928).

19. Baron de Grenus (*Notices biographiques*) describes François Grenus as a native of Morges, in the Pays de Vaud; but H. Lüthy, *La Banque protestante en France*, I (Paris, 1959), 38, 42, refers to him as an immigrant from Armentières.

dustry of Switzerland was created almost entirely by immigrants, the most spectacular of them, perhaps, being the converted Jew, Marcus Perez, who offered to make Basel the new economic centre at the cost of his abandoned home-town of Antwerp.[20] In the Calvinist Palatinate it was the same.[21] Even in Scotland, where the Calvinist clergy vigorously opposed any economic enterprise, it was Flemish immigrants who, in 1588, sought to establish that basis of modern industrial capitalism, the cloth industry.[22]

It would be easy to multiply instances. The general pattern is clear. When Weber observed, as evidence for his thesis, that in Hamburg the oldest entrepreneurial family was a Calvinist, not a Lutheran family, or when Slingsby Bethel recorded that it was "the Reformed," not the Lutherans, who were the active businessmen in the north German cities with which he was familiar, they are merely recording the fact of the Dutch, or rather Flemish, dispersion. And although the men thus dispersed were largely Calvinists, they were not necessarily Calvinists. Their local origins were more constant than their religion. Thus the richest of all the refugees who came to Frankfurt were the so-called Martinists, the Lutherans of Antwerp: a dozen of them, we are told, could buy up all the Calvinists put together. At any time from 1580 the richest man in Frankfurt was probably a Lutheran — but a Lutheran from Antwerp. In Hamburg, too, some of the immigrant Dutch merchants were Lutherans, like the de Meyers and the Matthiesens. In Cologne the two greatest immigrant entrepreneurs, Nicolas de Groote and Georg Kesseler, were not Calvinists but Catholics; but they came from Antwerp. Even in Calvinist Holland one of the greatest of the

20. On the immigrants into Switzerland, see J. C. Möriköfer, *Geschichte der evangelischen Flüchtlinge in der Schweiz* (Leipzig, 1876), pp. 30–42; A. E. Sayous, "Calvinisme et capitalisme à Genève," in *Annales d'histoire économique et sociale*, 1953; Walter Bodmer, *Der Einfluss der Refugianteneinwanderung von 1500–1700 auf die schweizerische Wirtschaft* (Zürich, 1946); and the histories of Basel by T. Geering (1886), R. Wackernagel (1907–16) and Paul Burckhardt (1942).

21. See Eberhard Gothein, *Wirtschaftsgeschichte des Schwarzwaldes* (Strasbourg, 1892), I, 674 ff.; Richard Frei, *Die Bedeutung der niederländischen Einwanderer für die wirtschaftliche Entwicklung der Stadt Hanau* (Hanau, 1927); Paul Koch, *Der Einfluss des Calvinismus*.

22. For the opposition of the Church of Scotland to economic progress, see W. L. Mathieson, *Politics and Religion: A Study in Scottish History* (Glasgow, 1902), II, 202–3; H. G. Graham, *The Social Life of Scotland in the Eighteenth Century* (1906), pp. 159–62. For the introduction of "Flemyng wobsters" by the burgh of Edinburgh, see *Burgh Records of Edinburgh 1573–89* (Edinburgh, 1882), p. 530.

Flemish immigrants, Johan van der Veken, the entrepreneur of Rotterdam, was a Catholic—but a Catholic from Antwerp. Similarly, the founders of the new extractive industries were not necessarily Calvinists, but they were generally Liégeois. De Geer's father was a Catholic when he emigrated from Liège. The Biscayan iron industry was organized by that prince of Liégeois industrialists, Jean Curtius. The greatest pioneer of the extractive industry of the Rhineland, Jean Mariotte, was a Catholic—but a Catholic from Liège. Clearly all these men are more united by their Flemish or Liégeois origins than by their religious views.[23]

Once this fact is established, new lines of inquiry soon present themselves. Instead of looking primarily at the religion of the entrepreneurs, we may look at their local origins. And once we do that— once we cease to look only at the Calvinists among them—we soon find that they are not confined to Flanders. Analysing the entrepreneurial class of the new "capitalist" cities of the seventeenth century, we find that the whole class is predominantly formed of immigrants, and these immigrants, whatever their religion, come predominantly from four areas. First, there are the Flemings, by whose Calvinism Weber ultimately defended his thesis.[24] Secondly, there are the Jews from Lisbon and Seville, whom Sombart set up as rivals to Weber's Calvinists.[25] Thirdly, there are the south Germans, mainly from Augsburg.

23. For Frankfurt, see Dietz, *Frankfurter Handelgeschichte;* for Cologne, H. Thimme, "Der Handel Kölns am Ende des 16ten Jahrhundert und die internationale Zusammensetzung der Kölner Kaufmannschaft," in *Westdeutsche Zeitschrift für Geschichte und Kunst,* xxxi (1912); for van der Veken, E. Wiersum, "Johan van der Veken, koopman en banker te Rotterdam, 1583-1616," in *Verslagen der Maatschappij der Nederl. Letterkunde,* 1912. For Curtius, see J. Lejeune, *La Formation du capitalisme moderne dans la Principauté de Liège au 16ᵉ siècle* (Paris, 1939); for the Mariotte family, J. Yernaux, *La Métallurgie liégeoise et son expansion au 17ᵉ siècle* (Liège, 1939).

24. Weber afterwards stated that when he had said "that Calvinism shows the juxtaposition of intensive piety and capitalism, wherever found," he had meant "only Diaspora Calvinism" (*Archiv für Sozialwissenschaft u. Sozialpolitik,* xxv, 245 n. 5). But, in fact, apart from one sentence parenthetically quoted from Gothein, Weber, in his original work, never referred to Diaspora Calvinism and his arguments are drawn almost exclusively from English Puritan writers.

25. Or rather, we should say, the Peninsular *émigrés,* most of whom were Jews; for just as the Flemings who emigrated were not all Calvinists, so the *émigrés* from Lisbon and Seville were not all Jews. The Ximenes family, about whom Mr. Kellenbenz has written (*Unternehmekräfte,* pp. 146, 185, 253), were not Marranos: they were staunch Catholics, who had no religious need to emigrate.

Fourthly, there are the Italians, mainly from Como, Locarno, Milan and Lucca. From place to place the proportions vary. In Hamburg and the Baltic, where they have been systematically studied by Mr. Kellenbenz, the Flemings preponderate, followed by the Jews. Geography and the old Spanish connection easily explain this. In France we find a greater number of south Germans, who came through the branch offices of the great Augsburg family firms of the sixteenth century. Such were Barthélemy d'Herwarth, who came through Lyons, and the Catholic Eberhard Jabach, famous for his magnificent picture gallery, who came through Cologne.[26] In Switzerland the Italians predominated: Turrettini, Duni, Balbani, Arnolfini, Burlamacchi, Calandrini, Minutoli, Diodati, Appiani, Pellizari—these, not the local disciples of Calvin, were the first makers of modern Swiss prosperity; and they continued to make it, without much help from the bigoted natives, until they were replaced or reinforced by a new immigration: the immigration of the French Huguenots.

Antwerp, Liège, Lisbon, Augsburg, Milan, Lucca . . . we only have to recite these names to see what has happened. These are great names in European economic history. On the eve of the Reformation they were the heirs of medieval capitalism, the promising starters of modern capitalism. For large-scale capitalism, before the industrial revolution, depended on long-distance trade and two great industries, cloth and minerals. In the Middle Ages, thanks to the long-distance trade of Italy, the cloth industry had been built up in Italy and its northern depot, Flanders. From the financial accumulation thus created, the capitalists of both Italy and Flanders had been able to mobilize the still more costly, but ultimately still more profitable extractive industry of Europe. By 1500 all the techniques of industrial capitalism were concentrated in a few cities strung along the old Rhineland route from Flanders to Italy. At one end was Antwerp, heir to Bruges and Ghent, commanding the old Flemish cloth industry and financing the extractive industry of Liège; at the other end were the Italian cities, the commercial and financial cities of Venice and Genoa, the industrial cities of Milan and Florence. To these had recently been added two new centres: Augsburg, whose cloth industry raised the huge financial super-

26. For the south Germans in Lyon, see K. Ver Hees, "Die oberdeutsche Kaufleute in Lyon im letzten Viertel des 16ten Jahrhundert," in *Vierteljahrschrift für Sozial- und Wirtschaftsgeschichte*, 1934. There was also a colony in Marseilles: see A. E. Sayous, "Le Commerce de Melchior Manlich et Cie d'Augsbourg à Marseilles," in *Revue historique*, CLXXVI (1935), 389–411.

structure of the Fugger and other families and enabled them to rival even Antwerp, concentrating in their hands the extractive industry of central Europe; and Lisbon, the capital of a new world-wide commercial empire, with possibilities of long-distance trade undreamed of before. These were the centres of European capitalism in 1500. In some way or other, between 1550 and 1620, most of these centres were convulsed, and the secret techniques of capitalism were carried away to other cities, to be applied in new lands.

This is not, of course, the German view. Marx, Weber, Sombart all believed that a new form of capitalism was created in the sixteenth century. Medieval production, they believed, was "petty production" only. It was not till the Reformation, they believed, that large-scale industrial production was possible. Then Reformation, industrial capitalism and the economic rise of the Protestant powers synchronized. After that it was easy to see causal connections. But today few scholars believe in this sudden sixteenth-century break-through of industrial capitalism. We know too much about medieval Italian and Flemish capitalism.[27] The enterprises of Benedetto Zaccaria in Genoa, of Roger de Boinebroke in Ghent, of the great cloth-merchants and bankers in Florence, were as "rational" in their methods, as "bureaucratic" in their structure, as any modern capitalism;[28] and if the founders of

27. It is interesting to observe the narrowly German origin of Weber's theory. Its antecedents were German too. It was W. Endemann, in his great work *Studien in der romanisch-kanonistischen Wirtschafts- u. Rechtslehre* (Berlin, 1874–83), I, 371 ff., who wrote that it took the Protestant revolt to free European capitalism from the repressive grip of the Catholic Church, and it was L. Goldschmidt, in his *Universalgeschichte des Handelsrechts* (Stuttgart, 1891), p. 139, who gave currency to the misleading statement that, in the Middle Ages, *homo mercator vix aut numquam potest placere Deo*. Endemann's statement was criticized at the time by Sir W. Ashley, *Introduction to Economic History*, II (1893), 377 ff.; but it still runs its course, as is shown by the extreme statement of the case in Benjamin N. Nelson, *The Idea of Usury* (Princeton, 1949). The fatal dissemination of Goldschmidt's statement, once it had been taken up by Pirenne, is shown in J. Lestocquoy, *Les Villes de Flandre et d'Italie* (Paris, 1952), pp. 195–96. Weber's immediate starting-point—the only factual evidence set out in his work—was a statistical study of Catholic and Protestant education in Baden by Martin Offenbacher. These statistics have been questioned by Kurt Samuelsson, *Ekonomi och Religion* (Stockholm, 1957), pp. 146–57. The exclusively German application of Weber's theory is pleasantly remarked by A. Sapori, *Le Marchand italien du moyen âge* (Paris, 1944), pp. xxix–xxx.

28. For Zaccaria, see R. S. Lopez, *Genova marinara nel dugento: Benedetto Zaccaria, ammiraglio e mercante* (Messina, 1933); for Boinebroke, G. Espinas, "Jehan Boine Broke, bourgeois et drapier douaisien," in *Vierteljahrschrift für Sozial- u. Wirtschaftsgeschichte*, 1904.

these medieval enterprises were sometimes outrageous characters—
"Jewish adventurer-capitalists" rather than "worldly ascetics"—why, so
(we now find) were the Calvinist de Geers and de Wittes of the seventeenth century. The idea that large-scale industrial capitalism was ideo-
logically impossible before the Reformation is exploded by the simple
fact that it existed. Until the invention of the steam engine, its scope
may have been limited, but within that scope it probably reached its
highest peak in the age of the Fugger. After that there were convulsions
which caused the great capitalists to migrate, with their skills and their
workmen, to new centres. But there is no reason to suppose that these
convulsions, whatever they were, created a new type of man or enabled
a new type of capitalism to arise, impossible before. In fact the techniques of capitalism applied in Protestant countries were not new. The
century from 1520 to 1620 is singularly barren of new processes. The
techniques brought by the Flemings to Holland, Sweden, Denmark, by
the Italians to Switzerland and Lyons, were the old techniques of medieval capitalism, as perfected on the eve of the Reformation, and applied
to new areas. That is all.

And yet, is it quite all? In saying this we may have cleared the
air; but we have not solved the problem. We have merely changed it.
For Marx, Weber, Sombart, who regarded medieval Europe as non-
capitalist, the problem was to discover why capitalism was created in
the sixteenth century. For us, who believe that Catholic Europe, at least
up to the Reformation, was perfectly able to create a capitalist economy, the question is, why, in the sixteenth century, did so many of
the essential agents of such an economy—not only entrepreneurs, but
also workers—leave the old centres, predominantly in Catholic lands,
and migrate to new centres, predominantly in Protestant lands? And
this is still largely a problem of religion. We may point to many non-
religious reasons: the pressure of guild restrictions in the old centres;
the ease with which entrepreneurs and workers (unlike landlords or
peasants) can migrate; the new opportunities which were already pre-
senting themselves in the north. But these reasons, which can explain
individual cases, cannot explain the general movement. For, after all,
the majority of these men, though they might leave easily, did not leave
willingly. They were expelled. And they were expelled for religion. The
Italians who fled over the Alps from Milan or Como were largely cloth-
merchants and cloth-workers who feared persecution for their religious views. The Italians of Lucca who founded the silk industry of
Switzerland were silk-merchants who felt the pressure of the Roman

Inquisition not on their looms, but on their "heretical" views.[29] The Flemings who left the southern Netherlands for the north were either workers from the rural cloth industry fleeing from Alba's Tribunal of Blood or Antwerpers to whom Alexander Farnese gave the alternative of Catholicism or exile.[30] All these men, who had worked, or whose ancestors had worked, peacefully in Catholic Flanders and Italy in the past, now found themselves unable to reconcile themselves to Catholicism any longer: economic reasons might point the direction, but religion gave them the push. The question we have to ask is, what had happened to create this new gulf between sixteenth-century Catholicism and the sixteenth-century entrepreneurs and workers: a gulf quite unknown to the medieval Church and the medieval entrepreneurs and workers?

In face of this question, it is convenient to ask, what was the religious attitude of those actively engaged in economic life in 1500? Basically we can define it, for lack of a better word, as "Erasmianism." I wish I could find a better word—one more obviously applicable to Italy as well as to northern Europe (for the characteristics were general)—but I cannot. Let me therefore make it clear that by Erasmianism I mean not specifically the doctrines of Erasmus, but those general views to which the early reformers, and Erasmus in particular, gave a clear form. These Erasmians were Christian and Catholic, but they rejected or ignored a great deal of the new external apparatus of official Catholicism: an apparatus which, since it absorbed energy, consumed time and immobilized property, without having any necessary connection with religion, was equally disliked by educated, by pious, and by active men. So, instead of "mechanical religion," and of monasticism which had come to represent it, the Erasmians extolled "primitive Christianity," private devotion, the study of the Bible; and they believed intensely in the sanctification of lay life. Against the exaggerated pretensions of the clergy,

29. For the emigration from Lucca, see A. Pascal, "Da Lucca a Ginevra," in *Rivista Storica Italiana*, 1932–35.

30. Examination of the places of origin of the *émigrés* from Flanders to Frankfurt, Hamburg, etc., shows that the poor immigrants were largely workers from the Walloon clothing and mining towns, while the rich immigrants came predominantly from Antwerp. The massive migration of the cloth-workers of Hondschoote to Leiden is the subject of Mr. E. Coornaert's study, *Un Centre industriel d'autrefois: la draperie-sayetterie d'Hondschoote* (Paris, 1930).

claiming that the clerical or monastic condition was, by itself, holier than the lay condition, the laity exalted the married state as being not a mere concession to base human nature, but a religious state no less holy than clerical celibacy; and they exalted the lay calling as being, if sanctified by inner faith in its daily exercise, no less holy than the clerical office. This belief in the positive religious value of a lay calling was seized upon by Weber as the essence of the "Protestant ethic," the necessary condition of industrial capitalism. In keeping with his view of a new, revolutionary idea in the sixteenth century, Weber ascribed it, in its verbal form, to Luther and, in its real significance, to Calvin. But in fact, although Weber was no doubt right to see in the idea of "the calling" an essential ingredient in the creation of capitalism, he was undoubtedly wrong in assuming that this idea was a purely Protestant idea. His philological reasoning is known to be wrong. And, in fact, the idea was a commonplace before Protestantism. It occurs constantly in the works of Erasmus, who regularly extols the real, inner piety of the active layman in his calling above the complacency of the indolent monks who assume a greater holiness because of the costume they wear or the "mechanical devotions" which they practise.

In all this there is, of course, nothing explicitly heretical. Pressed to extremes, Erasmianism could be subversive of the clerical establishment. Put into practice, it would have diminished the number of the clergy, reduced their influence over the laity, cut down their means of propaganda, blocked the sources of their wealth. But as it was provoked only by the indecent number of the clergy, their indecent power and wealth, so, in normal times, it was unlikely to be pushed to extremes. Nor was it exclusively a doctrine, or rather a mental attitude, of the mercantile classes. It was an attitude which appealed to the educated laity in general. Erasmus had friends and patrons among princes and their officers, even among the clergy, as well as among the mercantile classes. Nevertheless there was a sense in which it was peculiarly the attitude of the *bourgeoisie*. In a time of crisis, Erasmian princes (like Charles V) would remember their "reason of state": they might (like him) carry their private Erasmianism to the grave, but they would hesitate before attacking the vested interests of the Church, which were so involved with those of the throne—and indeed of the social order. Erasmian officers and lawyers, as a class, would follow their prince. Erasmian clergy, as a class, would go with the Church. Among the educated classes, the urban, mercantile classes—not the great tax-farmers or contractors, economically tied to the Crown or the Church, but the really independent, self-confident entrepreneurs—were most free to follow their philosophy to its logical conclusion, if they were forced to do so.

In the decades of the Reformation they were forced to do so. In those years the abuses of the Church drove its critics into extremity and the Erasmians, wherever they were, found themselves obliged either to surrender at discretion or to admit themselves heretics. If they chose the latter course, they became Calvinists. For Calvin, far more than is generally admitted, was the heir of Erasmus: the heir in a more intolerant age, it is true, the heir who has to fight for his legacy, and whose character is changed by the struggle, but still, in essentials, the heir. If we follow his career, or read his works, we are constantly reminded of Erasmus. Calvin was nurtured on Erasmian teaching. He published his great work in the last city of Erasmus. Some of his writings are almost plagiarisms of Erasmus. Like Erasmus, unlike Luther, Calvin believed in a reformed visible Church: the hierarchy was not to be destroyed but purified, made more efficient, more dynamic. And everywhere the Erasmian *bourgeoisie*, if it did not renounce its Erasmian views altogether, turned to Calvinism as the only form in which it could defend them. The mercantile aristocracy of Venice, preserving inviolate their republican constitution, were able to keep their old character, neither Papist nor Protestant. But their colleagues in Milan, Como, Lucca were not. So the most independent of them slid gradually into Calvinism, or at least, as they slipped over the Alps into Switzerland, accepted (with whatever private reservations) the public leadership of the Calvinists, the only International which could give protection and coherence to a group of urban minorities whose own strength lay not in numbers but in their moral and intellectual quality.

So the change took place. It was not that Calvinism created a new type of man, who in turn created capitalism; it was rather that the old economic *élite* of Europe were driven into heresy because the attitude of mind which had been theirs for generations, and had been tolerated for generations, was suddenly, and in some places, declared heretical and intolerable. Had the Roman Church and the Spanish State not suddenly resolved to persecute the views of Erasmus and Vives, Ochino and Vermigli, Castellio and Sozzini, the mercantile aristocracies of Antwerp, Milan, Lucca, even Seville[31] would no doubt have continued, like that

31. Seville, the only great mercantile city of Spain, was also the last centre of Spanish "Erasmianism." This was crushed in 1558–59, with the great purge of the Jerony-

of Venice, to preserve their orthodoxy, wearing it, as of old, with a slight difference. In fact, this was not so. The abuses of Rome drove the merchant aristocracies into a position which the terrified Court of Rome saw as positively heretical. Justification by faith, this Pauline orthodoxy which consecrated "interior religion," the religion of the layman without priests — was not this the same doctrine which Luther was using to proclaim a revolt throughout Europe, a revolt from Rome?

We can see why Rome panicked. But to leave the question thus, as if reaction to a temporary crisis created a major shift in European economy for three centuries, would be unpardonably superficial. For why, we must ask, did the lay princes forward this priestly panic? And why did the fugitive Calvinist entrepreneurs so easily, and so permanently, leave the economic centres of Europe? For after all, the era of panic was relatively brief. Catholic princes (as the case of de Witte shows) were prepared to make concessions to economically valuable heretics, and after a generation most of the Calvinist entrepreneurs had lost their doctrinal purity. If de Witte was prepared to serve Wallenstein and have his son baptized as a Catholic, if the merchants of Hamburg were prepared to work for the King of Spain, there is no reason to suppose that they would have absolutely refused to return to their old allegiance in a more tolerant age. Besides, they were not always comfortable in Calvinist countries. Calvinism might have begun as Erasmianism armed for battle; in its first generation it might have attracted the *élite* of Europe; but soon, as it widened its base, it changed its character and lowered its standards. By 1600 Calvinism was the religion not only of the educated laity, but also of ambitious noblemen and rural squireens; it was controlled, often, by fanatical clergy, little better than the monkish inquisitors against whom it had once been a protest. To escape from such company the original intellectual Calvinists turned aside to Arminianism in Holland, to undenominational lay Puritanism in England. Besides, on the Catholic side, a new order had arisen which sought to recapture the *élite* of the laity: the Jesuits whom, in their first generation, the old clerical orders, the Dominican and Franciscan last-ditchers against reform, had rightly seen as dangerous continuators of that hated message, attenuators of clerical apparatus, flatterers of lay piety — in fact, Erasmians.

To pose this question is to go far outside the field of mere doc-

---

mite monastery of S. Isidoro, and the flight of eighteen of its monks abroad, mostly to Geneva.

trine. It is to ask large, hitherto unanswered questions of sociology. It is to ask, not why the ideas of an Erasmus or an Ochino were alarming to the Court of Rome in the days of Luther's revolt, but what was the structure of the Counter-Reformation State, which crushed out that revolt. For always we come back to this: the Calvinist and for that matter the Jewish entrepreneurs of northern Europe were not a new native growth: they were an old growth transplanted. Weber, in seeing the "spirit of Capitalism" as something new, whose origins must be sought in the sixteenth century, inverted the problem. The novelty lay not in the entrepreneurs themselves, but in the circumstances which drove them to emigrate. And they were driven out not merely by priests, on doctrinal grounds, though these supplied the pretext and the agency of expulsion, but—since the religion of State is a formulation of social ideology—by societies which had hardened against them. In the sixteenth century Italy and Flanders, for centuries the home of commercial and industrial capitalism, so changed their social character that they would no longer tolerate those men who, in the past, had made them the economic heart of Europe. The expulsion of Calvinists from the area of Spanish dominion or patronage—for both Flanders and Italy had passed, by 1550, under Spanish control—is a social fact comparable with the expulsion from Spain, in the same period, of those other socially unassimilable elements, the Moors and the Jews.

In other words, we must look for the explanation of our problem not so much in Protestantism and the expelled entrepreneurs as in Catholicism and the expelling societies. We must ask what was the social change which came over Catholic societies in the sixteenth century. It was a change which occurred predominantly in countries of the Spanish clientele. For instance, it did not occur in France—at least until Louis XIV expelled the Huguenots, with consequences, both to the expelling society and to the rest of Europe, remarkably similar to those of the sixteenth-century expulsions. On the other hand, it was not confined to the Spanish empire, for we find a similar withdrawal, if not positive expulsion, from some other Catholic countries. For instance, there was a gradual exodus from the independent prince-bishopric of Liège.[32] Nor was it exclusively dependent on religion. This is shown in Italy where the Catholic entrepreneurs who had contrived to keep within the bounds of orthodoxy nevertheless believed that the conditions of their prosperity were incompatible not with the doctrines, but

32. See J. Yernaux, *La Métallurgie liégeoise*, pp. 99–105.

with the social forms of the Counter-Reformation. The great instance, of course, is Venice. The Catholic merchant society of Venice fought with surprising solidarity against successive attempts to introduce the social forms of the Counter-Reformation. The resistance of the republic in the early seventeenth century, against the combined pressure of Pope and Spain, is a struggle not between two religions, but between two social forms. When the Republic finally weakened about 1630, the Counter-Reformation moved in and commercial life shrank. The same antithesis can be seen, on a smaller scale, in the republic of Lucca. Cosimo I of Tuscany was restrained from the conquest of Lucca because, having seen the flight of so many of the great silk-merchants under papal pressure, he had no wish to scare away the rest. It was not that they were heretical or that he would willingly have driven them into heresy. The Medici dukes of Tuscany were famous for their encouragement of merchants, whether they were natives, foreigners or even heretics. What Cosimo feared was that, if the republic of Lucca were incorporated in the princely state of Tuscany, the merchants would flee *"come fecero i Pisani."* Therefore, though he could easily have captured the city, he refrained, because, he said, he could never capture the men who made the wealth of the city.[33]

"The republic" . . . "the princely state" . . . Already in defining the problem we have suggested the answer. In the remainder of this essay I can still only suggest it, because the subject obviously requires longer treatment than I have space for. But I will try to outline the process as I believe that it happened. If, in doing so, I only reveal the gaps in our knowledge, perhaps that will encourage someone to supply those gaps.

The capitalism of the Middle Ages was the achievement, essentially, of self-governing city-republics: the Flemish and Hanseatic towns in the north, the Italian towns in the Mediterranean, the Rhineland and south German towns between them. In these republics, the merchants who governed them were orthodox, even devout Catholics: the Pope, after all, was the patron of the Italian cities against the Emperor, and the Florentine capitalists, as afterwards the Fugger of Augsburg, were the economic agents of the Pope. But they were Catholics in their own way. Their piety, their charity, was positive, constructive, sometimes even lavish; but it did not create, directly or indirectly, obstacles to their own mercantile enterprise. They might feed monks with

33. See E. Callegari, *Storia politica d'Italia, preponderanze stranieri* (Milan, 1895), p. 253.

their superfluous profits, but they did not immobilize mercantile wealth in monasticism. They might put a proportion of their sons into the Church, but within reason: they saw to it that the main enterprise of the republic was not impeded by a stampede into the Church.[34] They might subscribe to the building of churches, and fine churches too, but not on an extravagant scale: there is a difference between the duomo of Florence and the stupendous cathedrals of the north. And this care of the Church was combined with a parallel care of the State. The State, after all, was their instrument: they did not wish it to develop too many organs of its own, or become their master. Nor did they wish either Church or State to become too costly: to impose, through taxation, direct or indirect, an insupportable burden on commerce and manufacture, the nourishment of the city. For the city-republics, or at least those of them that were centres of international commerce, were not solid societies: they were international merchant colonies, and were kept in being by the constant afflux of "foreign" merchants, drawn to them by favourable circumstances. As such they were extremely sensitive to cost. Even a slight rise in the burden of taxation, a slight fall in the margin of profit, could cause a flight of capital to other more convenient centres—from Siena to Florence, from Ulm to Augsburg. This was a fact which, in episcopal cities like Liège, bishops had to recognize. It was a fact which conditioned the religious outlook of the city aristocracies themselves. In the fifteenth century, when the Church, in its opposition to Conciliar reform, set out to increase its strength by the multiplication of regular clergy and their propagandist and fiscal devices, it was not for nothing that the movement which would culminate in Erasmianism, the positive formulation of opposition to all these processes, found its natural supporters in the educated *bourgeoisie* of the old free cities. They recognized, even at its beginning, the process which, for some of them, would bring prosperity to an end.

Of course there was always an alternative process. A mercantile class could find profit—at least short-term profit—in yielding to the times. In the fifteenth century the cities were being swallowed up by the princes, and the princes, to sustain their new power, were enlisting the support of the rural aristocracy and the Church, and creating

34. In general, the mercantile cities seem to have prevented the building up of large estates in mortmain by the Church. See, for instance, C. M. Cipolla, "Comment s'est perdue la propriété ecclésiastique dans l'Italie du Nord entre le XIe et le XVIe siècle?" in *Annales: économies, sociétés, civilisations*, 1947, pp. 317–27.

around their thrones a new class of "officers," expensively paid out of indirect public taxes or impositions of trade. Some of the old mercantile families profited by this change. They became court financiers or monopolists, and because the free-trade area within which they operated was larger than before, they sometimes made spectacular fortunes. But except when whole cities obtained exceptional monopoly positions in the new empires—like Genoa in the Spanish empire—these individual gains of state capitalists were offset by losses among private capitalists, who, since they no longer controlled the State, were powerless to redress it. Naturally, they drew the consequences. If one great merchant saved himself by becoming court purveyor or financier to the prince, others brought up their sons to be not merchants but "officers" of the new Court, or of the expanding Church, thus contributing to the burden which was crushing their class; and they invested their capital more heavily in land. Those who did not, and felt the added burden of those who did, retreated into critical, Erasmian doctrines and looked for other mercantile opportunities in freer, less taxed lands.

For already, at the beginning of the sixteenth century, new difficulties were pressing at home, new opportunities were beckoning abroad. In some towns of Flanders, Switzerland and Germany the craft-guilds had strengthened their power and, to protect their own employment, were impeding technical change. Even without religious pressure, the entrepreneurs of those towns were beginning to seek new bases, and the unprivileged workers willingly followed them. We see this change, unconnected with religion, in England, where capital and labour moved from the old towns of the east coast to the "new towns" farther inland. And the great entrepreneurs were looking still farther afield. The Fugger, having built up their mining organization in the mature economy of the south, were already applying it in the hitherto unexploited mineral wealth of Scandinavia. Even without the Reformation, there were purely economic reasons for a shift.

Then, in the 1520s, came the great revolt: the revolt of Luther. It was not a revolt within the old, mature economy of Europe: it was a revolt of the "underdeveloped," "colonial" areas of northern and central Europe, long taxed, frustrated and exploited (as they felt) to sustain the high civilization of the Mediterranean and the Rhine. Like all great social revolts, it used ideas which had been developed in the more advanced societies against which it was directed. The Erasmian criticism of the mercantile republics was adopted by the revolutionaries of the north. But, of course, it was adopted with a great difference. Al-

though the Erasmians might sympathize with part of the Lutheran programme, they could not go the whole way: that would be a betrayal of
their civilization. Poised between the new "bureaucratic" principalities with their hypertrophied organs, the object of their criticism, and
the anarchic, revolutionary doctrines of Luther, which ran far ahead of
their criticism, the Erasmians suffered a terrible crisis of conscience.
But as they were a minority, as the city-republics were no longer an independent force in politics, they had ultimately to choose. Either they
must surrender, be absorbed into the world they had criticized, at best
be tolerated within it, or they must themselves go forward into revolution. Fortunately in the time of their crisis, they did not have to submit to the anarchic revolution of Luther. In their old homes, in the
urban societies of the Netherlands, of the Rhine, of Switzerland, of
north Italy, the Erasmian message was being transformed, strengthened, sharpened, made capable of independence and resistance. Between the Catholic princes of the Mediterranean and Burgundy, fighting for the preservation of an old supremacy, and the Lutheran princes
of Germany, placing themselves at the head of national revolt, arose
that slender dynamic force of the surviving free cities of Europe: the
Calvinist International.

    With this great struggle we are not here concerned. What concerns
us is the structural change which the Catholic countries underwent in
the course of it. For in the end the revolt was stayed. If most of northern
Europe was lost, and ceased to be an economic colony of the Mediterranean, Catholicism survived in its old home. The dream of the reformers, of carrying revolution to Rome itself, was never realized, and
Rome reconquered even the Erasmian Calvinist cities of north Italy
and Flanders. But this victory was won at a heavy social cost. Just as
the papacy had triumphed over the Conciliar Movement in Europe by
multiplying its abuses, its costly apparatus of power and propaganda,
and becoming, for the sake of spiritual supremacy, more and more of
a secular monarchy, so, in the next century, it triumphed over the Reformation at home by a still further continuation of that process and
by a still more intimate alliance with the secular, princely State. The
Counter-Reformation, which animated that reconquest, may be seen
as a great spiritual revival: a new movement of mysticism, evangelism,
charity. But sociologically it represented an enormous strengthening
in the "bureaucratic" structure of society. The reformers had challenged clerical wealth, clerical mortmain and the swollen regular orders
which had sustained themselves and enriched the Church by "mechani-

cal devotions." At first, in the 1530s, the Church had recognized the justice of the challenge. It had contemplated conciliation, appeasement. But then the mood had hardened. The Counter-Reformation papacy, abandoning all thoughts of conciliation, turned to aggression on every threatened front. Clerical wealth, it declared, must be not diminished but increased; there must be not fewer but more regular orders, more lavish propaganda, more magnificent buildings, more elaborate devotions. Moreover, since the Church, to defend itself, needed the power of the princes, the princely bureaucracy, in return, was sustained by the clerical bureaucracy. Popery, as wavering Protestant kings were often reminded, was the only real guarantee of monarchy. And indeed, in a sense, it was. Would Charles I so easily have lost his throne if his fragile Court had been buttressed by a rich bureaucratic Church, with numerous offices and tempting perquisites for laymen, and, instead of Puritan lecturers, an army of friars evangelizing and preaching obedience among the people?

Of course, in its early stage, the weight of this enlarged apparatus might be carried. The new mysticism, the spiritual effort of the early Counter-Reformation, could refloat the old hulk which the reformers had vainly sought to lighten. The early Jesuits contrived to breathe into it some of the old Erasmian spirit. They cultivated the laity, modernized the philosophy of the Church, sought to reassure merchants and other laymen of the usefulness of their calling.[35] But the enthusiasm evoked by a heroic effort cannot outlast the generation which has sustained the effort; and by the seventeenth century the spirit of the Counter-Reformation was weary: what remained was the weight and

---

35. The economic modernity of the Jesuits has been emphasized by H. M. Robertson, *The Rise of Economic Individualism* (Cambridge, 1935). Mr. Robertson tends to emphasize only the Jesuit teaching and practice in matters of business morality. This not only involved him in irrelevant religious controversy: it also unnecessarily narrowed his argument, which I am sure is correct. (Long before it was attacked as a slander by an Irish Jesuit, it had been put forward as a vindication by an English Jesuit. See *Usury Explain'd, or conscience quieted in the case of putting out money at interest*, by Philopenes [John Dormer *alias* Hudleston, S.J.] London, 1695–96.) In fact, the argument for Calvinism, as put forward by Weber, is that the central, positive message of Calvinism, the sanctity of secular work—not merely peripheral teaching on such subjects as usury or business ethics—led indirectly to capitalism. But this same central message can be found among the Jesuits too. I have not found a copy of the work, but the title of a book by a Spanish Jesuit—*Los bienes de honesto trabajo y daños de la ociosidad*, by Pedro de Guzmán (Jérez, 1614)—seems clear enough. The economic modernity of the early Jesuits is only part of their general modernity: their determination to recapture from heresy the *élite* of the laity.

Louis de Geer at the age of sixty-two

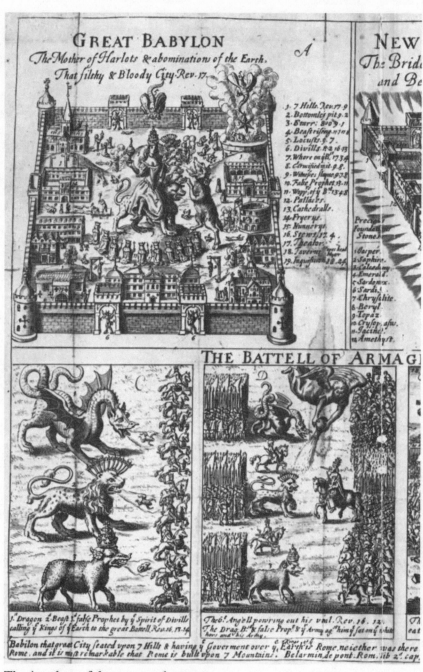

The Apocalypse of the seventeenth century

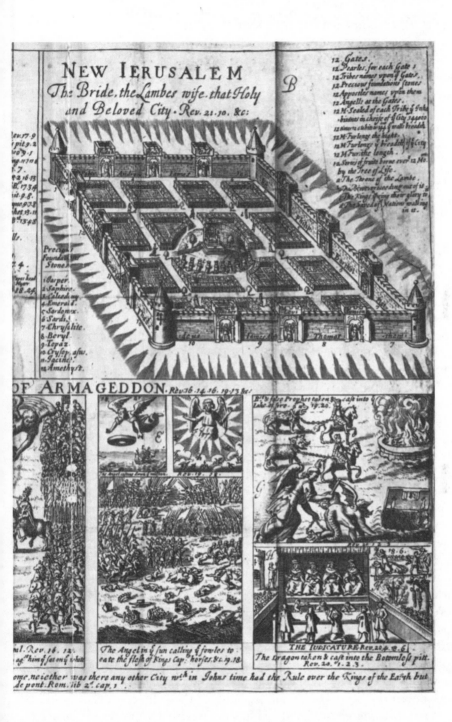

cost of the new machinery. And if the old princely bureaucracy had tended to squeeze out the mercantile life of urban societies, how much more was that likely to happen when the princely bureaucracies had been doubled by the addition, the inextricable addition, of clerical bureaucracies, no less costly, no less contemptuous of economic life which was not subservient to their needs?

Nor was it merely a question of cost: of the taxes which the new State imposed on the private capitalist class. The new State entailed a new society and the new social forms gradually strengthened themselves by investing in themselves. For any society which does not apprehend revolution tends to invest in itself. A capitalist society invests in capitalism, a bureaucratic society in bureaucracy. The public ethos of society—the order in which it values the various professions—and the opportunities for placing its capital both tend in the same direction. In medieval Flanders or Italy the mercantile profession led to power in the city oligarchies and to public respect. If a merchant built up a great fortune, how was he likely to use it? Whatever spiritual and worldly insurance policy he might take out in the form of gifts to the Church or the poor and the purchase of land or annuities for his dependants, his charity would not be at the expense of a future commercial life. A great part of it would be in favour of urban commercial institutions. He would keep the bulk of his fortune in commerce, and if he would show his orthodoxy by putting some of his family into the Church, he would put those on whom its worldly fortune would depend into business. Thus the wealth and manpower of society would be directed into commerce and industry and the Church would be the consecration of a business community. But in seventeenth-century Flanders and Italy it would be different. Even if a man had made a great fortune in commerce or industry, when he came to invest it for the future of his family he would look to the society around him and draw the appropriate conclusions. That society, he would observe, was no longer a mercantile urban society: it was a courtly, bureaucratic society, and its values and its opportunities were quite different. For his spiritual salvation, and for his dependants, he would still take out an insurance policy. He would still give his tithe to the Church, buy land or *rentes* for his widow. But for those of his sons on whom the worldly hopes of the family rested he would use his capital accumulation to buy offices in the administration of Church or State. Under the pashalik of the prince, officers would never starve: merchants might. Thus the wealth and power of society would be directed into office and the Church would be the consecration not of a mercantile but of an official society.

Thus the Counter-Reformation State gradually created, even in the old mercantile cities which it conquered, a new kind of society: a society, moreover, which then strengthened itself by its own social momentum. In Venice, because it was not absorbed by or converted into a princely State, in Amsterdam, because it continued the republican society which had been suppressed in Antwerp, the old character was preserved. The merchant of Amsterdam invested his fortune and placed his sons in continuing business, partly because it was honourable, partly because it was profitable — unlike a prince, a self-governing city-state could be trusted not to adopt laws or a policy ruinous to business — partly because there were fewer alternatives. In Milan and Antwerp the reverse happened. There independent capitalism wilted. The only great profits in business were the profits of state capitalism. But as even state capitalism generally begins with private capitalism, the great state capitalists of the princely states are often found to have made their first fortunes abroad. And even the state capitalists, if they plant their families and invest their fortunes within the State, tend to invest their profits in office and land, not commerce. The Genoese plutocracy, tolerated as a self-governing urban enclave in order to be the state financiers of the Spanish empire, and investing their profits in offices, titles and land within that empire, are typical of this history. So is Hans de Witte, an immigrant into Bohemia who became the state capitalist of the Emperor and invested in office, titles and land in Bohemia. As for the native capitalists, absorbed by conquest into the Counter-Reformation States, they turned necessarily the same way. If we take any great Counter-Reformation city in 1630 and compare it with its own condition in 1530, the pattern of change is similar. Outwardly the difference may not be obvious. The number of rich men may not have perceptibly diminished. There may be as many fine town houses, as many carriages, as much — perhaps even more — evidence of private spending. There is still a prosperous, conspicuous *haute bourgeoisie*. But when we look behind this front we find that the source of wealth is different. The spending in 1530 had been predominantly by an *élite* of merchants and manufacturers. In 1630 it is predominantly by an *élite* of "officers."[36]

The Counter-Reformation State was generalized in Europe, above all, by the power of Spain. It is one of the great accidents, perhaps

36. This is shown, for Belgium, by Pirenne; for Como by B. Caizzi: *Il Comasco sotto il dominio spagnolo* (Como, 1955). Cf. E. Verga, *Storia della vita milanese* (1931), pp. 272–78.

misfortunes, of history that it was the Castilian monarchy, that archaic "feudal" society accidentally raised to world power by American silver, which stood out, in the sixteenth century, as the champion of the Catholic Church, and thus fastened something of its own
character upon both Church and State wherever their combined patronage prevailed. The Roman Catholic religion, as medieval history
had shown, was perfectly compatible with capitalist expansion. The
growth of princely States in the advanced capitalist societies undoubtedly, in itself, marked an economic regression, whether those States
were patronized by Spain or not. Rome, with its swollen clerical bureaucracy, would have been an unmercantile city at any time. But the
Spanish patronage, by its own character and by the necessities of State,
imposed the pattern in a yet more extreme form. Moreover, it was
fatally successful. The wealth and military support of Spain enabled
the princely States under its protection to work: to seem economically
viable even if they were not; and this illusion lasted long enough for
the new system to become permanent. In 1610 the patronage of Spain
was the natural sustenance of every princely Court which felt itself no
longer secure: even a Protestant Court, like that of James I, was its pen-
sionary. Conversely, every mercantile society, even if it were Catholic,
like Venice, regarded Spain as its enemy. By 1640 Spanish patronage
could be of little help to anyone; but by then the societies of Counter-
Reformation Europe had been fixed: fixed in economic decline.[37]

A general tendency is sometimes illustrated by its exceptions. I have
suggested a general pattern of change in Counter-Reformation States.

---

37. This general antithesis between two alternative systems—the "bureaucratic"
system of the princes which may encourage state capitalism, but squeezes out free
enterprise, and the mercantile system of the free cities, which is not incompatible with
a more flexible type of monarchy—may be illustrated also in Chinese history. In China
the bureaucratic society which had been strengthened by the earlier dynasties was
loosened in the ninth century A.D. with the massive secularization of monastic property. Thereafter, under the Sung dynasty, came a great efflorescence of science and
technology. "Wherever one follows up any specific piece of scientific or technologi-
cal history in Chinese literature," says Dr. Joseph Needham, in his *Science and Civilisation in China*, I (Cambridge, 1954), 134, "it is always at the Sung dynasty that one
finds the major focal point." But with the Ming dynasty, the old bureaucratic structure
was restored and the great Chinese inventions—including the three which, according
to Francis Bacon, "have changed the whole face and state of things throughout the
world," viz. printing, gunpowder and the compass—were followed up not in China but
in Europe. The force of this parallel has been impressed upon me by the studies of the
late Mr. Étienne Balasz.

First, there is the reanimation not only of Catholic dogma but also of the whole structure of the Church: a wave of mysticism reinvigorates the old, decadent machinery, which the reformers have attacked. New religious orders are founded. New forms of charity, new devotions, new methods of propaganda bring new resources to the Church and increase its possessions in mortmain. This reinvigoration of the Church is a reinvigoration also of the State which accepts it and which, by definition, is a princely State; for urban republics are opposed to such large subtractions from economic life. But when a generation has passed and this spirit has evaporated, the burden of this great increase is both felt and resented. The newly established society, feeling itself vulnerable and threatened, becomes intolerant and turns against the uncomfortable, unassimilated elements in its midst. The obstinate survivors of the old reforming party are expelled, and the State settles down to enjoy its security, which it celebrates by pullulation of offices in the happily united Church-State. Such is the general rule which I have posited. It can easily be illustrated in Italy, Spain, Flanders, Bavaria, Austria. The apparent exception is France. But once we look below the surface we soon find that this exception is more apparent than real. For obvious reasons, the Counter-Reformation came late to France; but when it came the consequences were the same. It is only the timing that is different.

As the great power opposed to Spain, France found itself opposed to the Counter-Reformation, which, in its first century, had been so openly associated with Spanish power. Consequently, in France, the social repression of the Counter-Reformation was long unfelt. Henri IV might outdo many other Catholic princes in gestures of papalism (for he had a past to bury), but the apparatus of the Counter-Reformation State was not adopted in his time. The France of Richelieu contained Huguenots and Jansenists; it received the fugitives of the Roman and Spanish Inquisitions; it published the works suppressed by the Roman censorship; and it benefited by the vast sales of Church lands carried out in the Wars of Religion. But this happy state did not last long. Even in the time of Richelieu, the pro-Spanish party of the *dévots*, defeated in politics, was gaining ground in society. It was then that the new Catholic mysticism flowed in from Spanish Flanders and led to the foundation of new religious orders; then that the structure of the French Church was at last reformed. In the early years of Louis XIV the two opposite tendencies were fully revealed. Colbert, the heir to Richelieu's economic policy, preached a mercantilist doctrine of consecrated work, containment of Church lands, reduction of venal offices in the State, diminution of monks and nuns. But the monarchy which Louis XIV set out to establish was not of that kind, and he preferred to base it on the Spanish model, consecrated by the Counter-Reformation Church. So, with the death of Colbert, offices were multiplied as never before, regular clergy were increased, and as the burden and the repression became apparent, the old remedy was applied. In 1685 the Huguenots were expelled. A new Dispersion, comparable with the dispersion of the Flemings and the north Italians, fertilized the economy of Protestant Europe. And just as the Habsburgs, in the Thirty Years War, had to seek their state capitalists among the private capitalists whom they had previously expelled from their dominions as heretics, so the Bourbons, in the eighteenth century, had to finance their wars by applying to the Swiss financiers who, in fact, were not Swiss at all but French Huguenots whom earlier Bourbon kings had expelled from France.[38]

Such was the effect on society of the fatal union of Counter-Reformation Church and princely State. What of its effect on the Church? In the Middle Ages the Church, which had been the organ of a feudal, rural society, adapted itself to the growth of commercial and industrial capitalism. This had entailed some difficult adjustments, for neither the merchant employers nor the industrial workers—that is, primarily, the weavers and the miners—had been content with the doctrines elaborated for a society of landlords and peasants. The entrepreneurs had disliked external "works," had rejected the ban on usury. But the Church met them half-way and all was well. The industrial workers, brought together by their conditions of work, listened to radical preachers urging mystical faith, community of life and "primitive Christianity." The Church was alarmed and sometimes declared

---

38. See Lüthy, *La Banque protestante en France*, I. In general it is interesting to note the criteria of urban success adopted by the social propagandist of the Counter-Reformation, Giovanni Botero. In his treatise on the Greatness of Cities, he assumes, as the cause of wealth, the residence of princes and noblemen, the presence of government offices and law courts and—very parenthetically—state-controlled industry; but the cities in which free capitalists assembled and formed merchant oligarchies receive short shrift. Taking Geneva and Frankenburg as types, he describes them as the asylums of rebels and heretics "unworthy to be commemorated by us as cities." And yet these and such cities were the true heirs of the medieval communes, with their cosmopolitan merchant colonies, composed, in the first instance, of "foreign" refugees (*Cause della Grandezza delle Città*, 1588, II, i).

them heretics. It drove out of its communion the followers of Arnold of Brescia, the Poor Men of Lyons, the Waldenses, the Lollards, the Taborites. But others it met half-way. The Beghards in Bruges, the Umiliati in Milan, the Brethren of the Common Life in the north continued within the fold of an expanded orthodoxy.[39] Thus the medieval Church, by its relative elasticity, by its toleration and accommodation—however limited—of new tendencies, remained the universal Church not only geographically, as the Church of all western Europe, but socially, as the Church of all classes. But after the Reformation this changed. In its years of panic, the bloated, rigid Church of the inquisitors and the friars saw the Erasmianism of the entrepreneur as a form of German Lutheranism: *Erasmus posuit ova, Lutherus eduxit pullos;* and it saw the "primitive Christianity" of weavers and miners as a form of German Anabaptism. So it drove both out of the fold. In the 1550s the popes of the Counter-Reformation drove the Italian Erasmists over the Alps and closed down the Order of the Umiliati (much changed from their former poverty) in Rome. In the late sixteenth and seventeenth centuries the Catholic Church was not only, in politics, the Church of the princely system, and, in society, the Church of a "feudal," official system: it was also exclusively tied to these systems. Its old elasticity had gone, intellectually and spiritually as well as politically. While the Protestant Churches (or some of them) contained within them a wide range of ideas and attitudes—liberal Calvinism for their merchants and entrepreneurs, Anabaptism and Mennonism for their industrial workers—the Catholic Church no longer had anything similar. Without heresy, without variety, it was the Church of one form of State and one form of society only. It was not without reason that the theorists of the Counter-Reformation States, like Botero, harped on the essential unity of Church and State. The Catholic Church was the Church of their State. Equally it was not for nothing that Paolo Sarpi, the theorist of the one genuine mercantile republic which sought to remain within the Catholic Church, constantly and trenchantly insisted on the separation of Church and State. The Catholic Church was no longer the Church of his State: if it was to survive in Venice without destroying Venetian society, it must be kept rigorously distinct. Nor was it for nothing that the most famous work of Paolo Sarpi, the greatest of Catholic historians, a Servite friar of unimpeachable doctrinal ortho-

---

39. For the Umiliati, see L. Zanoni, *Gli Umiliati* (Milan, 1911).

doxy, remained unpublished in any Catholic country until the eighteenth century.[40]

Of course, this was not the end of the story. By the eighteenth century the economic and intellectual failure of the Counter-Reformation States was obvious, and the statesmen and thinkers of those States began to draw the consequences. Society, they agreed, must be loosened. Its "feudal" structure must be lightened. The Church must both itself share in this lightening and cease to consecrate the present heaviness. So the Spanish reformers of the eighteenth century preached a Catholic reform indistinguishable from the old Erasmianism which

40. The same general point which I have made about economic enterprise—that it was the Counter-Reformation State which extruded it from society, not Calvinist doctrine which created it, or Catholic doctrine which stifled it, in individuals—can be made also in respect of another phenomenon closely related to economic enterprise: scientific advance. Both Weber and his followers argued that Calvinist doctrine led, as Catholic or non-Calvinist doctrine did not, to the empirical study of Nature; and this theory has become an orthodoxy in America and elsewhere (cf. the influential works of Robert K. Merton, "Puritanism, Pietism and Science," in *Sociological Review*, XXVIII, 1936, and "Science, Technology and Society, in seventeenth-century England," *Osiris*, IV (1938), and R. F. Jones, *Ancients and Moderns* (St. Louis, 1936); R. Hooykaas, "Science and Reformation," in *Cahiers d'histoire moderne*, III, 1956–57, pp. 109–39). But it seems to me that such conclusions can only be reached either by concentrating all study on Calvinist ideas and Dutch or Huguenot scientists, while ignoring the contemporary development of similar ideas in other Churches (e.g., among the Catholic Platonists and the Jesuits) and their no less successful application by Catholic, Lutheran and Anglican scientists like Galileo, Kepler and Harvey, or by "saving the phenomena" with the aid of elaborate explanations, comparable with Ptolemaic epicycles, such as the suggestion that Bacon was "really" a Puritan (Hooykaas), or may have derived his ideas from "his very Puritan mother" (Christopher Hill, "Protestantism and the Rise of Capitalism," in *Essays . . . in Honour of R. H. Tawney*, Cambridge, 1961, p. 31). If these relevant facts are fairly included in the study, it seems to me that the exclusive causal connection between Calvinism and science necessarily dissolves. What remains is the irreducible fact that whereas Pico and Ficino died in the aura of Catholic sanctity, and Copernicus' work was dedicated to and accepted by the Pope, the Jesuits found it necessary to limit their scientific studies, and Bruno, Campanella and Galileo were all condemned south of the Alps. In other words, ideas which were perfectly entertainable in Catholic societies before the Counter-Reformation, and by individual Catholics thereafter (Galileo protested that "no saint could have shown more reverence for the Church, or greater zeal"), were repudiated by Counter-Reformation society. For it was not the theology of the Pope, it was Counter-Reformation reason of State and the social pressure of the religious orders which forced the condemnation of Galileo, just as they had forced the condemnation of Erasmus, whom Pope Paul III would have made a cardinal (cf. my article, "Galiléo et l'Église romaine: un procès toujours plaidé," in *Annales: économies, sociétés, civilisations*, 1960, pp. 1229–34).

had been so ferociously extinguished in the Spain of Charles V and Philip II. In France and Italy the new Jansenists preached a very similar message. Their recommendations were not entirely without effect. Statistics are hard to come by, but it seems that in both France and Spain the weight of the Church, measured in the number of regular clergy, having increased throughout the seventeenth century, diminished again in the eighteenth. But it did not diminish fast enough. So the reformers called for political action. The call was heard. First, reforming princes intervened. Throughout Catholic Europe the Jesuits were expelled. Febronianism was the new Erasmianism of State. Joseph II, like Henry VIII, defied the Pope and dissolved the monasteries. Then came the revolution and after it, the reaction: a reaction in which the hope of reform seemed, for a time, to be finally lost.

However, it was not lost. A generation later the attack was renewed. When it was renewed, its character had changed. South of the Alps, it was openly anti-clerical. But in France, the home of Calvin, which had once had a strong Protestant party, the battle was fought, once again, in familiar form. In the reign of Louis-Philippe, and even more in the reign of Napoleon III, the economy of France was revolutionized by Protestant entrepreneurs. But once again it was not because they were Calvinists, and therefore animated by the "capitalist spirit," that these men were able to achieve the *Wirtschaftswunder* of the Second Empire and the Third Republic. They were not the authentic French Protestants, the true believers who, since 1685, had preserved the Calvinist faith in the "Churches of the Desert" in Languedoc. If we examine closely the great Protestant entrepreneurs of nineteenth-century France we find that, once again, they are nearly all immigrants. They are either Calvinists from Switzerland—the descendants of those earlier refugees, Italians of the 1550s or Frenchmen of 1685—or Lutherans from Alsace: Alsace which, as an imperial fief, had been outside the reach of the Edict of Nantes, and so also of its Revocation. In either case the pattern is the same. In the sixteenth and seventeenth centuries the underdeveloped countries which had revolted from Rome offered opportunities to the entrepreneurs of the old industrial centres, Flanders, Italy and south Germany; in the nineteenth century the underdeveloped Catholic countries offered opportunities to the heirs of those entrepreneurs to return. In the first period the hardening of the Counter-Reformation State had driven those men out; in the nineteenth the loosening of that State made it easy for them to return.

For in the nineteenth century the Counter-Reformation State at last dissolved. The ideas of the Enlightenment, the necessity of progress, the painful contrast with Protestant societies all contributed to the process. But in the long run perhaps another force was equally powerful. In the seventeenth century the Roman Catholic Church had suffered a general spiritual and intellectual contraction. After the effort of the Counter-Reformation, there had followed a long period of narrow bigotry. The humanism of the early Jesuits had been a flash in the pan: by 1620 they had settled down to be the mere sophists of the Counter-Reformation State. Even in the eighteenth century the union of Church and State was not denied: the Febronian princes sought to reform both, not to disunite them. But in the nineteenth century an effort was at last made to detach the Catholic Church from the Catholic princely State. Naturally enough, the attempt was made in France, the Catholic monarchy which was the last to admit and the first to disavow the fatal union. Naturally enough, it was most strongly resisted in Rome, the Church-State *par excellence*, driven into new postures of rigidity by the last struggle for the Temporal Power. But in the end it prevailed. That the countries of the Counter-Reformation could, in the end, catch up, economically, with those of the Reformation without a new revolt from Rome was due in part to the new elasticity which Catholicism acquired in the nineteenth century: to its painful severance from the *ancien régime*. The European Common Market of today, that creation of the Christian Democrats of Italy, Germany and France, owes something to Hugues de Lamennais.

2 | The General Crisis of the Seventeenth Century

The middle of the seventeenth century was a period of revolutions in Europe. These revolutions differed from place to place, and if studied separately, seem to rise out of particular, local causes; but if we look at them together they have so many common features that they appear almost as a general revolution. There is the Puritan Revolution in England which fills the twenty years between 1640 and 1660, but whose crisis was between 1648 and 1653. In those years of its crisis there was also the series of revolts known as the Frondes in France, and in 1650 there was a *coup d'état* or palace revolution, which created a new form of government in the United Provinces of the Netherlands. Contemporary with the troubles of England were those of the Spanish empire. In 1640 there was the revolt of Catalonia, which failed, and the revolt of Portugal, which succeeded; in 1641 there was nearly a revolt of Andalusia too; in 1647 there was the revolt of Naples, the revolt of Masaniello. To contemporary observers it seemed that society itself was in crisis, and that this crisis was general in Europe. "These days are days of shaking . . ." declared an English preacher in 1643, "and this shaking is universal: the Palatinate, Bohemia, Germania, Catalonia, Portugal, Ireland, England."[1] The various countries of Europe seemed merely the separate theatres upon which the same great tragedy was being

1. Jeremiah Whittaker, Εἰρηνοποιός, *Christ the Settlement of Unsettled Times*, a fast sermon before the House of Commons, 25 Jan. 1642–43. Cf. H. G., B.L.C., *England's Present Distractions parallel'd with those of Spaine and other foreign countries* (1642). Many other instances could be given.

simultaneously, though in different languages and with local variations, played out.

What was the general cause or character of this crisis? Contemporaries, if they looked beyond mere surface parallels, tended to find deep spiritual reasons. That there was a crisis they felt sure. For a generation they had felt it coming. Ever since 1618 at least there had been talk of the dissolution of society, or of the world; and the undefined sense of gloom of which we are constantly aware in those years was justified sometimes by new interpretations of Scripture, sometimes by new phenomena in the skies. With the discovery of new stars, and particularly with the new comet of 1618, science seemed to support the prophets of disaster. So also did history. It was at this time that cyclical theories of history became fashionable and the decline and fall of nations was predicted, not only from Scripture and the stars, but also from the passage of time and the organic processes of decay. Kingdoms, declared a Puritan preacher in 1643, after touching lightly on the corroborative influence of the comet of 1618, last for a maximum period of 500 or 600 years, "and it is known to all of you how long we have been since the Conquest."[2] From our rationalist heights we might suppose that the new discoveries of science would tend to discredit the apocalyptic vaticinations of Scripture; but in fact this was not so. It is an interesting but undeniable fact that the most advanced scientists of the early sixteenth century included also the most learned and literal students of biblical mathematics; and in their hands science and religion converged to pinpoint, between 1640 and 1660, the dissolution of society, the end of the world.[3]

This intellectual background is significant because it shows that the crisis of the mid-seventeenth century did not come by surprise, out of sudden accidents: it was deep-seated and anticipated, if only vaguely anticipated, even before the accidents which launched it. No doubt accidents made revolution longer or deeper here, shorter or more su-

---

2. William Greenhill, Ἀξίνη πρὸς τὴν Ῥίζαν, a sermon preached before Parliament, 26 April 1643. Similar views were common in Spain. See Sancho de Moncada, *Restauración Política de España* (Madrid, 1619), Discurso I. Moncada also touches on the comet.

3. It is enough to refer to J. H. Alsted, the scholar and educationalist of Herborn, who was also "the standard-bearer of millenaries in our age"; to his Bohemian pupil, J. A. Comenius; and to the Scottish mathematician Napier of Merchistoun, who invented logarithms in order to speed up his calculations of the number of the Beast.

perficial there. No doubt, too, the universality of revolution owed something to mere contagion: the fashion of revolution spreads. But even contagion implies receptivity: a healthy or inoculated body does not catch even a prevailing disease. Therefore, though we may observe accidents and fashions, we still have to ask a deeper question. We must ask, what was the general condition of western European society which made it, in the mid-seventeenth century, so universally vulnerable — intellectually as well as physically — to the sudden new epidemic of revolution?

Of course there are some obvious answers. Most obvious of all is the Thirty Years War, which began in 1618, the year of the comet, and was still raging in the 1640s, the years of revolution. The Thirty Years War, in the countries affected by it, undoubtedly prepared the ground for revolution. The burden of war-taxation, or military oppression, or military defeat, precipitated the revolts in Catalonia, Portugal, Naples. The dislocation of trade, which may have been caused by the Thirty Years War, led to unemployment and violence in many manufacturing or commercial countries. The destructive passage or billeting of soldiers led to regular peasant mutinies in Germany and France. One need only look at M. Roupnel's study of Burgundy in those years, or at the reports sent to the chancellor Séguier describing the constant risings of the French peasants under the stress of war-taxation, or at the grim etchings of Callot, to realize that the Thirty Years War was a formidable factor in the making of that discontent which was sometimes mobilized in revolution.[4]

And yet it is not a sufficient explanation. After all, the European wars of 1618–59 were not new phenomena. They were a resumption of the European wars of the sixteenth century, the wars of Charles V against François I and Henri II, of Philip II against Elizabeth and Henri of Navarre and the Prince of Orange. Those sixteenth-century wars had ended with the century, in 1598, in 1604, in 1609: in 1618 and 1621 and 1635 they had been resumed, consciously resumed. Philip IV looked back constantly to the example of Philip II, "mi abuelo y mi señor"; Prince Maurice and Prince Frederick Henry to William of Orange, their father; Oliver Cromwell to "Queen Elizabeth of glorious memory." Richelieu and Mazarin sought to reverse the verdict of Câteau-

---

4. See G. Roupnel, *La Ville et la campagne au XVIIe siècle dans le pays dijonnais* (Paris, 1955); Séguier's documents are printed, in French, in the appendix to B. F. Porshnev, *Narodnie Vosstaniya vo Frantsii pered Frondoi, 1623–48* (Moscow, 1948).

Cambrésis in 1559. And yet, in the sixteenth century these wars had led to no such revolutions. Moreover, the seventeenth-century revolutions were sometimes independent of the war. The greatest of those revolutions was in England, which was safely—some said ignominiously—neutral. In the country which suffered most from the war, Germany, there was no revolution.

I have said that the sixteenth-century wars had led to no such revolutions. Of course there had been revolutions in the sixteenth century: famous, spectacular revolutions: the religious revolutions of Reformation and Counter-Reformation. But we cannot say that those revolutions had been caused by those wars. Moreover, those revolutions, however spectacular, had in fact been far less profound than the revolutions of the next century. They had led to no such decisive breach in historical continuity. Beneath the customary wars of Habsburg and Valois, beneath the dramatic changes of the Reformation and Counter-Reformation, the sixteenth century goes on, a continuous, unitary century, and society is much the same at the end of it as at the beginning. Philip II succeeds to Charles V, Granvelle to Granvelle, Queen Elizabeth to Henry VIII, Cecil to Cecil; even in France Henri IV takes up, after a period of disturbance, the mantle of Henri II. Aristocratic, monarchical society is unbroken: it is even confirmed. Speaking generally, we can say that for all the violence of its religious convulsions, the sixteenth century succeeded in absorbing its strains, its thinkers in swallowing their doubts, and at the end of it, kings and philosophers alike felt satisfied with the best of possible worlds.[5]

How different from this is the seventeenth century! For the seventeenth century did not absorb its revolutions. It is not continuous. It is broken in the middle, irreparably broken, and at the end of it, after the revolutions, men can hardly recognize the beginning. Intellectually, politically, morally, we are in a new age, a new climate. It is as if a series of rainstorms has ended in one final thunderstorm which has cleared the air and changed, permanently, the temperature of Europe. From the end of the fifteenth century until the middle of the seventeenth century we have one climate, the climate of the Renaissance; then, in the middle of the seventeenth century, we have the years of change, the years of revolution; and thereafter, for another century and

5. This point—the growing social insensitivity of the sixteenth-century thinkers as monarchical, aristocratic society becomes more self-assured—is made by Fritz Caspari, *Humanism and the Social Order in Tudor England* (Chicago, 1954), pp. 198–204.

a half, we have another, very different climate, the climate of the Enlightenment.

Thus I do not believe that the seventeenth-century revolutions can be explained merely by the background of war, which had also been the background of the previous, unrevolutionary century. If we are to find an explanation, we must look elsewhere. We must look past the background, into the structure of society. For all revolutions, even though they may be occasioned by external causes, and expressed in intellectual form, are made real and formidable by defects of social structure. A firm, elastic, working structure—like that of England in the nineteenth century—is proof against revolution however epidemic abroad. On the other hand a weak or over-rigid social structure, though it may last long in isolation, will collapse quickly if infected. The universality of revolution in the seventeenth century suggests that the European monarchies, which had been strong enough to absorb so many strains in the previous century, had by now developed serious structural weaknesses: weaknesses which the renewal of general war did not cause, but merely exposed and accentuated.

What were the general, structural weaknesses of the western monarchies? Contemporaries who looked at the revolutions of the seventeenth century saw them as political revolutions: as struggles between the two traditional organs of the ancient "mixed monarchy"—the Crown and the Estates. Certainly this was the form they took. In Spain, the Crown, having reduced the Cortes of Castile to insignificance, provoked the Catalan revolution by challenging the Cortes of the kingdom of Aragon. In France, after the meeting of the Estates-General in 1614, Richelieu contrived to discontinue them, and they never met again till 1789; the Parlement of Paris struck back in the Fronde, but only to be defeated by Mazarin and reduced to the insignificance which was afterwards so bluntly rubbed in to it by Louis XIV. In Germany the Emperor challenged and reduced the Electoral College, even though the electors, as individual princes, reduced their own diets to insignificance. In England the Parliament challenged and defeated the king. At the same time the kings of Denmark and Sweden, struggling with or within their diets, ended by establishing personal monarchies, while the king of Poland, unable to imitate them, became the puppet of his. Altogether, we may say, the universal casualty of the seventeenth century was that Aristotelean concept, so admired in 1600, so utterly extinct in 1700, "mixed monarchy." The position was described summarily by the English political philosopher James Harrington, who, in 1656, diagnosed the general crisis which had produced such violent results in his own country of Oceana. "What," he asked, "is become of the Princes of Germany? Blown up. Where are the Estates or the power of the people in France? Blown up. Where is that of the people of Aragon and the rest of the Spanish kingdoms? Blown up. Where is that of the Austrian princes in Switz? Blown up. . . . Nor shall any man show a reason that will be holding in prudence why the people of Oceana have blown up their king, but that their kings did not first blow up them."

Now there can be no doubt that politically Harrington was right. The struggle was a struggle for power, for survival, between crowns and estates. But when we have said this, have we really answered our questions? If revolution was to break out otherwise than in hopeless rural *jacqueries*, it could be only through the protest of estates, parliaments, cortes, diets; and if it was to be crushed, it could be only through the victory of royal power over such institutions. But to describe the form of a revolution is not to explain its cause, and today we are reluctant to accept constitutional struggles as self-contained or self-explanatory. We look for the forces or interests behind the constitutional claims of either side. What forces, what interests were represented by the revolutionary parties in seventeenth-century Europe—the parties which, though they may not have controlled them (for everyone would agree that there were other forces too), nevertheless gave ultimate social power and significance to the revolts of cortes and diets, estates and parliaments?

Now to this question one answer has already been given and widely accepted. It is the Marxist answer. According to the Marxists, and to some other historians who, though not Marxists, accept their argument, the crisis of the seventeenth century was at bottom a crisis of production, and the motive force behind at least some of the revolutions was the force of the producing *bourgeoisie*, hampered in their economic activity by the obsolete, wasteful, restrictive, but jealously defended productive system of "feudal" society. According to this view, the crisis of production was general in Europe, but it was only in England that the forces of "capitalism," thanks to their greater development and their representation in Parliament, were able to triumph. Consequently, while other countries made no immediate advance towards modern capitalism, in England the old structure was shattered and a new form of economic organization was established. Within that organization modern, industrial capitalism could achieve its astonishing results: it was no longer capitalist enterprise "adapted to a generally feudal framework": it was capitalist enterprise, from its newly won island base, "transforming the world."

This Marxist thesis has been advanced by many able writers, but, in spite of their arguments, I do not believe that it has been proved or even that any solid evidence has been adduced to sustain it. It is, of course, easy to show that there were economic changes in the seventeenth century, and that, at least in England, industrial capitalism was more developed in 1700 than in 1600; but to do this is not the same as to show either that the economic changes precipitated the revolutions in Europe, or that English capitalism was directly forwarded by the Puritan "victory" of 1640–60. These are hypotheses, which may of course be true; but it is equally possible that they are untrue: that problems of production were irrelevant to the seventeenth-century revolutions generally, and that in England capitalist development was independent of the Puritan Revolution, in the sense that it would or could have occurred without that revolution, perhaps even was retarded or interrupted by it. If it is to be shown that the English Puritan Revolution was a successful *"bourgeois* revolution," it is not enough to produce evidence that English capitalism was more advanced in 1700 than in 1600. It must be shown either that the men who made the revolution aimed at such a result, or that those who wished for such a result forwarded the revolution, or that such a result would not have been attained without the revolution. Without such evidence, the thesis remains a mere hypothesis.

Now in fact no advocate of the Marxist theory seems to me to have established any of these necessary links in the argument. Mr. Maurice Dobb, whose *Studies in the Development of Capitalism* may be described as the classic textbook of Marxist history, consistently assumes that the English Puritan Revolution was the crucial "break-through" of modern capitalism. It bears, he says, "all the marks of the classic *bourgeois* revolution": before it, capitalism is cramped and frustrated, never progressing beyond a certain stage, a parasite confined to the interstices of "feudal" society; in it, the "decisive period" of capitalism reaches its "apex"; after it, the bonds are broken and the parasite becomes the master. Similarly, Mr. E. J. Hobsbawm, in his two articles on "The Crisis of the Seventeenth Century,"[6] consistently maintains the same thesis. "Had the English Revolution failed," he writes, "as so many other European revolutions in the seventeenth century failed, it is entirely pos-

6. In *Past and Present*, no. 5 (May 1954) and no. 6 (Nov. 1954); reprinted in *Crisis in Europe 1560–1660*, ed. Trevor Aston (1965).

sible that economic development might have been long retarded." The results of the Puritan "victory" were "portentous": nothing less than the transformation of the world. But it is to be observed that although Mr. Dobb assumes this position throughout his book, he nowhere gives any evidence to prove it. As soon as he reaches the "decisive period" of capitalism, he suddenly becomes vague. "The lines of this development," we learn, "are far from clearly drawn"; "the details of this process are far from clear and there is little evidence that bears directly upon it." In fact, not a single piece of documented evidence is produced for what is throughout assumed to be the crucial event in the whole history of European capitalism. And Mr. Hobsbawm is even more summary. He dwells at length upon the economy of Europe at the time of the revolutions. He assumes the "portentous" importance of the Puritan Revolution in changing the economy. But of the actual connection between the two he says not a word.[7]

Altogether, it seems to me that the Marxist identification of the seventeenth-century revolutions with "*bourgeois* capitalist" revolutions, successful in England, unsuccessful elsewhere, is a mere *a priori* hypothesis. The Marxists see, as we all see, that, at some time between the discovery of America and the Industrial Revolution, the basis was laid for a new "capitalist" form of society. Believing, as a matter of doctrine, that such a change cannot be achieved peacefully but requires a violent break-through of a new class, a "*bourgeois* revolution," they look for such a revolution. Moreover, seeing that the country which led in this process was England, they look for such a revolution in England.

---

7. As far as I can see, Mr. Dobb's only arguments of such a connection are the statements (1) that agricultural capitalists supported the Parliament while old-fashioned "feudal" landlords supported the Crown; (2) that "those sections of the bourgeoisie that had any roots in industry . . . were wholehearted supporters of the parliamentary cause"; and (3) that the industrial towns, particularly the clothing towns, were radical. None of these statements seems to me sufficient. (1) is incorrect: the only evidence given consists in undocumented statements that Oliver Cromwell was an improving agriculturalist (which is untrue: in fact having—in his own words—"wasted his estate," he had declined from a landlord to a tenant farmer), and that "Ireton his chief lieutenant was both a country gentleman and a clothier" (for which I know of no evidence at all). In fact some of the most obvious "improving landlords," like the Earl of Newcastle and the Marquis of Worcester, were royalists. (2) is unsubstantiated and, I believe, incorrect; wherever the industrial *bourgeoisie* has been studied—as in Yorkshire and Wiltshire—it has been found to be divided in its loyalty. (3) is correct, but inconclusive; the radicalism of workers in a depressed industry may well spring from depression, not from "capitalist" interest.

And when they find, exactly half-way between these terminal dates, the violent Puritan Revolution in England, they cry εὕρηκα! Thereupon the other European revolutions fall easily into place as abortive *bourgeois* revolutions. The hypothesis, once stated, is illustrated by other hypotheses. It has yet to be proved by evidence. And it may be that it rests on entirely false premises. It may be that social changes do not necessarily require violent revolution: that capitalism developed in England (as industrial democracy has done) peacefully, and that the violent Puritan Revolution was no more crucial to its history than, say, the fifteenth-century Hussite and Taborite revolutions in Bohemia, to which it bears such obvious resemblances.

If the crisis of the seventeenth century, then, though general in western Europe, is not a merely constitutional crisis, nor a crisis of economic production, what kind of a crisis was it? In this essay I shall suggest that, in so far as it was a general crisis—i.e., ignoring inessential variations from place to place—it was something both wider and vaguer than this: in fact, that it was a crisis in the relations between society and the State. In order to explain this, I shall try to set it against a longer background of time than is sometimes supposed necessary. For general social crises are seldom explicable in terms of mere decades. We would not now seek to explain the communist revolution in Russia against a background merely of the twelve years since 1905, nor the great French Revolution against the background merely of the reign of Louis XVI. For such a purpose we would think it necessary to examine the whole *ancien régime* which came to an end here in 1917, there in 1789. Similarly, if we are to seek an explanation of the general European crisis of the 1640s, we must not confine ourselves to the preceding decade, ascribing all the responsibility (though we must undoubtedly ascribe some) to Archbishop Laud in England or the Count-Duke of Olivares in Spain. We must look, here too, at the whole *ancien régime* which preceded the crisis: the whole form of State and society which we have seen continually expanding, absorbing all shocks, growing more self-assured throughout the sixteenth century, and which, in the mid-seventeenth century, comes to an end: what for convenience we may call the State and society of the European Renaissance.

The Renaissance—how loose and vague is the term! Defining it and dating it has become a major industry among scholars, at international congresses and in learned papers. But let us not be deterred by this. All general terms—"*ancien régime*," "capitalism," "the Middle Ages"—are loose and vague; but they are nevertheless serviceable if we use them only generally. And in general terms we know well enough what we mean by the European Renaissance. It is the sudden expansion of our civilization, the excited discovery of world upon world, adventure upon adventure: the progressive enlargement of sensitivity and show which reached its greatest extension in the sixteenth century and which, in the seventeenth century, is no more. Expansion, extension—these are its essential characteristics. For the sixteenth century is not an age of structural change. In technology, in thought, in government, it is the same. In technology, at least after 1520, there are few significant changes. The expansion of Europe creates greater markets, greater opportunities, but the machinery of production remains basically constant. Similarly, in culture, the great representatives of the European Renaissance are universal, but unsystematic. Leonardo, Montaigne, Cervantes, Shakespeare take life for granted: they adventure, observe, describe, perhaps mock; but they do not analyse, criticize, question. And in government it is the same too. The political structures of Europe are not changed in the sixteenth century: they are stretched to grasp and hold new empires, sometimes vast new empires, vaster than they can contain for long without internal change. Nevertheless, as yet, there is no such internal change. It is not till the seventeenth century that the structure of government is adjusted to cope with the territorial expansion of the sixteenth, in Spain, in France, in Britain.[8] Until then, the Renaissance State expands continuously without bursting its old envelope. That envelope is the medieval, aristocratic monarchy, the rule of the Christian prince.

It is a fascinating spectacle, the rise of the princes in sixteenth-century Europe. One after another they spring up, first in Italy and Burgundy, then all over Europe. Their dynasties may be old, and yet their character is new: they are more exotic, more highly coloured than their predecessors. They are versatile, cultivated men, sometimes bizarre, even outrageous: they bewilder us by their lavish tastes, their incredible energy, their ruthlessness and *panache*. Even when they are introverted, bigoted, melancholic, it is on a heroic scale: we think of Charles V solemnly conducting his own funeral at Yuste or Philip II methodically condemning millions of future lives to the treadmill of ceaseless prayer for his own soul. Undoubtedly, in the sixteenth century, the princes are everything. They are tyrants over past and future;

8. See my essay, "The Union of Britain in the Seventeenth Century," below, pp. 407–26.

they change religion and divine truth by their nod, even in their teens; they are priests and popes, they call themselves gods, as well as kings. And yet we should remember, if we are to understand the crisis at the end of their rule, that their power did not rise up out of nothing. Its extraordinary expansion in the early sixteenth century was not *in vacuo*. Europe had to make room for it. The princes rose at the expense of someone or something, and they brought in their train the means of securing their sudden, usurped new power. In fact, they rose at the expense of the older organs of European civilization, the cities; and they brought with them, as the means of conquest, a new political instrument, "the Renaissance Court."

Not much has been written about the eclipse of the European cities on the eve of the Renaissance; but it is an important phenomenon.[9] For how can we think of the Middle Ages without thinking of the cities, and yet who thinks of them after 1500? In the Middle Ages the free communes of Flanders and Italy had been the founders of Europe's trade and wealth, the centres of its arts and crafts, the financiers of its popes and kings. The German cities had been the means of colonizing and civilizing the barbarous north, the pagan east of Europe. These cities, moreover, had had their own way of life and had imposed upon Europe some of their own methods of government and standards of value. In its earliest form, the Renaissance itself had been a city phenomenon: it had begun in the cities of Italy, Flanders and south Germany before it was taken over, and changed, by princes and popes. And this early Renaissance had the character of the cities within which it was still contained. Like them it was responsible, orderly, self-controlled. For however great their wealth, however splendid their town halls and hospitals, their churches and squares, there is always, in the cities, a trace of calculation and self-restraint. It is the virtue of civic self-government, however oligarchically controlled: a spirit very different from the outrageous, spendthrift, irresponsible exhibitionism of the princes which was to come.

For between the fifteenth and the sixteenth centuries the princely suitors came, and one after another the cities succumbed. The rich cities of Flanders gave in to the magnificent dukes of Burgundy, the rich cities of Lombardy and Tuscany to the magnificent princes of Italy. The Baltic cities of the Hanse were absorbed by the kings of Poland or

9. M. Fernand Braudel has touched on it in his great work *La Méditerranée et le monde méditerranéen à l époque de Philippe II* (Paris, 1949), pp. 285–91.

Denmark or ruined themselves by vain resistance. Barcelona yielded to the King of Aragon, Marseilles to the King of France. Even those apparent virgins, Genoa and Augsburg, were really "kept cities," attached by golden strings to the King of Spain and the Emperor. The Doge of Venice himself became a prince, ruling over lesser cities in the *terra firma*. Only a few, like Geneva, remained obstinate spinsters; and that sour, crabbed city missed the gaiety of the Renaissance. Even the exceptions prove the rule. Accidental princely weakness, or indirect princely patronage, lies behind the new prosperity of Frankfurt, Ragusa, Hamburg, Danzig.

For as a rule surrender was the price of continued prosperity: how else could the cities survive, once the princes had discovered the secret of State? By subduing the Church, extending their jurisdiction, mobilizing the countryside, the princes had created a new apparatus of power, "the Renaissance State," with which they could tax the wealth of the cities, patronize and extend their trade, take over and develop their art and architecture. If the cities hope to thrive now, it must be by new methods. It must not be through independence: those days are past. It must be through monopoly, as the sole grantees of princely trade in these expanding dominions; as Lisbon and Seville throve on the grants of the kings of Portugal and Spain. Or they might thrive as centres of extravagant princely consumption, as royal capitals. For in some of the old cities the victorious princes would establish their new courts: courts which sucked up the wealth of the whole country and rained it down on the city of their residence. Essentially the sixteenth century is an age not of cities but of courts: of capital cities made splendid less by trade than by government. It was not as industrial or commercial cities, but as courts, that Brussels, Paris, Rome, Madrid, Naples, Prague achieve their splendour in the sixteenth century. And the brilliance of these courts is not the discreet, complacent self-advertisement of great merchants out of their calculated profits: it is the carefree magnificence of kings and courtiers, who do not need to count because they do not have to earn.

Of course the cities wriggled at first. Ghent resisted its Burgundian dukes. The old cities of Spain struck back against their foreign king. Florence sought to throw out the Medici. Genoa and Augsburg surrendered only after doubt and strife. But in the end each in turn was overpowered, subdued and then—if lucky—rewarded with the golden shower which fell not from trade, or at least not directly from trade, but from the Court. And with the cities the old city culture was transformed too. Erasmus, preaching peace and civic justice and denouncing the heedless wars and wasteful magnificence of princes, is a true figure of the first, the city Renaissance, cultivated, pious, rational; but he is swept up in the princely embrace and made a mascot of royal courts, until he flees to die in a free city on the Rhine. Sir Thomas More, whose Utopia was a league of virtuous, independent cities, is captured and broken by the splendid, cannibal Court of Henry VIII. Soon after 1500 the age of independent city culture is over. So is the age of careful accountancy. We are in the age of the Field of Cloth-of-Gold, of heroic conquests and impossible visions and successive state bankruptcies: the age of Columbus and Cortés, of Leonardo da Vinci and St. Francis Xavier, each, in his way, like Marlowe's hero, still climbing after knowledge infinite, or, like Don Quixote, pursuing unattainable mirages, heedless of mortal limitations. It is the age, also, whose fashionable handbooks were no longer civic or clerical, but were called *The Courtier, The Governour, The Prince, The Institution of a Christian Prince, The Mirror* (or *the Horologe*) *of Princes.*

How was this miracle possible? When we look back at that age, with its incredible audacities, its contemptuous magnificence in speculation and spending, we are amazed that it lasted so long. Why did not European civilization burst in the sixteenth century? And yet not only did it not burst, it continued to expand, absorbing all the time the most fearful strains. The Turks in the east wrenched away the outposts of Europe; Christendom was split asunder by religious revolution and constant war; and yet at the end of the century the kings were more spendthrift, their courts more magnificent than ever. The Court of Spain, once so simple, had been changed to a Burgundian pattern; the Court of England, once so provincial, had become, under Queen Elizabeth, the most elaborate in Europe; and the princes of Italy and Germany, with palaces and libraries, picture-galleries and *Wunderkammer*, philosophers, fools and astrologers, strove to hold their own. As the century wore on, social conscience dwindled, for social change seemed impossibly remote. Was ever an architect more effortlessly aristocratic than Palladio, or a poet than Shakespeare, or a painter than Rubens?

How indeed was it possible? One answer is obvious. The sixteenth century was an age of economic expansion. It was the century when, for the first time, Europe was living on Asia, Africa and America. But there was also another reason. The reason why this expansion was always under the princes, not at their expense, why the princes were always carried upwards, not thrown aside by it, was that the princes had allies who secured their power and kept them firmly in place. For the princes could never have built up their power alone. Whatever weaknesses in society gave them their opportunity, they owed their permanence to the machinery of government which they had created or improved, and to the vested interests which that machinery fostered. This machinery, the means and result of princely triumph, is the Renaissance State, and it is to this that we must now turn: for it was the Renaissance State which, in so much of Europe, first broke or corroded the old power of the cities and then, in its turn, in the seventeenth century, faced its own crisis and dissolved.

We often speak of the Renaissance State. How can we define it? When we come down to facts, we find that it is, at bottom, a great and expanding bureaucracy, a huge system of administrative centralization, staffed by an ever-growing multitude of "courtiers" or "officers." The "officers" are familiar enough to us as a social type. We think of the great Tudor ministers in England, Cardinal Wolsey, Thomas Cromwell, the two Cecils; or of the *letrados* of Spain, Cardinal Ximénez, the two Granvelles, Francisco de los Cobos, António Pérez; and we see their common character: they are formidable administrators, Machiavellian diplomats, cultivated patrons of art and letters, magnificent builders of palaces and colleges, greedy collectors of statues and pictures, books and bindings. For of course these men, as royal servants, imitated their masters, in lavishness as in other matters. But what is significant about the sixteenth century is not merely the magnificence of these great "officers," it is the number—the ever-growing number—of lesser officers who also, on their lesser scale, accepted the standards and copied the tastes of their masters. For all through the century the number of officers was growing. Princes needed them, more and more, to staff their councils and courts, their new special or permanent tribunals which were the means of governing new territories and centralizing the government of old. It was for this reason that the Renaissance princes and their great ministers founded all those schools and colleges. For it was not merely to produce scholars, or to advance learning or science, that old colleges were reorganized or new founded by Cardinal Ximénez or Cardinal Wolsey, by Henry VIII of England or John III of Portugal, or François I of France. The new learning, it is notorious, grew up outside the colleges and universities, not in them. The function of the new foundations was to satisfy the royal demand for officers—officers to man the new royal bureaucracies—and, at the same time, the public demand for office: office which was the means to wealth and power and the gratification of lavish, competitive tastes.

Thus the power of the Renaissance princes was not princely power only: it was also the power of thousands of "officers" who also, like their masters, had extravagant tastes and, somehow, the means of gratifying them. And how in fact were they gratified? Did the princes themselves pay their officers enough to sustain such a life? Certainly not. Had that been so, ruin would have come quicker: Cobos and Granvelle alone would have brought Charles V to bankruptcy long before 1556, and Henry VIII would have had to dissolve the monasteries fifteen years earlier to sustain the economic burden of Cardinal Wolsey. The fact is, only a fraction of the cost of the royal bureaucracy fell directly on the Crown: three-quarters of it fell, directly or indirectly, on the country.

Yes, three-quarters: at least three-quarters. For throughout Europe, at this time, the salaries paid to officers of State were small, customary payments whose real value dwindled in times of inflation; the bulk of an officer's gains came from private opportunities to which public office merely opened the door. "For the profits of these two great offices, the Chancellor and the Treasurer," wrote an English bishop, "certainly they were very small if you look to the ancient fees and allowances; for princes heretofore did tie themselves to give but little, that so their officers and servants might more depend upon them for their rewards." [10] What Bishop Goodman said of Jacobean England was true of every European country. Instances could be multiplied indefinitely.[11] Every officer, at every Court, in every country, lived by the same system. He was paid a trivial "fee" or salary and, for the rest,

10. Godfrey Goodman, *The Court of King James I* (1839 ed.), I, 279.

11. On this subject generally see Federico Chabod's essay "Y a-t-il un état de la Renaissance?" in *Actes du colloque sur la renaissance, Sorbonne, 1956* (Paris, 1958), and also, for Milanese instances, his "Stipendi nominali e busta paga effettiva dei funzionari nell' amministrazione milanese alla fine del cinquecento," in *Miscellanea in onore di Roberto Cessi II* (Rome, 1958) and "Usi e abusi nell' amministrazione dello stato di Milano a mezzo il 1500," in *Studi storici in onore di Gioacchino Volpe* (Florence, n.d.). For Naples, see G. Coniglio, *Il Regno di Napoli al tempo di Carlo V* (Naples, 1951), pp. 11–12, 246, etc. For France see R. Doucet, *Les Institutions de la France au XVIe siècle* (Paris, 1948), pp. 403 ff.; cf. Menna Prestwich, "The Making of Absolute Monarchy, 1559–1683," in *France: Government and Society*, ed. J. M. Wallace-Hadrill and J. McManners (1957). I have given some English instances in *The Gentry, 1540–1640* (*Economic History Review*, supp. no. 1, 1953). See also J. E. Neale, "The Elizabethan Political Scene,"

made what he could in the field which his office had opened to him. Some of these profits were regarded as perfectly legitimate, for no man could be expected to live on his "fee" alone: it was taken for granted that he would charge a reasonable sum for audiences, favours, signatures, that he would exploit his office to make good bargains, that he would invest public money, while in his hands, on his own account. But of course there were other profits which were generally regarded as "corruption" and therefore improper. Unfortunately the line dividing propriety from impropriety was conventional only: it was therefore invisible, uncertain, floating. It differed from person to person, from place to place. It also differed from time to time. As the sixteenth century passed on, as the cost of living rose, as the pressure of competition sharpened and royal discipline slackened, there was a general decline of standards. The public casuists became more indulgent, the private conscience more elastic, and men began to forget about that conventional, invisible line between "legitimate profits" and "corruption."

Let us consider a few instances which illustrate the system. In England, the Master of the Wards had a "fee" of £133 p.a., but even Lord Burghley, a conscientious administrator, made "infinite gains"—at least £2000 p.a.—out of its private opportunities, quite apart from its non-financial advantages. His son did far better. The Lord Treasurer's fee was £365 p.a., but in 1635 even Archbishop Laud, a notable stickler for administrative honesty, reckoned that that great officer had "honest advantages" for enriching himself to the tune of over £7000 p.a. The archbishop made this calculation because he had been shocked by the much larger sums which recent lord treasurers had been making at the expense of king and subject alike. In 1600 the Lord Chancellor's fee was £500 p.a., but in fact the office was known to be "better worth than £3000 p.a." To Lord Chancellor Ellesmere this did not seem enough, and, like many great men, he sighed that he could not make ends meet. He was thought conscientious: perhaps (like Burghley) he was also hypocritical. At all events, his successors had no such difficulty.

> How have the Lord Chancellors lived since [exclaimed Bishop Goodman], how have they flowed with money, and what great purchases have they made, and what profits and advantages have they had by laying

in *Proceedings of the British Academy*, xxiv (1948); K. W. Swart, *The Sale of Offices in the Seventeenth Century* (The Hague, 1949).

their fingers on purchases! For if my Lord desired the land, no man should dare to buy it out of his hands, and he must have it at his own price; for any bribery or corruption, it is hard to prove it: men do not call others to be witnesses at such actions.[12]

All writers of the early seventeenth century agree that the casual profits of office had grown enormously; and these casual profits were multiplied at the expense of the consumer, the country.

Thus each old office granted, each new office created, meant a new burden on the subject. Royal parsimony made little difference. Our Queen Elizabeth, we all know, was judged very parsimonious: far too parsimonious by her own officers. After her death, her parsimony became one of her great retrospective virtues: how favourably it compared with the giddy extravagance of James I, the fiscal exactions of Charles I! But she was not praised for her parsimony in her own time. For what in fact did it mean? "We have not many precedents of her liberality," says a contemporary, "nor of any large donatives to particular men. . . . Her rewards consisted chiefly in grants of leases of offices, places of judicature; but for ready money, and in any great sums, she was very sparing." [13] In other words, she gave to her courtiers not cash but the right to exploit their fellow subjects: to Sir Walter Ralegh the right to despoil the bishops of Bath and Wells and Salisbury and to interpose his pocket between the producer and consumer of tin; to the Earl of Essex the right to lease the monopoly of sweet wines to merchants who would recoup themselves by raising the cost to the consumer. Thanks to these invisible *douceurs* she contrived, at the same time, to keep her taxes low and her officers sweet.

Whether they kept taxes low or not, all European sovereigns did likewise. They had no alternative. They had not the ready money, and so, if they were to gratify their servants, reward their favourites, service their loans, they had to raise it at a discount or pay excessively in kind. They leased Crown lands at a quarter (or less) of their true value in order that "officers" or "courtiers" could live, as lessees, on the difference. They granted monopolies which brought in to the Crown less

12. See, for the Master of the Wards, J. Hurstfield, "Lord Burghley as Master of the Court of Wards," in *Transactions of the Royal Historical Society*, 5th ser., xxxi (1949); for the Lord Treasurer, P. Heylin, *Cyprianus Anglicus* (1668), p. 285; for the Lord Chancellor, Goodman, *The Court of King James I*, i, 279; *Manningham's Diary* (Camden Society, 1868), p. 19.

13. Sir R. Naunton, *Fragmenta Regalia*, ed. A. Arber (1870), p. 18.

than a quarter of what they cost the subject. They collected irrational old taxes, or even irrational new taxes, by imposing, fourfold, irrational burdens on the tax-payers. The King of France obliged his peasants to buy even more salt than they needed, in order to raise his yield from the *gabelle*. We all know what a burden wardship and purveyance became in the reigns of Queen Elizabeth and King James. Both visibly cost the subject four times what they brought to the Crown. Invisibly—that is, beyond that invisible line—they cost far more.[14]

Nor was it only the Crown which acted thus. The practice was universal. Great men rewarded their clients in exactly the same way. It was thus that those great empires of personal patronage were built up which at times threatened to disrupt the whole system of monarchy. In France, it was through his "clients"—that is, "le grand nombre d'officiers que son crédit avoit introduit dans les principales charges du royaume"— that the Duke of Guise was able to make royal government impossible, to control the Estates-General of France, and nearly place his own dynasty on the throne of the Valois. It was to prevent the recurrence of such a portent that Henri IV afterwards, by the institution of the *Paulette*, made offices hereditary, subject to an annual payment to the Crown. This did not cure the social fact, but it cured the aristocratic abuse of it.[15] In Elizabethan England the Earl of Leicester similarly built up a great system of patronage, "Leicester's Commonwealth," which rivalled Lord Burghley's *regnum Cecilianum*. Queen Elizabeth managed to control Leicester, but not his stepson, the heir to his ambi-

14. For the cost of monopolies, see W. R. Scott, *The Constitution and Finance of . . . Joint-Stock Companies to 1720*, I (1911). The cost of wardship appears clearly from Mr. Joel Hurstfield's studies. He concludes that "the unofficial profits from fiscal feudalism taken as a whole, were at least three times as high as the official ones": "The Profits of Fiscal Feudalism, 1541-1602," in *Economic History Review*, 2nd ser., VIII (1955- 56), 58. Of purveyance, Bacon wrote, "There is no pound profit which redoundeth to Your Majesty in this course but induceth and begetteth £3 damage upon your subjects, besides the discontentment" (*Works*, ed. J. Spedding *et al.* (1857-74), III, 185). The truth of this statement is clearly demonstrated in Miss Allegra Woodworth's excellent study, *Purveyance in the Reign of Queen Elizabeth* (Philadelphia, 1945). For Crown lands, Bacon told King James that, properly administered, they "will yield four for one" (*Works*, IV, 328): others put the proportion far higher, sometimes twenty to one. Cf. E. Kerridge, "The Movement of Rent," in *Economic History Review*, 2nd ser., VI (1953-54), 31-32. The Earl of Bedford similarly, in 1641, calculated that in some places the proportion was twenty to one (Woburn Abbey, Duke of Bedford's manuscripts).

15. See Cardinal de Richelieu, *Testament politique*, ed. Louis André, 7th ed. (Paris, 1947), pp. 233-34, 241-42.

tions, the Earl of Essex. Essex, for a moment, looked like the Guise of England. Like Guise, he had to be removed, surgically. Later the Duke of Buckingham would build up, by royal permission, a similar empire of patronage. He would be removed surgically too.

The Church, in this respect, was similar to the State: it was, after all, by now a department of State, and it must be seen, sociologically, as an element in the bureaucratic structure. Originally an attempt had been made to separate it from that structure. The Reformation movement, Catholic as well as Protestant, was in many respects a revolt against the papal "Court"—using the word "Court," as I always do, in the widest sense—that is, not merely a national revolt against a foreign Church, but a social revolt against the indecent, costly and infinitely multiplied personnel, mainly of the regular orders, which had overgrown the working episcopal and parish structure. We only have to read the history of the Council of Trent to see this: the exclusion of the Protestants from that assembly merely shows that, socially, Catholic demands were identical. Protestant societies, by revolution, disembarrassed themselves of much of the papal Court. But even Protestant princes, as princes, preferred to take over, rather than to destroy the bureaucracy of the Church. Catholic princes went further: they accepted both the existing clerical structure and the positive increase which was entailed upon it by the Counter-Reformation. For although, in one sense, the Counter-Reformation may have been a movement of moral and spiritual reform, structurally it was an aggravation of the bureaucracy. However, the princes found that it paid them to accept this aggravation, for in return for their allegiance it was placed under their control, and became at once an extended field of patronage and a social palliative. The Catholic princes had vast clerical patronage for laymen as well as clergy: the Church absorbed the potential critics: and the new or strengthened religious orders, by evangelization, reconciled society to the burden which they imposed upon it. Thus the Catholic princes of the Counter-Reformation were generally able to stifle the forces of change to which Protestant princes found themselves more nakedly exposed, and it became a truism, and perhaps a truth, that popery was the sole internal preservative of monarchy. But even in Protestant monarchies, the bureaucratic pressure of the Church was felt and resented. The Church, it was said, was burdened with absentee clergy, tithe-eating laity, a swollen number of ecclesiastical officers, and parasitic lessees who lived happily on "beneficial leases" of Church lands. For Church lands, like Crown lands, were regularly leased at absurd under-rents. It was not only the State: the whole of society was top-heavy.

Moreover, and increasingly as the seventeenth century succeeded to the sixteenth, this multiplication of ever more costly offices outran the needs of State. Originally the need had created the officers; now the officers created the need. All bureaucracies tend to expand. By the process known to us as Parkinson's Law, office-holders tend to create yet more offices beneath them in order to swell their own importance or provide for their friends and kinsmen. But whereas today such inflation is curbed by the needs of the Treasury, in the sixteenth century the needs of the Treasury positively encouraged it. For offices, in the sixteenth century, were not granted freely: they were sold, and—at least in the beginning—the purchase-price went to the Crown. If the Crown could sell more and more offices at higher and higher prices, leaving the officers to be paid by the country, this was an indirect, if also a cumbrous and exasperating, way of taxing the country. Consequently, princes were easily tempted to create new offices, and to profit by the competition which forced up the price. As for the purchaser, having paid a high price, he naturally sought to raise his profits still higher, in order to recoup himself, with a decent margin, for his outlay: a decent margin with which an ambitious man might hope, in the end, to build a house like Hatfield or Knole, entertain royalty to feasts costing thousands, retain and reward an army of clients, plant exotic gardens and collect *objets d'art* and pictures.

So "the Renaissance State" consisted, at bottom, of an ever-expanding bureaucracy which, though at first a working bureaucracy, had by the end of the sixteenth century become a parasitic bureaucracy; and this ever-expanding bureaucracy was sustained on an equally expanding margin of "waste": waste which lay between the taxes imposed on the subject and the revenue collected by the Crown. Since the Crown could not afford an absolute loss of revenue, it is clear that this expansion of the waste had to be at the expense of society. It is equally clear that it could be borne only if society itself were expanding in wealth and numbers. Fortunately, in the sixteenth century, the European economy was expanding. The trade of Asia, the bullion of Africa and America, was driving the European machine. This expansion may have been uneven; there may have been strains and casualties; but they were the strains of growth, which could be absorbed, individual casualties which could be overlooked. Occasional state bankruptcies clear off old debts: they do not necessarily affect new prosperity. War increases

THE GENERAL CRISIS 63

consumption: it does not necessarily consume the sources of wealth. A booming economy can carry many anomalies, many abuses. It could even carry—provided it went on booming—the incredibly wasteful, ornamental, parasitic Renaissance court and Churches.

Provided it went on booming . . . But how long would it boom? Already, by 1590, the cracks are beginning to appear. The strains of the last years of Philip II's wars release everywhere a growing volume of complaint: complaint which is not directed against constitutional faults— against the despotism of kings or the claims of estates—but against this or that aspect or consequence of the growth and cost of a parasitic bureaucracy. For of course, although war has not created the problem, war aggravates it: the more the costs of government are raised, the more the government resorts to those now traditional financial expedients— creation and sale of new offices; sale or long lease, at under-values, of Crown or Church lands; creation of monopolies; raising of "feudal" taxes: expedients which, on the one hand, multiply the already over-grown bureaucracy and thus the cost to the country, and, on the other hand, further impoverish the Crown.

But if the strains are already obvious in the 1590s, they are, as yet, not fatal: for peace comes first. A few opportune deaths—Philip II in 1598, Queen Elizabeth in 1603—hasten the process, and throughout Europe war after war is wound up. And then, with peace, what relief! The overstrained system is suddenly relaxed, and an era of pleasure and renewed extravagance follows. Was there ever an era of such lavishness as the time between the end of Philip II's wars and the outbreak of the Thirty Years War, the time when the world was ruled, or at least enjoyed, by Philip III and the Duke of Lerma in Spain, James I and the Duke of Buckingham in England, "The Archdukes" in Flanders, Henri IV and Marie de Médicis in France? It is a world of giddy expenditure, splendid building, gigantic feasts and lavish, evanescent shows. Rubens, when he came to the Duke of Buckingham's England, marvelled at such unexpected magnificence "in a place so remote from Italian elegance." No nation in the world, said a contemporary Englishman, spent as much as we did in building. We built houses, said another, thinking of Hatfield and Audley End, "like Nebuchadnezzar's." All "the old good rules of economy," said a third, had gone packing. But the Spanish ambassador, reporting to his king these costly Jacobean festivals, would only say that no doubt they would seem very impressive "to anyone who had not seen the grandeur and state with which we do such things in Spain"—as well he might, in the days when the Duke of

Lerma, the courtier of the almost bankrupt King of Spain, went forth to meet his future queen with 34,000 ducats' worth of jewels on his person, and another 72,000 ducats' worth carried behind him.[16]

Such is the character of the Renaissance courts in their last Indian summer after the close of the sixteenth century. And even this, of course, is only the conspicuous, still sunlit tip of the iceberg whose sides are hidden from us by intervening oblivion and whose greater base was always, even at the time, submerged. How, we may ask, could it go on? Even in the 1590s, even a far less expensive, more efficient bureaucracy had been saved only by peace: how could this much more outrageous system survive if the long prosperity of the sixteenth century, or the saving peace of the seventeenth, should fail?

In fact, in the 1620s they both failed at once. In 1618 a political crisis in Prague had set the European powers in motion, and by 1621 the wars of Philip II had been resumed, bringing in their train new taxes, new offices, new exactions. Meanwhile the European economy, already strained to the limit by the habits of peacetime boom, was suddenly struck by a great depression, the universal "decay of trade" of 1620. Moreover, in those twenty years, a new attitude of mind had been created: created by disgust at that gilded merry-go-round which cost society so much more than society was willing to bear. It was an attitude of hatred: hatred of "the Court" and its courtiers, hatred of princely follies and bureaucratic corruption, hatred of the Renaissance itself: in short, Puritanism.

In England we naturally think of our own form of Puritanism: extreme Protestantism, the continuation, to unbearable lengths, of the half-completed sixteenth-century Reformation. But let us not be deceived by mere local forms. This reaction against the Renaissance courts and their whole culture and morality was not confined to any one country or religion. Like the thesis, the antithesis also is general. In England there is an Anglican Puritanism, a "Puritanism of the Right." What greater enemy had English Puritanism, as we know it, than Archbishop Laud, the all-powerful prelate who drove it to America till it returned to destroy him? And yet he too illustrates this same reaction. Did English Puritans denounce "the unloveliness of lovelocks," gay

16. *Correspondencia oficial de D. Diego Sarmiento de Acuña, conde de Gondomar*, ed. A. Ballesteros y Beretta (*Documentos inéditos para la historia de España*), III (Madrid, 1944), 232. P. Mantuano, *Casamientos de España y Francia* (Madrid, 1618), pp. 124–25, quoted in Agustín Gonzales de Amezúa, *Lope de Vega en sus cartas* (Madrid, 1935), I, 70–71.

clothes, the drinking of toasts? The archbishop forbade long hair in Oxford, reformed clerical dress, waged war on ale-houses. In Roman Catholic countries it was the same. Did the English Puritans first denounce, then close the London theatres? In Spain—even the Spain of Lope de Vega—*pragmática* after *pragmática* denounced stage plays. In France the Jansenist Pascal disliked them hardly less. In Bavaria there was a Catholic prudery, and a police enforcement of it, as disagreeable as the worst form of English Puritanism. There was the same war against luxury too. In 1624 Philip IV of Spain cut down his household, published sumptuary laws, and banished the ruff—that symbol of sartorial magnificence—from Spain by decree, from Europe by example. In France Cardinal Richelieu was doing likewise. It was a sudden war, almost a crusade, against the old Renaissance extravagance. In Flanders Rubens would find himself surviving his old Court patrons and would turn to country landscapes. Literature reflects the same change. Of Castiglione's famous manual, *The Courtier*, at least sixty editions or translations were published between 1528 and 1619; after the latter date, for a whole century, none.

In the 1620s Puritanism—this general mood of Puritanism—triumphs in Europe. Those years, we may say, mark the end of the Renaissance. The playtime is over. The sense of social responsibility, which had held its place within the Renaissance courts of the sixteenth century—we think of the paternalism of the Tudors, the "collectivism" of Philip II—had been driven out in the early seventeenth century, and now it had returned, and with a vengeance. War and depression had made the change emphatic, even startling. We look at the world in one year, and there we see Lerma and Buckingham and Marie des Médicis. We look again, and they have all gone. Lerma has fallen and saved himself by becoming a Roman cardinal; Buckingham is assassinated; Marie de Médicis has fled abroad. In their stead we find grimmer, greater, more resolute figures: the Count-Duke of Olivares, whose swollen, glowering face almost bursts from Velázquez's canvases; Strafford and Laud, that relentless pair, the prophets of Thorough in Church and State; Cardinal Richelieu, the iron-willed invalid who ruled and remade France. In literature too it is the same. The fashion has changed. After Shakespeare, Cervantes, Montaigne, those universal spirits, with their scepticism, their acceptance of the world as it is, we are suddenly in a new age: an age here of ideological revolt, Milton's "jubilee and resurrection of Church and State," there of conservative pessimism, cynicism and disillusion, of John Donne and Sir Thomas Browne, of

Quevedo and the Spanish Baroque: for the baroque age, as Mr. Gerald Brenan says, "—one cannot say it too often—was a tight, contracted age, turned in on itself and lacking self-confidence and faith in the future."[17]

Such was the mood of general, non-doctrinal, moral Puritanism which, in the 1620s, launched its attack—here from within, there from without—on the Renaissance courts. There are differences of incidence, of course, differences of personality from place to place, and these differences could be crucial—who can say what would have happened if Archbishop Laud had really been, as Sir Thomas Roe thought, "the Richelieu of England"? There were also differences in society itself. But if we look closely we see that the burden on society is the same even if the shoulders which creak under it are different. For instance, in England the cost of the Court fell most heavily on the gentry: they were the tax-paying class: wardships, purveyance and all the indirect taxes which were multiplied by the early Stuarts fell heaviest on them. On the other hand in France the *noblesse* was exempt from taxation, and the *taille* and *gabelle*, which were multiplied by the early Bourbons, fell heaviest on the peasants. No doubt English landlords could pass some of their burdens on to their tenants. No doubt impoverishment of French peasants diminished the rents of their landlords. But the difference is still significant. It was a commonplace in England, where "the asinine peasants of France," with their "wooden shoes and canvas breeches," were regularly contrasted with our own, more prosperous yeomen. It is illustrated by the ultimate result: in England, when revolution came, it was a great revolution, controlled by the gentry; in France, there were, every year for the same twenty years, revolts—little but serious revolts—of the peasants. Nevertheless, if the rebels were different, the general grievance against which they rebelled—the character and cost of the State—was the same.

For wherever we look, this is the burden of all complaints. From 1620 to 1640 this is the cry of the country, the problem of the courts. We can hear the cry from the back benches of the English parliaments in the 1620s. We can see the problem in Bacon's great essays, written between 1620 and 1625, on "Sedition and Troubles" and "The True Greatness of Kingdoms." We hear the cry in Spain in the protests of the Cortes, see the problem in the pamphlets of the *arbitristas:* Sancho

17. Gerald Brenan, *The Literature of the Spanish People* (Cambridge, 1951), p. 272.

de Moncada's *Restauración Política de España;* in Fernández Navarrete's *Conservación de monarquías* with its wonderful analysis of the social ills of Spain, and in Olivares's long memorandum to Philip IV, outlining his new programme for the country,[18] all written in the critical years 1619–21. We see it in France, above all, in the *Testament politique* of Richelieu, written in 1629 and the early 1630s, the period when governments everywhere were facing these problems, or trying to face them, before it was too late. And these demands, these problems, are not constitutional, they are not concerned with monarchy or republic, Crown or Parliament. Nor are they economic: they are not concerned with methods of production. Essentially they are demands for emancipation from the burden of centralization; for reduction of fees; reduction of useless, expensive offices, including—even in Spain—clerical offices; abolition of the sale of offices ("for whosoever doth farm or buy offices doth bind himself to be an extortioner," and "they which buy dear must sell dear"); abolition of heredity of offices; abolition of those wasteful, indirect taxes which yield so little to the Crown but on whose superabundant "waste" the ever-expanding fringe of the Court is fed.

Thus the tension between Court and country grew, and the "revolutionary situation" of the 1620s and 1630s developed. But revolutionary situations do not necessarily lead to revolutions—nor (we may add) are violent revolutions necessary in order to create new forms of production or society. Society is an organic body, far tougher, far more resilient, than its morbid anatomists often suppose. The frontiers between opposing classes are always confused by a complex tissue of interests. Office-holders and *bourgeoisie*, consumers and producers, taxgatherers and tax-payers are not neatly distinguishable classes. On the contrary, men who think of themselves as "country" at one moment often discover that they are "Court" at another, and such discoveries may lead to unpredictable apostasy. For this reason, social tensions seldom if ever lead to a clean split: rather they lead to an untidy inward crumbling whose stages are determined not by the original social tensions but by intervening political events and political errors. Therefore, if we are to carry this study further, from revolutionary situation to revolution, we must take account of these intervening events and

18. Published in A. Valladares de Sotomayor, *Semanario erudito,* XI (Madrid, 1788). I owe this reference to Mr. J. H. Elliott.

errors: events and errors which, by definition, must vary from place to place, and whose variation will explain, in part, the difference between the revolutions in those different places.

Perhaps we can see the problem best if we consider the means of avoiding revolution. If the Renaissance courts were to survive, it was clear that at least one of two things must be done. On the one hand the parasitic bureaucracies must be cut down; on the other hand the working bureaucracy must be related to the economic capacity of the country. The first programme was one of administrative, the second of economic reform. The first was easy enough to define—any country gentleman could put it in two words—but difficult to carry out: it meant the reduction of a parasitic, but living and powerful class; and although this can be done without revolution, as it was done in nineteenth-century England—one only has to read the *Extraordinary Black Book* of 1831 to see the huge parasitic fringe which had grown again around the eighteenth-century Court—it is at best a delicate and difficult operation. The second was far more difficult to define: it meant the discovery, or rediscovery, of an economic system. Nevertheless, such a definition was not beyond the wit of seventeenth-century thinkers, and in fact several thinkers did point out, clearly enough, the kind of economic system which was required.

What was that system? It was not a "capitalist" system—or at least, if it was capitalist, there was nothing new about it. It did not entail revolution or a change in method of production or in the class structure. Nor was it advocated by revolutionary thinkers: in general, those who advocated it were conservative men who wished for little or no political change. And in fact the economic programme which they advocated, though applied to modern conditions, looked back for its example. For what they advocated was simply the application to the new, centralized monarchies of the old, well-tried policy of the medieval communes which those monarchies had eclipsed: mercantilism.

For what had been the policy of the medieval cities? It had been a policy of national economy—within the limits of the city-state. The city had seen itself at once as a political and as an economic unit. Its legislation had been based on its trading requirements. It had controlled the price of food and labour, limited imports in the interest of its own manufactures, encouraged the essential methods of trade—fishing and shipbuilding, freedom from internal tolls—invested its profits not in conspicuous waste or pursuit of glory, or wars merely of plunder, but in the rational conquest of markets and the needs of national economy: in technical education, municipal betterment, poor relief. In short, the city had recognized that its life must be related to its means of livelihood. In the sixteenth-century eclipse of the cities, in their transformation into overgrown, overpopulated capitals, centres merely of exchange and consumption, much of this old civic wisdom had been forgotten. Now, in the seventeenth-century eclipse of the spendthrift Renaissance Courts, it was being remembered. The economists wished to go farther: to reapply it.

Of course, they would reapply it in changed circumstances, to different national forms. The princes, it was agreed, had done their work: it could not be reversed. The new nation-states had come to stay. But, said the reformers, having come, let them now apply to their different conditions the old good rules of the cities. Let them not merely pare down the parasitic fringe that had grown around them, but also relate their power, in a positive sense, to economic aims. Let them favour a gospel of work instead of aristocratic, or pseudo-aristocratic *hidalguía*. Let them protect industry, guarantee food-supplies, remove internal tolls, develop productive wealth. Let them rationalize finance and bring down the apparatus of Church and State to a juster proportion. To reverse the Parkinson's Law of bureaucracy, let them reduce the hatcheries which turned out the superfluous bureaucrats: grammar schools in England, colleges in France, monasteries and theological seminaries in Spain. Instead, let them build up local elementary education: skilled workers at the base of society now seemed more important than those unemployable university graduates, hungry for office, whom the new Renaissance foundations were turning out. "Of grammar-schools," declared that great intellectual, Sir Francis Bacon, "there are too many": many a good ploughboy was spoiled to make a bad scholar; and he and his followers advocated a change in the type of education or the diversion of funds to elementary schools. Of colleges, declared the founder of the French Academy, Cardinal Richelieu, there are too many: the commerce of letters, if unchecked, would banish absolutely that of merchandise "which crowns states with riches" and ruin agriculture "the true nursing-mother of peoples." Of monasteries, declared the Catholic Council of Castile in 1619, there are too many, and it prayed that the Pope be asked to authorize their reduction, for although the monastic state is no doubt, for the individual, the most perfect, "for the public it is very damaging and prejudicial." Monasteries, protested the Cortes of Castile, have outgrown the needs of religion: they now contain persons "rather fleeing from necessity to the delights of indolence than moved by devotion." So, in country after country, the protest was raised. It was the backswing of the great educational impulse of the Renaissance and Reformation, the great religious impulse of the Counter-Reformation.[19]

To cut down the oppressive, costly sinecures of Church and State, and to revert, *mutatis mutandis*, to the old mercantilist policy of the cities, based on the economic interest of society—such were the two essential methods of avoiding revolution in the seventeenth century. How far were either of them adopted in the states of western Europe? The answer, I think, is instructive. If we look at those states in turn, we may see, in the extent to which either or both of these policies were adopted or rejected, some partial explanation of the different forms which the general crisis took in each of them.

In Spain neither policy was adopted. It was not for lack of warning. The Cortes of Castile, the Council of State, the *arbitristas*, individual statesmen continually pressed both for reduction of officers and clergy and for a mercantilist policy. In 1619 Philip III was urged to abolish, as a burden to society, the hundred *receptores* newly created six years earlier, even though that should mean repaying the price at which they had bought their offices. In the same year the greatest of Spanish ambassadors, Gondomar, whose letters show him to have been a consistent mercantilist, wrote that Church and Commonwealth were both endangered by the multiplication of clergy "since the shepherds now outnumber the sheep"; and he added that the same was true in the State, where "ministers of justice, *escribanos*, *comisarios* and *alguaziles*" were multiplying fast, but there was no increase of "ploughmen, ships or trade."[20] Two years later, under the pressure of economic crisis and the renewal of war, it seemed that something would at last be done. The reign of Philip IV began with the famous *capítulos de reformación*. The number of royal officers was fixed by law. Next year the king declared that since an excessive number of offices is pernicious in the State

---

19. For Bacon's proposal see his *Works*, ed. Spedding, IV, 249 ff.; for Richelieu, his *Testament politique*, ed. Louis André, pp. 204–5; for Spain the *Consulta del Consejo Supremo de Castilla*, published in P. Fernández Navarrete, *Conservación de monarquías* (Madrid, 1947, Biblioteca de Autores Españoles, XXV), p. 450; *Actas de las Cortes de Castilla*, XXII, 434, etc.

20. *Correspondencia oficial de* . . . II (Madrid, 1943), 140. Cf. the other letters of Gondomar printed in Pascual Gayangos, *Cinco cartas político-literarias de D. Diego Sarmiento, conde de Gondomar* (Madrid: Sociedad de Bibliófilos, IV, 1869).

("most of them being sold, and the officers having to make up the price they have paid"), and since a great number of *escribanos* is prejudicial to society ("and the number at present is excessive, and grows daily") the number of *alguaciles, procuradores* and *escribanos* in Castile must be reduced to one-third, and recruitment must be discouraged by various means.[21] For a moment, it seemed that the problem was to be faced. The leaders of the war-party themselves, implicitly, recognized the cause of Spain's weakness. The purpose of *las Pazes*—the successive treaties of peace in 1598, 1604, 1609—they said, had been to repair the strength of Spain; but in fact peace had strengthened the mercantilist Dutch and only weakened bureaucratic Spain.[22] Now war was necessary to redress the balance; but even to make war the structure of society must be reformed; the bureaucratic state had failed alike as a system of peace and as a system of war.

So spoke the reformers of the 1620s. But their voice was soon stifled, for there was no social or institutional force behind them to make their protest effective. The Castilian middle class was weak and penetrated by office-holders; the power of the old Cortes towns had been suppressed in their last rising against the Burgundian State a century before; and the Cortes of Castile was now an aristocratic body which hardly sought to do more than demur. Besides, war, which exposed the economic weakness of the bureaucratic system, equally prevented any reform of that system. A few reforms were attempted, or at least enacted on paper;[23] but the mood soon changed. The need for immediate funds caused the government to exploit the existing machinery, not to reform it for the sake of future efficiency. So all the projects of the reformers were soon forgotten, and in 1646 the Cortes of Castile would draw attention to their failure. In spite of all those protests and those efforts, offices had not diminished during the war: they had multiplied. Instead of one president and three councillors of the Treasury, there were now three presidents and eleven councillors; instead of three *contadores* and a *fiscal*, there were now fourteen *contadores;* in-

21. Archivo Histórico Español, *Colección de documentos inéditos para la historia de España y de sus Indias,* v (Madrid, 1932), 28, 281, etc.

22. A. Rodriguez Villa, *Ambrósio Spínola, primer marqués de los Balbases* (Madrid, 1904), pp. 342–48, 382 ff.; J. Carrera Pujal, *Historia de la economía española* (Barcelona, 1943), I, 485 ff.; Pascual de Gayangos, *Cinco cartas político-literarias.*

23. For a summary of these reforms see H. Bérindoague, *Le Mercantilisme en Espagne* (Bordeaux, 1929), pp. 85–104.

stead of four councillors at war there were now more than forty; and all these, salaried or unsalaried (for their salaries, their "fees," were anyway trifles), had entertainment, expenses, lodgings, privileges and perquisites at the expense of the subject.[24] The weight of this burden might have been redistributed a little within the country, but it had certainly not been reduced.[25] Nor had the Spanish economy been enabled to bear it. For meanwhile the national wealth of Spain had not increased: it had diminished. The voices of the mercantilists were stifled. The trade of Spain was taken over almost entirely by foreigners. The vitality of the country was crushed beneath the dead weight of an unreformed *ancien régime*. It was not till the next century that a new generation of *arbitristas*—philosophers inspired by English and French examples—would again have the strength and spirit to urge on a new dynasty the same reforms which had clearly but vainly been demanded in the days of Philip III and Philip IV.[26]

Very different was the position in the emancipated northern Netherlands. For the northern Netherlands was the first European country to reject the Renaissance Court, and the Court they rejected was their own Court, the greatest, most lavish Court of all, the Burgundian Court which, with the abdication of Charles V, had moved and made itself so fatally permanent in Spain. The revolt of the Netherlands in the sixteenth century was not, of course, a direct revolt of society against the Court. That is not how revolutions break out. But in the course of the long struggle the Court itself, in those provinces which freed themselves, was a casualty. There the whole apparatus of the Burgundian Court simply dissolved under the stress of war. So did the Burgundian Church, that huge, corrupt department of State which Philip II unskilfully sought to reform and whose abuses the great patrons of revolt, in the beginning, were seeking to preserve. Whatever

24. *Consulta* of the Cortes of Castile, 18 Aug. 1646, printed in Alonso Núñez de Castro, *Libro historico-politico, solo Madrid es Corte*, 2nd ed. (Madrid, 1669), pp. 84 ff. This whole book, first published in 1658, illustrates the process I am describing.

25. For the factual (though not legal) redistribution of fiscal burdens in Spain under Philip IV, see A. Domínguez Ortiz, "La desigualdad contributiva en Castilla en el siglo XVIII," in *Anuario de historia del derecho español*, 1952.

26. For these *arbitristas* of the eighteenth century, see Jean Sarrailh, *L'Espagne éclairée* (Paris, 1954): which does not, however, bring out the extent to which Ward, Jovellanos, Campomanes, etc., were repeating the programme of the early seventeenth-century Spanish mercantilists—e.g., of Sancho de Moncada, whose work (originally dedicated to Philip III in 1619) was reprinted, dedicated to Ferdinand VI, in 1746.

the causes or motives of the revolution, the United Provinces emerged from it incidentally disembarrassed of that top-heavy system whose pressure, a generation later, would create a revolutionary situation in other countries. Consequently, in those provinces, there was no such revolutionary situation. The new Court of the Princes of Orange might develop some of the characteristics of the old Court of the dukes of Burgundy, but only some: and as it started lean, it could better afford a little additional fat. There were crises no doubt in seventeenth-century Holland—the crises of 1618, of 1650, of 1672: but they were political crises, comparable with our crisis not of 1640 but of 1688; and they were surgically solved for the same reason: the social problem was no longer acute: the top-heavy apparatus of the State had been purged: society beneath was sound.

Moreover, if accident rather than design had rid the United Provinces of the Renaissance State, policy had also achieved there the other, economic reform of which I have written. It was not that there was a *bourgeois* or "capitalist" revolution in Holland.[27] Dutch industry was relatively insignificant. But the new rulers of Holland, seeking the means of guarding their hard-won freedom, set out to imitate the fortune and the methods of those older mercantile communities which had preserved their independence through centuries by rationally combining commercial wealth and maritime power. By adopting the techniques of Italy, welcoming the *émigré* experts of Antwerp, and following the old good rules of Venetian policy, Amsterdam became, in the seventeenth century, the new Venice of the north. The economic originality of seventeenth-century Holland consisted in showing that, even after the victory and reign of the Renaissance princes, whom they alone had driven out, the mercantilism of the cities was not dead: it could be revived.

Midway between completely unreformed Spain and completely reformed Holland lies what is perhaps the most interesting of all examples, Bourbon France. For France, in the seventeenth century, was certainly not immune from the general crisis, and in the Frondes it had a revolution, if a relatively small revolution. The result was, as in

27. That the economy of the United Provinces was not a new, revolutionary form of capitalism, but a return to the system of the medieval Italian cities, is argued by Mr. Jelle C. Riemersma in his article "Calvinism and Capitalism in Holland, 1550–1650," in *Explorations in Entrepreneurial History*, I (1), 8, and is admitted even by Marxists like Mr. Dobb and Mr. Hobsbawm. Mr. Hobsbawm indeed goes so far as to call the Dutch economy "a feudal business economy" (*Past and Present*, no. 6, 1954).

Spain, a victory for the monarchy. Triumphant over its critics and adversaries, the monarchy of the *ancien régime* survived in France, and survived for another century and a half. On the other hand the French monarchy of Louis XIV was not like the Spanish monarchy of Philip IV and Charles V. It was not economically parasitic. Industry, commerce, science flourished and grew in France, in spite of the "failure" of the *"bourgeois* revolution," no less than in England, in spite of its "success." To all appearances, in 1670, in the age of Colbert, absolutism and the *ancien régime* were perfectly compatible with commercial and industrial growth and power.

And indeed, why not? For what had hindered such growth in the past, what had caused the crisis in society, was not the form of government, but its abuses; and though these abuses might be removed by revolution, or might fall as incidental casualties of a revolution, their removal did not necessarily require revolution. There was always the way of reform. It is not necessary to burn down the house in order to have roast pig. And although France (like Holland) had had a fire in the sixteenth century, in which some of its burden of waste matter had been incidentally consumed, it did also, in the years thereafter, achieve some measure of reform. The fire, indeed, had prepared the ground. The French civil wars of the sixteenth century, if they had done much harm, had also done some good. They had burnt up the overgrown patronage of the great nobles and reduced the patronage of the Court to the patronage of the king. Henri IV, like the Prince of Orange, like Charles II of England after him, found himself at his accession disembarrassed of much ancient parasitism: he could therefore afford to indulge a little new. And on this basis, this *tabula partim rasa*, he was able to achieve certain administrative changes. The *Paulette*, the law of 1604 which systematized the sale of offices, did at least regulate the abuses which it has often, and wrongly, been accused of creating. Sully, by his *économies royales*, did keep down the waste around the throne. And Richelieu, in the 1630s, not only meditated a complete mercantilist policy for France: he also, even in the midst of war, succeeded— as Laud and Olivares, whether in peace or war, did not—in regulating that most expensive, most uncontrollable of all departments, the royal household.[28] Thanks to these changes, the *ancien régime* in France was

---

28. For Richelieu's mercantilism see H. Hauser, *La Pensée et l'action économique du cardinal de Richelieu* (Paris, 1944). For his reform of the royal household, see M. Roland Mousnier's article in vol. 1 of *Histoire de France*, ed. M. Reinhard (Paris, 1955).

repaired and strengthened. The changes may not have been radical, but they were enough—at least for the time being.

Of course the French solution was not permanent. The advantage of the French government, in the early seventeenth century, was simply that it had shed some of its burdens: it was less encumbered than the Spanish by the inheritance of the past. In the course of time the old weight would soon be resumed: the later reign of Louis XIV would be notorious for its plethora of offices and benefices, multiplied deliberately in order to be sold. And even in the earlier years, the pressure of war had the same effect. Again and again, as in Spain, there were demands that the venality of office be reformed or abolished; again and again the government considered such reform; but in the end, on each occasion, the French monarchy, like the Spanish, faced with the demands of war, postponed its projects and instead of reforming, positively strengthened the system.[29] Richelieu at first, like Olivares in Spain, sought to combine war and reform, but in the end (again like Olivares) sacrificed reform to war. Marillac would have sacrificed war to reform.[30] By the end of the seventeenth century, Louis XIV would be financing his wars by massive creations of useless offices. But at the beginning of the century the position was different. Richelieu and Mazarin no doubt had other advantages in their successful struggle to maintain the French *ancien régime* in the era of the Huguenot revolt and the Frondes. They had an army absolutely under royal control; they had taxes whose increase fell not on gentry, assembled and vocal in Parliament, but on scattered, inarticulate peasants; and they had their own political genius. But they had also an apparatus of state which had already undergone some salutary reform: a State which, in the mind of Richelieu and in the hands of his disciple Colbert, could become a mercantilist State, rationally organized for both profit and power.

Finally there is England. In England the Crown had not the same political power as in France or Spain, and the taxes fell on the gentry, powerful in their counties and in Parliament. In England therefore, it was doubly important that the problem be faced and solved. How far was it in fact faced? To answer this question let us look in turn at the two sides of the problem, administrative and economic.

In the sixteenth century the apparatus of the English State had

29. See Roland Mousnier, *La Vénalité des offices sous Henri IV et Louis XIV* (Rouen, n.d.), *passim*.

30. See Georges Pagès, "Autour du Grand Orage," in *Revue historique*, 1937.

neither suffered nor benefited from any such destructive accident as had befallen Holland or France. The Renaissance Court of the Tudors, whose parsimony under Elizabeth had been so unreal and whose magnificence and ceremony had so impressed foreign visitors, survived intact into the new century, when its cost and show were magnified beyond all measure by King James and his favourites. Already in 1604, Francis Bacon warned the new king of the danger. The Court, he said, was like a nettle: its root, the Crown itself, was "without venom or malignity," but it sustained leaves "venomous and stinging where they touch."[31] Two years later, King James' greatest minister, Robert Cecil, Earl of Salisbury, apprehended revolution against the same burden of the Court; and in 1608, on becoming Lord Treasurer, he applied all his energies to a large and imaginative solution of the whole problem. He sought to rationalize the farming of taxes and the leasing of Crown lands, to reform the royal household, liberate agriculture from feudal restrictions and abolish archaic dues in exchange for other forms of income whose full yield, or something like it, instead of a mere fraction, would come to the Crown. In 1610 Salisbury staked his political career on this great programme of reorganization. But he failed to carry it through. The "courtiers," the "officers" who lived on the "waste," mobilized opposition, and the king, listening to them, and thinking "not what he got but what he might get" out of the old, wasteful, irritant sources of revenue, refused to surrender them. Within two years of his failure, Salisbury died, out of favour with the king, completely unlamented, even insulted by the whole Court which he had sought to reform and, by reform, to save.[32]

After Salisbury, other reformers occasionally took up the cause. The most brilliant was Francis Bacon. He had been an enemy of Salis-

---

31. Francis Bacon, *Works*, ed. Spedding, III, 183.

32. Public justice has never been done to Salisbury's programme of reform in 1608-12, although the "Great Contract," which was only part of it, is well known. The evidence of it is scattered among the official papers of the time. Of contemporaries, only Sir Walter Cope and Sir William Sanderson, both of whom had been employed in it, sought to make it known and understood, but neither Cope's *Apology for the Late Lord Treasurer* (which was given to the king in manuscript) nor Sanderson's *Aulicus Coquinariae* was published at the time. Lord Ellesmere, Bishop Goodman and Sir Henry Wotton also appreciated it, but also did not publish their appreciation. See L. Pearsall Smith, *Life and Letters of Sir Henry Wotton* (1907), II, 487–89; Goodman, *The Court of King James I*, I, 36–42; and Ellesmere's paper entitled *Il dì loda la sera* in Huntington Library, Ellesmere MS. 1203.

bury, but once Salisbury was dead he sang the same tune. He diagnosed the evil—no man, perhaps, diagnosed it so completely in all its forms and ultimate consequences—but he could do nothing to cure it except by royal permission, which was refused, and he was overthrown. After his fall, in the years of the great depression, even the Court took alarm, and a new reformer seemed to have obtained that permission. This was Lionel Cranfield, Earl of Middlesex, who set out to carry through some at least of Salisbury's proposals. But permission, if granted, was soon, and conspicuously withdrawn. Cranfield, like Bacon, was ruined by Court faction, led from above by the royal favourite, the Duke of Buckingham, the universal manager and profiteer of all those marketable offices, benefices, sinecures, monopolies, patents, perquisites and titles which together constituted the nourishment of the Court. Thus when Buckingham was murdered and Strafford and Laud, the "Puritans of the right," came to power, they inherited from him an utterly unreformed Court.[33]

Did they do anything to reform it? Ostensibly they did. "The face of the court," as Mrs. Hutchinson wrote, "was changed." King Charles was outwardly frugal compared with his father: but such frugality, as we have seen in the case of Queen Elizabeth, was relatively insignificant. Laud and Strafford waged war on the corruption of the Court, whenever they perceived it; but they left the basic system untouched. Whenever we study that system we find that, in their time, its cost had not been reduced: it had grown. The greatest of Court feasts in Buckingham's days had been his own entertainment of the king in 1626, which had cost £4000; the Earl of Newcastle, in 1634, went up to £15,000. An office which was sold for £5000 in 1624 fetched £15,000 in 1640. Wardships, which had brought in £25,000 to the Crown when Salisbury had sought to abolish them in 1610, were made to yield £95,000 in 1640. And the proportion that ran to waste was no smaller. For every £100 which reached the Crown, at least £400 was taken from the subject. As Clarendon says, "The envy and reproach came to the King, the profit to other men."

33. Bacon's projects are scattered through his writings, which Spedding collected. One only has to compare his various proposals for reform of the Court, the law, education, the Church, the Crown estates, etc., with the demands of the radical party in the 1640s, to see the truth of Gardiner's statement (in *Dictionary of National Biography*, s.v. Bacon) that his programme, if carried out, might have prevented the revolution. For Cranfield's work, see R. H. Tawney, *Business and Politics under James I* (1958), Menna Prestwich, *Cranfield* (Oxford, 1966).

Thus in 1640 the English Court, like the Spanish, was still unreformed. But what of the English economy? Here the parallel no longer holds. For in England there was not that absolute divorce between Crown and *arbitristas* that was so obvious in Spain. The early Stuart governments did not ignore matters of trade. They listened to the City of London. By their financial methods, whether deliberately or not, they encouraged the formation of capital, its investment in industry. There were limits, of course, to what they did. They did not satisfy the systematic mercantilist theorists. They paid less attention to the base of society than to its summit. Nevertheless, in many respects, they favoured or at least allowed a mercantilist policy. They sought to naturalize industrial processes; they sought to protect supplies of essential raw-materials; they sought to monopolize the herring-fisheries; they protected navigation; they preferred peace abroad and looked to their moat. The years of their rule saw the growth of English capitalism, sponsored by them, on a scale unknown before. Unfortunately such growth entailed dislocation, claimed victims; and when political crisis increased the dislocation and multiplied the victims, the stiff and weakened structure of government could no longer contain the mutinous forces which it had provoked.

For in 1640 the leaders of the Long Parliament did not seek — they did not need to seek — to reverse the economic policy of the Crown. They sought one thing only: to repair the administration. The Earl of Bedford as Lord Treasurer, John Pym as Chancellor of the Exchequer, intended to resume the frustrated work of Salisbury: to abolish monopolies, wardships, prerogative taxes, cut down the "waste," and establish the Stuart Court on a more rational, less costly basis. Having done this, they would have continued the mercantilist policy of the Crown, perhaps extending it by redistribution of resources, and rationalization of labour, at the base of society. They would have done for the English monarchy what Colbert would do for the French. All they required was that the English monarchy, like the French, would allow them to do it.

For, of course, monarchy itself was no obstacle. It is absurd to say that such a policy was impossible without revolution. It was no more impossible in 1641 than it had been in the days of Salisbury and Cranfield. We cannot assume that merely human obstacles — the irresponsibility of a Buckingham or a Charles I, the reckless obscurantism of a Strafford — are inherent historical necessities. But in fact these human obstacles did intervene. Had James I or Charles I had the intelligence of Queen Elizabeth or the docility of Louis XIII, the English *ancien régime* might have adapted itself to the new circumstances as peacefully in the seventeenth century as it would in the nineteenth. It was because they had neither, because their Court was never reformed, because they defended it, in its old form, to the last, because it remained, administratively and economically as well as aesthetically, "the last Renaissance Court in Europe," that it ran into ultimate disaster: that the rational reformers were swept aside, that more radical men came forward and mobilized yet more radical passions than even they could control, and that in the end, amid the sacking of palaces, the shivering of statues and stained-glass windows, the screech of saws in ruined organ-lofts, this last of the great Renaissance Courts was mopped up, the royal aesthete was murdered, his splendid pictures were knocked down and sold, even the soaring gothic cathedrals were offered up for scrap.

So, in the 1640s, in war and revolution, the most obstinate and yet, given the political structure of England, the frailest of the Renaissance monarchies went down. It did not go down before a new "*bourgeois* revolution." It did not even go down before an old "mercantilist revolution." Its enemies were not the "*bourgeoisie*"—that *bourgeoisie* who, as a Puritan preacher complained, "for a little trading and profit" would have had Christ, the Puritan soldiers, crucified and "this great Barabbas at Windsor," the king, set free.[34] Nor were they the mercantilists. The ablest politicians among the Puritan rebels did indeed, once the republic was set up, adopt an aggressive mercantilist policy; but in this they simply resumed the old policy of the Crown and, on that account, were promptly attacked and overthrown by the same enemies, who accused them of betraying the revolution.[35] No, the triumphant enemies of the English Court were simply "the country": that indeterminate, unpolitical, but highly sensitive miscellany of men who had mutinied not against the monarchy (they had long clung to monarchist beliefs), nor against economic archaism (it was they who were the archaists), but

34. The preacher was Hugh Peter, as quoted in *State Trials*, v (1), 129–30.

35. Those who regard the whole revolution as a *bourgeois* revolution on the strength of the mercantile policy of the Rump between 1651 and 1653 might well reflect (*a*) that this policy, of peace with Spain, navigation acts, and rivalry with Holland over fishery and trade, had been the policy of Charles I in the 1630s, and (*b*) that it was repudiated, emphatically and effectively, by those who had brought the revolution to a "successful" issue—the Puritan army—and only revived at the Restoration of the monarchy.

against the vast, oppressive, ever-extending apparatus of parasitic bureaucracy which had grown up around the throne and above the economy of England. These men were not politicians or economists, and when the Court had foundered under their blows, they soon found that they could neither govern nor prosper. In the end they abdicated. The old dynasty was restored, its new mercantilist policy resumed. But the restoration was not complete. The old abuses, which had already dissolved in war and revolution, were not restored, and, having gone, were easily legislated out of existence. In 1661 Salisbury's "Great Contract," Bedford's excise, were at last achieved. The old prerogative courts—whose offence had been not so much their policy as their existence—were not revived. Charles II began his reign free at last from the inherited lumber of the Renaissance Court.

Such, as it seems to me, was "the general crisis of the seventeenth century." It was a crisis not of the constitution nor of the system of production, but of the State, or rather, of the relation of the State to society. Different countries found their way out of that crisis in different ways. In Spain the *ancien régime* survived: but it survived only as a disastrous, immobile burden on an impoverished country. Elsewhere, in Holland, France and England, the crisis marked the end of an era: the jettison of a top-heavy superstructure, the return to responsible, mercantilist policy. For by the seventeenth century the Renaissance Courts had grown so great, had consumed so much in "waste," and had sent their multiplying suckers so deep into the body of society, that they could flourish only for a limited time, and in a time, too, of expanding general prosperity. When that prosperity failed, the monstrous parasite was bound to falter. In this sense, the depression of the 1620s is perhaps no less important, as a historical turning-point, than the depression of 1929: though itself only a temporary economic failure, it marked a lasting political change.

At all events, the princely Courts recognized it as their crisis. Some of them sought to reform themselves, to take physic and reduce their bulk. Their doctors pointed the way: it was then that the old city-states, and particularly Venice, though now in decadence, became the admired model, first of Holland, then of England. And yet, asked the patient, was such reform possible, or even safe? Could a monarchy really be adapted to a pattern which so far had been dangerously republican? Is any political operation more difficult than the self-reduction of an established, powerful, privileged bureaucracy? In fact, the change was nowhere achieved without something of revolution. If it was limited in

France, and Holland, that was partly because some of the combustible rubbish had already, in a previous revolution, been consumed. It was also because there had been some partial reform. In England there had been no such previous revolution, no such partial reform. There was also, under the early Stuarts, a fatal lack of political skill: instead of the genius of Richelieu, the suppleness of Mazarin, there was the irresponsibility of Buckingham, the violence of Strafford, the undeviating universal pedantry of Laud. In England, therefore, the storm of the mid-century, which blew throughout Europe, struck the most brittle, most overgrown, most rigid Court of all and brought it violently down.

3 | The European Witch-craze of the Sixteenth and Seventeenth Centuries

I

The European witch-craze of the sixteenth and seventeenth centuries is a perplexing phenomenon: a standing warning to those who would simplify the stages of human progress. Ever since the eighteenth century we have tended to see European history, from the Renaissance onwards, as the history of progress, and that progress has seemed to be constant. There may have been local variations, local obstacles, occasional setbacks, but the general pattern is one of persistent advance. The light continually, if irregularly, gains at the expense of darkness. Renaissance, Reformation, Scientific Revolution mark the stages of our emancipation from medieval restraints. This is natural enough. When we look back through history we naturally see first those men, those ideas, that point forward to us. But when we look deeper, how much more complex the pattern seems! Neither the Renaissance nor the Reformation nor the Scientific Revolution are, in our terms, purely or necessarily progressive. Each has a Janus-face. Each is compounded both of light and of darkness. The Renaissance was a revival not only of pagan letters but of pagan mystery-religion. The Reformation was a return not only to the unforgettable century of the Apostles but also to the unedifying centuries of the Hebrew kings. The Scientific Revolution was shot through with Pythagorean mysticism and cosmological fantasy. And beneath the surface of an ever more sophisticated society what dark passions and inflammable credulities do we find, sometimes accidentally released, sometimes deliberately mobilized! The belief in witches is one such force. In the sixteenth and seventeenth centuries it was not, as the prophets of progress might suppose, a lingering ancient superstition, only waiting to dissolve. It was a new explosive force, constantly and fearfully expanding with the passage of time. In those years of apparent illumination there was at least one-quarter of the sky in which darkness was positively gaining at the expense of light.

Yes, gaining. Whatever allowance we may make for the mere multiplication of the evidence after the discovery of printing, there can be no doubt that the witch-craze grew, and grew terribly, after the Renaissance. Credulity in high places increased, its engines of expression were made more terrible, more victims were sacrificed to it. The years 1550–1600 were worse than the years 1500–1550, and the years 1600–1650 were worse still. Nor was the craze entirely separable from the intellectual and spiritual life of those years. It was forwarded by the cultivated popes of the Renaissance, by the great Protestant reformers, by the saints of the Counter-Reformation, by the scholars, lawyers and churchmen of the age of Scaliger and Lipsius, Bacon and Grotius, Bérulle and Pascal. If those two centuries were an age of light, we have to admit that, in one respect at least, the Dark Age was more civilized.

For in the Dark Age there was at least no witch-craze. There were witch-beliefs, of course—a scattered folk-lore of peasant superstitions: the casting of spells, the making of storms, converse with spirits, sympathetic magic. Such beliefs are universal, in time and place, and in this essay I am not concerned with them. I am concerned with the organized, systematic "demonology" which the medieval Church constructed out of those beliefs and which, in the sixteenth and seventeenth centuries, acquired a terrible momentum of its own. And when we make this necessary distinction between the organized witch-craze and the miscellaneous witch-beliefs out of which it was constructed, we have to admit that the Church of the Dark Age did its best to disperse these relics of paganism which the Church of the Middle Ages would afterwards exploit. Of course it was not entirely successful. Some of the pagan myths, like pagan gods and pagan rites, had crept into the Christian synthesis at an early date and had found lodgment in its outer crannies. St. Augustine in particular, with his baroque mind and African credulity, did much to preserve them: they form an incidental bizarre decoration of the huge doctrinal construction which his authority launched into western Christendom. But in general, the

Church, as the civilizer of nations, disdained these old wives' tales. They were the fragmentary rubbish of paganism which the light of the Gospel had dispelled.

So, in the eighth century, we find St. Boniface, the English apostle of Germany, declaring roundly that to believe in witches and were-wolves is unchristian.[1] In the same century Charlemagne decreed the death penalty for anyone who, in newly converted Saxony, burnt supposed witches. Such burning, he said, was "a pagan custom."[2] In the next century St. Agobard,[3] Bishop of Lyon, repudiated the belief that witches could make bad weather, and another unknown Church dignitary declared that night-flying and metamorphosis were hallucinations and that whoever believed in them "is beyond doubt an infidel and a pagan." This statement was accepted into the canon law and became known as the *canon Episcopi* or *capitulum Episcopi*.[4] It remained the official doctrine of the Church. In the eleventh century the laws of King Coloman of Hungary declined to notice witches "since they do not exist,"[5] and in the twelfth century John of Salisbury dismissed the idea of a witches' sabbat as a fabulous dream.[6] In the succeeding centuries, when the craze was being built up, all this salutary doctrine would have to be reversed. The laws of Charlemagne and Coloman would be forgotten; to deny the reality of night-flying and metamorphosis would be officially declared heretical; the witches' sabbat would become an objective fact, disbelieved only (as a doctor of the Sorbonne would write in 1609[7]) by those of unsound mind; and the ingenuity of churchmen

1. Sermon xv, cited in *Materials toward a History of Witchcraft collected by H. C. Lea*, arranged and edited by Arthur C. Howland, with an introduction by George Lincoln Burr (New York, 1957), pp. 178–82; hereafter cited as Lea, *Materials*. (See also below, p. 91.)

2. *Capitulatio de Partibus Saxoniae*, cap. 6. This decree, issued at Paderborn in A.D. 785, is printed in Wilhelm Boudriot, *Die alt-germanische Religion (Untersuchungen zur allgemeinen Religionsgeschichte*, ed. Carl Clemen, Heft 2, Bonn, 1928, p. 53).

3. In his *Liber contra insulsam vulgi opinionem de grandine et tonitruis*, written *c.* A.D. 820.

4. Lea, *Materials*, pp. 178–82.

5. Ibid., p. 1252.

6. Ibid., p. 172.

7. *Joannis Filesaci Theologi Parisiensis Opera Varia*, 2nd ed. (Paris, 1614), pp. 703 ff., "de Idololatria Magica Dissertatio," Dedication.

and lawyers would be taxed to explain away that inconvenient text of canon law, the *canon Episcopi*.

By the end of the Middle Ages this reversal would be complete. By 1490, after two centuries of research, the new, positive doctrine of witchcraft would be established in its final form. From then on it would be simply a question of applying this doctrine: of seeking, finding and destroying the witches whose organization has been defined.

The monks of the late Middle Ages sowed: the lawyers of the sixteenth century reaped; and what a harvest of witches they gathered in! All Christendom, it seems, is at the mercy of these horrifying creatures. Countries in which they had previously been unknown are now suddenly found to be swarming with them, and the closer we look, the more of them we find. All contemporary observers agree that they are multiplying at an incredible rate. They have acquired powers hitherto unknown, a complex international organization and social habits of indecent sophistication. Some of the most powerful minds of the time turn from the human sciences to explore this newly discovered continent, this America of the spiritual world. And the details which they discover, and which are continually being confirmed by teams of parallel researchers—field researchers in torture-chamber or confessional, academic researchers in library or cloister—leave the facts more certainly established and the prospect more alarming than ever.

Consider the situation as shown at any time in the half-century from 1580 to 1630: that half-century which corresponds with the mature life of Bacon and brings together Montaigne and Descartes. The merest glance at any report by the acknowledged experts of the time reveals an alarming state of affairs. By their own confession, thousands of old women—and not only old women—had made secret pacts with the Devil, who had now emerged as a great spiritual potentate, the Prince of Darkness, bent on recovering his lost empire. Every night these ill-advised ladies were anointing themselves with "devil's grease," made out of the fat of murdered infants, and, thus lubricated, were slipping through cracks and keyholes and up chimneys, mounting on broomsticks or spindles or airborne goats, and flying off on a long and inexpressibly wearisome aerial journey to a diabolical rendezvous, the witches' sabbat. In every country there were hundreds of such sabbats, more numerous and more crowded than race-meetings or fairs. There were no less than 800 known meeting-places in Lorraine alone. Some countries had national, some international centres. Such were the Blocksberg or Brocken in the Harz Mountains of Germany, the "delicate large meadow" called Blåkulla in Sweden and the great resort of La Hendaye in south-west France where no less than 12,000 witches would assemble for the gathering known as the *Aquelarre*. The meetings too were remarkably frequent. At first the interrogators in Lorraine thought that they occurred only once a week, on Thursday; but, as always, the more the evidence was pressed, the worse the conclusions that it yielded. Sabbats were found to take place on Monday, Wednesday, Friday and Sunday, and soon Tuesday was found to be booked as a by-day. It was all very alarming and proved the need of ever greater vigilance by the spiritual police.

And what happened when the witch had reached the sabbat? The unedifying details, alas, were only too well authenticated. First, she was surprised to observe nearly all her friends and neighbours, whom she had not previously suspected to be witches. With them there were scores of demons, their paramours, to whom they had bound themselves by the infernal pact; and above all, dominating them all, was the imperious master of ceremonies, the god of their worship, the Devil himself, who appeared sometimes as a big, black, bearded man, more often as a stinking goat, occasionally as a great toad. Those present recognized their master. They all joined to worship the Devil and danced around him to the sound of macabre music made with curious instruments—horses' skulls, oak-logs, human bones, etc. Then they kissed him in homage, under the tail if he were a goat, on the lips if he were a toad. After which, at the word of command from him, they threw themselves into promiscuous sexual orgies or settled down to a feast of such viands as tempted their national imagination. In Germany these were sliced turnips, parodies of the Host; in Savoy, roast or boiled children; in Spain, exhumed corpses, preferably of kinsfolk; in Alsace, fricassées of bats; in England, more sensibly, roast beef and beer. But these nice distinctions of diet made little difference: the food, all agreed, was cold and quite tasteless, and one necessary ingredient, salt, for some arcane demonological reason, was never admitted.

Such was the witches' sabbat, the collective orgy and communal religious worship of the new diabolical religion. In the intervals between these acts of public devotion, the old ladies had, of course, good works to do in the home. They occupied themselves by suckling familiar spirits in the form of weasels, moles, bats, toads or other convenient creatures; by compassing the death of their neighbours or their neighbours' pigs; by raising tempests, causing blights or procuring impotence in bridegrooms; and as a pledge of their servitude they were constantly having sexual intercourse with the Devil, who appeared (since even he abhors unnatural vice[8]) to she-witches as an *incubus*, to he-witches as a *succubus*.

What Gibbon called "the chaste severity of the Fathers" was much exercised by this last subject, and no detail escaped their learned scrutiny. As a lover, they established, the Devil was of "freezing coldness" to the touch; his embrace gave no pleasure—on the contrary, only pain; and certain items were lacking in his equipment. But there was no frigidity in the technical sense: his attentions were of formidable, even oppressive solidity. That he could generate on witches was agreed by some doctors (how else, asked the Catholic theologians, could the birth of Luther be explained?); but some denied this, and others insisted that only certain worm-like creatures, known in Germany as *Elben*, could issue from such unions. Moreover, there was considerable doubt whether the Devil's generative power was his own, as a Franciscan specialist maintained ("under correction from our Holy Mother Church"), or whether he, being neuter, operated with borrowed matter. A nice point of theology was here involved and much interested erudition was expended on it in cloistered solitudes. Some important theologians conjectured that the Devil equipped himself by squeezing the organs of the dead. This view was adopted (among others) by our King James.[9] Other experts advanced other theories, more profound than decent. But on the whole, Holy Mother Church followed the magisterial ruling of the Angelic Doctor, St. Thomas Aquinas, who, after St. Augustine, must be regarded as the second founder of demonological science. According to him, the Devil could discharge as *incubus* only what he had previously absorbed as *succubus*. He therefore nimbly alternated between these postures . . . There are times when the intellectual fantasies of the clergy seem more bizarre than the psychopathic delusions of the madhouse out of which they have, too often, been excogitated.

Such were the human witches, the fifth column of Satan on earth, his front-line agents in the struggle for control of the spiritual world. All through the sixteenth century, and for much of the seventeenth, men believed in the reality of this struggle. Laymen might not accept

8. Except, apparently, in Alsace. See R. Reuss, *L'Alsace au 17ᵉ siècle* (Paris, 1898), II, 106. Elsewhere "the nobleness of his nature" repudiates it (Lea, *Materials*, pp. 161, 380).

9. James VI, *Demonologie, in form of a Dialogue* . . . (Edinburgh, 1597), pp. 66 ff.

all the esoteric details supplied by the experts, but they accepted the general truth of the theory, and because they accepted its general truth, they were unable to argue against its more learned interpreters. So the experts effectively commanded the field. For two centuries the clergy preached against witches and the lawyers sentenced them. Year after year inflammatory books and sermons warned the Christian public of the danger, urged the Christian magistrate to greater vigilance, greater persecution. Confessors and judges were supplied with manuals incorporating all the latest information, village hatreds were exploited in order to ensure exposure, torture was used to extract and expand confessions, and lenient judges were denounced as enemies of the people of God, drowsy guardians of the beleaguered citadel. Perhaps these "patrons of witches" were witches themselves. In the hour of danger, when it almost seemed that Satan was about to take over the world, his agents were found to be everywhere, even in judges' seats, in university chairs and on royal thrones.

But did this campaign against the witches in fact reduce their number? Not at all. The more fiercely they were persecuted, the more numerous they seemed to become. By the beginning of the seventeenth century the witch-doctors have become hysterical. Their manuals have become encyclopaedic in bulk, lunatic in pedantry. They demand, and sometimes achieve, wholesale purges. By 1630 the slaughter has broken all previous records. It has become a holocaust in which lawyers, judges, clergy themselves join old women at the stake. That at least, if nothing else, must have enforced an agonizing reappraisal.

And indeed, it was in the wake of the greatest of all purges—perhaps in revulsion after it—that the solidity of the witch-hunters began to give way. In the middle of the seventeenth century—in the 1650s—scepticism, unavailing hitherto, begins at last to break through. Imperceptibly, the whole basis of the craze begins to dissolve, in Catholic and Protestant countries alike. By the 1680s the battle is effectively won, at least in the west. The old habits of mind may linger on; there will be pockets of resistance here and there, recurrence of persecution now and then, but somehow the vital force behind it is spent. Though the argument may go on, the witch-trials and witch-burnings have become once again mere sporadic episodes, as they had been before the Renaissance. The rubbish of the human mind which for two centuries, by some process of intellectual alchemy and social pressure, had become fused together in a coherent, explosive system, has disintegrated. It is rubbish again.

How are we to explain this extraordinary episode in European history? In the eighteenth century, when the men of the Enlightenment looked back on this folly of "the last age," they saw it merely as evidence of the "superstition" from which they had recently been emancipated, and the nineteenth-century historians, who approached it in a more detached, scientific spirit, interpreted their more abundant material in the same general terms. To the German Wilhelm Gottlieb Soldan,[10] the first historian of the craze, the witch-cult was a legacy of Greco-Roman antiquity, naturally developed, artificially preserved. To him, as to the Englishman W. E. H. Lecky, its gradual conquest was one aspect of the rise of "rationalism" in Europe.[11] To the American Andrew Dickson White it was a campaign in "the warfare of science with theology."[12] But none of these scholars sought to explain why the centuries of Renaissance and Reformation were so much less "rational," less "scientific" than the Dark and early Middle Ages. Even the profoundest of nineteenth-century historians of witchcraft, Joseph Hansen, the liberal, free-thinking archivist of Cologne, hardly faced this problem. In two important works[13] he collected a mass of documentary material and presented a lucid narrative of "the rise of the great witch-craze"; but as he aimed only to document its origins, he concluded his work once he had brought it to the early sixteenth century, when "the system of the new witch-craze had achieved its final form."[14] The fact that, in this final form, the craze was to last for two centuries, and those the centuries of Renaissance, Reformation and experimental science, did

---

10. W. G. Soldan, *Geschichte der Hexenprozesse* (Stuttgart, 1843). Soldan's pioneering work has been twice reprinted, each time with substantial additions and revisions: first by his own son-in-law Heinrich Heppe in 1879; secondly, under the double name of Soldan-Heppe, by Max Bauer in 1911. The differences between the first and the last edition are so great that in this essay I shall always distinguish them, citing the original work as Soldan and the later edition as Soldan-Heppe.

11. W. E. H. Lecky, *History of the Rise and Influence of the Spirit of Rationalism in Europe* (1865). My references to this work will be to the edition of 1900.

12. A. D. White, *A History of the Warfare of Science with Theology in Christendom* (New York, 1897).

13. Joseph Hansen, *Quellen und Untersuchungen zur Geschichte des Hexenwahns und der Hexenverfolgung im Mittelalter* (Bonn, 1901); *Zauberwahn, Inquisition und Hexenprozess im Mittelalter* (Munich, 1900); hereafter cited as *Quellen* and *Zauberwahn* respectively.

14. Hansen, *Zauberwahn*, p. 473.

indeed perplex him. He suggested that the explanation lay in the survival of "the medieval spirit." This answer, says the modern historian of magic, is "unconvincing."[15] But is his own explanation any more convincing? The witch-craze, says Lynn Thorndike (echoing Michelet[16]), grew naturally out of the misery of the fourteenth century, that century of the Black Death and the Hundred Years War. These disasters no doubt helped; but they do not explain. As Hansen had already observed, the craze gathered force before either of them had begun, and it continued, in its "final form," for two centuries after both were over: two centuries not of misery, but of European recovery and expansion.

While Hansen was writing about the witch-craze in Germany, another great historian was thinking about it in America. In his youth H. C. Lea had begun a work on "man's assumed control over spiritual forces" in which he hoped to deal with the whole question of witchcraft in the world; but illness interrupted it, and he afterwards deviated into what he described as the "bypath" of "a simpler and less brain-fatiguing amusement." In other words, he wrote his two monumental works on the medieval and the Spanish Inquisition.[17] But the Inquisition cannot be divorced from the subject of witchcraft and in both works Lea found himself brought up against it. In his history of the medieval Inquisition, he showed the gradual merging of sorcery and heresy, and in his Spanish studies he showed that in Spain, "thanks to the good sense of the Inquisition," the witch-craze "was much less dreadful than in the rest of Europe." It was not till he was eighty-one that Lea returned to his original subject. He collected, annotated and arranged a vast mass of material covering the whole history of witchcraft in Christendom; but when he died, the book itself was unwritten. His material, however, has been edited and published,[18] and his interpretation is clear from his notes, as also from his earlier works.

Lea is one of the greatest of liberal historians. It is inconceivable that his work on the Inquisition, as an objective narrative of fact, will ever be replaced. Its solidity has withstood all partisan criticism. His

---

15. Lynn Thorndike, in *Cambridge Medieval History*, VIII, § xxii, 686–87.

16. Jules Michelet, *La Sorcière* (Paris, 1862). My references are to the edition Garnier-Flammarion, 1966.

17. H. C. Lea, *The History of the Inquisition in the Middle Ages* (London and New York, 1888); *The History of the Inquisition in Spain* (New York, 1906).

18. See above, p. 85, n. 1.

"History of Witchcraft," had it been written, would no doubt have stood as firm. Nevertheless, as interpreters of social history, even the greatest of the nineteenth-century liberal historians now seem to date. Their philosophy was formed in the happy years before 1914, when men could look back on the continuous progress, since the seventeenth century, of "reason," toleration, humanity, and see the constant improvement of society as the effect of the constant progress of liberal ideas. Against such a background it was natural to see the witch-craze of the past, like the persecution of Moors and Jews, or the use of torture, or the censorship of books, as a residue of mere obscurantism which growing enlightenment had gradually dispelled, and which would now never return.

Unfortunately, we have seen them return. With the advantage of after-knowledge, we look back and we see that even while the liberal historians were writing, their olympian philosophy was being threatened from beneath. It was in the 1890s that the intellectual foundations of a new witch-craze were being laid. It was then that *The Protocols of the Elders of Zion* were forged in France and the grotesque mythology of anti-semitism was used to inspire the pogroms of eastern Europe. To the liberals of the time this new form of superstition was beneath contempt. At most, it was a lingering survival of past superstition. We who have seen its vast and hideous consequences cannot accept so comforting an explanation. Faced by the recrudescence, even in civilized societies, of barbarous fantasies in no way less bizarre and far more murderous than the witch-craze, we have been forced to think again, and thinking, to devalue the power of mere thought. Even intellectual history, we now admit, is relative and cannot be dissociated from the wider, social context with which it is in constant interaction.

This being so, we are prepared to admit, as our ancestors were not, that mental structures differ with social structures, that the "superstition" of one age may be the "rationalism" of another and that the explanation of intellectual change may have to be sought outside purely intellectual history. We cannot see the long persistence and even aggravation of the witch-craze merely as a necessary effect of clerical domination, or its dissolution as the logical consequence of release from religious fundamentalism. Therefore we may be forgiven for looking at this whole episode, whose basic facts, thanks to the work of our predecessors, are not in dispute, with eyes different from theirs. They saw, through all the centuries, a continuous dialogue between superstition, whose form constantly varied, and reason, which was always the same.

We agree with one of the most perceptive and philosophical of modern French historians, that the mind of one age is not necessarily subject to the same rules as the mind of another, that "dans sa structure profonde, la mentalité des hommes les plus éclairés de la fin du XVIe siècle, du début du XVIIe siècle, ait différé, et radicalement, de la mentalité des hommes les plus éclairés de notre temps."[19]

II

When Hansen wrote that the system of the new witch-craze had achieved its final form by the 1480s, he was referring to the two documents of that decade from which the centralized European witch-craze, as distinct from spasmodic local outbursts, can be dated. The first of these is the papal bull *Summis Desiderantes Affectibus*, issued by Pope Innocent VIII in December 1484, deploring the spread of witch-craft in Germany and authorizing his beloved sons, the Dominican inquisitors Heinrich Institor (Krämer) and Jakob Sprenger, to extirpate it. The second is the earliest great printed encyclopaedia of demonology, the *Malleus Maleficarum*, "the Hammer of Witches," published by these same two inquisitors two years later, in 1486. The relationship between these two documents is perfectly clear: they are complementary one to the other. The papal bull had been solicited by the inquisitors, who wished for support in their attempt to launch the witch-hunt in the Rhineland. Having obtained it, they printed it in their book, as if the book had been written in response to the bull. The book thus advertised to all Europe both the new epidemic of witchcraft and the authority which had been given to them to suppress it.

The importance of the papal bull of 1484 is incontestable. Apologists for the papacy have protested that it made no change: it was merely a routine document which authorized the Dominicans to go on doing what they were already doing and told other authorities—bishops and secular powers—not to obstruct their work.[20] No doubt it did this; but it also did something else, which was new. What the Dominicans had been doing hitherto was local. They had been persecuting and burning

19. L. Fèbvre, "Sorcellerie: sottise ou révolution mentale," in *Annales: économies, sociétés, civilisation*, 1948, p. 14.

20. This is the argument of Ludwig Pastor, *History of the Popes*, v, 2nd English ed. (1901), 347.

witches locally. From now on a general mandate was given, or implied. And the *Malleus*, which is inseparable from the bull, gave force and substance to that mandate. First, by its content, by gathering together all the curiosities and credulities of Alpine peasants and their confessors, it built up a solid basis for the new mythology. Secondly, by its universal circulation, it carried this mythology, as a truth recognized by the Church, over all Christendom. Finally, the *Malleus* explicitly called on other authorities, lay and secular, not merely not to obstruct, but positively to assist the inquisitors in their task of exterminating witches. From now on, the persecution, which had been sporadic, was—at least in theory—made general, and secular authorities were encouraged to use the methods and mythology of the Inquisition. Rome had spoken.

Why did Rome speak? Why did Innocent VIII, that worldly humanist, the patron of Mantegna and Pinturicchio, Perugino and Filippino Lippi, yield to these fanatical Dominican friars? The answer, obviously, is not to be sought in his personality. It is to be sought rather in circumstances: in the historical situation out of which the witch-beliefs had arisen and in the war which the Dominican inquisitors had long been waging against them. This question brings us at once to a particular area, the area in which these beliefs had always been endemic and in which, for two centuries, they had already been persecuted: the mountain areas of Catholic Europe, the Alps and the Pyrenees.

The mountain origin of the witch-craze is by now well established. So are the circumstances in which it was formulated, and in which the Dominicans came to be its great adversaries. These circumstances bring us back to the very foundation of the order, in the struggle between the Catholic Church and the heretics of the twelfth century, the Albigensians of Languedoc and the Vaudois of the Alps. It was to combat these heretics that the Inquisition and the Dominican order had been founded, and it was in the course of that "crusade" that the inquisitors had discovered, beneath the forms of one heresy, the rudiments (as they thought) of another. From an early date, therefore, they had pressed the Pope to grant them jurisdiction over witchcraft as well as over recognized theological heresy. To the Dominicans the two forms of error were inseparable: one continued the other, and the pursuit must not cease when the formal error had disappeared underground. They could still recognize it by its smell. So, although the form might seem to change, the old names persisted. By the fifteenth century we hear little of Vaudois or Cathari as theological terms: those errors had been burnt out, at least for a time. But in the Alps, in the Lyonnais and in

Flanders witches are known as *Waudenses* and their gatherings as a *Valdesia* or *Vauderye*, and in the Pyrenees we find them described as *Gazarii* or "Cathars."[21]

When the Dominicans pressed for inquisitorial power over witchcraft, the papacy had at first resisted. The old canons of the Church, and particularly the *canon Episcopi*, denied the reality of witches and forbade their persecution. Therefore, in 1257, Pope Alexander IV had refused these demands unless manifest heresy, not merely witchcraft, could be proved. But little by little, under constant pressure, the papacy had yielded. The great surrender had been made by the French popes of Avignon, and particularly by the two popes from southern France, John XXII and his successor Benedict XII, who had already, as bishops in Languedoc, waged war on nonconformity in the old Albigensian and Vaudois areas. John XXII, who declared heretical the Franciscan doctrine of the poverty of Christ (so dangerously akin to the old Vaudois ideas), also, by his constitution *Super illius specula* of 1326, authorized the full use of inquisitorial procedure against witches, of whom he lived in personal terror. For the next century and a half — until the Witch Bull of Innocent VIII, and indeed afterwards — the main effort of the inquisitors (although there were some spectacular "political" witchcraft trials in France, Burgundy and England) had been directed against the witches of the Alps and the Pyrenees.

At first the campaign was most vigorous in the Pyrenees. From the papacy of John XXII onwards, witch-trials were held all over the old Albigensian territory; but soon they spread to the Alps also. The sitting of the Council of the Church in Basel in 1435–1437 gave a great opportunity to the local witch-hunters, and it was in those years that a zealous inquisitor, John Nider, wrote what has been called "the first popular essay on witches."[22] It was called *Formicarius*, "the Ant-heap," and was based principally on confessions of Swiss witches collected by a Swiss magistrate, Peter of Berne. The *Formicarius* may be regarded as a little *Malleus*, and it had a similar effect in a more restricted field. Papal instructions were sent out to the witch-inquisitors to redouble their zeal, and in 1440, the deposed Pope Eugenius IV took the opportunity to de-

---

21. For instances of the use of the term *Vauderye*, see especially Hansen, *Quellen*, pp. 408–15; *Zauberwahn*, pp. 409–18. For *Gazarii*, see *Quellen*, pp. 118, 232.

22. G. L. Burr, "The Literature of Witchcraft," in *George Lincoln Burr: his Life and Selections from his Writings* (Ithaca, N.Y., 1943), p. 166. This volume will hereafter be cited as Burr, *Life*.

nounce his rival, "that eldest son of Satan, Amadeus, Duke of Savoy" — that is, the successful anti-Pope Felix V — as having given himself over to the witches "or Vaudois" who abound in his land.[23] In the next hundred years some famous inquisitors were busy in the Alpine valleys — Bernard of Como, Jerome Visconti, Bartolomeo Spina. In 1485, according to the *Malleus*, the inquisitor of Como burnt forty-one witches, all of whom confessed to sexual intercourse with *incubi*, and yet even so the practice was increasing. This was the point of time at which the Witch Bull and the *Malleus* were published.

Meanwhile the Pyrenean inquisitors, after a temporary lull, had resumed their activities. In 1450 they too produced a little *Malleus*. This was a tract by Jean Vineti, Dominican inquisitor of Carcassonne: the first work, it seems, to declare that witchcraft was a new heresy, unconnected with the old rural beliefs which the Church of the past had tolerated. This separation of the new witchcraft from the old was a point of great technical importance. Indeed, we can say that it gave the witch-craze its charter: for it enabled the inquisitors to get round the greatest obstacle in the way of witch-persecution: the *canon Episcopi*.[24] About the same time witch-beliefs were found to have spread to the Spanish slopes of the Pyrenees and the King of Castile was invited to take action against them.[25]

Thus by the time that the authors of the *Malleus* obtained the blessing of Pope Innocent VIII, the craze had already been in operation for nearly two centuries in the mountain areas, the old homes of heresy and centres of inquisitorial persecution. The two authors of the *Malleus*, the solicitors of the bull, were themselves natives of the Alpine regions, and all their examples and cases are drawn from upper Germany. The most active of the pair was Krämer, who was inquisitor in the Tyrol; he afterwards became inquisitor in Bohemia and Moravia, where he acted vigorously against the "Waldenses" of Bohemia as well as against witches.[26]

The Alps and the Pyrenees, the original cradle of the witch-craze,

23. Hansen, *Quellen*, p. 18.

24. For Vineti's *Tractatus contra Daemonum Invocatores*, see Lea, *Materials*, p. 272.

25. Julio Caro Baroja, *Las brujas y su mundo*, Madrid, 1961 (English trans. N. Glendinning, *The World of the Witches*, 1964, pp. 103, 143–45).

26. For the history of the *Malleus* and its authors, see Hansen, *Quellen*, pp. 360–407, *Zauberwahn*, pp. 473 ff.

would long remain its base. Individual witches, of course, might be found anywhere, and in certain circumstances might infect whole areas: for the old unorganized superstitions of the countryside were always there, always ready to be inflamed. Isolated rural societies anywhere — in the dreary flats of the Landes in France, or of Essex in England, or in the sandy plain of north Germany — would always be subject to witch-beliefs. Psychopathic disturbances, which could easily be rationalized as witchcraft, are independent of geography. Individual inquisitors, too, would discover or create beliefs in any area in which they happened to operate: Krämer and Sprenger would have plenty of counterparts among the Protestant clergy — and among the laity too, like Matthew Hopkins, the famous "witch-finder general" of the English civil war. But these are secondary developments, individual extensions. As a continuing social phenomenon, involving not merely individuals but whole societies, the witch-craze would always be associated particularly with the highlands. The great European witch-hunts would centre upon the Alps and their foothills, the Jura and the Vosges, and upon the Pyrenees and their extensions in France and Spain. Switzerland, Franche-Comté, Savoy, Alsace, Lorraine, the Valtelline, the Tyrol, Bavaria and the north Italian bishoprics of Milan, Brescia and Bergamo; Béarn, Navarre and Catalonia: these would be the primary centres. Here the new heresy had been discovered, hence it would be generalized. From the fantasies of mountain peasants, the Dominicans elaborated their systematic demonology and enabled or compelled Renaissance popes to denounce a new heresy in Europe. The heads of the old Albigensian and Vaudois heresy were sprouting again.

This prevalence of witchcraft, and of illusions that can be interpreted as witchcraft, in mountainous areas doubtless has a physical explanation. Rural poverty, as Michelet observed, naturally drives men to invoke the spirits of revenge.[27] The thin air of the mountains breeds hallucinations, and the exaggerated phenomena of nature — the electric storms, the avalanches, the cracking and calving of the mountain ice — easily lead men to believe in demonic activity.[28] But these explanations, by themselves, are not enough. Rural poverty, after all, was a commonplace of all centuries. So, no doubt, were some of the beliefs that it engenders. The superstitions of the mountain are but exaggerations of

27. "D'où date la sorcière? Je dis sans hésiter, des temps du désespoir." Jules Michelet, *La Sorcière*, Introduction.

28. Cf. Hansen, *Zauberwahn*, pp. 400–402; Lea, *Materials*, p. 245.

the superstitions of the plain. Why then, we ask, did the Dominicans wage such war on them? Why did they insist on seeing them as something different from the superstitions which, in the plain, the Church had so long tolerated or ignored? What was the underlying, permanent difference which the Dominicans rationalized as successive layers of "heresy"?

Sometimes, no doubt, it was a difference of race. The Basques, for instance, were racially distinct from the latinized Germans—Franks and the Visigoths—around them. But difference of race, though it may sharpen other differences, is not in itself decisive. It is only when it corresponds with difference of social organization that conflict or incompatibility arises; and then it is the social difference which decides. In the Middle Ages the men of the mountains differed from the men of the plains in social organization, and therefore they also differed in those customs and patterns of belief which grow out of social organization and, in the course of centuries, consecrate it. Theirs, we may almost say, were different civilizations.

Medieval civilization, "feudal" civilization, was a civilization of the plains, or at least of the cultivated lands which could sustain the manor and its organization. In the poor mountain areas, pastoral and individualist, this "feudalism" had never fully established itself. Sometimes Christianity itself had hardly penetrated thither, or at least it had not been maintained there in comparable form. Missionaries might have carried the Gospel into the hills, but a settled Church had not institutionalized it, and in those closed societies a lightly rooted orthodoxy was easily turned to heresy or even infidelity. M. Fernand Braudel, in his incomparable work on the Mediterranean, has commented, briefly but brilliantly, on this fact. He has pointed to isolated mountain societies long untouched, or only superficially touched, by the religion of state and easily—if as superficially—converted to the heresy of new evangelists or the religion of a sudden conqueror. The conversion of the mountains to Christianity—or, for that matter, to Islam—(he writes) was far from complete in the sixteenth century; and he refers to the Berbers of the Atlas mountains, and the highland Kurds in Asia, so slowly won for Mohammed, "while the highlands of Spain will preserve the religion of the Prophet in Christian Spain and the wild Alps of Lubéron protect the lingering faith of the Vaudois." [29]

29. Fernand Braudel, La Méditerranée et le monde méditerranéen à l'époque de Philippe II (Paris, 1949), pp. 12–15.

The mountains, then, are the home not only of sorcery and witch-craft, but also of primitive religious forms and resistance to new orthodoxies. Again and again they have to be won back to sound religion; for missionaries come and go and the established Church does not easily take root in such poor soil. We see this in England, where the north and west, "the dark corners of the realm," would have to be re-evangelized by Puritan missionaries a century after the Reformation, and in Scotland, where the Highlands would relapse into "paganism" and would need to be recovered by a new Puritan movement in the eighteenth century. What would happen in Britain after the Reformation had happened in Europe before it. The Dominicans were the evangelists of the "dark corners" of Europe where the Catholic Church was not permanently established. As such they carried the gospel of "feudal" Christian Europe into the unfeudal, half-Christian societies of the mountains, and inevitably, in that different world, found that their success was transitory: that ancient habits of thought reasserted themselves, that social incompatibility clothed itself in religious heresy, and that when formal heresy had been silenced or burnt out, the same fundamental incompatibility took, or seemed to take, another form. The old rural superstition, which had seemed harmless enough in the interstices of known society, assumed a more dangerous character when it was discovered, in strange, exaggerated form, among the barely subdued "heretics" of the highlands. Thanks to that social gulf, that social unassimilability, witchcraft became heresy.

Once we see the persecution of heresy as social intolerance, the intellectual difference between one heresy and another becomes less significant. Innocent VIII was the persecutor of Bohemian Hussites and Alpine "Vaudois" as well as of witches, just as John XXII had persecuted Fraticelli as well as witches. Social persecution is indivisible, or at least does not stop at mere intellectual frontiers. But if we wish to see this point more strikingly illustrated, it is useful to turn from one form of Inquisition to another. Only four years before the worldly, humanist Pope, Innocent VIII, yielded to the German Dominicans and launched his bull against the witches of Germany, his predecessor, the even more worldly humanist Pope Sixtus IV, had yielded to the Spanish Dominicans and approved the new Inquisition in Spain. It is difficult entirely to separate these two gestures, so close in time, so similar in consequence, so distinct in place and circumstance; and in fact, by looking at them together, we may be able to shed some light upon them both.

For the Spanish Inquisition, like the medieval Inquisition, was ostensibly set up to deal with formal heresy, and therefore neither the Jews nor the Moors of Spain, at the time of its creation, were subject to it. Heresy is a crime of Christians: the Jews and Moors were then "unbelievers." But gradually both Jews and Moors were brought under the control of this organ of social conformity, just as witches had been brought under the control of the medieval Inquisition. The witches had been brought under this control by the device of an extended definition of heresy; the Jews and Moors were brought under that of the Spanish inquisitors by the device of compulsory conversion to Christianity. In both cases the engine of persecution was set up before its future victims were legally subject to it. In both cases, once legally subject to it, the original pretext of their subjection was forgotten. Both witches and converted Jews were first subjected to the Inquisition as heretics; but before long both were being burnt without reference to ideas, the former as witches, the latter as Jews.

Moreover, in both cases the persecutors were the same. It was the Dominicans who, from the start, had persecuted the witches in the Alps and the Pyrenees. It was the Dominicans also who, with some help from the Franciscans, had been the great persecutors of the Jews. This too had been, at first, a sporadic persecution. It had broken out in Germany during the Black Death, when the Jews were accused of poisoning the wells and were burnt in hundreds by angry crowds and petty magistrates. It had broken out in Italy, where the stern Franciscan St. Bernardino of Siena had inflamed the mobs against the usurious crucifiers of Christ. From 1391 pogroms had been constant in Spain where the Catalan demagogue, the Franciscan St. Vicente Ferrer, had rivalled the exploits of St. Bernardino in Italy. The establishment of the Inquisition in Spain was a triumph of the Spanish Dominicans, the expulsion of the unconverted Jews (which left the rest of them subject to the Inquisition) a triumph for the Franciscan Cardinal Ximénez. Both these campaigns can be seen as part of a general evangelical crusade by the friars. That crusade would culminate, in the reign of Innocent VIII's successor, Alexander VI, with the attack on the "pagan" papacy itself by the Dominican friar Savonarola.

The similarity between the persecution of Jews and the persecution of witches, which reached their climax in different places at the same time, suggests yet again that the pressure behind both was social. The witch and the Jew both represent social nonconformity. At first both are persecuted sporadically, without much reason given; for the witch is not condemned by the old law of the Church, and the Jew, as an unbeliever, is outside it. Then legal grounds are devised to prosecute both: the former by a redefinition of terms, the latter by enforced baptism, is made liable to a charge of heresy. Finally, when that charge is no longer convenient, it is no longer used. The witch, as we shall see, is persecuted simply for "being a witch," the Jew for "being a Jew," for reasons not of belief but of blood, for defect of *limpieza de sangre*. Thus the reasons vary but the persecution continues: clear evidence that the real reason lies deeper than the reason given.

Moreover, it sometimes seems that these two types of social nonconformity are interchangeable. In its periods of introversion and intolerance Christian society, like any society, looks for scapegoats. Either the Jew or the witch will do, but society will settle for the nearest. The Dominicans, an international order, hate both; but whereas in the Alps and Pyrenees they pursue witches, in Spain they concentrate on Jews. It is not that there are no witches in Spain. The Pyrenees, after all, are as much Spanish as French, and in the fourteenth and fifteenth centuries, when the Roman Inquisition operated in Aragon, the witches of northern Spain supplied many of its victims. The earliest of all general treatises on witchcraft was written in 1359 by a Dominican inquisitor-general in Aragon,[30] and in the next century Spanish witches—*bruxas* and *xorguinas*—gave as much trouble to the champions of orthodoxy as Spanish Jews.[31] Numerous works on demonology were produced in Spain in the fifteenth and early sixteenth centuries, and Spanish expertise in such matters was exported to other countries.[32] But once the Inquisition had been firmly established, the local order of priority asserted itself. With Jews and Moors on their hands, the inquisitors had very little time for witches, and so they have won glowing tributes for their "firmness" and "temperate wisdom" in this respect.[33]

30. Nicolas Eymeric, *Tractatus contra Daemonum Invocatores* (see Lea, *The Inquisition in the Middle Ages*, II, 175).

31. See, for instance, Hansen, *Quellen*, pp. 71, 124, 238–39, 246–51. The Spanish Franciscan Alonso de Espina, in his *Fortalicium Fidei* (Nuremberg, 1494), denounces Jews and witches (whom he calls by their Spanish names) with equal ferocity.

32. Thus at the end of the sixteenth century Juan Maldonado and Martín del Rio, both Spaniards, taught demonology in France and Flanders respectively, and in the mid-seventeenth century we find the Spanish terms, *xurguminae* and *bruxae*, used in a work published in Hungary (J. C. Mediomontanus, *Disputatio Theologica de Lamiis et Veneficis*, Grosswardein, 1656, cited in Lea, *Materials*, p. 1254).

33. Lea, *History of the Inquisition in Spain*, IV, 217–18. For witchcraft cases in Spain

In Germany, on the other hand, the priorities are reversed. There, outside the Alpine regions, there is little or no persecution of witches in the fourteenth and early fifteenth centuries; but those are the years of terrible anti-Jewish pogroms. About 1450 the inquisitors begin to extend the witch-hunt down the Rhine, and this, of course, is the immediate purpose of the *Malleus*.[34] In the sixteenth century the witch gradually replaces the Jew, and in the seventeenth the reversal is almost complete. If the universal scapegoat of the Black Death in Germany had been the Jew, the universal scapegoat of the Wars of Religion will be the witch. There were exceptions to this generalization, of course. The Rostock jurist Dr. Gödelmann, for instance, at the end of the sixteenth century, evidently hated Jews more than the witches about whom he explicitly wrote. He would suspend his liberal utterances about the latter in order to vent his hatred of the former: a blasphemous, impious race rightly expelled from their dominions by many Christian rulers.[35] Perhaps he was merely behind the times. And really good Germans (like Luther) would contrive to hate both together: at the close of the sixteenth century the Catholic Elector of Trier and the Protestant Duke of Brunswick would set out to exterminate both. But in general the emphasis fell either on one or on the other. In our own days it has fallen back upon the Jews.

This interchangeability of victims, which suggests that both Jews and witches were persecuted rather as types of social nonconformity than for doctrinal or other given reasons, can be illustrated in many ways. In medieval Hungary, for instance, witches were sentenced, for a first offence, to stand all day in a public place, wearing a Jew's hat.[36] Witchcraft was one of the charges often made against the Jews. But the neatest instance of alternative priorities between the same two social groups is shown by the events on either side of the Pyrenees in the years 1609–10.

In those years there was a sudden panic of denunciation in the old

---

outside the Basque provinces, see also Sebastián Cirac Estopañán, *Los procesos de hechicerías en la inquisición de Castilla la Nueva* (Madrid, 1942) and the excellent introduction by Agustín Gonzales de Amezúa to his edition of Cervantes, *El casamiento engañoso y el coloquio de los perros* (Madrid, 1912).

34. Soldan-Heppe, I, 229, 245–46.

35. J. G. Gödelmann, *de Magis, Veneficis et Lamiis . . . Libri III* (Frankfurt, 1591), pp. 51–54.

36. Lea, *Materials*, p. 1253.

kingdom of Navarre, which had once straddled the Pyrenees but was now divided into two parts, one governed from Paris, the other from Madrid. The King of France, Henri IV, who was also King of Navarre, in response to the clamour of the noblemen and syndics of the Pays de Labourd, issued a commission to the president of the parlement of Bordeaux and to the counsellor of the parlement, Pierre de l'Ancre, to deal with the matter. In four months these energetic officials, both bigoted Catholics, burnt nearly a hundred witches, including several priests. But in describing his triumphs afterwards, and in denouncing the practices which he and his colleague had so gloriously repressed, de l'Ancre did not stop at witches. A whole section of his work is devoted to denunciation of the Jews: their absurd and indecent rites and beliefs, their cruelty, their greed, their poisoning of Christian wells, their forcible circumcision and ritual murder of Christian children. The Jews, says de l'Ancre, "by their filth and stink, by their sabbaths and synagogues," are so disgusting to God that he has not only withdrawn from them his grace and his promise: he has also condemned them to creep about the world "like poor snakes," deprived of every kind of office, dignity or public employment. The Jews, he adds, are ordinarily great magicians: they turn themselves into wolves by night; they can never be converted into good Christians. In other words, they behave just like witches.[37]

Thus in French Navarre the stereotype of the enemy of society is the witch: but the Jew is not forgotten. He comes second, to take the fag-end of persecution, or at least of denunciation. On the Spanish side of the Pyrenees the persecution is no less, but the order of priority is reversed. There in this same year, 1609, the Inquisition had achieved one of its great triumphs: the expulsion from Spain, as unassimilable heretics, of the whole Morisco population. Next year, in 1610, the Inquisition in Navarre, where there were no Moriscos, dealt with its local tensions. At a great *auto-de-fé* in Logroño, fifty-three persons were presented. Many of them were Jews, but no less than twenty-nine were presented as witches. But when the Spanish Inquisition reached the humble category of witches, its appetite was already slaked. Of those twenty-nine, six were burnt alive; another six, having died in prison, were burnt in effigy. The remaining eighteen, having confessed and repented, were spared. As Lea remarks, under any other jurisdiction they would have been burnt. And even this relatively merciful sentence led

---

37. Pierre de l'Ancre, *L'Incrédulité et mescréance du sortilège pleinement convaincue* (Paris, 1622), pp. 446–501.

to a commission of inquiry which concluded, in effect, that all witch-craft was an illusion, so that Spanish witches enjoyed thereafter an even greater immunity. As Michelet wrote, the Spanish Inquisition, "exter-minatrice pour les hérétiques, cruelle pour les Maures et les Juifs, l'était bien moins pour les sorciers." Having chosen its victims elsewhere, it could afford to overlook the base, even bestial deviations of Pyrenean goatherds.[38]

So, in 1609-10, as in 1478-84, the persecution of witches can be seen as part of the same process as the persecution of Jews. That perse-cution was not doctrinal: it was not (whatever excuse might be given) because the victims were "heretics." It was not launched merely by the personal decision of a bigot in the papal chair. Neither Sixtus IV nor Innocent VIII was a bigot—nor were Leo X and Clement VII, the Medici popes, who continued the process. Nor was the established Church bigoted. In general the established Church is opposed to the persecution. In the 1480s the established authorities—bishops and sec-ular clergy as well as princes and city governments—disliked it. The authors of the *Malleus* found themselves obstructed by the ecclesias-tical establishment in Germany and they were reduced to forging the approbation of the University of Cologne.[39] The Archbishop of Trier resisted the bull, declaring that there were no witches in his diocese.[40] (A century later it would be very different.) Even when the persecu-tion was in full swing, the distinction is still perceptible. The Galli-can Church would oppose it in France,[41] the Anglican Church in En-gland,[42] the Catholic Church at its headquarters, Rome.[43] The pressure throughout came from a lower level, from the missionary orders who moved among the people, on the sensitive social frontier between dif-fering communities, whether in the heart of a multi-racial society, as in

38. Lea, *History of the Inquisition in Spain*, iv, 225-39; Jules Michelet, *La Sorcière*, p. 172.

39. See the careful examination by Hansen (summarized in Lea, *Materials*, pp. 337 ff.).

40. Soldan-Heppe, ii, 1.

41. Lea, *Materials*, p. 1287.

42. See below, p. 130-31.

43. Practically no witches were burnt in Rome in the whole period of the witch-craze. See Nikolaus Paulus, *Hexenwahn und Hexenprozess, vornehmlich im 16ten Jahr-hundert* (Freiburg-im-Breisgau, 1910), pp. 260 ff.

Spain, or in frontier areas, the areas of missionary activity. The popes might authorize, but the pace was set by the tribunes of the people, and the tribunes in their turn responded to popular pressure, seeking a scapegoat for social frustration.

For no ruler has ever carried out a policy of wholesale expulsion or destruction without the co-operation of society. To think otherwise, to suppose that a ruler, or even a party in the state, can thus cut out part of the living tissue of society without the consent of society, is to defy the lesson of history. Great massacres may be commanded by tyrants, but they are imposed by peoples. Without general social support, the organs of isolation and expulsion cannot even be created. The social resentment of the Spanish *pueblo*, not the bigotry of Spanish kings, lay behind the foundation of the Spanish Inquisition. Spanish society approved the persecution of the Jews and welcomed the expulsion of the Moriscos. French society applauded the massacre of the Huguenots in 1572 and their expulsion in 1685. German society supplied Hitler with the means of destroying the Jews. Afterwards, when the mood has changed, or when the social pressure, thanks to that blood-letting, no longer exists, the anonymous people slinks away, leaving public responsibility to the preachers, the theorists and the rulers who demanded, justified and ordered the act. But the historian must present to it too its share of the account. Individually that share may be infinitesimal but collectively it is the largest of all. Without the tribunes of the people, social persecution cannot be organized. Without the people, it cannot be conceived.[44]

So it was with the persecution of witches. If the Dominicans, by their constant propaganda, created a hatred of witches, they created it in a favourable social context. Without that context their success is inexplicable. But within that context, these tribunes played an essential part. From the very beginning it was they who detected the social pressure. It was they who mobilized it. And in order to mobilize it, they also supplied the mythology without which it could never have become a European movement. To this mythology we must now turn.

44. Is it necessary to document these statements? Then let the reader refer to the works of Américo Castro for the Spanish Inquisition; let him observe the conflict between personal humanity and social fear, in respect of the expulsion of the Moriscos, in the contemporary works of Cervantes and the Spanish *arbitristas;* let him read M. Jean Orcibal's *Louis XIV et les protestants* (Paris, 1951); and let him digest the profound and terrible book of Mr. Raul Hilberg, *The Destruction of the European Jews* (Chicago, 1961).

"A Witches'
Sabbat"

III

The mythology of the witch-craze, I have suggested, was the articulation of social pressure. In a religious society such articulation generally takes the form of heresy. But before examining any heresy it is useful to ask who in fact articulated it. Was it the heretics themselves, or was it the inquisitors who articulated it for them? This is an important question, applicable to many historic heresies. It applies, among others, to the Albigensians and to the Vaudois. So, when the inquisitors discovered a new "heresy" beneath the ruins of Albigensianism, we naturally ask the same question. Did they really discover this new heresy, or did they invent it?

It has been argued by some speculative writers that the demonology of the sixteenth century was, in essence, a real religious system, the old pre-Christian religion of rural Europe which the new Asiatic religion of Christ had driven underground but never wholly destroyed. But this is to confuse the scattered fragments of paganism with the grotesque system into which they are only long afterwards arranged. The primitive peoples of Europe, as of other continents, knew of charms and sorcery, and the concept of night-riding "with Diana or Herodias" survived into the early Christian centuries; but the essential substance of the new demonology—the pact with Satan, the witches' sabbat, the carnal intercourse with demons, etc., etc.—and the hierarchical, systematic structure of the kingdom of the Devil, are an independent product of the later Middle Ages.[45] All the evidence makes it clear that the new mythology owes its system entirely to the inquisitors themselves. Just as anti-semites build up, out of disconnected titbits of scandal, their systematic mythology of ritual murder, poisoned wells and the world-wide conspiracy of the Elders of Zion, so the Hammerers of Witches built

---

45. The idea that witch-beliefs were lingering relics of a systematic pre-Christian religion was first advanced by Jacob Grimm, who, in his *Deutsche Mythologie* (Göttingen, 1835), argued that the witch-cult was no other than the ancient Teutonic religion. In this form it was refuted by Soldan, who argued that, in so far as it contained pagan concepts, those concepts could be traced to Roman (and so to Greek and Oriental), not to Germanic paganism (Soldan, p. 494). The distinction may be too fine: possibly some of the coarser ingredients, though justified from literary sources, were directly derived from German paganism (see below, p. 171). But however that may be, the demonological system, as distinct from the particular details incorporated in it, is demonstrably scholastic and medieval. The fancies of the late Margaret Murray need not detain us. They were justly, if irritably, dismissed by a real scholar as "vapid balderdash" (C. L. Ewen, *Some Witchcraft Criticisms*, 1938).

up their systematic mythology of Satan's kingdom and Satan's accomplices out of the mental rubbish of peasant credulity and feminine hysteria; and the one mythology, like the other, once launched, acquired a momentum of its own. It became an established folk-lore, generating its own evidence, and applicable far outside its original home.

How that folk-lore was established is clear enough to anyone who reads the successive manuals of the inquisitors. Fighting against the enemies of the Faith, they had easily divided the world into light and darkness, and having systematized the kingdom of God in a *Summa Theologiae*, what was more natural than to systematize the kingdom of the Devil in a *Summa Daemonologiae?* The method was the same: the only difference lay in the nature of the material. The basic evidence of the kingdom of God had been supplied by Revelation. But the Father of Lies had not revealed himself so openly. To penetrate the secrets of his kingdom, it was therefore necessary to rely on indirect sources. These sources could only be captured members of the enemy intelligence service: in other words, confessing witches.

So the Dominicans set to work and their efforts were soon rewarded. Since a system was presupposed, a system was found. The confessions—those disconnected fragments of truth hardly won from the enemy—were seen as the few visible projections of a vast and complex organization, and so every new confession supplied fresh evidence for deductive minds. The same logic which had constructed the great work of the Angelic Doctor would construct a series of demonological manuals confirming and extending each other. The climax, because of its timing and distribution, would be the *Malleus*. When it was published, it carried on its title-page the bold epigraph, *Haeresis est maxima opera maleficarum non credere* ("to disbelieve in witchcraft is the greatest of heresies"). It was the exact opposite of the ruling of the Church in the Dark Ages. Since the ninth century, the wheel had come full circle.

But if the theory of Satan's kingdom, with its hierarchy of demons and witches, rested ultimately on the confessions of witches, how were those confessions obtained? This question is crucial. If the confessions were freely given, we have to admit at least the "subjective reality" of the experiences confessed, and then the remarkable identity of those confessions, which converted many a sixteenth-century sceptic, becomes a real problem. On the other hand, if the confessions were obtained by torture, that problem hardly exists. The similarity of answers can be explained by a combination of identical questions and intolerable pain. Since some of the most distinguished historians of witchcraft have adopted this explanation,[46] we must clearly examine the whole question of the part played by judicial torture in the trial of witches.

Judicial torture had been allowed, in limited cases, by Roman law; but Roman law, and with it judicial torture, had been forgotten in the Dark Ages. In the eleventh century Roman law had been rediscovered in the west, and torture had soon followed it back into use. In 1252 Innocent IV, by the bull *Ad Extirpanda*, had authorized its use against the Albigensians. By the fourteenth century it was in general use in the tribunals of the Inquisition, and it was used, particularly, in cases of witchcraft, where evidence was always difficult to find. In 1468 the Pope declared witchcraft to be *crimen exceptum* and thereby removed, in effect, all legal limits on the application of torture in such cases. It was not, as yet, used by the secular courts; and Lea points out that certain of the more extravagant and obscene details of witches' confessions do not, at first, appear before secular tribunals, but only before the tribunals of the Inquisition. In other words, they were obtained only by the courts which used torture. But this distinction between lay and clerical practice did not last for long. At the time of the Renaissance the medieval Inquisition was everywhere in decay and, north of the Alps at least, the secular courts had taken over many of its functions. Thus cases of witchcraft in Germany and France were judged by secular lords who had higher jurisdiction. But at the same time the procedures of Roman law were adopted in the criminal law of all countries of western Europe except England. Thus England alone escaped from the judicial use of torture in ordinary criminal cases, including cases of witchcraft.[47] It may also be observed that some of the more extravagant and obscene details remain absent from the confessions of English witches.[48] When we consider all these facts, and when we note that

46. Soldan, Lea and Soldan's twentieth-century editor, Max Bauer, ascribed a great deal of demonological science, but not all, to torture. Lea's disciple and biographer, G. L. Burr, seems, in his essays on witchcraft, to have gone further and to have supposed that torture created witchcraft (cf. *Life*, pp. 177–78).

47. There were exceptions—e.g., for high treason—and the English common law provided *peine forte et dure*, or pressing to death, for refusal to plead. But these exceptions are not germane to the present argument. There was also some non-judicial torture in ill-regulated cases: e.g., during the civil wars, when Matthew Hopkins and his assistants used the *tormentum insomniae*. See Wallace Notestein, *A History of Witchcraft in England, 1558–1718* (New York, 1909), pp. 204–5.

48. England was unique in another respect too. English witches, unlike those of Europe and Scotland, were not burnt (as for heresy), but hanged.

the rise and decline of the European witch-craze corresponds generally with the rise and decline of judicial torture in Europe, we may easily conclude that the two processes are interdependent: that the Dark Ages knew no witch-mania because they lacked judicial torture and that the decline and disappearance of witch-beliefs in the eighteenth century is due to the discredit and gradual abolition of torture in Europe. We may also observe that, since torture has been revived in certain European countries, absurd confessions have returned with it.

That this general conclusion is true, is, I believe, undeniable. The evidence supplied by Lea clearly shows that the witch-craze grew by its own momentum; that witches' confessions became more detailed with the intensification of inquisitorial procedure; and that the identity of such confessions is often to be explained by the identity of procedure rather than by any identity of experience: identical works of reference, identical instructions to judges, identical leading questions supported by torments too terrible to bear. This natural inference is also supported by positive evidence. Accused witches often admitted to their confessors that they had wrongly accused both themselves and others, and these admissions are the more credible since they brought no advantage to the accused—unless they were willing, as they seldom were, to make a formal retraction, which meant submitting to torture again. Some judges refused to allow testimony because they knew that it had been created by torture and was therefore unreliable; and it was the increasing recognition of this fact which, more than anything else, ultimately discredited the whole science. As Sir George Mackenzie, the Lord-Advocate of Scotland, declared of the Scottish witches who were still being burnt in his time, "most of all that ever were taken were tormented after this manner, and this usage was the ground of all their confession."[49]

It might well be. When we consider the fully developed procedure at continental or Scottish witch-trials we can hardly be surprised that confessions were almost always secured. For such a crime, the ordinary rules of evidence, as the ordinary limits of torture, were suspended. For how could ordinary methods prove such extraordinary crimes? As Jean Bodin would write, not one in a million would be punished if the procedure were governed by ordinary laws. So, in the absence of a "grave *indicium*," such as a pot full of human limbs, sacred objects, toads, etc.,

49. Sir George Mackenzie of Rosehaugh, *The Laws and Customs of Scotland in Matters Criminal* (1678), p. 9.

or a written pact with the Devil (which must have been a rare collector's piece),[50] circumstantial evidence was sufficient to mobilize the process. And the circumstantial evidence need not be very cogent: it was sufficient to discover a wart, by which the familiar spirit was suckled; an insensitive spot which did not bleed when pricked; a capacity to float when thrown into water; or an incapacity to shed tears. Recourse could even be had to "lighter *indicia*," such as a tendency to look down when accused, signs of fear, or the mere aspect of a witch, old, ugly or smelly. Any of these *indicia* might establish a *prima facie* case and justify the use of torture to produce the confession, which was proof, or the refusal to confess, which was even more cogent proof and justified even more ferocious tortures and a nastier death.

Of the tortures used, we have plenty of evidence. Basically they were the same throughout the lands of Roman law. There were the *gresillons* (in Scottish *pennywinkis*), which crushed the tips of fingers and toes in a vice; the *échelle* or "ladder," a kind of rack which violently stretched the body; and the *tortillon* which squeezed its tender parts at the same time. There was the *strappado* or *estrapade*, a pulley which jerked the body violently in mid-air. There was the leg-screw or Spanish boot, much used in Germany and Scotland, which squeezed the calf and broke the shin-bone in pieces—"the most severe and cruel pain in the world," as a Scotsman called it—and the "lift" which hoisted the arms fiercely behind the back; and there was the "ram" or "witch-chair," a seat of spikes, heated from below. There was also the "Bed of Nails," which was very effective for a time in Styria. In Scotland one might also be grilled on the *caschielawis*, and have one's finger-nails pulled off with the *turkas* or pincers; or needles might be driven up to their heads in the quick. But in the long run perhaps nothing was so effective as the *tormentum insomniae*, the torture of artificial sleeplessness which has been revived in our day. Even those who were stout enough to resist the *estrapade* would yield to a resolute application of this slower but more certain form of torture, and confess themselves to be witches.[51] Once a

50. It is gravely mentioned as an *indicium* by Carpzov (cited in Lea, *Materials*, p. 826).

51. Lists of tortures are given in many of the sixteenth- and seventeenth-century manuals—e.g., Benedict Carpzov, *Practica Rerum Criminalium* (1635), quoted in Lea, *Materials*, p. 823. They are also mentioned in reports of trials, e.g., Robert Pitcairn, *Criminal Trials in Scotland* (1833), I, pt. 2, 215–23. Summaries may be found, for Alsace, in Reuss, *L'Alsace au 17ᵉ siècle;* for Lorraine in Ch. Pfister, "Nicolas Rémy et la sor-

witch had confessed, the next stage was to secure from her, again under torture, a list of all those of her neighbours whom she had recognized at the witches' sabbat. Thus a new set of *indicia* was supplied, clerical science was confirmed, and a fresh set of trials and tortures would begin.

It is easy to see that torture lay, directly or indirectly, behind most of the witch-trials of Europe, creating witches where none were and multiplying both victims and evidence. Without torture, the great witch-panics of the 1590s and the late 1620s are inconceivable. But can we ascribe the whole craze, in effect, to torture, as some liberal writers seem to do? Can we suppose that witchcraft had no other basis than the fanaticism and prurience of the inquisitors, spellbound by their own inventions? I must confess that I find this difficult to believe. The problem seems to me more complex than that. If the confessions were merely a response to torture we should have to explain why even in England, where there was no judicial torture, witches confessed to absurd crimes;[52] why the people were so docile in the face of such a mania; and above all, why some of the most original and cultivated men of the time not only accepted the theory of witchcraft, but positively devoted their genius to its propagation. For, as Lucien Fèbvre said, although we may dismiss Henri Boguet and many others as "imbeciles," we have to stop before the great figure of Bodin: Bodin the Aristotle, the Montesquieu of the sixteenth century, the prophet of comparative history, of political theory, of the philosophy of law, of the quantitative theory of money, and of so much else, who yet, in 1580, wrote the book which, more than any other, reanimated the witch-fires throughout Europe.[53] To turn over the pages of Bodin's *De la démonomanie des sorciers*, to see

cellerie en Lorraine à la fin du 16e siècle," in *Revue historique*, 1907; for Germany, in B. Duhr, *Geschichte der Jesuiten in den Ländern deutscher Zunge* (Freiburg-im-Breisgau, 1907-21), ii, ii, 482. For the use of *tormentum insomniae* to extract false confessions in our own time see Z. Stypulkowski's account of his own experiences in his book *Invitation to Moscow* (1951).

52. "Note also," Reginald Scot wrote, "how easily they may be brought to confess that which they never did, nor lieth in the power of man to do." (*Discovery of Witchcraft*, 1584, epistle to Sir Thomas Scot, J.P.)

53. L. Fèbvre, in *Annales: économies, sociétés, civilisations*, 1948, p. 15. By an unfortunate misprint, the word "Boguet" has here been printed as "Bossuet," and this error has since been redoubled in an attempt to make it more plausible. In the posthumously published collection of Fèbvre's essays, *Au cœur religieux du XVIe siècle*, the phrase "un imbécile?" has been changed into "Bossuet?" No doubt the editor thought that the master had gone too far in describing Bossuet as an imbecile; but in fact it was only the

this great man, the undisputed intellectual master of the later sixteenth century, demanding death at the stake not only for witches, but for all who do not believe every grotesque detail of the new demonology, is a sobering experience. After such an experience it is impossible, absurd, to suppose that the confessions of witches were mere clerical fabrications, imposed upon reluctant victims by instruments of torture.

Nor is the coincidence in time of judicial torture and the witch-craze in any way decisive. When we look closely at the dates, we find that the abolition of torture did not precede but often followed the disintegration of witch-beliefs. Torture was not abolished in Prussia till 1740 (although it had been brought under strict control in 1714); but the Prussian Land Law of 1721 had already declared that no belief could be placed in the pact with the Devil, night-riding to the sabbat, metamorphosis, intercourse with demons, etc.; and since the law always lags behind the fact, we can assume that the belief had already faded.[54] In Bavaria the decisive blow to the belief was struck by the Theatine monk Ferdinand Stertzinger in 1766, but torture was not abolished till 1806.[55] In France witch-beliefs died before the Revolution, torture after it. In general, it seems clear that it was the growing disbelief in confessions produced by torture which brought torture into discredit: in other words, that the disintegration of witch-beliefs led to the abolition of torture, not *vice versa*.

What then is the explanation of those confessions, and of their general identity? When we read the confessions of sixteenth- and seventeenth-century witches, we are often revolted by the cruelty and stupidity which have elicited them and sometimes, undoubtedly, supplied their form. But equally we are obliged to admit their fundamental "subjective reality." For every victim whose story is evidently created or improved by torture, there are two or three who genuinely believe in its truth. This duality forbids us to accept single, comprehensive, rational explanations. "Rationalism," after all, is relative: relative to the general intellectual structure of the time. The sixteenth-century clergy and lawyers were rationalists. They believed in a rational, Aristotelean universe, and from the detailed identity of witches' confessions they

---

printer who had done so. The "imbecillity" quoted is from Henri Boguet, *Examen des sorciers* (Lyon, 1602), Dedication to the Vicar-General of Besançon.

54. Lea, *Materials*, pp. 1133, 1431–35.

55. Lea, *Materials*, pp. 1459–61.

logically deduced their objective truth. To the "patrons of witches" who argued that witches were "aged persons of weak brains" whose melancholy natures were exploited by the Devil, the Rev. William Perkins could reply with confidence that, if that were so, each would have a different fantasy; but in fact men of learning had shown "that all witches throughout Europe are of like carriage and behaviour in their examinations and convictions." Such international consistency, he argued, was evidence of central organization and truthful testimony.[56] The liberal scholars of the nineteenth century were also rationalists. They knew that, objectively, the confessions of witches were worthless. Therefore they found another explanation of their identity. They ascribed it to the identity of the questions and the pressure of torture. But we in the twentieth century are not rationalists—at least in our approach to human behaviour and human belief. We do not look only for external causes of identical expression or identical illusion. We look also for internal causes, and we find them in human psychology and psychopathology.

That external suggestion alone does not account for witches' confessions is clear when we descend to detail. Again and again, when we read the case histories, we find witches freely confessing to esoteric details without any evidence of torture, and it was this spontaneity, rather than the confessions themselves, which convinced rational men that the details were true. It was because he had heard confessions given without torture that Paolo Grillandi, a judge of witches in central Italy in the early sixteenth century, was converted to the belief that witches were transported bodily to the sabbat. Bodin too assures us that the confession which converted him to the science of demonology and inspired him to become its most formidable propagandist was made "sans question ny torture"; and yet the woman, Jeanne Harvellier of Verbery near Compiègne, had been remarkably circumstantial. Not only had she compassed the death of man and beast: she had also had the Devil for her paramour for thirty-eight years, during which he had visited her "en guise d'un grand homme noir, outre la stature des hommes, vestu de drap noir," coming to her by night, on horseback, booted and spurred, with a sword at his side. She had also described her visits to the sabbat in copious detail; and here too the detail had exactly con-

56. William Perkins, *A Discourse of the Damned Art of Witchcraft* (Cambridge, 1608), pp. 187–93. The "patron of witches" whom Perkins is attacking is clearly Reginald Scot. The same point had been made by Bodin.

firmed the science of the demonologists: the long and tiring journey which left her utterly exhausted, the adoration of a big black man whom they called Belzebuh, the sexual promiscuity. Bodin admits that such a story seemed strange and almost incredible at second-hand. But he had heard it himself; he was a man of the world; and he was personally convinced of its spontaneity. Who are we to doubt his conviction?[57]

Or take the case of Françoise Fontaine, the servant-girl whose interrogation at Louviers by Loys Morel, *prévôt-général* of Henri IV in Normandy, was discovered and published in full in 1883. Here there was no question of torture: the *prévôt* was a humane man, and the story was elicited by patience, not pressure. And yet the story is the standard story, even down to the details: the visit of the Devil through the window, in the guise of "un grand homme tout vestu de noir, ayant une grande barbe noire et les yeux fort esclairantz et effroyables"; the large promises made; the oppressive solidity of his attentions, the lack of pleasure derived from them, the ice-cold contact . . . In his introduction to the document, the Vicomte de Moray has shown, from the evidence of the Salpêtrière hospital in Paris, that every detail of Françoise Fontaine's experience has its parallel today: the diabolic incubus is only the sixteenth-century form of a kind of sexual hysteria familiar to every twentieth-century psychiatrist.[58]

Only . . . ? No, not quite. For there is, in these numerous sixteenth-century and seventeenth-century cases, one ingredient which has since disappeared: the Devil. Today, every psychopath has his or her private obsession. The supposed *incubi* and *succubi* vary from patient to patient. In the past the neurotics and hysterics of Christendom centralized their illusions around the figure of the Devil, just as the saints and mystics centralized theirs around the figure of God or Christ. So, while the pious virgins, having vowed themselves to God, felt themselves to be the brides of Christ, the less pious witches, having bound themselves to Satan, felt themselves to be his concubines. The former, like St. Theresa or Madame Guyon, enjoyed ecstasies of glowing pleasure piercing their inmost entrails as they clung to the mystical body of their Saviour; the latter, like Françoise Fontaine or a hundred others who were dragged before their judges, felt joyless pangs as they lay crushed

57. Paolo Grillandi, *Tractatus de Sortilegiis*, 1536 (Lea, *Materials*, pp. 401–5). Jean Bodin, *De la démonomanie des sorciers* (Paris, 1580), Preface.

58. *Procès-verbal fait pour délivrer une fille possédée par le malin esprit à Louviers*, ed. Armand Bénet (Paris, 1883), pp. 38–44, 87–92.

in the embrace of that huge black figure who "jettoit quelque chose dans son ventre qui estoit froid comme glace, qui venoit jusques au dessus de l'estomac et des tétins de ladite respondante." In the former the psychopathic experience was sublimated in the theology of the Fathers, and they might be canonized; in the latter it ran into disorder in the folklore of the demonologists, and they might be burnt.[59]

Here, surely, we see what the Dominican inquisitors had done, what their successors would do. They did not, of course, discover a concealed world of demons, objectively there (as they supposed). They did not even discover a systematic illusion, a false religion of paganism behind the true religion of Christ. Doubtless there were some pagan survivals in witchcraft just as there were some pagan survivals in Christianity. In Lorraine, for instance, the sabbat was ascribed, incidentally, to the old "high places" of pre-Christian worship.[60] But what was taken over was mere fragments, not a system: it was the inquisitors who supplied the system. Nor did those inquisitors invent a purely imaginary system, in the ordinary sense of that verb: they may have used their ingenuity to create the system, but they did not create the basic evidence on which it rested. They found it in the confessions of supposed witches; and as those confessions seemed genuine to the witches who made them, we can hardly blame the inquisitors for supposing them to be genuine too. What was "subjective reality" to the penitent was "objective reality" to the confessor. Out of those fragments of truth, spontaneously given if also amplified by suggestion and torture, a total picture of Satan's kingdom could, by logic, by the "rationalism" of the time, be built up.

Thus the genesis of the sixteenth-century witch-craze can be explained in two stages. First, there is the social tension. Just as systematic anti-semitism is generated by the ghetto, the *aljama*, not by the individual Jew, so the systematic mythology of the witch-craze was generated not by individual old women casting spells in scattered villages — these had always been tolerated — but by unassimilable social groups

59. There is no need to press the comparison: it is obvious to anyone who faces the evidence. Compare, for instance, the evidence in any sexual witch-trial with the evidence given in J. H. Leuba, *The Psychology of Religious Mysticism* (1925), or the grotesque treatises of the sixteenth- and seventeenth-century demonologists with the hardly less grotesque lives of the baroque saints. The point is also made by the Vicomte de Moray, in *Procès-verbal*, pp. lxxxi–lxxxvii.

60. See Étienne Delcambre, *Le Concept de la sorcellerie dans le duché de Lorraine au XVIe et XVIIe siècle* (Nancy, 1948–51), fasc. 1, pp. 149–53.

who, like the Jews and Moors of Spain, might be persecuted into outward orthodoxy but not into social conformity, and who therefore became, as the others did not, objects of social fear. It was out of this
tension that the frustrated evangelists began to manufacture the new
mythology of Satan's kingdom. That that mythology was entirely fantastic need not here concern us. We may merely observe that, in this
respect, it is not unique. Some of the ideas and practices ascribed to
the Albigensians, and before them to other esoteric sects,[61] had been
no less fantastic, and the absurdity of inquisitorial demonology should
be a salutary warning to us never to trust the accounts which a persecuting society has drawn up of any esoteric heresy with which it is
at war. But once the mythology had been established, it acquired, as it
were, a reality of its own. Ideology is indivisible, and those who believed
that there were devil-worshipping societies in the mountains soon discovered that there were devil-worshipping individuals in the plains. So
the second stage of the witch-craze developed out of the first. The
new mythology provided a new means of interpreting hitherto disregarded deviations, an explanatory background for apparently innocent
nonconformity. Whatever seemed mysterious and dangerous (like the
power of Joan of Arc), or even mysterious and merely odd, could best
be explained by it. Nonconformists themselves, in search of a sustaining ideology, even deliberately took up the newly revealed doctrines;
sadists like Gilles de Raïs dignified their brutalities by giving them a
satanic impulse; helpless victims of society clutched at it for relief; and
psychopaths co-ordinated their delusions about its central theme.

In a climate of fear it is easy to see how this process could happen:
how individual deviations could be associated with a central pattern.
We have seen it happen in our own time. The McCarthyite experience

61. Anyone who supposes that the absurd and disgusting details of demonology
are unique may profitably look at the allegations made by St. Clement of Alexandria
against the followers of Carpocrates in the second century A.D. (*Stromata*, III, 5-10),
or by St. Epiphanius against the Gnostic heretics of the fourth century A.D. (in his
Panarion), or by St. Augustine against certain Manichaean heretics (*c. Faustum*, xv, 7;
xxii, 30; xx, 6; *de Moribus*, ii, 65; *de Natura Boni*, 47; *de Haeresibus*, 46), or indeed at the
remarks of Tacitus on the early Christians (*Annals*, xv, 44) or of the orthodox Catholics
on the Albigensians and Vaudois of the twelfth century and the Fraticelli of the fourteenth (see the remarks of Juan Ginés de Sepúlveda quoted in Lea, *Materials*, p. 203).
In these recurrent fantasies the obscene details are often identical, and their identity
sheds some light on the psychological connection between persecuting orthodoxy and
sexual prurience. The springs of sanctimony and sadism are not far apart.

of the United States in the 1950s was exactly comparable: social fear, the fear of a different kind of society, was given intellectual form as a heretical ideology and suspect individuals were then persecuted by reference to that heresy. In the same way, in the fourteenth and fifteenth centuries, the hatred felt for unassimilable societies was intellectualized as a new heresy and politically suspect individuals were brought to judgment by reference to it. The great sorcery trials in France and England at that time—the trials of the Templars and Joan of Arc, of the Duchess of Gloucester and the Duchess of Bedford—were political exploitations of a social fear and a social ideology, whose origins were to be found at a deeper level and in another field. The difference was that whereas McCarthyism in America lasted only a few years (although it may yet recur), the European witch-craze had a far longer history. The new ideology reached its final form in the 1480s. From the publication of the *Malleus* onwards, its basic content never changed. There was no further development. And yet equally there was no disintegration. It formed a reservoir of monstrous theory from which successive persecutions were fed: persecutions which did not diminish but were positively intensified in the course of the next two hundred years.

IV

The duration of the witch-craze is certainly surprising, for whatever forces may have created it there were others which would seem naturally to undermine it. In the fourteenth century, that century of plague and depression and social dislocation, the mental climate might be congenial;[62] but the later fifteenth century, which saw the craze formally launched, was the beginning of a period of new European expansion. Nor was the craze, even then, firmly accepted. The established Church—the bishops and the secular clergy—had no great love of the friars and their fanatical doctrines. The educated urban laity of Europe were in no mood to swallow the Alpine credulities, the monkish phantasmagoria of excited missionaries. City governments, even in what were to become the classic lands of witchcraft, resisted

62. The spread of witchcraft in fifteenth-century France is explicitly connected with the devastation of the Hundred Years War by Petrus Mamoris, canon of St. Pierre of Saintes and Regent of the University of Poitiers, in his *Flagellum Maleficorum*, written about 1462 and published, without date or indication of place, about 1490 (sig. a ii verso, "Ingressus ad Rem").

the craze, with varying success, even at its height.⁶³ Civil lawyers, the professional rivals of the clergy, were at first highly sceptical of these new doctrines. Besides, the Witch Bull and the *Malleus* appeared in an age of enlightened criticism. It was the time of Renaissance humanism, when Lorenzo Valla and Erasmus and their disciples, under the protection of princes and free cities, were using human reason to dissolve ancient superstitions and established errors. At a time when the older forgeries of the Church were being exposed and the text of Scripture critically examined, why should new absurdities escape scrutiny? Surely the Donation of Constantine and the apostolic authorship of the Apocalypse were not more obviously improbable than *succubi* and the sabbat.⁶⁴

63. Thus the magistrates of Metz, in the witch-ridden duchy of Lorraine, at least resisted the claims of the Dominican inquisitor to be sole judge in 1456 (Lea, *Materials*, p. 235). The Senate of Venice similarly opposed the operations of the Dominican inquisitors in the dioceses of Bergamo and Brescia (see the bull *Honestis petentium votis* of Leo X in 1521; cf. Soldan-Heppe, I, 555–57). The city of Cologne successfully kept down the persecution until 1629 (see below, p. 145). The city of Nuremberg was an island of safety for witches in Bavaria throughout the period (see Burr, *Life*, p. 185). The city of Strasbourg was another such island in Alsace (see R. Reuss, *La Sorcellerie au 16ᵉ et 17ᵉ siècles, particulièrement en Alsace*, Strasbourg, 1871, pp. 178–81). The city of Lübeck survived the sixteenth century almost untouched by the craze (Soldan-Heppe, I, 526–27).

64. The attitude of Erasmus towards witchcraft is disputed. His references to it are few, and their interpretation (since he never explicitly affirms or questions its reality) depends on the amount of irony which can be detected in the tone of his voice; which in turn depends on the reader. A letter of 14 Jan. 1501 concerning a sorcerer of Meung-sur-Loire (*Des. Erasmi Opus Epistolarum*, ed. P. S. Allen, I, 1906, 334–41) has been interpreted as showing scepticism by some (e.g., Thomasius, *de Origine ac Progressu Processus Inquisitorii contra Sagas*, Halle, 1729, pp. 52–53; Soldan, p. 321; G. Längin, *Religion und Hexenprozess*, Leipzig, 1888, p. 73), credulity by others (e.g., Paulus, *Hexenwahn und Hexenprozess*, p. 18, who is followed by Bauer in Soldan-Heppe, I, 414). But I find it difficult to read Erasmus' accounts of the witches near Freiburg-im-Breisgau, one of whom caused a village to be burnt down, while the other conducted an amour with an inn-keeper's daughter and inundated a village with fleas, as written in a serious spirit. Erasmus himself described such stories as *vulgi fabulas* (op. cit., x, 275, 316, 324). In any case, it is clear that the general philosophy of Erasmus was sceptical, and it seems safer, with him as with Grotius, Selden, Bacon, etc. (see below, p. 166), to deduce his particular views from his known general ideas than to seek to extract evidence of belief from casual and elliptical references.

Moreover, the very silence of Erasmus is expressive. In his *Annotations on the New Testament* he avoids every opportunity of encouraging the demonologists. On all those passages from which Catholics and Protestants alike deduced the power of the Devil to

So we are not surprised to find, at the beginning, a good deal of dissent. When the Archduke Sigismund of Austria learned of the new doctrines which were to be extirpated from his Tyrolean lands, he consulted a learned civil lawyer, a doctor of Padua, now professor in Constance, to give him advice; and the lawyer, Ulrich Müller (alias Molitor), replied with a treatise in which he insisted that although there were witches who listened to the suggestions of the Devil and who therefore deserved to die, nevertheless these witches had none of the powers which they claimed but were the victims of despair or poverty or village hatreds.[65] Such opinions were widely repeated. Lawyers like Andrea Alciati and Gianfrancesco Ponzinibio, philosophers like Cornelius Agrippa of Nettesheim and Girolamo Cardano, medical men like Antonio Ferrari, called Galateo, even Franciscan Schoolmen like Samuel de' Cassini all agreed that the powers claimed by witches, or ascribed to them, were largely illusions. They were the hallucinations of melancholy, half-starved persons; they should be interpreted by lay science — the science of medicine and law — not theology; and their proper cure was not fire but hellebore, the classical cure for mere human insanity.[66] Such a view had already been advanced two centuries before by the famous medieval physician of the University of Padua, Peter of Abano, who now became widely quoted by all the enemies of the witch-craze — and as widely attacked by its promoters. Indeed, the University of Padua, the centre of Renaissance science, became the citadel of

---

intervene in human affairs (Matt. iv. 5, Luke iv. 2, Rev. xii. 12), Erasmus is almost ostentatiously unhelpful. "Diaboli nomen," he says firmly, in connection with the temptation of Christ (and the Devil's power to transport Christ to the pinnacles of the Temple was one of the stock proofs of his power to transport witches to the sabbat) ". . . non spiritum impium sed simpliciter delatorem aut calumniatorem significare videtur." In this, as in so much else, he is followed by Grotius. And since Erasmus regarded the encounters of the Desert Fathers, Paul and Anthony, with the Devil, though described by St. Jerome, whom he revered, as imaginary, he is unlikely to have given more credit to the similar encounters of witches, as described by monks, whom he hated. De l'Ancre, incidentally, included Erasmus among the sceptics whose incredulity had culpably weakened the crusade against witches (L'Incrédulité, p. 23), and Weyer, the greatest opponent of the craze, was a disciple of Erasmus. See below, p. 135.

65. Ulricus Molitor, Tractatus de Pythonicis Mulieribus (Strasbourg, 1489).

66. Andrea Alciati, Parergon Juris (Lea, Materials, p. 374); Gianfrancesco Ponzinibio, Tractatus de Lamiis et Excellentia Juris Utriusque (ibid., p. 377); Girolamo Cardano, de Subtilitate (1550) and de Rerum Varietate (1557), ibid., p. 435; Samuel de' Cassini, Question de le strie (1505), ibid., p. 366.

common sense against the new mythology: its doctors appealed from the new Aristotle of the Schoolmen to the original Aristotle of Stagira, and in that process the philosophical basis of witchcraft dissolved. Agostino Nifo, doctor of Padua and physician to el Gran Capitán, Gonzalo de Córdoba, and to Pope Leo X, showed that, in a true Aristotelean universe, there was no room for demons. The greatest of the Paduans, Pietro Pomponazzi, went further. Cautiously, and hedging his meaning with pious lip-service to orthodoxy (for his work on the immortality, or rather mortality, of the soul had already been publicly burnt in Venice), he argued that all the marvels which the vulgar, and the Church, ascribed to demons could be explained away by other influences. Those influences were not yet purely "natural" forces: they were celestial bodies and hidden powers. But at least they were not diabolic interventions. Pomponazzi maintained that apparitions were natural phenomena and that men "possessed by the devil" were merely melancholic. "Had his views prevailed," writes the greatest authority on Renaissance magic, "there would hardly have been any witchcraft delusion and persecution or religious wars."[67]

If the revived and purified Aristoteleanism of the Renaissance pointed one way out of the satanic cosmology, another very different way was pointed by the revived Platonism, or rather neo-Platonism, of Florence. The scientific revolution of the sixteenth and seventeenth centuries, it is now generally agreed, owed more to the new Platonism of the Renaissance, and to the Hermetic mysticism which grew out of it, than to any mere "rationalism" in the modern sense of the word. Ficino with his "natural magic," Paracelsus for all his bombast, Giordano Bruno in spite of his "Egyptian" fantasies, did more to advance the concept and investigation of a regular "Nature" than many a rational, sensible, Aristotelean scholar who laughed at their absurdities or shrank from their shocking conclusions. It was precisely at the time of the Witch Bull that Platonic ideas were adopted in Italy and it was during the next century and a half that they provided the metaphysical impulse to the exploration of Nature. Nature, to the neo-Platonists, might be filled with "demons" and charged with "magical" forces, operating by sympathies and antipathies. It might not exclude the existence of "witches"—creatures who, by arcane methods, contrived to short-circuit or deflect its operations. But at least it had no need of such vulgar mechanism as particular satanic compacts, with their ridiculous concomitants of carnal intercourse, "imps," broomsticks and the witches' sabbat. It is no accident that "natural magicians" like Agrippa and Cardano and "alchemists" like Paracelsus, von Helmont and their disciples were among the enemies of the witch-craze, while those who attacked Platonist philosophy, Hermetic ideas and Paracelsian medicine were also, often, the most stalwart defenders of the same delusion.[68]

Thus it might seem that the dogmas so magisterially formulated by the *Malleus* would soon crumble against the corrosive ideas of the new century. However, they did not. The sceptics spoke only to be instantly overpowered by the defenders of faith. Those who deny the existence of *incubi* and *succubi*, declared the Dominican inquisitor of Lom-

---

68. Agrippa and Cardano were both frequently attacked as being themselves witches (e.g., by Bodin and James VI). So was the greatest critic of the witch-craze, Johann Weyer, who had been a pupil of Agrippa. Among Weyer's supporters was Dr. Johann Ewich, a physician, who was also an advocate of "natural magic" (although both he and Weyer opposed Paracelsus). On the other side Thomas Erastus of Heidelberg impartially attacked Paracelsus on medicine—in his *Disputationes de Medicina Nova Paracelsi* (1572)—and Weyer on witches—in his *Disputatio de Lamiis* (1578)—and the Provençal physician Jacques Fontaine of St.-Maximin was equally extreme in his diatribes against witches and against Paracelsus (see *Jacobi Fontani Sanmaxitani . . . Opera*, Cologne, 1612, pp. 313–25, "Magiae Paracelsicae Detectio," and cf. Thorndike, *History of Magic and Experimental Science*, VI, 554). The French Huguenot Lambert Daneau showed himself an obscurantist Aristotelean scientist in his *Physice Christiana* (1580) and an obscurantist witch-hunter in his *de Veneficis . . . Dialogus* ([Geneva], 1574). So did the Dutch Calvinist oracle Voëtius. The French scholar Gabriel Naudé, in his *Apologie pour les grands personnages . . . soupçonnez de magie* (Paris, 1625), shows himself an admirer of the Platonists, Hermetics and Paracelsians and an opponent of witch-beliefs. The same is true of the English physician John Webster (see his *Displaying of Supposed Witchcraft . . . 1677*).

The Englishman Richard Franck, who went on a fishing expedition to Scotland in 1656–57 and expressed scepticism about witches, was also a Helmontian naturalist (see his *Northern Memoirs*, ed. Sir Walter Scott, Edinburgh, 1820, pp. 158–59).

This equation of Platonists and "natural magicians" with critics of the witch-craze is not constant and some Platonists—like the "Cambridge Platonists" Henry More and Joseph Glanvill—were also believers in witchcraft. But logically it seems to me that Renaissance Platonism and Paracelsianism were incompatible with the crude form of witch-belief which had been established on the basis of scholastic Aristoteleanism. For this reason I am not convinced by the suggestion of Fèbvre (*Annales: economies, sociétés, civilisations*, 1948, p. 13) that Renaissance Platonism, merely because it postulated a world of demons, positively contributed to witch-beliefs. They were a very different kind of demons. I am grateful to my friend Mr. Pyarali Rattansi for illuminating discussions on this abstruse matter.

bardy, Sylvester Mozzolino, "catholice non loquuntur." These lawyers, protested Mozzolino's disciple Bartolomeo Spina, referring to Ponzinibio, are altogether ignorant of theology: they should be prosecuted by the Inquisition as the chief cause of the increase of witches. The robust Dominican Vincente Dodo announced that he would pursue the wavering Franciscan Cassini with a brandished sword. Afterwards the lay judges who inherited the mantle of the inquisitors would speak with the same voice. Peter of Abano and Alciati and Agrippa and all their followers, and all lenient judges, Bodin would write, were themselves witches, inspired by Satan in order to divert attention from their own kind and so enable them to multiply in peace.[69]

All through the sixteenth and seventeenth centuries this dialogue continued. The voice of scepticism—the scepticism of common sense, the scepticism of Paduan science, the scepticism of Platonic metaphysics—was never stilled. Every orthodox writer pays reluctant tribute to it by his hysterical denunciations of the unbelievers thanks to whom witches are multiplying so terribly in the world. Nevertheless, at least until the middle of the seventeenth century, the orthodox always prevailed. The voice of dissent was powerless to stay the persecution. It could hardly be uttered in safety. Romances of chivalry could be laughed out of existence, but no Don Quixote dared to kill, by ridicule, the bizarre novelettes which the grave lawyers and divines of all Europe published about Satan's kingdom.

Why was this? Some explanations easily offer themselves. The new intellectual forces were themselves ambivalent. The humanist spirit might be critical in a Valla or an Erasmus, but it could be uncritical in others to whom the very fables of Greece and Rome were as Holy Writ: and those fables—of Circe, of Pegasus, of the amours of gods with men—could be called in to sustain the witch-beliefs. The pseudo-Aristoteleanism of the Church had the support of a vested interest which the true Aristoteleanism of Padua had not. The gulf between the neo-Platonic demons, which filled and animated all Nature, and the diabolic hierarchy of the inquisitors might be very deep and logically impassable, but to the common eye—and even to some uncommon eyes—it was also very narrow and could be jumped. When Ficino and Pico della Mirandola, Reuchlin and Cardano, Copernicus and Paracel-

---

69. For Mozzolino, known as Prierias, see Lea, *Materials*, 354 ff.; for Spina, ibid. pp. 385 ff.; for Dodo, ibid. p. 367. Bodin's attack on Peter of Abano and Alciati is in his *De la démonomanie des sorciers*, Preface.

sus, Giordano Bruno and Campanella all believed, or seemed to believe, that men, by arcane knowledge, might make angels work for them and so control the movements of heaven, it was not unreasonable for ordinary men to suppose that witches, by a baser acquisition of power, might make devils work for them and so interfere with events on earth.

However, in matters of ideology, it is not generally the ideas which convince. Between two interpretations of any philosophy it is often external events which make the decision. Therefore if we are to ask why the witch-craze, established in its final form in the 1480s, was proof against all criticism for nearly two hundred years, we should perhaps turn back again from its intellectual content to its social significance. We may begin by considering its history: the timing, in relation to external events, of its great outbreaks.

Once we do this, we soon see that a pattern emerges. The fourteenth and fifteenth centuries had been periods of spectacular individual persecutions, but not, outside the Alps and the Pyrenees, of mass-crazes. What we have seen, in those centuries, is the formulation of doctrine on the basis of Alpine and Pyrenean experience and the application of it in particular trials, often of a political character. The Witch Bull and the *Malleus* mark the final presentation of the doctrine and help to extend it beyond its original frontiers. They demand a renewed crusade in the mountain areas, but at the same time they carry it outside those areas and call upon the support of secular as well as clerical authorities. In particular, they extend it, or seek to extend it, to lower Germany: that Germany which is already showing signs of the impending revolt from Rome, and in which the great adversaries of Luther would be the Dominicans.[70]

In the immediately following generation we can see the results. The crusade against the Alpine peoples is renewed. There is intenser persecution in Styria and the Tyrol. Then, from 1500 to 1525, there is a real social war, disguised as witch-hunting, in the Italian Alps. According to the Dominican inquisitor in the diocese of Como, a thousand witches were tried and a hundred burnt in his area every year. In the end the population took up arms and appealed to the bishop. The bishop sent a lawyer to report, and the lawyer convinced himself, and told the bishop, that very few of the persecuted peasants were really witches. In

70. For the leading part played by the Dominicans in the struggle against Luther in Germany, see especially Nikolaus Paulus, *Die deutschen Dominikaner im Kampf gegen Luther 1518–1563* (Freiburg-im-Breisgau, 1903).

1520 this crusade in the mountains was extended from the Alps to the Apennines and a long persecution soon began in the diocese of Bologna. Simultaneously it spread to the Pyrenees and Spanish inquisitors set to work in Guipúzcoa and Vizcaya. Meanwhile, in Germany, obedient to the bull, the secular powers began to take up the task which the inquisitors had been powerless to carry out.[71]

But apart from occasional activity in Germany, the first half of the sixteenth century, outside the Alps and Pyrenees, was a period of relative calm. The witch-hunt, it seemed, had passed its peak, or perhaps the sceptics were prevailing. In France, after the spectacular trials of the fifteenth century, witchcraft seemed forgotten.[72] Even in Germany, in spite of the *Malleus* and the inquisitors, the persecution remained slight.[73] Moreover, the law refused to make witchcraft in itself punishable by death. Luther and the Dominicans might vie with each other in credulous ferocity, but the imperial constitution of 1532, the *Constitutio Criminalis Carolina*, if it generalized the Roman law against witchcraft, also insisted on the old Roman distinction between the "good" and the "bad" witch. Punishment could only be for harm done by witchcraft: merely to be a witch was not enough.[74] Even in Switzerland, in those years, persecution was negligible. Geneva, that mercantile city, the seat of international fairs and an educated *bourgeoisie*, had long been

71. For the crusade in the Alps and Apennines, see Hansen, *Zauberwahn*, pp. 500–501, *Quellen*, pp. 310–12. The lawyer was Andrea Alciati, who describes his mission in *Parergon Juris*, printed in his *Opera* (Basel, 1558). For the inquisitors in the Spanish Pyrenees, see J. Caro Baroja, *The World of the Witches*, pp. 145–52.

72. For the increase in witch-trials in Germany after the bull, see G. Längin, *Religion und Hexenprozess*, pp. 76 ff. Bodin implies that witchcraft was of recent introduction in France in his time (Lea, *Materials*, p. 576). Similarly the author of the pamphlet *Les Sorcelleries de Henri de Valoys et les oblations qu'il faisoit au Diable dans le bois de Vincennes* (Paris, 1587) says that France was free from the abominable science of magic in the time of François I and Henri II, and indeed until the time of Henri III and the *Sainte Ligue*.

73. Sigmund Riezler, *Geschichte der Hexenprozessen in Baiern* (Cotta, 1896). Weyer states that, before 1562, the craze had died down in Germany (*de Praestigiis Daemonum*, 1563, Dedication).

74. The *Carolina* was based on the *Constitutio Bambergensis* of 1507, which had been compiled by Johann Freiherr zu Schwarzenberg u. Hohenlandsberg. The article of the Carolina on witchcraft (art. 109) was taken bodily from the Bambergensis. The relevant Roman law is the law of Constantine *de Maleficis et Mathematicis*, incorporated in the Code of Justinian.

free from witch-trials. In Schwyz they were unknown till 1571. Zürich, under Zwingli, was mild: Zwingli himself never showed any sign of belief in witchcraft. Erasmian Basel listened to the witch-stories of the surrounding mountains with polite amusement.[75]

But if the sceptics thought that they were prevailing, they were soon to know better. If the Catholic evangelists had launched the craze, the Protestant evangelists would soon revive and extend it. Already, in the 1540s, there had been warning signs. In 1540, in Luther's Wittenberg, four witches were burnt. On this subject Luther himself was as credulous as any Dominican, and as he grew older, he contrived to believe more: *succubi, incubi*, night-flight and all. Witches, he declared, should be burnt even if they did no harm, merely for making a pact with the Devil.[76] In Zürich, Zwingli's successors did not imitate his restraint.[77] In Geneva, Calvin held the same language as Luther. "The Bible," he declared, preaching to the Elect on the Witch of Endor, "teaches us that there are witches and that they must be slain . . . God expressly commands that all witches and enchantresses shall be put to death; and this law of God is an universal law." The law of God was stated most explicitly in Exodus xxii. 18: "thou shalt not suffer a witch to live." On this savoury text the Protestant clergy—Lutheran, Calvinist, Zwinglian— were to preach, with grim relish, for the next century; and they did not fail to point out that the law of God, unlike the law of the Emperor, made no exception in favour of "the good witch."[78]

75. For Zürich, see Paul Schweizer, "Der Hexenprozess und seine Anwendung in Zürich," in *Zürcher Taschenbuch*, 1902; Nikolaus Paulus, *Hexenwahn und Hexenprozess*, § VIII, "Der Hexenwahn bei den Zwinglianern des 16ten Jahrhundert." (But Paulus' attempt to prove Zwingli a persecutor *ex silentio* seems to me special pleading.) For Schwyz, see A. Dettling, *Die Hexenprozesse im Kanton Schwyz* (Schwyz, 1907).

76. Paulus, *Hexenwahn und Hexenprozess*, § II, "Luthers Stellung zur Hexenfrage," shows the growing credulity of Luther. Luther based his beliefs explicitly on the Bible and old wives' tales, but he was, of course, a renegade friar, and although he does not avow such a source, he was no doubt familiar with the more systematic demonology of the inquisitors.

77. Paulus, *Hexenwahn und Hexenprozess*, § VIII. The decline of the Zwinglian Church from the liberalism of its founder is further emphasized in the next century. See the account of Bartholomäus Anhorn, *Magiologia* (Basel, 1674), in Lea, *Materials*, p. 747.

78. Paulus, *Hexenwahn und Hexenprozess*, § IV, "Die Bibel als Autorität für protestantische Hexenverfolgung," gives many instances of the use of this happy text. For the undeniable effect of Calvinism, see the summary in G. L. Burr, "New England's Place

Wherever they went, they carried the craze with them. It was Lutheran preachers who first brought it to Denmark,[79] Calvinist missionaries who implanted it in Transylvania.[80] Like the Dominicans before them, the Protestant evangelists introduced the systematic mythology of the Inquisition into countries which hitherto had known only the disconnected superstitions of the countryside. It was Lutheran preachers who brought the witch-craze in the 1560s into Brandenburg, Württemberg, Baden, Bavaria, Mecklenburg. It was the Calvinist revolution which brought the first witch-law to Scotland in 1563 and thus inaugurated a century of terror. In the previous year the first general witch-law had been passed by the English Parliament. In both Scotland and England the pressure came from the "Marian exiles"—the Protestant clergy who, in the days of persecution, had sat at the feet of Calvin or other Reformers, in Switzerland and Germany.[81]

The responsibility of the Protestant clergy for the revival of the witch-craze in the mid-sixteenth century is undeniable. It has led some commentators to argue that Protestantism has a special responsibility

---

in the History of Witchcraft," in *Proceedings of the American Antiquarian Society*, 1911, reprinted in Burr, *Life*, pp. 352–77.

79. The Danish oracle was Niels Hemmingsen (Hemmingius), who published his *Admonitio de Superstitionibus Magicis Vitandis* at Copenhagen in 1575. He had studied at Wittenberg under Luther's successor, Melanchthon, and shows some of the good sense of his master. But he is firm on the subject of the "good" witch; "similis est impietas nocere et prodesse arte magica"; and he explicitly rejects the old distinction of Roman Law.

80. F. Müller, *Beiträge zur Geschichte des Hexenglaubens und des Hexenprozesses in Siebenburgen* (Brunswick, 1854), pp. 16 ff.

81. For Scotland, see G. F. Black, "Witchcraft in Scotland 1510–1727," in *Bulletin of the New York Public Library* XLI, no. 11 (Nov. 1937). For England, Notestein, *History of Witchcraft in England*. Notestein points out that the first prosecutions under the new law were explicitly related, by the magistrate concerned, to the opinions brought by Jewel from Switzerland: "there is a man of great cunning and knowledge come over lately unto our Queen's Majesty which hath advertised her what a company and number of witches be within England; whereupon I and other of her Justices have received commission for the apprehending of as many as are within these limits" (p. 46). It may be added that the first manual of witch-beliefs to be published in England also came from Switzerland. It was Lambert Daneau's *de veneficis . . . Dialogus*, of which Thomas Twyne published a translation in 1575. Daneau's work had been written at Gien, near Orléans, where he was a Huguenot pastor; but it was published in Geneva, whither he had fled after the massacre of St. Bartholomew and where he had formerly learned his doctrines from Calvin himself.

for such beliefs. But this is absurd: it is to judge on far too narrow a basis. To dispose of such a conclusion, we need only look back to the Dominicans. We may equally look forward to the Jesuits.

For if the Dominicans had been the evangelists of the medieval Counter-Reformation, the Jesuits were the evangelists of the sixteenth-century Counter-Reformation, and if Protestant evangelists carried the craze to the countries which they conquered for Reform, these Catholic evangelists carried it equally to the countries which they re-conquered for Rome. Some of the most famous of Jesuit missionaries distinguished themselves in propagating the witch-craze: St. Peter Canisius, the apostle of Germany; Peter Thyraeus, the oracle of the witch-burning Archbishop of Mainz; Fr. Schorich, the court-preacher of the Duke of Baden; Gregor von Valentia, the theologian of Ingolstadt; Jerome Drexel, court-preacher to the insatiable Duke of Bavaria; Georg Scherer, the court-preacher of the Emperor in Vienna. It was the Catholic reconquest which brought the witch-craze in a terrible form to Bavaria, where dukes William V and Maximilian I, great patrons of the Jesuits, kept the witch-fires burning. It was the Catholic reconquest which decimated the Rhineland in the 1590s, and the Jesuits who stood behind its greatest executioners, the Archbishop of Trier and his terrible suffragan, Bishop Binsfeld. It was the Catholic reconquest which introduced witch-burning into Flanders, and the Jesuit del Rio who would keep it up. Philip II's letters patent of 1590, declaring witchcraft the scourge and destruction of the human race, inaugurated a long reign of terror in Flanders. The Counter-Reformation brought the witch-craze to Poland as the Reformation had brought it to Hungary. The restitution of clerical power in 1600 led to the renewal of witch-trials in Franche-Comté. Special powers granted by the Pope in 1604 enabled the Duke Maximilian to intensify the crusade in Bavaria. Pierre de l'Ancre, the gleeful executioner of the Pays de Labourd in 1609, gloried in his Jesuit education.[82]

Thus, if we look at the revival of the witch-craze in the 1560s in its

82. For the Jesuits in Germany, see especially Duhr, *Geschichte der Jesuiten in den Ländern deutscher Zunge*, II, ii, 498, etc.; Riezler, *Geschichte der Hexenprozessen in Baiern*. The admissions of the Jesuit historian are as telling as any of the accusations of the Protestant. For Franche-Comté, see the documents published by F. Bavoux in *La Sorcellerie en Franche-Comté: Pays de Quingey* (Monaco, 1954) and *Hantises et diableries dans la terre abbatiale de Luxeuil* (Monaco, 1956). See also Lea, *Materials*, pp. 1218–19. For Flanders, see J. B. Cannaert, *Procès des sorcières en Belgique sous Philippe II et le gouvernement des archiducs* (Ghent, 1847). For Poland, Soldan-Heppe, I, 427.

context, we see that it is not the product either of Protestantism or of Catholicism, but of both: or rather, of their conflict. Just as the medieval Dominican evangelists had ascribed witch-beliefs to the whole society which resisted them, so both the Protestant and Catholic evangelists of the mid-sixteenth century ascribed the same beliefs to the societies which opposed them. The recrudescence of the absurd demonology of the *Malleus* was not the logical consequence of any religious idea: it was the social consequence of renewed ideological war and the accompanying climate of fear. The parties drew on a mythology which was already there, elaborated out of a similar situation by their medieval predecessors. Perhaps, on the eve of the Reformation, that mythology was on the way out. Who can say what might have happened if Erasmus had triumphed instead of Luther and Loyola? Then the Renaissance might have led direct to the Enlightenment and the witch-craze have been remembered as a purely medieval lunacy. But that was not to be. The frontal opposition of Catholics and Protestants, representing two forms of society incompatible with each other, sent men back to the old dualism of God and the Devil and the hideous reservoir of hatred, which seemed to be drying up, was suddenly refilled.

The recrudescence of the witch-craze from about 1560 can be documented from innumerable sources. We can trace it geographically, watch it, country by country, as the Protestant or the Catholic missionaries declare war on the obstinate. We can see it in literature, in the series of grotesque encyclopaedias in which writer after writer repeated and amplified the fantasies of the *Malleus*. We can see it in its legal form, in the gradual change of law and practice to meet the alleged multiplication of witches, and in the gradual acquiescence of the lawyers in a new and profitable branch of their business.[83] One of the new practices was the "cold-water test," the throwing of a suspected witch into a pond or river to see whether she would float or not.[84] If she

83. It is interesting to observe the change in the legal attitude towards witchcraft in the course of the sixteenth century. At first the lawyers were generally hostile to the new mythology—as Mozzolino (see above, p. 123), Francisco de Vitoria (*Relectiones XII Theologicae*, ch. x, cited in Hansen, *Quellen*, pp. 354–57) and others admit. But from mid-century they generally support the witch-hunters, and by 1600 they are more savage and pedantic than the clergy. The same conservative spirit which had once resisted the novelty now venerated the established doctrine.

84. So called to distinguish it from the "hot-water test," which involved thrusting the suspect's arm into boiling water and measuring guilt or innocence by the effect.

did, diabolic aid was proved and she was burnt as a witch. If she sank, innocence could be presumed, although perhaps, by that time, she had drowned. The literature of the time shows that this test was invented, or revived, in the 1560s.[85] At the same time the law itself received an important modification: under clerical pressure it abandoned the old and humane distinction between the "good" and the "bad" witch.

In 1563 the Scottish witch-law, obedient to the voice of Calvin, prescribed death for all witches, good or bad, and for those who consulted them.[86] In 1572 Augustus the Pious, Elector of Saxony, introduced a new criminal code, the *Consultationes Saxonicae*, according to which even the "good" witch was to be burnt, merely for having made a pact with the Devil, "even if she has harmed nobody with her sorcery." This provision was the result of organized pressure by the lawyers and clergy of Luther's Wittenberg.[87] The same provision was adopted ten years later in the Palatinate by its Lutheran Elector Ludwig, and by a number of other princes. Where the Catholic, Lutheran or Calvinist Churches ruled the practice was the same.[88] In Elizabethan England the law preserved the old distinction and indeed the Anglican Church has

85. See the controversy on the subject provoked by Adolf Schreiber (Scribonius), *de Examine et Purgatione Sagarum . . . Epistola* (Lemgo, 1583). Schreiber was a physician of Marburg and advocated the test as scientific. His critics included Johann Ewich, state physician of the city of Bremen, and Hermann Neuwaldt, a physician of Brunswick. Ewich described the cold-water test as "indicium recens repertum sed nunc quoque passim usitatum" (*De Sagarum . . . Natura, Arte, Viribus et Factis*, Bremen, 1584, sig D.3); Neuwaldt as a test which he had observed "nunc denuo vires resumere" (*Exegesis Purgationis sive Examinis Sagarum*, Helmstedt, 1585). It is mentioned in Weyer's *de Praestigiis Daemonum* (Lea, *Materials*, pp. 524–25). Most lawyers—even Bodin—condemned the cold-water test (see Gödelmann, *de Magis*, i, ch. v, nn. 21, 23, 26–30). But their condemnation was vain: the custom, once adopted, became a new sport with country people, as popular as bear- or bull-baiting. See Francis Hutchinson, *An Historical Essay on Witchcraft* (1718), p. 175. For its use in France, see *Papiers d'état du chancelier Séguier* (Paris, 1964), i, 636–37. I owe this last reference to Mrs. Menna Prestwich.

86. *Acts of the Parliament of Scotland*, ii, 539.

87. Paulus, *Hexenwahn und Hexenprozess*, pp. 55–57.

88. Thus Melchior Goldast, a Calvinist lawyer, in a memorial submitted to the Catholic Elector of Trier in 1629, declares that witches, whether harmful or not, must be burnt, and gives a list of princes and cities, Catholic, Lutheran and Calvinist, that have adjusted their laws accordingly (*Rechtliches Bedencken von Confiscation der Zauberer- und Hexen-Güther*, Bremen, 1661). See also Lea, *Materials*, p. 805; Paulus, *Hexenwahn und Hexenprozess*, p. 78.

an honourable record of sanity and moderation.[89] Its teacher had been Bucer, the disciple of Erasmus, whose influence also kept Strasbourg as an island of sense in the Rhineland. But even in England the Calvinist clergy pressed for conformity with the pure "schools of Christ" abroad. Their oracle was the Cambridge preacher and casuist William Perkins, who lectured on the subject in Emmanuel College in the 1590s. He impressed upon his hearers—and indirectly on the founding fathers of New England Puritanism, who were to prove apt pupils[90]—the standard view of the godly that by the law of Moses, "the equity whereof is perpetual," and from which there are no exceptions, the witch must be put to death. Whoever has made a pact with the Devil, even to do good, must die. Indeed, said Perkins, "the good witch" was "a more horrible and detestable monster than the bad"; so if "death be due to any," as we know that it is due to all, "then a thousand deaths of right belong to the good witch."[91] A few years later, the royal demonologist, James VI of Scotland, came to reign in England. Brought up as a good Calvinist and committed to all the absurdities of continental science, he did not like the mild Elizabethan law. He "found a defect in the statutes," we are told, ". . . by which none died for witchcraft but they only who by that means killed, so that such were executed rather as murderers than witches." So he had the law changed. Henceforth death was the legal penalty, even in England, for the "good" witch.[92]

That this recrudescence of the witch-craze in the 1560s was directly connected with the return of religious war is clear. It can be shown from geography: every major outbreak is in the frontier-area where religious

89. "The singularly favourable contrast which the Anglican Church presents both to continental Catholicism and to Puritanism" is mentioned both by W. E. H. Lecky, *History of the Rise and Influence of . . . Rationalism in Europe*, i, 124–26, and by White, *The Warfare of Science with Theology*, i, 362. Lest religious bias be suspected, it may be added that White was a Baptist. The same point had been made by Francis Hutchinson, *An Historical Essay on Witchcraft*, Dedication: "in the main, I believe, our Church of England and its clergy, have as little to answer for, in this respect, as any." The Erasmian *via media*, the lukewarmth of a non-evangelizing Church, has something to commend it. For Strasbourg, see Lea, *Materials*, pp. 1081, 1208; Reuss, *La Sorcellerie*, pp. 178–81.

90. For the influence of Perkins on the New England Puritans, see Burr, *Life*, p. 366.

91. Perkins, *A Discourse on the Damned Art of Witchcraft*, pp. 173–78, etc.

92. For the witch-law of James I, passed in 1604, see Notestein, *History of Witchcraft in England*, pp. 101–4.

strife is not intellectual, a dissent of opinion, but social, the dissidence of a society. When Bishop Palladius, the Reformer of Denmark, visited his diocese, he declared those who used Catholic prayers or formulas to be witches; and witches, he said, "in these days of pure Gospel-light," must be burnt.[93] When Bishop Jewel, fresh from Switzerland, told Queen Elizabeth that witches and sorcerers "within these last few years are marvellously increased within this your Grace's realm," and demanded action against them, he was declaring Protestant war on the Catholic England of Mary Tudor.[94] The persecution in England was sharpest in Essex and in Lancashire—two counties where Catholicism was strong and the Puritan evangelists particularly energetic. The Scottish Calvinists, when they obtained their witch-law, were similarly declaring war on Catholic society. Germany and Switzerland were also countries where the two religions faced each other in sharp social opposition: in Germany the persecution remained most persistent in Westphalia, the seat of medieval heresy and sixteenth-century Anabaptism,[95] while in Switzerland the Calvinist cities made war on the obstinate peasantry of the country.[96] In France the geographical antithesis was no less clear. The same areas which had accepted the medieval heresies became, in the sixteenth century, the solid base of the Hugue-

93. See J. Janssen, *A History of the German People at the Close of the Middle Ages*, trans. by M. A. Mitchell and A. M. Christie (1896–1925), xvi, 307.

94. Notestein, *History of Witchcraft in England*, p. 116.

95. H. A. Meinders, writing in Lemgo (Westphalia) in 1716, refers to terrible abuses in witch-prosecutions in Westphalia from 1600 to 1700 in which whole towns, especially Herford and Lemgo, have been laid waste (cited in Lea, *Materials*, p. 1432; cf. also the remarks of Jacob Brunnemann, ibid. p. 429). But the persecution had begun well before 1600. It was in Lemgo, in 1583, that Scribonius had published his arguments in favour of the cold-water test, now generally used "in hisce nostris regionibus, praesertim vero in Westphalia." He dedicated his works to the magistrates of Lemgo and Osnabrück whom Ewich and Neuwaldt afterwards accused of "iniquity and injustice" against witches. The Westphalian jurist Anton Praetorius, who wrote against the craze in 1598–1602, had been driven to protest by the executions he had witnessed there. (See Paulus, *Hexenwahn und Hexenprozess*, § x, "Der calvinische Prediger Anton Praetorius, ein Bekämpfer der Hexenverfolgung"). For statistical evidence of the persecution in Osnabrück in the 1580s and 1590s, see Hansen, *Quellen*, p. 545, n. 1.

96. Thus, in the areas ruled by the Protestant, German-speaking city of Bern, the victims came principally from the Catholic, French-speaking Pays de Vaud: see F. Treschsel, *Das Hexenwesen im Kanton Bern* (1870) and H. Vuilleumier, *Histoire de l'Église réformée du Pays de Vaud sous le régime bernois* (Lausanne, 1927–33), ii, 642–721.

nots: in the Wars of Religion the Protestant south opposed the Catholic north and the last redoubt of Protestantism was the last redoubt of Albigensianism, Languedoc. It was therefore natural that witches should be found in Protestant islands like Orléans or Normandy; that by 1609 the entire population of "Protestant" Navarre should be declared to be witches;[97] and that the capital of the witch-burners should be the great centre of vindictive Catholic orthodoxy, Toulouse.[98]

The same connection can be shown from chronology. The recrudescence in the 1560s marks the period of Protestant evangelism. Thereafter, almost every local outbreak can be related to the aggression of one religion upon the other. The Wars of Religion introduce the worst period of witch-persecution in French history. The outbreak in the Basque country in 1609 heralds the Catholic reconquest of Béarn. The terrible outbreaks in Germany, in Flanders and the Rhineland in the 1590s, and again in 1627–29, mark the stages of Catholic reconquest. Understandably, the Catholic historians of Germany dwell with unction on the persecutions of the 1560s and 1570s, when the witch-burners

97. This is repeatedly stated by de l'Ancre, *L'Incrédulité*.

98. Toulouse has preserved a constant character of intolerance. It was the centre from which the Albigensian heresy was exterminated; it played a sanguinary part in the suppression of the Huguenots of Languedoc; and it was no less brutal in the war against witches. The first witch known to have confessed to sexual intercouse with the Devil was burnt in Toulouse in 1275 (Lea, *Inquisition in the Middle Ages*, III, 384). From the time of Pope John XXII, it was the scene of continual and ferocious witch-trials (Lea, *Materials*, pp. 222, 230–32, etc.); and in the single year 1577, according to Pierre Grégoire, a civil lawyer of Toulouse (*Syntagma Juris Universi* . . . Lyon, 1582), the parlement of Toulouse burnt 400 witches. The same authority would burn Giulio Cesare Vanini for intellectual heresy in 1619 and break Jean Calas on the wheel for being a Huguenot in 1762. The cathedral of Albi, the University of Toulouse, and the thaumaturgical apparatus of Lourdes mark the successive triumphs of an intolerant orthodoxy over spirit, mind and common sense.

The same character of intolerance, regardless of the nature of the heresy, can be detected in Bavaria. The oppressive nature of the Counter-Reformation in Bavaria is well known. Max Bauer, the editor of Soldan-Heppe's *Geschichte der Hexenprozesse*, printed as motto to the book a peculiarly revolting song of Bavarian orthodoxy:

Die Teutschen wurden wohlgemut,
Sie giengen in der Ketzer Plut
Als wers ein Mayentawe.

(The Germans were high-spirited: they waded in the blood of heretics as though it were summer dew.) In our time Bavaria was the cradle of Nazism.

were Protestant.[99] Protestants can take their revenge by looking back to the Dominican campaign of the later Middle Ages, or forward to the Catholic triumphs of the early seventeenth century.

Was there any difference between the Catholic and the Protestant craze? Theoretically, yes. The Catholics inherited the whole medieval tradition of the later Fathers and the Schoolmen while the Protestants rejected everything which a corrupt papacy had added to the Bible and the primitive Fathers. Theoretically, therefore, they should have rejected the whole demonological science of the Inquisitors; for no one could say that *succubi* and *incubi*, "imps" or werewolves, cats or broomsticks were to be found in the Bible. This point was constantly made by isolated Protestant critics, but it had no effect on their official theorists. Some Calvinist writers might be more intellectual and austere in detail,[100] but in general Catholics and Protestants vied with each other in credulity. The authority of Luther transmitted all the fantasies of the Dominicans to his disciples, and the confessions of witches were regarded as an untainted supplement to Holy Writ. So, in the end, Catholics and Protestants agreed on the facts and drew on each other for details. The Catholic Binsfeld cites the Protestants Erastus and Daneau; the Calvinist Voëtius and the Lutheran Carpzov cite the Dominican *Malleus* and the Jesuit del Rio. They all also agreed in denouncing those infamous sceptics who insisted on telling them that supposed witches were merely deluded, "melancholic" old ladies and that the Bible, in denouncing death to "witches," had not referred to persons like them. From either side, terrible denunciations fell upon these neuters in the holy war, these "patrons of witches," who, together with lenient judges, were regularly declared to be witches themselves, equally deserving of the bonfire and the stake.

99. Thus the burden of all Nikolaus Paulus' scholarly essays, printed as *Hexenwahn und Hexenprozess*, is to show (*a*) that before the Reformation all men, including the humanists, believed in witchcraft, so that the Catholic inquisitors deserve no special blame; (*b*) that in the late sixteenth century the Protestants were great burners of witches. Although Paulus carries his interest in Protestant persecution down to the end of the seventeenth century, he shows no interest in the persecutions from 1590 to 1630, which were mainly Catholic.

100. Thus Perkins (*A Discourse on the Damned Art of Witchcraft*) does not mention *succubi* or *incubi*—which are absent also from English witch-trials—and rejects anything which might be regarded as popish "conjuring"; but he accepts the pact with the Devil and the power of the Devil, by God's permission, to work whatever miracles he likes; from which all else can logically flow, even without the Dominican learning.

And who were these sceptics? The most famous of them was Johann Weyer, a survivor from the civilized days of Erasmus, a pupil of the Platonist Cornelius Agrippa of Nettesheim, a doctor of medicine who had studied in the humanist France of François I and practised in Erasmian Holland. In 1550 he had been invited to Cleves by the tolerant, Erasmian Duke of Cleves-Jülich-Berg-Marck, William V,[101] and it was under his protection, and with his encouragement, that he wrote, in 1563, at the age of forty-eight, his famous, or notorious work, de Praestigiis Daemonum. In this, while accepting the reality of witchcraft and the whole Platonic world of spirits, he argued that all the activities to which witches confessed, and for which they were now being burnt throughout Germany, were illusions created in them either by demons or by disease. Having written his work, Weyer sent copies to his friends and awaited the reaction.

The reaction was formidable. Weyer had chosen to publish his book precisely at the moment when the witch-craze, after a long lull, was beginning again. That, indeed, was what had provoked him to write. But this Erasmian Platonist—"the father of modern psychiatry" as he has been called—was no longer heard by a generation that had repudiated Erasmus. A fellow-physician might hail him as a prophet of enlightenment, a Hercules triumphant over superstition,[102] but his other readers thought differently. Weyer was told by his friends that his book must be destroyed or rewritten; by his enemies that he was a "Vaudois," a Wycliffite, a lunatic. His work was denounced by the French Calvinist Lambert Daneau, burnt by the Lutheran University of Marburg, and put on the Index by the Catholic governor of the Netherlands, the Duke of Alba, who would ultimately secure Weyer's

101. William V's father, John III, had carried out an Erasmian reform in his duchies, and had secured, as William's tutor, Erasmus' friend Conrad von Heresbach (see A. Wolters, Conrad von Heresbach, Elberfeld, 1867). Carl Binz, Doctor Johann Weyer . . . 2nd ed. (Berlin, 1896), p. 159, describes William V as "der in den Grundsätzen des Erasmus erzogene Herzog." Weyer's own attitude is illustrated by the fact that the whole of his chapter xviii is an extract from Erasmus' Apologia adversus articulos aliquot per monachos quosdam in Hispaniis exhibitos (Basel, 1529). Weyer was himself a Protestant, but his Protestantism has to be deduced: it is never stated either by him or his enemies—further evidence of his Erasmian moderation. (See Janssen, A History of the German People, XVI, 320–21.) On Weyer see also Leonard Dooren, Doctor Johannes Wier, Leven en Werken (Aalten, 1940).

102. This fellow-physician was Johann Ewich, whose letter was printed by Weyer. See above, p. 130, n. 85.

Jean Bodin

dismissal from the Court of Cleves. However, the book was read, and in 1577 Weyer published a sequel in which he had congratulated himself on its salutary effect. Unfortunately, he had to add, the tyrants had now resumed their murderous persecution, and so he sought, once again, to expose their errors. This second book happened to come into the hands of Jean Bodin just as Bodin was working himself into a lather of indignation at the leniency of French judges and the infamous neutrality of the French court: the "Erasmian," "Platonic" Court of Catherine de Médicis.[103] As if he had not written rubbish enough, Bodin hastily added an appendix denouncing Weyer as an infamous patron of witches, a criminal accomplice of the Devil.

There were sceptics after Weyer, but none of them improved materially on his work. Just as the demonology of the witch-hunters, Catholic or Protestant, was laid down in final form in the *Malleus*, so the basic philosophy of the sceptics, Catholic or Protestant, was laid down by Weyer, and neither the one nor the other was modified by the argument of a century. Every champion of demonological science from Daneau and Bodin onwards took care to attack the "vain ravings" of Weyer; no sceptic, at least in print, did more than repeat his arguments. The most famous of his successors, the Englishman Reginald Scot, if he was inspired by his own experiences, accepted the arguments of Weyer, and thereafter Weyer and Scot feature together, as an infamous couple, in the books of the orthodox. King James VI of Scotland himself wrote his treatise on *Demonologie* to refute Weyer and Scot; when he came to the English throne one of his earliest acts was to have Scot's work sent to the bonfire; and the Dutch Calvinist Voëtius, equally enraged against both sceptics, is able to dismiss their arguments by appealing to unassailable authority: Weyer was refuted by King James and Scot "by the public burning of all copies of his book."[104]

103. Bodin attacked Charles IX as a patron of witches in his *De la démonomanie des sorciers*. Henri III was regularly attacked on the same grounds in the *Ligueur* pamphlets of 1589. See, for instance, *La Vie et faits notables de Henri de Valois; L'Athéisme de Henri de Valoys; Les Sorcelleries de Henri de Valoys; Charmes et caractères de sorcelleries de Henri de Valoys trouvez en la maison de Miron, son premier médecin*. The Erasmianism of the Court of Catherine des Médicis is well brought out by Frances Yates, *The Valois Tapestries* (*Studies of the Warburg Institute*, 1959), pp. 102–8. For Henri III as patron of Platonic "magicians," see Frances Yates, *Giordano Bruno* (1964), p. 180.

104. *Gisberti Voetii Selectarum Disputationum Theologicarum . . . Pars Tertia* (Utrecht, 1649), pp. 539–632, "de Magia." It is amusing to note this stern Calvinist's

The enemies of Weyer, Scot and other sceptics always accused them of denying the reality of witchcraft. Their defenders impatiently insisted that this was not true. Nor was it. Weyer believed implicitly in the power of Satan, but not that old women were his agents. "Truly I deny not that there are witches," Scot had written, ". . . but I detest the idolatrous opinions conceived of them." To the end of the witch-craze, although we always hear it said that there are some who disbelieve the very existence of witches,[105] we never actually hear the denials. To the last the most radical argument against the witch-craze was not that witches do not exist, not even that the pact with Satan is impossible, but simply that the judges err in their identification. The "poor doting women," as Scot called them, who are haled before the law courts, and who may confess—whether through torture or delusion—to being witches, have not in fact made any pact with the Devil, or surrendered to his charms, or harmed man or beast. They are "melancholic." This was a very tiresome doctrine, and it drove successive orthodox commentators into tantrums of indignation. It could not be refuted. But equally it could not refute the witch-craze. Logically, it left it untouched.

The powerlessness of the critics, a full century after the Witch Bull, is clearly shown by the terrible events which accompanied the Catholic reconquest in Germany. If the Protestant princes and petty lords had waged war on witches in Württemberg and Baden, Brandenburg and Saxony, in the 1560s, "out of respect for law and evangelic piety,"[106] the Catholic princes and prince-bishops (who exercised the same power) outdid them in their turn from 1580 onwards. In one German state after another the hunt was then taken up, and no prince was too in-

---

deference to public authority: he never mentions Scot without adding "eius liber titulo *Discoverie of Witchcraft* in Anglia combustus est," "fuit tamen liber ille publica auctoritate combustus," or some such phrase: e.g., pp. 544, 451, 564.

105. "Witches, if there be such creatures" is a phrase which crops up in casual records—e.g., in the remarks of an English soldier in Scotland (see *Letters and Papers illustrating the Relations between Charles II and Scotland in 1650*, Scottish History Society, 1894, p. 136). Edward Fairfax, in *A Discourse of Witchcraft . . .* (1621), refers to such as "think that there be no witches at all," of whom he has heard that there are many, "some of them men of worth, religious and honest." But this absolute disbelief is not found in reasoned writing.

106. It was "aus habendem Recht und evangelischer Frommigkeit" that the Protestant Count Ulrich and Count Sebastian von Helfenstein tortured and burnt sixty-three witches in 1562–63 (see Paulus, *Hexenwahn und Hexenprozess*, p. 110).

significant to qualify for the competition. The Prince-Abbot of Fulda, for instance, Balthasar von Dernbach, had been driven out by his Protestant subjects. When he came back in 1602, he took his revenge. He gave a free hand to his minister, Balthasar Ross, who styled himself *Malefizmeister* or "witchmaster" and conducted "a travelling inquisition" round the principality, falling unexpectedly on villages where he scented a rich prey. He invented new tortures, was paid by results, and in three years, out of 250 victims, had made 5393 gulden.[107] Other instances could be given. But perhaps the most spectacular example, in those first years of reconquest, was given by the pious Archbishop-Elector of Trier, Johann von Schöneburg.

Johann von Schöneburg began his reign in 1581. "Wonderfully addicted" to the Jesuits, for whom he built and endowed a splendid college, he showed his devotion in militant fashion too. First he rooted out the Protestants, then the Jews, then the witches: three stereotypes of nonconformity. Thanks to his patronage the campaign of Trier was "of an importance quite unique in the history of witchcraft." In twenty-two villages 368 witches were burnt between 1587 and 1593, and two villages, in 1585, were left with only one female inhabitant apiece.[108] Among the victims were men, women and children of noble birth and public position. Such was Dietrich Flade, rector of the university and chief judge of the electoral court. Unconvinced by the confessions which had been extracted by torture, he judged the victims leniently. Consequently the prince-archbishop had him arrested, accused of witchcraft himself, tortured till he confessed whatever was put to him, strangled and burnt. This put a stop to leniency by judges, and the population of Trier continued to shrink. As it shrank, the executioner, like some solitary cannibal, swelled in pride and sleekness, and rode about on a fine horse, "like a nobleman of the court, dressed in silver and gold, while his wife vied with noblewomen in dress and luxury."[109]

107. Lea, *Materials*, pp. 1075, 1079, 1232; Soldan, pp. 312–13.

108. *Gesta Trevirorum*, ed. J. H. Wyttenbach and M. F. J. Müller (Trier, 1839), III, 47–57. This fearful account of the persecution in Trier is by a canon of the cathedral who was shocked by its excesses. Parts of it are quoted by Soldan, pp. 358–61; Lea, *Materials*, pp. 1188–91; G. L. Burr, *Translations and Reprints from the Original Sources of European History: The Witch Persecutions* (Philadelphia, 1897). The remark about the unique significance of the persecution in Trier is by Burr.

109. For the persecution in Trier, see Lea, *Materials*, pp. 1075, 1189–90; G. L. Burr, "The Fate of Dietrich Flade," *American Historical Association Papers*, v (1891), 3–57

The craze in Trier was spectacular; but it was by no means isolated. All through the Rhineland and in south Germany, in those years, the example was followed, and the unrestrained secular and clerical juris- diction of the princes was capable of terrible abuse. Moreover, like the good kings of Israel whom they strove to emulate, each prince also had his prophet to fire his zeal and keep it on fire. The Arch- bishop of Trier had his suffragan Peter Binsfeld, whose two sangui- nary works, published in 1589 and 1591, were of great help in sustain- ing and guiding the persecution. The Archbishop of Mainz had his Jesuit Peter Thyraeus, who went to press in 1594. The Duke of Lorraine had the lawyer Nicholas Rémy, whose *Daemonolatreia*, published in 1595, was hailed as the greatest Catholic encyclopaedia of witchcraft since the *Malleus*. The Cardinal-Archbishop of Besançon in the Span- ish Franche-Comté had another lawyer, Henri Boguet, whose *Examen des sorciers* was published in 1602, its soundness attested by the rector of the Jesuit College of Besançon. Meanwhile the Spanish authorities in Flanders were encouraged by the huge success of their local prod- uct. This was the massive encyclopaedia of Martín del Rio, Spaniard turned Fleming, lawyer turned Jesuit. It was first published in 1599– 1600, at Louvain, and quickly replaced Rémy's work as the new Catho- lic *Malleus*. When we consider that these same years, 1580 to 1602, the years from Bodin to Boguet, also saw the Protestant *Demonologie* of King James in Scotland, the work of the Calvinist Perkins in En- gland, the translation of Bodin's work into Latin by the Dutch Calvinist Franciscus Junius,[110] and the Lutheran manuals of Henning Gross in Hanover and Johann Georg Gödelmann in Mecklenburg, as well as a hundred lesser works, we see what batteries of learning were ready to quench the thin and feeble voice of dissent.

To read these encyclopaedias of witchcraft is a horrible experience. Each seems to outdo the last in cruelty and absurdity. Together they in- sist that every grotesque detail of demonology is true, that scepticism must be stifled, that sceptics and lawyers who defend witches are them- selves witches, that all witches, "good" or "bad," must be burnt, that no excuse, no extenuation is allowable, that mere denunciation by one

---

(partly reprinted in Burr, *Life*, pp. 190–233). For the similar prosperity of the execu- tioner in Schongau, Bavaria, see Riezler, *Geschichte der Hexenprozessen in Baiern*, p. 172. Other instances in Soldan, pp. 314 ff.

110. Franciscus Junius (François du Jon) was French by birth, but naturalized in the Netherlands.

witch is sufficient evidence to burn another. All agree that witches are multiplying incredibly in Christendom, and that the reason for their increase is the indecent leniency of judges, the indecent immunity of Satan's accomplices, the sceptics. Some say, writes Binsfeld, that the increase of witches is an argument for leniency. What a suggestion! The only answer to increased crime is increased punishment: as long as there are witches, enchanters, sorcerers in the world, there must be fire! fire! fire! Rémy thought that not only the lawyers but also the law was too mild. By law, children who were said to have attended their mother to the sabbat were merely flogged in front of the fire in which their parent was burning. Rémy would have had the whole seed of witches exterminated and pointed (to show that Catholics too could quote the Bible) to the fate of the irreverent children whom Elisha had very properly caused to be devoured by bears. Boguet was reduced to an agony of hysteria when he thought of the fate of Christendom unless the epidemic were checked. Already, he calculated, the witches of Europe could raise an army bigger than that which Xerxes had led into Europe. And all around him he saw signs of their increase. Germany was almost entirely occupied in building bonfires for them—he was looking, no doubt, towards Trier and Mainz. Switzerland had had to wipe out whole villages in order to keep them down—in the last decade at least 311 witches had been burnt, in steadily increasing batches, in the Pays de Vaud alone.[111] Travellers in Lorraine may see thousands and thousands of stakes—the stakes to which Nicolas Rémy was sending them. "We in Burgundy are no more exempt than other lands . . . Savoy has not escaped this pest": indeed, it was from the mountains of Savoy that they descended into Franche-Comté—Savoy, as the Calvinist Daneau had written, which could produce an army of witches able to make war and defeat great kings.[112] All over Europe, cried Boguet, "that miserable and damnable vermin" "was multiplying on the land like caterpillars in a garden . . . I wish they all had but one body, so that we could burn them all at once, in one fire!"

When we read these monstrous treatises, we find it difficult to see their authors as human beings. And yet, when we look at their biographies, what harmless, scholarly characters they turn out to be! Rémy

---

111. Vuilleumier, *Histoire de l'Église réformée*, ii, 655–56.

112. Daneau, *de Veneficis . . . Dialogus*, p. 11. Savoy was still one of the main centres of the craze a century later. See P. Bayle, *Réponse aux questions d'un provincial* (Rotterdam, 1704), i, 285.

was a cultivated scholar, an elegant Latin poet, the devoted historian
of his country. When he died in 1616, having sent (we are told) between two and three thousand victims to the stake, he was universally
respected. His dedication of his *Daemonolatreia* to Cardinal Charles
of Lorraine showed touching personal solicitude: the cardinal suffered
from rheumatism, which he ascribed to the machinations of witches.[113]
Boguet was similarly a scholar, widely read in the classics and in history.
De l'Ancre, the hammer of the Basque witches, is an enchanting writer
who gives us an idyllic account of his country house at Loubens, with its
grotto and chapel of oyster-shells, poised on a hill overhanging the Garonne, "the Mount Parnassus of the Muses." This old anti-semite and
witch-burner, who had retired thither to devote himself to the Muses,
was desolated when gout detained him at Bordeaux and prevented him
from showing his "chapel of grottos and fountains" to Louis XIII.[114]
The Jesuit del Rio was also a universally respected figure, dedicated to
quiet scholarship from his earliest days, when he had provided himself
with a specially constructed combination of desk and tricycle in order
to dart, with all his papers, from folio to folio in great libraries. Thanks
to such labour-saving devices, he produced an edition of Seneca at the
age of nineteen, citing 1100 authorities, and was hailed by no less a
scholar than Justus Lipsius as "the miracle of our age." He knew nine
languages, was marvellously chaste, refusing, when young, to share the
bed of a very illustrious man, was devoted to the Virgin Mary, was
feared as much by heretics as Hector by the Greeks or Achilles by the
Trojans, and died, almost blind with the intensive study which he had
devoted to the detection and exposure of witches.[115]

   Society, it is clear, approved of Rémy and Boguet, de l'Ancre and del
Rio, and they themselves were entirely content with their work. They,
after all, were the scholars, the rationalists of the time, while the sceptics were the enemies of reason. Such sceptics were Platonists, Hermetics, Paracelsians—in which case they were witches themselves and
deserved to be burnt, as Giordano Bruno and Vanini were—or they
were "Epicureans," "libertines," "Pyrrhonists," who distrusted human

---

113. For an account of Rémy, see Ch. Pfister, in *Revue historique*, 1907.

114. P. de l'Ancre, *L'Incrédulité*, Dedication, etc.

115. See *Martini Antonii Delrio e Soc. Jesu . . . Vita brevi commentariolo expressa* (Antwerp, 1609).

reason and reduced its finest constructions to a powder of doubt. Such was Montaigne, who, having attended a witch-burning at some petty court in Germany, remarked that "it is rating our conjectures highly to roast people alive for them." [116] Against such fancies the guardians of reason and education naturally stood firm, and orthodoxy was protected, impartially, by the miracle of Catholic learning, the Jesuit del Rio, and the Protestant Solomon, King James.

Indeed, the more learned a man was in the traditional scholarship of the time, the more likely he was to support the witch-doctors. The most ferocious of witch-burning princes, we often find, are also the most cultured patrons of contemporary learning. The Catholic Prince-Bishop of Würzburg, Julius Echter von Mespelbrunn, who introduced the craze into his territory in the 1590s, was a universal man of the time, polite, learned and enlightened—with the enlightenment of the Counter-Reformation. [117] His Protestant contemporary, Heinrich Julius, Duke of Brunswick, is described as "unquestionably the most learned prince of his time"—and he was a contemporary of our James I. He was skilled in mathematics, chemistry, natural science, Latin, Greek and Hebrew. He was a jurist who preferred the Pandects to the Bible and read the Codex rather than a romance; an architect who designed the buildings of his new University of Helmstedt; a poet and a playwright. In his plays he dwelt with unction on the moral duty of princes to burn witches, and throughout his reign (which he began by expelling the Jews from his state) he never failed in that duty. In his lifetime, says a chronicler, the Lechelnholze Square in Wolfenbüttel looked like a little forest, so crowded were the stakes; works of gross superstition were gratefully dedicated to him; [118] and at his death, his court-preacher, enumerating his virtues, dwelt especially on his zeal in burning witches "according to God's word." [119]

116. Montaigne, *Essais*, liv. III. § 11.

117. See Götz Freiherr von Pölnitz, *Julius Echter von Mespelbrunn* (Munich, 1934).

118. E.g., Henning Gross (Grosius), *Magica seu mirabilium historiarum de Spectris . . . Libri II* (Eisleben, 1597). In his dedication Gross, a Hanoverian bookseller, offers servile gratitude to the prince for his exterminating justice against witches in these days when Satan is more than ever discharging his abominable poison through Christendom.

119. A. Rhamm, *Hexenglaube und Hexenprozesse, vornämlich in den braunschweigischen Landen* (Wolfenbüttel, 1882). Cf. Soldan-Heppe, II, 59 ff.

The European witch-craze of the 1590s, which elicited so many screams of orthodoxy, did at least elicit one protest. In 1592, eight years after Scot's protest in England, Cornelis Loos, a devout Catholic, ventured to suggest that night-flying and the sabbat were imaginary, that *incubi* and *succubi* did not exist, and that confessions extracted by torture were a means of shedding innocent blood. But Loos, unlike Scot, never reached the public. The Cologne printer to whom he offered his book sensed the danger. Loos was denounced, imprisoned and forced to a humiliating recantation. The good Bishop Binsfeld was present at his recantation and the good Jesuit del Rio published the text of it as a prophylactic "lest some evil demon should succeed" in printing the views which the benevolent authorities had so far suppressed. In fact the prophylactic was unnecessary. In spite of repeated efforts, which cost him further imprisonment, until death by plague saved him from the stake, Loos' book was never published. It remained locked up for three centuries in the Jesuit college at Trier and his shocking views were known only from his officiously published recantation.[120]

But if the orthodox contrived to suppress the critics, they did not succeed in reducing the witches. After 1604 the campaign abated, at least for a time: the return of peace to Europe no doubt helped, and King James himself, having settled down in England, gradually forgot his Scottish ferocity against witches.[121] In those years the main persecution was once again in the Pyrenees. But the reservoir of fear remained even when it was not in use; those mountain streams continued to feed it; and when religious war returned to Europe the witches were suddenly found, once again, to have increased alarmingly during the years of peace. In the 1620s, with the destruction of Protestantism in Bohemia and the Palatinate, the Catholic reconquest of Germany was resumed. In 1629, with the Edict of Restitution, its basis seemed complete. Those same years saw, in central Europe at least, the worst of all witch-persecutions, the climax of the European craze.

All over Europe (as a Jesuit historian admits) the witch-trials multiplied with the Catholic reconquest.[122] In some areas the lord or bishop

120. The manuscript was discovered in 1886 by G. L. Burr. See his account published in *The Nation* (New York), 11 Nov. 1886.

121. For King James' conversion, see Notestein, *History of Witchcraft in England*, pp. 137–45.

122. Duhr, *Geschichte der Jesuiten*, II, ii, 498. The point had already been made, in an indirect way, by the witch-burning Bishop Forner of Bamberg, when he inquired,

was the instigator, in others the Jesuits. Sometimes local witch-committees were set up to further the work. Among prince-bishops, Philipp Adolf von Ehrenberg of Würzburg was particularly active: in his reign of eight years (1623–31) he burnt 900 persons, including his own nephew, nineteen Catholic priests, and children of seven who were said to have had intercourse with demons.[123] The years 1627–29 were dreadful years in Baden, recently reconquered for Catholicism by Tilly: there were 70 victims in Ortenau, 79 in Offenburg. In Eichstatt, a Bavarian prince-bishopric, a judge claimed the death of 274 witches in 1629. At Reichertsofen an der Paar, in the district of Neuburg, 50 were executed between November 1628 and August 1630. In the three prince-archbishoprics of the Rhineland the fires were also relit. At Coblenz, the seat of the Prince-Archbishop of Trier, 24 witches were burnt in 1629; at Schlettstadt at least 30—the beginning of a five-year persecution. In Mainz, too, the burnings were renewed. At Cologne the City Fathers had always been merciful, much to the annoyance of the prince-archbishop, but in 1627 he was able to put pressure on the city and it gave in.[124] Naturally enough, the persecution raged most violently in Bonn, his own capital. There the chancellor and his wife and the archbishop's secretary's wife were executed, children of three and four years were accused of having devils for their paramours, and students and small boys of noble birth were sent to the bonfire.[125]

The craze of the 1620s was not confined to Germany: it raged also across the Rhine in Alsace, Lorraine and Franche-Comté. In the lands ruled by the abbey of Luxueil, in Franche-Comté, the years 1628–30 have been described as an "épidémie démoniaque." "Le mal va croissant chaque jour," declared the magistrates of Dôle, "et cette malheureuse engeance va pullulant de toutes parts." The witches, they said, "in the hour of death accuse an infinity of others in fifteen or sixteen other villages." [126]

---

in his *Panoplia Armaturae Dei* (see below, p. 146, n. 127), why it was that there were so many witches in Catholic lands and so few in Protestant. And cf. Soldan-Heppe, ɪ, 426–27.

123. See Friedrich Merzbacher, *Die Hexenprozesse in Franken* (Munich, 1957).

124. Lea, *Materials*, pp. 1203–4.

125. This was reported by a correspondent of Count Werner von Salm. The document is quoted in W. v. Waldbrühl, *Naturforschung u. Hexenglaube* (Berlin, 1867).

126. See Bavoux, *Hantises et diableries dans la terre abbatiale de Luxueil*, pp. 128–29.

But the worst persecution of all, in those years, was probably at Bamberg. There the prince-bishop was Johann Georg II Fuchs von Dornheim, known as the *Hexenbischof* or "Witch-bishop." He built a "witch-house," complete with torture-chamber adorned with appropriate biblical texts, and in his ten-year reign (1623–33) he is said to have burnt 600 witches. He, too, had his Court-prophet, his suffragan, Bishop Forner, who wrote a learned book on the subject.[127] One of their victims was the bishop's chancellor, Dr. Haan, burnt as a witch for showing suspicious leniency as a judge. Under torture he confessed to having seen five burgomasters of Bamberg at the sabbat, and they too were duly burnt. One of them, Johannes Julius, under fierce torture confessed that he had renounced God, given himself to the Devil, and seen twenty-seven of his colleagues at the sabbat. But afterwards, from prison, he contrived to smuggle a letter out to his daughter Veronica, giving a full account of his trial. "Now my dearest child," he concluded, "you have here all my acts and confessions, for which I must die. It is all falsehood and invention, so help me God. . . . They never cease to torture until one says something. . . . If God sends no means of bringing the truth to light, our whole kindred will be burnt." [128]

Johannes Julius' *cri de coeur*, which must represent hundreds of unuttered cries from inarticulate victims, found one response. The terrible persecution of the 1620s caused a crisis within the very order which did so much to direct it: the Jesuits. Already, in 1617, Adam Tanner, a Jesuit of Ingolstadt, had begun to entertain very elementary doubts which had raised an outcry against him in his order. Now another Jesuit, Friedrich Spee, was more radically converted by his experience as a confessor of witches in the great persecution at Würzburg. That experience, which turned his hair prematurely white, convinced him that all confessions were worthless, being based solely on torture, and that not a single witch whom he had led to the stake had been guilty. Since he could not utter his thoughts otherwise—for, as he wrote, he dreaded the fate of Tanner—he wrote a book which he intended to circulate in manuscript, anonymously. But a friend secretly conveyed it to the Protestant city of Hameln and it was there printed in 1631 under the title *Cautio Criminalis*.

127. *Panoplia Armaturae Dei adversus . . . Magorum et Sagarum Infestationes* (1625).

128. For the persecution in Bamberg, see Johann Looshorn, *Geschichte des Bisthums Bamberg* (Munich, 1886), v, 55; Merzbacher, *Die Hexenprozesse in Franken*, pp. 42 ff.

Spee's work was not the only critical work produced by the massacres of the 1620s;[129] but it was the most eloquent protest against the persecution of witches that had yet appeared. Like Tanner and all the early enemies of the craze, he did not doubt the reality of witchcraft. But he was convinced that, although "all Germany smokes everywhere with bonfires which obscure the light," he had not yet seen a real witch, and that "however much the Princes burn, they can never burn out the evil." It was torture, and torture alone, which caused denunciation and confession. The whole "science" of the witch-doctors was based on torture. "All that Rémy, Binsfeld, del Rio and the rest tell us is based on stories extracted by torture." Torture proves nothing, nothing at all. "Torture fills our Germany with witches and unheard-of wickedness, and not only Germany but any nation that attempts it. . . . If all of us have not confessed ourselves witches, that is only because we have not all been tortured." And who, he asked, were the men who demanded these tortures? Jurists in search of gain, credulous villagers and "those theologians and prelates who quietly enjoy their speculations and know nothing of the squalor of prisons, the weight of chains, the implements of torture, the lamentations of the poor—things far beneath their dignity." We think at once of Nicolas Rémy, writing elegant verses in his fine house at Les Charmes in Lorraine, of Pierre de l'Ancre retiring with his Muses to the grotto of his *cottage orné* on the Garonne, of Fr. del Rio in his devout cell, growing blind with study of the Fathers and stiff with prayer to the Virgin.

We might also at this time think of another, and this time a Lutheran scholar. In 1635, four years after the publication of Spee's book, Benedict Carpzov published his great work, *Practica Rerum Criminalium*, dealing with the trial of witches. Carpzov had probably read Spee. He admitted that torture was capable of grave abuse and had led to thousands of false confessions throughout Europe. But he concluded that, *suadente necessitate*, it should still be used, even on those who seemed innocent; and his view of innocence was not liberal. He maintained that even those who merely believed that they had been at the sabbat should be executed, for the belief implied the will. From "the

129. Other protests include Theodor Thumm, *Tractatus Theologicus de sagarum impietate . . .* (Tübingen, 1621); the anonymous *Malleus Judicum*, of about 1626 (Lea, *Materials*, p. 690; but see also Paulus, *Hexenwahn und Hexenprozess*, pp. 193–94); Justus Oldekop, *Cautelarum Criminalium Sylloge* (Brunswick, 1633), on which see Burr's note in Lea, *Materials*, p. 850.

faithful ministers of the Devil, who bravely defend his kingdom"—i.e., sceptics like Weyer with their "frivolous" arguments—he appeals to the Catholic authorities: the *Malleus*, Bodin, Rémy, del Rio. And having thus restated the sound doctrine—his book became "the *Malleus* of Lutheranism"—he would live to a ripe old age and look back on a meritorious life in the course of which he had read the Bible from cover to cover fifty-three times, taken the sacrament every week, greatly intensified the methods and efficacy of torture, and procured the death of 20,000 persons.

Thus Spee, for all his eloquence, achieved no more than Loos or Scot or Weyer before him. His attack, like theirs, was not upon the belief in witches—indeed, he was less radical than Weyer, who, though the earliest, was the boldest of them all. By his personal influence he may have reduced the savagery of the persecution in the next generation, for the most enlightened of seventeenth-century prince-bishops of Würzburg, Johann Philipp von Schönborn, Elector of Mainz, the friend and patron of Leibniz, was convinced by him and worked to undo the damage wrought by his predecessors.[130] But if the witch-craze of the 1620s died down in the 1630s that was largely due to extraneous causes: war and foreign domination. The French in Lorraine and Franche-Comté, the Swedes in Mecklenburg, Franconia and Bavaria, put a stop to this social war among the natives, just as the English, in the 1650s, would do in Scotland. They did so not necessarily because they were more liberal—the spectacular French witch-trial of Urbain Grandier took place in the 1630s, Matthew Hopkins would have a free hand in England in the 1640s, and the witch-craze would break out in Sweden in the 1660s—but simply because they were foreign, and witch-trials were essentially a social, internal matter. And anyway, the stop was not permanent. Once the hand of the foreigner was removed, the natives would return to their old ways. As in Scotland, relieved of English occupation in the 1660s, so in Mecklenburg after the withdrawal of the Swedes, so in Lorraine after the departure of the French, the old persecution would break out again. Indeed, in some areas the persecution was worse at the end of the seventeenth than at the end of the sixteenth century. In 1591 the Rostock professor of law, J. G.

---

130.   According to Leibniz, Philipp von Schönborn "fit cesser ces brûleries aussitôt qu'il parvint à la Régence; en quoi il a été suivi par les ducs de Brunswic et enfin par la plupart des autres princes et états d'Allemagne" (*Théodicée*, I, 144-45, § 97).

Gödelmann, had urged liberalism and clemency on the Mecklenburg judges. A century later his successor Johann Klein asserted in print the reality of *succubi* and *incubi* and demanded (and secured) death by burning for those who were accused of intercourse with them, and his arguments were supported in print by the dean of the faculty of theology at Rostock thirty years later. As late as 1738 the dean of the faculty of law at Rostock demanded that witches be extirpated by "fire and sword" and boasted of the number of stakes he had seen "on one hill." [131]

Thus the intellectual basis of the witch-craze remained firm all through the seventeenth century. No critic had improved on the arguments of Weyer; none had attacked the substance of the myth; all that successive sceptics had done was to cast doubt on its practical interpretation: to question the value of confessions, the efficacy of torture, the identification of particular witches. The myth itself remained untouched, at least in appearance. Artificial though it was, recent though it was, it had become part of the structure of thought, and time had so entwined it with other beliefs, and indeed with social interests, that it seemed impossible to destroy it. In happy times men might forget it, at least in practice. In the early sixteenth century there had seemed a good chance that it might be forgotten—that is, dissolve again into scattered peasant superstitions. But those happy times had not lasted. The ideological struggle of Reformation and Counter-Reformation—that grim struggle which was so disastrous in European intellectual history—had revived the dying witch-craze just as it had revived so many other obsolescent habits of thought: biblical fundamentalism, theological history, scholastic Aristoteleanism. All these had seemed in retreat in the age of Erasmus and Machiavelli and Ficino; all returned a generation later to block the progress of thought for another century.

Every crucial stage in the ideological struggle of the Reformation was a stage also in the revival and perpetuation of the witch-craze. In the 1480s the Dominicans had made war, as they thought, on the relics of medieval heresy. That was the time of the Witch Bull and the *Malleus*, and the renewed persecution in those "Alpine valleys cold" in which del Rio would afterwards see the eternal source of witchcraft and Milton the ancient cradle of Protestantism. In the 1560s the Protes-

---

131. Paulus, *Hexenwahn und Hexenprozess,* § vi; Ernst Boll, *Mecklenburgische Geschichte . . . neu bearbeitet von Dr. Hans Witte,* ii (Wismar, 1913), pp. 123 ff.

tant missionaries had set out to evangelize the countries of northern Europe whose rulers had accepted the new faith, and at once the witch-hunt had been renewed by them. From 1580 the Catholic Counter-Reformation had begun to reconquer northern Europe and the persecution became, once again, a Catholic terror, with the new Jesuits replacing the old Dominicans as evangelists. It was then that the Spaniard Francisco Peña, a canon lawyer in the Roman Curia, collected and summarized the conclusions of the Roman inquisitors: for no subject, he wrote, was now more frequently discussed by the Catholic clergy than sorcery and divination.[132] Finally, the Thirty Years War, the last stage of the ideological struggle, brings with it the worst persecution of all: the "epidémie démoniaque" which reached its climax in the year of Catholic restoration, 1629.

Admittedly there are exceptions to this general rule. In England, for instance, the persecution of witches was always trivial by continental standards[133] and its closest student has been able to detect no pattern in it. "There was in fact," writes Ewen, "no clearly defined periodic wave of witch-mania sweeping through the country, but rather a succession of sporadic outbreaks. The underlying current of superstition, always present, manifested itself unpleasantly whenever and wherever fanaticism was unusually rampant, the influence of one man being sufficient to raise the excess of zeal to the danger point."[134] Perhaps this may safely be said of England, where persecution, thanks to the absence of judicial torture, never became a craze. But does not such an

132. "Nulla est fere hodie frequentior disputatio quam quae de sortilegiis et divinationibus suscipitur." For Peña, see Hansen, *Quellen*, pp. 357–59. He concluded that *incubi* and *succubi* were real and that the night-flight to the sabbat was proved beyond doubt.

133. The figures commonly given for the execution of witches in England are grotesquely exaggerated. Lea himself, in his *History of the Inquisition in Spain*, IV, 247, estimated the number of victims in Britain as 90,000, "of whom about a fourth may be credited to Scotland." But Mr. C. L. Ewen's careful study of the records of the Home Circuit has discredited all such wild guesses. He concludes that between 1542 and 1736 "less than one thousand" persons were executed for witchcraft in England (*Witch Hunting and Witch Trials*, 1929, p. 112). The executions in Scotland, where torture was used, were not less but far more numerous: probably 4400 in the ninety years from 1590 to 1680 (see Black, in *Bulletin of New York Public Library*, XLI, no. 11 (Nov. 1937), p. 823).

134. Ewen, *Witch Hunting and Witch Trials*, p. 113.

answer, even there, beg the question? For why was fanaticism, at some times, "unusually rampant"? Why did "one man," like Matthew Hopkins, appear in 1645 rather than in 1635? In fact, when we compare England with the Continent, we see that the rhythm of English persecution follows very closely that of the continental craze of which it is a pale reflection. On the Continent, the great persecutions are after 1560, when the Protestant evangelists carry it northwards; after 1580 as the Counter-Reformation overtakes them, and especially in the 1590s, those years of general economic depression and European plague; and in the 1620s, during the Catholic reconquest of the Thirty Years War. In England persecution similarly begins in the 1560s with the return of the Marian exiles; it similarly takes new life in the 1580s and 1590s, the years of Catholic plots, war and fear; and thereafter, if its course is different—if it virtually ceases for the duration of the Thirty Years War—this very divergence is perhaps the exception which proves the rule. For England—to her shame, cried the Puritans—was uninvolved in the Thirty Years War. In the 1640s, when civil and ideological war came to England, witches were persecuted in England too.[135]

Another exception which may yet prove the general rule is supplied by Sweden. The Swedish Lutheran Church, like the Anglican Church, was neither a persecuting nor a proselytizing body, at least in its first century. When it came in contact with the Lapps of the north, it found—as the Roman Church had found in the Pyrenees and the Alps—a different society, racially as well as socially different, half-

135. The trials of witches in England fell off markedly after 1617, when James I, in Fuller's words, "receding from what he had written in his *Demonologie*, grew first diffident of, and then flatly to deny, the workings of witches and devils, as but falsehoods and delusions." (Notestein, *History of Witchcraft in England*, pp. 142–44; Ewen, *Witch Hunting and Witch Trials*, pp. 98 ff.; but see also G. L. Burr's review of Ewen in *American Historical Review*, xxxv, 1929–30, 844 ff.) Under the personal rule of Charles I executions for witchcraft ceased altogether in England, at least in the counties of the Home Circuit (Ewen, op. cit.), and were at least severely cut down in Scotland: one of the articles of complaint against the Scottish bishops in 1638 was for "staying" such proceedings (W. L. Mathieson, *Politics and Religion. A Study in Scottish History from the Reformation to the Revolution*, Glasgow, 1902, ii, 157–59). However, the events of 1640 changed all that in both countries. The Scottish General Assembly of 1640, having got rid of the bishops, required all ministers to nose out witches and urge the enforcement of the law against them (ibid. p. 159), which they did, to some tune; and in 1645 more witches were executed in England than in any year before or since (see the statistics in Ewen, op. cit., pp. 102–8, 221–31).

pagan in religion, given over, it seemed, in that Arctic cold, to bizarre witch-beliefs.[136] But as it did not seek to assimilate these harmless dissenters, their beliefs were not persecuted, and the Lapland witches remained always outside the general European witch-craze. In 1608 Sweden, like other Lutheran countries, adopted the Mosaic penalties for offences previously punished by the Church courts; but even this provision, which was used to justify witch-burning elsewhere, had no such consequence in Sweden. There witch-trials remained sporadic and episodic, and no great native witch-doctor, like King James in Scotland, or Perkins in England, or Hemmingsen in Denmark, or Gödelmann in Mecklenburg, sought to erect in Sweden the full-blown demonology of Europe. Indeed, as we have seen, in the Thirty Years War the Swedish generals, obeying explicit orders from Queen Christina, suppressed the witch-fires in Germany. It was not till the 1660s that a change came to Sweden, and then it was in circumstances which recall the European outbreaks.

For in the 1660s the established Lutheran Church in Sweden became intolerant. Like the established Calvinist Church in Scotland, it had shaken itself free from alliance with other, more liberal Protestant parties, and its Puritan leaders prepared to advertise their purity by a great witch-hunt. In 1664 it branded as heretical the Syncretist Movement—the movement of Pan-Protestantism which had been so useful in the Thirty Years War. In 1667 it put out a new declaration of orthodoxy, "the most rigorous of the century," against the subtle menace of Cartesianism: that Cartesianism which Descartes himself had brought to the Court of Queen Christina. Now that Queen Christina was an exile in Rome, the frightened Church of Sweden resolved to assert itself; its preachers became zealots of their faith, eager to sniff out and condemn heresy; and in the same year the witch-mania was fired by panic fears in the province of Dalårna. "It is something more than an accident," writes Hr. Sundborg, "that the victory of orthodoxy in 1664 was followed so closely by the outbreak of the persecutions."[137] The same might be said of all the previous European crazes.

136. The Lapland witches were first reported in Olaus Magnus, *de Gentibus Septentrionalibus* (Rome, 1555), pp. 119–28; thereafter they became famous in Europe. Cf. Milton, *Paradise Lost*, II, 665.

137. Bertil Sundborg, "Gustaf Rosenhane och Trolldomsväsendet," in *Lychnos* (Uppsala), 1954–55, pp. 203–64. I am indebted to Professor Michael Roberts for his help in interpreting the Swedish evidence.

Why did social struggle, in those two centuries, invariably revive this bizarre mythology? We might as well ask, why has economic depression in Germany, from the Middle Ages until this century, so often revived the bizarre mythology of anti-semitism: the fables of poisoned wells and ritual murder which were spread at the time of the Crusades, during the Black Death, in the Thirty Years War, and in the pages of Julius Streicher's Nazi broadsheet, *der Stürmer?* The question is obviously not simple. It carries us beyond and below the realm of mere intellectual problems. We have here to deal with a mythology which is more than a mere fantasy. It is a social stereotype: a stereotype of fear.

Any society is liable, at times, to collective emotion. There is the exalted "messianism" which is common in rural societies in medieval Europe; in southern Italy, Spain and Portugal in early modern times; in modern Brazil. There is also the undefined "great fear," such as ran through rural France at the beginning of the revolution of 1789. And these emotions tend to take stereotyped form. How such stereotypes are built up is a problem in itself; but once they are built up, they can last for generations, even centuries. The stereotype in German society has long been the Jewish conspiracy. In England, from the days of the Spanish Armada till the days of the "Papal Aggression" of 1851 and the "Vaticanism" of 1870, it has been the Popish Plot.[138] In America today it seems to be the Red scare. In continental Europe, in the two centuries after the Witch Bull, it was the witch-craze. So firmly had the mythology of Satan's kingdom been established in the declining Middle Ages that in the first centuries of "modern" Europe—to use a conventional notation of time—it became the standard form in which the otherwise undefined fears of society became crystallized. Just as psychopathic individuals in those years centred their separate fantasies (or, as the seventeenth-century doctors would say, their "melancholy") on the Devil, and thus gave an apparent objective identity to their subjective experiences, so societies in fear articulated their collective neuroses about the same obsessive figure, and found a scapegoat for their fears in his agents, the witches. Both the individual and the society made

138. Apart from the Gunpowder Plot of 1605 and the Popish Plot of 1678, there was the imaginary Popish Plot reported by Andreas ab Habernfeld in 1640, which was kept alive for many years afterwards; the Irish Massacre of 1641 which still curdled the blood of John Wesley in the next century; the *canard* that it was the Papists who had burnt London in 1666; the myth of the Warming-pan in 1688; the Gordon Riots of 1780; etc., etc.

this identification because the Devil, his kingdom and his agents had been made real to them by the folk-lore of their times; but both, by this identification, sustained and confirmed the same centralizing folk-lore for their successors.

Thus the mythology created its own evidence, and effective disproof became ever more difficult. In times of prosperity the whole subject might be ignored except on a village level, but in times of fear men do not think clearly: they retreat to fixed positions, fixed prejudices. So social struggle, political conspiracy, conventual hysteria, private hallucination were all interpreted in the light of a mythology which, by now, had been extended to interpret them all, and the craze was renewed. At each renewal, some bold and humane dissenter would seek to challenge the collective hysteria and cruelty. Ponzinibio would challenge the Dominican inquisitors, Weyer the Protestant persecutors of the 1560s, Loos and Scot the Catholic and Protestant persecutors of the 1590s, Spee the Catholic torturers of the 1620s and 1630s. But none of these would do more than question the esoteric details of the myth and the identification of the victims. The basis of the myth was beyond their reach. They might convince educated princes, as Weyer convinced the Duke of Cleves and Spee, the future Prince-Bishop of Würzburg and Elector of Mainz; and no one should underestimate the influence that a prince might have to extend or suppress the effect of the craze.[139] But their opponents appealed against them to a lower level—to petty magistrates and clerical tribunes [140]—and on that lower level kept the

139. Thus Weyer states that witches were not burnt in the dominions of the Duke of Cleves, and he names several other princes who were equally firm and equally effective, e.g., the Elector Frederick of the Palatinate and Duke Adolf of Nassau. The princes of Hesse, Philip the Magnanimous and William V, the Wise, similarly controlled the persecution in their lands. Cf. the effect of James I's conversion in England. On the other hand the extension of the persecution when princes gave free rein, or positively encouraged it, is obvious: perhaps nowhere so obvious as in the prince-bishoprics of Germany.

140. Thus, while Weyer relied on the Duke of Cleves and Weyer's supporters Johann Ewich and Hermann Neuwaldt on Count Simon of Lippe-Redtburg and (vain hope!) Heinrich Julius of Brunswick-Lüneburg, their critic Schreiber dedicated his works to the magistrates of Lemgo and of Osnabrück "dominis suis et fautoribus optimis." In general, local magistrates remained the guarantors of the craze, while the best hope of reformers was to secure the support of a prince. Cf. the statements of the magistrates of Dôle, in Franche-Comté (above, p. 145) and the protests of the parlement of Rouen against Colbert's order prohibiting witch-trials (Lecky, *History of the*

craze alive. It remained alive until the eighteenth-century Enlightenment, defended by clergymen, lawyers and scholars, and capable of being reanimated by any sudden coincidence of forces, when politicians or judges surrendered to social fear. The great outbreaks in Sweden in 1668–77, in Salzburg in 1677–81, in Mecklenburg after 1690 and in colonial New England in 1692 show that if the Thirty Years War was the last occasion of international mania, national mania could still be aroused. The fire still lurked beneath the cinders.

Nevertheless, after the Thirty Years War something had happened. It was not merely that the war was over. The stereotype itself had weakened. In Protestant and Catholic countries alike the myth has lost its force. In the 1650s Cyrano de Bergerac could write in France as if it were already dead, at least among educated men.[141] Twenty years later, in 1672, the law would recognize its death when Colbert abolished the charge of *sorcellerie sabbatique*. In Cromwellian England the 1650s saw an outbreak of books repudiating witch-trials; the frequent discovery and execution of witches, Francis Osborne told his son in 1656, "makes me think the strongest fascination is encircled within the ignorance of the judges, malice of the witnesses, or stupidity of the poor parties accused."[142] In Calvinist Geneva, once so ferocious, the last witch was burnt in 1652: the urban aristocracy had by now reduced the clergy to order. At the same time the magistrates of Bern issued an ordinance to restrain the witch-judges. In 1657 even the Church of Rome, which had put all critical books on the Index, issued "a tardy *instructio* urging her inquisitors to circumspection."[143] From now on, in spite of local recrudescence and intellectual support, the climate of opinion has changed, and the assertors of witchcraft, but recently so confident, find

---

Rise and Influence of . . . Rationalism in Europe, I, 98–99). In Mecklenburg—as in Scotland—the triumph of the witch-burners coincided with the triumph of the Estates over the prince. The Swedish outbreak of 1667 took place while the power of the Crown was in abeyance.

141. See Lucien Fèbvre, in *Annales: économies, sociétés, civilisation*, 1948, p. 15.

142. Francis Osborne, *Advice to his Son* [1656], ed. E. A. Parry (1896), p. 125. Among books against witch-trials at that time are [Sir Robert Filmer], *An Advertisement to the Jury-men of England touching Witches* (1653); Thomas Ady, *A Candle in the Dark* (1656).

143. Lea, *Materials*, pp. 743–44; Burr, *Life*, p. 186. For the effect of the Roman Instruction in Poland, see Lea, *Materials*, pp. 1232, 1273.

themselves on the defensive. While the social stereotypes of the Jew in Germany and the Popish Plot in England retain their plausibility, that of the witch is failing, and we have to ask, how did this happen? Why did a mythology which, against all likelihood, had been prolonged for two centuries, suddenly lose its force? For although the old laws may remain on the statute book and the old beliefs will linger in school and cloister, the systematic mythology and the social force which it inspired, is crumbling. By 1700 the "craze" is over: the infidels, as John Wesley was to lament, "have hooted witchcraft out of the world."

V

The decline and apparently final collapse of the witch-craze in the late seventeenth century, while other such social stereotypes retained their power, is a revolution which is surprisingly difficult to document. We see the controversies continue. Important names appear on both sides—but the greater names, at least in England, are on the side of the craze, not against it. How can the obscure and tipsy Oxford scholar John Wagstaffe or the crochety Yorkshire surgeon-parson John Webster compete with the names of Sir Thomas Browne and Richard Baxter and the Cambridge Platonists Ralph Cudworth, Henry More and Joseph Glanville? And yet on neither side are the arguments new: they are the arguments which have always been used. On the side of orthodoxy some caution can be observed: the grosser and more preposterous details of the demonologists are silently dropped (although continental and Scottish lawyers and clergy continued to assert them) and the argument is given a more philosophic base. But on the sceptical side there is no advance. Webster is no more modern than Weyer. Nevertheless, without new argument on either side the intellectual belief quietly dissolved. The witch-trials, in spite of a few last outbursts, came to an end. The witch-laws were repealed, almost without debate.

It has been pointed out that, in this reform, Protestant countries led the way. England and Holland were regarded, in 1700, as countries long since emancipated while the Catholic prince-bishops of Germany were still burning away. Inside Germany, says a German scholar, the Protestant states abandoned persecution a full generation before the Catholic.[144] In mixed societies, like Alsace, the Catholic lords had always been

---

144. Riezler, *Geschichte der Hexenprozessen in Baiern*, p. 282.

fiercer than the Protestant.[145] And certainly Catholic manuals continued to insist on demonological doctrine when the Protestant writers had conveniently forgotten it. However, in view of the undoubted part played by the Protestant Churches in forwarding the craze after 1560, we should perhaps be chary of claiming any special virtue for Protestantism in resisting it after 1650. Calvinist and Lutheran doctrines were as uncompromising, Calvinist and Lutheran clergy as ferocious as Catholic; and where the Calvinist or Lutheran clergy had effective power—as in Scotland or Mecklenburg—the craze continued as long as in any Catholic country. To the very end, honours remained even between the two religions. If the last witch-burning in Europe was in Catholic Poland in 1793, that was an illegal act: witch-trials had been abolished in Poland in 1787. The last legal execution was in Protestant Glarus, in Switzerland, in 1782. Appropriately the craze which had been born in the Alps retreated thither to die.

But if the power of the clergy, Protestant or Catholic, prolonged the craze, their weakness hastened its end; and the clergy were undoubtedly weaker in some Protestant than in most Catholic countries. This was particularly true in the United Netherlands. The Dutch Calvinist clergy, the *Predikants*, were notoriously intolerant; but unlike their Scottish brethren, they were never allowed to exercise or influence jurisdiction. This was discovered even during the national revolution. In 1581 Lambert Daneau, the most important Huguenot preacher after his masters Calvin and Beza, and incidentally, like them, a formidable witch-hunter, received a call to a chair in the new University of Leiden. He answered the call. But he had not been long in Leiden before his theocratic pretensions brought him into trouble. The Council of Leiden, he was told, would resist the inquisition of Geneva no less than that of Spain; and he found it prudent to leave the Netherlands to rule over a more submissive flock in Pyrenean France.[146] In the next century the Dutch Calvinist clergy continued to demand death for witchcraft. Their intellectual oracles, Junius, Rivetus, Voëtius, were unambiguous on this point.[147] The greatest and latest of them was Voëtius, professor

145. Reuss, *L'Alsace au 17e siècle*, II, 105.

146. P. de Félice, *Lambert Daneau, sa vie, ses ouvrages, ses lettres inédites* (Paris, 1882).

147. Both Junius and Rivetus expressed their views in commentaries on Exod. xxii. 18: Franciscus Junius, *Libri Exodi Analytica Explicatio* (Leiden, 1598); Andreas Rivetus, *Commentarius in Exodum* (Leiden, 1634). Junius also translated Bodin's *Démonomanie*.

and rector of the University of Utrecht. He denounced, with equal assurance, the theories of Galileo, Harvey and Descartes and marshalled a series of massive arguments to show that there are witches and that they should not be suffered to live. It particularly infuriated him that Scot's work, though rightly burnt in England, had been translated into Dutch and had corrupted many readers in the republic, already only too full of "libertines" and "semi-libertines." [148] He was no doubt thinking of "Arminians" like Hugo Grotius, who would put authority in matters of religion in the hands of lay magistrates and declared that the Mosaic penalties were no longer binding; or Episcopius, who denied the reality of the witch's pact with Satan, the very basis of witchcraft; or Johann Greve, who, like Weyer, came from Cleves and urged the abolition of torture in witch-trials.[149] It was an Arminian too, "the Arminian printer" Thomas Basson, the printer of Grotius and Arminius himself, who had translated Scot's book and published it in Leiden; and it was the Arminian historian Pieter Schrijver, or Scriberius, who had set him on.[150] The Calvinist clergy succeeded in condemning Arminianism, procured the exile of Grotius and hounded Greve from his parish at Arnhem. But they were never able to capture criminal jurisdiction from the lay magistrates, and it was clearly for this reason, not because of any virtue in their doctrine, that no witch was burnt in Holland after 1597 and witch trials ceased in 1610.[151]

Was the collapse of the witch-craze then due merely to the victory of the laity over the clergy: a victory that was more easily won in Protestant countries, where the clergy had already been weakened, than in Catholic countries where it had retained its power? The inference is natural, and no doubt partly true: but it can only be partly true. For whence did the laity acquire their ideas? The witch-craze may have been first formulated by the clergy, but by 1600 it was being

148. *Gisberti Voëtii Selectarum Disputationum Theologicarum . . . Pars Tertia*, pp. 539–632, "de Magia." Voëtius, who dominated Utrecht till his death in 1678, at the age of eighty-seven, first wrote this work in 1636 and amplified it in later editions. His arguments were repeated with approval by Johann Christian Frommann, *Tractatus de Fascinatione Novus et Singularis* (Nuremberg, 1675).

149. See Johann Greve [Graevius], *Tribunal Reformatum* (Hamburg, 1624). Greve was influenced by Weyer whom he often quotes. See Binz, *Doctor Johann Weyer*.

150. J. A. von Dorsten, *Thomas Basson, 1555–1613, English Printer at Leiden* (Leiden, Sir Thomas Browne Institute, 1961), pp. 49–54.

151. Jacobus Scheltema, *Geschiedenis der Heksenprocessen* (Haarlem, 1828), p. 258.

perpetuated by the lawyers. Bodin, Boguet, de l'Ancre, Carpzov were lay magistrates, not clergymen. We have seen the lay magistrates of Lemgo, in Westphalia, imposing the new cold-water test, and those of Dôle, in Franche-Comté, demanding fiercer penalties for the growing pest of witchcraft. It was the lay magistrates of Essex, under the chairmanship of the Puritan Earl of Warwick, who in 1645 condemned a record number of witches to death at Chelmsford assizes and it was the lay magistrates of Rouen who protested against Colbert's order suspending witch-trials. When we compare these laymen with clergy like the Arminian Greve or the Jesuit Spee, or the Anglican bishops of James I and Charles I, or the Gallican bishops of Richelieu and Mazarin,[152] we have to admit that there are laity and laity, clergy and clergy. No doubt the independent laity of mercantile cities or great courts have a more liberal outlook than the legal caste of provincial towns or petty principalities. But is not the same true of the clergy? Ultimately, the difference is a difference of ideas. The independent laity—educated merchants, officials, gentry—may be freer to receive new ideas than clergy or lawyers; they may give social content and social force to such ideas; but the ideas themselves, as often as not, are generated among the clergy. The Reformation itself, that great social revolution, began as "une querelle de moines."

We can see the resistance of the laity to the witch-craze all through its course. It was a resistance to which every witch-doctor paid indignant tribute. But it was a limited resistance: a resistance of scepticism, of common sense, not of positive disbelief or opposite belief. Men revolted against the cruelty of torture, against the implausibility of confessions, against the identification of witches. They did not revolt against the central doctrine of the kingdom of Satan and its war on humanity by means of demons and witches. They had no substitute for such a doctrine. And because that doctrine was established, even accepted, it had provided the central pillar around which other doctrines, other experiences had entwined themselves, adding to its strength. Sceptics might doubt. They might even protest. But neither doubt nor protest was enough. In fair weather the luxury of scepticism might be allowed; but when the storm returned, men fell back again on the old faith, the old orthodoxy.

152. See, for instance, the enlightened letter sent by Léonor d'Estampes de Valençay, Archbishop and Duke of Reims, to the chancellor, Séguier, on 28 July 1644, quoted in *Lettres et mémoires du chancelier Séguier*, ed. Roland Mousnier (Paris, 1964), i, 636–37.

If the witch-craze were to be attacked at its centre, not merely doubted at its periphery, it was clearly necessary to challenge the whole conception of the kingdom of Satan. This neither Weyer nor Scot nor Spee had done. All through the sixteenth and seventeenth centuries it had been an axiom of faith that the Church was engaged in a life-and-death struggle with Satan. The writers of the *Malleus* had referred, in lamentable tones, to the impending end of the world whose disasters were everywhere visible,[153] and the Protestant writers, reactionary in this as in all else, had used, and intensified, the same language. In the early seventeenth century millenary ideas, forgotten since the Middle Ages, were revived, and the greatest discovery of a scientific century was declared to be the calculation, by a future Fellow of the Royalist Society, of the hitherto elusive number of the Beast.[154] But at the very end of the century one writer did attempt to challenge the whole idea of Satan's kingdom. This was the Dutch minister Balthasar Bekker, who in 1690 published the first version of the first volume of his *de Betoverde Weereld*, "the Enchanted World."

Both at the time and since Bekker was regarded as the most dangerous enemy of witch-beliefs. The orthodox denounced him in unmeasured tones. Like Greve, seventy years before, he was persecuted by the Calvinist clergy of Holland and ultimately, though protected by the city of Amsterdam, driven out of the ministry. The first two volumes of his book, it is said, sold 4000 copies in two months and it was translated into French, German and English. Pamphlets were poured out against him. He was held responsible for the cessation of witch-burnings in England and Holland[155] — although witches had never been burnt in England and burnings had long ceased in Holland. Bekker, it has been regularly said, struck at the heart of the witch-craze by destroying belief in the Devil.[156]

Perhaps he did in theory; but did he in fact? When we look closer,

153. "Cum inter ruentis seculi calamitates, quas (proh dolor!) non tam legimus quam passim experimur . . . mundi vespere ad occasum declinante et malicia hominum excrescente . . ." etc., etc. *Malleus Maleficarum* (Apologia).

154. See the lyrical exclamations of the celebrated Puritan divine William Twisse in his Preface to Joseph Mede's *Key of the Revelation* (1643) and cf. Twisse's letter to Mede in Mede's *Works*, ed. John Worthington (1664), II, 70–71.

155. Jacob Brunnemann, *Discours von betrüglichen Kennzeichen der Zauberey* (Stargard, 1708), cited in Lea, *Materials*, p. 1427.

156. This point was made by Soldan in 1843 and has been repeated ever since.

we find reasons for doubt. Bekker's foreign reputation seems largely a myth. The controversy over his work was conducted almost entirely in the Dutch language.[157] And that controversy was evidently soon over. In 1696 a Frenchman declared that Bekker's disciples were already falling away, disappointed by his later volumes; and this opinion is confirmed by the fact that the English translation never got beyond the first volume.[158] An Englishman who wished to refute Bekker a few years later, and who sent to Holland "for all that was writ against him and any replies he had made," could obtain only one small volume in French.[159] The German translation was declared by a good judge to be worthless: the translator, it was said, understood neither Dutch nor German nor his author.[160] By 1706 Bekker seemed forgotten. His work had enjoyed a *succès de scandale* only. And anyway, he had not repudiated belief in the Devil. He merely believed that the Devil, on his fall from Heaven, had been locked up in Hell, unable further to interfere in human affairs. This purely theological point was not likely to cause a revolution in thought. In his particular arguments about witches Bekker was inspired, as he admitted, by Scot, and did not go beyond Scot.

Moreover, Bekker's radicalism was disowned by later, and perhaps more effective, opponents of the witch-craze. If any group of men destroyed the craze in Lutheran Germany it was the Pietists of the University of Halle whose leader, in this respect, was Christian Thomasius, the advocate of the vernacular language. In a series of works, beginning with a university thesis in 1701, Thomasius denounced the folly and cruelty of witch-trials. But he was careful to dissociate himself from Bekker. There is a Devil, Thomasius protests, and there are witches: this "cannot be denied without great presumption and thoughtless-

157. A. van der Linde, *Balthasar Bekker Bibliographie* (The Hague, 1869), lists 134 contemporary works concerning Bekker. Apart from one in French (see next note) and two in Latin, all are in Dutch.

158. Benjamin Binet, *Traité historique des dieux et des démons* (Delft, 1696). The English translation of Bekker's work appeared under the title *The World turn'd upside down* . . . (1700).

159. John Beaumont, *An Historical, Physiological and Theological Treatise of Spirits* (1705). This work is not mentioned by van der Linde.

160. Eberhard David Hauber, *Bibliotheca Acta et Scripta Magica* (Lemgo, 1739), i, 565. Hauber was a liberal Lutheran clergyman whose work—reprints of earlier texts illustrating the witch-craze—helped to liberalize the public opinion of Germany. But, like Thomasius, he was critical of Bekker.

ness." But Weyer and Scot and Spee have shown that the witches who are tried in Germany are quite different from those witches whose death is prescribed in the Bible, that the demonology of the Church is a mixture of pagan and Jewish superstition, and that confessions produced by torture are false. Again and again Thomasius protests that he is falsely accused of disbelieving in the Devil. He believes in the Devil, he says, and that he still operates, externally and invisibly: he only disbelieves that the Devil has horns and a tail; and he believes in witches: he only disbelieves in their pact with the Devil, the sabbat, *incubi* and *succubi*. When we examine his arguments we find that neither he nor his friends at Halle went beyond Scot or Spee or those English writers, Wagstaffe and Webster, whose works they caused to be translated into German.[161] And yet it is equally clear that the arguments which had been advanced in vain by Scot and Spee were effective when advanced by Thomasius. The witch-craze did not collapse because Bekker dislodged the Devil from his central position: the Devil decayed quietly with the witch-belief;[162] and why the witch-belief decayed—why the critical arguments which were regarded as unplausible in 1563 and in 1594 and in 1631 were found plausible in 1700—is mysterious still.

The nineteenth-century liberal historians did indeed offer an answer. They saw the controversy as a straight contest between superstition and reason, between theology and science, between the Church and "rationalism." The Englishman Lecky, the Americans White, Lea and Burr, the German Hansen, write as if the irrationality of the witch-beliefs had always been apparent to the natural reason of man and as if the prevalence of such beliefs could be explained only by clerical bigotry allied with political power. This bigotry, they seem to say, was artificially created. The persecution began, says Burr, because the Inquisition, having fulfilled its original purpose of destroying the Albigensian

161. A German translation of Wagstaffe's *Question of Witchcraft Debated* (1669) was published at Halle, dedicated to Thomasius, in 1711. Thomasius himself wrote a preface to a German translation of Webster's *The Displaying of Supposed Witchcraft*, which was also published at Halle in 1719.

162. How little Bekker had to do with the destruction of belief among the Dutch laity is shown by the remarks of a French officer who visited Holland with the Prince de Condé in 1673—nearly twenty years before Bekker wrote. He reported that at that time most Dutchmen regarded Hell as a "phantom" and Paradise as "an agreeable chimera" invented by the clergy to encourage virtue. See G.-B. Stoppa, *La Religion des Hollandois* . . . (Paris, 1673), p. 88.

heretics, found itself with nothing to do and so "turned its idle hands to the extirpation of witches." [163] From that time onwards, these writers suggest, the "rationalists" fought a long battle against clerical and conservative bigotry. At first it was a losing battle, but at last persistence brought its reward: the tide turned and the battle was ultimately won. And yet, these writers seem to be saying, even now it is not quite won. As long as there is religion, there is a danger of superstition, and superstition will break out in these and such forms. The world—so Hansen ended his great work—will not be free till the still undefeated residue of superstition has been expelled from the religious systems of the modern world.

Today such a distinction between "reason" and "superstition" is difficult to maintain. We have seen the darkest forms of superstitious belief and superstitious cruelty springing again not out of half-purged religious systems, but out of new, purely secular roots. We have seen that social stereotypes are more lasting than religious systems—indeed, that religious systems may be only temporary manifestations of a more deep-seated social attitude. We have also come to distrust too rational explanations. The picture of the Inquisition using up its idle machinery against witches simply to prevent it from rusting cannot convince us. Finally, we can no longer see intellectual history as a direct contest between reason and faith, reason and superstition. We recognize that even rationalism is relative: that it operates within a general philosophic context, and that it cannot properly be detached from this context.

The liberal historians of the nineteenth century supposed that it could be so detached: that those men who, in the sixteenth and seventeenth centuries, were revolted by the cruelty of witch-trials, or rejected the absurdities of witch-beliefs, ought to have seen that it was not enough to protest against these incidental excesses: they should have seen that the whole system had no rational basis. In their impatience with the critics of the past, these liberal historians sometimes seem to us absurdly anachronistic. When he examines the work of Weyer, Lea becomes positively snappish. Why, he asks, is Weyer so "illogical"? Why cannot he see "the fatal defect" in his own reasoning? Weyer, he exclaims, was "as credulous as any of his contemporaries": his work is an extraordinary mixture of "common sense" and "folly"; "nothing can exceed the ingenious perversity" of his views, his belief in magic

163. Burr, *Translations and Reprints*, p. 1.

and demons while he rejects the sabbat and *succubi*. No wonder "his labours had so limited a result." [164] It is clear that, to Lea, "reason," "logic," is a self-contained, independent system of permanent validity. What is obvious in nineteenth-century Philadelphia must have been equally obvious in sixteenth-century Germany. We are reminded of Macaulay's remark that "a Christian of the fifth century with a Bible is neither better nor worse situated than a Christian of the nineteenth century with a Bible" and that the absurdity of a literal interpretation was "as great and as obvious in the sixteenth century as it is now." [165]

But the difficulty of the men of the sixteenth and seventeenth centuries was that witch-beliefs were not detachable from their general context. The mythology of the Dominicans was an extension, with the aid of peasant superstition, feminine hysteria and clerical imagination, of a whole cosmology. It was also rooted in permanent social attitudes. In order to dismantle this grotesque mental construction, it was not enough—it was not possible—to look at its component ideas in isolation. They could not be so isolated, nor was there yet an independent "reason" detached from the context of which they too were a part. If men were to revise their views on witchcraft, the whole context of those views had to be revised. Then, and then only, this extension—the weakest part of it, but theoretically essential to it—would dissolve. Until that had happened, all that men could do was to doubt its more questionable details. Even then, even when that had happened, the repudiation would not be complete: for it would be merely intellectual. Unless there were also a social transformation, the social basis of the belief would remain—although a new stereotype would have to be devised in order to express the hostility which it had embodied.

How inseparable the witch-beliefs were from the whole philosophy of the time is clear when we look at the demonologists as a class, and at their whole intellectual output, not merely at their treatises on witches and witchcraft. Some of them, of course, are specialists, like Boguet, or are concerned, as lawyers, with witchcraft as an object of the criminal law. But the majority of them are philosophers in a wider field. To St. Thomas Aquinas, the greatest of medieval Dominicans, as to Francisco de Vitoria, the greatest of Spanish Renaissance Dominicans, [166] demon-

---

164. Lea, *Materials,* pp. 494–96, 511, etc.

165. The passage is in Macaulay's essay on Ranke's *History of the Popes.*

166. Vitoria was the greatest of the philosophers of Salamanca: see Marjorie

ology is but one aspect of the world which they seek to understand. Scribonius, who defended the cold-water test, was a professor of philosophy who wrote on natural science and mathematics. The Zwinglian Erastus was a physician, a theologian, a political philosopher as well as a writer on witches. The Lutheran Heinrich Nicolai, professor of philosophy at Danzig in the mid-seventeenth century, wrote on "the whole of human knowledge" before coming to the specialized department of witchcraft.[167] The Calvinists Daneau and Perkins and Voëtius were the encyclopaedists of their party in France, England and Holland: Daneau wrote on Christian physics and Christian politics as well as on witches and every other subject; Perkins was an oracle on all moral questions; Voëtius, like Bacon, took all learning for his province—only, unlike Bacon, in every direction, he resisted its advancement. Bodin was the universal genius of his age. King James and del Rio were men of multifarious, if conservative learning. When we look at the work of these men as a whole, we see that they wrote upon demonology not necessarily because they had a special interest in it, but because they had to do so. Men who sought to express a consistent philosophy of nature could not exclude what was a necessary and logical, if unedifying extension of it. They would not have agreed with the modern historian of magic that "these off-scourings of the criminal courts and torture-chamber, of popular gossip and local scandal, are certainly beneath the dignity of our investigation." [168] Rather, they would have agreed with Bertrand Russell that to flinch from such necessary consequences of their professed beliefs, merely because they were disagreeable or absurd, would be a sign of "the intellectual enfeeblement of orthodoxy."

Equally, those who questioned witch-beliefs could not reject them in isolation. Pomponazzi, Agrippa, Cardano are universal philosophers, Weyer and Ewich medical men with a general philosophy of Nature. If they reject witch-beliefs, it is because they are prepared to question the accepted philosophy of the natural world, of which witch-beliefs were an extension, and to envisage a completely different system. But

---

Grice-Hutchinson, *The School of Salamanca* (Oxford, 1952). He dealt with witchcraft in his *Relectiones XII Theologicae* (Relectio X "de Arte Magica"), written about 1540 and first published at Lyon in 1557.

167. H. Nicolai, *de Cognitione Humana Universa, hoc est de omni scibili humano* (Danzig, 1648); *de Magicis Actionibus* (Danzig, 1649). Nicolai was a "syncretist," and therefore relatively liberal.

168. Thorndike, *History of Magic and Experimental Science*, v, 69.

few men, in the sixteenth century, were prepared to make that effort. Failing such an effort, there were only two ways in which a man could express his dissent from the orthodox demonologists. He could accept the basic philosophic orthodoxy of his time and confine his criticism to the validity of particular methods or particular interpretations. This was the way of Scot and Spee, who believed in witches, but not in the modern methods of identifying them. Or he could recognize that the science of demonology rested firmly on human reason, but doubt the infallibility of such reason and so reserve a liberty of "Pyrrhonist" scepticism. This was the way of Montaigne, who dared to refer to the unanswerable conclusions of scholastic reason as "conjectures."

Neither of these methods was radical enough, by itself, to destroy the intellectual belief in witches. The criticism of a Scot or a Spee might be acceptable in fair times, but it did not touch the basis of belief and with the return of a "great fear" it would soon be forgotten. The scepticism of a Montaigne might undermine orthodoxy, but it could equally sustain it—as it often did—by undermining heresy. Montaigne himself was claimed as an ally by his witch-burning friend de l'Ancre.[169] The greatest of French sceptics, Pierre Bayle, left the witch-craze exactly where he found it, and his English contemporary, Joseph Glanvill, used scepticism positively to reinforce belief in witchcraft.[170] What ultimately destroyed the witch-craze, on an intellectual level, was not the two-edged arguments of the sceptics, nor was it modern "rationalism," which could exist only within a new context of thought. It was not even the arguments of Bekker, tied as they were to biblical fundamentalism. It was the new philosophy, a philosophical revolution which changed the whole concept of Nature and its operations. That revolution did not occur within the narrow field of demonology, and therefore we cannot usefully trace it by a study which is confined to that field. It occurred in

169. P. de l'Ancre (*Tableau de l'inconstance des mauvais anges et démons*, Paris, 1613, p. 77) remarks that "le coeur et l'âme du sieur de Montaigne" was the fashionable Jesuit Maldonado, who used scepticism only in the cause of orthodoxy. Maldonado preached against witches in Paris and was the acknowledged teacher (*meus quondam doctor*) of del Rio. See Martin del Rio, *Disquisitionum Magicarum Libri VI*, Louvain, 1599–1600, "Proloquium," and I, 210; J. Maldonado, "Praefatio de Daemonibus et eorum praestigiis," printed in H. M. Prat, *"Maldonat et l'Université de Paris"* (Paris, 1856), pp. 567 ff.; Clément Sclafert, "Montaigne et Maldonat," *Bulletin de Littérature Ecclésiastique* LII (Toulouse, 1951), pp. 65–93, 129–46.

170. P. Bayle, *Réponse aux questions d'un provincial*, ch. xxxv–xliv; J. Glanvill, *Some Philosophical Considerations touching the being of witches* (1666); etc.

a far wider field, and the men who made it did not launch their attack on so marginal an area of Nature as demonology. Demonology, after all, was but an appendix of medieval thought, a later refinement of scholastic philosophy. The attack was directed at the centre; and when it had prevailed at the centre, there was no need to struggle for the outworks: they had been turned.

This, it seems to me, is the explanation of the apparent silence of the great thinkers of the early seventeenth century, the philosophers of natural science, natural law, secular history. Why, we are asked, did Bacon, Grotius, Selden not express disbelief in witchcraft? Their silence, or their incidental concessions to orthodoxy, have even been taken, by some, to argue belief. But this, I suggest, is a wrong inference. The writers who make it are, once again, treating the subject in isolation. If we wish to interpret reticence, the correct method is not to examine, with rabbinical exactitude, particular breaches of reticence, but first to consider the whole context of a man's thought. When we do that, the explanation, I believe, becomes clear. Bacon, Grotius, Selden may have been reticent on witches. So, for that matter, was Descartes. Why should they court trouble on a secondary, peripheral issue? On the central issue they were not reticent, and it is in their central philosophy that we must see the battle that they were fighting: a battle which would cause the world of witches, ultimately, to wither away.[171]

Nevertheless, what a struggle it had been for the centre! No mere scepticism, no mere "rationalism," could have driven out the old cosmology. A rival faith had been needed, and it therefore seems a little unfair in Lea to blame the earliest and greatest opponent of the craze for being hardly less "credulous" than his adversaries.[172] The first rival

---

171. Bacon's few observations on witches, noncommittal in general, incredulous in particular, are cited in Lea, *Materials*, p. 1355. For his positive views on "magic," see P. Rossi, *Francesco Bacone, dalla magia alla scienza* (Bari, 1951). Selden has been credited with reactionary beliefs on account of one lawyerly observation in his *Table-Talk*, which in fact indicates scepticism, not belief: his real "Platonic" views on Nature can be seen in his *de Diis Syris* (1617), Syntagma, i, cap. 2. Grotius not only believed generally in a universal order of Nature: specifically he rejected the penalties of the Mosaic law, which were the basis of witch-persecution in Protestant countries (*de Jure Belli ac Pacis*, lib. i, cap. i, xvi "Jure Hebraeorum numquam obligatos fuisse alienigenas"); repudiated biblical fundamentalism (much to the indignation of good Calvinists); and in his Annotations on the Old and New Testament followed the example of Erasmus in omitting to comment on the passages customarily cited in support of witch-beliefs.

172. Lea's lack of sympathy with any rationalism but his own is shown by his re-

faith had been Renaissance Platonism, "natural magic": a faith which filled the universe with "demons," but at the same time subjected them to a harmonious Nature whose machinery they served and whose laws they operated. Ultimately, Renaissance Platonism had been left with its demons, and the Cambridge Platonists, insulated in their fenland cloister, were to provide some of the last intellectual defenders of witch-beliefs.[173] But the impulse which it had given was continued by other philosophers: by Bacon with his "purified magic," by Descartes with his universal, "mechanical" laws of Nature, in which demons were unnecessary. It was Descartes, Thomasius and his friends agreed, who dealt the final blow to the witch-craze in western Europe[174]—which perhaps explains, better than the original Protestantism of Colbert, the early suspension of witch-trials in France. Queen Christina of Sweden, who ordered the witch-trials to cease in the Swedish-occupied parts of Germany,[175] had herself been the pupil of Descartes. Gustaf Rosenhane and the physician Urban Hiärne, who resisted the great Swedish witch-craze of 1668–77, were both Cartesians.[176] So was Bekker himself in Holland, though his critics insisted that he had muddled the teaching of his master.[177] But the final victory, which liberated Nature from the biblical fundamentalism in which Bekker himself had still been imprisoned, was that of the English deists and the German Pietists,[178] the

marks on Erastus and Paracelsus. Erastus, he says, "was superior to many of the superstitions of the age, as is shown in his criticism of Paracelsus, and yet a believer in witchcraft" (*Materials*, p. 430). It evidently did not occur to Lea that the rationalism of Erastus entailed belief in witchcraft, while the "superstition" of Paracelsus might create the context of a new rationalism which would dispense with it.

173. The Cambridge Platonists adopted neo-Platonic ideas just at the time when Platonism, from a liberating, was turning into a reactionary force. But Cambridge itself was in many ways cut off from the Baconian and Cartesian ideas which were accepted in Oxford in the 1650s. Even Newton was in many ways imprisoned in the backward-looking Puritan theology of Restoration Cambridge.

174. Thomasius, *de Crimine Magiae* (Halle, 1701, § XLVII). Cf. F. M. Brahm, *Disputatio Inauguralis* . . . (1701), in Lea, *Materials*, p. 1406.

175. See her order of 1649 in Hauber, *Bibliotheca* . . . *Magica*, III, 250.

176. Bertil Sundborg, in *Lychnos*, 1954–55, pp. 204–64.

177. Even the sympathetic Hauber made this criticism (op. cit. I, 565).

178. It is perhaps unfair to isolate Thomasius from the other Pietists, just as it would be unfair to isolate Bekker from other Cartesians. The founder of the Pietist movement, P. J. Spener, had preceded Thomasius in opposing witch-beliefs in his

heirs of the Protestant heretics of the seventeenth century, the parents of that eighteenth-century Enlightenment in which the duel in Nature between a Hebrew God and a medieval Devil was replaced by the benevolent despotism of a modern, scientific "Deity."

VI

I have suggested that the witch-craze of the sixteenth and seventeenth centuries must be seen, if its strength and duration are to be understood, both in its social and in its intellectual context. It cannot properly be seen, as the nineteenth-century liberal historians tended to see it, as a mere "delusion," detached or detachable from the social and intellectual structure of the time. Had it been so—had it been no more than an artificial intellectual construction by medieval inquisitors—it is inconceivable that it should have been prolonged for two centuries after its full formulation; that this formulation should never afterwards have been changed; that criticism should have been so limited; that no criticism should have effectively undermined it; that the greatest thinkers of the time should have refrained from openly attacking it; and that some of them, like Bodin, should even have actively supported it. To conclude this essay I shall try to summarize the interpretation I have offered.

First, the witch-craze was created out of a social situation. In its expansive period, in the thirteenth century, the "feudal" society of Christian Europe came into conflict with social groups which it could not assimilate, and whose defence of their own identity was seen, at first, as "heresy." Sometimes it really was heresy: heretical ideas, intellectual in origin, are often assumed by societies determined to assert their independence. So Manichaean ideas, carried—it seems—by Bulgarian missionaries, were embraced by the radically distinct society of Pyrenean France and "Vaudois" ideas, excogitated in the cities of Lombardy or the Rhône, were adopted in the Alpine valleys where "feudal" society could never be established. The medieval Church, as the spiritual organ of "feudal" society, declared war on these "heresies," and the friars, who waged that war, defined both orthodoxy and heresy in the process. We

---

Theologische Bedencken (1700); Gottfried Arnold, who defended the heretics of the past in his *Unparteyische Kirche- und Ketzerhistorie* (1699), co-operated with Thomasius; and it was from the university press of Halle, the centre of Pietism, that nearly all the German books against the witch-craze were sent forth.

know that the doctrines which they ascribed both to the Albigensians and to the Vaudois are not necessarily the doctrines really professed by those "heretics," whose authentic documents have been almost entirely destroyed by their persecutors. The inquisitors ascribed to the societies which they opposed at once a more elaborate cosmology and a more debased morality than we have any reason to do. In particular, they ascribed to the Albigensians an absolute dualism between God and the Devil in Nature, and orgies of sexual promiscuity—a charge regularly made by the orthodox against esoteric dissenting societies. Both these charges would be carried forward from the first to the second stage of the struggle.

For the first stage was soon over. Orthodox "feudal" society destroyed the "Albigensian" and reduced the "Vaudois" heresies. The friars evangelized the Alpine and Pyrenean valleys. However, the social dissidence remained, and therefore a new rationalization of it seemed necessary. In those mountain areas, where pagan customs lingered and the climate bred nervous disease, the missionaries soon discovered superstitions and hallucinations out of which to fabricate a second set of heresies: heresies less intellectual, and even less edifying, than those which they had stamped out, but nevertheless akin to them. The new "heresy" of witchcraft, as discovered in the old haunts of the Cathari and the Vaudois, rested on the same dualism of God and the Devil; it was credited with the same secret assemblies, the same promiscuous sexual orgies; and it was described, often, by the same names.

This new "heresy" which the inquisitors discovered beneath the relics of the old was not devised in isolation. The Albigensians, like their Manichaean predecessors, had professed a dualism of good and evil, God and the Devil, and the Dominicans, the hammers of the Albigensians, like St. Augustine, the hammer of the Manichees, had adopted something of the dualism against which they had fought. They saw themselves as worshippers of God, their enemies as worshippers of the Devil; and as the Devil is *simia Dei*, the ape of God, they built up their diabolical system as the necessary counterpart of their divine system. The new Aristotelean cosmology stood firmly behind them both, and St. Thomas Aquinas, the guarantor of the one, was the guarantor of the other. The two were interdependent; and they depended not only on each other, but also on a whole philosophy of the world.

The elaboration of the new heresy, as of the new orthodoxy, was the work of the medieval Catholic Church and, in particular, of its most active members, the Dominican friars. No argument can evade or circumvent this fact. The elements of the craze may be non-Christian, even pre-Christian. The practice of spells, the making of weather, the use of sympathetic magic may be universal. The concepts of a pact with the Devil, of night-riding to the sabbat, of *incubi* and *succubi*, may derive from the pagan folk-lore of the Germanic peoples.[179] But the weaving together of these various elements into a systematic demonology which could supply a social stereotype for persecution was exclusively the work, not of Christianity, but of the Catholic Church. The Greek Orthodox Church offers no parallel. There were peasant superstitions in Greece: Thessaly was the classic home of ancient witches. There were encyclopaedic minds among the Greek Fathers: no refinement of absurdity deterred a Byzantine theologian. The same objective situation existed in the east as in the west: Manichaean dualism was the heresy of the Bogomils of Bulgaria before it became the heresy of the Albigensians of Languedoc. But even out of the ruins of Bogomilism, the Greek Orthodox Church built up no systematic demonology and launched no witch-craze. By the schism of 1054 the Slavonic countries of Europe—with the exception of Catholic Poland, the exception which proves the rule—escaped participation in one of the most disreputable episodes in Christian history.[180]

Such, it seems, was the origin of the system. It was perfected in the course of a local struggle and it had, at first, a local application. But the intellectual construction, once complete, was, in itself, universal. It could be applied anywhere. And in the fourteenth century, that century of increasing introversion and intolerance, among the miseries of the Black Death and the Hundred Years War in France, its application was made general. The first of the Avignon popes, themselves bishops from recalcitrant Languedoc, gave a new impulse to the craze. The weapon forged for use against nonconformist societies was taken up to destroy nonconformist individuals: while the inquisitors in the Alps and the Pyrenees continued to multiply the evidence, the warring

179. This is stated by Weiser-Aall in Bächtold-Stäubli, *Handwörterbuch des deutschen Aberglauben III* (Berlin and Leipzig, 1930–31), pp. 1828 ff., s.v. "Hexe."

180. This point is made by Riezler, *Geschichte der Hexenprozessen in Baiern*, p. 51, and by Hansen, *Quellen*, p. 71. It may be remarked that the one great Church Father who wrote before the schism and who provided an intellectual basis for the later witch-craze, St. Augustine, had little or no influence in Byzantium. This was no doubt partly because he wrote in Latin. Without Augustine, without Aquinas, the Greek Church lacked the cosmological infrastructure of the witch-craze.

political factions of France and Burgundy exploited it to destroy their enemies. Every spectacular episode increased the power of the myth. Like the Jew, the witch became the stereotype of the incurable non-conformist; and in the declining Middle Ages, the two were joined as scapegoats for the ills of society. The founding of the Spanish Inquisition, which empowered the "Catholic Kings" to destroy "judaism" in Spain, and the issue of the Witch Bull, which urged cities and princes to destroy witches in Germany, can be seen as two stages in one campaign.

Even so, the myth might have dissolved in the early sixteenth century. The new prosperity might have removed the need for a social scapegoat. The new ideas of the Renaissance might have destroyed its intellectual basis. We have seen that in the years 1500–50, outside its Alpine home, the craze died down. In those years the purified Aristoteleanism of Padua corrected the extravagance of scholastic physics; the neo-Platonism of Florence offered a more universal interpretation of Nature; the new criticism of the humanists pared down medieval absurdities. All these intellectual movements might, in themselves, be ambivalent, but they might, together, have been effective. In fact they were not. In the mid-sixteenth century, the craze was revived and extended and the years from 1560 to 1630 saw the worst episodes in its long history. It seems incontestable that the cause of this revival was the intellectual regression of Reformation and Counter-Reformation, and the renewed evangelism of the rival Churches. The former gave new life to the medieval, pseudo-Aristotelean cosmology of which demonology was now an inseparable part. The latter carried into northern Europe the same pattern of forces which the Dominicans had once carried into the Alps and Pyrenees—and evoked a similar response.

The Reformation is sometimes seen as a progressive movement. No doubt it began as such: for it began in humanism. But in the years of struggle, of ideological war, humanism was soon crushed out. The great doctors of the Reformation, as of the Counter-Reformation, and their numerous clerical myrmidons, were essentially conservative: and they conserved far more of the medieval tradition than they would willingly admit. They might reject the Roman supremacy and go back, for their Church system, to the rudimentary organization of the apostolic age. They might pare away the incrustations of doctrine, the monasticism, the "mechanical devotions," the priestcraft of the "corrupted" medieval Church. But these were superficial disavowals. Beneath their "purified" Church discipline and Church doctrine, the Reformers retained the whole philosophic infrastructure of scholastic Catholicism. There was no new Protestant physics, no exclusively Protestant view of Nature. In every field of thought, Calvinism and Lutheranism, like Counter-Reformation Catholicism, marked a retreat, an obstinate defence of fixed positions. And since demonology, as developed by the Dominican inquisitors, was an extension of the pseudo-Aristotelean cosmology, it was defended no less obstinately. Luther might not quote the *Malleus;* Calvin might not own a debt to the Schoolmen; but the debt was clear, and their successors would admit it. Demonology, like the science of which it was a part, was a common inheritance which could not be denied by such conservative Reformers. It lay deeper than the superficial disputes about religious practices and the mediation of the priest.[181]

But if the Reformation was not, intellectually, a progressive movement, it was undoubtedly an evangelical movement. Like the Dominicans of the Middle Ages the Lutheran and Calvinist clergy set out to recover for the faith—for their version of the faith—the peoples of northern Europe whom the Catholic Church had almost lost. In the first generation after Luther this evangelical movement had hardly begun. Luther's appeal was to the Christian princes, to the Christian nobility of Germany. As in the England of Henry VIII, Reform had begun as an affair of state. But by 1560 the princes, or many of them, had been won, and the immediate need was for preachers to establish religion among their people. So the second generation of Reformers, the missionaries formed in Wittenberg or Geneva, poured into the lands of hospitable princes or estates and the Word was preached not only in the ears of the great but in rural parishes in Germany and Scandinavia, France, England and Scotland.

Of course the triumph of the preachers was not always easy. Sometimes they found individual opposition; sometimes whole societies seemed obstinately to refuse their Gospel. Just as the Dominican missionaries had encountered stubborn resistance from the mountain

181. Paulus (*Hexenwahn und Hexenprozess,* § iv), in his attempts to spare the medieval Catholic Church, argues that the Protestant Reformers derived their demonology not from their Catholic predecessors but direct from Germanic mythology. This argument (which is also used by the Catholic apologist Janssen) depends, once again, on an improper isolation of witch-beliefs from general cosmology. If Luther had rejected the Aristotelean cosmology while accepting witch-beliefs, then it *might* be said that he derived those beliefs from pagan sources—although even then the argument would be very strained. But since he, like Calvin, accepted the basic cosmology of the medieval Church, there is no need for such ingenuity. When the front door is wide open, why make a detour in search of a back passage?

communities of the Alps and Pyrenees, so the Protestant missionaries found their efforts opposed by whole communities in the waste lands of the neglected, half-pagan north. The German preachers found such dissidence in Westphalia, in Mecklenburg, in Pomerania: areas, as a German physician later observed, where the peasants live miserably on thin beer, pig's meat and black bread;[182] the more tolerant Swedish clergy found it, though they did not persecute it, in the racially distinct societies of Lapland and Finland; the Scottish Kirk found it, and persecuted it, among the Celtic Highlanders. Sometimes this opposition could be described in doctrinal terms, as "popery." The Scottish witches who set to sea in a sieve to inconvenience King James were declared to be "Papists," and Lancashire, of course, was a nest of both Papists and witches. Sometimes it was too primitive to deserve doctrinal terms, and then a new explanation had to be found. But this time there was no need to invent a new stereotype. The necessary stereotype had already been created by the earlier missionaries and strengthened by long use. The dissidents were witches.

With the Catholic reconquest a generation later, the same pattern repeats itself. The Catholic missionaries too discover obstinate resistance. They too find it social as well as individual. They too find it in particular areas: in Languedoc, in the Vosges and the Jura, in the Rhineland, the German Alps. They too describe it now as Protestant heresy, now as witchcraft. The two terms are sometimes interchangeable, or at least the frontier between them is as vague as that between Albigensians and witches in the past. The Basque witches, says de l'Ancre, have been brought up in the errors of Calvinism. Nothing has spread this pest more effectively through England, Scotland, Flanders and France, declares del Rio (echoing another Jesuit, Maldonado) than *dira Calvinismi lues*. "Witchcraft grows with heresy, heresy with witchcraft," the English Catholic Thomas Stapleton cried to the sympathetic doctors of Louvain.[183] His argument—his very words—were

182. Friedrich Hoffmann, *Dissertatio Physico-Medica de Diaboli Potentia in Corpora* (Halle, 1703), quoted in Lea, *Materials*, p. 1466; and see Lea's note *ad loc.* Cf. also Brunnemann, *Discours von betrüglichen Kennzeichen der Zauberey*, cited in Lea, *Materials*, p. 1429, which also gives Westphalia, Pomerania and Mecklenburg as the home of witches.

183. "Crescit cum magia haeresis, cum haeresi magia." Thomas Stapleton's dissertation on the question "Cur magia pariter cum haeresi hodie creverit," delivered on 30 Aug. 1594, is printed in *Thomae Stapleton Angli S.T.D. Opera Omnia* (Paris, 1620), II, 502–7.

afterwards repeated, with changed doctrinal labels, by Lutheran pastors in Germany.[184] Whenever the missionaries of one Church are recovering a society from their rivals, "witchcraft" is discovered beneath the thin surface of "heresy."

Such, it seems, is the progress of the witch-craze as a social movement. But it is not only a social movement. From its social basis it also has its individual extension. It can be extended deliberately, in times of political crisis, as a political device, to destroy powerful enemies or dangerous persons. Thus it was used in France in the fourteenth and fifteenth centuries. It can also be extended blindly, in times of panic, by its own momentum. When a "great fear" takes hold of society, that society looks naturally to the stereotype of the enemy in its midst; and once the witch had become the stereotype, witchcraft would be the universal accusation. It was an accusation which was difficult to rebut in the lands where popular prejudice was aided by judicial torture: we have only to imagine the range of the Popish Plot in England in 1679 if every witness had been tortured. It is in such times of panic that we see the persecution extended from old women, the ordinary victims of village hatred, to educated judges and clergy whose crime is to have resisted the craze. Hence those terrible episodes in Trier and Bamberg and Würzburg. Hence also that despairing cry of the good senator de l'Ancre, that formerly witches were "hommes vulgaires et idiots, nourris dans les bruyères et la fougière des Landes," but nowadays witches under torture confess that they have seen at the sabbat "une infinité de gens de qualité que Satan tient voilez et à couvert pour n'estre cognus." [185] It is a sign of such a "great fear" when the *élite* of society are accused of being in league with its enemies.

Finally, the stereotype, once established, creates, as it were, its own folk-lore, which becomes in itself a centralizing force. If that folk-lore had not already existed, if it had not already been created by social fear out of popular superstition within an intellectually approved cosmology, then psychopathic persons would have attached their sexual

---

184. Hauber (*Bibliotheca . . . Magica*, II, 205) states that he possessed a copy of Stapleton's dissertation as emended for delivery in a Lutheran university during the great witch-craze of the late 1620s. The words "Luther" and "Lutherans" had been changed into "the Pope" and "the Jesuits"; otherwise no alteration had been thought necessary: a nice commentary on the intellectual originality of both sides. The good Lutheran had left Stapleton's abuse of the Calvinists intact.

185. P. de l'Ancre, *Tableau de l'inconstance des mauvais anges et démons* (Paris, 1613), dedication to Mgr. de Sillery, chancelier de France.

hallucinations to other, perhaps more individual figures. This, after all, is what happens today. But once the folk-lore had been created and had been impressed by the clergy upon every mind, it served as a psychological as well as a social stereotype. The Devil with his nightly visits, his *succubi* and *incubi*, his solemn pact which promised new power to gratify social and personal revenge, became "subjective reality" to hysterical women in a harsh rural world or in artificial communities — in ill-regulated nunneries as at Marseilles, at Loudun, at Louviers, or in special regions like the Pays de Labourd, where (according to de l'Ancre) the fishermen's wives were left deserted for months. And because separate persons attached their illusions to the same imaginary pattern, they made that pattern real to others. By their separate confessions the science of the Schoolmen was empirically confirmed.

Thus on all sides the myth was built up and sustained. There were local differences of course, as well as differences of time; differences of jurisdiction as well as differences of procedure. A strong central government could control the craze while popular liberty often let it run wild. The centralized Inquisition in Spain or Italy, by monopolizing persecution, kept down its production, while north of the Alps the free competition of bishops, abbots and petty lords, each with his own jurisdiction, kept the furnaces at work. The neighbourhood of a great international university, like Basel or Heidelberg, had a salutary effect,[186] while one fanatical preacher or one over-zealous magistrate in a backward province could infect the whole area. But all these differences merely affected the practice of the moment: the myth itself was universal and constant. Intellectually logical, socially necessary, experimentally proved, it had become a *datum* in European life. Rationalism could not attack it, for rationalism itself, as always, moved only within the intellectual context of the time. Scepticism, the distrust of reason, could provide no substitute. At best, the myth might be contained as in the early sixteenth century. But it did not evaporate: it remained

---

186. The University of Heidelberg deserves particular credit, for it maintained critical standards in a strongly Calvinist country. In 1585, or just before, the faculty of law at Heidelberg opposed the death penalty for witchcraft, saying that it was "billicher zu Seelsorgern führen dann zur Marten und zum Todte" — better to cure the soul than to torture and kill the body (cited in Binz, *Doctor Johann Weyer*, pp. 101–2). One of the most powerful opponents of the craze, the Calvinist Hermann Wilchen or Witekind, who wrote under the name "Lerchheimer von Steinfelden," was professor of mathematics at Heidelberg (see Janssen, *A History of the German People*, XVI, 326). On the other hand the famous Thomas Erastus, professor of medicine, was a firm believer.

at the bottom of society, like a stagnant pool, easily flooded, easily stirred. As long as the social and intellectual structure of which it was a part remained intact, any social fear was likely to flood it, any ideological struggle to stir it, and no piecemeal operation could effectively drain it away. Humanist critics, Paduan scientists, might seek to correct the philosophic base of the myth. Psychologists—medical men like Weyer and Ewich and Webster—might explain away its apparent empirical confirmation. Humane men, like Scot and Spee, by natural reason, might expose the absurdity and denounce the cruelty of the methods by which it was propagated. But to destroy the myth, to drain away the pool, such merely local operations no longer sufficed. The whole intellectual and social structure which contained it, and had solidified around it, had to be broken. And it had to be broken not at the bottom, in the dirty sump where the witch-beliefs had collected and been systematized, but at its centre, whence they were refreshed. In the mid-seventeenth century this was done. Then the medieval synthesis, which Reformation and Counter-Reformation had artificially prolonged, was at last broken, and through the cracked crust the filthy pool drained away. Thereafter society might persecute its dissidents as Huguenots [187] or as Jews. It might discover a new stereotype, the "Jacobin," the "Red." But the stereotype of the witch had gone.

187. Thus in 1685 Louis XIV expelled the Huguenots from France as an unassimilable group, but as far as I know, the charges of witchcraft so furiously hurled at the Huguenots of the south in 1609 were not repeated. The Huguenot became again, *per se*, the stereotype of social hatred, and so remained long afterwards, as shown by the Calas affair in 1762. The social significance of that affair is well brought out in David D. Bien, *The Calas Affair: Persecution, Toleration and Heresy in 18th-century Toulouse* (Princeton, 1960).

4 | The Religious Origins of the Enlightenment

I

It is commonly said that the intellectual, no less than the industrial revolution of modern Europe has its origins in the religious Reformation of the sixteenth century: that the Protestant Reformers, either directly, by their theology, or indirectly, by the new social forms which they created, opened the way to the new science and the new philosophy of the seventeenth century, and so prepared the way for the transformation of the world. Without the Protestant Reformation of the sixteenth century, we are told, we should have had no Enlightenment in the eighteenth century: without Calvin we should have had no Voltaire.

This theory has often been questioned, but it is hard to destroy. Generation after generation finds in it an irresistible plausibility. It is part of the philosophy of action without which any study of history seems remote and academic. In the past it has been a Whig theory. In the nineteenth century the "Whig" Protestant writers—Guizot in France, Macaulay in England—looking forward to change in the future, transferred their ideas into the past and saw the Protestants of the sixteenth century, the Whigs of the seventeenth, not merely as the party of radical action (which is one thing), but also as the party of economic, social and intellectual progress (which is another). Today the same theory is a Marxist theory. The Marxists, having replaced the Whigs as the party of radical action, similarly look to their pedigree, and attach themselves to an older radical tradition. In order to replace the Whigs, they borrow their philosophy. To them too progress is synonymous with political radicalism—and progress includes intellectual progress. Whoever is politically radical, they seem to say, is also intellectually right.

It is interesting to observe the continuity, in this respect, between the political radicals of yesterday and today: to see the torch, so nearly dropped from the failing hands of the last Whigs, skilfully caught and carried on by their successors, the first Marxists. This transfer of the same formula to different hands, this neat theoretical lampadophory, occurred at the close of the last century. It was then that the theory of the exclusively Protestant origin of progress, of modern thought, of modern society, having long been argued in political terms by the *"bourgeois"* thinkers of Europe, received its new, social content from the work of Max Weber and, being thus refloated, sailed triumphantly into the new age. Today, in this new form, it is as strong as ever. The Puritan Revolution in England, we are now assured, was not merely the "constitutional" revolution: it was also the *"bourgeois"* revolution: and the *bourgeois* revolution was, in turn, the intellectual revolution. The new science, the new philosophy, the new historiography, the new economy were all the work of "radical Protestants"—the more radical the more progressive;[1] and a distinguished non-Marxist modern historian, reviewing a history of modern Scotland, can casually remark, as a truism that needs no argument, that the Scottish Enlightenment of the eighteenth century, the Scottish industry of the nineteenth century, would have been inconceivable in an episcopalian country.[2]

How simple history would be if we could accept these convenient rules of thumb! But, alas, I find that I cannot. Admittedly the new philosophy was established in England in the 1650s. Admittedly Scotland was Presbyterian in the seventeenth century, enlightened in the eighteenth. But before we conclude that one fact determines the other, that *post hoc* is the same as *propter hoc*, it is essential to test the links of the argument. Is it clear that the new philosophy would not have triumphed in England in the 1650s if Charles I had continued to rule? Is it certain that Scotland would have remained backward, even in the eighteenth century, if its Church had continued to be governed by bishops, as

1. See, for instance, Christopher Hill, *Intellectual Origins of the Puritan Revolution* (Oxford, 1965). I have expressed my criticisms of Mr. Hill's argument in *History and Theory*, v, 1 (1966).

2. A. J. P. Taylor, review of George Pryde, *Local and Central Government in Scotland since 1707* (1960), in the *New Statesman*.

under Charles I and Charles II? These hypothetical questions are perhaps unanswerable in themselves; but they cannot be entirely jumped. We must at least consider them. Even if a direct answer is impossible, there is always the comparative method. Before accepting a conclusion on the imperfect evidence of one society, we can look aside to the evidence of another. We may note that the new philosophy triumphed in France in the 1650s although Louis XIV crushed the Fronde. Why then, we may ask, should the ruin of Charles I have been a necessary condition of its triumph, at the same time, in England? Calvinism did not create Enlightenment in seventeenth-century Transylvania, nor did episcopacy stifle it in the England of Wren and Newton. Why then should we leap to conclusions about eighteenth-century Scotland?

So we may object; and yet, to our objections, we can already foresee the answers. They are the answers which the men of the Enlightenment themselves would have given. Voltaire might not have had much good to say of the Protestant Reformers or the Protestant clergy. He might detest Calvin, "cet âme atroce"; he might dismiss the founding fathers of the Reformation as "tous écrivains qu'on ne peut lire"; and he might prefer the society of sophisticated Parisian *abbés* to the dull, worthy prelates of Protestant England. But objective facts had to be faced. Intellectual life was undeniably freer, heresy was undeniably safer in Protestant than in Catholic countries. This had always been true, and it was no less true in the eighteenth century. The exceptions did but prove the rule. Giannone might succeed in publishing his great work in Naples, but what a scandal followed its publication, what disastrous consequences to author and printer alike! To avoid persecution, and to reprint his work, Giannone was ultimately driven to take refuge in Protestant Geneva, only to be treacherously lured into Catholic Savoy, kidnapped by Catholic agents, and to disappear for the rest of his life into a Catholic prison. Montesquieu and Voltaire might escape such physical dangers, but they took no risks. Voltaire saw his *Lettres philosophiques* burnt in Paris and thought it prudent to live abroad, or at least within easy reach of the Swiss frontier. Montesquieu sought to meet trouble half-way by squaring the censors—and failed at the last. And both published their works in Protestant cities, in Calvinist Holland or Calvinist Switzerland. Admittedly discussion was free in Catholic countries. Admittedly the censorship was imperfect. Admittedly social eminence limited clerical power. But the basic fact remained. Hume might insist that as much real freedom could be found in Catholic France as in Calvinist Scotland. It was difficult to argue with him, since he had experience of both. But in the end, when the best has been said about the one and the worst about the other, the difference between the intellectual life of the two societies cannot be overlooked. It was the difference which caused Gibbon to describe the exceptions to the rule as "the *irregular* tendency of papists towards freedom" and "the *unnatural* gravitation of protestants towards slavery." [3]

Moreover, if we look at the stages of the Enlightenment, the successive geographical centres in which its tradition was engendered or preserved, the same conclusion forces itself upon us. The French Huguenots, we are told—Hotman, Languet, Duplessis-Mornay and their friends—created the new political science of the sixteenth century. Calvinist Holland brought forth the seventeenth-century concept of natural law and provided a safe place of study for Descartes. Cromwellian England accepted the scientific programme of Bacon and hatched the work of Hobbes and Harrington. The Huguenots in Calvinist Holland—Pierre Bayle, Jean Leclerc—created the Republic of Letters in the last years of Louis XIV. Switzerland—Calvinist Geneva and Calvinist Lausanne—was the cradle of the eighteenth-century Enlightenment in Europe: it was in Geneva that Giannone and Voltaire would seek refuge; it was a Calvinist pastor of Geneva, Jacob Vernet, who would be the universal agent of the movement: the correspondent of Leclerc, the friend and translator of Giannone, the friend and publisher of Montesquieu, the agent of Voltaire; and it was to Calvinist Lausanne that Gibbon would owe, as he would afterwards admit, his whole intellectual formation. Finally, after Switzerland, another Calvinist society carried forward the tradition. The Scotland of Francis Hutcheson and David Hume, of Adam Smith and William Robertson carried on the work of Montesquieu and created a new philosophy, a new history, a new sociology. Thither, as Gibbon wrote, "taste and philosophy seemed to have retired from the smoke and hurry of this immense capital," London;[4] and Thomas Jefferson would describe the University of Edinburgh and the Academy of Geneva as the two eyes of Europe.

Calvinist Holland, Puritan England, Calvinist Switzerland, Calvinist Scotland . . . If we take a long view—if we look at the continuous

---

3. E. Gibbon, *Vindication* . . . , in *Miscellaneous Works* (1814), I, 75.

4. *The Letters of Edward Gibbon*, ed. J. E. Norton (Oxford, 1956), II, 100.

intellectual tradition which led from the Renaissance to the Enlightenment — these Calvinist societies appear as the successive fountains from which that tradition was supplied, the successive citadels into which it sometimes retreated to be preserved. Without those fountains, without those citadels what, we may ask, would have happened to that tradition? And yet how easily the fountains might have been stopped, the citadels overrun! Suppose that the Duke of Savoy had succeeded in subjugating Geneva — as so nearly happened in 1600 — and that the Bourbons, in consequence, had imposed their protectorate on the remaining French cantons of Switzerland. Suppose that Charles I had not provoked an unnecessary rebellion in Scotland, or even that James II had continued the policy of his brother and perpetuated a high-flying Tory Anglican government in England. If all this had happened, Grotius, Descartes, Richard Simon, John Locke, Pierre Bayle would still have been born, but would they have written as they did, could they have published what they wrote? And without predecessors, without publishers, what would have happened to the Enlightenment, a movement which owed so much of its character to the thought of the preceding century and to its own success in propaganda and publicity?

No doubt this supposition is unfair, as all hypothetical questions, except the simplest, always are. The easy answer is that if Catholicism had triumphed in Europe, the whole terms of the problem would have been different: the ideological struggle would have been relaxed in victory, and ideas which had been excluded and suppressed by a society in tension might well have been tolerated by a society at ease. But on the facts it is clear that there is at least a *prima facie* case for the view that Calvinism was in some way essential to the intellectual revolution which led to the Enlightenment. The question therefore remains, in what way? Was it a direct or an accidental connection? Did Calvinism provide an essential mental or moral discipline? Did its theological doctrines, when translated into secular terms, produce a new philosophy? Or is the connection rather a social connection, independent of ideas? In order to answer these questions it is best to begin not by presupposing the connection, but by asking what was the religious tradition which led to the Enlightenment. What philosophical precursors did the men of the Enlightenment themselves recognize? When we have answered this question, when we have defined the continuing intellectual tradition, we may examine the relation between this tradition and the equally continuous tradition of European Calvinism.

II

The answer to this first question is, I think, reasonably clear. When Voltaire looked back in history, he recognized, of course, numerous predecessors at all times for various elements in his philosophy. But when he sought the beginnings of modernity, of his modernity, of the process which gradually and unevenly built up the new philosophy of which he was the prophet, he found them not in the Reformation, which he hated, but in the period before the Reformation, "the century which ends with Leo X, François I and Henry VIII": in other words, in the period of the late Renaissance and the Pre-Reform, the age of Valla and Erasmus, Machiavelli and Guicciardini, that liberal era which was overwhelmed and eclipsed by the hateful struggles of religion. That was the time, Voltaire wrote, when a new spirit, spreading over Europe from Italy, caused a revival of letters, an efflorescence of the arts, a softening of manners. The human mind, in those years, experienced a revolution "which changed everything, as in our own world."[5]

Unfortunately it did not last. With the Reformation came the Wars of Religion, which destroyed all, or nearly all, the intellectual achievements of the recent past, making the second half of the century frightful and bringing upon Europe "une espèce de barbarie que les Hérules, les Vandales et les Huns n'avaient jamais connue." It was not till the end of the sixteenth century, till the reign of Voltaire's constant hero, Henri IV, that the progress of mankind, which those wars had interrupted, could be resumed. This was the second stage of the Renaissance, the time when "philosophy began to shine upon men" with the discoveries of Galileo and the enlarged vision of Lord Chancellor Bacon. But this second stage, Voltaire lamented, was also cut short by wars of religion. The quarrels of "two Calvinist doctors" about grace and free will brought enlightened Holland back to dissension, persecution and atrocity. The newly restored civility of Europe foundered in the Thirty Years War. In England, polished and enlightened under James I, "les disputes du clergé, et les animosités entre le parti royal et le parlement, ramenèrent la barbarie."[6]

Throughout the middle years of the seventeenth century, as Voltaire saw them, barbarism prevailed. It was not till the personal reign of

---

5. Voltaire, "Conseils à un journaliste sur la philosophie, l'histoire, le théâtre," in *Mélanges*, ed. L. Moland, tome I, vol. XXII, 241; *Essai sur les moeurs*, ch. cxviii, cxxi.

6. *Essai sur les moeurs*, ch. cxxi, clxxix, clxxxvii.

Louis XIV that it began to give way. Then, in the generation immediately preceding his own, Voltaire discovered the period of victory. In the middle of the seventeenth century "la saine philosophie commença à percer un peu dans le monde"; by the end of it, thanks above all to the great English writers Locke and Newton, the Moderns had won their "prodigieuse supériorité" over the Ancients. Today, wrote Voltaire, there is not a single ancient philosopher who has anything to say to us. They have all been superseded. Between Plato and Locke, there is nothing, and since Locke, Plato is nothing.[7]

To Voltaire, in effect, there are three periods since the gothic Middle Ages which he can recognize as pointing forward to the "philosophy" and civilization of the Enlightenment. These are, first, the period before the Reformation; then the brief era of Henri IV and James I; and finally the period from the later seventeenth century onwards. These three periods can be summarized as the age of Erasmus, the age of Bacon and the age of Newton.

From France we turn to England, from Voltaire the propagandist to Gibbon the philosopher of history. Gibbon's attitude to the past was different from that of Voltaire. He had more respect for scholarship, a greater sense of the relativity of ideas, less confidence in the universal validity of "reason." But his interpretation of the stages of modern "philosophy" is precisely the same as that of Voltaire. When he traces the development of "philosophic history," of that "philosophy and criticism," that "reason" which achieved its fulfilment in "the full light and freedom of the eighteenth century," the essential links are the same. Machiavelli and Guicciardini, he writes, "with their worthy successors Fra Paolo and Davila," are justly esteemed the founders of modern history "till, in the present age, Scotland arose to dispute the prize with Italy herself." Again, in theology, he writes, "Erasmus may be considered as the father of rational theology. After a slumber of a hundred years it was revived by the Arminians of Holland, Grotius, Limborch and Leclerc; in England by Chillingworth, the latitudinarians of Cambridge, Tillotson, Clarke, Hoadly, etc."[8] Again and again, in his footnotes and miscellaneous observations, Gibbon shows the pedigree of his philosophy, and we see his masters grouped, mainly, in three periods. First, there is the age of the Pre-Reform, of Erasmus, Machiavelli,

7. Voltaire, *Siècle de Louis XIV* (1751), ch. xxxiv, xxxvi.

8. Gibbon, *Decline and Fall of the Roman Empire*, ed. J. B. Bury (1909), vi, 128, and vii, 296.

Guicciardini. Then there is the beginning of the seventeenth century, the age of Grotius and Bacon, Paolo Sarpi and de Thou. Finally there is the end of the same century and the beginning of the next: the age of Newton and Locke, Leibniz and Bayle. These three periods are distinct phases of light separated from each other, the first two by "a slumber of a hundred years," the second and third by the heart of the seventeenth century.

What is the common character of these three periods in which the men of the Enlightenment agreed to recognize their predecessors? The first and most obvious fact is that they are all periods of ideological peace. The first period, the age of Erasmus, is the last age of united Christendom in which the rational reform of an undivided Church seemed possible. The second period, the age of Grotius, the Dutch heir of Erasmus, is the period of *las Pazes*, the lull between the wars of Philip II and the Thirty Years War. The last age, the age which merges in the eighteenth-century Enlightenment, begins with the end of that war. It is not a period of peace, any more than the age of Erasmus had been; but the wars of Louis XIV were not, like the wars of the late sixteenth and early seventeenth centuries, ideological wars: they were not characterized by that shrivelling of the mind, that narrowing of vision and severance of communication which is the peculiar quality of doctrinal strife.

Secondly, we may observe that these three periods are periods, and their intellectual leaders are often protagonists, not only of ideological peace but of theological reconciliation. Erasmus wore himself out preaching peace and a reform of the Church which would forestall and prevent the violent schism threatened by Luther. Grotius worked for a reunion of the Churches on an Arminian—that is, an Erasmian—base. Leibniz devoted much of his universal energy to the same end and was supported by allies in all countries and of all religions: the Catholic Spinola and Molanus, the Anglican Archbishop Wake, the Lutheran Praetorius, the Calvinist Jablonski, the Arminian Leclerc. In these projects of reunion, as in so much of the public activity of Leibniz, there was much of state policy also. But the spirit behind them was that which led ultimately to the deism of the eighteenth century, enabling Gibbon, and many others, to acquiesce "with implicit belief in the tenets and mysteries which are adopted by the general consent of Catholics and Protestants."

Finally, these three periods, so happily exempt from ideological war, hot or cold, were all, for that reason, periods of cosmopolitan intellectual correspondence. The correspondence of Erasmus knew no frontiers, geographical or ideological. It extended from Scotland to Transylvania, from Poland to Portugal. The struggles of the later sixteenth century broke up this intellectual unity, but the peace of the early seventeenth century restored it. The Jacobean age—if we may use this parochial but convenient term—was indeed one of the great ages of free exchange in the intellectual world. Lipsius and Casaubon, de Thou and Sarpi, Camden and Grotius, Gruter and Peiresc were nodal points in a vast network of intellectual contact which took no account of national or religious differences. It was then that the phrase "the Republic of Letters" first came into use. It was a phrase which, at that time, had a missionary content. The *élite* of that new Republic, like the Erasmian *élite* before them, knew that they were not merely enjoying a delightful international conversation: they were also working together to lay the intellectual foundations of a new world. To Bacon, the reign of James I in England coincided with a European Renaissance comparable only with the golden ages of Greece and Rome. It was a time when ancient literature had been revived, when "controversies of religion, which have so much diverted men from other sciences," had happily dried up, and peace, navigation and printing had opened the prospect of infinite progress. "Surely," he wrote, "when I set before me the condition of these times, in which learning hath made her third visitation, I cannot but be raised to this persuasion, that this third period of time will far surpass that of the Grecian and Roman learning—if only men will know their own strength and their own weakness both, and take, one from the other, light of invention, not fire of contradiction."[9]

Unfortunately, as Bacon's life drew to its close, the fire of contradiction broke out again. In the revolution of Holland Grotius escaped from prison into lifelong exile; in the Thirty Years War Rubens in Antwerp lamented the collapse of the golden age; and a little later the English disciples of Grotius at Great Tew would be broken up by what one of them, Clarendon, would describe as "this odious and unnecessary civil war."

Nevertheless, even the odious ideological wars of the mid-seventeenth century did not destroy the society of Europe. When they were over, the Republic of Letters was reconstituted, stronger than ever. The scholars and thinkers of Europe resumed their contacts. As Vol-

---

9. F. Bacon, *Advancement of Learning*, in *Works*, ed. J. Spedding *et al.* (1857–74), III, 476–77.

taire would write, "Jamais la correspondance entre les philosophes ne fut plus universelle: Leibniz servait à l'animer." [10] Leibniz, Locke and Newton were indeed the law-givers of the Republic, but its great propagandists, the men who gave currency to the name and popularity to the concept, were the two great rivals in Amsterdam, Bayle and Leclerc: Bayle, the sceptical Encyclopaedist, the "Pyrrhonist" who looks back to Montaigne and Charron in the second of our two periods, to Erasmus—or at least to one aspect of Erasmus—in the first; Leclerc, the Arminian disciple of Grotius, the editor of his *de Veritate Religionis Christianae*, who was also the admirer of Erasmus, the producer of the greatest edition of his works: an edition which a German publisher has thought worth reproduction *in toto* today.

The first major point which I wish to make in this essay is already, I hope, clear. To those who would say that the ideas of the European Enlightenment were hammered out in the strife of ideological revolution and civil war, it can be replied—and the men of the Enlightenment would themselves have replied—that, on the contrary, those ideas were worked out in periods of ideological peace and *rapprochement*, and were only interrupted and delayed, not furthered, by the intervening periods of revolution. Revolution may have shifted the balance of political or social power. It may have been necessary to preserve, here or there, the basis of intellectual advance. That is another matter. But on the substance of thought it had no discernible direct effect. The new ideas which were conveyed by devious channels through two centuries and which finally overturned the old orthodoxies of Europe were generated not in the heat of war or under the stress of revolution—that heat and that stress do not provoke new thought: rather they drive men back into customary, defensive postures, causing them to reiterate old slogans— but in the mild warmth of peace, the gentle give-and-take of free and considered international discussion.

Where then is the function of Calvinism: that Calvinism, that "radical Protestantism," for which such large claims have been advanced and for whose claims, I have admitted, a *prima facie* case can be made? The immediate answer is clear. Not one of the "philosophers" to whom the men of the Enlightenment looked back, and whose names I have quoted, was an orthodox Calvinist. The doctrines of Calvin, as far as we can see, had no direct influence on any of the ideas which led to

10. Voltaire, *Siècle de Louis XIV*, ch. xxxiv.

the Enlightenment. Whatever debt the philosophers of the eighteenth century might owe to Calvinist cities, Calvinist universities, Calvinist societies, we have yet to discover any evidence of obligation to Calvinist Churches or Calvinist ideas. Our problem, the connection between Calvinism and the Enlightenment, is a problem still.

III

How are we to resolve this problem? Obviously, we can approach the answer only if we tread very cautiously. We must not hastily presume a logical connection where we can only demonstrate a local coincidence, however regular. Before basing any conclusions on that local coincidence, we must examine the local circumstances. This means that we must look at the separate Calvinist societies a little more closely than the confident political or sociological theorists have done. We must also look at them comparatively, remembering that Calvinism in one society is not necessarily the same as in another. One name may cover a variety of forms.

For international Calvinism was not an abstraction. Like any other international movement it was localized, and transformed by local forces, in a number of very different societies, and these societies had their own histories, their own internal tensions. There were European powers like Holland; defensive federations like the cantons of Switzerland; city-states like Geneva and La Rochelle; isolated rural peninsulas like Scotland; exposed and aggressive principalities like the Palatinate; miniscule lordships or academic republics like Hanau, Herborn and Wesel, Saumur and Sedan. It is not enough to say that sixteenth-century Heidelberg, seventeenth-century Holland, Puritan England, Huguenot France, eighteenth-century Switzerland and Scotland—the successive seed-plots of the Enlightenment—were all Calvinist societies; or at least it is not enough, having said this as a fact, to leave it as a demonstration. The societies themselves were too different, and also too complex in themselves, for such easy generalizations. The terms we have used are too loose. We must look more closely into both the one and the other. We must analyse the character of the societies and look behind the loose, general terms.

When we do this, we soon discover a very important fact. We find that each of those Calvinist societies made its contribution to the Enlightenment at a precise moment in its history, and that this moment was the moment when it repudiated ideological orthodoxy. In fact, we may say that the separate Calvinist societies of Europe contributed to the Enlightenment only in so far as they broke away from Calvinism.

This may be connected with a change in the character of Calvinism. For there is no doubt that such a change took place. Calvinism in the sixteenth century may have retained some traces of the intellectual distinction of its founder, some residue of the Erasmianism which lay behind it. But in the next century it is very different. Read (if you can) the writings of the great doctors of seventeenth-century Calvinism, the heirs of Calvin and Beza, Buchanan and Knox. Their masters may have been grim, but there is a certain heroic quality about their grimness, a literary power about their writing, an intellectual force in their minds. The successors are also grim, but they are grim and mean. Perkins and "Smectymnuus" in England, Rivetus and Voëtius in Holland, Baillie and Rutherford in Scotland, Desmarets and Jurieu in France, Francis Turrettini in Switzerland, Cotton Mather in America—what a gallery of intolerant bigots, narrow-minded martinets, timid conservative defenders of repellent dogmas, instant assailants of every new or liberal idea, inquisitors and witch-burners! But however that may be, the facts can hardly be denied. Once we look at the circumstances in which each of those societies I have named became in turn the home of the pre-Enlightenment, we discover that in every instance the new ideas which interest us spring not from the Calvinists but from the heretics who have contrived to break or elude the control of the Calvinist Church: heretics whom the true Calvinists, if they could, would have burnt.

But in order to illustrate this conclusion, let us look briefly and in turn at the Calvinist societies which I have enumerated, and the circumstances of their enlightenment.

First Holland. Here the facts are well known. The rise of liberal ideas in Holland, which was to make Leiden the seminary and Amsterdam the refuge of advanced thinkers in all the sciences, was made possible not by the Calvinist Church, but by its critics, its heretics: first the "libertines," then the Arminians and their clients the Socinians. Every Dutch philosopher whose ideas look forward to the Enlightenment suffered persecution of one kind or another from the local Calvinist clergy. Fortunately, in the Netherlands, the Calvinist clergy never had complete power. The lay power, however precariously, was always supreme. Calvin himself might have Servetus, an early Socinian, burnt in Geneva, but Calvin's followers raged in vain against the followers of Servetus in Holland. When the French Calvinist Lambert

Daneau, the disciple of Calvin and Beza, the greatest Calvinist doctor of his time, was "called" to the ministry at Leiden in 1581, he soon discovered the difference between Dutch and Swiss Calvinism. He was told that the citizens of Leiden would no more tolerate the Inquisition of Geneva than the Inquisition of Spain; and he returned in a huff to a more docile flock in rural Gascony. Wisely, the Arminians in Holland insisted on the supremacy of the civil power over the clergy. The civil power was their only protection against the fanatical *Predikants*. But at times of crisis, when the civil power was at bay against a foreign enemy and needed the support of the people, it was driven into alliance with the Calvinist Church. Such times were always fatal to the Arminians. In 1618 there was such a crisis, and it led to their immediate ruin. Their statesman Oldenbarnevelt was judicially murdered, their philosopher Grotius imprisoned and exiled. At the Synod of Dordt, a strict, repressive Calvinism was imposed on the Church of the United Provinces. However, the tyranny of the orthodox was not permanent; when the political crisis was over, the Arminians recovered their freedom and the Socinians—those "most chymical and rational" of sectaries, as an Englishman called them [11]—throve under their protection. The universal oracle of orthodox Calvinism, Gisbert Voëtius, might denounce liberal ideas and new ideas of all kinds, and especially the ideas of Descartes, but the new philosophy was preserved and continued by Arminian patronage. From Arminius and Grotius, the spiritual and the secular disciples of Erasmus, the line of descent leads, through Episcopius, Limborch and Leclerc, unmistakably to the Enlightenment.

Exactly the same pattern can be seen in England. The struggle between the English "Presbyterians" and the Independents in the 1640s, complicated though it is by changing political issues, is in one sense— the intellectual sense—a struggle between Calvinists and Arminians. The English "Presbyterians," even their clergy, might not be good Calvinists as seen from Holland or Scotland, but at least they were better than the Independents. For the Independents were true Arminians—as indeed they were often called: believers in free will, in religious toleration, and in lay control of the Church. The victory of the Independents over the "Presbyterians" may have been, in immediate politics, the victory of radicals over moderates, but in social matters it was the victory of the laity over the clergy, and therefore in intellectual

11. Francis Osborne, *Advice to a Son* [1656], ed. E. A. Parry (1896), p. 112.

matters the victory of lay ideas over clerical ideas. Scholastic Aristo-teleanism—the old philosophy of the Catholic Church which Reforma-tion and Counter-Reformation had alike refurbished and reimposed—went down in England not when English Prynne and Scottish Baillie triumphed over Archbishop Laud, but when the Erastians like Selden—some of whom were "Presbyterian" just as the Dutch Arminians were also Calvinists—refused to set up in England a "presbytery" accord-ing to the word of God. It was then that the ideas of Descartes came into England, then that the ideas of Bacon triumphed, then that Oxford became the capital of the "New Philosophy."

It happened in Scotland too. In Scotland the Calvinist Church had succeeded in doing what it had not been able to do in England or Hol-land—what it could do only where the laity was weak and at the mercy of the clergy: that is, in relatively undeveloped rural societies like Scot-land or New England, or in small, defenceless communities surrounded by a hostile world, like the Huguenot Churches of France after 1629. It had stamped out all forms of dissent. First it had crushed Arminian deviation. That indeed had been easy, for Scottish Arminianism was a feeble growth. Its most famous, perhaps its only advocate within the Kirk, was John Cameron. He was soon forced into exile. Then, having crushed its heretics, the Kirk turned to do battle with its external ene-mies, the bishops. By the 1640s its triumph was complete. Its intellec-tual character in those years of triumph is clear from the copious cor-respondence of Robert Baillie, the most learned (and by no means the most illiberal) of the party, denouncing in turn lay control, toleration, free will, the "Tridentine popery" of Grotius, the "fatuous heresy" of Descartes and the "insolent absurdity" of Selden. Baillie in Glasgow is an echo of Voëtius in Utrecht. But in the 1650s, with the English con-quest, the Calvinist Kirk was broken, and for a few years a brief, partial flicker of Enlightenment hovered over its ruins. Unfortunately it did not last. There was no native basis for it, and when the foreign armies were withdrawn, the Kirk soon recovered its power and snuffed it out.[12]

A generation later it was the turn of the French Huguenots. In the sixteenth century the French Calvinist community had contained some of the most advanced and original thinkers in France: Hotman, Duplessis-Mornay, Agrippa d'Aubigné, Bernard Palissy, Pierre de la Ramée, Ambroise Paré, Isaac Casaubon, Joseph Justus Scaliger . . .

12. For this first flicker of enlightenment in Cromwellian Scotland, see my essay, "Scotland and the Puritan Revolution," below, pp. 359–406.

The list could be continued. Catherine de Médicis herself admitted that three-quarters of the best educated Frenchmen of her time were Huguenots. But after 1629, when the pride and autonomy of the Huguenots were broken, the independent laymen gradually disappear from among them, and French Protestantism, like Scottish Protestantism, is dominated by a clergy which becomes, with time, increasingly narrow and rigid: crabbed prudes and Puritans, haters of literature and the arts, stuck in postures of defence. There were exceptions of course; but the great exception—the aristocratic Academy of Saumur—only proves the rule. For the Academy of Saumur, which shocked the Calvinist establishment by admitting Cartesianism into its teaching, was Arminian. John Cameron, the Scottish Arminian whom the Kirk of Scotland had expelled, had gone to Saumur and had there succeeded the formidable Dutch Calvinist Gomar. From that day onwards Saumur was the centre of Protestant enlightenment in France, an affront to good Calvinists everywhere.[13] As the *intendant* of Anjou wrote to Louis XIV in 1664, "elle réunit tout ce qu'il y a de gens d'esprit dans le parti protestant pour le rendre célèbre";[14] and a later historian, looking back, can write that "à la base de presque tout libéralisme protestant au 16e siècle, on retrouve Saumur."[15] But Saumur was suspect among the Huguenots of France, and the other Protestant academies took good care to avoid such suspicion. There the laity remained obedient to the clergy, and the clergy obeyed the strict Calvinist rules of the Synod of Dordt.

From this subjection the French Protestant laity were ultimately released—little though he intended it—by Louis XIV. For the expulsion of 1685—as the late Erich Haase has shown—was destined to be the intellectual salvation of the French Protestants. In exile, in sympathetic Protestant societies, they escaped at last from the rigid clericalism to which, as a persecuted minority in Catholic France, they had perforce succumbed. Among the Arminians and Socinians of Holland and the Latitudinarians of England they discovered a new freedom. So,

13. Compare, for instance, the sour remarks of Robert Baillie on Moïse Amyraut, the Arminian successor of Cameron at Saumur, whose "fancies," "vanity and pride" were "troubling" the Churches of France (*Letters and journals of Robert Baillie* (Edinburgh, 1841–42), II, 324, 342, and III, 311, etc.).

14. P. Marchegay, *Archives d'Anjou* (Angers, 1843), p. 127.

15. Annie Barnes, *Jean Leclerc et la République des Lettres* (Geneva, 1938), p. 46. Cf. Joseph Prost, *La Philosophie à l'académie protestante de Saumur, 1606–1685* (Paris, 1907).

leaving their self-appointed spiritual director, "the Grand Inquisitor of the Dispersion," Pierre Jurieu, to castigate their backsliding and denounce them as Socinians or infidels, they followed the more seductive teaching of the Arminian Leclerc, the sceptical Bayle.[16]

A few years later a similar change took place in Switzerland. With the opening of the eighteenth century Switzerland began to replace Holland as the geographical headquarters of the Enlightenment. Balthasar Bekker, the Cartesian clergyman who was hounded from the Church of Holland for disbelieving in witches, was the last European figure of the native Dutch Enlightenment of the seventeenth century. Thereafter it was French-speaking Huguenots who re-created the Republic of Letters. And if they made its first capital in Amsterdam and Rotterdam, they soon made its second capital in Geneva and Lausanne. If the doctrines of Descartes had been received in Holland, those of Locke were received in Switzerland; and Switzerland would retain its supremacy for the rest of the century. When Gibbon decided to retire to Lausanne, his English friends thought him mad. How could a man who had enjoyed the polite society of London and Paris bury himself in a provincial Swiss city? But Gibbon knew Lausanne and he knew his own mind, which had been fashioned there. He never regretted his decision.[17]

But once again, when we look at the social background to this intellectual change, we find that this Swiss enlightenment has followed on an internal change, and that internal change is the defeat of Calvinism. In the seventeenth century the Calvinist Church in Switzerland had accepted the decrees of the Synod of Dordt. The Academy of Geneva had indeed suffered an Arminian infiltration and had found itself threatened by the invading "doctrine of Saumur." But its resistance had been successful. Fear of Savoy had been to Geneva what fear of Spain had been to Amsterdam: it had given a reserve of power to the party of resistance, the bigots of the Church. The *Consensus Helveticus* of 1674 marked the triumph of the strict Calvinist party: it was the Swiss equivalent of the Synod of Dordt, and it was imposed on universities and academies throughout Calvinist Switzerland. The works of Grotius and all his disciples were banned, and the young Leclerc left the *cachot* of Geneva for the freedom of Saumur. By 1685 all the Swiss

---

16. Erich Haase, *Einführung in die Literatur der Refuge* (Berlin, 1959).

17. See Gibbon's letter to Lord Sheffield in *The Letters of Edward Gibbon*, III, 58–59.

Philippe Duplessis-Mornay, founder of the Protestant Academy at Saumur

academies were in decline. Basel, once an international university, had become purely provincial. At Lausanne, jealously controlled by the oligarchy of Bern, the printing industry was dead and the canton de Vaud could be described as "pays, sinon de barbarie, pour le moins du monde peu curieux et éloigné du beau commerce."

From this intellectual stagnation Switzerland was raised by a new, and this time successful, Arminian revolt. In Geneva this revolt was begun by Jean-Robert Chouet, a Cartesian who returned from Saumur to Geneva in 1669. It was continued by his pupil J.-A. Turrettini. Thanks largely to the energy of Turrettini, the *Consensus Helveticus* was finally defeated in Geneva. From 1706 it was no longer imposed on the clergy; and from that date Turrettini's exiled friend Jean Leclerc would date the enlightenment of Geneva. In the next generation Geneva, to the Encyclopaedists, was a Socinian city. The ministers of religion, wrote d'Alembert, have pure morals, faithfully obey the law, refuse to persecute dissenters, and worship the supreme being in a worthy manner: the religion of many of them is "a perfect Socinianism." This was a change indeed. The tables had been turned on history, and the Socinian Servetus had triumphed in the very capital of his grim enemy, Calvin.[18]

In Lausanne the same battle was fought, with a different result and by different means. The battle there was more complicated because Lausanne was not, like Geneva, self-governing: it was a subject city, governed by the distant—and orthodox—oligarchy of Bern. Against that control the Arminians of Lausanne struggled hard. There was Daniel Crespin, the professor of eloquence, yet another product of Saumur, whose pupils were formally denounced for Arminianism in 1698. There was Jean-Pierre de Crousaz, Arminian and Cartesian, who had studied in Paris and Leiden and known Malebranche and Bayle. There was Jean Barbeyrac, the Arminian translator of Grotius, Puffendorf and Archbishop Tillotson. And there were others who, with them, sought to mitigate or evade the severity of the *Consensus*, its explicit condemnation of "Pietism, Socinianism and Arminianism." But while their colleagues in Geneva prevailed, the philosophers of Lau-

18. The suppression and final victory of Arminianism in Geneva is well described in Miss Annie Barnes' valuable work, *Jean Leclerc et la République des Lettres*. The Encyclopaedists' references to the Socinianism of Geneva—which caused a great stir in the city—are in the article "Genève." See also Francesco Ruffini, *Studi sui riformatori italiani* (Turin, 1955), pp. 444 ff.

sanne struggled in vain against an orthodoxy supported from without by the magistrates of Bern. Ten years after the victory of heresy in Geneva, Bern resolved to crush it in Lausanne, and when resistance mounted, the pressure was increased. Finally, in 1722, the oligarchs of Bern struck. They resolved to dismiss all clergy and teachers who refused to accept the *Consensus* in its strict sense, with its oath to oppose Socinianism and Arminianism. The liberal world was outraged. The kings of England and Prussia wrote letters of protest. But their Excellencies of Bern were resolute. They imposed their wishes. They broke the spirit of de Crousaz, now Rector of the Academy. And when protests continued to be raised, and Major Davel even threatened to lead a revolt against the domination of Bern, they issued a positive order forbidding further discussion of the subject. Orthodoxy, it seemed, had triumphed: the debate was closed.

And yet in fact, from that very date, the heretics had triumphed in Lausanne. The forms and oaths might be maintained for another generation, but their force was spent. The last antics of orthodoxy had made it ridiculous. As the young Gibbon wrote, whether through shame, or pity, or the shock of Davel's attempt, the persecution ceased, and if Arminians and Socinians were still denounced by the self-righteous, they suffered, from now on, only social discrimination. Intellectually they had won; and their victory inaugurated what a modern Italian historian has called the "risveglio culturale losannese." Long afterwards, looking back on the formation of his own mind, Gibbon would avow his debt to that cultural revival, and above all to de Crousaz, whose "philosophy had been formed in the school of Locke, his divinity in that of Limborch and Leclerc," whose lessons had "rescued the Academy of Lausanne from Calvinistic prejudice," and who had diffused "a more liberal spirit among the clergy and people of the Pays de Vaud." [19]

Finally, from Switzerland we return to Scotland again. There the brief flicker of enlightenment in the 1650s had been quickly extin-

---

19. The struggle between Arminianism and Calvinism in Lausanne is traced in the noble work of Henri Vuilleumier, *Histoire de l'Église réformée du Pays de Vaud sous le régime bernois* (Lausanne, 1927–33), III. See also Philippe Meylan, *Jean Barbeyrac 1674–1744* (Lausanne, 1957). The Italian historian is Giuseppe Giarrizzo, *Edward Gibbon e la cultura europea del settecento* (Naples, 1954), pp. 29–34. Gibbon's early essay is his preceptive "Lettre sur le gouvernement de Berne" (*Miscellaneous Works*, II; edited also by Louis Junod in Université de Lausanne, *Miscellanea Gibboniana*, 1952, pp. 110–41). His remarks on de Crousaz are in his autobiography.

guished. The Stuart Restoration and the "Killing Times" had driven the Kirk back into postures of defensive radicalism—just as persecution by Louis XIV had driven the French Huguenots. The narrow bigotry of the Kirk, the messianic gibberish of the outlawed Cameronians, are the Scottish equivalents of the spiritual police system of Jurieu and the hysteria of "the French prophets," the Camisards of the "Desert." But the peace imposed on the Kirk by William III had some of the effects of the peace formerly imposed by Cromwell, and the union with England in 1707, which opened new economic opportunities and new intellectual horizons to the Scottish laity, undermined the clergy in the same way in which exile in Holland and Switzerland had undermined the Huguenot pastors. Henceforth the Scottish laity would be, as Baillie had complained of the English in his time, "very fickle and hard to be keeped by their ministers." The liberalism which in the 1650s had rested on English regiments could now rest on a native Scottish base.

The solvent effects, first of the Orange Settlement, then of the union with England, were soon clear. Arminianism raised its head again in the Scottish Church. By the Revolution Settlement of 1689–90 the Calvinist Church did indeed recover its formal structure. The bishops once again disappeared. The General Assembly, dissolved since 1653, was revived. The ejected ministers returned. But while the forms of the old Calvinism were thus restored, its internal strength was undermined. Episcopalian ministers were allowed to retain their livings simply by taking an oath of allegiance to the Crown. The covenants—the National Covenant of 1638 and the Solemn League and Covenant of 1643, the shibboleths of the strict Calvinists—were quietly dropped. Thus the Scottish Church too was set free from its Synod of Dordt, its *Consensus Helveticus*. In 1712 the Patronage Act, the work of the English Tories, put Scottish Church appointments effectively under educated lay patronage, and guaranteed the Church, at last, against the bigotry of the past century.[20] Twenty years later the strict defenders of the Covenants, long resentful of such backsliding, decided to secede from the Church on this issue. Having seceded, they showed the strength of their convictions by a solemn protest against the abolition of witch-burning. This "Original Secession" was to be the first of a series of secessions

20. For the civilizing effect of the Patronage Act, see the memorandum by the Rev. Alexander Carlyle quoted from the Carlyle MSS. in H. G. Graham, *Scottish Men of Letters in the Eighteenth Century* (1908), pp. 86–87. It was, of course, an anti-democratic Act. That does not prevent it from being liberal.

which, by draining away the fanatics, strengthened the new, moderate, laicized party in the Kirk. By the time when foreigners looked in admiration to the Enlightenment of the north, the Scottish Kirk had been de-Calvinized: it was governed, for thirty years, by the Arminian historian William Robertson, the friend of Hume, Gibbon and Adam Smith.

Thus we now see that if the new philosophy was forwarded in successive Calvinist societies, it was forwarded, in each instance, not by Calvinism but by the defeat of Calvinism. Arminianism or Socinianism, not Calvinism, was the religion of the pre-Enlightenment. Calvinism, that fierce and narrow re-creation of medieval scholasticism, was its enemy: the last enemy which died in the last ditches of Holland, England, Switzerland, Scotland.

IV

Still, it may be objected, these "heresies" are Calvinist heresies. Arminianism grew out of Calvinism. Socinianism was regarded by Catholics and Protestants alike as a radical movement, a deviation to the extreme Left. If the Calvinist thesis is untenable in the strict sense, may it not remain tenable in a modified sense? Instead of "Calvinism" may we not read "radical Protestantism," Puritanism on the left wing of Calvinist orthodoxy? Unfortunately even this modification is, I believe, untenable. It is untenable partly because such terms as Left and Right, however useful they may be in political history, have no meaning in intellectual history: ideas cannot be ranged, like political parties, in a continuous spectrum according to the energy or violence with which men are prepared to go in one of two directions. But even if such crude categories are admitted, it is still untenable because neither Arminianism nor Socinianism was in fact necessarily a radical movement.

Arminianism is generally regarded as a right-wing deviation from Calvinism. The Dutch Arminians were attacked by the Dutch Calvinists as opening the way to popery. Oldenbarnevelt was accused of appeasing Catholic Spain. Grotius was regularly denounced as a crypto-Papist. The constant cry of alarm of the Dutch Calvinists was that "the Arminian was himself a disguised papist, a concealed Jesuit." [21] Exactly the same was said of the English Arminians. "If you mark it well," cried

21. P. Geyl, *The Netherlands in the Seventeenth Century* (1961), i, 45.

the Cornish Puritan Francis Rous in the last, tumultuary session of the early parliaments of Charles I, "you shall see an arminian reaching out his hand to a papist, a papist to a Jesuit." Crypto-popery was the regular charge made against the Arminian clergy in England and Scotland, the followers of Archbishop Laud.

It is true, historians have tried to separate English from Dutch Arminianism in order to admit the Anglo-Catholicism of the former while saving the Protestantism of the latter. Arminianism in England, they say, is a mere nickname: it was applied, almost accidentally, to a clerical party in the Anglican Church and does not entail the same doctrinal content as in Holland; and in support of this they cite the *bon mot* of George Morley, who, when asked "what the Arminians held," replied that they held "all the best bishoprics and deaneries in England." But this distinction between Dutch and English Arminianism is an arbitrary separation which does not survive closer scrutiny. In fact, English and Dutch Arminianism are closely connected. Grotius admired the Church of England of his time — the Church of Laud — above all other Churches: "body and soul he professeth himself to be for the Church of England," a diplomatic colleague wrote of him; and he personally admired Archbishop Laud.[22] Grotius' English followers in religion were Anglicans: Lord Falkland and his circle at Great Tew — Chillingworth, Hales, Clarendon, George Sandys; Henry Hammond, the chaplain of Charles I, who was to be the chief propagandist of "the Grotian religion" in the 1650s; Clement Barksdale, the royalist High Anglican parson who wrote the biography of Grotius and translated his works. Conversely, Laud himself, for all his clericalism, was liberal in theology: he was the patron of Chillingworth and Hales, the friend of Selden. And the Laudian bishops in Scotland, if we can see past the libels of the good Scotch Calvinists, denouncing them as monsters spawned in the foul womb of Antichrist, are found to be liberal, tolerant and enlightened men, true Arminians in the spirit of Grotius.[23] The most famous of

22. See "Testimonia de Hugonis Grotii adfectu erga ecclesiam Anglicanam," printed at the end of Leclerc's edition of Grotius' *de Veritate Religionis Christianae*. The diplomatic colleague was Lord Scudamore, English ambassador in Paris when Grotius was Swedish ambassador there: a strict Laudian who shocked even so good an Anglican as Clarendon by his refusal to communicate with the French Huguenots.

23. See W. L. Mathieson, *Politics and Religion. A Study in Scottish History from the Reformation to the Revolution* (Glasgow, 1902).

Scottish Arminians, John Cameron, perfectly illustrates the indivisibility, the universality, of the Arminian movement. Like the Laudians he supported the introduction of episcopacy into Scotland and was attacked for his Arminian doctrines by the detestable Rutherford. But he remained a liberal within the Calvinist Church and when driven out of Scotland went to create the liberal tradition of Saumur, the saving spirit of the French Huguenots.

The case of Socinianism is similar. Because the Socinians were attacked as the most outrageous heretics by orthodox Catholics and Protestants alike, they are often regarded as "radical Protestants," on the extreme Left. But this is too simple a view. Socinianism in the seventeenth century was a heresy of the Right before it was a heresy of the Left—if indeed we can use such terms at all. It was regularly associated with Arminianism. In Holland only the Arminians accepted the Socinians into communion. In England Archbishop Laud and several of his bishops were accused of Socinianism.[24] So were the Laudian bishops in Scotland.[25] So were later Anglican bishops like Stillingfleet and Tillotson.[26] So was Grotius.[27] So were the disciples of Grotius: Falkland, Hales and Chillingworth in England; Episcopius, Limborch and Leclerc in Holland. Indeed Arminianism and Socinianism are often interchangeable terms, at least as terms of abuse. Of course there may have been Socinians on the Left too—for Socinianism is only the application of secular, critical, human reason to religious texts and religious problems—and certainly, during the Puritan Revolution, both Arminianism, the Arminianism of John Milton, and Socinianism, the

24. H. J. McLachlan, *Socinianism in Seventeenth-century England* (Oxford, 1951), p. 97. Cf. Bishop Goodman's complaint to Laud that Laud had raised to the episcopate men like Howson, Montagu, Curll and Mainwaring and "some others whom you favoured and whom I suspected to be Socinians" (quoted in G. Soden, *Godfrey Goodman*, 1953, pp. 152–53). Sir Edward Peyton, in his *Divine Catastrophe of the House of Stuart* (1652), also accused the Laudian clergy of Socinianism.

25. See, for instance, the attacks on John Maxwell, Bishop of Ross, Laud's principal agent in Scotland, in Samuel Rutherford's *Lex Rex* (1644), Preface. Rutherford accused Maxwell of "popery, socinianism, tyranny etc."

26. Stillingfleet was attacked as a Socinian by the Catholic convert Hugh Cressy (formerly Lord Falkland's chaplain) in his pamphlet, S[erenus] C[ressy], *Fanaticism Fanatically imputed to the Catholic Church by Dr. Stillingfleet* (1672); Tillotson in Charles Leslie, *The Charge of Socinianism against Dr. Tillotson considered* (1695), etc.

27. E.g., in John Owen, *Vindiciae Academicae* (1655).

Socinianism of John Bidle, appeared as Puritan movements. But historically both had been movements within the Anglican establishment before they became movements in Puritan society; and when the Anglican establishment was restored, they took their place in it again.

In general we are too prone to suppose that the Independency of the Puritan Republic was intellectually a radical movement. Once again this results from a confusion of political with intellectual terms. Because the Independents, the Cromwellians, were prepared to cut off the king's head, while the Presbyterians, the followers of Denzil Holles, wished to keep it on, it is easy to suppose that the former were more "radical" than the latter. But this is not necessarily true, even in politics. After their radical gesture, the Independents showed themselves, in many ways, the more conservative party. They were the English party, who resented Scottish dictation in English affairs, and their ultimate ideal was an Elizabethan monarchy, with a moderate, lay-controlled Church, not a stadholderate and a theocracy. Once the Independents were established in power, they soon discovered their continuity with Anglican royalists. In Scotland, the old royalists preferred the regicide English Independents to the royalist Scottish Presbyterians, and in England Cromwell openly confessed that he preferred "a royalist interest to a Scotch [i.e., Presbyterian] interest." The execution of Charles I is to some extent, in the distinction between "Presbyterians" and Independents, a red herring. Independency was not, in itself, a radical movement: it was the continuation, on a new political base, of a liberal tradition which had previously been embodied in Anglicanism, and which had to reassert itself against the illiberal Calvinism of the Scots.

Even in small matters this continuity can be seen. Those who see the Independents as Puritan fanatics, more extreme than the "Presbyterians," tend to overlook the inconvenient evidence that contemporaries saw the position (at least outside politics) in reverse. They saw the "Presbyterians" as the sour, Puritan party and the Independents as the gay, "libertine" successors of the cavaliers. To Anthony Wood, the Presbyterians "seemed to be very severe in their course of life, manners or conversation, and habit or apparel," constantly preaching damnation, whereas the Independents, clergy and laity alike, were "more free, gay, and with a reserve frolicsome"; of a gay habit, preaching liberty. The Independent minister John Owen, for instance, when vice-chancellor of Oxford, "instead of being a grave example to the university," went about "in quirpo like a young scholar," with powdered hair, lawn bands and tasselled bandstrings, flowing ribbons, "Spanish leather boots with large lawn tops, and his hat mostly cocked."[28] In Scotland similarly the good Calvinist Baillie complained of the flamboyant elegance, lavish expense and courtly manners of his own hated rival, Owen's friend, the Independent Patrick Gillespie.[29] In Scotland, as in England, the Independents—or some of them—were the un-Calvinist, free, gay party: the heirs of the royalists.

Thus the Arminian-Socinian movement which, by breaking Calvinist rule in one society after another, released the forces of the new philosophy, was, if anything, a right-wing movement; royalist and Anglican in England and Scotland, "crypto-Catholic" in Holland, "libertine" in Switzerland. Nor is this in any way surprising. For in fact this movement is not an extension of Calvinism, as is so often supposed, nor a deviation from it, either to right or to left. It is an independent movement, with a distinct origin, a continuous tradition, and a pedigree longer than that of Calvinism. Indeed, Calvinism can be seen as an outgrowth of it, an obscurantist deviation from it, rather than *vice versa*. In order to see this, and to follow the two-hundred-years dialogue between the two movements, we must go back to the figure who stands at the source of both of them as of so much else: Erasmus.

V

If Arminianism is free will in theory, tolerance in practice, within a reformed, primitive, visible, Christian Church, Erasmus is the first Arminian; and indeed the Dutch Arminians recognized the fact. So did their English disciples: Erasmus was the inspiration not only of Arminius and Grotius but also of Grotius' disciples at Great Tew. Equally if Socinianism is the application of critical, solvent human reason to religious texts and to religious problems, within a similar Church, Erasmus is the first Socinian, and this paternity was recognized too. The Swiss and Italian *émigrés* who founded the Socinian movement in Switzerland and carried it to Poland—Castellio, Acontius, Lelio Sozzini himself—were disciples of Erasmus. Even in the nar-

28. Anthony Wood, *Life and Times*, anno 1648, 1657, 1659; *Athenae Oxonienses*, ed. P. Bliss (1813–21), IV, 98.

29. See below, pp. 387 ff. Owen declared his "long Christian acquaintance and friendship" with Gillespie in his preface to Gillespie's posthumously published *The Ark of the Covenant Opened* (1667).

row sense of the word, the sense in which its enemies used it, Socinianism derives from Erasmus. For the peculiar tenet of the early Socinians, the particular result of their application of reason to Scripture, was the rejection of the doctrine of the Trinity, and so of the divinity of Christ; and although Erasmus had not exposed himself on this topic, any more than many later Socinians were to do, it was his textual scholarship which was the basis of their rejection. He demonstrated, with a cogency that was proof against his own later half-hearted withdrawals, that the only biblical text which could be used to support that doctrine was spurious. It can therefore be said that Sozzini and Arminius merely gave their names to particular developments of a philosophy which they had received from Erasmus. This philosophy preceded Calvinism as Erasmus preceded Calvin. It was violently attacked by Calvin, who assailed the believers in free will as "libertines" and had Servetus burnt for rejecting the Trinity. Nevertheless, at certain times, it was subsumed in Calvinism and became a solvent force within it.

How Erasmianism was subsumed in Calvinism is easy to see. Erasmus himself preached his doctrines from the Right, to the Establishment. But he did not capture the Establishment, and in the generation after his death, his disciples had to reconsider their position. Either they must surrender to the Catholic Church which meant that they must give up their essential philosophy, or they must take up arms against that Church and, in so doing, accept radical leadership and the transformation of that philosophy. The choice was disagreeable, but could hardly be avoided—unless one were to seek a refuge outside the area of struggle, in distant Transylvania or anarchical Poland. The boldest spirits chose the second alternative. They decided to take up arms. Admittedly, in taking up arms, they had to surrender part of their philosophy, but it was better to surrender part than to surrender all. If they submitted to the leadership of a militant Protestant sect which, at that time, was still young and malleable, they might yet hope to control or influence it. At the very least they might preserve and reassert, after victory, the doctrines which, for the time being, must be muted. Submission to Rome, it seemed at that time, was quite different. Rome was old and strong. It did not bargain or compromise; and submission to it was total and final.

The militant Protestant sect to which the Erasmians naturally submitted was Calvinism. Calvinism might be, in many ways, fundamentally opposed to Erasmianism. Calvinism was intolerant, fundamentalist, scholastic, determinist, while Erasmianism was tolerant, sceptical, mystical, liberal. But Calvinism itself had Erasmian origins. Unlike Lutheranism, it presupposed a reformed, visible, primitive Church; it was also austere, scholarly, scientific; and in its earliest days it appealed to the same class in the same areas—the educated official and mercantile classes of Latin Europe. In submitting to Calvinism the Erasmians of Europe saw rather the common origin than the separate development of their movements. They were like those European Liberals who, in the 1930s, rather than surrender to Fascism, accepted Communist leadership of the Popular Front. Like these twentieth-century successors, they would soon find their relations with the Party uncomfortable, and afterwards—in happier times—they would seek the way out.

This slide of the Erasmians into Calvinism is easy to document. Wherever there was a centre of Erasmianism in the 1520s and 1530s— in the cities of France and Switzerland, the Rhineland and the Netherlands, in the princely Courts or noble households of Navarre, Transylvania, Poland—there we shall find a centre of Calvinism in the 1550s and 1560s. We can even watch the process happening. In the 1550s, when the Court of Rome seemed committed to blind reaction and all the works of Erasmus were put on the Index, the humanists of Europe were driven to the Left, driven into the arms of the only organization which seemed capable of preserving, at whatever price, the residue of their philosophy. It was then that the English humanists, fleeing from Marian persecution, accepted the leadership of Geneva; then that the humanists of the Netherlands, persecuted under the *Plakaten*, turned to the Calvinism that was to provide the discipline of their later revolt; then that the French humanists—the sceptical *littérateurs* of the days of François I—chose the road that would end, for many of them, with the massacre of St. Bartholomew; then that George Buchanan, who was one of them, would return at last to Scotland and become the intellectual leader of Calvinist revolution. Thanks to such men Calvinism, whose real social strength came from the urban artisanate, organized and disciplined by an indoctrinated clergy, could be said to have attracted the intellectual *élite* of Europe.

However, attraction is not absorption. This intellectual *élite* never formed the core of the Calvinist Church. Always the two intellectual elements of the Calvinist Church—the clergy who controlled its force and the humanists who merely attached themselves to it—remained separable, and often there was tension between them. The degree of tension varied with the structure of society around them. In monarchical countries with a developed, independent laity, the Calvinist Church could not prevail. Erasmian princes—Queen Elizabeth, William of Orange, Catherine de Médicis—might use the Church at times, but would always prefer to be independent of it, and looked to the laity to provide that independence. In petty principalities or city-states the Church would be proportionately stronger—especially if such states were politically weak and vulnerable and needed to draw on a reservoir of fanaticism. In such states the lay power would still seek to be independent of the Church. In Geneva there was a continuing struggle between the Venerable Company of Ministers and the City Council. In the Palatinate princely patronage was independent of the Church. But, in fact, in both societies, since they lived in fear of conquest, the Church exercised great power. In backward countries, like Scotland or Navarre, where an educated, independent laity hardly existed, the Church was without a rival: the prince had nothing to balance against it—unless, like James I or Henri IV, he had external patronage: the patronage of England or France. On the other hand, in eastern Europe, where an anarchical noble liberty prevailed, Erasmianism could still maintain itself independently of Calvinism—at least to the end of the sixteenth century. Hence Poland and Transylvania were the home of Socinianism in the second half of the sixteenth century.[30] Finally, the international Protestant universities preserved something of the liberty of the old communes. In great monarchies the universities might be brought to conformity with the established Church; but where a university was a powerful international centre, it could be a centre of intellectual heresy. The great days of the Protestant University of Heidelberg were those in which it rose above the cramping orthodoxy of the Palatinate and was the western centre of Socinianism.[31]

This distinction between the intolerant, predestinarian, scholastic doctrines of the Calvinist clergy and the tolerant, sceptical rationalism of the Erasmians whom political necessity had joined to them must

30. See Stanislas Kot, *Socinianism in Poland* (Boston, 1957); A. Pirnát, *Die Ideologie der Siebenbürger Antitrinitarier in den 1570-er Jahren* (Budapest, 1961); F. Pall, "Über die sozialen und religiösen Auseinandersetzungen in Klausenburg (Cluj) in der zweiten Hälfte des 16ten Jahrhunderts und ihre polnisch-ungarischen Beziehungen," in *La Renaissance et la Réformation en Pologne et en Hongrie* (*Studia Historica Academiae Scientiarum Hungaricae*, LIII, Budapest, 1963), pp. 313–28.

31. C.-P. Clasen, *The Palatinate in European History 1559–1660* (Oxford, 1963), pp. 35–42.

be emphasized if we are to understand the religious context of Protestant intellectual history in the seventeenth century. For the two movements were never completely fused. They never could be. Only the pressure of fear—the fear of Catholic subversion or foreign conquest or both—kept them united. It was this fear which had brought them together in the beginning. The same fear would bring them together again and again, whenever freedom had to be sacrificed to discipline, private criticism to common faith. But whenever that fear was suspended the two parties to the alliance naturally drew apart. In times of security why should the rational, sceptical, mystical heirs of Erasmus accept the leadership of intellectual reactionaries, scholastical bigots, blinkered Augustinians, Hebraic fundamentalists? They could afford to stand on their own.

Once this distinction is recognized, the relationship between Arminianism and Calvinism becomes much clearer. Arminianism is not a Calvinist heresy. Inherently, it has nothing to do with Calvinism. It is only accidentally connected with Arminius.[32] Essentially it is an independent movement which precedes Calvinism. Its apparent emergence out of Calvinism in Holland, Switzerland, Scotland, its appearance as a movement in the Anglican Church in opposition to the Calvinism of the Elizabethan clergy, is in fact merely the assertion of independence by an earlier tradition which had been temporarily merged with Calvinism.

It had been merged under the pressure of politics. The same political conjuncture which had first compelled the humanist Erasmians to join the Calvinist Church was to recur again and again. It was to recur in the 1580s, when the threat of Spanish conquest hung over the Netherlands and the Erasmians of Holland, in self-defence, would yield to the Calvinist *Predikants* whom many of them hated. At the same time, under the same threat, the English Calvinist clergy would become, for a time, the articulators of English resistance and, in that fortunate conjuncture, would attempt to impose their leadership on the Church. This was the time of the Marprelate Tracts and of John Field's attempt to capture control of the Church of England from within. In both countries, England and Holland, the Calvinists would be protected by that

32. Thus in England Arminianism was first advanced by the French *émigré* Peter Baro, Lady Margaret Professor of Divinity at Cambridge, in 1595—fifteen years before Arminius published his theses in Holland. See H. C. Porter, *Reformation and Reaction in Tudor Cambridge* (Cambridge, 1958), ch. xvii.

unscrupulous political adventurer, the Earl of Leicester, who was indeed the patron of "radical Protestants" everywhere, but not necessarily, therefore, of original ideas. The same threat would create a similar alliance in France; but there the fact of civil war, and the nice balance of forces, would enable many of the humanists to preserve a middle position between the Churches. Those who in England and Holland were liberals within the Calvinist fold, in France might be Huguenots—but might equally be Catholic *politiques*. In either case, their loyalty to their religious party was conditional. When the external danger was removed, they would assert their independence.

At the end of the sixteenth century that danger was removed. By 1600 the first assault of the Counter-Reformation had been successfully resisted, and the Erasmians no longer needed to submerge their identity within a disciplined party. So they re-emerged. But because they had once been submerged, they re-emerged with a difference, at least of name. Their continuous identity had been forgotten and they took, or were given, the names of their new leaders. Arminius in Holland seemed a heretic within the Calvinist Church, although in fact he did but reassert the old doctrines of Erasmus. Fausto Sozzini, through whom "rational" theology came back to western Europe, seemed the founder of a new "Polish" sect, although in fact he did but repeat the ideas of the Swiss and Italian disciples of Erasmus, displaced for a generation; and because that sect made itself known in Holland and disconcerted the clergy of the established Calvinist Church, it too seemed to be a Calvinist heresy. So Socinianism was described as a "radical Protestant" movement, on the "extreme Left" of Protestantism. But these terms are meaningless. Or at least, if they have meaning, it is only if we admit that Calvinism itself was a reactionary movement, a revival of the scholastic theology, providential history and Aristotelean science which Erasmus, Machiavelli and the Platonists of Florence had threatened to undermine.

So dawned the second phase of the Enlightenment, the golden "Jacobean" age of Bacon and Grotius: a phase which was rudely interrupted as one society after another shrank into itself before the threat of renewed ideological war. In 1618 the fear of war, of Spanish and Catholic reconquest, came to Holland, and once again the Calvinist preachers, the propagandists of resistance, asserted their power. The Arminians were crushed, or recognized the greater danger and came willingly to heel. In other countries the same pattern was repeated, with local variations. If Grotius was imprisoned in Calvinist Holland, Bacon was posthumously puritanized in England. The advocates of the Puritan origins of science would puritanize him still. It was not till the end of the ideological wars of Europe—that is, till the 1650s—that liberal, rational ideas could begin to emancipate themselves, once again, from their alliance with Calvinism: that oppressive alliance which political necessity had forced upon them in order to escape the even more oppressive clericalism of the Counter-Reformation.

VI

But if Arminianism and Socinianism, the religious movements which led to the Enlightenment, thus looked back past Calvin to the days of Erasmus and the Pre-Reform, the days of an undivided Catholic Church, what of the other half of that Church, the half which remained Catholic? For the Catholic Church also had its Erasmists. Not all of them surrendered unconditionally to the forces of the Counter-Reformation. Some at least had supposed, or hoped, that the critical, liberal spirit could be preserved within the Catholic Church: that surrender to the new dogmatism of the Council of Trent was a mere temporary necessity, and that afterwards they too could look back past the new orthodoxy to the ideas which it seemed to extinguish. In this they were perhaps mistaken, for the clericalism of the Counter-Reformation was more powerfully armed than the clericalism of the Protestant Churches. But we should not blame them for that. In their hatred of the excesses of the Reform—the vulgarity, the vandalism, the blind revolutionary spirit which it enlisted—they did not foresee the future. They did not calculate, in the 1550s, that the aggressive revolutionary, dynamic Calvinist clergy would gradually lose their grip while the Catholic clergy, the defenders of a weakened tradition, would gradually strengthen theirs.

So even in Catholic countries, beneath the forms even of Counter-Reformation orthodoxy, we can discover a persistent tradition of liberalism, waiting to reassert itself. It does not show itself in organized parties or distinct sects, like the Arminian and the Socinian parties in the Protestant Churches. The Catholic Church does not allow parties or sects: diversity of opinion within it must be expressed more vaguely, in "movements." But as a movement it is visible enough, at least in certain societies. Admittedly, it is difficult—though not altogether impossible—to see it in Spain and in the countries dominated by Spain: Italy,

Flanders and Portugal. There the engines of clericalism were fully developed and were backed by a strong central power. It is equally difficult to see it in "recusant" societies: Catholic communities living insecurely under Protestant rule. Such hunted minorities in Holland or England would be as narrow in their orthodoxy, as submissive to their clergy, as the Protestants of France under Louis XIII and Louis XIV. But in Catholic countries where there was no effective Inquisition and a strong, educated laity, able to influence their clergy, the tradition remains firm, even if submerged, even if disguised; and when the pressure of social and ideological struggle is released it will soon break out.

The most obvious of such societies, at least in the first century of the Counter-Reformation, were France and Venice. In France the secular power was perforce tolerant of its numerous Huguenot subjects. In Venice the old republican independence was asserted and the Counter-Reformation was kept at bay. Consequently both France and Venice were natural centres of Catholic humanism. That humanism was not snuffed out by the Catholic reaction of the 1550s. It survived the anarchy of the Wars of Religion, and revealed itself openly in the years of reduced ideological tension which I have described as the second phase of the Enlightenment: the generation before the full impact of the Thirty Years War.

The great names in this period are obvious enough. If the years 1590–1625, in the Protestant world, are the age of Bacon and Selden and Grotius, in the Catholic world they are the age of Montaigne and de Thou, Davila and Sarpi. All these were recognized as precursors by the men of the Enlightenment. Montaigne was the heir to the scepticism of Erasmus, the father of that seventeenth-century Pyrrhonism which relaxed the dogmas of the Churches and the Aristotelean cosmology behind them.[33] De Thou, Davila and Sarpi are named by Gibbon as the second founders, after Machiavelli and Guicciardini, of "philosophic history." Davila is indeed the Machiavelli of the seventeenth century, the favourite reading of "civil historians" and philosophic statesmen. De Thou, the most Protestant of Catholic historians—the founder, according to modern Catholic writers, of the persistent "Protestant bias" in sixteenth-century French historiography[34]—was an admirer of Erasmus: indeed, his greatest crime in the eyes of the Church was that

33. On this subject, see especially Richard H. Popkin, *The History of Scepticism, from Erasmus to Descartes* (Assen, Netherlands, 1964).

34. Cf. Lucien Romier, *Le Royaume de Catherine de Médicis* (Paris, 1925), p. xxxii.

in his *History* he not only mentioned the forbidden name of Erasmus but described him as *grande huius saeculi decus*, "the great glory of this century." And as for Sarpi, how can we think of that generation without him? At every turn we find ourselves faced by that indefatigable polymath: the Servite friar who corresponded with the Protestants of Europe in order to create a solid, non-doctrinal front against papal aggression; the historian who sought to show that European history had taken a false turn at the Council of Trent; the statesman who insisted, alone among Catholics, on the Socinian doctrine of the separation of Church from State; the social scientist whose analysis of the economic power of the Church improves upon that of Selden, foreshadows that of Giannone, and was hailed by Gibbon as "a golden volume" which would survive the papacy itself, "a philosophical history and a salutary warning."[35]

Most of these "Catholic Erasmians" of the early seventeenth century were heretics within their Church, just as the Arminians were heretics in the Protestant Churches. De Thou, in spite of a determined rearguard action, saw his work condemned by Rome in 1609. At his death his last volume was preserved from destruction only by the devotion of his secretary, Pierre Dupuy, who sent the manuscript abroad to be published in Geneva. The devotion of his heirs would have burnt it. Sarpi, of course, was the hated enemy of the papacy, and his great work was smuggled to England for publication: it was never published in a Catholic country till the eighteenth century. Even Montaigne, whose Pyrrhonism could be and was used as a means to defend traditional Catholicism, did not survive unscathed: his essays were finally condemned in Rome in 1676. And if the greatest religious thinker of seventeenth-century France, Cardinal Bérulle, the founder of the Oratory, contrived to combine the ideas of Erasmus and Montaigne with the Catholicism of the Counter-Reformation,[36] his disciples, the French Oratorians, soon found themselves in difficulty.

For the Oratorians, in the second half of the seventeenth century, would be the heretics within the Catholic fold. In Saumur the Catholic Oratory would compete with the Huguenot Academy in teaching the ideas of Descartes, condemned by the orthodox of both Churches. The

35. Gibbon, *Decline and Fall of the Roman Empire*, VII, 99.

36. For Bérulle, whom Mr. Popkin describes (*History of Scepticism*, p. 178) as "perhaps the most important religious thinker of the Counter-Reformation in France," see especially Jean Dagens, *Bérulle et les origines de la restauration catholique* (Bruges, 1950).

Oratorian Malebranche would reconcile Cartesianism with Catholicism. The Oratorian Bernard Lamy—another Cartesian of Saumur—would draw the young Leclerc from Calvinism to Arminianism. And above all, there would be the greatest of seventeenth-century biblical scholars, the Oratorian Richard Simon, who reintroduced Socinian rationalism into the study of Scripture.

Richard Simon was a devout Catholic. If he demolished the sacred text of the Bible, he did it, no doubt, for good Catholic purposes. He wished to turn the tables on the Protestant controversialists who had demolished the Fathers and fallen back on the Bible as the sole source of truth. But he demolished it all the same, and the Trinity to boot. For he too, like Erasmus and Socinus, rejected the famous verse, i John v. 7, on which the doctrine of the Trinity was held to depend. For his critical method Simon looked back to Erasmus. His immediate models were the Protestant scholars Scaliger, Buxtorf, Cappel and Bochart. And he provided material for Voltaire. No wonder the orthodox—Protestant as well as Catholic—hated him. No wonder Bishop Bossuet, the paladin of Catholic orthodoxy, the defender of the monolithic Roman (or rather, Gallican) tradition against the multiple, changing heresies of Protestantism, was haunted to his death by the thought of this infamous priest. For Simon's work, published by Protestant printers in Amsterdam and sent to the bonfire by Bossuet in Paris, showed irrefutably that the supposed monolith, for all its superficial smoothness and apparent strength, was itself no less complex, no less uncertain, no less variable than the enemy which beset it. The grandiose synthesis of established Counter-Reformation Catholicism was worm-eaten with heresy—Socinian heresy—too.[37]

Thus throughout the seventeenth century the Erasmian tradition —to use a convenient phrase—survived in the Catholic as well as in the Protestant Church, and by the end of the century it was challenging the established orthodoxy there too. Under different names it was undermining or transforming the Aristotelean certainties which had been restated and reimposed by Catholics and Protestants alike. Ultimately it would undermine even the new system which, for a time, had seemed to threaten both Churches, but which had gradually been absorbed into

---

37. For the Oratorians, see Haase, *Einführung in die Literatur der Refuge*, pp. 66, 379–80; for Richard Simon, Henri Margival, *Essai sur Richard Simon et la critique biblique au XVIIe siècle* (Paris, 1900); also Henri Hazard, *La Crise de la conscience européenne 1650–1715* (Paris, 1935), pt. ii, ch. iii, iv.

the state-Catholicism of France and had supplied it with a new articulation and a new defence against Pyrrhonism: the system of Descartes. Giannone would turn from Descartes to de Thou, Montaigne, Bacon and Newton.[38] Voltaire would reject Descartes for Bacon, become the prophet of Locke and Newton—both Socinians in religion—and draw on the work of English Quakers and deists, French Oratorians and Jesuits: for the Jesuits too, for a brief time, were "heretical" in the eyes of the Church, critics attenuating doctrinal difficulties, anthropologists preaching a religious relativity which would lead them into trouble and scandal in the great affair of Chinese ceremonies.[39] Gibbon's intellectual progress typified the pre-history of the Enlightenment. First, he would succumb to the majestic system of Bossuet: "the English translations of the two famous works of Bossuet, bishop of Meaux, achieved my conversion," he would write, "and I surely fell by a noble hand." Then, following the example of the Socinian Chillingworth and the Pyrrhonist Bayle, whose "acute and manly understandings" had been entangled in the same sophistries, he returned to his native Protestantism and was finally re-educated in Lausanne by Arminian teachers and the works of emancipated Huguenot scholars of the Dispersion.[40]

In all this, where is Calvinism? Where is "radical Protestantism"? Except as enemies of the Enlightenment they are nowhere to be found. Their part, it seems, is no more positive than that of the Dominican and Franciscan inquisitors in the Roman Church—except that their repression was, happily, less effective. Indeed, where Calvinism was strongest—in Scotland—we find the seeds of Enlightenment not so much in its Arminian deviationists, whom it was able to suppress, as in its open enemies, who hid from it in secluded corners or fled to safety abroad. For the Scottish Enlightenment—that wonderful, unexplored subject which Scottish historians have disowned in order to reiterate old party

---

38. P. Giannone, *Vita scritta da lui medesimo*, ed. Sergio Bertelli (Milan, 1960), pp. 22-23, 36-41; [L. Panzini] *Vita*, in P. Giannone, *Opere postume* ("Italia" [i.e., London], 1821), pp. 149-50; Giuseppe Ricuperati, "Le Carte Torinesi di Pietro Giannone," *Memorie dell' Accademia delle Scienze di Torino* (Turin, 1962), pp. 23-27.

39. For the Jesuit influence on Voltaire, see Réné Pomeau, *La Religion de Voltaire* (Paris, 1956).

40. In his *Memoirs of my Life and Writings* Gibbon declares his debts to his intellectual predecessors. It is interesting to observe how many of the writers who influenced him—like Bayle and Leclerc, Jacques Basnage, Isaac de Beausobre, Jean Barbeyrac, Jean-Pierre de Crousaz—were exiled Huguenots.

war-cries about the battle of Bannockburn and the dubious virtue of Mary Stuart—perhaps owed more to Scottish Jacobites, even to Scottish Catholics, than to Scottish Presbyterians: to the Jacobite physician Archibald Pitcairne, denounced as a deist or atheist and more at home in Leiden than in Edinburgh; to the Jacobite scholar William Ruddiman secluded in his protective library; to the episcopalian north-east captured by the mysticism of Antoinette Bourignon; to the Catholic lairds who nourished heretical ideas in isolated castles and peel-towers and the Catholic hedge-priests who visited them. The founder of critical history in Scotland, Thomas Innes, was an *émigré* Catholic priest in the service of the Pretender. The chevalier Ramsay, precursor of the encyclopaedists, began as one of the mystics of the north-east, became the secretary of the Catholic Quietist Madame Guyon and ended as a Catholic deist, tutor of the young Pretender. The 10th Earl Marischal, friend of Frederick the Great, patron of Rousseau, was an *émigré* Jacobite. David Hume was a Jacobite till 1745; his friend Lord Kames remained one thereafter. And without these, what is the Scottish Enlightenment?[41]

VII

Thus, when we look into the religious origins of the Enlightenment we do not discover them in any one Church or sect. They are to be found in both Churches and in several sects. What is common to the men who express such ideas is that all of them are, in some sense, heretical: that is, they either belong to dissident groups within their Churches or are themselves regarded as unorthodox. The orthodox Churches—Catholic, Lutheran, Anglican, Calvinist—look askance at them.[42] Moreover, the heretical tradition which they share is not only

41. For some sidelights on these Jacobite and Catholic influences, see A. D. MacEwen, *Antoinette Bourignon, Quietist* (1910); G. D. Henderson, *Mystics of the North East* (Aberdeen, Spalding Club, 1934) and *Chevalier Ramsay* (1952); Franco Venturi, *Le origini dell' Enciclopedia* (Milan, 1962), pp. 16–26; and, for Innes, *Registrum de Panmure*, ed. John Stuart (Edinburgh, 1874).

42. I have not concerned myself with Lutheranism in this essay, but I believe that the same general point could be made in respect of it, viz.: that it was "heretical" Pietism, not orthodox Lutheranism, which opened the way to the Enlightenment in Germany. The rigid structure of clerical Aristoteleanism was undermined and destroyed by the Pietists Spener and Thomasius; the Pietists were attacked by the ortho-

independent of the Reformation from which it is so often supposed to have sprung. It precedes the Reformation; and the Reformation, though it may at first have liberated it, has soon become a repressive movement, positively fragmenting and obstructing it. The intellectual tradition of scepticism, mysticism, critical scholarship, lay reason, free will, which was united in Erasmus was broken up and driven underground by the ideological struggles of the sixteenth and seventeenth centuries. What had once been a general movement within a united society, acceptable in the courts of princes and in the cathedrals of the established Church, became, under the impact of successive ideological struggles, a number of separate heresies, labelled with sectarian names and equally condemned by all right-minded members of the several religious establishments. In times of ideological peace, olympian minds like those of Grotius or de Thou or Bacon would seek to reunite these ideas, to restore to them their original respectability, and to develop them further. Once again princes and higher clergy would listen to them. But the return of religious war gave power to the radicals of orthodoxy; to the Calvinists who condemned Grotius in Holland, to the friars who condemned Galileo in Italy. The movement which might have been reunited was once again splintered: what might have been the orthodoxy of a united society became again the heresies of divided Churches. The eighteenth-century Enlightenment, when it came, would be a reunion of all the heretics, the reintegration of a movement which religious revolution had arrested and transformed, but could not destroy.

And yet, when we have said this, we have not said all. The ghost of Calvinism cannot so easily be exorcised. For if Calvinism was intellectually retrograde and repressive, a positive, vindictive enemy of enlightenment, politically it nevertheless performed an essential service. It is not enough to say that the Enlightenment would have come sooner had there been no ideological war in the sixteenth and seventeenth centuries. The fact is that there was such war; and once we accept

---

dox as Pelagians (i.e., Arminians), Papists and Socinians; and the great Pietist defence of heresy, Gottfried Arnold's *Unparteyische Kirche- und Ketzerhistorie*, afterwards inspired the greatest figure of the German Enlightenment, Goethe. The Pietists, like the Arminians and the Socinians, looked back behind the (Lutheran) orthodoxy of the state Church to Valentin Weigel and Sebastian Franck and, through them, to Erasmus, the neo-Platonists and the Rhenish mystics; cf. A. Koyré, *Mystiques, spirituels, alchimistes* (Paris, 1955).

that fact, we have to admit that Calvinism played an important, perhaps a vital part in it. It gave to the Netherlands the spiritual force which transformed an aristocratic resistance into a national revolution and created a new political phenomenon in Europe. It gave to Scotland the power to assert and preserve its national identity. It gave to the city of Geneva the power to resist covetous enemies. Without that resistance the Counter-Reformation might well have triumphed in Europe, and although we may admit that the Erasmian tradition survived even under the heavy weight of the new Catholicism, we have to admit also that its survival was very precarious and that without the resistance and example of Protestant Europe, it might have been extinguished. Certainly this was the view of contemporaries. We cannot overlook the general view of the humanists of the mid-sixteenth century to whom the choice seemed to be either total surrender of the intellect to Catholicism or merely partial surrender to Calvinism. The discipline of Calvinism could be seen as the temporary discipline of necessary war; that of Counter-Reformation Catholicism seemed the permanent discipline of a police-state. And certainly it was in the societies in which the Counter-Reformation had not triumphed that intellectual independence was soonest resumed.

This conviction of contemporaries that Calvinism, however intellectually reactionary, was the necessary political ally of intellectual progress is shown most clearly by the attitude of the Roman Catholic precursors of the Enlightenment. Jacques-Auguste de Thou was a good Catholic who lived and died in the profession of his faith. But he was also, as he continually observed, devoted to historical truth, and historically he saw the Huguenots as the defenders of Erasmian reform and progress. For this he was denounced in Rome. To avoid condemnation he adopted every device, every compromise, every concession — except the only one which would have served him. He refused to retract his opinions. Consequently he was condemned. The drama of de Thou's long-drawn-out battle with Rome, the whole tenor of his *History*, a "Protestant" history by a Catholic writer, and the evidence of his correspondence with his intimate friends in the Calvinist party — Jerome Groslot de Lisle, whose father had perished in the massacre of St. Bartholomew; Isaac Casaubon, who had fled to England to escape the *convertisseurs;* Georg Michael Lingelsheim, the tutor and councillor of the Calvinist Count Palatine — all this shows that, for de Thou, even Catholic enlightenment depended on the help of the Calvinist resistance.

Even more vivid is the evidence of de Thou's great contemporary, Paolo Sarpi: the Catholic friar who led the intellectual resistance of Europe, and the political resistance of Venice, against the aggression of the Counter-Reformation. Sarpi's whole life made him an ally of the Protestant world, and there is no need here to document the details of his alliance with it. But one fact deserves special mention. Soon after the Synod of Dordt, Sarpi wrote to the Dutch scholar and poet Daniel Heinsius declaring his own position in the religious controversies of Holland. That position, at first sight, surprises us. For Sarpi gave his support not, as we should expect, to the Arminians, the party of liberal Calvinists who were the natural allies of liberal Catholics, but to the Contra-Remonstrants, the extreme Calvinists, the persecutors of Grotius, the bigots of Predestination. On merely intellectual grounds this action is unintelligible. It assumes significance only if we see it in a political light. On the eve of renewed ideological war, the greatest Catholic historian recognized that the extreme Calvinists, the party of uncompromising, unconditional resistance, were the essential allies of all those Catholics who sought to preserve the intellectual freedom so nearly smothered by the Council of Trent.[43]

Politically, therefore, Calvinism may well have been necessary to the intellectual progress of Europe in the seventeenth century. This we may concede, just as we may concede that politically the Whig party was necessary to the securing of English liberty in the same century. But there is a difference between political and intellectual truth. The fact that Whig resistance broke Stuart despotism does not mean either that the Whig theories of the constitution and of liberty were intellectually right or even, in themselves, progressive. Nor does it mean that such theories, of themselves, entailed the consequences which followed the victory of the party professing them. Similarly, the fact that Calvinist resistance was necessary to the continuation and development of an intellectual tradition does not entail any direct or logical connection between them. A philosopher, in a time of crisis, may have to put on a suit of armour. To that suit of armour he may owe his life, and his capacity to go on philosophizing. But that does not make the armour the source of his philosophy. Indeed, while it is being worn it may well impede free speculation, which can be resumed only when the battle is over and it has been put off. The virtue of Calvinism, in respect of

43. See Boris Ulianov, "Sarpiana: la Lettera del Sarpi allo Heinsius," in *Rivista Storica Italiana*, 1956.

the Enlightenment, may perhaps be reduced to this. As a suit of armour it proved serviceable in battle, and though more uncomfortable to wear, proved easier to discard than the archaic, ornamentally encrusted chain-mail which protected, but also stifled the philosophers of the rival Church.

5 | Three Foreigners: The Philosophers of the Puritan Revolution

In November 1640 the Long Parliament met in London. The members who gathered at Westminster were angry, determined men. They had been kept out of Parliament for eleven years, and during those years they had suffered public and private grievances and humiliations. They disapproved of the government's foreign policy which had been one of peace with ignominy while the cause of Protestantism was going down abroad and profitable opportunities of privateering lay neglected in the West Indies. They disapproved of its home policy, which had consisted in a frontal war on the gentry, the laity of England, in order to sustain, at their expense, a swollen, parasitic court and a reinforced, reactionary clerical estate. They disapproved of the government itself, which was unsympathetic to all their views, and of its means of sustaining itself, which had been by imprisoning its critics, even to death, without legal trial or just cause. And they were particularly enraged by its last desperate venture: for six months earlier it had summoned Parliament only to dissolve it again in an arrogant, humiliating fashion, and to plunge in a desperate military gamble whose success (all agreed) would have meant the end of Parliament altogether. Fortunately it had failed; and because of that failure the leaders of the opposition had been able to force upon the government a new Parliament: a Parliament of angry men who were determined to make an end of this system of government, hold an inquest on its misdeeds, and punish the great gambler, Strafford.

All this is well known. It is also well known how Strafford resolved, even now, to break the Parliament; how the leaders of Parliament struck first against him; how for months all other business was interrupted by the trial of Strafford; how the judicial murder of Strafford poisoned relations between the king and Parliament and led to civil war between them; and how that civil war turned ultimately to revolution, regicide, republic, military despotism, anarchy and, at last, restoration. And yet we also know that none of these consequences was intended by the Parliament. However angry men had been in November 1640, they had not wished for anything like this. They were all of them deeply conservative men. Most of them—especially those who opposed the Court— were elderly men. They were all of them royalists: even three years later, after a year of civil war, they would unanimously send to the Tower a member who only hinted at republicanism. What then, we may ask, did they really want? What would have been their course if the great rock of Strafford's case had not thrust itself up, at the very beginning of their journey, and diverted them from the smooth waters in which they had intended to sail into the headlong torrent and foaming cataracts which carried them to disaster? It is easy to see what they did not want. They did not want wardship and purveyance, ship-money and monopolies, prerogative taxes and prerogative courts, clericalism and Star Chamber. But what were their positive aims? What sort of a brave new world did they envisage, and confidently envisage, in that brief period, those few days, between the meeting of Parliament on 3 November and the sudden, irremediable diversion of their course by the menace of Strafford on the eleventh?

At first sight it seems easy enough to answer this question, for did not the English gentry themselves express their aims? We look at their professed demands, the demands of their leaders: of the great patrons who had brought them into Parliament, of the common lawyers who had long formulated their demands, of the "Calvinian" clergy who preached to them and for them; and looking at these demands, we say that what the English gentry wanted was regular parliaments, constitutional guarantees, a "Presbyterian" Church. But at second glance— when we observe what they did to Parliament, the constitution, "Presbyterianism"—we find that this answer will not do. No doubt they wanted these things, but they did not want them as ends: they wanted them as means to other things, and when they did not lead to those other things, then they were rejected. So were the leaders who advocated them. Already in 1641 Oliver Cromwell, in Parliament, was attacking the patronage of the peers: in 1644 he would sigh for the day when there would be never a nobleman in England; in 1649 he would abolish the House of Lords. At the same time the cry of the Puritan gentry would swell against those "insatiable cannibals" the common lawyers, whose robes Colonel Pride, after the battle of Dunbar, would have hung up, with the captured Scots flags, as spoils of victory in Westminster Hall. And as for the "Presbyterian" clergy, we know how they fared. "Old priests writ large," they were used and thrown aside; they never, at any moment, controlled the Puritan Revolution.

Therefore, if we are to discover the positive aims of the English gentry—not merely the Puritan gentry, but the "country party" which in 1640 was united against the Court (though not against the king)—we must not listen to their leaders only: we must listen to themselves. We must place our ear not in the corridors of Westminster, nor in aristocratic palaces, nor in law courts and churches, but to the ground of rural England and Wales, in the counties from which these gentry came. We must discover, if we can, the voices not of metropolitan officials, but of dim squires, men who, more often than not, never raised their voices to speak publicly across the centuries, who did not publish theories, or make set speeches in Parliament, but who were nevertheless the angry men in Parliament and behind Parliament, the men who, from behind, struck down their lukewarm, politic, legalistic, aristocratic and clerical leaders and pushed on, over their bodies, to destruction.

Can we ever discover the aims of such men, men who, by definition, are inarticulate? Well, we can try. Enough of them left some record— whether in diaries or commonplace-books, casually recorded ejaculations or pious, ungrammatical devotions—for us to risk some generalization. In this essay I intend to take this risk. I intend to isolate, if possible, the positive, constructive aims not of the politicians, the front-benchers, but of the unpolitical back-benchers who at first followed those leaders and then, by going on when they had stopped, made the revolution.

Of course this is not easy. The language these men used is not always the language of politics or even of sense. Sometimes their demands seem absurdly parochial: they are using the nation's Parliament, and demanding a national revolution, in order to change their village parson or village schoolmaster. Sometimes they seem absurdly metaphysical: they will mobilize the train-bands or sit in committee to halt the course of Antichrist or discover the number of the Beast. Nevertheless, by reducing these demands to some common content, by generalizing the parochial and condensing the metaphysical, I believe we can come to some conclusions. No doubt many of their conclusions were negative, but with those negative conclusions I am not here concerned. I am concerned only with positive, constructive aims. These I propose to state; and having stated them I hope to show that they were not entirely forgotten even in the anarchy which overtook them. Through twenty years of what Cromwell called "blood and confusion," the gentry of England lurched and stumbled; but in the brief intervals between bloody noses and confused noises they still saw, and were led on by, a vision of society which they hoped somehow, at the end of it, to attain: a vision, moreover, made vivid to them by three philosophers, none of whom was English, but who together may perhaps be called, both in their limited, practical aims and their wild, bloodshot mysticism, the real philosophers, the only philosophers, of the English Revolution.

The social programme of the country party, as it was formed in the 1630s, in the years of Strafford and Laud, and as it emerges indistinctly from these records, can be easily summarized. Beneath the continued rule of a royal and episcopal government, which they took for granted (only demanding that it govern in harmony with the people, as under "queen Elizabeth of glorious memory"), they demanded two things: decentralization and laicization. For throughout the last century the English people had seen a constant process of centralization. There had been centralization of the State—what else was Tudor government, the "new monarchy" with its bureaucratic organization? There had been centralization—or rather, recentralization—of the Church: the Reformation had been a protest against Roman centralization; but that protest had only half succeeded, and now central power was being built up again by Canterbury and the country parishes remained neglected and starved. There had been centralization of economy: London had constantly drained business, wealth, population from the old provincial towns. And the country gentry—the best of them, those who did not merely mope at home or clamour to be in on the racket—wished to see this process reversed. They wished to see their counties, their local towns, their parishes raised out of the squalor and neglect and indignity into which they had been allowed to slide, thereby becoming mere backwaters, areas of emigration to the City and the Court. In wanting this, the "country" wanted also a continuation, or rather a resumption, of the Protestant Reformation: that Reformation which had originally meant not a centralized state Church, "a patriarch at Canterbury instead of a pope at Rome," but the dissolution of parasitic corporations, the redistribution of locked-up resources, the settlement of adequately paid, useful, preaching ministers in the parishes, the foundation of municipal institutions, local almshouses, local schools.

We can see this policy in numerous details, if we look for it. We can see it in the law. Many of the demands for reform of the law which became so loud during the Puritan Revolution were essentially for decentralization. Why, men asked, should all the law courts be in London? Why should "a mass of money" be thus "drawn from the veins into the ulcers of the kingdom"? Why should there not be local courts, giving speedier justice, not in "brackish French," but in the plain English tongue? And since lawsuits were generally about land, why should the titles to land be discoverable only in London? Why should there not be registries, one in each county; and all land, of course, held by simple tenure, in free socage, free from the control of another central, abusive court, the Court of Wards?[1]

Then there was education. Higher education for the gentry was the essential road to employment: why should it be centralized in the (to many of them) distant and costly towns of Oxford and Cambridge? The gentry demanded universities or colleges in York, Bristol, Exeter, Norwich, Manchester, Shrewsbury, Durham, Cornwall, the Isle of Man, wherever they themselves happened to live. And not only universities. Grammar schools were no doubt many, but their location was arbitrary, according to the residence or whim of their founders. There were demands for "an Eton college in every county." And, at a humbler level, there was a great demand for uniform, decentralized primary education. If the "country" was to raise itself up out of its seedy, neglected state, it must be, men said, on the base of an educated, industrious artisanate. The Elizabethan gentry and middle class, says Dr. Rowse, "believed in education for their children," and took steps to ensure it; but "they thought education less important for the people, and they were right." But were they right? The best of them, by the seventeenth century, thought that they were not: that the educational system of the

1. The quotation is from Milton, *Of Reformation touching Church Discipline* (1641). The swelling demand for "county registers" can be traced in the voluminous pamphlets on law reform. It was raised in the reign of James I by one Henry Miles (who brought it up again in 1647; see G. H. Turnbull, *Hartlib, Dury and Comenius*, Liverpool, 1947, p. 85), and again in 1641 by Richard Lloyd of Esclus (see A. H. Dodd, *Studies in Stuart Wales*, Cardiff, 1952, p. 67). In the 1640s and 1650s it is a regular part of the "country" programme. See, for instance, *Certain Proposals for Regulating the Law* (n.d.; *Somers Tracts*, 1811, v, 534); William Sheppard, *England's Balm* (1656); William Cole, *A Rod for the Lawyers* (1659).

IOHAN·AMOS COMENIVS, MORAVVS. Aᵒ ÆTAT. 50: 164.

Ex sump: M: S:

G: Glouer. fe:

Loe, here an Exile! who to serue his God,
Hath sharely tasted of proud Pashurs Rod;
Whose learning, Piety, & true worth, being knowne
To all the world, makes all the world his owne.

F: Q:

J. A. Comenius

The Pansophic Enlightenment

country, like its government and Church, was top-heavy and that the balance must be restored.[2]

It must be restored also in the Church. Nothing was so obvious to the conscientious country gentry of the 1630s as the unbalance in the Church. The Reformers had dissolved monasteries, abolished costly superstitions, redistributed wealth; but how disappointing the result now seemed! Had the tithes of the monasteries been returned to the parish clergy from whom they had originally been filched? Had the gospel, liberated from its former constriction, been carried into the neglected north and west of England? Had the wealth of the Church been redistributed within the Church? The answer was, no, or not enough. All men realized that, not least Archbishop Laud. Unfortunately Laud sought to repair the base of the Church by repairing the summit first. He would first re-create clerical power, clerical wealth at the top, and then use that power and that wealth to enforce changes at the bottom. And his method of change was to be not co-operation with the laity, and lay piety—that great new force which lay behind the whole Reformation—but frontal war on it. Naturally the laity did not co-operate. They were eager to help—their achievement in augmenting the value of livings was in fact far greater than Laud's—but not in that way.[3]

For the programme of the country party was not merely one of decentralization. It was also one of laicization. For in spite of the Reformation it now seemed to them that religion, education, the law had all become professionalized. They had fallen, or fallen back, into the hands of complacent corporations which were converting them, more and more, into private monopolies with mysterious, private rules, the means of perpetuation. But by now "the country" had begun to sus-

2. Proposals for local universities and colleges are to be found in *The Fairfax Correspondence, Memoirs of the Reign of Charles I*, ed. G. W. Johnson (1848), II, 275; John Brinsley, *A Consolation for our Grammar Schools* (1622); Samuel Harmar, *Vox Populi* (1642); John Milton, *Of Education* (1643); *Stanley Papers*, III, iii (Chetham Society, 1867), pp. 14–15; Benjamin Nicholson, *The Lawyer's Bane* (1647); George Snell, *The Right Teaching of Useful Knowledge* (1649); Hugh Peter, *Good Work for a Good Magistrate* (1651); John Lewis, *Contemplations upon these Times* (1646) and εὐαγγελιόγραφα . . . (1656); William Dell, *The Right Reformation of Learning, Schools and Universities* (1653). The demand for an Eton College in every county is in William Vaughan, *The Golden Grove* (1600), pt. III, ch. 37. Dr. Rowse's remark is in his *The England of Elizabeth* (1950), p. 494.

3. For evidence of this paragraph, need I do more than mention Mr. Christopher Hill's excellent book, *Economic Problems of the Church* (Oxford, 1956)?

pect the validity of these rules and the motives behind them. The lawyers' "brackish French," the "paramount" Aristoteleanism of the universities, the new "superstition" of the Anglican Church now seemed to be merely the mumbo-jumbo of social conservatism, the meaningless argument against useful change. But the country did not despair of change, and if the professionals were imprisoned in their own categories, the laity were prepared to reject those categories. Society would be changed, they said, by lay energy, using lay science: a simple, rational approach to law—the law of Selden or Hale; a simple, rational approach to learning—the learning of Bacon; a simple, rational approach to religion—the religion not of Puritanism, which could so easily become a new clericalism, but of latitudinarianism, whether Anglican or Puritan: the "layman's" religion of Chillingworth or Hales.

Such, in general, was the philosophy of the country party. Of course I have simplified it, and idealized it. In practice it ran into many difficulties, as the opposition of vested interests was discovered; and naturally it had many less reputable supporters, whose interests tainted its simplicity. It was also carried to unexpected lengths. In the course of the revolution the demands for decentralization—decentralization of Parliament, decentralization of trade—became sometimes ruinous, sometimes ridiculous; and extreme laicization sometimes led merely to anarchy. Still, if we are to see the practical philosophy of the country party at its best, this, I believe, is it. And once we have seen it in this form, we can see it also in another. This philosophy of the country, of the enemies of the Court, of the austere, religious, parochial men who would become Puritans, rebels, republicans, was, in almost every respect, the philosophy of that greatest of courtiers, that extravagant, metropolitan sceptic, that "peremptory royalist" (as he called himself), Francis Bacon.

It is a paradox, and yet how can we deny it? Look at Bacon's works, look at his addresses to the lawyers, his memorials to the king, his memoranda on education, his speeches in Parliament, his declarations on science. It is all there. The country party, or at least their leaders in Parliament, did not listen to Bacon in his day. They lined up behind his great rival, the crabbed, pedantic, unimaginative idolator of the existing common law with all its obscurities and abuses, the greatest profiteer of its centralization, Sir Edward Coke. And yet, if we look closely, or look later, how wrong they were! All the reforms of the law which would be loudly and angrily demanded by a rebellious people in the

1640s had been lucidly and loyally demanded, a generation before, not by Coke, never by Coke, but always by Bacon. It was the same in education. Bacon, the greatest advocate of lay reason and lay religion, would have reformed the universities, dethroned Aristotle, introduced natural science; he would have stopped the growth of grammar schools and built up elementary education; he would have decentralized charitable foundations, whether schools or hospitals, for "I hold some number of hospitals with competent endowments will do far more good than one hospital of exorbitant greatness"; he would have decentralized religion, planting and watering it in the forgotten "corners of the realm"; and he would have decentralized industry, trade, wealth, for "money is like muck, not good except it be spread." When we read this evidence — evidence which is obvious, inescapable, constant throughout his writings — we can easily agree with the greatest of English seventeenth-century historians, S. R. Gardiner, that if only Bacon's programme had been carried out, England might have escaped the Great Rebellion.[4]

But how could the country gentry of England know this? How could Francis Bacon speak intelligibly to them? A double gulf separated them from him. First, there was a social gulf, the gulf between the great intellectual courtier of an outrageous, spendthrift Court and the serious-minded, parsimonious, provincial country squires to whom, in fact, he had seldom addressed himself: for as a conservative reformer he had preached privately to the king, not publicly to them. Secondly, and perhaps even more significantly, there was a gulf in time: a very narrow gulf, it is true, but also a very deep gulf; for it was the gulf between 1620 and 1630 in which a whole world, a whole philosophy of life, had irretrievably foundered and sunk.

For if we are to understand changes in human history, human philosophy, we must always remember the importance of single generations. One generation of men may be bound together by common experiences from which its fathers and sons are exempt; and if those experiences have been signal, terrible, inspiring, they will give to that generation a character distinctive to itself, incommunicable to other men. How can we who lived through the 1930s, whose minds and attitudes were formed by the terrible events of those days, understand

---

4. For Bacon's views on the Church, see, for instance, his *Works*, ed. Spedding *et al.* (1857–74), iii, 49, 124, 103 ff.; on education, iv, 249–55; on law reform, v, 84; vi, 59–70, 182–93; and vii, 181 ff., 358–64. But such instances could be multiplied. Gardiner's verdict is in his article on Bacon in the *Dictionary of National Biography*.

or be understood by men to whom those events are mere history, reduced to the anodyne prose of textbooks? Of course not every generation has common experiences sufficient to mark it out in this way;
the experiences, if they are to have this effect, must be powerful, formidable, inspiring. But if they are inspiring, then there are such generations. Spaniards, in their history, talk of "the generation of '98" as
an enormous, significant fact which alone gives meaning to a part of
its course. In Europe the generation of the 1930s may well prove similar. And in seventeenth-century Europe, and particularly Protestant
Europe, the generation of the 1620s was the same.

The 1620s had been a terrible decade. For most of Europe it had
been a decade of economic depression leading into new absolute power
and European war. For Protestant Europe it had also been a decade of
total defeat on all fronts: by 1629 the complete extinction of the whole
European Reformation seemed in sight, and its intellectual leaders envisaged flight into uninhabitable wastes or imaginary islands. And in
England, if the suffering was less, the shame was greater. To Englishmen the 1620s was a decade of irresponsible government and economic
crisis at home and the betrayal, the fatal betrayal, of a great tradition
abroad. When they looked back on history, Englishmen saw Queen
Elizabeth giving leadership, strength, victory to European Protestantism. Now, when they looked out, they saw only feeble English intervention and then withdrawal into timid neutrality. And what was the
result of this weakness? As English fleets and armies returned in defeat and disgrace from ill-managed expeditions, the whole Protestant
cause collapsed. From Gibraltar to Danzig, from the Channel ports to
Hungary, the ideological enemy struck down every citadel of Protestantism in turn; and from Bohemia, Poland, the Palatinate of the Rhine,
La Rochelle, a stream of refugees arrived on these still safe but igno-
minious shores. Amid such a series of catastrophes the whole climate of
opinion in Protestant Europe was convulsed. It was the end of an era,
the end perhaps of an illusion. The age of the Renaissance, that age of
unbounded optimism, olympian speculation, carefree *douceur de vivre*
was over. Armageddon had arrived. How, in these last convulsions of
the world, could men breathe the atmosphere or think the thoughts of
the past, even the immediate past? Was it not rather a time to count the
few remaining days of the world, to expect the conversion of the Jews,
to listen for the last, or at least the penultimate Trump, to calculate the
abstruse and fugitive number of the Beast?

In the 1630s the serious-minded gentry of England indulged in a great deal of such calculation, and their home-grown scholars were assisted by many a crack-brained European refugee. In many an English manor-house, in many a vicarage or college cell, old computations were revised and new elaborated. There was the old work of Thomas Brightman, a Puritan clergyman who had lived in the household of the Osborne family. His application of the Apocalypse to current affairs had been sent to the bonfire by the obedient bishops of Queen Elizabeth, but had been taken up eagerly abroad. There was the later work of the German encyclopaedist Johann Heinrich Alsted, "the standard-bearer of millenaries in our age," written in Herborn in 1627, shortly before its author fled from the calamities of Germany to Protestant Transylvania. But most important of all were the researches of the Cambridge scholar Joseph Mede, the tutor of John Milton. Mede had worked out his "synchronisms," as he called them, by rigorous intellectual method, uninfluenced by external events. But when applied to external events, they fitted (as it seemed at the time) marvellously. His *Clavis Apocalyptica*, also published in 1627, became the handbook of all who wished to interpret current affairs by biblical prophecy. During his lifetime (he died in 1639) numerous well-known clergymen consulted him as an oracle on these abstruse matters, and after his death "learned Mr. Mede" remained for a generation the undisputed authority on them: in thirty years, wrote one of them, there had been no apocalyptic work of significance "but what hath been lighted at his flame." The laity were no less impressed. Sir Nathaniel Rich, cousin and political agent of the Earl of Warwick, was one of Mede's admirers; a Shropshire country gentleman and Member of Parliament, Richard More, would translate his work into English; and in 1639, from the depths of Herefordshire, a gentlewoman would write to her son at Oxford solemnly reminding him that this was the year in which "many are of opinion that Antichrist must begin to fall."

This new climate of opinion, generated by the disasters of the 1620s, necessarily affected the context of men's thought, and the context, in turn, affected its character. Even Baconianism was transmuted by it. The English country gentry had accepted "Baconian" ideas as the formulation of their mundane hopes and interest. But in such a climate they could not accept the pure Baconianism of Francis Bacon. Baconianism must be changed to meet them. It must put off its courtly Jacobean clothes, its patrician elegance, its metropolitan urbanity and scepticism, its traces of the galleries and aviaries of York House, the gardens and fishponds of Gorhambury, and become instead a "country Baconianism," acceptable in the new world of the 1630s. It must be serious, Puritan, dull, only with its dullness lit up here and there by lunatic flashes: millenary calculations, messianic hopes, mystical philo-semitism.[5]

The need produced the men. Just at this moment the essential agents of this metabolism appeared. And they appeared, appropriately, out of the maelstrom of central Europe. Just as the first Protestant Reformation in England, the Reformation of Edward VI, though an English movement, had been animated by foreign thinkers, seeking a new asylum and new base, so its seventeenth-century continuation, though also a purely English movement, was to seek inspiration from three displaced foreigners: foreigners who would inject into the "Baconian" empiricism of England the high-flown metaphysics of the Thirty Years War. These three foreigners were Samuel Hartlib, John Dury and Jan Amos Komenský, the famous Comenius.[6]

Samuel Hartlib was a Prussian, from Polish Prussia. His father had been "merchant royal" to the King of Poland, and his home was in

5. Brightman's work was *Apocalypsis Apocalypseos* (Frankfurt, 1609). An English translation was printed at Leiden in 1616 and in London in 1644. That Brightman was maintained by the Osborne family is stated by Francis Osborne, *Traditional Memoirs on the Reign of King James* (1658), p. 34. Alsted's apocalyptic work was *Diatribe de Mille Annis Apocalypticis* (1627), which was translated into English by William Burton and published as *The Beloved City* (1643). For Mede, see his *Works*, ed. John Worthington (1664); John Worthington, *Diary and Correspondence*, ed. J. Crossley, II (Chetham Society, 1855), p. 69; *The Letters of Lady Brilliana Harley* (Camden Society, 1854), p. 41. The English translation by More appeared in 1643, entitled *The Key of the Revelation Searched and Demonstrated*, with a preface by Dr. Twisse, one of Mede's friends and correspondents. For messianism and philo-semitism in Europe during the Thirty Years War, see also Michael Roberts, *Gustavus Adolphus*, I (1953), 521–27; H. J. Schoeps, *Philosemitismus im Barock* (Tübingen, 1952), especially pp. 18–45.

6. For biographies of these three men, see G. H. Turnbull, *Samuel Hartlib* (Oxford, 1920); J. M. Batten, *John Dury, Advocate of Christian Reunion* (Chicago, 1944); J. Kvačala, *J. A. Comenius, sein Leben u. seine Schriften* (Leipzig, 1892); R. F. Young, *Comenius in England* (Oxford, 1932). On all three men and their work, new light has been shed by the rediscovery, in 1945, of Hartlib's papers, which had been lost since 1667 and are now in the possession of Lord Delamere. From their rediscovery until his death in 1961, they were worked upon by the late Professor G. H. Turnbull, whose book *Hartlib, Dury and Comenius* is largely an account of their contents. Turnbull also published a series of articles based on them, which I shall cite where relevant. I would here like to express my appreciation of the generous help which I received from Mr. Turnbull when working on this subject.

Elbing, on the Baltic sea. He seems to have studied when young in Cambridge and there to have been captivated by Baconian ideas; but he returned to Elbing, and it was only in 1628, with the Catholic conquest of Elbing, that he came, with other refugees, permanently to England. There he threw himself into works of charity, collected money for Protestant refugees from Poland, Bohemia and the Palatinate, set up a short-lived school on Baconian principles at Chichester, and finally, in 1630, moved to London and lived permanently in Duke's Place, Holborn. The rest of his life and fortune was spent in a "super-abundant charity to his neighbours and to God, in a faithful adventure much tending to his glory": in other words in relieving his fellow-refugees, encouraging practical, lay piety and, more particularly, in disseminating useful knowledge interfused with messianic speculations.

For essentially Hartlib believed in "useful knowledge." As a Baconian, he was convinced that a whole world of such knowledge was at hand, if only men would seek it, and that it could be applied, if only they would distribute it. And how profitably it could be applied, even by governments! "The public aims," he once wrote, "of those that are over the affairs of state, to reform and direct them towards the good of all, may be infinitely improved," if only such leaders will learn how to make use of the statistical, economic and other information which could so easily be supplied to them. And he himself was ready to supply it. All he required was co-operation. To ensure co-operation he advocated a union of all good men, bound together in an "invisible college" by religious pacts and devoting themselves to collective undertakings. They should improve husbandry, teach languages, forward inventions, compile statistics, educate the Red Indians, the Irish, the poor, recommend domestic servants, welcome—perhaps convert—the Jews, interpret the Apocalypse. They should put at the service of the State an "engine" for "the settlement of the felicity thereof." Such a union, he believed, could easily be achieved in a tolerant Protestant society. Once the ideological enemy had been destroyed and Protestantism had been established, or re-established, throughout Europe, it would be possible, by such means, to regenerate the whole world.[7]

That general victory of Protestantism would no doubt come. Meanwhile, while waiting and working for it, one could plan. One could begin with a "model": a practical experiment in a limited field.

7. S. Hartlib, *A Further Discovery of the Office for Public Address for Accommodation* (1648), in *Harleian Miscellany* (1745), vi, 13.

The idea of such a model had been put forward in the early seventeenth century by a German thinker whom Hartlib much admired, Johann Valentin Andreae, the founder of the Rosicrucians. Ever since 1620—the year of disaster in Bohemia, the year in which Andreae published his most influential work—Hartlib and his friends had dreamed of establishing such a "model." They called it "Antilia" or "Macaria" (the former name came from Andreae's work,[8] the latter from More's *Utopia*); and they imagined it in distant islands or peaceful enclaves, shut off from the hostile world. At one time it was to be in Virginia; at another in Lithuania, on the estates of the Protestant Prince Radziwill; or again in Livonia, on an island belonging to Count Jacob de la Gardie; or in Prussia, on the land of Freiherr von Stein. But gradually, as the Counter-Reformation triumphed in Europe, it was in England that Hartlib saw his opportunity. So it was in England that he set up his headquarters and offered himself as universal secretary of the union of good men. There he would advertise, solicit, publish, co-ordinate, lubricate. In fact it was to his "great and unwearied zeal for learning" that England owed Milton's essay on education, Pell's *Idea of Mathematics*, Evelyn's *Sylva*, the work of Weston on husbandry, of Petty on "political arithmetic," and a dozen other manuals of general improvement. He was "the great intelligencer of Europe," himself unoriginal, but the friend of every thinker in his adopted country, the means of contact and correspondence with the Protestant Dispersion; and the basis of all his friendships was his zeal for Baconian science, Baconian methods, combined with that inevitable addition of the 1620s: Protestant unity, apocalyptic prophecy and "the final overthrow of Antichrist in Europe."

With Hartlib we must always associate John Dury. Dury also came from Elbing. The son of an exiled Scottish minister, he had studied in Holland, taught in a Huguenot household in France and then become a minister in Elbing, where he had met Hartlib and discovered that he also was a Baconian. Then, when the Jesuit reconquest squeezed him too out of Elbing, he had become a wandering missionary, preaching Protestant union as a means of political survival, Baconian methods as the hope of social regeneration. He presented himself to Gustavus Adolphus, the sudden saviour of the Protestant cause. He was taken up

8. For the concept of "Antilia," see Margery Purver, *The Royal Society, Concept and Creation* (1967), pp. 219–27. For Andreae, see Felix Emil Held, *Christianopolis, an Ideal State of the Seventeenth Century* (New York, 1916).

by Sir Thomas Roe, the advocate of English intervention in the Thirty Years War. To the English Court he argued that Protestant union was the only effective means of reinstating the king's nephew in his hereditary dominions: "Protestant unity," he wrote, "will be more worth to the Prince Palatine than the strongest army that His Majesty can raise him."[9] He even pressed his cause on Archbishop Laud, who treated him very shabbily, sending him on fool's errands first to Devonshire, then to Germany, to be rid of him. But no one could get rid of Dury. He was indefatigable, an idealist, a crusader. "Methinks I see you," wrote one of his English patrons,

> clambering up that laborious and rugged way after St. Paul, in journeyings often, in perils of water, of robbers, of false brethren, in perils both in city and in country, in weariness and painfulness, in watching often, in want and necessities, and besides all these conflictations, labouring under the daily care of the churches.

Whenever we catch a glimpse of him he is in one of these postures: he is in Germany, in Holland, in Denmark, in Sweden, beset with poverty, selling his father's books to buy bread, waiting in the ante-rooms of warring princes and generals, indifferent bishops, querulous theologians; he is writing on education; collecting Bacon's works for German princes or the young Queen of Sweden; interpreting the Apocalypse; counting the number of the Beast. And all the time, as he travels incessantly over Europe, his rear is protected by the "agitation and cooperating industry" of his constant friend in London, Samuel Hartlib, "the boss of the wheel," as Dury called him, "supporting the axle-tree of the chariot of Israel."[10]

The third member of this remarkable triumvirate was a much more famous, and even stranger man. Comenius was a Bohemian, a minister of the pietist Church of the Bohemian Brethren. He too had fled from place to place as the Habsburgs and the Jesuits reconquered his native land. In 1628, after many displacements, he had arrived, with his community, on the estate of a Polish devotee, Count Raphael Lescyński, at Leszno in Poland. There he too had discovered the works of Bacon

9. G. H. Turnbull, "Letters written by John Dury in Sweden 1636-8," in *Kyrkohistorisk Årsskrift* (Stockholm), 1949.

10. For Dury's reunionist activity in the 1630s, see especially Gunnar Westin, *Negotiations about Church Unity, 1628–1634* (Uppsala Universitets Årsskrift, 1932), and the same writer's *Brev fran John Durie dren 1636–1638* (Uppsala, 1933).

and had at once become an enthusiast. Bacon and Campanella, he once wrote, were the two heroes who had conquered the giant Aristotle. But like Hartlib, Comenius also accepted Bacon with a difference. At the Academy of Herborn, he had been a pupil of the millenarian J. H. Alsted. He had also, like Hartlib, been deeply influenced by Andreae. It was to Andreae's "golden book," he afterwards wrote, that he owed "almost the very elements" of the ideas which he was to make famous from his place of refuge at Leszno. These ideas he summarized under the name "Pansophia."

Like Hartlib, like Bacon, Comenius believed in the unity of knowledge. He was an encyclopaedist. He believed that all knowledge could be mastered and shared, and being so mastered and so shared could change the world. But in order to make knowledge common, he believed that universal peace must be secured: that new, simplifying techniques of learning must be devised and generalized; and that new truths must be extracted from Scripture. To him, as to Hartlib and Dury, universal peace meant peace among non-Catholics—unity of Protestants, reception of Jews—and the means of pursuing it was by "models." Learning was to be simplified by "didactic" processes and generalized by means of a new educational system. The new truths of Scripture were to be extracted by applying mathematical and astronomical science to the prophetic books of the Bible. So Comenius too subjected his fragmented Baconian science to a fashionable non-Baconian purpose: to the expectation of the Millennium, the calculation of the number of the Beast, the elucidation of the Apocalypse.

In the 1630s, in Leszno, Comenius was busy preaching Pansophia. He wrote books on the reform of teaching-methods and the creation of new schools. He was already an enthusiast for the Millennium, the Messiah and the Jews. In Leszno he wrote his first works on education. At once they were pirated in England.[11] But before long the pirates were overtaken by a disinterested admirer, who wrote to him from England offering to send him some of Bacon's manuscripts, to collect money for his work, to look after his disciples in England, to procure him an amanuensis. This disinterested admirer was, of course, that universal agent, Samuel Hartlib.

Comenius was charmed by Hartlib's advances. How could he fail

11. Comenius' *Janua Linguarum* was published in England in 1631 by John Anchoran and was at once welcomed in several schools. Another unauthorized edition, Wye Saltonstall's *Clavis ad Portam*, was published at Oxford in 1634.

to respond to such unexpected "Christian charity towards me, albeit unknown, and towards us, whom the world had cast off"? He sent his works to England, where Hartlib published them. Soon afterwards Hartlib put him in touch with Dury, and Dury, now in Sweden, saw to it that his books and ideas were distributed there. Dury also put him in touch with new patrons. For in Sweden at this moment there were two great men who seemed natural patrons alike of the Protestant reunionist and the educational reformer. One was the king, Gustavus Adolphus, the leader and saviour of European Protestantism, who was also the founder of Uppsala University and the educator of Sweden. The other was his indispensable financier, the greatest, most enlightened Protestant merchant, banker and industrialist of his day, the founder of the Swedish copper and iron industries, the patron of scholars, the Liégeois immigrant, Louis de Geer.

When Gustavus and Louis de Geer beckoned Dury and Comenius to settle under their patronage in Sweden, it seemed inevitable that they should yield. Sweden was then the leader of European Protestantism. Its armies were reconquering Europe after the disasters of the 1620s. Its Court was at once the motor of social reform at home and the magnet which attracted the messianic prophets displaced from the fallen citadels of Prague and Heidelberg. Dury, for his Protestant reunion, Comenius for his educational programme, both for their mystical aspirations, looked naturally to the power of Gustavus Adolphus and to his chancellor, Axel Oxenstjerna, who continued that power after the king's death at Lützen. And Louis de Geer, as no one else, could finance their operations. But in fact they did not yield. For Hartlib, in England, had already built up for them a rival group of patrons. That group consisted of their natural disciples, the inarticulate, intellectually leaderless country party of England.

Perhaps it sounds extravagant to represent these three foreigners as the intellectual cement of the English country party. That party, it can be said, had other, non-intellectual bonds: it was held together by patronage, by kinship, by the great Puritan "cousinage" of which we read so much. And yet was this really so? The bonds of patronage were soon snapped; kinship united men across party divisions as well as within them; and the lines of "cousinage" were far less clear or exclusive than historians pretend. No doubt Oliver Cromwell was related to John Hampden and Hampden to Sir Thomas Barrington and Barrington to the Earl of Warwick, and all these were Puritan leaders; but what of Sir Oliver Cromwell and Alexander Hampden and Warwick's brother

the Earl of Holland, who were also in the "cousinage" and were all royalists? No, within the cousinage, within the patronage-group, there is
another, more exclusive bond: the bond of common ideas. And if we
make a list of all those men who were acknowledged leaders of the country party in 1640, clergy and lay, and then ask what common intellectual influence they acknowledged, the answer is clear. Whatever other
interests may have divided them, they were all united in the patronage
of our three philosophers, Hartlib, Dury and Comenius.

Let us glance at that list. First there are the clergy. Their most important clerical patron was John Williams, Bishop of Lincoln and Dean
of Westminster, formerly Lord Keeper of England, now the leader of
clerical opposition to Archbishop Laud. Williams had been the friend,
the successor in office, the executor of Francis Bacon; he held Baconian views and lived (much to the irritation of Laud) with Baconian
magnificence. He founded libraries, patronized schools, enriched colleges, encouraged teachers of the new learning. Already in 1630 Hartlib
and Dury were in touch with him, and he was liberal to them both. In
1632 — it seems — he put Hartlib in charge of his "academy" of young
noblemen at his palace of Buckden.[12] Other bishops soon followed his
example: Archbishop Ussher of Armagh, bishops Davenant of Salisbury, Hall of Exeter, Morton of Durham. These were notoriously the
"anti-Laudian" bishops, the men whom the country party praised as
the type of "moderate" bishop required in a reformed Church. Not a
single "Laudian" bishop appears among the patrons of Hartlib, Dury
and Comenius: such patronage was a badge of the country party in the
Church.

It is a badge also in the State. For who are the lay patrons of these
three foreigners? At the head of the list is Elizabeth, Queen of Bohemia,
the king's sister, the royal figurehead of opposition, the pensioner of
the Parliament throughout the Civil Wars. With her are her diplomatic
supporters, Sir William Boswell, another executor of Francis Bacon,

12. Comenius, whose *Great Didactic* (quoted in Young, *Comenius in England*, p. 84)
is our source for this episode, does not name the great patron who gave Hartlib a
"castle" as his academy. Young himself suggests that it was either Williams or the Earl
of Warwick. Turnbull (*Hartlib, Dury and Comenius*, p. 20) suggests that it may have
been Lord Brooke, who certainly placed Hartlib for a time at his house at Hackney.
But the remarkable agreement of Comenius' account with the account, by his chaplain,
of Bishop Williams' academy for young noblemen at Buckden (see J. Hacket, *Scrinia
Reserata*, 1693, II, 38) suggests to me that Williams was the patron and Buckden the
"castle."

now ambassador at The Hague, where the exiled queen kept her Court, and Sir Thomas Roe, former ambassador to Gustavus Adolphus. Then we find the great peers, who would force the king to summon the Parliament of 1640, and their clients, who would fill it: the Earl of Pembroke with his followers, John Selden and Sir Benjamin Rudyerd; the Earl of Bedford, with John Pym and Oliver St. John; the Earl of Warwick with Lord Brooke and Lord Mandeville, Sir Nathaniel Rich, Sir Thomas Barrington and Sir John Clotworthy. All these would be famous in Parliament, and every one of them on the "Puritan" side. Only when we go out of politics, below the level of politics, do we discover an occasional "royalist" among the patrons of these three men, and even then they are "country" royalists, not courtiers: Sir Justinian Isham of Lamport, Sir Christopher Hatton of Holmby; men hardly distinguishable from their unpolitical supporters on the other side, Sir Cheney Culpeper of Leeds Castle, Kent, or Nicholas Stoughton of Stoughton, Surrey.[13] These men were interested not in politics but in practical improvements and their estates—or in the Apocalypse and Armageddon. They planted trees or were concerned about village schools, and they clutched at the three philosophers as possible re-creators of rural society. "Truly," as Culpeper wrote, "I shall value myself by nothing more than in that it may please God to give me a heart and the honour of contributing my mite towards them."

To us perhaps the most interesting of all is the link with John Pym. We know so little about Pym, he is so pure a politician, so elusive a personality, and yet so decisive a figure in our history, that any light on his private views is welcome. And here is a little, oblique and yet illuminating shaft. For Pym, that uncommunicative, unintellectual, friendless man, was not only an admirer of Bacon,[14] he was also deeply interested in education—he endowed a free school at Brill[15]—and he was one of the earliest and most constant supporters of Hartlib, Dury and Comenius. He had "intimate and familiar acquaintance" with Hartlib,

13. Nicholas Stoughton (whom Young, and others following him, wrongly calls Sir Nicholas) had been a Member of Parliament in the 1620s, and was a member again in 1645–48; but I can find no evidence that he ever spoke there, and so feel safe in calling him unpolitical.

14. In his *Ephemerides*, under the year 1634, Hartlib wrote: "Mr. P[im] judged it [Bacon's *Novum Organum*] if one read it and consider all, else not be able to judge of the excellency."

15. W. K. Jordan, *The Rural Charities of England* (1960), p. 57.

with whom he often corresponded, subscribed money to Dury's ventures, offered support to Comenius and maintained one of his disciples at Cambridge.[16] He was so affected, he wrote, to the undertakings of Dury and Comenius that if he were able he would support them alone; as it was, he prayed that richer men than he would swell that support. We shall soon see the practical way in which Pym sought to achieve the object of his prayers.

Thus we may fairly describe Hartlib, Dury and Comenius as the philosophers of the English country party in the 1630s. Peers and bishops, Parliament-men and country gentry, all who were bound together by opposition to the rule of Strafford and Laud, were also bound together in support of these three men. They recognized them as the prophets and articulators of Baconian reform. It was Baconian reform with a difference, of course, Baconianism for new times, and brought down to a lower level. We may call it "vulgar Baconianism," for it lacked the range and power of the true Baconian message. Bacon's great philosophical synthesis had been fragmented: his "experiments of light" had been transformed into inflamed apocalyptic speculations, his "experiments of fruit" into the uncontrolled elaboration of gadgets. Still, it was Baconianism of a kind, and the men of the country party took it seriously. As the rule of Laud and Strafford came to an end they listened more attentively than ever to the prophets of the new divine revelation and the new social reform.

The first publication of the new gospel came in 1639. One of the supporters who had been won over by Hartlib was John Stoughton, minister of St. Mary's, Aldermanbury, in London. Stoughton was one of the many clerical clients of the Earl of Warwick, the greatest noble patron of the opposition to Charles I. In 1639 Stoughton, dying, bequeathed to Hartlib a strange, rhapsodical pamphlet which he had written for a Hungarian Protestant about to return to Transylvania, and Hartlib published it, with a dedication to George Rakóci, Prince of Transylvania. Rakóci, at this time, was the white hope of the scattered Protestants of south-eastern Europe, their only champion now

16. It was Daniel Erastus whom, according to Dury, "Mr. Pym maintained at Cambridge" (see Turnbull, *Hartlib, Dury and Comenius*, p. 371). Erastus was one of Comenius' community, and was sent by him, together with Samuel Benedictus, to England in 1632, where Hartlib took charge of them. Benedictus went to Sidney Sussex College, Erastus to St. Catherine's College, Cambridge (see Young, *Comenius in England*, p. 33).

that Bohemia had been reconquered and the Swedes had drawn back
to the Baltic coast, and Stoughton's pamphlet preached to this distant
champion the messianic gospel of international Protestantism at bay.
Europe was in ruins, he admitted, the faithful were scattered, the disaster seemed universal; nevertheless the tide was about to turn, the
Princes of the World would rise up in arms against the popish Babylon and her protector, the House of Austria, and she would fall. And
who, he asked, would be the agents of this change? Suddenly, in the
midst of a jumble of learned gibberish, the talismanic names appear:
the sacred efforts of our Dury, the lofty achievements of your neighbour Comenius, the heaven-blest message, the *documenta lucifera, ex-
perimenta fructifera*, of that universal hero Lord Verulam. These were
to be the means whereby the popish Babylon was to be overthrown and
the last golden age before the Millennium settled in felicity. Bacon,
Dury and Comenius were represented by Stoughton—or perhaps by
his editor Hartlib—as the founding fathers of the new Church, about
to be established: Comenius the Polycarp, Dury the Irenaeus, Bacon
the golden-mouthed Chrysostom.[17]

Stoughton's turgid metaphysics were published in the days of opposition. More interesting are the efforts of our philosophers and their
patrons once the Long Parliament had met and the chance had come for
more constructive action. With practical opportunity came practical
responsibility and from November 1640 onwards we look for evidence
of practical policy. We turn from diffuse exhibitions of somewhat lurid
light to more limited experiments of fruit.

Where shall we look for evidence of such policy? At first sight it
is not obvious. Throughout the period of the Puritan Revolution, immediate politics take precedence and long-term policy is submerged
or pushed aside. Nevertheless there are moments when it is revealed.
One such moment, I have suggested, is at the very beginning of the
Long Parliament, before the danger of violent dissolution and the trial
of Strafford absorbed all energy. Another is in the summer of 1641,
between the execution of Strafford, which men thought had liberated
them from that danger, and the Irish rebellion, which brought it formi-
dably and permanently back again. There were also later moments—
brief interludes of apparent "settlement" in the long, painful history of

17. John Stoughton, *Felicitas Ultimi Saeculi* (1640). That Stoughton was a protégé
of the Earl of Warwick is apparent from the dedication (by his widow) of his posthumously published sermon, *The Christian's Prayer for the Church's Peace* (1640).

"blood and confusion"—when it seemed possible, with whatever differences of circumstance or temper, to return to the original programme. But first of all let us look at the first moment, when circumstances were still happy and tempers relatively sweet. Is there any evidence, in those early November days of 1640, of the ultimate social intentions which the Lords and Commons had hoped to realize if immediate political danger had not intervened?

I believe there is. In general, in the Great Rebellion, it is difficult to know the real purpose of politicians. Events quickly took control, and men's statements of policy are too often immediate responses to those events. Sometimes they are tactical; sometimes over-passionate; seldom can we be sure that they represent deliberate, long-term aspirations. But there is one source which has not been much used and which, I believe, does give us, on certain occasions, the agreed "party line." I refer to the fast sermons preached before the Parliament, and particularly before the House of Commons.

At first on special occasions only, but later at monthly intervals, the two Houses of Parliament held a "solemn fast" at which they listened to two sermons, one in the morning, one in the afternoon. The preachers were specially appointed in advance, on the nomination of some member, and afterwards they were officially thanked and generally invited to have their sermons printed and published. From the names of the members of the House of Commons who proposed the preachers, or who conveyed the thanks of the House, or from other evidence, we can generally deduce which preachers were put forward by the leaders of Parliament, and on such occasions we can be reasonably sure that the preachers were briefed. Pym, like his great heroine Queen Elizabeth, did not neglect the art of "tuning the pulpits." Frequently, in the course of the Parliament, we can see this happening. The opening of the iconoclastic campaign, the revival of the impeachment of Laud, the attack on the queen—all these changes of policy were first foreshadowed in fast sermons. Such sermons, therefore, when we have them and know their sponsors, can be valuable pointers to general policy; and we naturally ask whether such a pointer exists for the early days of November 1640.[18]

The answer is, yes. At the very beginning of the Parliament, before any other business was undertaken, two fast days were arranged

18. For a fuller treatment of this subject see my essay "The Fast Sermons of the Long Parliament," below, pp. 273–316.

and preachers chosen. One of the days was to be "Queen Elizabeth's day," 17 November, upon which the clergy would seasonably remind members of their duty to resume the great queen's interrupted work.[19] The other day, a day made more solemn by a collective taking of the sacrament, was to be a few days later, and the preachers chosen for it were George Morley, afterwards Bishop of Winchester, and John Gauden, afterwards famous as the author of *Eikon Basiliké*. For our purposes Morley is unimportant: he was most probably proposed by Hyde and Falkland, and his sermon was so little liked by the leaders of the House that he alone was not invited to print it. We therefore can (indeed must) ignore him.[20] But Gauden is different. He was one of the protégés of the Earl of Warwick, and the thanks of the House were conveyed to him by Warwick's kinsman, Pym's ally Sir Thomas Barrington. We can be reasonably certain that Gauden was proposed and briefed, in our crucial period, by Pym and his friends. His sermon may therefore supply the evidence we seek of Pym's long-term policy.

Gauden's sermon was entitled *The Love of Truth and Peace*. In general it was an invitation to peaceful reformation. But for our purpose the interesting part of it is the end. For the preacher concluded by commending to the favour of the House

> the noble endeavours of two great and public spirits who have laboured much for truth and peace: I mean, Comenius and Duraeus, both famous for their learning, piety and integrity and not unknown, I am sure, by the fame of their works, to many of this honourable, learned and pious assembly.

Who, asked Gauden, had done more for truth than Comenius? Or for peace than Dury? "But alas," he added, "both these noble plants are like to wither to a barrenness for want of public encouragement"; and therefore he urged his hearers

19. This was the anniversary of Queen Elizabeth's accession, and became, after her death, a day of Protestant rejoicing. See J. E. Neale, *Essays in Elizabethan History* (1958), pp. 9–20.

20. Anthony Wood, *Athenae Oxonienses*, ed. P. Bliss (1813–21), iv, 149–50. Wood's account has led later writers (including William Hunt in the *Dictionary of National Biography*, s.v. Morley) to suppose that Morley's suppressed sermon was in 1642; but this is an error. See below, p. 278, n 9.

to consider whether it were not worthy the name and honour of this state and church to invite these men to you, to see and weigh their noble and excellent designs, to give them all public aid and encouragement to go on and perfect so happy works, which tend so much to the advancing of truth and peace.

It seems improbable that Gauden himself was familiar with Dury, Comenius and their work.[21] What he said was simply what he had been told to say. And it seems that the proposal which he made excited some questions, for when he came to publish his sermon he added, as a necessary answer to such questions, a fact which had evidently not been known to him at the time. It might not seem easy, he now wrote, to fetch Comenius and Dury to England, "the one being in Poland, the other in Denmark." However, it was easier than it seemed, for "there is a fair, easy and safe way of addresses to them both, opened by the industry and fidelity of Mr. Hartlib, whose house is in Duke's Place, London . . ."

The hint was taken. Hartlib was approached. He was told to invite both Dury and Comenius in the name of "the Parliament of England." And he duly set to work. He was not more eager to fetch them than they were to come. In Denmark Dury lost no time in preparing for the journey. In Poland Comenius was filled with enthusiasm. Far away in England he saw the dawn breaking, and he longed to be there. If only he could free himself from his duties in Poland . . . But he would free himself. Somehow or other he would come and play his part in the new reformation.

Unfortunately, by the time Dury and Comenius received their invitations, the English Parliament was preoccupied with other things. From mid-November 1640 to May 1641 all long-term plans were in temporary suspense. To the leaders of Parliament, for the time being, there was only one business. Public attention was concentrated upon that *cause célèbre*, that struggle upon which the fate of Parliament itself seemed to depend: the trial of Strafford. Only when that was over, only (cried the majority) when Strafford was dead, could the constructive

---

21. In Gauden's numerous writings there is no other reference to Hartlib, Dury or Comenius, and when all three were in England, in answer to his recommendation, he appears to have paid no attention to them or they to him. Hartlib told Comenius that he had been summoned by Parliament. He clearly regarded Gauden as a mere mouthpiece.

aims of Parliament be once again pursued. Meanwhile they were suspended.

On 12 May 1641 Strafford was executed. At last the long struggle was
over, the unbearable tension was suddenly released, and throughout
England there was a new mood of exhilaration. To us, who know the
consequences, who look back and see, from 1641 to 1660, nothing but
anarchy and bloodshed, useless victories and doomed experiments, this
may well seem paradoxical, and we easily overlook it. Prudent politicians, even at the time, foresaw these consequences: they realized that
Strafford's death might well ruin the prospect of bloodless reformation.
But at the time the prudent politicians were in eclipse. To the enthu-
siasts, the excited, the angry, the apprehensive men, the execution of
Strafford was like the execution, half a century before, of Mary Queen
of Scots. The great bogyman, whose life was a standing threat to liberty, religion, Parliament, had been destroyed; the nightmare of the
past had been dissolved; and from now on, it seemed, the great task of
reformation was easy, almost automatic.

While plans were made for reform in Church and State, Pym prepared to disband, as no longer needed, the forces he had mobilized to
achieve his power. In September he made peace with the Scots. The
armies of "our brethren of Scotland" had done their work; they were
sent home, and the church bells pealed through all England as they
had done on the defeat of the great Armada and on the return of
Prince Charles, uncommitted, from his Spanish journey. And Pym's
Irish allies had done their work too: they had helped to kill Strafford; now they too could be dropped. With supreme tactical skill Pym
double-crossed both Scots Presbyterians and Irish Catholics. He had
made them work for him, but had not paid their price. In the new England there would be neither a Presbyterian Church nor a toleration for
Catholics, but a purely English reformation. Who could then suppose
that to pursue that reformation Pym would find himself, before long,
imprisoned in the alliance of the planter-gentry of Ireland, buying back
(and this time paying the price of the English Church) the alliance of
"our brethren of Scotland"?

It is essential to remember the mood of exhilaration which possessed the spirits of Englishmen in the summer of 1641: it illustrated
many of the purposes of the revolution, and it explains much of the
depression and bitterness which followed in the years of failure afterwards. It was like the exhilaration which men felt in the early days of

the French Revolution. "Bliss was it in that dawn to be alive," wrote Wordsworth of those days; and in the summer of 1641 the greatest poet of Caroline England felt the same. For these were the months of Milton's great pamphlets, those marvellous works, so buoyant, so intoxicated, so rich in imagery, in which he saw England as a young man glorying in his strength, waking and shaking off his past torpor and bondage, and himself, its poet, singing, among "the hymns and hallelujahs of the saints," "the jubilee and resurrection of the state." And that same phrase, "jubilee and resurrection of church and state," was echoed again, from the pulpit of St. Margaret's, Westminster, by Pym's favourite preacher, Stephen Marshall, when Parliament, by another solemn fast, celebrated the peace with Scotland. For had not civil war been avoided? Was not the basis of reformation now truly laid? Stephen Marshall, on that morning, invited his congregation to look back on "the wonders (I had almost said the miracles), of the last year," so different from the fate of neighbour nations "when Germany remains a field of blood." Sixteen forty-one was "this year, this wonderful year, wherein God hath done more for us, in some kinds, than in fourscore years before"; and in the afternoon Jeremiah Burroughes assured the Commons that the great day, prophesied in Scripture, had now come, when swords should be beaten into ploughshares, spears into pruninghooks: 1641 was a more wonderful year even than 1588: "Babylon is fallen, it is fallen, so fallen that it shall never rise again in power." [22]

Such was the emotional background of politics in the summer of 1641, after Strafford's death. And who were the men who hoped to profit by this victory, to harness this emotion? The greatest, most constructive politician of 1641, the Earl of Bedford, was dead. He had died suddenly, prematurely, of smallpox, a few days before Strafford, whose life he had vainly tried to save. But he had his successors. In the House of Commons, of course, there was his client, his man of affairs, whom he had placed, with his own son, in his own pocket-borough of Tavistock, John Pym. In the House of Lords, which still at that time kept its ascendancy, there was another man who, like Bedford and Pym, would also ultimately fail in politics, but who, at that time, had an incontestable superiority: John Williams, Bishop of Lincoln.

22. For the exaltation of Milton in 1641, see E. M. W. Tillyard, *Milton* (1934), pp. 116–26. The phrase "jubilee and resurrection of the state" is in Milton's *Animadversions upon the Remonstrant's Defence* (July 1641), and in Stephen Marshall, *A Peace Offering to God . . .* (7 Sept. 1641); cf. J. Burroughes, *Sion's Joy* (7 Sept. 1641).

History has dealt hardly with Bishop Williams. He is remembered as the aristocratic *frondeur* of the Church under Laud, the clerical Kerensky of the revolution, a critic who could never construct, a reformer who was swept aside. And yet, when we look closely at that year of hope, that "wonderful year" 1641, we cannot avoid seeing something of his greatness. For now he had come into his own. He was the undoubted leader of the House of Lords. He was the only man, among the leaders of the country party, who had held high political office: for he had been the greatest officer of state under King James. He was indefatigable in public business: in this year, 1641, he sat on more committees of the Lords than any other peer. And one of these committees was the most important of all committees at that time. It was "Bishop Williams' committee" on religion, a committee of moderate, still undivided clergymen which was devising a constructive plan of ecclesiastical decentralization and institutional reform agreeable to all parties.[23] To lower religious passions, to create a basis for such reform, the indefatigable bishop was spending the summer recess visiting his diocese, ladling cold water (as his chaplain put it) over clerical heat. Never did his position seem so strong as in those confident summer months of 1641. Obviously, if reformation was to be achieved, now was the time, and Bishop Williams and John Pym (if only they would keep in step) were the men. And Bishop Williams and John Pym were certainly in step in some matters. Both (unlike the Earl of Bedford) had demanded the death of Strafford. Both were patrons, convinced and generous patrons, of Hartlib, Dury and Comenius.

Therefore, in this summer of 1641, we should not be surprised to learn that the plan to bring Dury and Comenius to England was revived. By the end of June Dury had arrived in London and had been given an honorary post as chaplain to Strafford's successor, the Parliament's nominee as Lord Deputy of Ireland, the Earl of Leicester. Next month Comenius, who was still in Poland, received three different letters from Hartlib. All three had been sent by different routes; all three conveyed the same message; all three breathed the excitement, the urgency, the exaltation of those summer days. "It is for the glory of God," Hartlib ended his appeal: "deliberate not with flesh and blood. Come! come! come!"

Comenius consulted his colleagues, the elders of the Bohemian and

23. On Bishop Williams' committee and its proposed reforms, see W. A. Shaw, *A History of the English Church . . . 1640–1660* (1900), I, 65–74.

Polish Churches then in session at Leszno. No one knew why or for how long he had been summoned, but it was agreed that he should go. He himself thought he knew the reason: he was to realize Bacon's *New Atlantis* in England. So, full of enthusiasm, he set out from Danzig. He had a dramatic journey. Off the coast of Norway his ship ran into a tempest and was driven back "over the whole Baltic sea for nearly a hundred miles by the force of gales." Comenius never forgot this first experience of the sea: long afterwards he would incorporate an account of it in his most popular religious work, his *Labyrinth of the World*, the Czech *Pilgrim's Progress*, which he had written seventeen years before when a refugee on the estate of a Protestant lord in Bohemia.[24] His ship returned battered to Danzig, and for a time Comenius doubted whether to persevere in his strange, unsought mission. But in the end his friends and his conscience both urged him on and he put to sea again. This time he had a smooth journey, and on 21 September he arrived in London. It was an appropriate moment. All England was rejoicing in the Scottish peace; with Parliament in recess and the king in Scotland, the acrimony of public argument was stilled; and there, in London, were Hartlib and Dury, who, with other admirers, English and foreign, had come to meet him. Thus, in London, in an atmosphere of universal euphoria, all three philosophers met together, for the first time, to launch the new reformation.

Their first public entertainment was appropriate too. Comenius was taken to lodge with Hartlib in Duke's Place; he was told that he was summoned by Parliament and was to spend the whole winter in England, planning the new golden age; and a tailor was fetched to make him a suit of English clothes. "Scarcely was the suit ready," says Comenius, in his own account of his visit, "when we were told that we were all invited to dinner by a mighty patron of the Pansophic Society." This mighty patron was the great Baconian, the heir of Bacon himself, the aristocratic politician of the hour, Bishop Williams; and the dinner, no doubt, was in his London house, the Deanery of Westminster.

It was an impressive dinner. Bishop Williams liked to impress. Like Bacon, he piqued himself on his magnificence: his houses, his hospitality, his gestures, his gratuities were always on the grand scale, even when he was in political eclipse. Four years earlier, when Laud had at

24. *The Labyrinth of the World*, written by Comenius in 1623, was first published in 1631, probably in Leszno. The description of the storm at sea first appears in the second edition (Amsterdam, 1663).

last (it seemed) ruined him, he had distributed £2500—a truly Baconian
gesture—to the servants he was forced to abandon, before setting off
for imprisonment in the Tower.[25] And now, at the height of his power,
he showed the same liberality, charming and dazzling his guests. Why,
he asked, had Comenius not brought his wife and family with him?
They should be fetched. Did someone refer to the expense? Before anything was publicly voted, the Bishop guaranteed £120 a year, and others,
he said, would add more. Hartlib and Dury urged Comenius to accept.
Comenius protested that in his Church there was community of goods:
he must consider, must consult his friends. But the bishop would not be
put off: "after dinner," says Comenius, "proffering me his right hand,
he placed ten Jacobus pieces into mine, a bounty so large that I greatly
marvelled at it."

   With such a patron Comenius had good reason to be delighted.
Williams, he wrote, was "the most learned, the most cultured, and
politically the most sagacious of all the bishops." Moreover, the king
himself recognized the fact. Shortly after the dinner party at Westminster, he made Williams Archbishop of York. Since the Archbishop
of Canterbury was discredited, under impeachment, in the Tower, this
meant that Williams was not only one of the two greatest politicians in
the State but also effective primate of the whole English Church.

   The other great politician, of course, was Pym: the leader of the
Commons as Williams was of the Lords. But happily Pym too was a
devoted supporter of Comenius and his friends. In the midst of business he took time to see Comenius, to discuss his plans of universal
elementary education. So did the other leaders of the country party.

   No wonder Comenius, always an enthusiast, even a fantast, walked
as in a trance through the streets of London. Everywhere he admired
the signs of literacy and educational zeal. He watched the London congregation taking shorthand notes of sermons, and admired the vast output of books. Even the fair at Frankfurt, he thought, had fewer book-
stalls than London. He noted a new edition of Bacon's *Advancement of
Learning*. And he, Hartlib and Dury all set to work, in these favourable
circumstances, to prepare their blueprints for the new society.

   Hartlib's work, which was published in October 1641, was a dialogue, *A Description of the Famous Kingdom of Macaria*.[26] It is very brief,

25. *The Fairfax Correspondence, Memoirs of the Reign of Charles I*, i, 338.

26. For an analysis of Hartlib's *Macaria*, see J. K. Fuz, *Welfare Economics in English
Utopias* (The Hague, 1952), pp. 18–33.

but important. For it was the ultimate realization—as he thought—of that utopia, that ideal model of a Christian society, which he had inherited from Andreae, which he had long sought to plant, and which, to the end of his days, he would see as the first step to "the reformation of the whole world."[27] In the summer of 1641, the high point of his enthusiasm, he saw Macaria about to be established in the greatest of European islands. More's *Utopia*, Bacon's *New Atlantis*—his avowed models—would be realized at last, in England.

Basically, Macaria is a welfare-state, in which the wealth of society, instead of being concentrated in the capital and consumed in extravagance or irresponsible policy, is carefully husbanded at its source and then distributed productively over the whole country. The key to this process is the rational utilization of all resources. Landed estates are no larger than can be well cultivated, fisheries are encouraged, and trade is increased by mercantilist methods. Taxation is also designed to further the same end. In particular there is a 5 per cent inheritance tax on all fortunes. Finally, at the base of society, there is a system of popular education, local public works, repair of highways and bridges, and a local health service in every parish, run by a clergy educated in modern science. How easy it would be, thought Hartlib, to create such a rational society, if only rulers would understand the mechanics of it! Thanks to a little "engine"—what he would afterwards call an "Office of Public Addresses" and his disciple, William Petty, would name "political arithmetic"—the whole kingdom of England could be made "like a fruitful garden."

While Hartlib was working on his *Macaria*, Dury and Comenius were also plying their pens. Dury's work, written like *Macaria* in September 1641, was in effect a supplement to it, and it was written for Hartlib to present to Parliament as soon as the recess should be over. In it Dury, like so many other men in that season of exaltation, looked back to the peace with Scotland as the end of England's troubles, and forward to a new age of complete reformation. With the happy conclusion of the Scottish war, he said, the fears of the past had been converted into hope for the future. What wonderful new opportunities lay ahead! Vast resources, material and human, lay ready to be mobilized. Learning and education could be reformed, and their reformation would lead to that "advancement of sciences which my Lord of St.

27. Hartlib to Boyle, 15 Nov. 1659, in *The Works of the Hon. Robert Boyle* (1744), v, 293.

Albans hath wished and saluted far off." On this basis a new Protestant unity could be created which would turn the tide in Europe, confound the Pope, regenerate Europe, restore the king's nephew to his Electorate on the Rhine. Nor was it only the divisions of Protestants that would be healed. A still older division could also be repaired. Now was the time, wrote Dury, for Protestants to advance God's kingdom by winning back that disregarded but important nation, the Jews.

That the time was ripe for all these projects was clear to Dury by several signs. Providence had now brought to England the essential agents of the new reformation. There was Dury himself, impatient to be at work. There was Comenius, fetched by the earnest persuasion of his friends and his love of England. And thirdly, there was a hitherto unknown scholar who, like them, had come from the eastern shores of the Baltic sea. This was Johann Stefan Rittangel, professor of Oriental languages at Königsberg. That it was Providence which had brought Rittangel to England was clear for, like Comenius, he had come reluctantly and through perils and adventures at sea: he had been on his way to Amsterdam when he had been captured, robbed and diverted by Dunkirk pirates. His value lay in his long and deep experience of the Jews of Europe, Asia and Africa, among whom he had lived for twenty years and of whose conversion he could surely now be the instrument. Dury ended, as he had begun, on a messianic note. God's purpose, he wrote, is now clearly "to bring forth a new birth of states in Europe" — what else could be the meaning of "these sudden, great and mighty changes" among the nations? To think that, in these great changes, the Church would remain the same is to ignore "the experience of all ages." God is now at work, Christ's kingdom is coming, Babylon is falling, and "the Church also is travailing in her pangs to bring forth the man-child who should rule over the nations when they shall be quieted." Of these changes the English Parliament was to be the midwife. "The eyes of all the other churches, and chiefly those of Germany, are upon you."[28]

Such was Hartlib's, such Dury's concept of the new reformation. That of Comenius was at once more detailed and more metaphysical. Soon after his arrival in England he wrote, but did not publish,

---

28. Dury's treatise is *England's Thankfulness or an Humble Remembrance presented to the Committee for Religion in the High Court of Parliament . . . by a faithful well-wisher to this Church and Nation*. It was published by Hartlib in 1642. For an account of it, and for the reasons for ascribing it to Dury, see G. H. Turnbull, "The Visit of Comenius to England," in *Notes and Queries*, 31 March 1951.

three drafts for the reform of English education, filled with mystical, millenary language.[29] "I presume we all agree," he wrote, "that the last age of the world is drawing near, in which Christ and his Church shall triumph"; and this age was to be "an age of Enlightenment, in which the earth shall be filled with the knowledge of God, as the waters cover the sea." But let us not suppose, he added, that this great cosmic revolution entails any political revolution. Scripture warrants no such assumption. Tyrants will disappear, but just kings will remain, and under them the new reformation, the reign of Light, will be brought about. Universal education will be set up, on the Comenian plan, with a central "Pansophical" college, Bacon's "House of Solomon," and a system of schools reaching down, by new methods, to the humblest levels and the outermost fringes of society. And where could this "Pansophical" college more appropriately be set up than in England? From England Drake had sailed round the world; in England Lord Chancellor Bacon had laid the foundations of universal reform; surely it was in England that "the plan of the great Verulam" should now be realized: England should be the centre from which the new age of Enlightenment should transform the whole world.

Such was the mood, such the projects, of September and October 1641. All through that time his parliamentary friends had kept Hartlib informed of their political plans and activity,[30] and in mid-October, when Parliament reassembled, hope was high. Hartlib and Comenius were told to hold themselves in readiness: a committee of Parliament would be appointed to consult with them. Meanwhile a site for the "Pansophical" college was being sought. The Savoy Hospital was considered; so was the Hospital of St. Cross at Winchester; so was the college of anti-papal controversy which King James had founded at Chelsea and which now stood, bleak and deserted, "like a lodge in a garden of cucumbers." Comenius studied the revenues of Chelsea College in anticipation. Everything seemed to be going smoothly. Then suddenly came ill news from Ireland. The Irish Catholics, double-crossed by Pym, had broken out in revolt. The king, in Scotland, hailed the

29. These three works are *Via Lucis*, which he published in 1668, and two briefer works, which have been printed from the manuscripts by G. H. Turnbull, "Plans of Comenius for his stay in England," *Acta Comeniana*, xvii, i (Prague, 1958).

30. These day-by-day accounts, which cover the period from 1 Sept. to 1 Nov. 1641, and end with the news of the Irish rebellion, are now in the British Museum, Sloane MS. 3317, pp. 24-54.

news with satisfaction. Here was his chance. The Parliament, in London, was filled with gloom. The tide had turned: the period of euphoria was over:

> ex illo fluere ac retro sublapsa referri
> res Danaum.

Of course it was not really as sudden as all that. All through the summer rifts had been opening up as it became clear that Charles I was not serious in his acceptance of the new order. There were rifts in the country, in the Church, in the Parliament. In particular there was the rift between Lords and Commons, between Williams and Pym.

Even Comenius had noticed this. The bishop, he had observed, was beginning to be criticized, and had himself spoken "most reservedly" to him about the future. But Comenius would not be discouraged: "I hope and believe," he had written home to his friends in Poland, "in better things for the good bishop." Given goodwill, given political skill, surely these little rifts in the party of reform could be repaired.

But now the Irish rebellion and its consequences burst them all wide open. In November, while the king returned from Scotland, Pym, feeling his power crumbling, moved to the Left and, with the Grand Remonstrance, launched a public, frontal attack on the Crown. It was a fatal act and one which, incidentally, gave the king what he had previously lacked: a party. Thus encouraged, the king struck back, even more fatally. From now on constructive reform was impossible. Such reform depended on an agreed, effective political structure, and such a structure, if there was to be no revolution, could only be a "mixed monarchy" of king and Parliament. "All reformations," Bacon himself had told King James, "are best brought to perfection by a good correspondence between the king and his parliament." By destroying Strafford, the great divider, the leaders of the country party thought they had achieved such a "good correspondence." Now it was clear that they had not. From now on men would fight about the constitution, destroy the constitution: the social reformation, which depended on a working constitution, must wait. As Comenius wrote long afterwards, "one unhappy day, bringing tidings of massacre in Ireland and of outbreak of war there" had ruined all.

Comenius spent the winter of 1641–42 in England, still hoping against hope. He circulated his blueprint in manuscript. His friends commissioned his portrait, which was engraved by a well-known English artist and exhibited for sale, with commendatory verses by Francis

Quarles, the emblematist.[31] But soon hope faded. The country party was split, hopelessly split. So were Comenius' own patrons. In December Pym, the leader of the Commons, launched an open attack on Archbishop Williams, leader of the Lords. Williams then made a tactical error, which was fatal. Isolated, circumvented, ruined, he was sent back to the Tower from which Pym, only a year before, had rescued him. In his attempt to reform and save Church and monarchy he had failed utterly, and the last years of this former Lord Keeper and archbishop would be spent as a discredited soldier of fortune in his native Wales. By the new year Pym was preparing not now for social reformation but for military rebellion, and by the spring both sides were openly preparing for civil war. In May Dury left England to serve as chaplain to the king's daughter Mary, Princess of Orange, at The Hague. Why then should Comenius tarry longer in this disappointing island? He had come reluctantly; he was getting nowhere; and meanwhile other, less distracted patrons were beckoning him away: Cardinal Richelieu to France, John Winthrop to New England, Louis de Geer to Sweden. In particular he was pressed to go to Sweden. Louis de Geer, said his foreign friends, would do more for him, give him greater opportunities, than the whole, chaotic Parliament of England.

On 21 June 1642 Comenius sailed from England. "It was decided," he wrote, "that I should go to Sweden, assent being given even by my greater friends—for so St. Augustine was wont to call his patrons—the Archbishop of York, Lord Brooke, Master Pym and others; but only on this condition, that when affairs in England were more tranquil, I should return." The last message to be sent to him from England was from John Pym. On 20 June, the day before Comenius left, Pym, who was even now mobilizing for civil war, wrote hastily to Hartlib. He had been approached by an aged scientist, a follower of Copernicus, who wished to create a new model of the universe for use in schools and thereby to teach astronomy "without all those chimaeras of epicycles and eccentrics by which the minds of young students are terrified rather than taught." In the midst of political and military distractions Pym did not hesitate to seize this opportunity. "If you think the matter of importance," he wrote to Hartlib, "I pray you come to me as speedily as you can, and consult with Mr. Comenius if he be not gone, as I hope he

---

31. See p. 224. This portrait, by George Glover, was the basis of a later portrait, executed ten years later by Wenceslaus Hollar, another Bohemian *émigré*, whom Comenius had also met in London in 1642.

is not; and to you both I present the affectionate respects of your very affectionate friend, John Pym."

Soon afterwards the Orientalist Rittangel also left England. "Our island," lamented one of the gentry patrons of the group, "is not yet worthy of that famous oriental professor." Dury himself was less charitable. Rittangel, he afterwards told Hartlib, was a learned Hebraist, but of such a disposition that there was no dealing with him. It was not through him, after all, that God would convert the Jews.

Thus the "wonderful year" 1641 ended in disillusion and despair. Instead of reformation and a new society, instead of a welfare-state and an age of enlightenment, came civil war and revolution and long years of "blood and confusion." The social reforms of the country party slipped ever further into the background: their mere interests, their destructive passions found expression. They destroyed their enemies: they never constructed more than a ramshackle skeleton of their new Macaria, their ideal state.

Nevertheless, it would be wrong to stop here, as if all hope was finally given up. We should not forget the condition on which Comenius was released from England, that when its affairs were "more tranquil," he should return. All through the following years, as men fought and fumbled, they looked forward to such a period of tranquillity or "settlement"; at intervals they seemed to catch a glimpse of it; and at each glimpse of it—in 1646, when the civil war was over; in 1649, when the republic was set up; in 1653, when the oligarchy of the Rump Parliament was overthrown—we see them harking back to that old programme and its prophets: the programme and the prophets whose triumph had seemed so near in 1641.

Consider the cries which break through the din of battle and revolution all through the next twelve years. Decentralization of government, a "more equal representative of the people": such was the object of all proposals of parliamentary reform. "Reform of the law"—how often that demand is reiterated, after each apparently final battle: after Naseby, after Preston, after Dunbar, after Worcester. Decentralization of law—it was the infinite obstruction by the lawyers of the bill to set up county registers that would make Cromwell despair of the Rump and appeal instead to a new Parliament.[32] Decentralization, laicization

32. County registers had been proposed by the parliamentary committee on law reform on 20–21 Jan. 1653. For the obstruction, see Edmund Ludlow, *Memoirs*, ed.

of religion—what else was Independency? Decentralization, laicization of education—in 1649 the gentry of the north would petition for a local university and George Snell would dedicate to Hartlib and Dury his plan of general educational reform with rural colleges teaching lay subjects in every county town. In 1653 would come the concerted attack on the Aristoteleanism of the universities and William Dell's proposals for local colleges, while the Act for the settlement of Ireland would provide for local schools and manufactures. In 1656 Pym's kinsman Sir John Clotworthy would plan to establish a free school in Antrim.[33] To the very end these would be the positive ideals of the Puritans. In 1659, when the revived republic was foundering in anarchy, there would be a new spate of pamphlets proposing law reform, educational change, new models of government. Lady Ranelagh, the sister of Lord Broghill and Robert Boyle, would devote her mind to the reformation of law and lawyers.[34] Harrington's "Rota" would be in full spin. Milton would propose "to erect . . . all over the land schools, and competent libraries to those schools"; and in 1660, on the very eve of the royal restoration, he would still insist that "the civil rights and advancement of every person according to his merit" could be best secured by a general policy of decentralization, making "every county in the land a little commonwealth."[35] Behind all the changing forms of the revolution, its social programme remained constant.

So did the articulators of that programme. All through those years of change Hartlib and Dury were kept in reserve, to be brought out and heeded whenever "settlement" should have come. Pym's death, in December 1643, did not affect them. In his last days, when the parlia-

C. H. Firth (1894), I, 333–34. That such an act was expected from the Barebones Parliament is clear from the objections to it printed in August 1653 (*Reasons against the Bill entitled an Act for County Registries*).

33. For references, see p. 226, n. 2, above. For the demand of the northern gentry, see *Writings and Speeches of Oliver Cromwell*, ed. W. C. Abbott (Cambridge, Mass., 1945), II. For the concerted attack on the universities, see also John Webster, *Examen Academiarum* (1653); William Dell, *The Trial of Spirits . . .* (1653); Seth Ward, *Vindiciae Academiarum* (1653); R. B[oreman], Παιδείας Θρίαμβος (1653), etc. For schools in Ireland, see C. H. Firth and R. S. Rait, *Acts and Ordinances of the Interregnum* (1911), II, 730. For Clotworthy's proposed school in Antrim, see *Letters and Journals of Robert Baillie* (Edinburgh, 1841–42), III, 312.

34. Hartlib to Boyle, 31 May 1659, in Boyle, *Works*, v, 290.

35. John Milton, *The Likeliest Means to remove Hirelings out of the Church* (1659); *the Ready and Easy Way to establish a Free Commonwealth* (1660).

mentary cause was at its nadir, Pym appointed Dury as a member of the Westminster Assembly, which was to remodel the Church after victory, and after Pym's death his successor, Oliver St. John, wrote to Hartlib to assure him that he would not suffer by "the death of some persons who loved you." He did not. Thanks to St. John's constant favour, Hartlib was a regular pensioner of the Parliament. He also received private support from Pym's step-brother, Francis Rous, and from other "noble and worthy instruments" whom St. John had "quickened." [36] And eighteen months later, when the battle of Naseby had made final victory certain, we are not surprised to see our old friends stepping again on to the public stage.

It was "about the time of the battle of Naseby" that Dury returned to England, and having returned, he was invited to preach to the House of Commons. So once again, "this unnatural war being at an end," he urged the victors to resume the task which it had interrupted. His message was unchanged. Parliament must settle and purge the universities so that the clergy learn "the true language of Canaan" instead of "the gibberidge of scholastical divinity"; it must reform the law and the law courts throughout the land; and it must embrace all native and foreign Protestants in a comprehensive Church.

At the same time Hartlib also was eager to show that a new day had dawned. He enlisted a team of translators. At Cambridge the poet John Hall was set to translate the utopias of Hartlib's master, Andreae. Another agent was instructed to translate the utopia of Campanella "the City of the Sun"—that Campanella whom Comenius venerated next to Bacon. And of course Comenius' own works were not forgotten. In 1645 Comenius had written a wild and windy tract "on the reformation of human affairs." It too was translated by Hall on the orders of Hartlib. Next year Comenius wrote to Hartlib to ask whether, now that peace was restored, the time had come to establish in England "the College of Light." [37]

---

36. The public moneys voted to Hartlib are recorded in *Commons' Journals*. For private benefactions see Turnbull, *Hartlib, Dury and Comenius*, pp. 25–29. That St. John was Hartlib's principal patron is explicitly stated by Hartlib in his epistle dedicatory to St. John, prefixed to his edition of [Abraham von Frankenberg], *Clavis Apocalyptica* (1651).

37. G. H. Turnbull, "John Hall's letters to Samuel Hartlib," *Review of English Studies*, 1953. Hall's translation of Andreae's two works was printed as *A Modell of a Christian Society* and *The Right Hand of Christian Love Offered* (1647), with a Preface

Hartlib was already seeking to establish it. He was busy devising particular reforms, and pressing his advice on the "Presbyterian" Parliament. Parliament, he now declared, was God's trustee, charged with the greatest power given to any Protestant State. As such it must now organize Macaria in England. It should set up a "Committee for Rules of Reformation" to seek out the general rules and maxims of policy. At its disposal there should be "offices of temporal addresses" compiling statistics in London, and an "office of spiritual addresses" lodged in an Oxford college, near "the great library" and endowed with confiscated Church property. And as "the main foundation of a reformed Commonwealth" there should be a four-tier educational system, complete with school-inspectors. On this basis the Parliament would be able to perform its social function: to resolve religious differences, to stir up piety and charity, to advance the sciences according to "Lord Verulam's designations," and "to help to perfect Mr. Comenius' undertakings." All this could be done, Hartlib insisted, within the framework of the new "Presbyterian" system which Parliament was making the new basis of Church-government: the local organizers could be the country gentry or "the presbyters in every *classis* throughout the kingdom."[38]

In fact the "Presbyterian" settlement of 1646–48 was no more lasting than the Anglican settlement of 1640–41. Once again "blood and confusion" intervened. But when all was over, Hartlib and Dury were still there, Hartlib as the pensioner of Parliament, Dury maintained by various offices—keeper of the royal library, tutor of the king's children—both eager to reformulate their programme in yet a third interlude of settlement, the Independent republic. And reformulate it they did. Pamphlets poured from their pens, on husbandry, workhouses, foreign intelligence, bee-keeping, land-settlement, university reform, the Apocalypse. Some parts of the programme were even, however fragmentarily, realized. Measures of decentralization were discussed in

---

by Hall to Hartlib. Comenius' work is *de Rerum Humanarum Emendatione Consultatio Catholica*. It was first printed, in part, for private readers only, at Amsterdam in 1657 (see Jaromir Červenka, "Die bisherigen Ausgaben des Originaltextes der comenianischen Panergesie und Panaugie," *Acta Comeniana*, xx, i, Prague, 1961). For Comenius' letter to Hartlib, see Turnbull, *Hartlib, Dury and Comenius*, pp. 371–72.

38. John Dury, *Israel's Call to March out of Babylon into Jerusalem* (26 Nov. 1645); [S. Hartlib], *Considerations Tending to the Happy Accomplishment of England's Reformation in Church and State* (1646); S. H[artlib], *The Parliament's Reformation* (1646).

Parliament. A series of legal reforms was carried out.[39] Detailed plans for a university college at Durham were made.[40] Scores of new elementary schools were founded, as occasion allowed.[41] "Propagators of the Gospel" set to work in the north and in Wales. And in 1650 something very close to Hartlib's "Office of Addresses" was set up by his friend Henry Robinson.[42] However, in the end even this republican experiment failed. The Independent Commonwealth too foundered through lack of a solid political base. Its reforms were abortive; the energy of its leaders was diverted into foreign war or internal faction; and it was not till 1654 that a period of relative and precarious stability was achieved under yet another political experiment: the Protectorate of Oliver Cromwell.

The Protectorate of Oliver Cromwell was at best a rickety settlement. Cromwell himself did not like it. It was forced upon him and he accepted it reluctantly. Still, from his point of view, it was something. "Forms of government," constitutions, to him were always of secondary importance, "indifferent things," "dung and dross compared with Christ." To him, as to most of the real Independents, the essential thing was policy, and any government—monarchy, aristocracy, Parliament, usurpation—was legitimate provided it was accepted and enabled a sound policy to be carried out. The English monarchy, the English aristocracy, the English Parliament had all in turn been overthrown, not because they were wrong in themselves but "because they had betrayed their trust." Therefore the English people had "accepted" (as he maintained) his usurpation. And this usurpation would justify itself by doing what its more legitimate predecessors had not done: it would, at last, after all these "windings and turnings," this generation in the wilderness, achieve what had seemed so near to achievement in that distant "wonderful year" 1641, only to founder in long anarchy thereafter: the new reformation, the social reformation of the country party.

39. For the legal reforms of the republic, see F. A. Inderwick, *The Interregnum* (1891), especially pp. 227–33.

40. *Commons' Journals*, VI, 589–90.

41. W. A. L. Vincent, *The State and School Education, 1640–1660* (1950) gives details of these foundations.

42. See W. K. Jordan, *Men of Substance* (Chicago, 1942), p. 250. Turnbull, *Hartlib, Dury and Comenius*, pp. 84–86. Robinson was also a friend of Dury (ibid. pp. 244, 255).

It is important to remember this if we are to understand Cromwell's impatience with his first Protectorate Parliament in 1654–55. All through the first nine months of his Protectorate, Cromwell had sought, by ordinance, to lay the basis of that reformation. He had reformed the law and the Church. And now that Parliament had met, he expected it to vote money and approve and continue his work. Instead it disputed the terms of his rule. To Cromwell such constitutionalism was exasperating, unintelligible. It was putting the cart before the horse. For what had been the purpose of the revolution? To change the constitution? Certainly not. The old constitution of King, Lords and Commons, the "mixed monarchy" of Queen Elizabeth, was far the best constitution—if only the Stuarts had been willing to work it—and ultimately Cromwell would try to return to it, with himself instead of a Stuart as king. The purpose of the revolution had been to find a constitution—any constitution—under which the social reformation of England could take place. At the moment they had the Protectorate. Perhaps it was not ideal, but what of that? Why could they not accept it, try to make it work and, instead of pulling it to pieces, disputing about "circumstantials," use it, such as it was, to achieve "fundamentals," the aims of the revolution? Unfortunately the leaders of Parliament did not see it thus. They insisted on "pulling the instrument to pieces" and thereby, in effect, on obstructing the reformation.

So Cromwell disposed of his parliaments, those tiresome interruptions of his work, and sought, in the intervals—whether by ordinance or through major-generals or otherwise—to realize the programme of that unpolitical country party which he still so perfectly represented. Ignoring the great London lawyers with their obstructive legalities, he fetched a country lawyer from Gloucestershire to advise him in reforming the law. Together they devised "provincial courts throughout the whole nation and a register in every county"; they "startled the lawyers and the City" by "courts of justice and equity at York," and sought to insist "that all actions be laid in their proper county wherein the cause did arise." [43] Cromwell also encouraged the movement for en-

43. Cromwell's country lawyer was William Sheppard, who, in the preface to his *England's Balm*, describes how he was "called by his Highness from my county to wait upon him to the end he might advise with me and some others about some things tending to the regulation of the law." For the plans for legal decentralization which followed, see *Clarke Papers*, iii (Camden Society, 1899), 61, 76, 80; and cf. T. Burton, *Parliamentary Diary* (1828), i, 8, 17.

dowing and planting resident preachers throughout the country, gave public grants—more than had ever been given before—to repair the long-neglected fabric of old churches, or build new, in remote or backward areas.[44] He sent commissioners to inquire into educational needs, took care for the founding or refounding of elementary schools, set up the new college at Durham. His son Henry would do the same in Ireland.[45] And as a logical corollary of this policy Cromwell turned again to the early philosophers of the reformation, the philosophers of the 1630s whom his predecessors had patronized, the architects of Macaria, of Protestant unity, and of the Way of Light: Hartlib, Dury and Comenius.

For the intellectual world which surrounded Cromwell was very largely the world of these three men, the "invisible college" of which they were the centre. His practical ideals were their ideals; and so, it must be added, were his illusions. He, like them, was essentially a man of the 1620s, that disastrous decade in which the whole Protestant cause in Europe seemed to be foundering, and foundering because—in so far as the cause was human—the Protestants of Europe would not unite, and there was no English Queen Elizabeth to give them the old leadership. From the fearful experiences of that decade, he, like them, had also drawn messianic conclusions: he had believed that a new heaven and a new earth were coming; that the Jews—that other persecuted race who were also expecting the Messiah—would be received into the Christian fold; and that Christian men had a duty, while reforming the society around them, and gathering up their strength to beat back the temporarily triumphant Antichrist, to seek the key to the Scriptures, which were now being fulfilled: the vials that were being poured out, the trumps that were being sounded, and the inscrutable number of the Beast.

Such had been the philosophy of the 1620s; and now, in the 1650s, though all these experiences were long past, it was the same. Protestantism, thanks to its glorious saviour Gustavus Adolphus and the armies of his daughter, the virgin queen, the new Elizabeth, Queen Christina, might now be secure. A number of grave miscalculations about the trumps and the vials, the Ancient of Days and the Beast, might have been exposed. But Cromwell could not change his mind. It had been

44. For church restoration, see W. K. Jordan, *Philanthropy in England* (1959), p. 320.

45. As shown in the Hartlib MSS. (kindly communicated by Mr. C. Webster).

moulded, fixed, and perhaps slightly cracked, in the grim and lurid furnace of the past. So now, as Lord Protector, he adopted a foreign policy that was thirty years out of date: the policy which (in his opinion, and the opinion of most of the country party) King James and King Charles should have adopted in the 1620s: Protestant reunion in Europe, Elizabethan war in the West Indies, and a top-dressing of ideological mysticism which included the reception of the Jews.

Who could be the agents of such a policy? Not everyone, by now, believed in it. Professional diplomatists, practical men, younger men, men who understood present politics or national interest, were aghast at such anachronisms. But Cromwell did not care. He listened not to such men, but to his own contemporaries, the *émigrés* of the 1620s, the men whose voice, first heard thirty years before, still echoed imperatively in his ears. His policy was their policy, and now that he had power, that was the policy which he would realize, whatever the new circumstances. Out of its scattered fragments he would re-create the Protestant interest in Europe. He would offer his alliance to Sweden, wind up the fratricidal, economic war which the wicked Rump had declared on the Dutch, offer his protection to the demoralized German princes, the Swiss cantons, the persecuted saints of Savoy. And for the organization of such a crusade, for the employment of suitable agents and emissaries in it, whom should he more naturally employ than the great crusader himself, the old apostle of Protestant reunion, the *Doctor Resolutus* of the 1630s, John Dury?

So in 1654, as soon as Cromwell's rule was settled, Dury set out again on his travels, as the Protector's special envoy to the Netherlands, Switzerland, Germany. With him, as a regular ambassador to the Swiss cantons, Cromwell sent another envoy from the same circle. This was the mathematician John Pell, Hartlib's earliest disciple, who had begun his career as a school-master at Hartlib's school at Chichester. Both Pell and Dury, in their travels, used Hartlib as their post-box at home, their source of information and their channel to Cromwell's Secretary of State, John Thurloe. Two years later, when Cromwell wanted to send a regular ambassador to the German princes, he again consulted the same circle. He applied to its organizing secretary, Hartlib, and Hartlib proposed Sir Cheney Culpeper—that unpolitical Kentish squire whose only fame (besides his interest in growing cherries) consists in his constant patronage of Hartlib, Dury and Comenius. It was an odd choice, but no odder than Pell; and anyway it was to implement an odd policy. But in fact Culpeper did not go: Cromwell's secretary took the precaution of seeking a second opinion—from Dury; and Dury, though personally favourable, doubted Culpeper's diplomatic gifts.[46]

Meanwhile Dury had put the Protector in contact with another strange figure. In Amsterdam he had run into his old friend, the Jewish philosopher and enthusiast Menasseh ben Israel. Both Hartlib and Dury were active philo-semites, and Dury had long acted as London agent for Menasseh, distributing his works and fostering his millenary views. Now, from Amsterdam, he wrote to England to warn Cromwell of Menasseh's impending visit: the famous visit which, if it did not secure, at least blessed and publicized the return, after four centuries, of the Jews to England.

Hartlib too was active in those years of the Protectorate. He was pensioned by Cromwell as he had been by Pym and St. John. As always, he was corresponding, proselytizing, publishing. He was the animating spirit behind every "Baconian" project. He hunted out lost manuscripts of Bacon's works. He encouraged Bacon's eccentric disciple, Thomas Bushell, to realize "my Lord Verulam's *New Atlantis*" in Lambeth Marsh. He planned schools in Ireland and a "standing council of universal learning" to be set up in Lord Newport's disestablished collegiate church at Fotheringhay. He was consulted in the setting up of Cromwell's new college at Durham. He was appointed to draft its statutes, and most of its original Fellows and professors were his friends: Ezerell Tonge, its most active projector, who would afterwards be the main inventor of the Popish Plot; Robert Wood, Fellow of Lincoln College, Oxford, who had suggested to Hartlib a decimal coinage; and the German J. S. Küffeler, whom Hartlib had fetched from Holland in order that England might acquire his secret weapon—an engine which would sink any ship at one blow and enable its fortunate possessor "to give the law to other nations." Hartlib also designed a public-health service at Durham—"a charitable physician or laboratory for the poor"; and on the eve of the Restoration he was drafting petitions to augment the revenues of Cromwell's college at Durham.[47]

46. For Dury's diplomatic activity under the Protectorate, see Karl Brauer, *Die Unionstätigkeit John Duries unter dem Protektorat Cromwells* (Marburg, 1907). Pell's activities are shown by his papers published in R. Vaughan, *The Protectorate of Oliver Cromwell* (1838).

47. Thurloe State Papers (1742), vi, 593, and vii, 481 (*bis*); Worthington, *Diary and Correspondence*, i (1847), 68, 151, 196; Boyle, *Works*, v, 262–63, 281–82; C. E. Whiting, *The University of Durham 1832–1932* (1932), pp. 19–29; G. H. Turnbull, "Oliver

Hartlib was no less active on the ideological front. With his disciple Robert Boyle he encouraged the propagation of the Gospel by means of translations: Chylinski's Lithuanian Bible; Pococke's Arabic version of that "excellent book," Grotius' *de Veritate Christianae Religionis*. He supplied Secretary Thurloe with a Bohemian chaplain. And he too urged the admission and conversion of the Jews, before which, he believed, "the world may not expect any happiness"—or if not all the Jews, at least the austere Jewish sect of the Caraites. Above all he pressed for the establishment in England of his welfare-state, Macaria, that model by which the whole world should be reformed. That permanent aim of his life, "the building of Christian societies in small models," never seemed so urgent to him as when the Puritan experiment in England was dissolving in anarchy. "It is scarce one day, or hour in the day or night," he wrote to Boyle, in November 1659, "being brim-full with all manner of objects of that public and most universal nature, but my soul is crying out

> Phosphore, redde diem; quid gaudia nostra moraris?
> Phosphore, redde diem."

Even in January 1660 he believed that Macaria would "have a more visible being" within three months.[48]

Meanwhile, what of Comenius? He had left England thirteen years before, pledged to return "when affairs were more tranquil." At first he had worked in Elbing, safe again for Protestants under Swedish occupation; then—with an interval of travel in Hungary and Transylvania—he had returned to his community at Leszno in Poland. When the Protectorate had been set up, Hartlib had suggested that he return to England: were not affairs now "more tranquil"? But after so many false dawns Comenius could reasonably be sceptical about the English enlightenment. He was now an old man; his enthusiasm had cooled;[49]

Cromwell's College at Durham," in *Research Review* (Research Publication of the Institute of Education, University of Durham), no. 3 (Sept. 1952), pp. 1-7.

48. Worthington, *Diary and Correspondence*, I, 156, 163, 169, 180, 250, etc.; Boyle, *Works*, v, 292, 293, 295; Stanisław Kot, "Chylinski's Lithuanian Bible, Origin and Historical Background," in *Chylinski's Lithuanian Bible*, II (Poznan, 1958).

49. Already in 1643 Comenius had affronted Hartlib by advising him to abandon his high aims and take a job, and in 1647 he received another rebuff for suggesting that Hartlib drop his plans "von einer Correspondenz-Cantzlei"—i.e., an Office of Addresses. See G. H. Turnbull, *Samuel Hartlib*, p. 60.

he had his duties to his own community; his "greater friends" in England—Williams, Pym, Brooke, Selden—were now dead; his reputation there had sunk in his absence—why, men asked, had he produced "so many *prodromuses*," instead of getting on to a concrete project?—and anyway in Louis de Geer he had found a patron more useful than Archbishop Williams or John Pym. Why then should he risk again that terrible sea-journey in order to receive a less enthusiastic welcome? After thirteen years of absence he saw no reason to leave the peace of Leszno for what might well prove an illusory calm in storm-tossed England. Besides, by 1655, the opportunities of reforming the world seemed greater in Poland than in England.

For in 1655 Charles X of Sweden suddenly invaded Poland and the Polish State collapsed, as it seemed, in ruin before him. To the Protestants of eastern Europe a new deliverer, a new Gustavus, seemed to have arisen and they turned to worship him. The Bohemian Brethren were, by profession, non-political; but Comenius had long since given up any pretence of political neutrality. In recent years he had become dottier than ever and had taken to publishing messianic prophecies about the imminent fall of Antichrist, whose champions he had imprudently identified too exactly. Now, in the triumph of Charles X, he saw the fulfilment of those prophecies. A vast new Swedish empire seemed to him suddenly to offer a new theatre for his universal reformation, and he prostrated himself, with vulgar servility, before the conqueror. In a *Panegyric* (which Hartlib promptly published in London) he hailed the King of Sweden as the Moses, the Joshua, the Gideon, the David of his times, the hero who would mobilize the Lord of Hosts, free the persecuted saints from Egyptian bondage, bring them back into the Promised Land, smite the Midianites and slaughter the Philistines. Charles X, declared Comenius, should conquer and colonize the rich lands of the Ukraine, richer and nearer than the Indies, and establish there a New Order in all Europe. Pansophia, it seemed, was about to be established—by the sword.[50]

Unhappily the golden moment lasted no longer in 1655 than it had

50. Comenius allowed himself to believe in the opaque, rhapsodical prophecies of Christopher Kotter, Nicolas Drabik and Christina Poniatova: three Central European crackpots. Undeterred by the obstinate nonconformity of events he published their prophecies in 1657 under the somewhat misleading title *Lux in Tenebris*. His *Panegyricus Carolo Gustavo, Magno Suecorum Regi* was written in 1655 and published in London by Hartlib before 11 Feb. 1655/6.

done in 1641. Within a year the Swedes had been driven out and the Poles were back at Leszno. Naturally they took their revenge, and the unfortunate Bohemian Brethren paid the price of their bishop's indiscretion. Their township was razed to the ground; the school and library which Comenius had made famous were totally destroyed; and he himself lost all his possessions, books and manuscripts, including his magisterial refutation of the errors of Copernicus. So once again the Bohemian Brethren were homeless, and the piteous lamentations of Comenius were published in England by Samuel Hartlib.

The disaster of Leszno was Cromwell's opportunity: for it stirred again all the old emotions of the 1630s—the Protestant cult of the King of Sweden, the Elizabethan championship of the European Reformation. Cromwell, like Comenius, idolized Charles X, "a man that hath adventured his all against the popish interest in Poland," and he had already set himself up as the defender of oppressed Protestants throughout Europe: the Huguenots of France, the Vaudois of Piedmont, the scattered colonies in eastern Europe. So he now responded at once to Hartlib's agitation. He ordered a public collection for the relief of the poor Bohemians, contributing £50 himself; and once again Comenius received a personal invitation to England.

Admittedly it was not quite the same as in 1641. The old enthusiasm had gone. No one now expected the jubilee and resurrection of the State from him or from anyone else. Milton by now was soured, Cromwell was disillusioned, and Comenius himself was devalued.[51] Still, there was a certain, somewhat paradoxical link with the old days. In 1641 the immediate cause of Comenius' failure in England had been, as he had recognized, "the massacre in Ireland and the outbreak of war there." But by now all that was over. The Irish rebellion had been crushed by Cromwell himself; yet another of Hartlib's early disciples, William Petty, had been appointed by Cromwell to survey the conquered country; and settlers were being invited to people the land. Already in 1652 Hartlib had proposed to Cromwell the replanting of the conquered country "not only with adventurers but haply by the calling in of exiled Bohemians and other Protestants."[52] Now occasion and

---

51. Even the natural allies of Comenius were so disgusted by his *Panegyric* that they abated their sympathy for him in his misfortunes. See, for instance, the remarks of Worthington in *Diary and Correspondence*, II, 87–89.

52. The proposal is made in Hartlib's epistle dedicatory to *Ireland's Natural History*. This work had been written in 1645 by Gerard Boate, a Dutchman resident in

need coincided. Cromwell proposed that Comenius bring his whole community to Ireland.

Hartlib conveyed the invitation to him; but it was not accepted. The Bohemians, Comenius replied, still hoped that one day they would return to their native land. Besides (though it was not he who made this obvious point), how would he ever find in Ireland a patron as munificent as Louis de Geer had been, or as his son Lawrence de Geer now was? "Truly," a friend remarked when he observed Lawrence de Geer's generosity, "I do daily admire God's singular providence in bringing Comenius to this new jewel. There is no prince or state in the world who would have assisted him so really and furthered all these things as he doth." Others expressed the same facts more dryly. Comenius, they said, had become "a *bourgeois* of Amsterdam," bamboozling rich patrons with messianic gibberish. Thus seduced, Comenius could afford to ignore English offers. In Lawrence de Geer's house in Amsterdam he had found a last refuge far more comfortable than the bogs of Munster.[53]

But if Comenius himself never returned to England, that did not mean that his work there was forgotten. Far from it. His early educational reforms, which in the exaltation of 1641 he had hoped to impose wholesale, were applied piecemeal. "Comenius societies" were founded in London. And if his universal "Pansophical" college was not set up in splendour in Winchester or Chelsea or the Savoy, nevertheless, from a more modest beginning, it had in the end a greater future.

When Comenius had arrived in London in 1641, one of those who had turned out to meet him had been another *émigré* scholar, Theodore Haak.[54] Haak was a refugee from the Palatinate, the agent and treasurer of the other refugees, and as such a familiar figure in the Protestant Dispersion. Parliament would afterwards employ him as translator and send him as its envoy to Denmark. After the departure of Comenius, Haak became, in London, the continuator of his influence. Around him

---

London. After Boate's death Hartlib obtained the manuscript from his brother Arnold Boate and published it with a dedication to Cromwell and Major-General Fleetwood, then commanding in Ireland.

53. See C. H. Firth, *The Last Years of the Protectorate* (1909), II, 244. Vaughan, *The Protectorate of Oliver Cromwell*, II, 430, 447-53. Turnbull, *Samuel Hartlib*, pp. 374-75. The sardonic views of Comenius' later life with Lawrence de Geer are quoted from Bayle, *Dictionnaire*, s.v. Coménius, Drabiclus, etc.

54. For Haak, see Pamela R. Barnett, *Theodore Haak F.R.S.* (The Hague, 1962).

there collected those "Baconian" thinkers and scientists, the friends of Hartlib and Dury and of their patrons in the country party. There was Pell; there was Petty; there was Christopher Wren, whose earliest piece of architecture was a transparent three-storied beehive for Hartlib; there was Cromwell's personal physician, Jonathan Goddard; and there was Cromwell's brother-in-law, John Wilkins. Wilkins was himself the grandson of a famous Puritan preacher and had been brought up in Pym's circle at Fawsley in Northamptonshire. He had been chaplain to the Elector Palatine; the Long Parliament made him warden of Wadham College; and under Cromwell he became effective ruler of Oxford University. Under his direction the "vulgar Baconianism" of Hartlib and his friends was quietly transformed, elevated again into the pure Baconianism of Bacon. Wilkins' house in Oxford became the centre of a new Baconian experimental society. And in the 1660s, when the new society had become famous under royal protection, Comenius himself, ignoring the intermediate transformation, would confidently claim that he was its founder. "Others have laboured, and you have entered into their labours," he would declare; and to prove his claim he would publish the *Via Lucis* which he had written in England in 1641 and would dedicate it to his supposed continuators, "the Torchbearers of this Enlightened Age," the Royal Society of London.[55]

The Royal Society—the title might seem ironical for the result of an anti-royal revolution; but in fact it would not have been disdained by the consistent members of the country party. After all, these men were not republicans, they were Baconians. In 1641, though they held forms of government to be ultimately indifferent, they had been royalists and Anglicans. Hartlib had attended the Anglican church in Duke's

---

55. The relationship (if any) between "the Pansophical college" of Comenius, the "invisible college" of Hartlib and the Royal Society, as indeed the origin of the Royal Society itself, is a matter of controversy. F. E. Held, in his *Christianopolis, an Ideal State of the seventeenth century*, and R. H. Syfret, "The Origins of the Royal Society" (*Notes and Records of the Royal Society*, v, 1948) have argued that there was such a connection; but G. H. Turnbull, "Samuel Hartlib's Influence on the Early History of the Royal Society" (ibid. x, 1953), has convinced me that there was no direct connection. Neither Hartlib nor Comenius was a scientist, and, as I have suggested, there is a great difference between their "vulgar Baconianism" and the true Baconianism from which the Royal Society drew its philosophy. But it remains true (*a*) that the founders of the Royal Society shared many interests and ideals with Hartlib and Comenius and used similar language with them, and (*b*) that, in consequence of this, Comenius himself believed that the Royal Society was the realization of his "Pansophic" project.

Place; so had Comenius when in England; and Dury had held an Anglican living. Pym, to his dying day, had been an outspoken monarchist. Cromwell had been unable to conceive of government without "something monarchical in it." It was only the impossibility of King Charles that had driven such men, in their despair, to look for another political system under which to pursue their unpolitical aims. Now they had found that no other system could sustain itself. Only a monarchy, complete with House of Lords and established Church, could provide that "tranquillity" which they needed for their work. And so, when the new half-monarchy of the House of Cromwell had failed, there was nothing for it but to go back to the old full monarchy of the House of Stuart, from the Baconianism of the country, of the Puritans, to the Baconianism of the Court, of Bacon himself. It was without any real inconsistency that the Pansophic Society, first blessed by Pym, would be gradually transformed into the Royal Society, blessed by Charles II; that Chelsea College, first earmarked by the Parliament for Comenius, should be given by the king to Wilkins;[56] that Petty would become, like Bacon, a courtier, and Wilkins, like Williams, a bishop.

But if the Stuart monarchy, in the end, provided the basis for a Baconian academy, how far did it sustain (as in theory it could) a Baconian society? Did the Merry Monarch realize the reformers' plans for a decentralized, laicized, reconstructed society?

Institutionally, we can only say that he did not. When a revolution is defeated, its achievements and aspirations, good and bad, go down together. In 1660 Durham College was dissolved. The new college for Dublin was forgotten. The decentralized Cromwellian parliamentary franchise was scrapped. The Cromwellian law reforms were abandoned. It was not till the nineteenth century that these various projects were resumed.[57] Similarly the new elementary schools in Wales disappeared. Elementary education after 1660 was fostered best in the Dissenters' schools, cut off from the Establishment. County regis-

---

56. Charles II at first gave Chelsea College to the Royal Society as its headquarters, but it proved unsuitable and was afterwards returned.

57. Durham University was founded in 1832, University College, Dublin, in 1851. The disfranchisement of rotten boroughs and the enfranchisement of industrial towns —both features of the Cromwellian parliamentary system—were re-enacted by the Reform Bill of 1832. Some of the Cromwellian law reforms were re-enacted in the mid-nineteenth century (see Inderwick, *The Interregnum*).

ters were no more heard of.[58] The parish clergy, if resident, remained largely ignorant and poor. Perhaps this was not mere reaction. Perhaps society had not yet the productive capacity to bear so ambitious a welfare-state as was suggested by these "utopian" reformers. At all events, the attempt, as a systematic attempt, was abandoned. On the other hand the means of change had been created, or at least the obstacles had been removed. The top-heavy administration, the prerogative courts, the swollen bureaucratic superstructure of the State and the Church had been shed. If the new wealth of England was not planted in the country by planned decentralization, at least it was allowed to flow thither, even (thanks to the triumph of the mercantilists, who saw that a prosperous commerce depends on a robust industry) to grow there. For the rational part of their programme Hartlib and his friends had plenty of disciples whom government, from now on, seldom obstructed. But to build up the English country they had to rely on state liberalism, not state control. This perhaps was true of "laicization."

The one universal casualty was the irrational, crusading, mystical part of the "country" philosophy. By 1660 that had gone, gone for ever with the generation out of which it had been born. In the new Europe there was no place, no need, for utopianism. In 1660 Hartlib would still sigh for Macaria, but Bermuda, not England, would now seem "the fittest receptacle for it." In England it had "proved a great nothing": "name and thing have as good as vanished."[59] Dury would admit that his Protestant reunionism was no longer wanted and would settle down in Germany, under the protection of the Landgräfin of Hesse-Cassel, to reinterpret the Apocalypse without reference to the external world.[60] Comenius in Amsterdam, grown comfortable and snappish in

58. In *Harleian Miscellany*, III, 320, there is one later proposal, viz.: "Reasons and Proposals for a Registry . . . to be had in every County" (1671), with a reply by William Pierrepoint.

59. Hartlib to Worthington, Oct. 1660, in Worthington, *Diary and Correspondence*, I, 211–12. Same to same 10 Dec. 1660, ibid. p. 239.

60. In 1674 Dury published, evidently at Cassel, a work *Touchant l'intelligence de l'Apocalypse par l'Apocalypse même*. This work is extremely rare and I have been unable to find a copy of it; but its content is described by Pierre Bayle (*Dictionnaire*, s.v. Duraeus), by C. J. Benzelius (*Dissertatio Historico-Theologica de Johanne Duraeo . . .* Helmstedt, 1744, pp. 68–71) and apparently by Hans Leube (*Kalvinismus und Luthertum im Zeitalter der Orthodoxie*, Leipzig, 1928, I, 236–37, as cited in Batten, *John Dury*, p. 196). In it, Dury insisted that all Scripture must be interpreted by certain rules which, he believed,

his *bourgeois* old age, would begin to doubt his own millennial vaticinations. The Jews would be welcomed in the London of Charles II, but
as Court financiers, not as elder brethren of the Christians. Hartlib and
Comenius might claim the Royal Society as their work, but even they
would deplore its ideological betrayal. Instead of a spiritual union for
the overthrow of Antichrist, the new society would be so deliberately
neutral in religion that it could even be accused of a plan to "reduce
England unto popery." [61]

It was not that Christian irenism had been rejected. Rather it had
been transformed. Freed from the special circumstances of the Thirty
Years War, it had recovered its original universality. Antichrist, who
had assumed so visible and terrifying an aspect in the 1620s, had now
evaporated again. He was out of date; and his rhapsodical, millenarian
enemies were out of date with him. This would be recognized by Dury
whose last works—works of undenominational piety which caused
some to regard him as a Quaker—hinted that Rome too might become
part of Christian unity.[62] It would be recognized, in the next generation, by Comenius' grandson, Daniel Ernst Jablonski, who, as Court-
preacher in Berlin, would work with Leibniz and Archbishop Wake for
general reunion.[63] But the life work of Comenius himself, as of Hartlib
and Dury, and all those enthusiastic prophets of the Protestant Millennium, would seem, after 1660, irrecoverably dated.

---

would eliminate controversy; and he chose to illustrate these rules by interpreting the
Apocalypse, that being the most obscure work of the whole Bible. One of his rules was
"d'éviter en méditant toute recherche des choses qui n'appartiennent point à la matière
de laquelle il s'agit ou qui sont curieuses et n'ont point un exprès fondement à l'Écriture
Sainte . . ." Such an interpretation is equivalent to a renunciation of the whole tradition
by which the language of the Apocalypse had been applied to the events of the Thirty
Years War: a tradition which Dury had himself previously supported, e.g., in his "Epis-
tolical Discourse" prefixed to Hartlib's edition of [Abraham von Frankenberg's] *Clavis
Apocalyptica*.

61. This was the argument of Henry Stubbe in his works, *Legends No Histories*
(1670) and *Campanella Revived* (1670).

62. Dury, *Touchant l'intelligence de l'Apocalypse*, as quoted in Bayle and Benzelius.
Dury's last work was *Le Vrai Chrestien* (1676), which even Bayle and Benzelius had not
seen. But it was known to the German Pietist P. J. Spener, "qui aliquoties eius non sine
laude meminit," and, evidently, to Elizabeth, Princess Palatine (Benzelius, *Dissertatio*,
p. 71).

63. D. E. Jablonski was the son of Peter Jablonski, alias Figuius, the secretary and
son-in-law of Comenius, who had also served Dury as secretary in Sweden.

For by 1660 the generation of the 1620s, of the Protestant débâcle, was dead or dying, at least in high places, and its ideological world was dying with it. With the death of Cromwell, whose power had artificially prolonged it, that world was found to have quietly dissolved. There is continuity in history, but there is also discontinuity: each generation profits by the acquisitions of its predecessors, but sheds its mood, the mere deposit of incommunicable experience. And so Wilkins and Petty, Boyle and Wren might continue the scientific or social philosophy of Hartlib, Dury and Comenius; but never having experienced the disasters of the 1620s, they were exempt from its peculiar metaphysics: they would not waste their time on the Millennium, the Messiah or the number of the Beast.

6 | The Fast Sermons of the Long Parliament

"It was an observation of that time," wrote Clarendon of the Puritan Revolution, "that the first publishing of extraordinary news was from the pulpit; and by the preacher's text, and his manner of discourse upon it, the auditors might judge, and commonly foresaw, what was like to be next done in the Parliament or Council of State."[1] Clarendon himself took a great interest in the techniques both of parliamentary management and of political preaching. He had himself, in the first eighteen months of the Long Parliament, ample opportunities of watching the "tuning of the pulpits" by Pym; and indeed, I shall suggest, his first tactical defeat by Pym may have been in one such matter. Though some of his particular illustrations are incorrect, his general statement is, I believe, true. In this essay I wish to show how the leaders of the Long Parliament, while there was effective leadership, used the pulpit both for strategic and for tactical purposes: both to declare long-term aims and to inaugurate temporary shifts of policy; and I shall do so particularly with reference to those sermons over which the parliamentary leaders had direct control, the regular "fast sermons" which were preached before Parliament on the last Wednesday of every month from 1642 to 1649.

General fasts, with appropriate sermons, were, of course, nothing new in 1640. Great occasions had always called them forth. There had been a general fast on the approach of the Armada in 1588, a weekly

---

1. Edward, Earl of Clarendon, *The History of the Rebellion*, ed. W. D. Macray (Oxford, 1888), IV, 194.

fast in 1603 until the plague was over, and another general fast for the great plague of 1625. More recently, fasts had also been held at the beginning of Parliament. There was always something a little distasteful to the Crown about such proposals: they emphasized the gravity of affairs and implied that Parliament, with God's support, provided the means of solution. Consequently Queen Elizabeth never allowed them. In 1580, when the House of Commons suggested a public fast for the preservation of the queen's life and the better direction of the actions of the House, she was furious. The proposal was very modest, and the House proposed to leave the choice of preacher entirely to the Privy Councillors in the House "to the end they might be such as would keep convenient proportion of time and meddle with no matter of innovation or unquietness." Even so, the queen expressed her great misliking and astonishment at such rashness and made the House eat the humblest of humble pie. That done, she graciously allowed that their rash, unadvised, and inconsiderate error had proceeded from zeal, not malicious intent, and forgave them provided that they never misbehaved in that sort again.[2]

They did not; and it was not till the last Parliament of James I that a more formidable House of Commons revived the proposal. On 23 February 1624 Sir Edward Cecil moved that there be a general fast, with a collection for the poor, as in Holland. The House was to choose the preachers. But of course the king must give the authority: Parliament could only prescribe for itself. So the Commons conferred with the Lords and together they moved the king. James I agreed, saying that he would consult the bishops as to the best time. After that the practice became regular. There were general fasts, proclaimed by the king on the motion of both Houses, at the beginning of each of the first four parliaments of Charles I.[3]

Apart from fasts, or "days of public humiliation" in times of crisis, there were also special sermons on certain anniversaries and on days of thanksgiving for great victories or deliveries. The accession-day of the reigning monarch was one such anniversary; another was 5 November, the day of the Gunpowder Plot; a third, which rose in popularity as the Stuarts fell, was 17 November, the accession-day of Queen Elizabeth.

2. Some early fast-days are mentioned in a later fast sermon by William Gouge, *The Right Way* . . . (1648). See also *Commons' Journals* (hereafter referred to as *C.J.*), I, 118 ff.

3. *C.J.*, I, 671, 715, 869, 873–74, 922–26.

This was an unofficial day of thanksgiving, on which the Stuart kings, not unnaturally, tended to frown.[4]

Thus when the Long Parliament met in November 1640, it was perfectly natural that one of its first acts should be to propose a general fast, and it was, by now, perfectly natural that the king should agree to it. It was also perfectly predictable that particular crises or particular triumphs might elicit special days of "public humiliation" or "thanksgiving." What few would have predicted was that such occasions would be converted into a regular system in order to sustain the unity of Parliament and the fulfilment of an ever more radical programme over several years; that Pym would learn to "tune the pulpits" as effectively as ever his heroine Queen Elizabeth had done; and that well-timed sermons would not only declare the general party line, but also, on particular occasions, prepare the way for dramatic episodes. They would foretell the death first of Strafford, then of Laud; declare the civil war; initiate the iconoclastic programme; and, finally, they would announce the most dramatic, most revolutionary gesture of all: the execution of the king himself.

The first episode in this history comes at the very beginning of the Parliament. When Parliament met, its very first act was to propose a general fast. The procedure followed the form which was now usual. Both Houses, in agreement, requested the king to authorize the solemnity. Each House chose its own preachers. All business was to be suspended. There were to be sermons morning and afternoon. The Lord Mayor was to make arrangements in the City. At the same time the House of Commons, following earlier precedents, also appointed a day on which all its members should take the sacrament and listen to further sermons. This was an internal matter requiring no royal authority. When these plans were agreed, the dates were chosen. Symbolically, the date chosen for the joint fast was 17 November, Queen Elizabeth's day; the date for the taking of the sacrament was to be 29 November. The preachers chosen by the Commons were, for the first ceremony, Stephen Marshall and Cornelius Burges; for the second, John Gauden and George Morley.

These arrangements were not casual. Nothing, in those early days of the Long Parliament, was casual. After all, this great meeting of Par-

4. For the celebration of "Queen Elizabeth's day" under the Stuarts, see J. E. Neale, *Essays in Elizabethan History* (1958), pp. 9–20.

liament had been planned long ago. For three years "the great contrivers," as Clarendon called them, had been planning their tactics, preparing their programme. They had a political programme and a social programme, and they intended to realize them both by certain clearly defined steps. First, they had to force the king to summon Parliament; then they had to secure the return of their friends to Parliament; then they had to dismantle the existing royal government; finally, they had to persuade the king to accept the reformers into his counsels. For this purpose the great peers—the earls of Warwick, Pembroke, Bedford— had used their clerical and borough patronage. For this purpose the great strategists—Bedford and his supports, Pym and St. John—had devised their strategy. Naturally, now that the moment for parliamentary action had come, they were not unprepared. The function of the first sermons was to lay down the policy of Parliament, and the preachers chosen already knew their parts.

By far the most important of the preachers was Stephen Marshall, minister of Finchingfield, Essex, the most famous political parson of the revolution. Like so many of the political clergy, Marshall was a client of the Earl of Warwick, and he had served his master well, preaching for his parliamentary candidates throughout Essex. He had already preached the fast sermon at the beginning of the Short Parliament, that first false start of the reforming programme.[5] In the Long Parliament he would emerge as the inseparable political and spiritual ally of Pym, the interpreter of Pym's policy after Pym's death. At every stage of the revolution we can see him. Now he is thumping his pulpit on great occasions; now he is meeting with Pym, Hampden and Harley to prepare parliamentary tactics; now he is bustling through Westminster Hall to push voters into the Parliament before the division; now he is retiring, exhausted, to recuperate in the well-appointed house of his good friend "my noble Lord of Warwick." Later he would be the Parliament's envoy to Scotland, its chaplain with the captive king; he would pass unscathed from Presbyterianism to Independency; and if he always appeared as the spokesman for the winning side, his changes can be explained by one consistent aim, which was also the aim of Pym: to preserve the unity of opposition against royal and clerical reaction.[6]

5. *Cal. S.P. (Dom.) 1639–40*, p. 609.

6. There is no adequate biography of Marshall, whose importance, at least as the spokesman of policy, seems to me greater than has been allowed. The particular details which I have mentioned come from two passages in the diary of Sir Simonds D'Ewes,

From beginning to end Marshall was the clerical tribune of the Parliament. Others accompanied him for stretches of the road only. At the beginning his constant companions were Cornelius Burges, who now preached with him on the fast-day, and Edmund Calamy. They too were both clients of the Earl of Warwick. As a political parson Burges at least was hardly less active than Marshall. His greatest achievement would be the ingenious financial device of "doubling" on bishops' lands to pay off the Scottish armies. That busy Scotch minister, the Rev. Robert Baillie, who so piqued himself on his political ability, recognized "good Mr. Marshall" and "my dear friend Dr. Burges" as kindred spirits—at least until he found that they were even sharper than he. From the opposite side Clarendon would also single them out. "Without doubt," he would write, "the archbishop of Canterbury had never so great an influence upon the counsels at court as Dr. Burges and Mr. Marshall had then upon the Houses."[7]

Thus from the start the stage was set. By the time that Burges and Marshall mounted their pulpits, their message was predictable. Strafford was in prison, his plans to break the Parliament frustrated, at least for a time. But for how long? All depended on the cohesion of Parliament, its refusal to be divided by royal manoeuvre or internal strains. This had always been Pym's message: from his earliest days in Parliament he had advocated a "covenant" among the enemies of popery and tyranny. Now both Burges and Marshall sang to the same tune. In the universal peril, said Marshall, all hope lay in a covenant such as had been made to defend religion in the days of Queen Elizabeth. It was not enough, added Burges, "to pull down and cut off some of the Nimrods" who had invaded English laws and liberties: "there must be a thorough joining of themselves to God by covenant." And each in turn looked back to the same day eighty-two years ago, "the auspicious entrance of our late royal Deborah (worthy of eternal remembrance and honour) into her blessed and glorious reign."[8]

Marshall and Burges laid down the political conditions of parliamentary survival. The next sermons, the sermons of 29 November, showed something of the social programme envisaged. They also gave a

---

both quoted in F. A. Shaw, *A History of the English Church . . . 1640–1660* (1900), i, 81–82, and from *A Copy of a Letter written by Mr. Stephen Marshall* (1643), p. 1.

7. Clarendon, *History of the Rebellion*, i, 401.

8. C. Burges, *The First Sermon Preached to the House of Commons . . .* (1640); S. Marshall, *A Sermon Preached before the House of Commons* (1640).

further glimpse of the mechanics whereby the pulpits were tuned. John Gauden was another clerical protégé of the Earl of Warwick. George Morley was, as far as we can see, unconnected with the "great contrivers." He was an intimate friend of Hyde and Falkland, an Anglican of Socinian views like Falkland himself, and a regular member of Falkland's circle at Great Tew. His future was to be as a royalist ally of Hyde. But in 1640 Hyde and Falkland were reformers and Morley had incurred the dislike of Laud: they could therefore propose him in a loyal but anti-Laudian Parliament, and he could be chosen along with the candidate of the "great contrivers," Gauden. But even at this early stage the distinction between the real party leaders and their "moderate royalist" allies was made apparent. When the sermons were over, the House voted its thanks to Gauden, and invited him to print his sermon. The thanks, and the request, were conveyed by Sir Thomas Barrington, the brother-in-law of the Earl of Warwick. But Morley fared differently. His sermon, we are told, "was so little to their gust and liking" that no such message was sent to him. His sermon was not printed and we do not know what he said.[9]

On the other hand, Gauden's sermon, the sermon which the leaders of Parliament blessed, is a very revealing document. It was a plea for a peaceful, social and religious reformation in England, and it ended with a positive suggestion. If Parliament wished, said Gauden, to carry out this reformation, it could not do better than to consult "two great and public spirits who have laboured much for truth and peace," John Dury, the apostle of Protestant unity, and John Amos Comenius, the Bohemian reformer of education, "both famous for their learning, piety and integrity and not unknown, I am sure, by the fame of their works, to many of this honourable, learned and pious assembly." In the published version of his sermon Gauden added a note. It might not seem easy, he

9. The fate of Morley's sermon is described by Anthony Wood, *Athenae Oxonienses*, ed. P. Bliss (1813–21), IV, 150. Wood does not date it precisely: after mentioning "the wars," which, he says, commenced *anno* 1641 [*sic*], he says "at the beginning of which he [Morley] preached one of the first solemn sermons before the Commons. . . ." Since "the wars" began in 1642, the *DNB* (s.v. Morley) says that his sermon was in 1642. But in fact Morley was never invited to preach after November 1640. The *Commons' Journals* for November 1640 show that he was then invited to print his sermon, but less warmly than Gauden. It therefore seems clear that this is the episode to which Wood refers. In writing "at the beginning of which" Wood was no doubt thinking rather of "the troubles" generally than "the wars" particularly.

wrote, to fetch these men to England since Comenius was in Poland and Dury in Sweden. However, "there is a fair, easy and safe way of addresses to them both": they could be reached via Samuel Hartlib of Duke's Place, London.

Certainly Hartlib, Dury and Comenius were "not unknown" to the leaders of Parliament: they were far better known to them than to the preacher who now uttered their names. Hartlib was a close friend of Pym, and for the last few years most of the "great contrivers" had been in touch with them, directly or indirectly, circulating their works, supporting their projects, supplying them with money. Those three men were the philosophers of the "country party," and in naming them Gauden was stating in advance the social programme of the parliamentary reformers. And once the programme had been thus indicated, the rest followed. Hartlib was requested to fetch Dury and Comenius to England in the name of "the Parliament of England." Next year they came; and although the deterioration of politics made it impossible to realize their reforms, and Comenius would retire, disillusioned, to Sweden and Holland, their names would never be far from the lips of the parliamentary leaders. Whenever political peace seemed (however falsely) to have returned, Hartlib and Dury would be summoned to draft the new social millennium; and when Oliver Cromwell had at last, among the débris of Crown and Parliament, established some kind of order, it was from their circle that he would accept advice on religious reform, social and educational policy, even foreign affairs.[10]

So much for the first fast sermons, the sermons of 1640. At that time there was no thought of repetition. The ceremonies were inaugural ceremonies; the sermons charted the course ahead; the rest should be plain sailing. Unfortunately it was not in fact plain sailing. What Bedford called the great rock of Strafford's case thrust itself up and threatened to wreck the Parliament. For the trial of Strafford did not go according to plan. The legal charges were hard to prove and yet it seemed suicide to acquit him. Bedford himself wished to spare Strafford for the sake of ultimate compromise with the king; but would the king ever compromise if he had Strafford to advise him? Was it not safer to knock that fatal adviser on the head as a beast of prey, even if it alienated the king for ever? That was the view of Bedford's more radical allies.

10. I have dealt more fully with this episode and its significance in my essay "Three Foreigners," above, pp. 219–71.

Between these two policies the parliamentary leaders wavered. Then, at the beginning of April, events occurred to decide them. On 1 April Bedford and Pym learned of the Army Plot, the plot to rescue Strafford from the Tower by force. At first Bedford, in his desire to keep tempers down, persuaded Pym to say nothing to the Commons. But Pym, it is clear, was now converted. On 3 April he caused the remaining Irish charges against Strafford to be hastily despatched so as to push forward the more damaging English charges; and next day, being Sunday, he once again used the pulpit to declare policy.

The preacher of this ordinary Sunday sermon was Samuel Fairclough, a country clergyman from Suffolk. The patron of his living there was Sir Nathaniel Barnardiston, a close ally of Pym; and the preacher himself acknowledged that only the favour and command of his patron could have brought him from his rural obscurity to address so exalted a congregation. When the sermon was over he would return to that obscurity and come to our notice again only twelve years later, when he would preach at his patron's funeral. Nevertheless, this demure and humble parson was not afraid, on this occasion, to pronounce a very remarkable sermon. It was about the "troubler of Israel," Achan, whose sins lay heavily on the whole people of God, until they were relieved of it by his prompt execution on the orders of Joshua. For "troublers of the state," said the preacher, though they must have the benefit of "due trial and examination," must always be despatched "without any unnecessary delays or procrastination." Thereupon, with revolting relish, he repudiated in turn every argument of justice or humanity. Death, only death, would satisfy the remorseless preacher, death without time for repentance on one side or for reflection on the other. And then, lest he should seem to be speaking of too abstract a case, he dropped the case of Achan, whose punishment was more apposite than his crime, and turned to other "troublers of Israel" who had deserved the same fate. In particular he turned to Achitophel, the treacherous councillor of King David, who, having wormed his way into his master's confidence, and then stirred up armed revolt, finally undertook himself to suppress the rebellion he had raised, in order "that, as he had been President of the Council in peace, so now he might feed his ambitious humour in making himself general of the forces in war." In this capacity Achitophel, said the preacher (who seemed remarkably well informed about Strafford's speech to the Privy Council on 5 May 1640), had urged "all haste and expedition, no further counsel but his own: he would not have the battle delayed one day." Therefore let there be no delay in his despatch, which will give such joy to the Church as Israel felt when the Egyptians were drowned in the Red Sea, when Sisera was beheaded, when Haman was hanged.[11]

At this time, it should be noted, Strafford, though on a capital charge, was still legally presumed innocent. The knowledge of the Army Plot was still confined (it seems) to Bedford and Pym. The details of Strafford's advice in Council would not be revealed to Parliament till the next day. It is hardly conceivable that this country clergyman, so submissive to his patron, so dazzled by his momentary publicity, should have dared, on his own initiative, to dictate to Parliament, while the great trial was still *sub judice*, a new and more sanguinary course. And yet from that date this was the course which would be followed. The conclusion is forced upon us that Fairclough's sermon was the means of declaring a new party line.

Perhaps it was the usefulness of that sermon which suggested to Parliament a more frequent use of solemn fast-days; for only a fortnight afterwards a proposal for another joint fast was referred to a committee, and the committee, on 28 April, reported that there indeed were grounds enough for such a solemnity. Notwithstanding the former day of public humiliation, progress had been slow, dangers and fears remained, plague threatened ... However, the proposal seems not to have been pursued. No doubt it was lost in the press of business. And when Strafford's head was at last off, and the king, it seemed, had surrendered on all issues, the occasion for sackcloth and ashes was over. In the summer of 1641 Pym even felt able to disband the Scottish armies on which Parliament had hitherto relied and which had now become a liability. The next special religious demonstration was therefore not a fast but a day of thanksgiving for the peace with Scotland. To celebrate that event, the sign of victory, the basis of a purely English reformation, on 7 September 1641 the church bells were rung all over England; and Parliament listened to ecstatic sermons from Stephen Marshall and Jeremiah Burroughes. To both of them 1641 was *annus mirabilis*, "this wonderful year," greater than 1588, the year of the Armada, the "return of the prayers of forty and forty years" since the accession of Queen Elizabeth: the year which had silenced all critics, would enable swords to

---

11. S. Fairclough, *The Troublers Troubled, or Achan Condemned and Executed* (1641).

be beaten into ploughshares and spears into pruning-hooks, and would begin "a very jubilee and resurrection of Church and State." [12]

The euphoria of that autumn was general. It was then that Milton's great pamphlets were written, then that Dury and Comenius met in England to plan the new social reformation for which the political basis, it now seemed, was secure. The disillusion caused by the Irish rebellion and its consequences was therefore profound. By the middle of December the affairs of Parliament looked blacker than ever. The king was now back in London. He had won over the City, the House of Lords, the "neuters" in the country. He was preparing to strangle the Parliament. So we need not be surprised to find the leaders of Parliament, on 17 December, proposing once again (as well as certain more practical measures) a "day of humiliation." This time it was to be not only a parliamentary but a general fast, to renew and re-emphasize the solidarity of Parliament and people. The fast was to be celebrated by the two Houses and the City on 22 December, by the country on 20 January. The preachers to the Commons were to be, as so often, Stephen Marshall and Edmund Calamy. The Lords and the City would choose their own preachers. The arrangements in the country were to be made by the local authorities on the instructions of their members of Parliament.

By the day of the parliamentary fast London was already in turmoil. Pym had won one great victory: the City elections had given him control, through his radical ally Alderman Penington, of the Common Council. The king had counter-attacked by putting a notorious cavalier in command of the Tower. At any moment, it now seemed, the crunch would come. If Parliament was to survive, it must keep left, disdain no weapons, draw on the radical spirit of the City mobs, exalt their radicalism by ideological gestures. In the previous winter Pym had contained the City mobs, diverted their attacks on episcopacy, on images, on "popish" ceremonies. Now he must appeal to these forces. The sermons of 22 December reflected this mood. While Calamy deplored the delay in reformation caused by the sins of the City, which made it, like Sodom, ripe for destruction, Marshall beat the drum ecclesiastic and urged his hearers to hunt out the sinners. They should remember good King Josiah, who not only broke down "all the images and reliques of idolatry," but also "executed the justice and vengeance of God upon the

12. Jeremiah Burroughes, *Sion's Joy* (1641); S. Marshall, *A Peace Offering to God* (1641).

instruments of the kingdom's ruin, the idolatrous priests, digging the bones of some of them out of their graves." No nice scruples of prudence or legality had hindered that good work. Josiah "consulted not with flesh and blood": it was God's work and he did it without question, "with zeal and fervency." Parliament should now go and do likewise.[13] For these seasonable sermons the preachers were duly thanked and voted a gratuity of £20 apiece in plate.

So the fierce struggle for London was launched. Massive processions demanded justice against "bishops and popish lords," the obstacles to reform; "images" were denounced and attacked, Westminster Abbey and the House of Lords invaded; the impeachment of the queen was threatened. The king retaliated with his attempt on the Five Members and, failing, left London, resolved to enter it again only as a conqueror.

To the leaders of Parliament the king's flight was a declaration of war. At the time neither side might be prepared for war, and it would take eight months before the necessity of it could be admitted and the armies raised. The great problem was created by the "neuters," that solid body of men throughout the country who insisted, and would long insist, that there was no cause for civil war and demanded that king and Parliament make concessions to each other to restore the old "mixed monarchy." All through these first eight months of 1642 the "neuters" bombarded both sides with their appeals. But on both sides the leaders had already decided. On the king's side, we see it if we look behind his formal statements to his private correspondence with the queen. On Pym's side we see it, once again, in his tuning of the pulpits, and, in particular, in the utterances of his spiritual oracle, the true amplifier of his master's voice, Stephen Marshall.

For on 24 December, at the height of the struggle for London, when Marshall's last sermon was still echoing in their ears, the Commons once again turned their attention to public fasts. Recognizing that they were now faced by a permanent crisis, and that their survival depended on continuous contact with the country, continuous propaganda, they invited the Lords to join them in proposing to the king that as long as the troubles in Ireland remained unsettled, there should be a regular monthly fast. The ground was well chosen. The Lords agreed; the king could not demur; and a royal proclamation was duly published. By its terms, the last Wednesday of every month was to be kept as a

13. Edmund Calamy, *England's Looking-Glass* (1641); S. Marshall, *Reformation and Desolation* (1641).

fast-day "as well by abstinence from food as by public prayers, preaching and hearing the word of God . . . in all cathedrals, collegiate and parish churches and chapels" throughout England and Wales. The fast already arranged for the country on 20 January was confirmed. Thereafter Parliament, City and country would celebrate the fast on the same day, beginning on 23 February 1642.[14]

The parliamentary sermons of 23 February thus marked the beginning of a new regular system, a standing covenant between Parliament and people. Ostensibly linked to the rebellion in Ireland, which king and Parliament pretended equally to deplore, it was in fact tied to the English crisis which was sustained by that rebellion. By agreeing to the system, Charles I had put into the hands of his enemies a means of co-ordination and propaganda to which he himself had no parallel. What kind of an engine it was would be shown from the very start, in the opening sermons of those two star performers of the Parliament, Stephen Marshall and Edmund Calamy.

As before, Edmund Calamy, the unpolitical clergyman, looked to the past. Hitherto, he pointed out, the new English reformation had been carried out in a peaceable, parliamentary way. While the other nations "travailed through blood to a reformation," the building of the new England had gone forward, like Solomon's Temple, without the noise of hammer or axe.[15] It was all very satisfactory—so far. But what of the future? At this point Stephen Marshall, the politician, took over. As before, he looked forward; and he looked forward, quite clearly, to war. The bloodthirsty sermon in which, six months before the outbreak of hostilities, he denounced the "neuters" and called for total war would become the most famous of all his works. It was also the sermon which he himself most admired. According to his own account, he afterwards preached it, up and down the country, sixty times, and it was several times printed. It caused him to be known as "the great incendiary of this unhappy war." When he published it, he entitled it *Meroz Cursed*.

For there are times, explained the minister of Christ, when "God's blessed servants must come down from mount Gerizim, the mount of blessing, and go up on mount Ebal, the mount of cursing, and there curse, and curse bitterly," as the angel of the Lord once cursed the men of Meroz for failing to join in the battle "against King Jabin and his gen-

14. For the proclamation, see John Rushworth, *Historical Collections* (1721), III, i, 494.

15. Edmund Calamy, *God's Free Mercy to England* (1642).

eral Sisera, who for twenty years had mightily oppressed the children of Israel." "For all people are cursed or blessed according as they do or do not help the Church of God in its need." Does not the Holy Writ expressly say, "cursed is he that doeth the work of the Lord negligently"? And what is this imperative work of the Lord? "The next words," replied the preacher, "will tell you: cursed is everyone that withholds his hand from shedding of blood." For the Lord, he explained, "acknowledges no neuters"; "he that is not with me is against me," and "public neuters" shall receive from the hand of Christ the same bloody doom and execution which Gideon very properly imposed upon the men of Succoth and Penuel when they refused to co-operate in catching and killing his enemies. Then, moving on from the barbarities of the Old Testament to the barbarities of the Middle Ages, Marshall invited his hearers to admire "that brave Bohemian captain," John Zizka, "who not only was willing to fight while he lived but bequeathed his skin, when he died, to be made a drum-head for the service of the war."

Meroz Cursed was the first of a long series of incendiary sermons which, from now on, scandalized royalists and moderate men alike. "No good Christian," wrote Clarendon, "can without horror think of those ministers of the Church who, by their function being messengers of peace, were the only trumpets of war and incendiaries towards rebellion." The scriptural phrases used by Marshall, the texts concerning the men of Meroz, the curses upon those who did the work of the Lord negligently or held back from the shedding of blood, would become the commonplaces of many a later preacher.[16] So would some other choice scriptural examples: the virtue of Phinehas, the grandson of Aaron, who did not wait for authority but slew the transgressors with his own hand and thus stayed the plague that had visited Israel; the vices of Saul, who ignored the orders of Samuel to hew Agag, King of the

---

16. "There was more than Mr. Marshall who, from the 23rd verse of the 5th chapter of Judges, *Curse ye Meroz* . . . presumed to inveigh against, and in plain terms to pronounce God's curse against all those who came not with their utmost power and strength to destroy and root out all the malignants who in any degree opposed the Parliament." (Clarendon, *History of the Rebellion*, II, 320–21.) Clarendon's editor, W. D. Macray, remarks on this passage that "prolonged search has failed to trace the other sermons to which Clarendon refers." In fact the curse upon Meroz for neutrality is explicitly repeated in numerous fast sermons, e.g., Thomas Wilson, *Jericho's Downfall* (28 Sept. 1642); Thomas Case, *God's Rising, His Enemies Scattering* (26 Oct. 1642); Charles Herle, *A Pair of Compasses for Church and State* (30 Nov. 1642); John Ley, *The Fury of War and Folly of Sin* (26 April 1643), etc.

Amalekites, in pieces, and of Ahab who similarly defied the orders of a prophet and spared Ben-Hadad, King of Syria. They were part of the horrible propaganda with which Pym found it necessary, at times, to rally his forces in order to resist, and bring into "a good correspondency" with Parliament, a king whose circumstances happily dispensed him from such disagreeable language.

Thus the regular series of "monthly fasts" began. They would continue for seven years. The routine was soon established. When one ceremony was over, the next would be prepared. The two Houses would separately choose and invite their preachers. The invitation of the Lords was impersonal, that of the Commons conveyed by named members—neighbours, friends, kinsmen: presumably their original sponsors. Sometimes, of course, there were refusals and substitutes had to be found. When the fast-day came, official parliamentary business was omitted or cut down to a minimum. The Lords normally gathered in King Henry VII's chapel of Westminster Abbey, the Commons in St. Margaret's, Westminster. The two preachers delivered the sermons, one in the morning, one in the afternoon. The ceremonies were open to all: unless expressly excluded by a parliamentary order, the public was free to attend and (according to the fashion of the time) to take notes of the sermons. Next day, or within a few days, votes of thanks would be passed and conveyed to the preachers, generally with a request to print their sermons, by named members, generally their original sponsors. Then the process was repeated. Similar ceremonies took place all over the country. Nor was it only on the last Wednesday of the month that Parliament subjected itself and the people to this heavy dose of religion. Special crises called forth special fasts also: fasts to celebrate the opening of the Westminster Assembly, to desire blessings on the parliamentary armies when in difficulty, to persuade God to remove "a great judgment of rain and waters" or "abundance of rain and unseasonable weather," and to abate such calamities as the miseries of Scotland during the triumphs of Montrose, the incidence of the plague, divers crying sins and enormities of the Church, the spread of heresies and blasphemies, etc. There were also, when occasion called for them, special days of thanksgiving. All these entailed special sermons, whose preachers were chosen, thanked and invited to print in the same way.

Of course the procedure looks smoother in the parliamentary journals than it was in fact. In fact the fasts were always regarded as party propaganda and, in consequence, were often resented in the country. From the beginning there were complaints. Even Members of Parliament were accused of forgoing abstinence and sermons in order to drink and dine in taverns, and royalist pamphleteers and poets made merry at the sleek, black-robed, well-paid Marshall who lifted his nose like a whale to spout, and beat and banged his pulpit as he thundered damnation to the absentees. In the country the inattention was even worse, and a constant stream of orders and ordinances, imposing new burdens of enforcement and new penalties for omission, showed that the parliamentary example was ill followed. Still, at the centre a good appearance was kept up. There was also, in London, a good supply of preachers. From the start, as "scandalous" ministers were ejected, country preachers, encouraged by their local Members of Parliament, poured in to compete for their places, and from 1643 the Westminster Assembly provided a constant reservoir of clerical talent, eager to display itself to the new, many-headed patron of the Church. For the first few years, therefore—as long as the Parliament was united—the system reflected parliamentary policy. It also reflected the shifts in that policy. Out of many possible instances, a few must suffice.

The first great test of Pym's leadership, after the outbreak of war, came in the early months of 1643. At first, both sides had expected a quick victory: neither was prepared for a long war. Consequently, when both had failed in their first objectives, the pressure towards compromise was irresistible and Pym was obliged to negotiate with the king. But as he had little faith in the king's peaceful intentions, it was essential that the "treaty of Oxford" should not be interpreted as a sign of weakness on the parliamentary side. If the conservatives on Pym's right were willing to accept a treacherous peace, he must rely on the radicals on his left and show that, with their support, he would fight on for a more stable settlement. This resolution was clearly shown, on the very eve of the negotiations, by one of the fast sermons of 25 January 1643. It was a sermon which might seem, to anyone unaware of the real situation at Oxford, singularly inappropriate to the opening of a peace treaty.

The preacher was John Arrowsmith, who had been proposed by Pym's step-brother, Francis Rous. His text was Leviticus xxvi. 25, "I shall bring a sword upon you, that shall avenge the quarrel of my covenant," and his message was that bloody civil wars were peculiar signs of God's blessing on a country, and that England, having now been singled out for this favour, must fight it out, exacting "like for like and, particularly, blood for blood (Rev. xvi. 5-6)." [17] After listing the sins which called most loudly for blood, and which included especially the neglect of God's covenant and disrespect for its messengers, the clergy, he gave his specific instructions. He reminded his hearers that the English victory over the Scots at Musselburgh, a century before, had been won at the hour when Parliament, in London, ordered the burning of "idolatrous images." Thus if Pym held out his right hand to treat with the king, with his left he pointed the way to a more radical war and a new campaign of iconoclasm. Five days later he emphasized his threat by pushing through Parliament an ordinance abolishing episcopacy and including the ratification of the ordinance in the terms of the treaty. No doubt this paper ordinance was as yet merely a threat, to be withdrawn if necessary: Pym would always have settled for "moderate episcopacy"; but such withdrawal presupposed a real settlement. At present he suspected the king's motives and was determined to negotiate only from the appearance of strength and radical resolve.

The event justified him. In fact the king had no intention of making peace. He was playing for time till the queen should arrive from Holland with the means of victory. And in fact, all through the first three weeks of the treaty, as he spun it out, he was waiting for news of her arrival at Newcastle upon Tyne. Finally, after a series of dramatic adventures at sea, her little fleet arrived at Bridlington. By that time Parliament had been able to draw the moral, and on 22 February, as she drew towards land, the fast-preachers made it clear. They were John Ellis, invited once again by Rous, and William Bridge, whom Bishop Wren had driven abroad, but who had now returned, like the queen, from Holland, to be "one of the demagogues of the Parliament."

Ellis was chiefly concerned to expose the dangers of "a false peace" —that is, one which did not guarantee the future by "putting Christ into the treaty." He urged his hearers to remember the message of his predecessor Mr. Arrowsmith and make no peace till the false brethren and enemies of Christ had been trodden down like straw in the dunghill. Bridge was more explicit. Kings, he explained, were sometimes, like King David, too indulgent to their families, and he thought it necessary to warn King Charles against this fault. "Sir," he exclaimed, "your Absalom and your Adonijah, you may love them well, but not better than your own peace, your own people. If the Queen of your

---

17. John Arrowsmith, *The Covenant's Avenging Sword Brandished* (1643).

bosom stand in competition with your kingdom, you must not love her better than us, than it." He then quoted an edifying story from Turkish history. A Turkish emperor, he said, was charged by his subjects with neglect of his kingdom, "moved thereto (as they alleged) by the too much love of a lady, his concubine; whom in a great assembly the emperor showed to all his people on a time, and they concluded that, in regard of her excellent beauty, they could not blame him for being misled. But, saith he, that you may know how little I regard her in comparison with you, he drew his scimitar and killed her before them all." [18] Such was the example, which Mr. Bridge held up to Charles I, preparing to welcome, after a year's absence, his beautiful queen.

So the attack was launched on the queen, as the fomenter of civil war, the irreconcilable enemy of "settlement." In March, while still formally treating with the king, Parliament invaded the queen's chapel, broke up its furniture, expelled its priests. Then, on 16 April, the treaty was broken off, and radical passions had to be enlisted in earnest for the renewal of a more desperate war. On 24 April Sir Robert Harley asked for a committee to destroy superstitious monuments in London churches and himself at once set about the work. Two days later it was among headless statues and shivered stained-glass windows that the Commons gathered in St. Margaret's to hear the monthly fast sermons. The first, appropriately enough, was by a protégé of Harley himself, a country clergyman from Cheshire who served up the now familiar texts "Curse ye Meroz" and "Cursed be he that keepeth his sword back from blood." The second was by William Greenhill, another of Bishop Wren's victims, famous for his commentary on Ezekiel. His sermon once again was a pointer to immediate policy. He chose the ominous text, "The axe is laid to the root of the tree."

Like Samuel Fairclough two years before, Greenhill demanded "justice on delinquents." Indeed he referred back explicitly to the execution of Strafford. "When your justice fell upon that great cedar-tree above a year and a half ago," he cried, "did not all England tremble?" And now too much time had passed without a second stroke. Though great "delinquents" still lived, the executioner's axe had culpably been allowed to rust. That was most improper. However, he added, regretfully, "if justice be at a stand and cannot take hold of living delinquents to keep the axe from rust, let justice be executed upon lifeless delin-

18. John Ellis, *The Sole Path to a Sound Peace* (1643); Wm. Bridge, *Joab's Counsel and King David's Seasonable Hearing It* (1643).

quents. Are there no altars, no high places, no crucifixes, no crosses in the open street that are bowed unto and idolized? Lay your axe to the roots and hew them down!"[19]

The message was clear, and was instantly obeyed. Two days after the sermon, the terms of Harley's committee were extended to include the destruction of idolatrous monuments in streets and open places. On 2 May Cheapside Cross, that bugbear of the Puritans, the pride and glory of the City, was at last ceremonially hewn down. Thereafter, Parliament turned to "living delinquents." There can be no doubt who was in the mind of Greenhill when he spoke of living delinquents whom justice could not yet reach. It was the queen. And sure enough, on 23 May, Henry Darley proposed her impeachment. Darley was Pym's oldest ally and agent, and Pym himself intervened often in the debate and finally himself carried the resolution up to the Lords. Another member who intervened was Sir Peter Wentworth, who stated that it was high time to lay the axe to the root. The reference to Greenhill's sermon is obvious; and indeed it was Sir Peter Wentworth who had proposed Greenhill as preacher to Parliament. A week later another more accessible "living delinquent" felt the consequences of the same sermon. In the small hours of the morning a party of musketeers commanded by the implacable William Prynne, breaking into his room in the Tower, seized the documents, the diary, even the devotions of the Parliament's forgotten prisoner, Archbishop Laud. His impeachment too, long laid aside, was now to be resumed.

The spring and summer of 1643 was Pym's most radical period. He had to be radical. The position of Parliament seemed desperate, and at times his own position in Parliament seemed desperate too. Unless he kept left, he would lose control of it to the real radicals, Henry Marten, Alderman Penington and their friends. But Pym by himself was not a real radical. Always he saw past the immediate radical gestures to the ultimate conservative settlement. Therefore he never yielded anything substantial to the radicals on his left. Radical gestures could be forgotten, radical ordinances reversed, broken windows repaired. In the autumn of 1643, thanks to the Scottish alliance and the failure of Waller's Plot—dramatically revealed in the middle of the monthly fast sermon[20]—Pym recovered his central position; his chief rival, Henry

19. William Greenhill, 'Αξίνη πρὸς τὴν 'Ρίζαν (1643).

20. Both Thomas May (*The History of the Parliament*, 1647, p. 45) and Clarendon (*History of the Rebellion*, III, 44) mention that the news of Waller's Plot was publicly

Marten, was expelled from Parliament; and a new policy could be adopted. When Pym died, in December 1643, nothing irrevocable had been done. The queen was still unimpeached, Archbishop Laud was still alive, the episcopal Church was destroyed on paper only. A stroke of the pen could restore it: its lands were unsold. So when Stephen Marshall preached his master's funeral sermon, its message was neither radical nor sanguinary. It did not need to be. It was merely a plea for perseverance in the long, just, necessary civil war.[21]

If 1643 had begun as the year of the radicals, 1644 began as the year of the Scots. In December 1643 the Scotch commissioners and Scotch ministers returned to London and at once showed their resolution by boycotting Pym's funeral sermon. In 1641 they had been sent empty away, but this time they meant business. "Nothing for nothing" was their rule. If they were to come as deliverers, they must receive the price; and the price had long ago been stated: in order to guarantee the revolution in Scotland, England too must adopt a full Presbyterian system, on "the Scots model." That meant, incidentally, that the English Parliament, like the Scotch, accept the orders of a General Assembly of the Church. The Westminster Assembly, from a mere advisory body, a reservoir of preachers chosen by the lay Parliament, must assume command. As practised hands in clerical and political intrigue, the Scotch ministers were confident that they could bring this about. They obtained seats in the Assembly; they organized a party, gave orders, reported home. And they secured invitations to preach not merely, as in 1640–41, to the gaping populace of London, but to the Parliament itself. This was an opportunity not to be missed.

The Scotch ministers preached to the Commons on the four successive fast-days after their arrival. The series was opened by Alexander Henderson, the framer of the National Covenant of Scotland. He

communicated to Pym during the monthly fast, and Clarendon emphasizes the ominous significance of the gesture: "The time when Mr. Pimm was made acquainted with it is not known, but the circumstances of the publishing it were such as filled all men with apprehensions. It was on Wednesday the 31st May, their solemn fast-day, when being all at their sermon in St. Margaret's church in Westminster, according to their custom, a letter or message is brought privately to Mr. Pimm, who thereupon with some of the most active members rise from their seats, and after a little whispering together remove out of the church: this could not but exceedingly affect those who stayed behind."

21. S. Marshall, Θρηνῳδία, *The Church's Lamentation* (1643).

delivered, according to his colleague Robert Baillie, "a most gracious, wise and learned sermon" urging the English legislature to repair its past errors and now, though late, build the house of the Lord in England. The other three ministers, Samuel Rutherford, Baillie himself and George Gillespie, pressed the same message. England, said Gillespie, had been culpably slow in following the good examples of Scotland. The whole nation was guilty of scandalous laxity in the past, still unredeemed. Why had not the idolatrous high places been taken away? The trouble was, England was intolerably Erastian: it put its trust in the laity, not the clergy: "it did even make an idol of this Parliament and trusted to its own strength and armies." No wonder God had been greatly provoked and had visited the guilty country with defeat, until it had drawn the correct deductions and appealed to Scotland. From now on, given due obedience, all would be well: "Christ hath put Antichrist from his outer works in Scotland and he is now come to put him from his inner works in England." Baillie, in printing his sermon, rubbed it in even deeper. He was astonished, he told Francis Rous, the chairman of Parliament's committees on religion in England, that "the wheels of the Lord's chariot should move with so slow a pace." This "wearisome procrastination to erect the discipline of God" was inexplicable "to mine and every common understanding." It caused millions to live in every kind of carnal sin "without the control of any spiritual correction." All this was the result of a deplorable freedom of speech in the Assembly. Such things could not happen in Scotland . . . By a happy irony, Baillie sent an inscribed presentation copy of the sermon to "the most lernit, his noble friend Mr. Selden, in testimony of his high respect," adding the words τὸ μέλλον ἀόρατον, "the future is invisible." It was indeed. Long and loud Baillie would afterwards lament the ruin of all his plans by "the insolent absurdity" of that "head of the Erastians," John Selden.[22]

So the Scots, from the parliamentary pulpit, laid down the new party line, their party line. Unfortunately, as they soon found, the line was not followed. They had been invited merely out of civility, and once civility was satisfied, they were ignored. Except for an invitation to Alexander Henderson to preach on the day of thanksgiving for Marston

22. Alexander Henderson, *A Sermon Preached to the House of Commons* (1643); S. Rutherford [same title] (1644); R. Baillie, *Satan The Leader in Chief* . . . (1644); G. Gillespie, *A Sermon before the House of Commons* (1644). Baillie's inscribed presentation copy to Selden is now in the Bodleian Library, Oxford.

Moor, a Scotch victory, they were never invited to preach to the Commons again; and their English successors were lamentably tame and Erastian. On one occasion, indeed, Baillie could report "two of the most Scottish and free sermons that ever I heard anywhere." This was in the autumn of 1644, on the special fast-day for the armies of the Lord General, Essex, then in straits in the west: the two preachers then "laid well about them and charged public and parliamentary sins strictly on the backs of the guilty." And frequently the London clergy, responding to Scottish pressure in the Assembly, and excited by the prospect of clerical power, let fly at the error of toleration, at antinomian doctrines or at preaching tradesmen. But in general the Scots found that their labours were in vain. They colonized the Westminster Assembly only to find the Assembly itself ignored by the Parliament. The Parliament insisted on choosing its own preachers; naturally it chose those whom it could trust; and the preachers thus chosen, as Baillie lamented, spoke "before the Parliament with so profound a reverence as truly took all edge from their exhortations and made all applications to them toothless and adulatorious."[23]

However, one occasion should be recorded which may be regarded as a Scottish victory. In the autumn of 1644, while the Scots could boast of Marston Moor, the English armies were everywhere in difficulties. At Westminster tempers were frayed, Cromwell was attacking his commanding general, the Earl of Manchester, and the Scots were throwing themselves eagerly into the quarrel. Some radical gesture was needed to emphasize ultimate solidarity, some scapegoat, on whom all could agree, must be sacrificed. It happened that, at this time, the long, desultory trial of Archbishop Laud had at last reached the point of decision. All the evidence had been heard, and it seemed that, legally, he must be acquitted. But in fact the old archbishop was too good a scapegoat to miss. Presbyterians and Independents alike hated him. The Scots, in particular, pressed for his death. So the leaders of Parliament decided that he must die. And once again, as with Strafford, their decision was made clear through official fast sermons.

A special fast for the union of the parliamentary armies was held on 22 October. On that day Laud's room in the Tower was once again vainly raided for evidence on which to destroy him. At the same time Edmund Calamy, preaching before the Commons, reminded them of "all the guilty blood that God requires you in justice to shed, and you

---

23. Baillie, *Letters and Journals* (Edinburgh, 1841–42), II, 220–21.

do spare." [24] A few days later "many thousand citizens" petitioned for "justice" on delinquents, and Members of Parliament who sought to reject the petition were voted down. Then, on 30 October, came the monthly fast. "When your gins and snares catch any of the bloody birds," cried the Rev. Henry Scudder, "dally not with them: blood will have blood; contract not their bloodguiltiness upon your own souls by an unwarranted clemency and mildness." Would God, exclaimed the Rev. Francis Woodcock, the robe of justice were often "dyed in a deeper colour with the blood of delinquents. It is that which God and man calls for. God repeats it, *Justice, Justice*; we, echoing God, cry *Justice, Justice*." [25]

These were the sermons to the Commons. But sentence must be passed by the Lords, and the Lords were still sticklers for legality. What preacher, in these circumstances, would the Lords choose? In fact, they found a way of evading the problem. For the fast-day of 30 October they did not choose their own preachers but, only five days before the ceremony, invited the Westminster Assembly to appoint them. [26] The Assembly, of course, was glad to do so; the Scots, naturally, were delighted by this unusual subservience of a lay body; and the Lords heard a predictable sermon. The Rev. Edmund Staunton admitted that he had had "short warning"; but he did not have to look far for his matter. The City petition for the blood of delinquents, he said, had suggested his subject. So he sang the praises of Phinehas, who did not wait for legal authority before spearing Zimri and the Midianite woman, and of the eunuchs who threw down Jezebel so that "her blood was sprinkled on the wall"; he lamented the wickedness of Saul who omitted to hew Agag in pieces; "and now," he ended, "could I lift up my voice as a trumpet, had I the shrill cry of an angel which might be heard from east to west, from north to south, in all the corners of the kingdom, my note should be *Execution of Justice, Execution of Justice, Execution of Justice!* That is God's way to pacify wrath: *Then stood up Phinehas and executed judgment, and so the plague was stayed*." [27]

Next day, with mechanical precision, the House of Commons

24. Edmund Calamy, *England's Antidote against the Plague of Civil War* (1644).

25. Henry Scudder, *God's Warning to England* (1644); Francis Woodcock, *Christ's Warning Piece* (1644).

26. *Lords' Journals*, VII, 44.

27. Edmund Staunton, *Phinehas' Zeal in Execution of Judgment* (1644).

dropped the impeachment of Laud and proceeded by way of attainder to destroy him, guilty or not, and cast his head before the king as a preliminary to the treaty of Uxbridge, just in case he should doubt their radical resolve.

But if the destruction of Laud represented a victory for the Scots, it was a very slight victory compared with the defeat inflicted on them in the same months by the internal revolution in the English Parliament. For those were the months in which Vane and Cromwell, the Independents, established their authority and, in the New Model Army, forged a weapon which would soon eliminate the Scots from England and defeat them in Scotland. How deeply the Scots committed themselves to the losing side in that internal English struggle is vividly shown in Baillie's letters, and much of the hatred of Cromwell for the Scots, and their consequent misfortunes, dated from those days when they had sought to have him impeached, like Laud, as an "incendiary" between the two kingdoms. The climax of the struggle came in December 1644 with the proposal of the Self-Denying Ordinance; and in the methods by which Vane sought to carry this crucial ordinance he showed himself, in tactics if not in spirit, the true disciple of Pym.

The immediate chain of events began on 9 December 1644. On that date a report was due from the committee to which the bitter quarrel between Cromwell and the Earl of Manchester had been referred. The chairman of the committee was Zouche Tate. Instead of reporting on the particular issue, Tate submitted a general conclusion "that the chief causes of our division are pride and covetousness." Thereupon Cromwell delivered his famous speech about the moral decline of Parliament and the necessity for self-denial; Tate proposed a resolution that no Member of Parliament should, during the war, hold military or civil office; Vane seconded the proposal; and in the mood of the moment it was accepted by the House. A committee was instructed to bring the resolution forward as an ordinance.

This was a good beginning, but as yet it was only a beginning. The ordinance still had to be framed and read three times by the Commons. Meanwhile the mood of the moment might pass. And even if the ordinance passed the Commons, the Lords would certainly see it as an attack upon their authority. It was therefore essential to Vane and his friends to prolong the confessional mood and to spread it, if possible, to the Lords. For such a purpose they resolved, in Clarendon's words, "to pursue the method in which they had been hitherto so successful, and to prepare and ripen things in the Church that they might afterwards, in due time, grow to maturity in the Parliament." On 11 December, the day on which the ordinance was first read, the Commons agreed to hold a solemn fast in which they would humble themselves for their "particular and parliamentary sins" and so secure divine support for their future measures. This fast was fixed only a week ahead—a sure sign of immediate political necessity. Moreover, it had certain special features. First, the Lords were invited to celebrate it together with the Commons: instead of choosing their own preachers, they would thus have to listen to the preachers already chosen by the Commons. This also entailed a change of place. Neither Henry VII's chapel nor St. Margaret's would hold both Houses together, and Lincoln's Inn chapel was finally chosen. Secondly, the whole service was invested with a peculiar secrecy. Cries for the blood of "delinquents" might serve to rally the people, but the sins of the Parliament could be opened only in private. Strict measures were therefore devised to exclude the public from Lincoln's Inn chapel on 18 December while Lords and Commons listened "for eight or ten hours" to Thomas Hill, Obadiah Sedgwick and the inevitable Stephen Marshall. And these preachers, though thanked by both Houses, were not invited to print, and did not print their sermons.

For this reason we do not know exactly what they said, but there is no reason to distrust the general account which has been preserved by Clarendon.[28] After appropriate preliminary orisons, the preachers, he tells us, delivered their sermons, in which, "let their texts be what they would," they told the Houses plainly and at great length that all their troubles sprang from private greed and ambition which was alienating the people and postponing all hope of reformation. Finally, "when they had exaggerated these reproaches as pathetically as they could . . . they fell again to their prayers, that God would take his own work into His hand, and if the instruments He had already employed were not worthy to bring so glorious a design to a conclusion, that He would

28. Clarendon, *History of the Rebellion*, III, 456–60. S. R. Gardiner (*Great Civil War*, 1901, II, 91) refers to Clarendon's "blundering account" which, he says, is "plainly inaccurate" because Clarendon presupposes a fast of which there is no record in the parliamentary journals and which could have taken place only on a Sunday, i.e., 8 Dec., a day "on which no fast was ever appointed." But this criticism, which suggests that Clarendon, on the basis of mere "Oxford gossip," invented a non-existent fast, is in fact based on a misunderstanding: a misunderstanding which is at once cleared up when it is realized that Clarendon has confused the initial debate of Monday 9 Dec. with the second debate, and passage of the Ordinance in the Commons, on Thursday 19 Dec. As so often, Clarendon has interpreted the situation correctly, in spite of confusion of detail.

inspire others more fit, who might perfect what was begun and bring the troubles of the nation to a godly period." Next day, in the Commons, Vane dwelt on the lesson of the preachers. If ever God had appeared to the Parliament, he said, it was in the exercises of yesterday. And having enlarged on the holy theme he sped the Self-Denying Ordinance through its third reading and passed it up to the Lords.

It was a brilliant manoeuvre; but in politics there are no short cuts, and the Lords, in spite of their heavy religious battering, were not stunned into submission. It would take another three months, and other methods, before they would finally accept a much modified Self-Denying Ordinance. Nevertheless, the struggle over the Self-Denying Ordinance marked a crucial stage in the eclipse of the Scots. From then onwards they were gradually pushed out of English politics and forced to witness the success of that "high and mighty plot of the Independents," which Baillie had foreseen, "to have gotten an army for themselves under Cromwell" and so to push on with a purely English revolution.[29]

The Scots did indeed find one opportunity of fighting back, at least from the pulpit. This came in the summer of 1645. By that time their own position had become very delicate. On the one hand they had, as they felt, triumphed in the Westminster Assembly and, through it, were demanding the instant, overdue establishment in England of a Calvinist theocracy, complete with all-powerful General Assembly, ruling elders, and full powers of excommunication. On the other hand, even as they pressed their claims abroad, their position at home was in jeopardy. While Cromwell was winning victory after victory in England, in Scotland Montrose was master of almost the whole country. It was therefore significant that at this moment the Commons appointed as fast-preacher a man who, in the Westminster Assembly, was already known as an Erastian friend of Selden, an enemy of Scotch claims. This was Thomas Coleman, formerly a rector in Lincolnshire, now—as once before—sponsored by the two members for his county, Sir John Wray and Sir Edward Ayscough. In his sermon Coleman urged that the lay legislature of England "establish as few things *jure divino* as can well be," allow no rules to have divine sanction without clear scriptural warrant, and "lay no more burden of government upon the shoulders of ministers than Christ hath plainly laid upon them." The clergy, he said, should be content to be secured in learning and supplied with main-

29. Baillie, *Letters and Journals*, ii, 246.

tenance: Church government they should leave entirely to Parliament, for "a Christian magistrate, as a Christian magistrate, is a governor in the Church." In this manner the English Parliament, triumphant at Naseby, gave its answer to the Scotch General Assembly, reeling under the victories of Montrose.[30]

Coleman was not an Independent. He explicitly opposed Independency. He was a "Presbyterian" — but an English "Presbyterian," and the Scotch Presbyterians were aghast at his doctrines. They had already been very busy in the Assembly: a "blasphemous book" had taken up much of their time "before we got it burnt by the hand of the hangman." Now they found themselves faced by Coleman. To be silent under such an attack was impossible; but where could they counter-attack? The House of Commons was no good: the majority there were "either half or whole Erastians." But by good luck another opportunity presented itself. The House of Lords, commiserating with the military disasters of the Scots, had invited the four dominies to preach at four successive fasts and the last of these occasions was still to come. It was to be on 27 August, and the preacher was to be the youngest, most learned, most argumentative of the four, George Gillespie.

Gillespie seized his opportunity. Instead of lamenting the miseries and perhaps acknowledging the sins of his country, as the occasion required, he turned on Coleman. Coleman, he said, had been neither active nor passive on the side of reformation "but will needs appear on the stage against it." His views struck at the root of all Church government, were contrary to the Word of God, the Solemn League and Covenant, the opinions of other Reformed Churches, and the votes of Parliament and Assembly. They had given no small scandal and offence ... But Gillespie soon found that he himself had caused no less scandal, especially by misusing such an occasion. The controversy thus roused rumbled on, with increasing acrimony, for six months. Sides were taken; pamphlets proliferated. But whatever the power-hungry clergy of London thought, inside the Parliament the views of Coleman prevailed. Never again, even in the period of "Presbyterian" domination, was a Scotsman invited to preach to the English Parliament.[31]

Indeed, 1645 saw the end of Scotch influence in England. As the English "Presbyterians" asserted themselves, it became clear that they were not

30. Thomas Coleman, *Hope Deferred and Dashed* (1645).

31. G. Gillespie, *A Sermon Preached before the House of Lords* (1645). See also Baillie, *Letters and Journals*, ii, 306; *Cal. S.P. Dom. 1645–7*, p. 127.

really Presbyterians at all—the Scots had merely imposed the label on them. Even Stephen Marshall, Baillie now discovered, was really little better than an Independent: he "miskens us altogether," Baillie lamented: "he is for a middle way of his own." And meanwhile, even Marshall was finding his position as the oracle of Parliament challenged by more radical preachers imposed upon Parliament by the triumphant Cromwell. In 1645–46, the year of final victory, new names begin to appear as fast-preachers. The old regulars, Calamy and Burges, Sedgwick and Case, and many others who will soon abandon the revolution, are joined by their future supplanters, William Strong, Peter Sterry, Thomas Goodwin, John Owen, Nicholas Lockyer, Walter Cradocke, William Dell, Hugh Peter.

Above all, Hugh Peter. What Marshall was to Pym, Hugh Peter is to Cromwell. If Marshall preached electioneering sermons before the Parliament of 1640, Peter would ride round the country "making burgesses for Parliament" before the "recruiting" elections of 1646. If Marshall declared the reforming, political programme of Pym in 1640, Peter would declare the radical, social policy of Cromwell in 1647. If Marshall preached the thanksgiving sermon for the peaceful victories of 1641, Peter would preach the thanksgiving sermon for the military victories of 1646. If Marshall holloa'd the parliamentary pack onwards into war in 1642, Peter, in 1647, would holloa the Army onwards into revolution. If Marshall pressed his unwanted spiritual services upon Archbishop Laud as he was led to the block in 1645, Peter would utter his hideous, vindictive texts in the ears of a yet greater victim, as he was sent to the block in 1649. Both were great emergency preachers. In delicate crises, when other men hung back, they would come forward. But the occasions were different. Marshall, like Pym, sought always to preserve the Parliament, to carry it forward, armed and united, on the old path to reform; Peter, like Cromwell, would seek, with new allies, to hack a shorter, bloodier way to what he valued above any political form: a new society.[32]

Only one of Peter's fast sermons was ever printed. It was the thanksgiving sermon for victory preached on 2 April 1646. Like Marshall in 1641, when the Parliament seemed to have won its bloodless victory, he announced the present year as *annus mirabilis*, the most glorious year since the year of the Armada. "Oh the blessed change we see, that can travel from Edinburgh to the Land's End in Cornwall, who not

32. For Peter, see especially R. F. Stearns, *Hugh Peter, The Strenuous Puritan* (Urbana, 1954).

long since were blocked up at our doors! To see the highways occupied again; to hear the carter whistling to his toiling team; to see the hills rejoicing, the valleys laughing!" Even Germany, by now, seemed to be "lifting up her lumpish shoulder"; even "the thin-cheeked Palatinate" looked hopeful; the "over-awed French peasant" was studying his liberty, and the Dutch remembered how they had "bought their freedom with many, many thousands of good old Elizabeth shillings." "All Protestant Europe seems to get new colour in her cheeks"; why then should not England too flourish again?[33] And just as Marshall's thanksgiving sermon had been followed by blueprints for the new society which men believed to be within their reach, so Peter's thanksgiving sermon also announced a new spate of social pamphlets. Hartlib and Dury, the original prophets of the "country party," rushed into print again; Dury had been invited to preach before Parliament; and Hugh Peter himself, in pamphlet after pamphlet, projected the new social reforms which could be achieved, if not by the Parliament, then directly, outside Parliament, by the Army.

As yet, these new preachers of 1645–46 had to be discreet. To the Parliament, political settlement came before social change, and the pace must not be forced. Peter kept his social pamphlets distinct from his parliamentary sermon. John Owen attached his scheme of Church government to his fast sermon only when printed. William Dell went too far and paid the price. He kept his fast sermon within bounds but then published it with an outrageous preface. He was summoned before the House of Commons and disciplined. Nor was he ever allowed to preach before Parliament again. Even the Rump Parliament, which made him Master of Caius College, refused to have him: when his name was suggested, the House, for the only time on such a matter, divided; and he was voted down.[34]

Political settlement or social reform, an imperfect political compromise as the basis for future reformation or a social reformation now, without tarrying for any—that was indeed the issue of 1646–47, the issue on which Parliament and Army ultimately divided and through whose division revolution came in. And in that revolution, which wrecked the Parliament, the old methods of parliamentary busi-

33. Hugh Peter, *God's Doing and Man's Duty* (1646).

34. Dell's sermon (25 Nov. 1646) was printed as *Right Reformation*; the *Commons' Journals* report the sequel (v, 10 etc.). The abortive attempt to invite Dell to preach to the Rump was made on 28 Jan. 1653 (*C.J.* VII, 252).

ness were wrecked too. Pym and his friends, even Vane, St. John and Holles, might "tune the pulpits" in order to keep Parliament and people together along a prepared line; but how could this be done when Parliament was at the mercy of its own warring parties, and of military force? By now the London clergy, the natural source of fast-preachers, were more "Presbyterian" than the "Presbyterians" in Parliament, and the Army was more radical, more Independent than the Independents in Parliament. In such circumstances clergymen hardly knew what to say. There were too many tuners and no agreement about the musical notes. This became painfully clear in June 1647 when the mutinous Army, having seized the king, was hovering ominously around London, uncertain as yet whether to strike.

One of the preachers for the June fast was Nathaniel Ward, recently returned from New England. He was, as he afterwards wrote, "truly unwilling to come upon any public stage, knowing how perilous and jealous the times are"; and in fact he contrived to give universal offence. He urged Parliament to restore the king to his authority and establish the Church on a sure basis: "till these two wheels be set right, all the lesser are like to go wrong"; and so he proposed that the Parliament pay off the Army, reassert military discipline, correct the extremer forms of heresy in the ranks, and remedy some obvious grievances. It was eminently sensible advice, but unfortunately timed: only two days earlier the Army had forced the eleven "Presbyterian" leaders to withdraw from the House and presented a series of much more radical demands. Ward's commiseration of the king did not please the "Presbyterians"; his proposals for dealing with the Army infuriated the Army. His sermon "gave offence" to a terrorized House; in the Army it was described as "worse than Edwards his *Gangraena*"; and he was neither thanked nor asked to print.[35]

Next month the fast-day was even worse timed. It was due to fall on 28 July. But on 26 July the City mob invaded the Parliament and forced the House of Commons to reverse its recent votes and recall the eleven members; after which both Houses adjourned themselves till 30 July. The preachers thus delivered their sermons in a moment of "Presbyterian" counter-revolution. How the London preachers took

35. *C.J.* v, 205, 228; Rushworth, *Historical Collections*, vi, i, 596; *Clarke Papers*, i (Camden Society, 1891), 150. The sermon was afterwards printed "without the knowledge, or consent of the author," but containing a "Letter to some Friends" signed by him (*A Sermon preached before the House of Commons*, 1647).

advantage of that counter-revolution is recorded in the diary of Lord Lisle, a Member of Parliament: "on that day Mr. Edwards and divers other ministers in London stirred up the people in their sermons to raise arms to suppress the army, abusing the day which was set apart for the calamities of bleeding Ireland and exciting the people to put this kingdom again into blood, and so to make it bleeding England also." [36] But two days later, the illusion of "Presbyterian" victory faded. The Speakers of both Houses fled to the protection of the Army, the Army marched on London, and by 4 August Parliament and City alike were in its power. Fortunately the parliamentary preachers seem to have been very prudent, for they were thanked not only by the "Presbyterian" Parliament of 2 August, but also (since the proceedings of those days were afterwards annulled) by the Independent Parliament of 25 August. They showed their prudence still further in omitting, though invited, to print any of their sermons. [37]

The man who did publish was Stephen Marshall, who once again, in a moment of crisis, emerged as the politician of the hour. Like other men who were neither Cromwellians nor radicals, [38] Marshall believed that, at that moment, the unity of Parliament and Army was all-important and that the alternative would be confusion leading to unconditional royal reaction. So, in these last days of July, he flung himself into action. He made a party in the Westminster Assembly, worked on the aldermen of the City, darted to and fro between Lords, Commons and Army headquarters, and finally, with seventeen supporters in the Assembly, presented a petition to Parliament and City offering to make their peace with the Army. His efforts were successful. The City militia offered no resistance, and the Army entered London without a struggle. When all was over, the defeated party recognized Marshall as the chief architect of their ruin. "In that nick of time," wrote Baillie, when "one stout look more" would have established Presbyterianism for ever, it was Mr. Marshall, "the main instrument" of the Solemn League and Covenant, who, with "his seventeen servants of

36. *Sidney Papers*, ed. R. W. Blencowe (1825), p. 26.

37. The preachers on 28 July were, to the Lords, Christopher Love and Henry Langley and, to the Commons, Benjamin Whichcote and Thomas Jaggard.

38. E.g., like the Earl of Manchester, who had strong personal grounds for opposing Cromwell and who is generally regarded as a "Presbyterian," but who nevertheless joined the Army on this occasion and, being Speaker of the House of Lords, gave it the authority which it needed to overpower the Parliament.

the Synod ... put presently in the Army's power both Parliament, City and nation"; and Denzil Holles, the twice-purged leader of the "Presbyterians" in Parliament, never failed to denounce the former zealot for "Presbyterianism" who, on that occasion, became "a principal instrument" of Cromwell "... going and coming between Westminster and the headquarters, or the Parliament doors soliciting the members of both Houses, persuading them by all manner of arguments, sometimes assurances, sometimes terrifyings, to agree to those things which the Army desired." To Skippon, the commander of the City militia, and "to his chaplain Marshall," wrote Holles, "we must attribute all the evil that has befallen king and kingdom." Naturally, when the purged Parliament obediently voted a day of thanksgiving "for the restoration of the honour and freedom of the Parliament"—i.e., for its rescue by the Army from the "most horrible and abominable rape and violence" of the City mob—it was Stephen Marshall who was invited to preach the main sermon; and he preached it, as we should expect, to some tune. "That apostate," commented Holles, who now found himself accused of dividing king from Parliament, Parliament from City, and City from Army, "went beyond Ela, making the deliverance a greater one than the Gunpowder Treason, as I have been credibly informed by those that heard him."[39]

To Marshall it seemed that the old unity of Parliament had been restored. Once again, thanks to the Army, the old policy of his master, Pym, could be pursued. In fact it was not so. In fact the intervention of the Army proved the end of Parliament as an effective body in politics. This breach is indicated, incidentally, in the fast sermons. For five years the system had worked smoothly. Every month preachers had been chosen, had preached, had been thanked, had been invited to print their sermons, and had printed them. But from that date onwards all changes. Preachers are harder to find; refusals are more frequent; the Parliament becomes more dependent on a few reliable servants. Until 1647 no preacher had preached to either House of Parliament more than once a year, except Marshall and his understudy, the learned Greek and Hebrew scholar Joseph Caryl,[40] who had sometimes

39. For Marshall's part in the events of July–Aug. 1647, see *Lords' Journals*, IV, 368; Baillie, *Letters and Journals*, III, 17, 302, 306; Denzil Holles, *Memoirs* (1699), pp. 88, 110, 123, 143, 160, 168. S. Marshall, *A Sermon Preached to the Two Houses of Parliament* ... (1647).

40. Caryl accompanied Marshall as chaplain to Charles I at Holdenby House. He

preached twice or thrice. But in 1648 Marshall would be called upon seven times, Caryl four times and one other clergyman four times.[41] Finally, even those clergymen who could be prevailed upon to preach fast sermons showed a remarkable reluctance to print them. From the beginning of the monthly system until June 1647 every preacher had been asked to print his sermon, and had printed it. Nathaniel Ward, on 30 June 1647, was the first not to receive such an invitation. Even so, he printed his sermon. But from then on, though invitation remained the rule, printing was the exception. Only five out of the last fourteen fast sermons of 1647 were published, and thereafter the proportion steadily declined.[42] From July 1648 even Marshall forbore to print. It is clear that, from the revolution of 1647, the fast sermons, like the Parliament itself, had lost their purpose.

Nevertheless, on one last occasion the system returned to life. First in April 1641, when Pym had decided to change from legal impeachment to political attainder in order to destroy the life of Strafford, then in October 1644 when Vane had decided, in the same way, to destroy the life of Laud, the preachers had been brought in to announce, and to justify, this fearful change; and how could the grim masters of the Parliament now do less when the victim was both greater and, by now, in their eyes, guiltier than either Strafford or Laud? This time, because of that difference, the pace was slower, the pressure stronger; but the method was the same. The same careful choice, the same exact timing, the same bloodthirsty message indicated the continuity of technique between the judicial murder of the servants and of the master.

It was on 16 November 1648 that the Council of Officers, gathered at St. Albans, received from Henry Ireton the *Remonstrance of the Army*, which he had drawn up during Cromwell's absence in the north. It demanded that the king, as the sole and capital author of all the troubles of the kingdom, be speedily brought to trial. On the very next day the House of Commons had to appoint a preacher for the next fast, for the preacher nominated over a fortnight ago had suddenly withdrawn. This defaulting minister was that same Samuel Fairclough who,

---

was one of the very few ministers who, like Marshall, preached regularly to Parliament during the whole period from 1642 to 1653.

41. The other clergyman was John Bond. Caryl and Bond remained, with John Owen and William Strong, the main preachers of the Rump.

42. Only 13 out of 48 such sermons were printed in 1648, and only 10 out of 56 for the years 1649–53.

in 1641, had first called for the death of Strafford, and who had now, once again, been nominated by his patron. But in the face of these new developments his patron found himself more conservative, and perhaps Fairclough shrank from such a double triumph. In his place a radical Member of Parliament proposed a young clergyman, George Cokayne, minister of St. Pancras, Soper Lane. This was a famous Independent church whose minister was appointed by the parish and whose parishioners included the three pillars of radicalism in the City: Rowland Wilson, who would become sheriff, and Robert Tichborne and John Ireton, who would become lord mayors of the republic. John Ireton was the brother of Henry Ireton, the moving spirit of the revolution. Three days later, Henry Ireton presented the *Remonstrance* to a trembling Parliament, which sought to bury it by postponement. Then, on 29 November, came the fast-day, and the newly appointed Cokayne followed his senior colleague Obadiah Sedgwick into the pulpit.

His message was predictable. In every respect it echoed the *Remonstrance*. From the procrastinating Parliament, Cokayne demanded judgment and that quickly. "Delay not to act for the people's good who have intrusted you." He did not predetermine the method—"we leave that entirely to your wisdom"—nor the sentence—justice should still be "mingled with mercy"; but then neither did his brief, the *Remonstrance*. But his language, like that of the *Remonstrance*, was ominously firm: he reminded the Commons, as they had by now been reminded *ad nauseam*, of Saul and Ahab, who had "ventured God's displeasure" by sparing their captive kings. "Honourable and worthy, if God do not lead you to do justice upon those who have been the great actors in shedding innocent blood, never think to gain their love by sparing of them."[43] When the sermon was over, the thanks of the intimidated House were boldly conveyed by Cokayne's parishioner Rowland Wilson.

The order was given; from now on the events followed. On 1 December 1648 the person of the king was seized. On 6 December the Parliament was purged of its resisting members. It was the greatest purge of all, Pride's Purge. On the very next day the machinery was put in motion. A special fast was declared, and it was declared at once. There was to be no question of waiting for the ordinary monthly fast, whose

---

43. George Cokayne, *Flesh Expiring and the Spirit Inspiring* (1648). The full and laudatory biography of Cokayne by John B. Marsh, *The Story of Harecourt, being the History of an Independent Church* (1871), curiously omits any reference to this part of his sermon, or to any detail which links him with the trial of the king.

preachers had already been appointed before the Purge, no chance of counter-organization. The fast was to be on the morrow, on 8 December; and the preachers were carefully chosen. They were Stephen Marshall and Joseph Caryl, the two preachers most acceptable to the Army, and "the grand journey- or hackney-man of the Army," the "stalking-horse and setting-dog of the grandees of the Army," Hugh Peter.

None of the three sermons was afterwards printed, but the gist of them is clear from contemporary newspaper reports. Marshall and Caryl, the old parliamentary preachers, urged the broken remains of the Parliament, now as in 1647, to preserve harmony with the Army. Hugh Peter, more bluntly, told them to obey their masters. In particular, he advised them "to adjourn till Monday or Tuesday, that they may know how to steer their debates by the resolutions of the soldiery." The Rump of Parliament recognized the voice of its ruler. It adjourned for four days, till Tuesday.[44]

All through the next month Hugh Peter worked hard in favour of the Army and its violent proceedings. This was the time when he earned his sinister reputation as a tribune of revolution, a buffoon-preacher who dragged religion through the gutter and used it to sanctify every incidental indecency of naked power. His next opportunity to preach to the Parliament came on 22 December. This was a special fast-day, hastily appointed "for removing the heavy judgment of God now upon the kingdom." It was celebrated by both Houses together, in St. Margaret's (they could all fit into it comfortably now). The whole churchyard was filled with musketeers and pikemen, to guard the Parliament, and soldiers surrounded the pulpit to guard the preacher. Our accounts of the sermon are imperfect and perhaps exaggerated: they come from contemporary pamphlets and later recollections; but in substance they are no doubt true.[45]

Once again Peter gave the Rump of Parliament its immediate orders. He bade it (as if it had any alternative) put its trust in the Army, which would lead England out of its Egyptian bondage. But how was that to be done? it might be asked. "That," replied Peter, "is not yet revealed to me." Then, placing his head on the pulpit-cushion, he pretended to sleep until a voice from Heaven awoke him with a start, and

44. Stearns, *Hugh Peter*, p. 328. *C.J.* vi, 95.

45. Theodorus Verax [Clement Walker], *Anarchia Anglicana* (1648), *or the History of Independency*, part ii, pp. 49–50: "The Trial of Hugh Peter," in *An Exact and Most Impartial Accompt of the Indictment . . . of 29 Regicides . . .* (1660).

with the answer. "Now I have it," he exclaimed, "by Revelation! Now I shall tell you. This Army must root up monarchy, not only here but in France and other kingdoms round about. This is to bring you out of Egypt. This Army is the corner-stone cut out of the mountain, which must dash the powers of the earth to pieces." As for the objection that such a revolution was "without precedent," Peter soon disposed of that. The Virgin Birth was also without precedent, but it happened. "This is an age to make examples and precedents in." Then the preacher showed what precedent he would establish. He demanded the immediate trial of the king. The citizens of London, the London preachers, were all opposed to such a trial. Peter soon dealt with them. "Those foolish citizens," he said, were like the people of Jerusalem at the time of Christ's crucifixion: "for a little trading and profit they will have Christ (pointing to the redcoats on the pulpit-stairs) crucified and this great Barabbas at Windsor released; but I do not much heed what the rabble says. . . . My Lords, and you noble gentlemen of the House of Commons, you are the Sanhedrin and the Great Council of the Nation, therefore you must be sure to do justice and it is from you we expect it. . . . Do not prefer the great Barabbas, murderer, tyrant and traitor, before these poor hearts . . . the Army, who are our saviours." [46]

Next day the gentlemen of the House of Commons at least obeyed their orders. They set up a committee to consider how to proceed by way of justice against the king. But only four days later, before that committee could report, and before Cromwell himself had made up his mind, another fast-day had come round. This time it was the regular monthly fast, whose preachers, unlike those of 22 December, had been chosen a month before—in fact, before Pride's Purge. This, as it turned out, was unfortunate: it showed that, in revolutionary times, special fast-days, at short notice, were safer than an independent regular routine.

46. Mr. Stearns (*Hugh Peter*, pp. 330–32) makes two separate sermons out of this material, ascribing the passage about Barabbas to a later sermon preached at the time when the Rump was hesitating to pass the Act setting up the High Court of Justice— i.e., between 3 and 6 Jan. But the source—a Mr. Beaver, who heard the sermon and gave evidence at Peter's trial in 1660—is quite clear. He says that the occasion was "a fast at St. Margaret's" in Dec. 1648 "a few days before the House of Commons made that thing called an Act for his [the King's] Trial" (i.e., the ordinance which passed the Commons on 28 Dec.). It is also clear from the text that Peter was preaching to both Houses. All this evidence points conclusively to Peter's official fast sermon of 22 Dec.

One of the ministers chosen proved sound. He was Thomas Brookes, a radical minister whose sponsor, Sir John Bourchier, would survive the purge and become a regicide. Brookes preached a fire-eating sermon demanding justice, whatever the cost. Parliament, he declared, should ignore the clamour of kindred and friends, ignore the "ignorant, sottish people who think that the doing of justice will undo a land," and recognize that, on the contrary, neglect of justice will provoke God "to throw all your religious services as dung in your faces." He therefore recommended to them the classic examples of holy murder and impious clemency: Phinehas who did not wait for judgment; Saul and Ahab who spared the kings whom God had commanded them to kill.[47]

So spoke the morning preacher. It was an echo of the sanguinary sermons of Fairclough, calling for the blood of Strafford, of Scudder and Woodcock and Staunton calling for the blood of Laud; and the Rump Parliament duly approved his sermon. But in the afternoon a different, discordant voice was heard. Thomas Watson, pastor of St. Stephens, Walbrook, was a "Presbyterian" who had been proposed by the "Presbyterian" London merchant John Rolle. But the revolution which had occurred since he had been nominated, and which had probably excluded his sponsor from the House, did not deter him. To a congregation of furious or frightened men, hurrying or hurried blindly forward, he preached one of the boldest sermons that was ever uttered to the Long Parliament. It was a sermon against hypocrisy, and the preacher sketched, in apposite detail, the character of the hypocrite. The hypocrite, he said, is "zealous in lesser things and remiss in greater . . . zealous against a ceremony, a relic or painted glass . . . but in the meantime lives in known sin, lying, defaming, extortion, etc." He is zealous against popery, but makes no conscience of sacrilege, starving out the ministry, "robbing God of his tithes." Then he drew nearer and struck deeper. The hypocrite, he declared, "makes religion a mask to cover his sin." So "Jezebel, that she may colour over her murder, proclaims a fast." Already the congregation of parliamentary saints must have begun to tremble for what would come next. And well they might, for it came hot and strong, even personal. "Many," said the preacher (and there could be no doubt of whom he was thinking), "make religion a cloak for their ambition. Come see my zeal, saith Jehu, for the Lord. No Jehu, thy zeal was for the kingdom. Jehu made religion hold

47. Thomas Brookes, *God's Delight in the Progress of the Upright* (1648).

the stirrup till he got into the saddle and possessed the Crown. This is a most exasperating sin."

Predictably, the Rump did not thank Watson, or invite him to print his sermon. Even the Levellers, who would soon echo his sentiments about Cromwell's "hypocrisy," rejected such an ally. "This Presbyterian proud flesh," they said, "must down with monarchy, one being equal in tyranny with the other." But Watson ignored the implied veto. He published his sermon himself. He had no difficulty in finding a printer. The sermon came out under the same *imprimatur* as the *Serious and Faithful Representation*, the protest of the London clergy against the trial of the king and against the charge that they, by their opposition, had ever intended the destruction of the monarchy.[48]

Immediately after the fast-day, Cromwell made up his mind, and on 28 December the obedient Rump passed the ordinance for the king's trial. Two days later it chose its preachers for the next fast, which was due to fall on 30 January 1649. This time there was to be no chance of error. The two preachers were proposed by two safely radical members, Gilbert Millington and Francis Allen, both of whom would sign the king's death warrant. They were John Cardell and John Owen.

So the most dramatic month of the whole revolution began. At every stage the courage of the regicides was sustained by the shrill voice of the preacher, and the preacher, in that month, was always the same; for if there were several ministers who would press the Parliament to try the king, there was only one who would openly demand his execution. Between 26 December and 30 January there was no official parliamentary fast, but there were plenty of unofficial opportunities, and Peter used them to the full. Every stage of the personal tragedy of Charles I was punctuated by his gleeful exclamations. When the king was fetched from Windsor to St. James's Palace, Peter rode before his coach "like a bishop-almoner . . . triumphing." Himself placed in charge of the palace, he pestered the king to confess his crimes, as he had pestered Archbishop Laud at his trial and the Marquis of Winchester in the smouldering ruins of Basing House. At the solemn fast with which the High Court of Justice began its proceedings he exclaimed rapturously that, "with old Simeon," he could now cry *Nunc dimittis*; for after twenty years of prayer and preaching his eyes had seen salvation. Then he preached his famous sermon on the 149th Psalm:

---

48. Watson's sermon was published as *God's Anatomy upon Man's Heart*. The Leveller comments are from *The Moderate* (no. 25, p. 235, and no. 26, p. 248).

> Let the saints be joyful in glory: let them sing aloud upon their beds.
> Let the high praises of God be in their mouth, and a two-edged
>   sword in their hand;
> To execute vengeance upon the heathen, and punishments upon the
>   people:
> To bind their kings with chains and their nobles with fetters of
>   iron . . .

At critical moments in the trial Peter preached to the soldiers, encouraging them to hope for a bloody verdict; he gave them cues to drown all murmurs of dissent with rhythmical cries of "Justice, Justice!" or "Execution, Execution!"; and when sentence had been given, he preached a final sermon at St. James's Palace itself, choosing as his text Isaiah's famous denunciation of the King of Babylon:

> All the kings of the nations, even all of them, lie in glory, every
> one in his own house.
> But thou art cast out of thy grave like an abominable branch, and
> as the raiment of those that are slain, thrust through with a sword, that
> go down to the stones of the pit: as a carcase trodden under feet.
> Thou shalt not be joined with them in burial, because thou hast destroyed thy land, and slain thy people: the seed of evildoers shall never
> be renowned.

This savoury text Peter had hoped to utter to the face of the king himself; but, as he afterwards regretted, "the poor wretch would not hear me." Three days later the monthly fast was postponed for one day in order that London might witness a more spectacular ceremony: the execution of the king.

Next day the more prudent clergy emerged again. Messrs. Cardell and Owen duly congratulated the Rump on its great act of justice; they paraded, in retrospective vindication, the old gory texts about the wicked kings of Israel; and then they looked forward to the long-delayed reformation, the social reformation of which men had dreamed in 1640, in 1641, in 1646–47, only to be blocked by recurrent obstacles: Strafford, the Irish rebellion, the revolutionary crisis, and the second civil war. Now at last, it seemed, all the obstacles, even the greatest, had been destroyed: the way was clear. The Rump, said Owen, was God's instrument of justice which it was sin to resist; and when he published his sermon he appended to it a treatise on the religious reforms which were required in order to vindicate this title. The kingdom, said Cardell, was "an old ruinous house," ready, unless repaired or rebuilt, "to drop down upon your heads": there were "worm-eaten beams," "rotten posts and studs . . . that will never serve again, that must of necessity be removed."[49]

On the same day Stephen Marshall preached to the Lords. Unlike his colleagues, he was too prudent to print his sermon, but we can hardly doubt its gist. Marshall had travelled the whole way with the revolution hitherto. The spiritual ally of Pym had become the spiritual ally of Cromwell. From a "Presbyterian" he had become an Independent. Like Cromwell, like all the Independents, he was indifferent to "forms of government."[50] By agreeing to preach on the very morrow of regicide, even though it was to the reluctant Lords, he to some extent condoned the act. As the Presbyterian Robert Baillie afterwards wrote, "he was more satisfied with the change of government, both civil and ecclesiastical, than many of his brethren"; and the moderate royalist Thomas Fuller, no unfriendly biographer, noted that "he was of so supple a soul that he brake not a joint, nay sprained not a sinew, in the alteration of the times."[51]

Marshall's sermon to the House of Lords was its epitaph. When Cardell had spoken to the Commons of the rotten posts and studs of the kingdom which must be removed, there could be little doubt of his meaning. In fact, within a week, the House of Lords was abolished; but the House of Commons went on, and Marshall went on with it. But how different it must have seemed to him since the great days when, with Calamy and Burges, he had laid down its tactics and preserved the unity of its 400 members: when he had instructed them in St. Margaret's how to vote and then shepherded them busily into Westminster to register their votes; when he had trumpeted them into war and carried them, dwindling but still united, through the years of misfortune! By now all his old colleagues had fallen away. Calamy and Burges had joined the "Presbyterian" opposition; Gauden had passed through "Presbyterianism" to royalism, and had compiled the most famous, most effective of

49. J. Owen, *A Sermon Preached to the House of Commons* . . . (1649); J. Cardell, *God's Wisdom Justified and Man's Folly Condemned* (1649). Owen's sermon, in the preface to which, as Wood says (*Athenae Oxonienses*, IV, 103), "he doth insolently father the most hellish notion of the preceding day," was among the books formally condemned and burnt by the University of Oxford in 1685.

50. As he put it in *A Letter to a Friend in the Country* (1643), "among the divers kinds of lawful governments, monarchy, aristocracy and democracy, no one of them is so appointed of God as to exclude the other from being a lawful government."

51. Fuller, *The History of the Worthies of England* (1672), II, 52.

royalist tracts. In order to find fast-preachers, Parliament now had to draw on radical Army chaplains and furious sectaries. And in any case, it might be asked, what was the point of regular fast sermons now? Parliament had shrunk to a mere handful of commoners. Marshall himself had done his best to stay the shrinkage. He had protested against Pride's Purge—though, as always, he had clung to the winning side.[52] He would be used by Cromwell to woo back the "Secluded Members," but in vain.[53] Those who now sat at Westminster were so firmly held together by common interest, even common crime, that the old device of parliamentary sermons seemed hardly necessary.

Indeed, at such a time, political sermons were an added risk. The Rump had had one taste of the danger in Watson's sermon of 26 December. It had another on 25 February when Thomas Cawton, a London minister, publicly prayed before the Lord Mayor and Aldermen for Charles II and all the royal family. For this "treasonable prayer" the Council of State promptly sent him to the Gatehouse. Meanwhile *Eikon Basiliké* was circulating everywhere to encourage misguided religious devotion to the Stuarts. Nor was it only the royalist and Presbyterian enemies of the republic whose views were expressed in religious form. Levellers and Anabaptists on the left of the precarious new government were already preaching a "second revolution." Faced by this double danger, the Rump Parliament began to think that political sermons had lost something of their charm. Like so many revolutionary parties, it decided that liberty of expression was a luxury to be allowed only in the days of opposition; and at the end of March it acted accordingly. On 28 March it decided to bring in an Act ordering preachers in London not to meddle with matters of government but "only to apply themselves to their duty in preaching Jesus Christ and his Gospel for the edification of their congregations." A convenient precedent for such a measure had been given by the states of Holland and West Friesland which had acted a month ago to forbid the expression of any political opinion by the clergy.[54] Next day a timely pamphlet reinforced

52. That Marshall remonstrated against Pride's Purge appears from a marginal note in *A Serious and Faithful Representation of . . . Ministers of the Gospel within The Province of London* (1648), p. 1.

53. Wood, *Athenae Oxonienses*, III, 964.

54. *C.J.* VI, 175. The orders of the states of Holland and West Friesland had been procured by de Witt in consequence of clerical denunciations of the execution of Charles I. They were published in England on 26 Feb. 1649 as *An Extract out of the Register of the Resolution of the States of Holland, etc.*

this decision. It was by John Dury, one of the original prophets of the social reformation which was now, at last, to be realized; and it was entitled, *A Case of Conscience Resolved, concerning Ministers meddling with State Matters in their Sermons.*

Dury admitted that the "Court chaplains" of Charles I had preached political sermons, and that since 1640 "the popular preachers have paid them back in their own way"; but in the end what good, he asked, had come of all this political preaching, this confusion of the minister with the magistrate? On both sides it had "wrought nothing else but animosities and confusion." To those who insisted—and how often the Puritan preachers had insisted!—that men must not be lukewarm neuters, but zealous in the cause of God and for the public good, Dury replied that we must also beware lest we mistake the cause of God. It was the voice of religion disgusted with politics: the voice which would ultimately lead so many disillusioned men, and Dury himself, towards the new, quietist gospel of Quakerism.[55]

In all these circumstances we can hardly be surprised that doubts began to assail the Rump as to the desirability of continuing the regular monthly fast. After the king's execution, the old procedure was followed and the usual preparations were made for a fast on 28 February. Stephen Marshall was once again invited, but refused. So did another clergyman. Two preachers were ultimately found, and preached, but did not print their sermons. Then the House decided to change the date of the next fast to 22 March, and set up a committee, including Scot, Ireton and Cromwell, to draw up reasons for the change. Ten days later the committee was strengthened and the date of the fast was postponed to 5 April. On 17 March an Act was brought in accordingly, but in discussion the date was once again postponed, this time to 19 April. With this change the Act was published; but at the same time the committee was ordered to bring in, with all convenient speed, another, more general Act. On 23 April this Act was duly brought into the House. It was an Act to repeal the Act for the observation of the monthly fast.

The reasons given were no doubt true enough. The Parliament of England, it was said, had found by sad experience that the observation of the monthly fast had, for divers years, in most parts of the Commonwealth, been wholly neglected and in other places had been very imperfectly celebrated. Therefore, from now on, the said fast was abolished

---

55. Dury's tract inevitably landed him in controversy. He amplified it next year in *A Case of Conscience concerning Ministers Meddling with State Matters in or out of their Sermons, resolved more satisfactorily than before.*

and all men should, on the last Wednesday of the month, follow their lawful callings. In future, instead of the regular fast, there would only be such special fasts as might from time to time be ordered. In particular, there was to be a special fast on 3 May in the London area, and on 17 May in the country, to pray God to pardon the sins of the nation, its unthankfulness for recent mercies, its proneness and endeavour to relapse into its former tyranny and superstition, and "the iniquities of the former monthly fast-days."

Meanwhile the Parliament was concerning itself with political preaching in general. All through the early months of 1649 both royalists and radicals continued to use their opportunities. At first the great danger had been counter-revolution; but before long the threat of a second revolution seemed more imminent, as the Levellers roused their followers against the new "juggling junto" of Cromwell and Ireton. To a timid spirit even some of the official fast sermons might seem dangerously radical. The preachers on 19 April, for instance, gloried in the prospect of further convulsions and looked forward to the triumph of radical heresy and the cause of the poor.[56] On the special fast-day of 3 May, the sermons were even more radical. The preachers, we are told, declared "that after the oppressor was taken away, the oppression ought not to be continued" and that true patriots would prefer "to be poor in a rich Commonwealth than rich in a distracted, poor and almost ruined nation." At the time of the last Leveller mutiny these radical sentiments were not relished and the preachers, though thanked, were not invited to print their sermons. Next day Parliament ordered that the Act prohibiting the clergy from meddling in politics be reported. The Levellers believed that this Act was directed against them;[57] but in fact, when it was passed, on 9 July, the threat from that side was over; the last Leveller mutiny had been crushed, and the text was openly directed only against royalist propaganda and, more generally, against those who directly or indirectly preached or prayed against the power, authority or proceedings of the Parliament.[58]

With these two measures of 1649, the abolition of the regular monthly fast and the order against political preaching, we may con-

56. John Owen, Οὐρανῶν Οὐρανία, The Shaking and Translating of Heaven and Earth (1649); John Warren, The Potent Potter (1649).

57. The Moderate, no. 43 (1–8 May 1649), p. 492.

58. Resolves of the Commons concerning such ministers as shall preach or pray against the Present Government (9 July 1649).

clude this study of the political sermons of the Long Parliament. Of course it was not a final end. If the monthly fast had ceased, special fast-days or days of thanksgiving continued to be declared, and it would soon be clear that political sermons were by no means extinct. It was not even a tidy end. The monthly fast had originally been designed to continue as long as the troubles in Ireland. How much more satisfactory it would have been if it could have been kept going for those few remaining months! For, in fact, now that the troubles of England, however temporarily, were settled, the Irish troubles would soon be ended. On 1 November 1649 Parliament would learn of Cromwell's sack and massacre of Drogheda and Marshall and Sterry would be appointed to preach at the day of thanksgiving. If only the monthly fasts could have been kept up till then, they could have been called off with a ceremonious, triumphant flourish. But perhaps their premature end was really more appropriate. The connection with Ireland was, after all, accidental. The real purpose of the monthly fast had been to provide a constant sounding-board of parliamentary policy, a regular means of contact with, and propaganda to, the people. By the spring of 1649 none of those purposes could be fulfilled. A Parliament which had shrunk into an oligarchy no longer needed such a sounding-board, and an oligarchy which had lost touch with the people could no longer exploit the means of propaganda. Though we have few texts of the special fast sermons or thanksgiving sermons preached from 1649 to 1653, the circumstances in which they were preached sufficiently show the changed spirit behind them. The careful preparation, the narrow definition, the penalties threatened for nonconformity, all indicate a defensive spirit very different from that which had animated a national Parliament fighting for liberty; and by ceasing even to authorize the printing of the sermons, Parliament renounced the hope of using them to influence the country. In the hands of Hesilrige and Scot, Pym's broadcast propaganda had become a private lecture.[59]

Meanwhile others were taking up the discarded weapon. Already, during the rule of the Rump, the new political preachers were emerging. Once again, as in 1645–47, it was in Cromwell's army—that moving, restive body of men, rendered nervous by constant tension, exalted by successive victory—that they discovered their power. They were the

59. Formal thanks and invitations to print were the rule until March 1651, though preachers seldom took advantage of the invitations. From March 1651 thanks are rare and invitations to print rarer still, gradually ceasing altogether.

Anabaptist chaplains, the Fifth Monarchy Men. Stepping into the gap left by the ruin of the Levellers, these men quickly captured the old machinery of propaganda. Thanks to the patronage of Harrison, they even penetrated into St. Margaret's and uttered their disconcerting doctrines to the Parliament. Just as Cromwell, in 1645–46, had introduced Hugh Peter and Peter Sterry to alarm the followers of Holles and Stapleton, so Harrison now brought in the revolutionary Fifth Monarchy tribunes to alarm the followers of Hesilrige and Scot. It was he who sponsored Vavasour Powell in February 1650, John Simpson in March 1651 and Christopher Feake in October 1652. The Parliament shrank away from these radical preachers. It voted down a proposed vote of thanks to Simpson, avoided offering one to Feake; and in January 1653, when Harrison proposed the radical William Dell, it divided to defeat him. But the radicals, at the beginning of 1653, were not to be defeated by mere parliamentary votes. They had patrons more powerful than Hesilrige and Scot, congregations more numerous than the Rump; and they were determined to use both. If Parliament would not use them, they would overturn Parliament itself.

On 3 March 1653 the Long Parliament held what was to be its last solemn fast: a fast to implore God's blessing on the counsels and armed forces of the Commonwealth. The preacher, once again, was Stephen Marshall. That faithful servant, "the arch-flamen of the rebellious rout," "the trumpet by whom they sounded their solemn fasts," had begun the long series; now, accidentally, he was to end it: to pronounce the epitaph of the House of Commons as he had already done for the House of Lords. We do not know what he said. But while he uttered to his diminished congregation his unthanked, unrecorded sermon, a new force was mustering out of doors. In the churches and open places of London, Vavasour Powell, Feake and Simpson would soon be addressing massive audiences demanding the end of Parliament and a new system of government in which the pulpits should not be tuned by any man, but all power should be exercised direct by the preachers, the Saints.

7 | Oliver Cromwell and His Parliaments

Oliver Cromwell and his parliaments—the theme is almost a tragi-comedy. Cromwell was himself a Member of Parliament; he was the appointed general of the armies of Parliament; and the Victorians, in the greatest days of parliamentary government, set up his statue outside the rebuilt Houses of Parliament. But what were Cromwell's relations with Parliament? The Long Parliament, which appointed him, he first purged by force and then violently expelled from authority. His own Parliament, the Parliament of Saints, which to a large extent was nominated by his government, was carried away by hysteria, rent by intrigue and dissolved, after six months, by an undignified act of suicide. Of the parliaments of the Protectorate, elected on a new franchise and within new limits determined by the government, the first was purged by force within a week and dissolved, by a trick hardly distinguishable from fraud, before its legal term; the second was purged by fraud at the beginning and, when that fraud was reversed, became at once unmanageable and was dissolved within a fortnight. On a superficial view, Cromwell was as great an enemy of Parliament as ever Charles I or Archbishop Laud had been, the only difference being that, as an enemy, he was more successful: he scattered all his parliaments and died in his bed, while theirs deprived them of their power and brought them both ultimately to the block.

Nevertheless, between Cromwell and the Stuarts, in this matter, there was a more fundamental difference than this; for even if he could never control his parliaments in fact, Cromwell at least never rejected them in theory. This is not because he was deliberately consistent with his own parliamentary past. Cromwell was deliberately consistent in nothing. No political career is so full of undefended inconsistencies as his. But he was fundamentally and instinctively conservative, and he saw in Parliament part of the natural order of things. He did not regard it, as Archbishop Laud had regarded it, as "that hydra" or "that noise": he regarded it as the necessary legislature of England; and it was merely, in his eyes, an unfortunate and incomprehensible accident that his own particular parliaments consistently fell below the traditional standard of usefulness. Therefore again and again he summoned and faced them; again and again he wrestled with the hydra, sought to shout down the noise; and again and again, in the end, like the good man in a tragedy, caught in the trap of his own weakness, he resorted to force and fraud, to purges, expulsions and recriminations. He descended like Moses from Sinai upon the naughty children of Israel, smashing in turn the divine constitutions he had obtained for them; and the surprised and indignant members, scattered before their time, went out from his presence overwhelmed with turbid oratory, protestations of his own virtue and their waywardness, romantic reminiscences, proprietary appeals to the Lord, and great broken gobbets from the Pentateuch and the Psalms.

Why was Oliver Cromwell so uniformly unsuccessful with his parliaments? To answer this question we must first look a little more closely at the aims and character both of Oliver Cromwell and of that opposition to the Court of Charles I of which he was first an obscure and ultimately the most powerful representative: an opposition not of practised politicians (the practised politicians of 1640 were dead, or had lost control, by 1644), nor of City merchants (the great London merchants were largely royalist in 1640),[1] but of gentry: the backwoods gentry who, in 1640, sat on the back benches of Parliament, but who, as war and revolution progressed, gradually broke through the crumbling leadership which had at first contained them: the Independents.

Now these Independent gentry, it is important to emphasize, were

1. Mrs. Valerie Pearl, in her valuable work, *London and the Outbreak of the Puritan Revolution* (Oxford, 1961), has shown the strength of royalism in the effective City government until the internal revolution of Dec. 1641: a revolution described by Clarendon, *History of the Rebellion* (1843), pp. 149–50, and in the anonymous *Letter from Mercurius Civicus to Mercurius Rusticus* (1643), printed in *Somers Tracts* (1811), iv, 580.

not, as a class, revolutionary: that is, they did not hold revolutionary ideas. There were revolutionaries among the Independents, of course. There were revolutionaries in Parliament, men like "Harry Marten and his gang" — Henry Neville, Thomas Chaloner and others: intellectual republicans who had travelled in Italy, read Machiavelli and Botero and cultivated the doctrine of *raison d'état*; just as there were also revolutionaries outside Parliament: the Levellers and the Fifth Monarchy Men. But if these men were the successive sparks which kindled the various stages of revolution, they were not the essential tinder of it. The majority of the Members of Parliament, who at first accidentally launched the revolutionary movement and were afterwards borne along or consumed by it, were not clear-headed men like these. They were not thinkers or even dreamers, but plain, conservative, untravelled, country gentlemen whose passion came not from radical thought or systematic doctrine but from indignation: indignation which the electioneering ability of a few great lords and the parliamentary genius of John Pym had contrived to turn into a political force, and which no later leaders were able wholly either to harness or to contain. These were the men who formed the solid stuff of parliamentary opposition to Charles I: men whose social views were conservative enough, but whose political passions were radical, and became more radical as they discovered depth below depth of royal duplicity. These were the men who became, in time, the Independents; and Cromwell, though he transcended them in personality and military genius, was their typical, if also their greatest, representative.

Why were these men, in 1640, so indignant? They were indignant, above all, against the Court. Curiously it was the Court of James I rather than the Court of Charles I which aroused their strongest moral feelings; but then most of them were now middle-aged and those of them who had previous parliamentary experience had necessarily acquired it before 1628 — the younger men, brought up under Charles I, tended to be royalist.[2] It was the corrupt, extravagant Court of James I and the Duke of Buckingham, whose lavish expenses, "so vast and unlimited by the old good rules of economy,"[3] first insulted their own necessarily careful estate-management, and whose open, vulgar immo-

2. This point — that the royalist members were, on an average, ten years younger than the parliamentarians in 1640 — is clearly illustrated by D. Brunton and D. H. Pennington, *Members of the Long Parliament* (1954), pp. 14–20.

3. Clarendon, *History of the Rebellion*, ed. W. D. Macray, I, 12.

rality further scandalized their severe Puritan spirits.[4] But James I, by combining with his faults a certain political canniness, had postponed the impact of this indignation, and the very extravagance of his Court, with its sinecures and monopolies and pensions, had often bribed the potential leaders of opposition into silence. His son had corrected the moral abuses,[5] but by his political faults had nourished and increased and armed that indignation which those abuses had first engendered. Indeed, by his very parsimony Charles I hastened his own failure: for by cutting down the extravagance of the Court he had cut down the alleviating perquisites which had previously divided the opposition, and by raising the revenue from wardships he had rendered "all the rich families of England . . . exceedingly incensed and even indevoted to the Crown."[6] By 1640 political and moral indignation were combined against the House of Stuart and were together a powerful force in the hands of those practical politicians who perhaps shared it, who could certainly exploit it and who thought (but wrongly) that they could also control it.

And what were the positive ideals of these outraged but largely unpolitical conservative gentry? Naturally, in the circumstances, they were not very constructive. These men looked back, not forward: back from the House of Stuart which had so insulted them to the House of Tudor of which their fathers had spoken; and in the reign of Elizabeth they discovered, or invented, a golden age: an age when the Court had been, as it seemed, in harmony with the country and the Crown with its parliaments; an age when a Protestant queen, governing parsimoniously at home and laying only tolerable burdens on "her faithful Commons," had nevertheless made England glorious abroad—head of "the Protestant interest" throughout the world, victor over Spain in the Indies, protector of the Netherlands in Europe. Since 1603 that glorious position had been lost. King James had alienated the gentry, abandoned Protestantism for "Arminian" policy at home and popish alliances abroad, made peace with Spain and surrendered, with the

4. For the indignation which even courtiers, brought up at the orderly Court of Queen Elizabeth, felt at the vulgarity and immodesty of the Court of James I, see the letters of Lord Thomas Howard and Sir John Harington printed in N. E. McClure, *Letters and Epigrams of Sir John Harington* (Philadelphia, 1930), pp. 32–34, 118–21.

5. As even the Puritan Mrs. Hutchinson vividly admits. See her *Memoirs of Colonel Hutchinson* (Everyman edition), p. 67.

6. Clarendon, *History of the Rebellion*, 1, 199.

"cautionary towns," the protectorate over the Netherlands. When the religious struggle had broken out anew in Europe, it was not the King of England who had inherited the mantle of Queen Elizabeth as defender of the Protestant faith: it was a new champion from the north, the King of Sweden. In the 1630s, when Gustavus Adolphus swept triumphantly through Germany, he became the hero of the frustrated, mutinous English gentry; and when he fell at Lützen, scarcely an English squire but wrote, in his manor-house, a doggerel epitaph on the new pole-star of his loyalty, "the Lion of the North."

Such were the basic political views, or prejudices, of the English back-benchers who poured into Parliament in 1640. But they had social views also, and these too led them back to the same golden age of the Protestant queen. First there was the desire for decentralization—the revolt of the provinces and of the provincial gentry not only against the growing, parasitic Stuart Court, but also against the growing, "dropsical" City of London; against the centralized Church, whether Anglican or "Presbyterian"; and against the expensive monopoly of higher education by the two great universities. All this was implied in the Independent programme.[7] And also, what we must never forget, for it was a great element in the Protestant tradition, there was the demand for an organic society responsible for the welfare of its members. Ever since, among the first Reformers, "the Commonwealth Men," had protested against the irresponsibility, the practical inhumanity, the privileged uselessness of the pre-Reformation Church, the English Protestants had laid emphasis upon the collective nature of society and the mutual obligations of the classes which make it up.[8] Under Elizabeth, and especially in the long reign of Lord Burghley, something more than lip-service had been paid to this ideal; but under the Stuarts, and particularly in the reign of James I (that formative era of English Puritanism), the ideal had again been eclipsed as Court and Church became once again openly parasitic upon society. Those were the years in which the cry for social justice had become insistent and the Common Law, so

---

7. I have touched upon this aspect of the Independent programme in my essay, *The Gentry 1540–1640* (Economic History Society, 1954), p. 43.

8. I do not mean to imply that such views were not held in the Catholic Church *after* the Reformation. The revolt was European, and both Protestant and Catholic Churches inherited it, and competed with each other in formulating it. Similar "collectivist" doctrines were formulated by the Jesuits in Spain; but in England, being Protestant, it was part of the Protestant tradition.

extolled by its most successful practitioner, Sir Edward Coke, became, in other eyes, one of the most oppressive of social burdens. When the Anglican Archbishop Laud had failed in his desperate, purblind, but in some respects heroic, efforts to reform society centrally and from above, the Puritan opposition inherited much of his programme and sought to realize it in another form, as a decentralized, Independent commonwealth. The radicals would have achieved such reformation violently and devised new paper constitutions to secure and preserve it. The conservative Puritans, who were radical only in temper, not in their social or political doctrines, shied away from such novel remedies. Believing just as sincerely in a better, more decentralized, more responsible society, they looked for its achievement not to Utopia or Oceana but, once again, to a revived Elizabethan age.[9]

Such was the common denominator of positive philosophy shared by many of the back-bench Members of Parliament in 1640, as it emerges, by way of protest, from their pamphlets, their diaries, their letters to their patrons, their parliamentary ejaculations both before and after that crucial date. It is astonishing how faithfully it is reflected in the letters and speeches, as afterwards in the groping policy, of Oliver Cromwell. "Reformation of law and clergy," social justice for the "poor people of God" secured not by radical revolution but by patriarchal benevolence, a revival of the glories of "Queen Elizabeth of famous memory"—a protectorate over the Netherlands, a privateering war in the West Indies, and the leadership of "the Protestant interest" in Europe—all these recur in his later policy. Even the uncritical worship of Gustavus Adolphus is there. Perhaps nothing is more tragicomic in Cromwell's romantic foreign policy than his cultivation of the robber-empire in the Baltic, to which he would have sacrificed English commercial interests, and, in particular, of Queen Christina, whom he fondly courted with a pompous embassy, rich gifts and his own por-

---

9. Most recent writers—and not only Marxists and Fabians, for the same bias is to be found in the Roman Catholic W. Schenk's book, *The Concern for Social Justice in the Puritan Revolution* (1948)—have tended to find the evidence of such an interest in social reform only among the radical sects, who certainly made most noise about it. But I believe that just as much interest, in a more practical, less doctrinaire way, was shown by the conservative Independents. It can be discovered in their projects for law reform and Church matters, in their educational work (on which see especially Mr. W. A. L. Vincent's excellent study, *The State and School Education, 1640–1660*, 1950), in the ordinances of the Protector and Council between Dec. 1653 and Sept. 1654 and in the social policy carried out in the period of administration by major-generals.

trait. For was she not both a Protestant heroine and a virgin queen—her father, the great Gustavus, and "Queen Elizabeth of famous memory" rolled into one? In fact she was not. Even as he wooed her, that flighty Nordic blue-stocking was secretly being converted to popery by Jesuit missionaries, and Cromwell had to transfer his uncritical devotion to her successor.

But this was in the future. In 1640 Oliver Cromwell was still, like the other country gentry who had followed their patrons to Westminster, a mere back-bencher, a lesser ally of his kinsmen the Barringtons, John Hampden and Oliver St. John, a client of the Earl of Warwick. He never dreamed that his views would one day have more power behind them than theirs, or that the views which they all shared would be expressed otherwise than by the remonstrances of a faithful if indignant Parliament to a wayward but, they hoped (once his "evil counsellors" were removed), ultimately amenable king. None of them dreamed, in 1640, of revolution, either in Church or in State. They were neither separatists nor republicans. What they wanted was a king who, unlike Charles I, but like the Queen Elizabeth of their imagination, would work the existing institutions in the good old sense; bishops who, unlike the Laudian bishops, but like Bishop Hall or Archbishop Ussher, would supervise their flocks in the good old sense of "the sweet and noble" Anglican, Richard Hooker.[10] At first they hoped that King Charles would adjust himself, would jettison a few Stuart innovations, give a few guarantees, and become such a king of the State, such a supreme governor of the Church. It was only when King Charles had shown himself

---

10. The conservatism of the opposition in secular matters is generally admitted. In Aug. 1643 Henry Marten was sent to the Tower, without a division, for expressing republican sentiments. In Church matters the "Presbyterian" clergy and the extreme sectaries naturally expressed clear anti-Anglican sentiments; but the laity (as the history of the Westminster Assembly showed) had no intention of submitting to such clerical extremists. In fact, the spiritual advisers of the Independents, William Ames, Thomas Hooker, Hugh Peter, etc., were "non-separating congregationalists," who never disowned the Anglican Church (see Perry Miller, *Orthodoxy in Massachusetts*, Cambridge, Mass., 1933, pp. 177 ff.; R. P. Stearns, *Hugh Peter*, Urbana, 1954, p. 12, etc.). It was Henry Parker, a formidable Independent thinker, whose praise of Hooker I have quoted. Parker also described Bishop Hall as "one of the greatest assertors, and in that the noblest, of episcopacy" (W. K. Jordan, *Men of Substance*, Chicago, 1942, pp. 70–71). When in power, Cromwell granted far greater liberty to Anglicans than the revengeful Anglicans of the Restoration were disposed to admit (see R. Bosher, *The Making of the Restoration Settlement*, 1951, pp. 9–14), and appointed for Archbishop Ussher a State funeral in Westminster Abbey, with an Anglican service.

quite unadjustable that revolution, though unwanted, took place, generating its own momentum and driving basically conservative men to radical acts such as they would never have imagined before and would shudder to recollect afterwards, and facing them with fundamental problems of which they had never previously thought. It was only by an extraordinary and quite unpredictable turn of events that one of these back-benchers, Oliver Cromwell, having ruined all existing institutions, found himself, in 1649, faced with the responsibility of achieving, or restoring, the lost balance of society. It was a formidable responsibility for one so arbitrarily brought to eminence, but Cromwell took it seriously, for he was essentially a serious and a modest man; the question was, how could it be carried out?

The radicals, of course, had their plans: they were the intellectuals, or the doctrinaires, the new men and the young men of the revolution. They intended to continue the revolution, to create new engines of force, and to impose thereby new and untried but, in their eyes, hopeful constitutions. But Cromwell was not a radical or an intellectual or a young man. He did not want to continue the revolution, which had already, in his eyes and in the eyes of his fellow-gentry, got out of control. He wanted to stop it, to bring it under control, to bring "settlement" after an unfortunate but, as it had turned out, unavoidable period of "blood and confusion." Nor did he believe in new constitutions, or indeed in any constitutions at all. He did not believe, as some of his more wooden colleagues believed, in the divine right of republics any more than in the divine right of kings. Forms of government were to him "but a mortal thing," "dross and dung compared with Christ," and therefore in themselves quite indifferent. He was not, he once said, "wedded or glued to forms of government": had not the ancient Hebrews, God's own people, fared equally well, according to circumstances, under patriarchs, judges and kings?[11] Acceptability, or, as

---

11. *Clarke Papers*, i (Camden Society, 1891), 369. This indifference to forms of government, which implied a rejection of Charles I's rule without any particular constitutional alternative, was a commonplace among the Cromwellian Independents. Sir Henry Vane similarly held that "it is not so much the form of the administration as the thing administered wherein the good or evil of government doth consist" (*The People's Case Stated* in *The Trial of Sir Henry Vane, Kt.*, 1662, p. 106). Cf. Stephen Marshall, *A Letter to A Friend in the Country* (1643): "Among the divers kinds of lawful governments, monarchy, aristocracy and democracy, no one of them is so appointed of God as to exclude the other from being a lawful government"; and Hugh Peter, *Mr. Peter's Message with the Narration of the taking of Dartmouth* (1646), p. 2: "For it is certain that good

he called it, "acceptance," was to him the only test of right government. In his indignation against Charles I he might denounce monarchy, but in cooler moments he would admit that a government "with something monarchical in it" was probably the most acceptable, and therefore the best. In his indignation against the Earl of Manchester he might express his hope of living "to see never a nobleman in England"; but in cooler moments he could insist that "a nobleman, a gentleman, a yeoman" were "the ranks and orders of men whereby England hath been known for hundreds of years," and that "nobility and gentry" must be kept up.[12] Fundamentally, in his eyes, it was the fault of persons, not of institutions, which had been fatal to the *ancien régime:* "the King's head was not taken off because he was King, nor the Lords laid aside because Lords, neither was the Parliament dissolved because they were a Parliament, but because they did not perform their trust."[13] In politics Oliver Cromwell was not a theorist or a doctrinaire, but an opportunist.

Opportunists who do not believe in the necessity of particular constitutions take what lies nearest to hand, and what lay nearest to Cromwell's hand when he found himself called upon to restore his ideal Elizabethan society was naturally the surviving *débris* of the Elizabethan constitution. Parliament had been savaged—and by none more than himself—but its rump was there; the king had been destroyed, but he himself stood, if somewhat incongruously, in his place. Naturally he saw himself as a new Queen Elizabeth—or rather, being a humble man, as a regent for a new Queen Elizabeth; and he prepared, like her, to summon a series of deferential parliaments. Surely, since he was one of them, and since they all earnestly pursued the same honest ideal, the members would agree with him, just as they had agreed with "that Lady, that great Queen"? Surely he had only to address them in the Painted Chamber, to commend them in a few eloquent phrases, to leave them to their harmonious deliberations, and then, having received from them

---

men may save a nation when good laws cannot"; and *A Dying Father's Legacy* (1660), p. 110: "I nowhere minded who ruled, fewer or more, so the good ends of government be given out . . ." Cf. the similar views of other Independents quoted in E. Ludlow, *Memoirs*, ed. C. H. Firth (1894), I, 184–85, and T. Burton, *Parliamentary Diary* (1828), III, 260, 266.

12. B. Whitelocke, *Memorials* (1853), III, 374; *Camden Miscellany*, VIII (1883), 2; W. C. Abbott, *Writings and Speeches of Oliver Cromwell* (Harvard, 1937–47), III, 435, and IV, 273.

13. MS. Tanner, III, 13, quoted in *Clarke Papers*, III (1899), p. viii, n. 1.

a few "good laws," to dismiss them, in due time, amid applause, complimentingly, with a "Golden Speech"?

Alas, as we know, it did not happen thus. It was not with golden speeches that Cromwell found himself dismissing his parliaments, but with appeals to Heaven, torrents of abuse—and force. This was not merely because the basis of legitimacy and consent was lacking: Queen Elizabeth, like Cromwell, was disputed in her title, and Cromwell, like Queen Elizabeth, was personally indispensable even to those extremists who chafed at his conservatism. The fatal flaw was elsewhere. Under Oliver Cromwell something was missing in the mechanics of parliamentary government. It was not merely that useful drop of oil with which Queen Elizabeth had now and then so gracefully lubricated the machine. It was something far more essential. To see what that omission was, we must turn from the character to the composition and working of those uniformly unfortunate assemblies.

The methods by which Queen Elizabeth so effectively controlled her parliaments of—for the most part—unpolitical gentry are now, thanks to the great work of Sir John Neale and Professor Notestein, well known.[14] They consisted, first, in electoral and other patronage and, secondly, in certain procedural devices among which the essential were two: the presence in Parliament of a firm nucleus of experienced Privy Councillors, and royal control over the Speaker. Now these methods of control are of the greatest importance in the history of Parliament, and if we are to consider Oliver Cromwell as a parliamentarian it is necessary to consider his use both of this patronage and of these procedural devices. This, I think, has not before been attempted. My purpose in this essay is to attempt it. I believe it can be shown that it was precisely in this field that Cromwell's catastrophic failure as a parliamentarian lay. In order to show this it will be necessary to take Cromwell's parliaments in turn and to see, in each case, how far the patronage of the government and its supporters was used, and who formed that essential nucleus of effective parliamentary managers, that compact "front bench" which, under the Tudors, had been occupied by the royal Privy Council.

Of course, Cromwell did not inherit the system direct from Queen

14. Wallace Notestein, *The Winning of the Initiative by the House of Commons* (British Academy Lecture, 1924); J. E. Neale, *The Elizabethan House of Commons* (1949); *Elizabeth I and her Parliaments* (1953).

Elizabeth. In the intervening half-century there had been many changes—changes which had begun even before her death. For in the last years of Elizabeth both methods of royal control had been challenged: the Puritans had developed a formidable parliamentary "machine" independent of the Privy Council, and the Earl of Essex had sought to use aristocratic patronage to pack the House of Commons against the queen's ministers. But in the event, thanks to the parliamentary ability of the two Cecils, neither of these challenges had been successful. It was only after the death of the queen, and particularly after the rejection of Robert Cecil by James I, that the indifference of the Stuart kings and the incompetence of their ministers had enabled a parliamentary opposition to develop and to organize both patronage and procedure against the Crown. By 1640, when the Long Parliament met, the tables had been completely turned. In that year the opposition magnates—the earls of Bedford, Warwick and Pembroke—showed themselves better boroughmongers than the royal ministers, and the failure of Charles I to secure the election to Parliament, for any constituency, of his intended Speaker could be described by Clarendon as "an untoward and indeed an unheard of accident, which brake many of the king's measures and infinitely disordered his service beyond a capacity of reparation." [15] Thus in 1640 both patronage and procedure

15. R. N. Kershaw, "The Elections for the Long Parliament," in *English Historical Review*, 1923; Clarendon, *History of the Rebellion*, I, 220. The extent to which the party of opposition in 1640 was an aristocratic party, controlled by certain great boroughmongering lords, has, I think, been insufficiently emphasized by historians, although Clarendon, as a contemporary, takes it for granted. Pym was a client of the Earl of Bedford ("wholly devoted to the earl of Bedford," Clarendon, op. cit. I, 245); those who afterwards became Independents were largely (like the Independent preachers) clients of the Earl of Warwick, to whom Cromwell himself remained a constant ally, even when their rôles were reversed (ibid. p. 544). For the Earl of Warwick as head of a political party, see A. P. Newton, *The Colonising Activities of the Early Puritans* (New Haven, 1914), *passim*. For some of his electioneering activities, see J. H. Hexter, *The Reign of King Pym* (Cambridge, Mass., 1941), pp. 44–45. For the electioneering activities of the earls of Pembroke, see Violet A. Rowe, "The Influence of the Earls of Pembroke on Parliamentary Elections 1625–1641," in *English Historical Review*, 1935, p. 242. On the other hand, the electioneering feebleness of the government is shown by Archbishop Laud's refusal to avail himself of the borough-patronage at his disposal at Reading, or, apparently, at Oxford (see Laud, *Works*, 1847–60, VI, 587; M. B. Rex, *University Representation in England, 1604–1690*, 1954, p. 145). And yet, if Laud had chosen to recommend Sir Thomas Gardiner for Reading, there would have been a sound royalist Speaker instead of Lenthall, and the disaster so emphasized by Clarendon would

were firmly in the hands of the opposition. But this turning of the tables did not entail any change in the system by which Parliament was operated. It merely meant that the same system which had formerly been operated by the Crown was now operated against it. John Pym, the ablest parliamentary manager since the Cecils, resumed their work. He controlled the patronage, the Speaker, and the front bench. From 1640 until 1643 Parliament, in his hands, was once again an effective and disciplined body such as it had never been since 1603.

With the death of Pym in 1643 his indisputable empire over Parliament dissolved and lesser men competed for its fragments. First St. John, then Vane among the radicals, Holles among the conservatives, emerged as party leaders; but they cannot be described as successful party leaders: the machine creaked and groaned, and it was only by disastrously calling in external force—the Army—that the Independents were able, in the end, to secure their control. On the other hand, once Parliament had been purged and the king executed, a certain unity of counsel and policy returned. The Rump Parliament, which governed England from 1649 to 1653, may have been justly hated as a corrupt oligarchy, but it governed effectively, preserved the revolution, made and financed victorious war, and carried out a consistent policy of aggressive mercantile imperialism. Its rule was indeed the most systematic government of the Interregnum; and since this rule was the rule not of one known minister but of a number of overlapping assemblies operating now as Parliament, now as committees of Parliament, now as Council of State, while some of the administrative departments were notoriously confused and confusing, it is reasonable to ask who were the effective managers who made this complex and anonymous junta work so forcefully and so smoothly. This is a question which, in my opinion, can be answered with some confidence.

We have, unfortunately, no private diaries of the Rump Parliament which can show who managed its business or debates, but we have later diaries which show at least who claimed to have managed them; and from this and other evidence I believe we can say that, at least after 1651, the policy of the Rump was controlled by a small group of determined and single-minded men. Up to the summer of 1651 the ascendancy of these men is not so apparent, but with the policy which prevailed after that date it can, I think, be clearly seen. For in 1651, with the passing of

---

never have occurred. It is difficult to over-estimate the consequences which might have flowed from so slight an exertion.

the Navigation Act and the declaration of war against the Netherlands, the old Elizabethan ideal of a protectorate over the Netherlands was jettisoned in favour of a new and opposite policy, a policy of mercantile aggression against a neighbouring Protestant power. Furthermore, this policy, we are repeatedly told, was the policy not of the whole Parliament but of "a very small number," with allies in the City of London, "some few men" acting "for their own interest," "some few persons deeply interested in the East India trade and the new Plantations." [16]

Now the identity of these few men, or at least of their parliamentary managers, can hardly be doubted, for they never tired of naming themselves. They were Sir Arthur Hesilrige and Thomas Scot. In the later parliaments of the Interregnum, whose proceedings are fortunately known to us, Hesilrige and Scot appear as an inseparable and effective parliamentary combine. Together they head the list of those republicans whom Cromwell twice excluded from his parliaments. Together they are named by Ludlow as the principal champions of sound republican doctrine. Together they appear, in the *Commons' Journals*, as tellers for strictly republican motions. Moreover, not only did they repeatedly claim for themselves all the republican virtue of the Rump Parliament in general, but, in particular, the policy for which they most extolled the Rump was always precisely that policy of mercantile aggression which had been launched in 1651 with the triumphant but, in the eyes of serious-minded Protestants, fratricidal war against the Netherlands.

For Hesilrige and Scot were not only republicans. They were also, to use a later term, "Whigs." If republics were to them the best of all forms of government, that was not merely because of classical or biblical precedents, nor because of the iniquity of particular kings: it was because republics alone, in their eyes, were the political systems capable of commercial empire. Like the later Whigs, who were also accused of a preference for "oligarchy," they found their great example in the mercantile republic of Venice. "Is there anything but a Commonwealth that flourishes?" asked Scot: "Venice against the pride of the Ottoman Empire";[17] and he never ceased to urge a reversion to the aggressive

16. These statements concerning the fewness of the makers of Rump policy, made by Pauluzzi the Venetian resident, Daniel O'Neil the royalist agent, and the later Dutch ambassadors, are quoted by S. R. Gardiner, *History of the Commonwealth and Protectorate* (1894), II, 120 n.

17. The fashionable cult of Venice reached its height under the Commonwealth. The republicans Harrington and Neville made it their ideal; the anonymous tract, *A*

commercial policy of 1651–53. "We never bid fairer for being masters of the whole world." "We are rival for the fairest mistress in the world—Trade." "It is known abroad—the Dutch know—that a Parliament of England can fight and conquer too." "You never had such a fleet as in the Long Parliament," echoed Hesilrige; "all the powers in the world made addresses to him that sat in your chair"; "trade flourished, the City of London grew rich, we were most potent by sea that ever was known in England." When Cromwell expelled the Rump, he afterwards declared, "there was not so much as the barking of a dog or any general or visible repining at it"; and his gentry-supporters agreed with him: "there was neither coroner nor inquest upon it." But some squeaks there were, and it is interesting to see whence they came. At the crucial moment, when an agreed solution was almost in sight, it was Hesilrige who swept down from seventy miles away and by his presence and oratory prevented the other members from surrendering to less than force; and when they had been expelled by force, it was from the City of London that the only plea for their restoration came: a petition whose paternity is easy to recognize—for six years later it was implicitly claimed by Thomas Scot.[18]

Now it is interesting to note that this policy, the "Whig" policy of mercantile aggression which I have ascribed to Hesilrige and Scot and their allies in the City, though it was carried out by an Independent Parliament carefully purged of unsympathetic elements, was flatly contradictory to the declared views and prejudices of those ordinary Independent gentry whom Cromwell represented and who, in their general attitude, foreshadowed rather the Tory squires than the mercantile Whig pressure-group of the next generation.[19] Cromwell him-

Persuasive to a Mutual Compliance (1652), prophesies for the Rump a future comparable with that of Venice (Somers Tracts, VI, 158); James Howell's laudatory Survey of the Signorie of Venice, of her admired policy and method of government, was published in 1651; etc., etc.

18. Abbott, Writings and Speeches of Oliver Cromwell, III, 453; Burton, Parliamentary Diary, III, 97, 111–12, etc.

19. This distinction between the "Whig" policy of the Rump and the "Tory" policy of the Cromwellian Independents is well illustrated in the person of a prominent champion of the former and enemy of the latter, Slingsby Bethel. In his pamphlet The World's Mistake in Oliver Cromwell (1668) he attacked Cromwell precisely because he had reversed the mercantilist policy of the Rump; in his Interest of Princes and States (1680) he attacks the gentry as the chief obstacle everywhere to rational mercantile

self always favoured the Elizabethan policy of an alliance with and a protectorate over the Netherlands, and it was this policy which Oliver St. John had, until 1651, pressed upon the Dutch government at The Hague. The defection of St. John in 1651 had enabled the "Whig" party to carry their war policy, but in 1653, when Cromwell had expelled the Rump, he lost no time in ending the war they had begun. Further, Cromwell and his colleagues had revolted, in part, against the centralization of trade in the City of London, which had caused the decay of local boroughs and local industry: they had no wish to fight (and pay for) mercantile wars in the interest of the City; and afterwards, when they denounced the Rump, they "cast much dirt and unsavoury speech" on it as "a trading Parliament."[20] Decentralization, the provinces against the City, and the Protestant interest—these were their political slogans, the slogans which they had uttered in the 1630s and 1640s and would utter again after 1653, but which went altogether unheeded by those Rumpers who had temporarily seized control of the revolution. Finally, the Rump Parliament—and this was one of Cromwell's greatest grievances against it—showed itself increasingly indifferent to that Protestant "concern for social justice" which loomed so large in the Independent programme. War on Protestants abroad in the interest of City merchants was accompanied at home, in those years, by a privileged scramble for public property which seemed a mockery of Puritan ideals. The republic of Hesilrige and Scot might call itself a "Commonwealth," but in fact, said a real republican, "it was an oligarchy, detested by all men that love a Commonwealth";[21] or, if it were a commonwealth, it was only, according to the sour definition of Sir Thomas More: "a certain conspiracy of rich men procuring their own commodities under the name and title of a Commonwealth."

Thus the policy of the Rump in the years 1651-53—the years, that is, when the Army's resentment was mounting against it—was not only the policy of a small managing group which had obtained control of the

---

policy; and in the days when Whigs and Tories existed in fact, not merely in embryo, he was Whig sheriff of London in the year of the Popish Plot.

20. Burton, *Parliamentary Diary*, I, pp. xxv, xxviii. For Independent complaints against the growth of the City of London and its monopoly of trade, see ibid. I, pp. cx, 177, 343-44. For the same complaint resumed by a Tory back-bencher a generation later, see *The Memoirs of Sir John Reresby* (1875), p. 333.

21. Burton, *Parliamentary Diary*, III, 134.

assembly: it was also a policy essentially opposed to the aims of those Independents who had made the revolution. For all their insistence upon decentralization, social justice and Protestant alliances, those Independents had proved quite incapable of making such a policy even in their own Parliament which their own leader had purged in their interest. Unable, or unfitted, to exercise political power, they seemed doomed to surrender it to any organized group, however small, which was capable of wielding it—even if that group used it only to pursue policies quite different from their own. Though the "Tory" Independents had made the revolution and, through the Army, held power in the state, the "Whigs" had contrived to secure power in Parliament. To correct this and create a government of their own, the Independents had the choice between two policies. Either they could preserve the republican constitution and beat the "Whigs" at their own game—or, if that was too difficult for natural back-benchers, they could remove their rivals by force and place over Parliament a "single person," like-minded with themselves, to summon, dismiss and, above all, guide and regulate their assemblies. This latter course was entirely consistent with their general political philosophy; it was also the easier course; and consequently they took it. The crucial question was, did the new "single person" understand the technique of his task? He had in his hands all the power of the State; but had he in his head the necessary knowledge of parliamentary management: that is, patronage and procedure to prevent another usurpation of the vacant front benches? Would he now fill them with his Privy Councillors and thus cement, as Queen Elizabeth had done, the natural harmony between the faithful, if somewhat inarticulate, Commons and the Throne?

If this was what Cromwell hoped to do, his first opportunity after the expulsion of the Rump was perhaps his best, for the Parliament of Saints, the Barebones Parliament of 1653, was, after all, largely a nominated, not an elected, assembly. And yet, as it turned out, this experiment proved to be Cromwell's most humiliating failure. The Barebones Parliament is a classic example of an unpolitical assembly colonized from within by a well-organized minority. It was so colonized not merely because the majority of its members were unpolitical—that is true of most assemblies—but because Cromwell himself, in summoning it, was quite unaware of the real inspiration behind it, and made no attempt to convert it, by preparation or organization, into a useful or even workable assembly. As he afterwards admitted, it was a tale not only of the members' weakness but of his own: "the issue was not answerable to the simplicity and honesty of the design." [22]

The evidence for this is sadly plain. For what was in the minds of Cromwell and his conservative allies when they decided, or agreed, to summon the Barebones Parliament? We look, and all we find is a well-meaning, devout, bewildered obscurity. The Independents had no political theories: believing that forms of government were indifferent, they counted simply on working with the existing institutions, and now that the existing institutions—first monarchy, then republic—had been destroyed, they were at a loss. "It was necessary to pull down this government," one of them had declared on the eve of the expulsion, "and it would be time enough then to consider what should be placed in the room of it"; and afterwards it was officially stated that "until the Parliament was actually dissolved, no resolutions were taken in what model to case the government, but it was after that dissolution debated and discussed as *res integra*." [23] In other words, having expelled the Rump Parliament which had betrayed the Independent cause, the Independent officers found themselves in a quandary. They had acted, as Cromwell so often acted, not rationally nor with that machiavellian duplicity with which his victims generally credited him, but on an impulse; and when the impulsive gesture had been made and the next and more deliberate step must be taken, they were quite unprepared.

Over the unprepared the prepared always have an advantage. In this case the prepared were the new radical party which had replaced the broken Levellers: the extreme totalitarian radicals, the Anabaptists and their fighting zealots the Fifth Monarchy Men. These men had already established themselves in the Army through their disciplined tribunes, the chaplains; they already controlled many of the London pulpits; and for the capture of direct power they had two further assets: an organization, in the form of the Committee for the Propagation of the Gospel in Wales, which was now totally controlled by their energetic Welsh leader, Vavasour Powell, and his itinerant missionaries; and a patron at the highest level in Major-General Harrison, the commissioner in charge of the Welsh Propagators and—what was now more important—the *alter ego* of the unsuspecting Cromwell. In the

22. Abbott, *Writings and Speeches of Oliver Cromwell*, IV, 489.

23. Ludlow, *Memoirs*, I, 351; [Anon.] *A True State of the Case of the Commonwealth* (1654), quoted by Firth in Ludlow, op. cit. I, 358, n.

Rump Parliament, which after all had been the residue of a parliament of gentry, lawyers and merchants, these radical zealots had had little influence. Indeed, they had been its most violent enemies, for the Rump, unlike Cromwell, had been well aware of their subversive activities and had for some time been preparing, in spite of constant obstruction, to discontinue the Welsh Propagators who formed their essential committee. It was largely to forestall, or avenge, so crucial a blow that Harrison had urged Cromwell to expel the Parliament.[24] When he had expelled it, Cromwell had played into the hands of the radicals. They had used him to destroy their enemy for them; and they now looked forward to using him still further, as a means of achieving direct political power.

As so often in the history of Oliver Cromwell, there is something at once tragic and comic in the manner of his deception by the Fifth Monarchy Men. To him they were merely good religious men, and when he found that his own exalted mood of indignation against the Rump was shared by them, he followed their advice, little suspecting what deep-laid political schemes lurked behind their mystical language. "Reformation of law and clergy": was not that precisely his programme? A milder, cheaper, quicker law; a decentralized, godly, Puritan clergy; were not these his ambitions? How was he to know that by the same phrase the Anabaptists meant something quite different and far more radical: wholesale changes in the law of property, abolition of tithe, the extension over England of the closely organized, indoctrinated religious tribunes who had already carried their gospel over Wales "like fire in the thatch"? Oliver Cromwell suspected no such thing. When Harrison urged him to expel the Rump as the persecutors of the "poor saints in Wales," he innocently acquiesced; and when he found that the refusal of the Rump to renew their authority had left the Welsh Propagators without a legal basis, he as innocently supplied them with a substitute, writing to them to ignore strict legality and "to go on cheerfully in the work as formerly, to promote these good things." Months afterwards the greatest crime of the Rump would still seem to him to be its attempt to disband those Welsh Propagators, "the poor people of God there, who had men watching over them like so many wolves, ready to

24. The history of the struggle over the Welsh Propagators can be followed in T. Richards, *The Puritan Movement in Wales* (1920). See also Alan Griffith, *A True and Perfect Relation of the whole Transaction concerning the Petition of the Six Counties*, etc. (1654).

catch the lamb as soon as it was brought out into the world." [25] This romantic view of a knot of Tammany demagogues, who concealed their sharp practices behind lachrymose Celtic oratory, was soon to be sadly dispelled.

As soon as they had secured the expulsion of the Rump, the Fifth Monarchy Men were ready for the next step. What they required was a legislature nominated by the supposedly "independent" churches, some of which had been completely penetrated and were now safely controlled by them. Only in this way could so unrepresentative a party achieve power. Therefore when Cromwell remained poised in doubt, he soon found himself besieged by willing and unanimous advisers. "We humbly advise," the Saints of North Wales wrote to him from Denbigh (the letter was composed by the local Fifth Monarchy panjandrum Morgan Llwyd), "that forasmuch as the policy and greatness of men hath ever failed, ye would now at length, in the next election, suffer and encourage the saints of God in his spirit to recommend unto you such as God shall choose for that work." [26] Another Fifth Monarchy preacher, John Rogers, was even more precise. He urged that an interim junto of twelve, "like to Israel's twelve Judges," be first set up; that a Sanhedrim of seventy men "or else one of a county" be then nominated, in which "the righteous of the worthies of the late Parliament" might also be included; and that in all cases of doubt the General should "consult with the Saints (Deuteronomy i. 13) and send to all discerning spirited men for their proposals." [27] Through Harrison, these proposals were urged in the council of officers;[28] under this double pressure, direct and indirect, Cromwell easily yielded; and the Barebones Parliament, when it was summoned, was, in fact, a body constituted almost exactly as required in the Fifth Monarchy programme. The twelve councillors were appointed, and the members of the new Parliament were to be elected by the local churches[29] which the radicals had often

25. Abbott, *Writings and Speeches of Oliver Cromwell*, III, 13, 57.

26. *Milton State Papers*, ed. J. Nickolls (1743), p. 120; cf. J. H. Davies, *Gweithiau Morgan Llwyd* (Bangor, 1899 and 1908), II, 264.

27. John Rogers, *A Few Proposals*, quoted in Edward Rogers, *Life and Opinions of a Fifth Monarchy Man* (1867), p. 50.

28. See Harrison's letters on this subject in the Jones correspondence (see below, n. 31; also Ludlow, *Memoirs*, I, 358; *Clarke Papers*, III, 4).

29. Since this essay was written, Mr. Austin Woolrych, in an interesting article on "The Calling of Barebones Parliament," in *English Historical Review*, July 1965, has

penetrated. Some few members were to be nominated directly by the council.

Whom would the churches elect? Cromwell's own demands were moderate and sensible. He called for "known men of good repute" —that is, respectable Puritan, even if unpolitical, gentry; and such were the men he himself seems to have nominated: Lord Lisle, his own kinsmen, his own medical man Dr. Goddard, etc.[30] But the radicals had more definite, more positive, views: they were determined to send to Parliament only reliable radical party-members. The chance survival of the correspondence of one of their Welsh sympathizers, Colonel John Jones of Merionethshire, clearly shows their electioneering tactics:[31] for in Wales at least there were now no "independent" churches, only Vavasour Powell's dragooned itinerant missionaries. Consequently even the formality of election was there unnecessary. "I presume," Harrison wrote to Colonel Jones, "brother Powell acquainted you our thoughts as to the persons most in them to serve on behalf the Saints of North Wales: Hugh Courtney, John Browne, Richard Price out of your parts." In other words, the three members for North Wales were simply nominated in London by Harrison and Powell and their names communicated, as a courtesy, to a prominent supporter in the district. It need hardly be added that all three were prominent Fifth Monarchy Men, and all were duly "elected." No doubt

---

argued that whatever demands or suggestions were made, the Members of that Parliament were not "elected" by the Churches, but nominated by the Council of Officers, and that the various letters from the Churches, proposing particular members, were not replies to requests but unsolicited proposals. Although convinced by Mr. Woolrych's argument, I have not altered my text. The effective difference is anyway slight, since the Council naturally would be in many cases, and demonstrably was in others, guided by the local Saints. Mr. Woolrych's conclusions make the achievement of the Fifth Monarchy Men in "colonizing" a purely "nominated" assembly even more remarkable.

30. Lord Lisle was evidently nominated by the council, since he sat for Kent but had not been nominated by the churches of Kent, whose list of nominees survives (*Milton State Papers*, p. 95).

31. Some of these letters were published in the *Transactions of the Lancashire and Cheshire Historical Society* (1861), pp. 171 ff. (The originals are now MS. 11440 in the National Library of Wales.) Colonel Jones afterwards separated himself from the Fifth Monarchy Men, married Cromwell's sister and supported the Protectorate; but at this time, as his letters show, he was a complete fellow-traveller with Harrison and Vavasour Powell.

the three members for South Wales—Vavasour Powell's own district—were similarly chosen. Two of them also appear to have been Fifth Monarchists.[32] Similarly in England, wherever radical preachers controlled the churches, radical politicians were recommended to the council as Members of Parliament, and Harrison, on the council, saw to it that they were approved.[33] So the Fifth Monarchists and their fellow-travellers, a compact minority, moved *en bloc* to Westminster. It was machine-politics, and it worked like magic. Complacently Harrison could write to a friend that "the Lord had now at last made the General instrumental to put the power into the hands of His people"; but that, he added, "was the Lord's work, and no thanks to His Excellency."[34] The innocent Cromwell was still quite unaware of the revolutionary movement which he was sponsoring.

Thus the Barebones Parliament was "elected," and when it met, on 4 July 1653, Cromwell addressed it in his most exalted style. Now at last, he thought, he had a Parliament after his heart, a Parliament of godly men, gentry of his own kind, back-benchers, not scheming politicians—with a sprinkling, of course, of Saints. He had a sound Speaker too, Francis Rous, a gentleman, a religious man and a typical Cromwellian: elderly, unpolitical, "Elizabethan," a step-brother of Pym and a friend of Drake. Surely so pure a body could be trusted to make good laws. Having urged them to do so, he withdrew altogether from the scene and waited for the good laws to emerge. He did not seek to control Parliament; though elected to its committees he did not sit on them; in an honest attempt "to divest the sword of all power in the civil administration" he drew aside, as Queen Elizabeth and her Privy

32. The three members for South Wales were James Phillips, John Williams and Bussy Mansell. According to J. H. Davies, *Gweithiau Morgan Llwyd*, II, p. lxiii, two of them were Fifth Monarchists. Louise Fargo Brown, *Baptists and Fifth Monarchy Men* (Washington, D.C., 1912), p. 33, only identifies one of them, viz. John Williams, as a Baptist or Fifth Monarchy Man; but whether formally enrolled in the party or not, Bussey Mansell certainly voted with the radicals and was one of the last-ditchers on the radical side who were ultimately turned out by force (see his letter in *Thurloe State Papers*, 1742, I, 637).

33. Apart from the Welsh seats, I deduce that other constituencies were thus "colonized" from the few surviving lists sent in by the churches. Thus, although the churches of Norfolk and Gloucester proposed miscellaneous names, many of which were not accepted by the council, the churches of Suffolk and Kent proposed solid lists of radical voters (*Milton State Papers*, pp. 92–95, 124–25).

34. S. R. Gardiner, *History of the Commonwealth*, II, 222.

Council had never done, from the business of managing Parliament, and waited for results.

The results were as might have been expected. The Cromwellian back-benchers were as clumsy old bluebottles caught in the delicate web spun by nimble radical spiders. The radicals were few—there were only eighteen definitely identifiable Anabaptists or Fifth Monarchy Men,[35] of whom five were from Wales; but it was enough. They made a dash for the crucial committees;[36] Harrison, unlike Cromwell, sat regularly both in the House and on its committees; and outside the clerical organizers of the party had the London pulpits tuned. The oratory of Blackfriars created for the radicals that outside pressure which in the past had enabled Pym to intimidate the royalists and Vane to intimidate the "Presbyterians." Within six months the radicals had

35. Brown, *Baptists and Fifth Monarchy Men*, p. 33. It is often stated that the extremists had a "party" of about sixty (e.g., by H. A. Glass, *The Barebones Parliament*, 1899; Brown, op. cit., p. 33, and *The First Earl of Shaftesbury*, New York, 1933, p. 55; Margaret James, "The Tithes Controversy in the Puritan Revolution," in *History*, 1941); but I do not think that so definite a statement can properly be made. It rests on the numbers in divisions, as recorded in the *Commons' Journals* and on two (slightly different) voting-lists for the last crucial debate, one of which is quoted from Thomason E. 669 by Gardiner, *History of the Commonwealth*, III, 259 (it is also in *Thurloe State Papers*, III, 132), and the other, without reference, by Glass. But divisions were not always on a straight conservative-radical issue and it is not proper to label members permanently as "Cromwellians" or "radicals" on the basis of one imperfectly recorded division (Glass's list gives Squibb as a conservative, which is ridiculous, and the lists anyway do not distinguish, among those who did not vote on the conservative side, between radicals, abstainers and absentees). Further, many of those who voted as radicals in 1653 afterwards, when separated from the radical leaders, conscientiously served the Protectorate, having no doubt been—like Cromwell himself—innocent fellow-travellers with the extremists. From a critical study of the tellers in divisions, and from other sources, it is certainly possible to identify the leaders on both sides: Sir Anthony Ashley Cooper, Sir Charles Wolseley, Sir Gilbert Pickering, Alderman Tichborne, on the conservative side; Harrison, Samuel Moyer, Arthur Squibb, Colonel Blount, John Ireton and Thomas St. Nicholas on the radical side. No doubt there were others—like the solid bloc of Baptists and Fifth Monarchists—whose position can be as clearly defined. But it is likely that the ordinary back-benchers belonged to no "party," but voted according to the occasion, and that the success of the radicals consisted in managing floating voters as well as in having control over disciplined voters.

36. The committees most heavily colonized by the radicals were, naturally, those concerned with the essential parts of their programme, viz. tithes and the law. The Committee for a New Model of the Law contained all the principal radicals, and out of its eighteen members no less than thirteen voted on the radical side in the crucial last debate.

such control over the whole assembly that the Cromwellian conservatives, panic-stricken at their revolutionary designs, came early and furtively to Whitehall and surrendered back to the Lord General the powers which, through lack of direction, they had proved incapable of wielding.

Who were the parliamentary managers of the Barebones Parliament who thus filled the vacuum left by Cromwell's inability or refusal to form a party? Once again, I think, they can be identified. Arthur Squibb, a Fifth Monarchy Man, was a London lawyer with Welsh connections,[37] and Samuel Moyer, a Baptist, was a London financier and member of the East India Company who had recently been added—no doubt by Harrison—to the Council of State. Both were sincere radicals in politics and religion, as they afterwards showed in their eclipse; both had done well out of the revolution; they had worked together on important financial committees, particularly on the permanent Committee of Compounding; they are named together among the earliest public spokesmen for the Barebones Parliament;[38] and in the end, when Cromwell had discovered how he had been abused, it was Squibb and Moyer who, with Harrison and the preachers, were singled out for his revenge.[39] In the committees of the Barebones Parliament, where the radicals concentrated their strength, Samuel Moyer, their link with the Council of State, headed the list by sitting, as no other man did, on seven standing committees; and we know from Cromwell himself that

37. He had begun his career in the office of a Welsh lawyer, Sir Edward Powell, and was connected by marriage with the Welsh judge John Glyn.

38. After Cromwell's opening speech, the members adjourned till 8 a.m. next day for "a day of humiliation for a blessing upon their meeting, not any minister speaking before them (as was proposed), only themselves. Amongst the rest was Mr. Squibb and Samuel Moyer" (*Clarke Papers*, III, 9).

39. After the institution of the Protectorate, Squibb was forced to give up his offices as keeper of the prison at Sandwich and teller of the exchequer (*Cal. S.P. Dom. 1654*, pp. 116, 272). He was involved in Venner's Fifth Monarchy rising of 1656 (*Thurloe State Papers*, VI, 185). At the Restoration he and his brothers sought in vain to recover the tellership of the exchequer (*Cal. S.P. Dom. 1661–2*, p. 369; *1663–4*, pp. 121, 582; *1666–7*, pp. 182–83, 535). He was imprisoned in the Tower in connection with a Fifth Monarchy sermon in 1671 (*Cal. S.P. Dom. 1671*, p. 357). Moyer disappeared from the Council of State and all official positions at the same time. He reappeared to present the republican and Fifth Monarchy petition in Feb. 1659 (*Commons' Journals*, 9–15 Feb. 1659; Burton, *Parliamentary Diary*, III, 288) and again another petition on 12 May 1659 (*Commons' Journals*, s.d.).

Squibb's house in Fleet Street was the central office of the party, "and there were all the resolutions taken that were acted in that House day by day; and this was true *de facto*—I know it to be true."[40] Against this highly organized party-machine—the Welsh electioneering machine of Vavasour Powell, the publicity-making machine of the London pulpits now controlled by the party, and the parliamentary caucus of Harrison, Squibb and Moyer—Cromwell, for immediate purposes, had nothing: nothing, that is, except the ultimate basis of his rule—force.

It was by force, in the end, that the little group of radicals who refused to accept the suicide of the majority were expelled. While Speaker Rous, that "old bottle," as the radicals called him, who was unable to contain the new wine, went off "with his fellow old bottles to Whitehall" to surrender their authority, some thirty radical members remained in the House at Westminster. Too few to count as a quorum, they could not legally act as a parliament; but they called Samuel Moyer to the mace and began to register their protests. They were interrupted by two colonels who ordered them to leave and then, meeting with no compliance, "went out and fetched two files of musketeers and did as good as force them out; amongst whom," says a saddened Welsh radical, "I was an unworthy one."[41] "And why should they not depart," retorted a conservative pamphleteer, "when their assembly was by resignation dissolved, since they were but one degree above a conventicle, and that place, famous for the entertainment of so many venerable assemblies, was not so fit for them as Mr. Squibb's house, where most of their machinations were formed and shaped."[42]

Cromwell's reply to the collapse of the Barebones Parliament was not to devise—he never devised anything—but to accept a new constitution. Just as, after his impulsive dismissal of the Rump, he had accepted the ready-made plans of Major-General Harrison and his party of Saints for a Parliament of their nominees, so now, after the sudden disintegration of that Parliament, he accepted from Major-General Lambert and his party of conservative senior officers the newly prefabricated constitution of the Instrument of Government. By this the new Protectorate was set up, and Cromwell, as Lord Protector, care-

---

40. Abbott, *Writings and Speeches of Oliver Cromwell*, iv, 489.

41. *Thurloe State Papers*, i, 637; cf. [? Samuel Highland] *An Exact Relation of the late Parliament*, 1654 (*Somers Tracts*, vi, 266–84); *Clarke Papers*, iii, 9–10.

42. *Confusion Confounded, or a Firm Way of Settlement Settled* (1654).

fully limited by a council of senior officers, was required, after an interval of nine months, to summon a new parliament based on a new franchise. Since this new franchise was, basically, the realization of the plan already advanced by the conservative senior officers seven years earlier in Ireton's *Heads of Proposals*, it must be briefly analysed: for if ever the Independent gentry got the kind of parliament for which they had fought, it should have been in the two parliaments of the Protectorate elected on the franchise which they had thus consistently advocated. If social composition were sufficient to secure a harmonious and working parliament, that success should now be assured.

The most obvious feature of the new franchise is that while preserving property qualifications, and thus substantially the same social level of representation, it notably altered the distribution of membership, drastically cutting down the borough representation and greatly increasing the county representation. Compared with these facts, the creation of four new boroughs or three new county seats are insignificant adjustments of detail. In fact, the new franchise, in spite of these four new boroughs, reduced the total number of parliamentary boroughs in England and Wales from 212 to 106 and the total number of borough members in Parliament from 413 to 133. At the same time the county representation was increased from 90 out of 509 seats to 264 out of 400 seats. In other words, whereas in previous parliaments borough members had occupied 83 per cent and county members 17 per cent of the seats, in Cromwell's parliaments borough members were now to occupy 34 per cent and county members 66 per cent. The county representation was thus quadrupled, the borough representation more than halved.

What is the significance of this sweeping change? The Victorian writers who saw in Cromwell an early nonconformist Liberal supposed that he had in some way "modernized" the franchise. Had he not disfranchised rotten boroughs and enfranchised new boroughs? But the overall change, the gigantic switch from borough seats to county seats, seems to me more significant than such modifications of detail. Modern Marxist historians, believing that the Protectorate was a device of the rich, a forcing-house of capitalism, suppose that the new franchise was "designed to bring the electoral system into something like correspondence with the property-distribution in the country."[43] But where was the wealth of England? Much of the new wealth was wealth from trade,

43. C. Hill and E. Dell, *The Good Old Cause* (1949), p. 445.

concentrated—as the Independent gentry indignantly complained—more and more in the City of London. Even if we consider landed wealth only, it can hardly be argued that its distribution was better represented by the new members than by the old. Landed wealth was distributed among noblemen, merchants and gentry. Cromwell's parliaments under the new franchise contained no English peers and very few merchants.[44] They were parliaments of gentry, and not necessarily of the richer gentry either. The chief difference between the new and the old members was that whereas the old had been predominantly borough gentry the new were predominantly county gentry. What does this difference between "borough gentry" and "county gentry," in fact, mean?

A glance at English parliamentary history at any time between 1559 and 1832 provides the answer. The borough gentry were client gentry; the county gentry were not—they were, or could be, independent of patronage. It was largely through the boroughs that patrons and parliamentary managers had, in the past, built up their forces in Parliament. It was through them that Essex had built up a party against Cecil and Cecil against Essex, through them that Charles I might have resisted the opposition magnates and the opposition magnates were, in fact, able to resist him. Further, at all times, it was through the boroughs that able men—lawyers, officials, scholars—got into Parliament as the clients of greater men and provided both the Administration and the opposition with some of their most effective members. The "rotten" boroughs, in fact, performed two functions: first, they made Parliament less representative of the electors than it would otherwise have been; secondly, they made it less inefficient as an instrument of policy.

Now, if, as I have suggested, the Independent gentry were, in fact, the rural "back-bench" gentry, such as were afterwards represented in the Tory party of Queen Anne and the first two Georges, it is clear that they, like the later Tories, would be opposed to the borough system as being, by definition, a device of the front-bench politicians to evade the "equal representation" of "the people"—that is, of the country gentry—and to introduce "courtiers" instead of honest country gentry into parliament. It is true, many of them had themselves been returned in this manner in 1640; but their own front-bench leaders, the "Pres-

44. For merchant representation in Cromwell's parliaments, see M. P. Ashley, *Commercial and Financial Policy of the Protectorate* (1934), pp. 6–8.

byterian" magnates, had then deserted them, and by 1647 they were clamouring for decentralization in Parliament as in government, law, Church and education. They demanded a Parliament not of untrustworthy "courtiers" or experts but of sound, honest, representative men like themselves: a "more equal representative" of real Independents, uncontrolled by any professional caucus; and since, in their own language, "it was well understood that mean and decayed boroughs might be much more easily corrupted than the numerous counties and considerable cities,"[45] they sought it by a reduction of "corrupt" borough seats and a multiplication of "independent" county seats.[46]

That had been in 1647, when the Independents had been in opposition. Now they were in power; but their philosophy had not changed. It was not merely that they were committed by their past: that would be too cynical an interpretation. Their philosophy was genuinely held: experience had not yet shown the inherent impossibility of a completely back-bench Parliament or the inherent difficulty of decentralization by a revolutionary central government; and Cromwell no doubt supposed that honest, Independent country gentlemen, freely elected from within the Puritan fold, would naturally agree with the aims and methods of his rule. Further, from the point of view of Cromwell and his council, there were certain compensations. If, by disfranchising the boroughs, the government had deprived itself of a system of patronage, it had equally denied that system to opponents who might, like the opponents of Charles I, be more skilful in using it. Besides, to make doubly sure, the new government prudently added to the English Parliament a new system of exclusively government patronage which had not been, and indeed could not have been, considered in 1647. The sixty new Scotch and Irish seats created by the Instrument of Government

45. Ludlow, *Memoirs*, II, 48. The same argument was a commonplace among the later Tories.

46. Mr. Ivan Roots, in his book *The Great Rebellion* (1966), p. 182, criticizes this part of my essay on the ground that the Instrument of Government, which changed the parliamentary franchise, was the work not of "Independent country gentry" but of "a group of officers." But this is to ignore the previous history of the reforms. The Instrument of Government merely put into effect changes which had been advocated by Independent members of Parliament, and their constituents, since 1645 (and indeed before), and which had been worked out in detail in the Rump Parliament in 1650–51. The "group of officers" realized what the "Independent country gentry" had long demanded.

were not, of course, designed for genuine representatives of the newly conquered Scots or Irishmen: they were safe pocket-boroughs for government nominees.

A Parliament of congenial, unorganized, Independent county gentry, like-minded with himself, reinforced by sixty direct nominees and saved, by the franchise, from the knavish tricks of rival electioneers—surely this would give Cromwell the kind of Parliament he wanted. Especially after the radical scare of 1653, on which he was now able to dwell, and which had made him appear, even to many of those "Presbyterians" who shuddered at his regicide past, a "saviour of society." Therefore, when the members had assembled in September 1654, and had listened to a sermon on the arrival of the Israelites, after their years in the Wilderness, at their Land of Rest, Cromwell felt able to apply the text to them and to congratulate them too on having at last, "after so many changings and turnings," arrived at a period of "healing and settling." Furthermore, he assured them, they were now "a *free* Parliament"; just as he had not sought to control the elections, so he would not in any way control or interfere with their deliberations. Instead, he urged them to discover among themselves "a sweet, gracious and holy understanding of one another"; and having so urged them, he once again swept off to Whitehall to await, in olympian detachment, the results of their deliberations.

He did not have to wait long. Able men can work any system, and even under the new franchise the experienced republicans had contrived to re-enter parliament. Once in, they moved with effortless rapidity into the vacuum created by the Protector's virtuous but misguided refusal to form a party. The speed with which they operated is astonishing: one is forced to conclude either that Hesilrige and Scot were really brilliant tacticians (a conclusion which the recorded evidence hardly warrants), or that Cromwell had no vestige of an organization to resist them. At the very beginning they nearly got their nominee—the notorious regicide John Bradshaw—in as Speaker. Having failed they displaced the rival Speaker by the old dodge of calling for a Committee of the Whole House. At once Hesilrige and Scot were in control of the debates; the floating voters drifted helplessly into their wake; and the whole institution of the Protectorate came under heavy fire. Within a week Cromwell had repented of his words about "a free Parliament," and all the republican members, with Hesilrige, Scot and Bradshaw at their head, had been turned out by force. Legislation was then handed back to the real back-benchers for whom the Parliament had been intended.

Ironically, the result was no better. Again and again Cromwell, by his own refusal to organize and his purges of those who organized against him, created in Parliament a vacuum of leadership; again and again this vacuum was filled. A pure parliament of back-benchers is an impossibility: someone will always come to the front; and since Cromwell never, like the Tudors, placed able ministers on the front benches, those benches were invariably occupied from behind. The first to scramble to the front were always the republicans: they were the real parliamentary tacticians of the Interregnum. But when they were removed, a second group advanced into their place. It was this second group who now, by their opposition, wrecked Cromwell's first Protectorate Parliament.

Who were they? As we look at their programme, shown in their long series of successive amendments to the new constitution which had been imposed upon them, we see that, basically, it is the programme of the old "country party" of 1640. The voice that emerges from those "pedantic" amendments, as Carlyle so contemptuously called them, is the voice of the original opponents of Charles I, the voice even of Cromwell himself in his days of opposition. It protests, not, of course, against the decentralization which by his ordinances he had been carrying out, which was still his policy, and of which the new franchise itself was one expression, but against the machinery of centralization whereby this policy was declared: against the new Court, the new arbitrariness, the new standing army, the new taxes of that Man of Blood, Oliver Cromwell. Cromwell was caught up in the necessities and contradictions of power and found himself faced by his own old colleagues in opposition. In his days of opposition he too, like them, had demanded a parliament of back-benchers. Now he had got it—when he was in power. By a new franchise and a new purge he had confined Parliament to the old country party just at the time when he had himself inherited the position, the difficulties and the necessities of the old Court.

But who were the leaders who gave expression and direction to this new country party? A study of the tellers in divisions, which is almost all the evidence we possess, enables us to name the most active of them. There was John Bulkley, member for Hampshire, Sir Richard Onslow, member for Surrey, and, above all, Colonel Birch, member for Hereford; and the interesting fact about these men is that they were all old "Presbyterians"—men who had been arrested or secluded in Pride's Purge. Thus, when the republicans had been removed, it was not the Independents who had occupied the vacant front benches—that indeed would have been contrary to their nature: it was the "Presbyterians." Heirs of the original front-bench opposition of 1640, first expelled by the army, then disgusted by the act of regicide, they had now decided to stomach the usurper as the only immediate guarantee against the even greater evil of social revolution; but they were not going to accept him on his terms: they were going to fight for their own.

And did no one seek to serve the cause of Independency against these new, revived "Presbyterian" opponents? Yes, the new Government had its champions, but it is interesting to note that they too were not Independents. In the Barebones Parliament it was Sir Anthony Ashley Cooper, a former royalist, since turned "Presbyterian," who had now come back to politics as a Cromwellian and had sought in vain, and without support from Cromwell, to organize parliamentary resistance against the radical extremists. He had been by far the most active parliamentarian on the "conservative" side, one of their elected representatives on the Council of State, their regular teller in controversial divisions; and when his efforts had been in vain, it was another former royalist, Sir Charles Wolseley, who had proposed and carried out the act of resignation whereby the radicals had been cheated of their victory. Now, in the Parliament of 1654, the same two ex-royalists emerged again as the opponents of the new "country party." Only this time their roles were reversed. Leaving Sir Charles Wolseley to inherit his position as the champion of Cromwellian government, Cooper, a far abler man, now appeared less as a protagonist than a mediator: he sought not to preserve the Protectorate in the new authoritarian form in which it stood, but to make such compromises with the opposition as would make it a tolerable form of government, a form of government such as the original Independents had always demanded. Consistently with that original programme, he even sought to civilize the institution by making Cromwell king. But once again Cromwell, aloof at Whitehall, never supported this voluntary ally who now foreshadowed the only practical solution of his problem and was afterwards to prove the most formidable parliamentary tactician of the next reign; and before the abrupt end of the session Cooper drew the consequences. Despairing of Cromwell, he crossed the floor and joined Colonel Birch in opposition. A fortnight later the Protector, now dependent entirely on the Army officers, came suddenly down to Westminster prematurely to dissolve yet another parliament. "I do not know what you have been doing," he declared, "I do not know whether you have been alive or dead!"—it is difficult to conceive of Queen Elizabeth or Lord Burghley making such an admission—and with the usual flood of turbid eloquence, hysterical abuse and appeals to God, he dissolved prematurely what was to have been his ideal parliament.

For the next year Cromwell surrendered entirely to his military advisers. He still hankered after his old ideals—it is a great mistake, I think, to suppose that he ever "betrayed" the revolution, or at least the revolution for which he had taken up the sword. But he resigned himself to the view that those ideals could best be secured by administration, not legislation. After all, "forms of government" were to him indifferent: one system was as good as another, provided it secured good results; and now it seemed to him that the ideals of the revolution—honest rule such as "suits a Commonwealth," social justice, reform of the law, toleration—would be better secured through the summary but patriarchal rule of the major-generals than through the legal but wayward deliberations of even an Independent Parliament. And, in fact, the major-generals did attempt such things: as Cromwell afterwards admitted, even while he attacked them, "you, Major-Generals, did your parts well."[47] Unfortunately, like Archbishop Laud before him, he was soon to discover that in politics, good intentions are not enough. The major-generals, like the Laudian bishops, might seek to supervise J.P.s, to reform manners, to manage preachers, to resist enclosures; but all this was expensive, and when the Spanish war, like Laud's Scottish war, proved a failure, the major-generals themselves begged Cromwell, for financial reasons, to do what even Laud had had to do: to face a Parliament. If Cromwell, like Laud, had apprehensions, the major-generals comforted him. Confident, as military men so often are, of their own efficiency, they assured him that they, unlike the bishops, could control the elections and secure a Parliament which would give no trouble. So, in the autumn of 1656, after the most vigorous electioneering campaign since 1640, a Parliament was duly elected.

The result was not at all what the major-generals had expected. Ironically, one of the reasons for their failure was that very reduction of the borough seats which the Independents had themselves designed. In the interest of decentralization, Cromwell and his friends had cut

47. Burton, *Parliamentary Diary*, I, 384.

down a system of patronage which now at last they had learned to use. In the period of direct rule by the major-generals, the government had "remodelled" the boroughs and converted them into safe supporters;[48] but alas, thanks to the new franchise, the boroughs were now too few to stem the tide, and from the uncontrollable county constituencies, which the new franchise had multiplied, the critics of the government — genuine Independent critics of a new centralization — were returned, irresistible, to Westminster. The major-generals had secured their own election, but little more: thanks to their own new franchise, their heroic electioneering efforts had proved vain; and Cromwell, when he saw what they had done, did not spare them. "Impatient were you," he told them, "till a Parliament was called. I gave my vote against it; but you were confident by your own strength and interest to get men chosen to your hearts' desire. How you have failed therein, and how much the country hath been disobliged, is well known."[49] He might well rub it in, for one of the first acts of the Parliament thus called was to vote out of existence the whole system of the major-generals.

Thus, in spite of vigorous efforts to pack it, Cromwell's second and last Protectorate Parliament consisted largely of the same persons as its predecessor; and in many respects its history was similar. Once again the old republicans had been returned; once again, as not being "persons of known integrity, fearing God and of good conversation," they were arbitrarily removed. Once again the old back-benchers, the civilians, the new country party, filled the vacuum. But there was one very significant difference. It was a difference of leadership and policy. For this time they were not led by the old "Presbyterians." A new leadership appeared with a new policy, and the Independents now found themselves mobilized not against but for the government of Oliver Cromwell. Instead of attacking him as a "single person," they offered now to support him as king.

The volte-face seems complete, and naturally many were surprised by it; but, in fact, it is not altogether surprising. The new policy was simply the old policy of Sir Anthony Ashley Cooper, the policy of civilizing Cromwell's rule by reverting to known institutions and restoring, under a new dynasty, not, of course, the government of the Stuarts, but the old system from which the Stuarts had so disastrously devi-

48. See B. L. K. Henderson, "The Cromwellian Charters," in *Transactions of the Royal Historical Society*, 1912, pp. 129 ff.

49. Burton, *Parliamentary Diary*, I, 384.

ated. For after all, the Independents had not originally revolted against monarchy: the "Whig" republicans, who now claimed to be the heirs of the revolution, had, in fact, been belated upstarts in its course, temporary usurpers of its aims. The genuine "Tory" Independents, who had now reasserted themselves over those usurpers, had merely wanted a less irresponsible king than Charles I. Nor had they wanted new constitutions. They had no new doctrines: they merely wanted an old-style monarch like Queen Elizabeth. Why should they not now, after so many bungled alternatives, return to those original limited aims? Why should not Cromwell, since he already exercised monarchical power, adjust himself more completely to a monarchical position? In many ways the policy of the "Kingship party" in Parliament—however denounced by the republicans as a betrayal of the revolution which they sought to corner—was, in fact, the nearest that the Puritans ever got to realizing their original aims. Consequently it found wide support. The country party and the new court at last came together.

Who was the architect of this parliamentary *coup*? There can be no doubt about his identity. Once again, it was a former royalist. Lord Broghill, a son of the 1st Earl of Cork, was an Irish magnate who had become a personal friend and supporter of Cromwell. He was now Member of Parliament for County Cork, and his immediate supporters were the other members for Ireland, whom, no doubt, as Cromwell's Irish confidant, he had himself helped to nominate. There was Colonel Jephson, member for Cork City and Youghal, where Broghill's family reigned; there was Colonel Bridge, member for Sligo, Roscommon and Leitrim; there was Sir John Reynolds, member for Tipperary and Waterford; and there was Vincent Gookin, member for Kinsale and Bandon, Surveyor-General of Ireland. In other words, Lord Broghill was a great parliamentary manager, like the earls of Warwick and Bedford in 1640. While the major-generals, as officials, had organized the attenuated boroughs of England in their support, Broghill, a private landlord, wedded to an entirely different programme, had organized another area of influence, in Ireland. If the "Presbyterians' had been, in some respects, a Scottish party, and the Fifth Monarchy Men a Welsh party, the "Kingship-men" were, in their first appearance, an Anglo-Irish party.[50]

Once again the remarkable thing is the ease with which the new

50. The Irish basis of the "Kingship party" was pointed out by Firth, "Cromwell and the Crown," in *English Historical Review*, 1902, 1903.

leadership secured control over Parliament. Just as the eleven "Presbyterian" leaders, whenever they were allowed to be present in 1647–48, had always been able to win control of the Long Parliament from Vane and St. John; just as, after 1649, the little group of republicans dominated every parliament to which they were admitted; just as a score of radical extremists dominated the Barebones Parliament of 1653, or a handful of old "Presbyterians" the Purged Parliament of 1654, so the little group of "Kingship-men" quickly took control, against the protesting major-generals, of the Parliament of 1656. Their success illustrates the complete absence of any rival organization, any organization by the government—and, incidentally, the ease with which Cromwell, if he had taken the trouble or understood the means, could have controlled such docile parliaments.

For there can be no doubt that Cromwell himself, though he stood ultimately to gain by it, was at first completely surprised by Broghill's movement. As he afterwards said, he "had never been at any cabal about the same."[51] Indeed, when Broghill's party first made itself felt in Parliament, it was positively opposed to the declared policy of the Protector; for Cromwell was still committed to the system of government by major-generals, and his faithful shadow, Secretary Thurloe, had already drafted a speech urging the continuation of that system— a speech which the sudden, belated conversion of his master and himself to the "Kingship party" left undelivered in his files.[52] Furthermore, the previous advocate of kingship, Sir Anthony Ashley Cooper, had been firmly excluded from the present Parliament by order of Cromwell himself. We are obliged to conclude that Cromwell at first genuinely intended to support the major-generals, and that, in jettisoning them, he did not follow any deliberate course. He simply wearied of them, as he had wearied in turn of the king, of the "Presbyterians," of the Levellers, of the Rump, of the Saints; and having wearied, he surrendered once again to a new party, just as, in the past, he had surrendered in turn to Vane, to Ireton, to Harrison, to Lambert—successive

51. Burton, *Parliamentary Diary*, I, 382.

52. The draft is in *Thurloe State Papers*, v, 786–88, where it is described as "minute of a speech in Parliament by Secretary Thurloe"; but, in fact, I can find no evidence that it was ever delivered, and I presume that it is a draft. In any case, delivered or undelivered, it shows that Thurloe, and therefore Cromwell, had intended to continue the major-general system, which, in fact, they jettisoned.

mentors who had successively promised to lead him at last out of the "blood and confusion" caused by their predecessors to that still elusive elixir, "settlement."

Having captured a majority in Parliament, the "Kingship party" set methodically to work. The government of the major-generals was abolished; the kingship, and the whole political apparatus which went with it—House of Lords, Privy Council, State Church, and old parliamentary franchise—was proposed. Except for the Army leaders, whom such a policy would have civilized out of existence, and the obstinate, doctrinaire republicans, all political groups were mobilized. The officials, the lawyers, the Protectoral family and clients, the government financiers—all who had an interest in the stability of government— were in favour. At last, it seemed, Cromwell had an organized party in Parliament. He had not made it: it had made itself and presented itself to him ready-made. It asked only to be used. What use did Cromwell make of it?

The answer is clear. He ruined it. Unable to win over the Army leaders, he wrestled with them, rated them, blustered at them. "It was time," he protested, "to come to a settlement and leave aside these arbitrary measures so unacceptable to the nation." [53] And then, when he found them inexorable, he surrendered to them and afterwards justified his surrender in Parliament by describing not the interested opposition of serried brass-hats but the alleged honest scruples of religious Nonconformist sergeants. Of course, he may have been right to yield. Perhaps he judged the balance of power correctly. Perhaps he could not have maintained his new monarchy without Army support. There was here a real dilemma. And yet the Army could certainly have been "remodelled"—purged of its politicians and yet kept strong enough to defend the new dynasty. As Monck afterwards wrote, and by his own actions proved, "there is not an officer in the Army, upon any discontent, that has interest enough to draw two men after him, if he be out of place." [54] Cromwell's own personal ascendancy over the Army, apart from a few politically ambitious generals, was undisputed. Instead of pleading defensively with the "Army grandees" as an organized party, he could have cashiered a few of them silently, as examples to the rest,

53. Burton, *Parliamentary Diary*, I, 382.
54. *Thurloe State Papers*, VII, 387.

and all opposition to kingship would probably have evaporated; for it was nourished by his indecision. The total eclipse first of Harrison, then of Lambert, once they had been dismissed—though each in turn had been second man in the army and the State—sufficiently shows the truth of Monck's judgment.

Be that as it may, Cromwell never, in fact, tried to solve the problem of army opposition. After infinite delays and a series of long speeches, each obscurer than the last, he finally surrendered to it and accepted the new constitution only in a hopelessly truncated form: without kingship, without Lords, without effective Privy Council. Even so, in the view of Lord Broghill and his party, it might have been made to work. But again, Cromwell would not face the facts. Neither in his new Upper House nor in his new Council would he give the "Kingship-men" the possibility of making a party. Spasmodic, erratic gestures now raised, now dashed their hopes, and led ultimately nowhere; the leaders of the party wrung their hands in despair at the perpetual indecision, the self-contradictory gestures of their intended king; and in the end, in January 1658, when the Parliament reassembled for its second session, the old republicans, readmitted under the new constitution, and compacted by their long exile, found the "Kingship-men" a divided, helpless, dispirited group, utterly at their mercy.

At once they seized their opportunity. The lead was given by their old leader, Sir Arthur Hesilrige. Why, he asked, had the preacher, in his opening address, said nothing in praise of "that victorious Parliament," the Rump? "I cannot sit still and hear such a question moved and bide any debate." Whereupon that other oracle of the republicans, Thomas Scot, "said he could not sit still but second such a notion, to hear one speak so like an Englishman to call it a victorious Parliament." From that moment the incorrigible combine was at work again, each seconding the other, filibustering unchecked with long, irrelevant speeches on the horrors of the *ancien régime*, boastful personal reminiscences, the divine right of parliaments, the virtue of regicide, the glories of the Rump. Hesilrige, who once spoke for three hours on past history, beginning with the Heptarchy, prophesied a two months' debate and "hoped no man should be debarred of speaking his mind freely, and as often as he pleased." As for himself, "I could speak till four o'clock." Within ten days all constructive business had become impossible: the Parliament, the French ambassador reported to his government, "était devenu le parlement de Hesilrige," and as such Cromwell angrily dis-

solved it, "and God judge between you and me."[55] Before he could summon another, he was dead.[56]

If Oliver Cromwell's parliaments were thus consistently hamstrung
through lack of direction, the one Parliament of his son Richard was,
if anything, more chaotic—and that in spite of immense efforts to prepare it. For weeks before it met, Secretary Thurloe and the Council, on
their own admission, did "little but prepare for the next Parliament."[57]
The old franchise, and with it the old opportunities of borough patronage, was restored. The Council, as Ludlow sourly remarks, "used
their utmost endeavours to procure such men to be chosen as were their
creatures and had their dependencies on them."[58] But the result was as
unsatisfactory as ever. The "Kingship party" was now dead: they would
have fought to make Oliver king, but who would fight to put the crown
on Richard's head rather than on that of Charles II? Lord Broghill did
not even sit in the new Parliament. On the other hand, the republicans
were full of confidence. The demoralization of the Cromwellians gave
them hope; in organization they were supreme; and when the Parliament met it was soon clear that Hesilrige and Scot were once again its
masters.

55. Burton, *Parliamentary Diary*, iii, 874, 117, 141, and ii, 437 (and cf. iii, 140); Bordeaux to Mazarin, 18 Feb. 1658, cited in F. Guizot, *Histoire de la république d'Angleterre*
(Paris, 1864), ii, 629.

56. For the failure of the "Kingship party" in Cromwell's last year see the analysis of their tactics in R. C. H. Catterall, "The Failure of the Humble Petition and
Advice," in *American Historical Review*, Oct. 1903 (ix, 36–65). Catterall concludes that
Cromwell was wiser than the "Kingship-men" and was working, more slowly, more
prudently and more patiently than they, to the same result: "Time was the essential
requisite. . . . Time, however, was not granted." What one thinks of Cromwell's plans
and prospects of success must depend on one's estimate of his character as revealed by
his previous career, and here I must dissent from Catterall. I cannot agree that patience
was "a quality always at Oliver's disposal and always exercised by him," nor find, in his
career, evidence of a slow and prudent progress towards a clearly envisaged political
aim. Rather he seems to me to have successively borrowed and then impatiently discarded a series of inconsistent secondhand political systems; and I see no reason to
suppose that he was any nearer to a final "settlement" at the time of his death than at
any previous time in his history of political failure.

57. *Thurloe State Papers*, vii, 562.

58. Ludlow, *Memoirs*, ii, 49, and references there cited, cf. *Calendar of State Papers*
(*Venetian*), xxxi, 276–77, 282, 284, 285.

Masters for what? Certainly not to lead it to constructive legislation. Republicanism in England, except in their fossilized minds, was dead: perhaps it had never been alive outside that limited terrain. Certainly it had not inspired the beginning of the rebellion, and certainly it was extinct at the end of it. From 1653 onwards, when the "Whig" policy which they had grafted on to the revolution had been repudiated, Hesilrige and Scot and their friends were simply obstructionists. They had a doctrine and a parliamentary organization. Thanks to that doctrine, and that organization, and the absence of any rival organization, they had achieved power for a time; but when their policy had been rejected, and they proved incapable of modifying it or making it acceptable, they could never recover power and they could use their clear, hard, narrow doctrine and their unrivalled parliamentary organization solely to destroy every rival party in Parliament, until the enemy they hated most of all, the monarchy of the Stuarts, returned to crush them and their rivals alike. From 1653 onwards the republicans were simply the saboteurs of every Parliament to which they could gain admittance. The weakness of the executive was their opportunity: an opportunity not to advance a cause, but simply to destroy their own rivals; and in no Parliament was that weakness so tempting to them, or that destruction so easy, as in the Parliament of Richard Cromwell, who was too feeble to adopt his father's methods and expel them.

Consequently the record of Richard's Parliament makes pitiful reading—even more pitiful than that of Oliver's parliaments, which at least is enriched by the serious purpose and volcanic personality of the Protector. In vain Richard's Speaker, regularly rebuked for his inability to control the debate, protested at the irrelevancy of members: "we are in a wood, a wilderness, a labyrinth. Some affirmative, some negative, which I cannot draw into one question. . . . The sun does not stand still, but I think you do not go forward." Even a new and more forceful Speaker, who himself pitched into the debate, answering everyone and laying about him "like a Busby among so many school boys," proved hardly more effective.[59] Most pitiful of all was the fate of Mr. Secretary Thurloe, the chief representative of the Protector in his Parliament, the man who was accused of having packed the Parliament with at least eighty of his nominees. If only he had done so, as it was his duty to have

59. Burton, *Parliamentary Diary*, iii, 192, 269–70, 281, 333, and iv, 205, 213, 234, 243.

done, the government might have fared better.[60] In fact, attempting to defend the indefensible, romantic, irrational foreign policy of the government, Thurloe found himself hopelessly left behind as one speaker after another carried the debate off into irrelevant byways. Before long, Thurloe, instead of defending his foreign policy, was defending himself against a charge of having sold English subjects into slavery in the West Indies; and in a debate on the constitution he even found himself in a minority of one.[61]

The Secretary of State in a minority of one! The mere thought of such a possibility would have made Mr. Secretary Cecil or Mr. Secretary Walsingham—if they could even have conceived such a thought—turn in their graves. And yet this is the man whom historians have supposed—merely on account of the number of letters which he either wrote or received or steamed open—to be the genius of Cromwellian government![62] When such a thing could happen it was clear that the old Elizabethan system of which the Cromwellians had dreamed, and indeed any parliamentary system, had indeed broken down.

Thus Oliver Cromwell's successive efforts to govern with and through Parliament failed, and failed abjectly. They failed through lack of that parliamentary management by the executive which, in the correct dosage, is the essential nourishment of any sound parliamentary life. As always with Cromwell, there is an element of tragic irony in his failure: his very virtues caused him to blunder into courses from which he could escape only by the most unvirtuous, inconsistent and indefensible expedients. And the ultimate reason of this tragic, ironical failure lies, I think, in the very character of Cromwell and of the Independency which he so perfectly represented. Cromwell himself, like

60. In fact, Thurloe protested, "I know not of three members thus chosen into the House." Burton, *Parliamentary Diary*, iv, 301.

61. Burton, *Parliamentary Diary*, iii, 399, 287; and cf. [Slingsby Bethel] "A True and Impartial Narrative . . . ," in *Somers Tracts*, vi, 481.

62. The political ability of Thurloe seems to me to have been greatly overrated by historians. His skill in counter-espionage is attested by his own state papers, and it excited such admiration at the time that it afterwards became legendary; but otherwise he seems to have been merely an industrious secretary who echoed his master's sentiments (and errors) with pathetic unoriginality. A good secretary is not necessarily a good Secretary of State.

his followers, was a natural back-bencher. He never understood the subtleties of politics, never rose above the simple political prejudices of those other backwoods squires whom he had joined in their blind revolt against the Stuart Court. His first speech in Parliament had been the protest of a provincial squire against popish antics in his own parish church; and at the end, as ruler of three kingdoms, he still compared himself only to a bewildered parish-constable seeking laboriously and earnestly to keep the peace in a somewhat disorderly and incomprehensible parish. His conception of government was the rough justice of a benevolent, serious-minded, rural magistrate: well intentioned, unsophisticated, summary, patriarchal, conservative. Such was also the political philosophy of many other English squires who, in the seventeenth century, turned up in Parliament and, sitting patiently on the back benches, either never understood or, at most, deeply suspected the secret mechanism whereby the back benches were controlled from the front. In ordinary times the natural fate of such men was to stay at the back, and to make a virtue of their "honesty," their "independency," their kinship rather with the good people who had elected them than with the sharp politicians and courtiers among whom they found themselves. But the 1640s and 1650s were not ordinary times. Then a revolutionary situation thrust these men forward, and in their indignation they hacked down, from behind, the sharp politicians and courtiers, the royalists and "Presbyterians," who had first mobilized them. Having no clear political ideas, they did not—except in the brief period when they surrendered to the republican usurpers—destroy institutions, but only persons. They destroyed parliamentarians and the king, but not Parliament or the throne. These institutions, in their fury, they simply cleaned out and left momentarily vacant. But before long the vacancy was refilled. By careful tests and a new franchise, Parliament was reopened—to Independents (that is, back-benchers) only; under careful reservations and a new title, the throne was reoccupied—by an Independent (that is, a back-bench) ruler. At last, it seemed, Crown and Commons were in natural harmony.

Alas, in political matters natural harmony is not enough. To complete the system, and to make it work, something else was necessary too: an Independent political caucus that would constitute an Independent front bench as a bridge between Crown and Parliament, like those Tudor Privy Councillors who gave consistency and direction to the parliaments of Henry VIII and Elizabeth. Unfortunately this was the one thing which Cromwell always refused to provide. To good Independents any political caucus was suspect: it smacked of sharp politicians and the Court. An Independent front bench was a contradiction in terms. Even those who, in turn, and without his support, sought to create such a front bench for him—Sir Anthony Ashley Cooper, Sir Charles Wolseley, Lord Broghill—were not real Independents, but, all of them, ex-royalists. Like his fellow-squires (and like those liberal historians who virtuously blame the Tudors for "packing" their parliaments), Cromwell tended to regard all parliamentary management as a "cabal," a wicked interference with the freedom of Parliament. Therefore he supplied none, and when other more politically minded men sought to fill the void, he intervened to crush such indecent organization. In this way he thought he was securing "free parliaments"—free, that is, from caucus-control. Having thus secured a "free parliament," he expected it automatically, as a result merely of good advice, good intentions and goodwill, to produce "good laws," as in the reign of his heroine Queen Elizabeth. He did not realize that Queen Elizabeth's parliaments owed their effectiveness not to such "freedom," nor to the personal worthiness of the parties, nor to the natural harmony between them, but to that ceaseless vigilance, intervention and management by the Privy Council which worthy Puritan back-benchers regarded as a monstrous limitation of their freedom. No wonder Cromwell's parliaments were uniformly barren. His ideal was an Elizabethan Parliament, but his methods were such as would lead to a Polish Diet. Consequently, each of his parliaments, deprived of leadership from him, fell in turn under other leadership and were then treated by him in a manner which made them feel far from free. Only in Cromwell's last year did a Cromwellian party-manager, without encouragement from him, emerge in the House of Commons and seek to save the real aims of the revolution; but even he, having been tardily accepted, was ultimately betrayed by his inconstant master. In that betrayal Cromwell lost what proved to be his last chance of achieving the "settlement" which he so long and so faithfully but so unskilfully pursued.

Thus it is really misleading to speak of "Cromwell and his parliaments" as we speak of "Queen Elizabeth and her parliaments," for in that possessive sense Cromwell—to his misfortune—had no parliaments: he only faced, in a helpless, bewildered manner, a succession of parliaments which he failed either to pack, to control or to understand. There was the Parliament of Hesilrige and Scot, the Parliament of Squibb and Moyer, the Parliament of Birch, the Parliament of Broghill, and the

Parliament of Hesilrige once again; but there was never a Parliament of Oliver Cromwell. Ironically, the one English sovereign who had actually been a Member of Parliament proved himself, as a parliamentarian, the most incompetent of them all. He did so because he had not studied the necessary rules of the game. Hoping to imitate Queen Elizabeth, who, by understanding those rules, had been able to play upon "her faithful Commons" as upon a well-tuned instrument, he failed even more dismally than the Stuarts. The tragedy is that whereas they did not believe in the system, he did.

8 | Scotland and the Puritan Revolution

Between the union of the crowns in 1603 and the union of the parliaments in 1707, the relations of England and Scotland were thoroughly unhappy. Unequal in strength, different in history, the two countries had enough similarity to force them together and yet enough diversity to make their contact always explosive. Moreover, each feared the other. To some Scots—to the "beggarly blue-caps" who streamed down to the golden Court of James I and set up dynasties in the north on the unearned profits of England—the union of crowns was a great gain; but to Scotland in general it was a great loss: the King of Scotland became an absentee captured by a foreign establishment, and able, if he wished, to use foreign resources against the liberties of his native country. For the same reason, England too had its apprehensions. The resources of Scotland might be slight, but they were not negligible. In internal English affairs they might give a narrow but decisive margin of superiority to the Crown over its opponents—as they afterwards did to its opponents over the Crown. From the earliest days of the union of crowns, the profoundest of English statesmen, Francis Bacon, foresaw that a revolution in England might well begin in Scotland.[1] A generation later, it did.

The English Puritan Revolution, at every stage, was affected by Scottish affairs. Without Scotland it could not have begun; having begun, without Scotland it might have been over in a year. But again

1. *The Letters and the Life of Francis Bacon*, ed. James Spedding, iii (1868), 73.

and again—in 1641, in 1643, in 1648, in 1651—Scotland reanimated the flames in which England was being consumed. Thereafter, when the revolution had triumphed in England, Scotland paid the price: the revolution was carried to it. The uneasy half-union of 1603 was completed, as even James I had not wished to complete it then, but as the statesmen of Queen Anne would be obliged to complete it afterwards, by a full union of parliaments. Indeed, the union of 1652 was far closer than that of 1707: for it was a union of Church and law as well. Moreover, I shall suggest, it entailed a social revolution in Scotland such as would not occur in fact till after 1745. Only it did not last. Within a few years all crumbled; yet another army set out from Scotland and ended by restoring, with the monarchy, the old half-union of 1603. With that restoration the last age of Scotland's independence, the darkest age in its history, began.

The character and effect of Scottish intervention in the English Revolution is well known. Everyone knows how the Scots were driven into revolt by Charles I's Act of Revocation and Archbishop Laud's liturgy; how the leaders of the Puritan opposition in England enlisted them as allies; how, thanks to that alliance, they were able to force Charles I to call a parliament and to prevent him from dissolving it; how Charles I, in the summer of 1641, by a personal visit to Scotland, sought and failed to reverse that alliance; how the English Parliament in 1643 renewed it, and brought a Scottish army, for the second time, into England; how Charles I, in reply, sought once again to raise up a rival party and a rival army in Scotland, and this time nearly succeeded; how the Marquis of Montrose, in his career of triumph, offered to lay all England as well as all Scotland at the feet of the king; but how, in fact, after his disaster at Philiphaugh and the surrender of the king not to his English but to his Scottish subjects, the Scottish Covenanters, in 1646, sought to impose their terms on both the king and the Parliament of England; how they were disillusioned and returned to Scotland, selling their king (as the royalists maintained) for £400,000 to the revolutionary English party which was to cut off his head; how the Scottish parties then sought, in vain, by yet other invasions of England, to stay or reverse the revolution: to snatch Charles I from the scaffold or to impose Charles II as a "covenanted king" on the throne; how Oliver Cromwell destroyed the first attempt at Preston, the second at Dunbar and Worcester; how all Scottish parties were thereafter pulverized by the victors, the Hamiltons executed, Argyll driven back to obscurity in Inveraray, the Committee of Estates rounded up, the General Assembly dissolved, and the whole country reduced to obedience, and blessed with order and tranquillity, for the remaining lifetime of the Protector.

All this is well known. Every English historian admits it. And yet, how many problems are left out of this summary! Even as we recite the facts, the questions force themselves upon us. For why did the Scots intervene so constantly, and at such cost, in English affairs? What springs of action prompted them again and again, in the 1640s, to impose a new pattern on a reluctant English society? And what was the nature of the revolution which, in the 1650s, was imposed on Scottish society by England? English historians, who have worked so intensively on the Puritan Revolution in the last half-century, have seldom asked these questions. To them, as to the English Independents of the time, the Scottish forces were "a mere mercenary army," which king and Parliament in turn summoned to their aid in their purely English struggle. They do not see them as the expression of social forces in Scotland. Indeed, they hardly look at the social forces of Scotland. Scotland, to them, is not an intelligible society responding to intelligible social forces. Like seventeenth-century visitors to Scotland, they tend to dismiss it as a barbarous country populated only by doltish peasants manipulated, for their own factious ends, by ambitious noblemen and fanatical ministers. And equally, they see the Union of 1652 as a mere military occupation, imposed, for the sake of order, on an exhausted land. Even Scottish historians have hardly sought to fill this gap. As far as published work is concerned, the sociology of seventeenth-century Scotland remains a blank.

Into such a blank it is rash for a foreigner to intrude, and in this essay I shall only offer, with prudent caution, some general suggestions. They concern the two problems which I have outlined above: the attempt of the Scots to impose Presbyterianism on England in the 1640s and the attempt of the English Puritans to carry through a social revolution in Scotland in the 1650s. But fundamental to both these problems, and to the failure of both attempts, is the pre-existing difference between the two societies: a difference which was masked, even at the time, by superficial similarities, but which was in reality profound: so profound that it made the attempt of the Scots to impose their own form of Presbyterianism on England futile, even absurd, and the attempt of the English to reform Scottish society in the 1650s premature and hopeless except under continuing force.

For in fact, behind all similarities, England and Scotland were poles apart. Consider the century before 1640, the century (some would say)

whose new strains, in England, gradually built up the pressures leading to revolution. In that century both England and Scotland had rejected the Roman supremacy. To that extent they were similar. But after
that similarity, what a difference! In England population, trade, wealth
had constantly increased. New industries had grown up and found new
markets in a richer, more sophisticated lay society at home. The economic growth of England had been extraordinary and had created,
however unequally, a new comfort and a new culture. But in Scotland
there had been no such growth. There was little trade, little industry,
no increase of population. Always poor and backward, it now seemed,
by contrast, poorer and more backward still. That contrast is vividly
illustrated by the comments of those who crossed the Tweed, in either
direction. We read the accounts of English travellers in Scotland. Their
inns, cries Sir William Brereton, are worse than a jakes; and he breaks
into a sustained cry of incredulous disgust at that dismal, dirty, waste
and treeless land. Then we turn to the Scottish travellers in England.
"Their inns," exclaims Robert Baillie, "are like palaces"; and Alexander
Brodie of Brodie, goggling at all the wicked fancies and earthly delights
of London, reminds us of a bedouin of the desert blinking in the bazaar
of Cairo or Damascus.[2]

Nor was the contrast merely one of material progress. Material
progress brings its strains. In England there had been a remarkable centralization, both of population and of wealth, in the twin cities of London and Westminster. There the new industrial wealth was centred,
there the swollen bureaucracy of government, the Court so resented
by the "country," was rooted. The population of London, in that century, had been quadrupled. Behind the political errors of the statesmen
and churchmen in the 1630s, these inescapable social facts provided the
solid substance of discontent. The "country," starved and drained (as
it felt) by a monopolist City and an anachronistic, parasitic Court, was
determined to assert its rights; and it felt able to do so because the same
century had bred up an educated lay estate, independent of Church and
government, and organized in a powerful institution: Parliament.

From all these new forces, and new strains, Scotland was exempt.
In Scotland, as there was no inflation, so there was no pressure; nor was
there any such concentration either of commerce or of government.

---

2. *Travels in Holland, the United Provinces, England, Scotland and Ireland 1634–5*
by Sir William Brereton (Chetham Society, I, 1844), 102–6. Robert Baillie, *Letters and
Journals* (Edinburgh, 1841–42), I, 271.

Edinburgh was, as it would long remain, destitute of mercantile spirit. There was no Court. While the other princes of western Europe had built up bureaucracies round the throne, the kings of Scotland had been the playthings of great, incorrigible feudatories from whom they had finally fled to England. Without merchants, without "officers," Scotland lacked altogether the new class of educated laymen on which the greatness of Tudor England had been built. For practical purposes its educated middle class consisted of lawyers and clergy, the two pillars of conservatism which the laity of England sought to reform. Consequently it lacked also their institutions. The Scottish Parliament was as feeble as the Castilian Cortes. It was because it represented so little that the country acquiesced, in 1707, in its ultimate migration to London.

Finally, there was a third difference. Scotland had already had a religious revolution. By an irony which seems also a law of history, the new religion of Calvinism, like Marxism today, had triumphed not in the mature society which had bred it, but in underdeveloped countries where the organs of resistance to it were also undeveloped. And because it had triumphed in backward countries, it had adapted itself to the circumstances of such countries. It had become dictatorial, priestly, theocratic. In England, in the reign of Edward VI, the Calvinist clergy (John Knox among them) had sought to determine the nature of the Reformation. They had failed and, in the reign of Mary, had been forced to flee abroad. On the accession of Elizabeth, they had returned eager for the power which seemed to await them. But the self-confident laity of England had soon reduced them to order. Only in moments of crisis—as in 1588—did the organized Calvinist clergy seem temporarily to represent the English people. But in Scotland, where there was no such laity, the Calvinist clergy had established their hold on society. They saw themselves as the educated *élite* which would impose a new doctrine, a new Church, a new morality on an indifferent people, and drag them upwards. And the laity of Scotland, recognizing its own weakness, accepted them, largely, as such. Kings and courtiers might dislike these insufferable dominies. Individual Scotsmen of culture might prefer the more tolerant, more civilized clergy of the Anglican Church. But those who wished to mobilize the people in Scotland had to use the tribunes of the people; and by 1640 those tribunes were the most highly organized force in Scottish life. If the Scottish Parliament, the organ of the Scottish laity, was a poor thing, the General Assembly, the organization of its clergy, was not. In times of crisis it could be, like the lay Parliament of England, the voice of the nation.

Thus between England and Scotland there was, by 1640, an immense social gulf, which the preceding century had widened. Beneath their common Protestantism and common language, concealed by their common opposition to the same threat, their whole structure differed. Because it had not shared the expansion of England, Scotland was exempt from the strains of growth. Because it had experienced a more radical religious reformation, it no longer felt certain ancient pressures. And because there was little or no independent, educated laity, the Calvinist clericalism, which in England or France might have been a transitory stage, in Scotland (as in New England) became a conservative tyranny. These different social facts entailed a radical difference of ideas. English Puritanism, though articulated by its clergy, was essentially a lay movement. It was also radical, looking forward to complete the half-reformation of the Tudors by a full emancipation of the laity. Scottish Presbyterianism, though sustained by its laity, was essentially clerical. It was also conservative, seeking not to go forward, to a lay society, but to secure, against the new, creeping episcopalianism of the Stuarts, the clerical reformation which had already been won. In 1640 this was a very real problem: it imposed on the Scots the need of a new, forward policy.

The policy of the Scottish Kirk in the 1640s was the natural result of its conservatism and its weakness. In this it did not differ from the other Calvinist societies of Europe. Everywhere, in 1640, established Calvinism was on the defensive. Having triumphed in weak and backward countries it had automatically exposed their weakness. For Calvinism, by then, had been rejected by all the military monarchies of Europe. Catholic, Lutheran and Anglican alike regarded it as a revolutionary doctrine and hoped, openly or secretly, to see it ultimately stamped out in the few, obscure corners where it still throve. The King of Spain longed to crush it in Holland; the Duke of Savoy dreamed of the destruction of Geneva; the French monarchy would not long tolerate the "republic" of La Rochelle; the King of England planned to undermine the Kirk of Scotland. Everywhere Calvinist rulers knew that their society was in danger from powerful neighbours, and to protect it they had, perforce, to adopt one of two policies. Either they must attenuate their Calvinism in order to secure the patronage of non-Calvinist princes, the enemies of their enemies, or, if such patronage were unattainable, they must fall back on themselves, call up their most radical preachers, appeal to the Calvinist International, and, in self-defence, carry the revolution abroad. In the sixteenth century the former policy was adopted by the Dutch, who needed the support of England and France; it was also adopted by the Scots, who sheltered under the wing of that useful, though Anglican neighbour, Queen Elizabeth. The latter was adopted by the Calvinists of the Palatinate and Bohemia in 1618–20; it was also, increasingly, adopted by the Scots when the successors of Queen Elizabeth, who were also their own kings, turned against them and left them isolated in the world.

At first, it was not necessary to adopt it in all its rigour. The Scottish Kirk, in 1638, might be threatened by the Crown of England and Scotland, but the errors of Charles I had given it powerful allies in both countries. The king might think that he had divided the classes in Scotland. He might suppose that by his "innocent Act of Revocation" he had freed the gentry from their "clientele and dependence" on the great lords. Many of the Scottish lairds, he claimed, had thanked him for their emancipation from that "intolerable bondage."[3] But in fact, as so often, he was wrong. Noble patronage was not broken; the gentry were not rendered independent; and by 1638 the former, as patrons, and the latter, as ruling elders, formed the strength of the National Covenant. Moreover, looking abroad, the architects of that Covenant could see, or thought they could see, a similar alliance of classes in England, all equally determined, with them, to bring the crown to reason. Thanks to this internal solidarity and to these external allies, the Scottish Covenanters were able to overthrow the new episcopacy which had been planted among them and "restore" the Kirk to its purest form.

Undoubtedly it was a great victory. But how long would it last? When the Scottish leaders looked about them, they had to admit that it had been a very close thing, the result of a remarkably favourable conjuncture such as could never be predicted, could hardly be expected to last, and might never recur. And of course, in changed circumstances, it might easily be reversed. Obviously, while the favourable conjuncture lasted, they must do whatever was necessary to make their victory permanent. And after the experience of the last generation they knew what was necessary. They must export their revolution. Theoretically the Scotch Kirk might co-exist with "moderate episcopacy" in England. It had done so in the previous century. But that was when Queen Elizabeth had reigned in England, and the two kingdoms had been

3. The king's view is expressed for him in [W. Balcanquhall], *A Large Declaration concerning the Late Tumults in Scotland* . . . (1639).

separate. King Charles and the union of crowns had changed all that. And anyway, how long would "moderate episcopacy" remain moderate? Episcopacy had been "moderate" in Elizabethan England and in Jacobean Scotland; but insensibly it had been transformed, as it could be transformed again. So the Scots leaders were clear. In England, as in Scotland, episcopacy must be rooted out. There must be no compromise, no return to the Elizabethan system. Only one form of Church-government in England was compatible with the permanence of Presbyterianism in Scotland: England must become Presbyterian too. The full-blown, bishopless, clerical Calvinism of 1639 must be accepted, *in toto*, by the stronger kingdom.

Moreover, thought the Scots, it could easily be done. There was no need of compulsion, hardly even of pressure. As they looked at England they saw only the resemblances, never the differences. Admittedly England was much richer and more powerful than Scotland, but the social and political structure, to their eyes, seemed exactly the same. Was not the parliamentary opposition, which had triumphed, there too bound together by noble patronage, inspired by "Calvinian" clergy, made solid by the gentry? Was there not a general outcry against the bishops? And did not the English, in that triumphant winter of 1640–41, looking back on the immediate causes of their triumph, "all everywhere profess" that, under God, they owed "their religion, liberties, parliaments and all they have" to the victorious army of their brethren the Scots? What wonder if, in the exaltation of the moment, with Charles I's policy in ruins, Strafford and Laud in the Tower, and the citizens of London submitting monster petitions for the abolition of episcopacy, the ever-complacent Scottish clergy overlooked the great social gulf which really separated the two countries, and supposed that "the Scots discipline" could be established in England by a mere hint from them, the experts, the teachers and the saviours of England?

So, that winter, four Scottish clergymen set out from Edinburgh to guide the grateful English towards the true doctrine and perfect system of Presbytery. It was a planned operation: each had his set task. One was to bring down "his little Grace" the Archbishop of Canterbury and the whole episcopal system; one was to destroy the Anglican ceremonies which accompanied it; the third was to define the Presbyterian system; the fourth to dish the sectaries who might have other ideas, of "the New England way"; and all four were to preach by turns to the Scots commissioners and all else who would come to hear the saving gospel from the north. The main advocate of Presbytery among these four evangelists was Alexander Henderson, the framer of the National Covenant. The alternating hammers of ceremonies and sectaries were George Gillespie and Robert Blair. The confident grave-digger of Anglicanism was the voluble, invaluable letter-writer, that incomparable Scotch dominie, so learned, so acute, so factual, so complacent, so unshakably omniscient, so infallibly wrong, Robert Baillie A.M. (Glasweg), regent of Glasgow University and minister of Kilwinning, Ayrshire.

The four clergymen set to work. They preached, they wrote, they lobbied; and always they saw the end of their labours just round the corner. Baillie's letters home are a continual purr of complacency. Of course, he admitted, the poor benighted English could not leap all at once up to the Scotch level; but he found them eminently teachable; and though his arms, as he said, were "full of my old friend, his little Grace," he was always ready to open his mouth too, to teach them. (Indeed, Baillie admitted that he opened his mouth "somewhat to his own contentment" and that it "weighted his mind" to keep it shut.) So on one occasion, he preached for an hour on God's singular mercies to the Scots, whereupon (he said) "many tears of compassion and joy did fall from the eyes of the English." Everywhere, he observed, there was not only a crying need, but also a general desire for Presbytery. There might be a few separatists, pursuing "the New England way," but "the far greatest part are for our discipline"; and anyway, it would be easy to use the separatists in the work of demolition and then discard them. Once the "rubbish" of Anglicanism was swept away, it would be easy to "build a new house": the house of the Lord according to John Calvin, John Knox and Andrew Melville. In May 1641, when the English Parliament signed the "Protestation" of solidarity against Strafford, it was, Baillie confidently declared, "in substance, our Scottish Covenant."

So Scot to Scot smugly blew his tribal trumpet; but the walls of the episcopal Jericho were strangely slow in falling. First there were excuses: the matter, said the English, must be deferred "till first we have gotten Canterbury down." The Scots took up the challenge. Baillie threw himself at "his little Grace," prepared to give him "the last stroke," and looked eagerly forward to his "funeral"; but somehow nothing happened. To hasten the matter, all four ministers wrote pamphlets, which, they felt, were "much called for": in particular, Alexander Henderson himself wrote "a little quick paper" against English bishops, giving "very good reasons for their removal out of the Church." The result was most unfortunate. The king, who had just publicly declared his faith in episcopacy, was "so inflamed as he was never before in his time for any other business." He told the Scots that, by such interference, they had forfeited their privileges; the English reformers maintained a prudent silence; and even "divers of our true friends" (lamented Baillie) "did think us too rash." Internal English affairs, the Scots were told, were an English matter: they should mind their own business. Thereupon, to Baillie's dismay, the House of Lords set up a committee to reform episcopacy: an infamous "trick," to "caulk the rotten hulk of episcopacy" and set it afloat again. The Scotch lay commissioners interposed discretion and, according to their instructions, submitted papers requesting a conformity of Church-government as a special means of preserving peace between the two kingdoms; but it made no difference. It was with difficulty that the English Parliament was prevented from telling them, too, to mind their own business. In the end they were simply told that the two Houses had already considered the reform of Church-government in England, and would proceed along their own lines "in due time, as shall best conduce to the glory of God and peace of the Church."[4]

So that was that. In the summer of 1641 the Scots were finally paid off and sent home. Pym had used them and dismissed them, just as he had used and then dismissed the Irish Catholic enemies of Strafford. Both had secured their immediate aims: Strafford was dead, and the king, that summer, ratified the Scottish revolution. But neither had obtained the long-term guarantees which they sought: there was to be no recognition of Catholicism in Ireland, and the Scottish revolution was not to be exported to England. And indeed, Pym could reply, why should it be? The English Church was the affair of Englishmen. The Scots had indeed been very useful, but they had been serving their own interest; they had been well paid; and they should be satisfied with what they had got: they had helped to restore, in England, that Elizabethan system which had protected the rear of the young Kirk of Scotland, and would do so still. So, in England, on 7 September, all the church bells were rung, to give thanks to God for a peace with Scotland, the departure of the Scots, and the basis laid for a purely English Church reformation.

Unfortunately history did not stop there. Those who call in foreign aid cannot complain if their enemies do so too. Charles I had not ac-

4. R. Baillie, *Letters and Journals*, I, *passim*; W. A. Shaw, *A History of the English Church . . . 1640–1660* (1900), pp. 127–33.

Roger Boyle, Lord Broghill, 1st Earl of Orrery

cepted the English reformation of 1641: and if the Scots and the Irish thought themselves double-crossed, why should he not exploit their resentment? In a year much had happened in Scotland; the unity of the Covenant was dissolving as the ambitions of Argyll showed through it. Much had happened in Ireland too since the great unifier of discontent, Strafford, had fallen. So in both Scotland and Ireland the king sought new allies to continue the struggle. In Scotland he failed: his personal presence there only served, in Clarendon's words, to make "a perfect deed of gift of that kingdom" to the Covenanting Party. But in Ireland the troubled waters yielded better fishing, and before long a train of events had begun which led insensibly to civil war in England, and thereby once again brought the English Parliament and the Scotch General Assembly together.

As soon as civil war appeared imminent, the English Parliament approached the General Assembly: would their brethren the Scots stand by the English Houses in their just struggle? But this time the Scots were not going to be double-crossed, as in 1641. Once bitten is twice shy, and they were resolved to have legal guarantees before they gave any help. The essential condition of help, they replied, was "uniformity of Kirk government." Prelacy must be "plucked up root and branch" in England, and Presbyterian government "by assemblies, higher and lower, in their strong and beautiful subordination" must be substituted for it. The English Parliament was prepared to renounce episcopacy, at least on paper; it was prepared to utter pious general formulas; but it absolutely refused to give any guarantee of Presbyterianism. It preferred to fight the king alone. At that time it thought it could win quickly. A little later, it had doubts, and applied again to the Scots. But still it said nothing about Presbyterianism. Baillie waxed sardonic about the strange "oversight." "It was a wonder," he wrote, "if they desired any help, that they denied to use better means for its obtaining." It was not till the summer of 1643, when the parliamentary cause seemed hopeless—when the king was preparing for the final onslaught, and the radicals in Parliament were in revolt—that Pym decided to seek a Scotch alliance even, if necessary, on Scotch terms. And those terms had not changed. They never would change. The Scots themselves, by 1643, were thoroughly apprehensive. They were almost as eager for an alliance as the English. But even so, they would stand out for the old price. As Baillie wrote, "the English were for a civil league"—mutual assistance without reference to religion—"we for a religious Covenant": a binding covenant of exact religious conformity.

Such was the origin of the Solemn League and Covenant. How hard the English fought against the Scotch condition, the Covenant, we know. Every phrase which alluded to it was contested in both Houses. All the verbal subtlety of Vane was needed to find a formula which could both mean and not mean it: mean it for the Scots, not mean it for the English. All the mental reservations of Cromwell were needed to slip out of that formula when it had been accepted. Pym himself, in his last recorded speech, pleaded sheer necessity as its only justification. Nevertheless, it was accepted; and because the name was accepted, the Scots, those incorrigible nominalists, supposed that the thing was accepted too. In December 1643 Robert Baillie, now a professor and more self-assured than ever, set out once again with his colleagues to London, confident, in spite of all past experience, that this time the cat was in the bag. All that was needed was to keep it there. And this now seemed easy. If only a "well-chosen committee," packed with Scots, were established in London, "they would soon get the guiding of all the affairs both of this state and church."

So the Scots set to work again. Their aim was constant and clear: "to abolish the great idol of England, the Service Book, and to erect in all the parts of worship a full conformity to Scotland." From the start there was to be no compromise. They refused to hear even Pym's funeral sermon, delivered by the pope of English "Presbyterianism," Stephen Marshall, "for funeral sermons we must have away, with the rest." In the Assembly of Divines as in Parliament "we doubt not to carry all clearly according to our mind." By adjuration from Scotland, reinforced by the Calvinists of France and Switzerland, all deviation from the true doctrine was to be forbidden; schismatics "and the mother and foster of all, the Independency of congregations" were to be suppressed; all suggestions of toleration were to be crushed. The English Parliament had double-crossed the Scotch General Assembly once. It must not do so again. Nor (thought the Scots) could it do so again. It was committed now by a greater need and chained in redoubtable syllables of assent.

Alas, even the most pedantic, professorial syllables cannot alter historic, social facts. In spite of the Covenant, in spite of Marston Moor, in spite of much ink and much breath, facts remained facts, and before many months had passed Baillie's letters became, once again, a series of anguished ejaculations. It was not only that Vane and St. John, "our former friends," the framers of the alliance, who owed all (said Baillie) to the Scots, had turned against them. Vane and St. John, it soon transpired, were acknowledged Independents. Even the professed English "Presbyterians," even Denzil Holles, their lay leader, even Stephen Marshall, their religious oracle, were no better. England, exclaimed Baillie, in a moment of truth, even parliamentary England, was either "fully episcopal" or "much episcopal"; Presbytery, to the English, was "a monster"; and the only hope of establishing "the Scots discipline" south of the Tweed was by means not of sermons or pamphlets, committees or advice, but of "our army at Newcastle." "If by any means we would get these our regiments, which are called near thirty, to 16,000 marching men," then "by the blessing of God, in a short time, we might ruin both the malignant party and the sectaries." Already, before the king was defeated, the Scots were thinking of a military conquest of England.

Vain hope! It was not the Scottish army that was to decide the English civil war. It is true, when the first war was over, an English party called the "Presbyterians" was in power. It is true, this party confirmed the abolition of episcopacy, putting the bishops' lands up for sale. It is true, the name and form of Presbyterianism were accepted to fill the void. But why were the bishops' lands sold? To raise money to get rid of the Scots who, once again, as in 1641, had served their turn and were to be sent home. And what was the Presbyterianism which was set up in the place of episcopacy? Was it "full conformity with the Kirk of Scotland"? Certainly not. It was, as Baillie himself lamented, "a lame erastian Presbytery" in which all the essentials of the Scottish system—the divine right of ruling elders, the judicial independence of the Church, its "strong and beautiful" internal structure, its formidable power of excommunication—had been sacrificed not only to the "sectaries" in Parliament and "the sottish negligence of the ministers and gentry in the shires," but also to the stubborn refusal of the so-called "Presbyterians" themselves.

For in fact—whatever compliance they made for the sake of Scottish help—the English "Presbyterians" were not Presbyterians. Perhaps no label has caused such political and historical confusion as the label "Presbyterian" attached to an English political party. Because of that label, seventeenth-century Scottish clergymen built up impossible hopes and modern historians have tied themselves in unnecessary knots. Why, asked the former, did the English "Presbyterians" not carry out the terms of the Solemn League and Covenant? Why, ask the latter, did the English "Presbyterians," whose Scottish brethren clung to their Church through thick and thin, become Independents in the 1650s and Anglicans in the 1660s? The answer to these questions is simple. Except for a few clergymen, tempted by clerical power, there were no English Presbyterians. Whatever history may call them, whatever events sometimes forced them to appear, the Englishmen who attempted to stabilize the revolution in 1646 were, as they had been in 1641, as they would be in 1660, "moderate Anglicans," believers, under whatever name, in a temperate, lay-controlled, Elizabethan episcopacy.

If we look at the men, if we look at their policy, always making allowances for circumstances, this is clear enough. Clarendon, going through the list of the "great contrivers," all of whom he had known, marvels to think of the damage done by these men, nearly all of whom, on examination, turned out to be so "well-affected" to the Anglican Church. John Pym himself, to his dying day, extolled "moderate episcopacy" as the ideal Church system, and the words in which he nevertheless urged his fellow "rebels" to swallow the Solemn League and Covenant show that he was addressing men who shared those ideals. Whatever words they might utter in the heat of the moment, whatever measures might be forced upon them by the necessity of war-finance or the mounting passions of civil war, those men would always have gladly settled for the system which divided them least. They might abolish episcopacy on paper, but all through the first civil war they took care not to abolish it irreversibly in fact. Even when, at long last, under Scottish pressure, the fatal step was taken and the bishops' lands were put up for sale, the consequences were not accepted. The English "Presbyterians," having got rid of the Scots and their absurd demands, were prepared to settle for a three-year probationary period which, as everyone knew, would be a half-way house to the restoration of episcopacy. Even the "Presbyterian" Lord Mayor of London of the time could afterwards be praised by a "Presbyterian" minister of the time, for his constant fidelity to the episcopal Church of England.[5] And as a matter of fact, those who became Independents were not very different in this. In 1647 when it was their turn to offer terms to the king, they offered to restore "moderate episcopacy." Oliver Cromwell himself, once the

5. See *The Royal Commonswealthsman* (1668), being the funeral sermon preached at the death of Thomas Adams, the "Presbyterian" Lord Mayor of London in 1646, by Nathaniel Hardy, whose own sermons in 1646–47 show him to have been a "Presbyterian."

violent years were over, sought to reunite the Anglican clergy in his Puritan Church[6] and gave a state funeral, with the Anglican liturgy, in Westminster Abbey, to the great figurehead of moderate episcopacy, Archbishop Ussher. For "moderate episcopacy" meant laicized episcopacy. Whatever form of Church structure (that is, of social structure) the English Puritans were prepared to accept, the one essential ingredient was laicization. If they could not have "moderate episcopacy," the next best thing might be called "Presbyterianism." It might borrow Presbyterian features. But essentially it would be Independency: a decentralized, laicized, Protestant Church.

To the Scots ministers this fact was never clear. Provincial, complacent men, accustomed to pontificate from their pulpits, tenacious of the dogma and discipline which had served them at home, inured to the nominalism of the Schools and accustomed to the docility of their flocks, they never dreamed that similarity of words could conceal such divergence of meaning. So they alternated between absurd confidence and righteous indignation. At one time—in 1646, when Montrose had been defeated in Scotland and the king in England, and the English "Presbyterians" had won control in the English Parliament—they would be triumphant. Total victory, it seemed, was theirs. In that year the General Assembly ordained that all Scotsmen who had been in arms with Montrose, or had dealt with him, or drunk his health, should be excluded from communion till they had made public confession of their sins; and the Commissioners of the Church insisted that, in all future treaties, they should be consulted as to the lawfulness of the terms. Meanwhile, at Newcastle, the Scots were demanding that the king accept the Covenant himself and enforce it in all England, and Baillie was confidently distributing the Church patronage of England among his friends. There was Mr. Lee, for instance, "a very able and deserving man," and very hot against Independency. Now was the time, Baillie instructed the English Parliament, to reward his merits: "the deanery of Christ Church is his due." But England, unlike Scotland, refused to accept these peremptory clerical commands; Mr. Lee was not made Dean of Christ Church; and before long Baillie would be expressing bitter, petulant disappointment. The "Presbyterians" in Parliament, he found, would not do his bidding: the "Presbyterian" aldermen were really "malignants" at heart; even the "Presbyterian" ministers turned out to be either royalists or Independents. When

6. See R. S. Bosher, *The Making of the Restoration Settlement* (1951), pp. 45–46.

Cromwell, with his "army of sectaries," overthrew the English "Presbyterians," who would have thought that half the "Presbyterians"—including Stephen Marshall himself—would have supported him? It was all most bewildering. It only showed, to Baillie, that almost everyone in England was extremely wicked, and that "no people had so much need of a Presbytery."[7]

So the Scottish intervention of 1643 proved, in the end, as vain as that of 1640. Each time the Scots had done their work; each time they had insisted on the same terms; each time they had been paid off in cash only. They had not exported their revolution. They had not done so because, between England and Scotland, there was a social difference which made Presbyterianism, in their sense, impossible; and by insisting on the impossible, by dragging the heirs of Pym further towards "the Scots model" than they would willingly go, they had ended by provoking a revolution and placing in power a party which was determined to have no more to do with them, but would settle England on an English model only: a model which, in the Church, might be laicized episcopacy—that is "moderate Anglicanism"—or might be laicized nonepiscopacy—that is Independency—but would not be Presbyterianism.

The importance of the Scottish failure in England can hardly be overestimated. Not only did it precipitate a revolution in England: it also, by its repercussions, opened the way to disaster in Scotland. From the moment of the Cromwellian revolution of 1647, the unity of the Scottish classes, forged in 1638, collapsed. After 1647 the Scots politicians, the "Engagers," recognized that the Presbyterianism of the Kirk could not be imposed on England. As far as religion was concerned, they would gladly have taken Scotland out of English politics. They would have settled for Presbyterianism at home and an allied, though not identical, Protestantism in England, as in the days of Queen Elizabeth. If they did in fact invade England in 1648, that was no longer to impose the Covenant: it was because the King of Scotland needed to be rescued from his English subjects. It was yet another fatal consequence of the union of crowns. On the other hand the Kirk still clung to its old policy. It opposed the invasion of 1648, not because it had given up a policy of coercion, but simply because this particular invasion was not consecrated by the old purpose. As Baillie wrote, "that Scotland at this

7. W. L. Mathieson, *Politics and Religion. A Study in Scottish History from the Reformation to the Revolution* (Glasgow, 1902), II, 82–83. Baillie, *Letters and Journals*, II, 177, 393.

time has a just cause of war against the sectarian army in England and their adherents, none of us do question": the English, by failing to erect a full Presbyterianism, had broken the Solemn League and Covenant and the Scots had every right to enforce its terms. For these reasons, he and his friends were "most cordial for a war." But this war of the Engagers was the wrong kind of war. At best it could only lead to "ane Erastian weak Presbytery with a toleration of Popery and episcopacy at court, and of divers sects elsewhere." That was no reason for the Kirk to go to war.[8]

So the forward policy of the Scottish Calvinists, like that of the Palatine Calvinists, ended only in catastrophe. They did not export their revolution: they only created a counter-revolution against their interference, and, as a result, brought division and disaster to themselves. One by one the Scottish parties were defeated: the politicians at Preston, the zealots at Dunbar, the nationalists at Worcester. By the autumn of 1651 Scotland lay prostrate before the arms of revolutionary England. All its national organs were destroyed. The king had fled abroad; the Committee of Estates had been seized; the General Assembly, "the glory and strength of our church upon earth," would soon be dissolved. Instead of the old Scottish revolution being forced upon England, the new English Revolution was about to be forced upon Scotland, now a part of the united, kingless Commonwealth of England, Scotland and Ireland. "Full conformity," with a vengeance, had come. Thus we come to the second chapter of our story: the policy not of the Scottish Presbyterians in an England which they had fondly hoped to manage, but of the English Independents in a Scotland which they had effectively conquered and which, for nine years, they ruled at will.

The rule of the English Commonwealth and Protectorate in Scotland is often regarded as a mere military operation. Certainly Scotland was governed, like England, by the sword. Certainly the Scottish nation and the Scottish Church had been defeated and were not reconciled to their defeat. Certainly the parliamentary union was not a free or equal union: the Scottish, like the Irish, members of Cromwell's parliaments were largely nominees of the English government. But it would be wrong to stop there, or suppose that the English government did nothing more positive in respect of Scotland than grant it freedom of trade, which it was too disorganized to use, and impose a welcome

8. Baillie, *Letters and Journals*, III, 25, 42, 52.

peace upon its Highland clans and Lowland factions. Within the English Revolution there was a positive social content, implied in the word "Commonwealth"; and this positive content it retained even when it was exported. Originally, of course, the English exported their revolution for the same reason which had impelled the Scots to export theirs: because it was insecure at home. As long as Charles II was accepted as King of Scots, as long as Catholic Ireland did not acknowledge the revolutionary government of England, that government did not feel safe against counter-revolution. Therefore Scotland and Ireland must accept the revolution too. But acceptance was not to be mere submission. It was to entail the same social content: Scotland and Ireland were to become "free commonwealths" too. In the midst of the fire and slaughter which they carried over Ireland, Cromwell's soldiers believed that they were engaged on a great constructive work, "the forming and framing of a commonwealth out of a corrupt, rude mass."[9] In Scotland there was less need of fire and slaughter; the mass was less corrupt, less rude; but the object was the same and it was pursued in the same messianic spirit. "When once the light breaks forth in this kingdom," wrote an English soldier in Scotland, "it will warm and heal apace, but the clouds must be broken first, the foundations of this old fabric must be shaken"; when that had been done, when Scotland had been "jussled up" to the level of the English Revolution, then "the poor, blind dead people shall see the light and feel the warmth of the sun (sweet liberty) to redeem them out of their present slavery."[10] A social revolution in Scotland comparable with that of England would be the basis of a stable union between the two countries, a natural defence not, this time, of the Scottish Kirk but of the English Commonwealth.

What was the nature of the social revolution which Cromwell sought to export to Scotland? In England that revolution was not essentially radical, though it had needed radical methods for its achievement. Essentially it was a seizure of power in the state by the classes who had been accustomed to power in the country but who, under the Stuarts, had been, or had felt themselves, more and more excluded by a parasitic Court and its Church: in other words, by the laity, the gentry. In opposition these men had demanded, and now in power they sought to realize, a general policy of decentralization and laicization. The feu-

9. The phrase is that of a Cromwellian soldier in Ireland, Colonel John Jones. (National Library of Wales MSS. 11440-D.)

10. *Clarke Papers*, II (Camden Society, 1894), 46.

dal taxes, the antique patronage which had sustained the Court and its peerage were to be abolished, together with the Court and the House of Peers: the Parliament was to be reduced to a parliament of gentry, and country gentry at that—the reduction of borough seats and the multiplication of county seats would achieve that purpose. Education was to be decentralized by the foundation of new local schools and colleges, and laicized by the reform of teaching and the adoption of new "Baconian" subjects. Religion was to be decentralized by the break-up of episcopal and capitular property, the redistribution of patronage, and the use of both for the "propagation of the Gospel" in remote, neglected areas. At the same time it was to be laicized by practical lay control and systematic toleration. Law was to be decentralized by breaking the monopoly of the London law courts and setting up "county registers" and "county judicatories," and laicized by the simplification of procedure and language. The whole policy was summarized as "reformation of law and clergy."

Of course there were differences of interpretation. Some men interpreted the policy in a conservative, some in a radical, even a revolutionary, spirit. Oliver Cromwell himself interpreted it in a conservative spirit. He believed that the policy should and must be carried out by the gentry. But equally he insisted that its benefits must be enjoyed by those humbler allies whose voices, in the counties and more democratic boroughs, had carried the Puritan gentry into Parliament in 1640 and whose arms, in the New Model Army, had since carried them through radicalism into power. All his life Cromwell would never betray "the godly party"—that is, the country party in depth, the alliance of gentle and simple which alone could preserve the gains of revolution—and many of his apparent inconsistencies, from his surrender to the Agitators in 1647 to his rejection of the crown in 1657, are to be explained by this genuine resolve never to betray his followers or split the "godly party."

But if Cromwell was always determined to earn the support of his radical followers, equally he would never adopt their radical policy. To him, the radicalism to which he had sometimes surrendered had always been a tactical necessity. It had been an inconvenient necessity because it had split the united front of 1640, driving some men into royalism, some into "Presbyterianism," some into Independency. Ultimately, Cromwell sought to restore that united front and, on the new basis of an England without Stuart kings, to continue the old reforming policy of 1640. The bigots of radicalism or republicanism might protest at his "reconciling" of royalists, "malignants," "cavaliers"; but he did not care. To him radicalism, republicanism, had been stages only; and, anyway, the original aims of the English Parliament were often better represented by men who, after 1640, had become royalists, like Anthony Ashley Cooper or Lord Broghill or Sir Charles Wolseley, than by the doctrinaires of a now obsolete radicalism, like the Levellers or the Fifth Monarchy men, or of a fossil republicanism, like John Bradshaw or Sir Arthur Hesilrige or Thomas Scot. So, from his basis in the Army and in the "godly party," whose vertical unity was his strength, Cromwell reached out horizontally to reunite the gentry whom war and revolution had divided, to find supporters among old "Presbyterians," even among old royalists, and so to realize at last, in new circumstances, the old policy of decentralization and laicization, "reformation of law and clergy."

Such was Cromwell's policy for England. If we wish to see the application of it we must not look at his parliaments, those sterile assemblies which (he complained) always cavilled at the admittedly questionable basis of his rule instead of making "good laws." We must look at his direct administration. This we can do particularly in two periods: in the nine months between the setting up of the Protectorate in December 1653 and the meeting of his first protectoral Parliament in September 1654, the great period of rule by ordinance of the Protector and Council; and in the period between his two protectoral parliaments, from the summer of 1655 to the end of 1656, the period of rule by major-generals. And the same is true for Scotland. For in Scotland too he could legislate by ordinance; there too he had military commanders. And so, if we look, we can see the same policy applied in Scotland too: not systematically of course (even in England it could not be applied systematically), but in the intervals of financial and military distractions, and yet with sufficient constancy to show the same positive aims as in England.

The parallel between Cromwell's policy in Scotland and in England can be seen, first of all, in the character of his advisers. If we wish to see the continuity and consistency of his English policy, we can look at the group of civilians whom he kept around him. These men who were his ablest supporters in his nominated Parliament, the Barebones Parliament, and who continued with him in the Council of State of the Protectorate, are first found as a group, significantly enough, in that committee for the reform of the law which Cromwell personally forced the Rump Parliament to set up. Similarly, in Scotland, the nucleus of Cromwell's closest advisers was formed by the three Scottish members of the joint commission for the administration of justice which the Rump, again undoubtedly under his pressure, set up in 1652. These three, with one addition, reappear as the nominated Scottish Members of the Barebones Parliament; and they continue as the Scottish members of the Scottish Council of State. In their common origin, as well as in their diverse past, these men illustrate both the consistent aim and the conciliatory method of Cromwell's policy.

The first three of these men, the commissioners for the administration of justice who, with four English colleagues, replaced the old Court of Session, were Sir William Lockhart of Lee, Sir James Hope of Hopetoun and Sir John Swinton of Swinton. If we may use such terms in Scotland, the first was a royalist, the second a Presbyterian, the third an Independent. Lockhart, from a servant of Charles I, an ally of Montrose, whose anti-clerical views he shared, was to become a firm "conservative" supporter of Cromwell, his best diplomatist, and a member, by marriage, of his family circle. The lands and offices with which he was rewarded in Scotland would draw sour comments from less yielding (or less tempted) compatriots. Hope was the son of Charles I's greatest law officer—the man who had framed the Act of Revocation, but then become a strong Covenanter. He was an enterprising and successful manager of his property, which included profitable lead-mines in Lanarkshire, and he believed in the improvement of Scotland untrammelled by English politics. He and his brother even urged Charles II to accept the English Revolution and be content with his Scottish crown. To this the king replied that he would first see both brothers hanged at one end of a rope and Cromwell at the other, and he sent them both to prison. Hope continued to press his advice and service on Charles II, but after Worcester saw that reform would never be achieved through him, and became a Cromwellian. Pressed by Cromwell to attend the Barebones Parliament, he at first refused; he would, he said, "own" the English government and act under it in Scotland; but he would not "go out of Scotland or meddle in state affairs." However, he was persuaded—although Cromwell afterwards regretted the persuasion. So Hope travelled up to London in the same coach with the third of "our triumvirs" among the judges, Sir John Swinton. Swinton was a Berwickshire laird of radical views: an extreme Covenanter who refused any compromise with the Stuarts. After Dunbar, he, like several other extremists, had seen that the old politics were useless and turned to Cromwell. For this he had been excommunicated by the Kirk and condemned to death by the Scottish Parliament; but such sentences had now lost their effect. Swinton accepted cordially the new situation and became, in Burnet's words, "the man of all Scotland most trusted and employed by Cromwell." [11]

These three were the original nucleus of Cromwell's Scottish advisers. In 1653 they were joined by a fourth, Alexander Jaffray. Jaffray was provost of Aberdeen, a city and county which had never much relished the Covenant. In his youth he had studied the cloth industry in England and been educated (like many Scotsmen, including Sir James Hope) among the Huguenots of France. In 1649, and again in 1650, he had been one of the commissioners from the Scottish Parliament sent to Holland to impose the Covenant on Charles II. Afterwards he was ashamed of the hypocrisy and compulsion involved: "we did sinfully both entangle and engage the nation and ourselves and that poor young prince to whom we were sent, making him sign and swear a covenant which we knew from clear and demonstrable reasons that he hated in his heart." Jaffray fought and was wounded at Dunbar, and after seeing "the dreadful appearance of God against us" there, and conversing, as a prisoner, with Cromwell and his chaplain, John Owen, he decided, like Swinton, that Presbyterianism was "not the only way of Christ." He even ventured to say so in writing to the Rev. Andrew Cant, the Presbyterian oracle of Aberdeen. This caused a predictable explosion, whose blast lodged Jaffray in the arms of Cromwell. [12]

Another Scotsman whom Cromwell summoned to his Parliament in London was Alexander Brodie of Brodie in Nairnshire. Brodie had accompanied Jaffray to Holland and Jaffray now urged him to accept Cromwell's invitation. But Brodie, a narrow, timorous spirit ("he is not a man of courage," he wrote of himself, "but faint and feeble and unstedfast, wavering, unclear-sighted and impure"), after much introspection and a family conclave, accepted advice from the Lord that the

11. For Lockhart's firm anti-clericalism, see *The Diary of Sir Archibald Johnston of Wariston* (Scottish History Society, 1911–40), III, 7. For criticism of him, see John Nicoll, *A Diary of Public Transactions . . . 1650–1667* (Edinburgh, 1836), p. 180; *The Diary of Mr. John Lamont of Newton 1649–71* (Edinburgh, 1830), p. 90. For Hope, see his *Diary*, 1646, ed. P. Marshall (Scot. Hist. Soc., 1958) and 1646–54, ed. Sir J. B. Paul (Scot. Hist. Soc., 1919); for Swinton, Burnet, *The History of My Own Time* (Oxford, 1897), I, 229.

12. For Jaffray, see his *Diary*, ed. J. Barclay (Aberdeen, 1833).

Covenant was still binding and that he must "eschew and avoid employments under Cromwell."[13]

These were the Scotsmen with whose aid Cromwell sought to carry the English social revolution, as he understood it, into Scotland: a revolution, there too, of "reformation of law and clergy." And what did this mean in fact, in Scottish circumstances? First of all, it meant reducing the power of those who, in the civil wars, in Scotland as in England, had frustrated the expression and application of such a policy: that is, of the great lords, with their oppressive patronage, and the intolerant Kirk, with its monopoly of the pulpit. It was the union of these two forces which had first launched the National Covenant and so made the English Revolution possible; but by now the same forces were the main obstacle to the progress of that revolution in their own land, and as such they must be broken. The English Commonwealth was determined to set up in Scotland, as in England, a gentry-republic, where all land was free of feudal burdens, where the patronage of the nobility was destroyed and where the Church had no coercive power over the laity. "Free the poor commoners," was the cry of hopeful Scots after the battle of Worcester, "and make as little use as can be either of the great men or clergy."[14]

The English Parliament did not need to be told. From the beginning, from the first proposal of union in the winter of 1651, this policy had been announced. "Forasmuch as the Parliament are satisfied," ran the opening declaration of its purpose, "that many of the people of Scotland who were vassals or tenants to, and had dependence on, the noblemen and gentry (the chief actors in these invasions and wars against England) were by their influence drawn into . . . the same evils," such persons who now put themselves under the protection of the Commonwealth were to be "set free from their former dependencies and bondage-services" and to live as tenants, freeholders and heritors, "delivered (through God's goodness) from their former slaveries, vassalage and oppressions." Thereupon the Republic declared the abolition of all jurisdictions other than those derived from Parlia-

13. For Brodie see his *Diary* (Aberdeen Spalding Club, 1863); also G. Bain, *Lord Brodie, his Life and Times* (Nairn, 1904). He refused office again in 1657 (*Thurloe State Papers*, 1742, VI, 351, 364).

14. *Mercurius Scoticus*, 14 Nov. 1651, cited in C. H. Firth, *Scotland and the Commonwealth* (Scot. Hist. Soc., Edinburgh, 1895), p. 339.

ment. All feudal tenures and all heritable jurisdictions were cancelled. "Justice," wrote a newswriter in the summer of 1652, "was wont to be open and free for none formerly but great men; but now it flows equally to all; which will in short time make them sensible from what bondage they are delivered." [15]

The Long Parliament declared; it was Cromwell who executed. In April 1654, in that first happy period of freedom from Parliament, so rich in legislation, the Protector's Council issued the Ordinance of Union abolishing, among other things, all feudal lordships, heritable jurisdictions, military services and wardship and all forfeitures and escheats except to the Lord Protector. Over two years later the ordinance was converted into an Act by the second Parliament of the Protectorate, and the Cromwellians who knew Scotland foretold a new era of peace when "all these unjust powers"—"the greatest hindrance to the execution of our laws" as James VI had called them—would be abolished "and justice will flow in an equal channel." From now on, they said, the great landlords would have to exchange patronage for wealth: instead of demanding from their tenants slavish personal attendance, they could demand improved economic rents, and so "nobles and gentles," as well as their tenants, "will be much happier than before." [16]

Hardly less formidable than the despotism of the great nobles was the despotism of the Church. The English Puritans had no intention of breaking the established Church of Scotland. They would accept it, just as they would have accepted the established episcopal Church of England, just as they had accepted the Presbyterian Church system which the events of the civil war had imposed on England—but on the same conditions. Just as English episcopacy was to be "moderate," and English "Presbyterianism" "Erastian," so Scottish Presbyterianism must be mitigated by lay claims. The power of the Church courts must be broken; the clergy must be under the civil law; the right of excommu-

15. The Declaration of 28 Oct. 1651 is printed in C. S. Terry, *The Cromwellian Union* (Scot. Hist. Soc., Edinburgh, 1902), p. xxiii. For the newsletter see ibid., pp. 180–81.

16. C. H. Firth and R. S. Tait, *Acts and Ordinances of the Interregnum* (1911), II, 871–75; T. Burton, *Parliamentary Diary* (1828), I, 12–18. Cf. Firth, *Scotland and the Protectorate* (Scot. Hist. Soc., Edinburgh, 1899), p. 333; *The Basilikon Doron of King James VI*, ed. J. Craigie, I (Scottish Text Society, 1944), pp. 88–89.

nication, which the English "Presbyterian" Parliament had absolutely refused to accept from its Scottish mentors, must now be reduced in Scotland; and there must be a large toleration. What Baillie had most feared from the restoration of the uncovenanted Stuarts in 1648—"ane weak Erastian Presbytery" with a large toleration beside it—was now to be set up by the republic. On this point, the republic was quite explicit. In its first declaration, it merely stated that it would promote the preaching of the Gospel in Scotland and advance the power of true religion and holiness, without defining who should be the preachers or what was true; but when its commissioners arrived in Edinburgh, they introduced, into this vagueness, an alarming clarity. Ministers, they said, whose consciences obliged them to wait on God according to the order of the Scottish Churches were to be protected and encouraged in their peaceable exercise of the same; but so also were others who "not being satisfied in conscience to use that form, shall serve and worship God in other Gospel way." That "great Diana of the Independents," a toleration, was to be established in Scotland.[17]

To break the power of great lords and established clergy was a negative act. The positive policy of the Commonwealth consisted in building up, in the vacuum thus created, a constructive reformation on the English model. We must now turn to examine this positive policy: a policy of reformation, as in England, of law and clergy.

The reform of Scottish law was to take place in two stages. First, there was to be a restoration of law and order, which had collapsed at the time of Dunbar, and which every Scottish county petitioned the conqueror to restore. That was done, and done effectively. But the Commonwealth intended to go further than that. It intended to assimilate the law of Scotland to that of England and thereby not only to make the union complete, but also to effect in Scotland that same decentralization of justice and simplification of law which was one of the most constant demands of the English country party and one of the greatest ambitions of Cromwell himself. In the earliest instructions given to the English commissioners sent to Scotland at the end of 1651, this aim is made clear. In order that the Scottish people may have right and justice duly administered to them, the commissioners were told to see the civil law of England put into execution "as near as the constitution and use of the people there and the present affairs will permit." For this

17. The Parliament's *Declaration* is printed in Terry, *The Cromwellian Union*, p. xxi; the commentary of the commissioners, ibid., p. xxvi.

purpose the commissioners could set up courts at will and appoint as law-officers both Englishmen and Scots.[18]

Within a few months, the English Council of State itself set up, to replace the old, hated Scottish Court of Session, a mixed board of four English and three Scottish "commissioners for the administration of justice." This was the board on which Lockhart, Hope and Swinton — "our three complying gentlemen," as Baillie called them — took their seats. Thereafter the particular reforms began. Legal fees, as in England, were regulated. The use of Latin in legal documents, as in England, was abolished. Legal language and procedure, as in England, were made easier. These were all measures of simplification. Decentralization was represented by the restoration, by ordinance, of local courts-baron to try petty cases (but with provision, here too, against heritable jurisdictions), and by the sending of English justices on circuit through the country; also by the establishment, in 1655, of justices of the peace on the English model. These had been instituted before, by James VI, but it was only under the Protectorate, with the abolition of "the regal power of their lairds of manors," that they began to "take some life." Finally, there were significant changes in the substance of the law. The severity of the law against debtors was mitigated, as in England. Church censures were frustrated. The burning of witches, that favourite sport of the Scotch clergy and judges, was interrupted. The Scottish diarists, who record with such lubricious relish the constant public executions for buggery, bestiality and sorcery, are forced sadly to admit that the English not only pulled down the stools of repentance in the churches but also gave to supposed witches "liberty to go home again upon caution." They were, as Baillie complained, "too sparing" in such matters; they even made inconvenient inquiries into the tortures which had made the poor women confess.[19]

---

18. Instructions to Commissioners, 4 Dec. 1651 in Firth, *Scotland and the Protectorate*, p. 395. Cf. the declaration of the Commissioners for regulating the universities, 1652, in which they state "that they intend, God willing, in convenient time, to alter and abolish all such laws . . . as shall be found inconsistent with the government of the Commonwealth of England." (Firth, *Scotland and the Commonwealth*, Scot. Hist. Soc., 1895, p. 44.)

19. For particular law reforms, see Terry, *The Cromwellian Union*, p. 176; Firth, *Scotland and the Commonwealth*, pp. 276–85, *Scotland and the Protectorate*, p. xxx; Nicoll, *Diary*, pp. 93, 96; Lamont, *Diary*, p. 42; and, in general, Aeneas Mackay, *Memoir of Sir James Dalrymple, Viscount Stair* (Edinburgh, 1873). For justices in eyre, see Nicoll, *Diary*, pp. 102–5; Lamont, *Diary*, p. 47. For J.P.s see Terry, *The Cromwellian Union*,

It was at the end of 1655 that the aims of the administration of justice in Cromwellian Scotland were most fully formulated. We can see them in the Protector's instructions to his Council in Edinburgh, and in that Council's instructions to the new J.P.s. We can also see them in the reports which the President of the Council sent home. Among instructions for raising men for West India expedition, and securing the country, Cromwell insisted that justice be restored and extended throughout Scotland, that vagabondage be controlled, that the endowment of hospitals be investigated and their rents strictly applied, and that every parish maintain its poor, so that none go begging. The instructions to the J.P.s defined these functions in detail, and the President of the Council himself set an example by regulating Heriot's Hospital in Edinburgh, reducing the cost by £600 p.a., and putting it "in as good a way for the end it was erected as ever." This policy is of a piece with the policy applied in England in the same months by the major-generals: it shows that Cromwell sought to enforce the same social policy in both countries — that the Puritan Revolution was, in his eyes, indivisible. That the policy was successful is shown by the testimony even of Presbyterians, lawyers and patriots from John Nicoll to Sir Walter Scott.[20]

There remained the reformation of the clergy. Here, far more than in England, the problem was to find, encourage and train liberal ministers. The existing ministers were divided by politics into "Remonstrants" or "Protesters" on one hand — men who refused any compromise with the Stuarts — and "General Resolutioners" on the other, who (with the General Assembly, while it lasted) were prepared to believe that Charles II could be a "covenanted king." But whatever their differences, the majority of both parties were rigid and intolerant Presbyterians, and the four universities of Scotland, where they were trained, were crusted cells of orthodoxy. The English Commonwealth was determined not only to "laicize" the established Church, but also, as in

---

pp. 180–81; Firth, *Scotland and the Protectorate*, pp. xxxviii, 98, 308–16, 403–5; *Thurloe State Papers*, IV, 741. For stools of repentance, see Lamont, *Diary*, p. 44; for witches, Baillie, *Letters and Journals*, III, 436; Lamont, *Diary*, pp. 44, 47; Firth, *Scotland and the Commonwealth*, p. 368.

20. *Thurloe State Papers*, IV, 127, 129, 525; Firth, *Scotland and the Protectorate*, p. 483; Nicoll, *Diary*, p. 104. Scott's observations ("Cromwell certainly did much to civilise Scotland . . ." etc.) are in his notes to Dryden's Heroic Stanzas on Oliver Cromwell, in *The Works of John Dryden* (Edinburgh, 1809).

England, to "propagate the Gospel" in undeveloped areas. For both purposes it needed to capture control of the universities; and so, from the beginning, it instructed its commissioners not only to promote preaching and secure maintenance for sound ministers, but also "to visit and reform the several universities, colleges, and schools of learning in Scotland," to alter, abolish and replace statutes, and to purge and appoint professors. These powers, confirmed afterwards to the Council of State in Scotland, opened the way to a fierce struggle. It began in Glasgow, the very citadel of the National Covenant, where (happily for us) the voluble Robert Baillie was virulently recording the changes which he vainly resisted.[21]

The key figure in the struggle for Glasgow was Patrick Gillespie, the brother of that George Gillespie who had been one of the four commissioners sent to England in the 1640s. Patrick Gillespie had originally been the leader of the Remonstrants, but now he was the leader of that minority among the Remonstrants whose hatred and distrust of the Stuarts drove them, in spite of their doctrinal purism, to welcome the English conquest. His position was thus the same as that of Sir John Swinton. In both capacities, both as a Remonstrant and as an anglophil, Gillespie was hated by Baillie and the other Resolutioners in Glasgow. Already, in the spring of 1651, Baillie and his party saw the danger ahead. There were vacant places to be filled in the University, and it was essential to fill them with sound Resolutioners. So the Resolutioners appealed to Charles II and to the Scottish Parliament to send visitors who would support them in making the appointments. But events moved too quickly. Within a few months Charles II and the Scottish Parliament would be scattered; the new English authorities would intervene; and the opportunity of the Resolutioners was lost. Baillie could only wring his hands and wail at the successful "impudence" of Gillespie who, thanks to this backing and the support of the local Remonstrants, in defiance of the rights of electors, soon got himself nominated principal of the university "for the poisoning of our seminary."

Once in power Gillespie never ceased to outrage his rivals. He introduced other professors—"young men," Baillie protested, of no learning or character, teachers of recondite heresies and blasphemous

---

21. Instructions to Commissioners, 1651, Firth, *Scotland and the Protectorate*, p. 393; Declaration by the Commissioners 4 June 1652, Firth, *Scotland and the Commonwealth*, pp. 44–45.

opinions; he interfered in other universities; he exerted the patronage of the university to stuff schismatic clergy into every position; he manufactured straw votes to consolidate his power; and, worst of all, he was so favoured by the English that he could never be defeated. In vain the General Assembly had deposed him: the General Assembly it was which perished. In vain the town council of Glasgow denounced him for neglect of duty and misappropriation of funds: his "good friend," Cromwell's other great ally in Scotland, Sir John Swinton, having shuffled off his own excommunication ("a strange enormity"), soon silenced such complaints. In the end Gillespie, by means of "his own silly creatures," got Cromwell's English Secretary of State, John Thurloe, made chancellor of the university and himself vice-chancellor — and then passed his office on to a creature "to be sure of a new vote." And in any crisis, he would sweep off to London, with outward pomp, live there in "a high, vain and sumptuous manner," beyond any bishop in Scotland, walk ostentatiously with Major-General Lambert, preach publicly before the Protector in an elegant velvet cassock, be closeted with him in Whitehall, and then return to Edinburgh in triumph, in a coach followed by twenty-five horsemen, with increased powers, an enlarged salary, and a huge bill for expenses to be met by the University of Glasgow.

The first of Gillespie's ominous visits to London took place in 1653 and lasted eleven months. When he returned, he brought with him a formidable document, which once again showed the unity of policy in the two countries. It was an ordinance "for the better support of the universities of Scotland and encouragement of public preachers there"; and it set up, among other things, a body of commissioners comparable with the English "triers" or "approvers," whose agreement was necessary before any minister could be presented to any living, and who had power to provide "out of the treasury of vacant stipends, or otherwise, as they shall think fit, a competent maintenance for such ministers who have gathered congregations in Scotland." These commissioners, of course, had been nominated by, and included, Gillespie and his friends; and the ordinance, at which the established clergy were "very much displeased," was known as "Mr. Gillespie's charter." [22]

Gillespie did not go alone to London. Cromwell invited with him five other clergymen; and although three of them refused to go (they

22. The ordinance is given in Nicoll, *Diary*, pp. 164–67, and thence in Firth and Rait, *Acts and Ordinances*, III, pp. cxii–cxiv.

belonged to the majority who would have no truck with the "sectaries"), two did. One of these two was John Menzies, professor of divinity at Marischal College, Aberdeen, whose excommunication by the Aberdeen synod had been stopped by the English garrison.[23] Through him, and through John Row, the intruded Independent principal of King's College, Cromwell's influence penetrated Aberdeen. There, according to Baillie, "all in both colleges"—with the exception of the formidable Andrew Cant—"have avowedly gone over to Independency and Separatism"; and from "Aberdeen's nest," "the apostates of Aberdeen," Gillespie fetched new professors and new votes to increase his power in Glasgow. At the same time Edinburgh was also won over. While Gillespie was being imposed on Glasgow, the town council of Edinburgh was instructed to "call," as principal of their university, a completely anglicized Scotsman who, suspiciously enough, had just returned from a visit to London, Robert Leighton. Like the Glasgow professors, the Edinburgh ministers tried to dissent. They said that "they were not satisfied with the manner of the call." They dissented in vain: Leighton was appointed. Only St. Andrews, the university of Andrew Melville, held out; but, as Baillie wrote to a friend there, "see to your colleges as you may: they are fully masters of Glasgow, Aberdeen, and almost of Edinburgh."[24]

It is easy, reading Baillie's letters, to see the struggle for the Scottish universities as merely an attempt to intrude English puppets, Protesters against Resolutioners in the bitter struggles of the Kirk. But when we look below the surface, we see a far more deliberate policy. The Cromwellian intruders were not mere political creatures. They were not orthodox Protesters—they were very different, for instance, from those fanatics of the Covenant James Guthrie and Sir Archibald Johnston of Wariston. They were men who had come to believe that the Church of Scotland must admit the laity, not merely into the formal structure of the Church, as "ruling elders," more clerical than the clergy,[25] but

23. The three who refused were the Remonstrants Robert Blair and James Guthrie and the leader of the Resolutioners, Robert Douglas. (See Firth, *Scotland and the Protectorate*, p. 102.) The one who accompanied Gillespie and Menzies was the Remonstrant John Livingstone—who however, afterwards, changed his mind.

24. For the capture of Aberdeen and Edinburgh, see J. Kerr, *Scottish Education* (1910), pp. 122, 134; Sir Alexander Grant, *The Story of Edinburgh University in its first 300 years* (1884); Baillie, *Letters and Journals*, iii, 244, 326-27.

25. The idea that ruling elders represented the laity was indignantly repudiated by

as an independent influence. To Resolutioners like Baillie, as to orthodox Protesters like Guthrie and Wariston, such an idea was anathema.
To them the structure of the Church was sacred, and to preserve it the
laity must be firmly kept in place. It must not become like the English
laity, "very fickle and hard to be keeped by their ministers." Baillie himself was a great inquisitor. He would have burnt books if he could—
"I am one of those," he wrote, "who would gladly consent to the burning of many thousand volumes of unprofitable writers"; and we know
what kind of books he would have burnt: the "insolent absurdity" of
John Selden, the great advocate of lay sense in religion; the "tridentine popery" of Hugo Grotius; and the trash of that "very ignorant
atheist," that "fatuous heretic," Descartes. To him the intellectual fare
of his flock must be as uniform, as monotonous and as unpalatable as
their unvarying daily diet of salt-beef and oatmeal. But the new Cromwellian churchmen were very different. Robert Leighton was a mystic
who detested religious formalism, believed in toleration and was accused of the usual heresies in consequence. He had already revolted
against the intolerance of the Church courts when he accepted the rule
of Edinburgh University. Behind Baillie's bitter phrases we can see that
the "ignorant young men" whom Gillespie brought to Glasgow were
similarly impatient of the old intolerance and formalism. Such, for instance, was Andrew Gray, fetched from St. Andrews and ordained in
Glasgow "over the belly of the town's protestation." Gray disgusted
Baillie by his "new guise of preaching, which Mr. Hew Binning and
Mr. Robert Leighton began." Instead of "exponing and dividing a text,"
and "raising doctrines and uses," this young man, said Baillie, "runs out
in a discourse on some common head, in a high, romancing, unscrip-
tural style, tickling the ear for the present, and moving the affections in
some, but leaving . . . little or nought to the memory and understanding." The formidable list of heresies of which Baillie accused Richard

---

the Scotch Kirk. James Guthrie, in his *Treatise of Ruling Elders and Deacons* (published
in 1699), refers contemptuously to those "who either out of ignorance or disdain do call
them *lay elders*, as if they were a part of the people only"; and cf. George Gillespie, *An
Assertion of the Government of the Church of Scotland* . . . (Edinburgh, 1641); S. Rutherford, *Lex Rex* (1644), p. 432. Ruling elders, all insisted, were *jure divino* and part of
the clerical structure. For this reason the whole institution was rejected by the English
laity, who scoffed at "that sacred beast, the ruling elder." As a nineteenth-century authority wrote: "the term *lay* elder is itself a term of scorn. . . . There is no such office.
The office of elder is an ecclesiastical one. He who holds it ceases to be a layman" (J. G.
Lorimer, *The Eldership of the Church of Scotland*, Glasgow, 1841, p. 44).

Robertson, another of Gillespie's supporters in Glasgow, points the same way.[26]

Having installed such men in positions of authority, and empowered them to "plant and dis-plant" ministers and teachers, Cromwell strengthened them in material ways. By "Gillespie's charter" he granted to the universities of Glasgow and Aberdeen a number of Church lands from the dissolved Scottish bishoprics (granted, but not conveyed, by Charles I in 1641), and added 200 marks sterling p.a. from the local customs for the support of students in theology and philosophy. When the "charter" was published in Scotland, Robert Leighton was sorry that he too had not been in London, with Gillespie and Menzies; so he hurried to repair the omission. Cromwell agreed to grant a like bounty to Edinburgh, and ordered the clause to be drawn; but afterwards, as Leighton reminded him, "you did not think the time fitting for its insertion, as Parliament was sitting" — that tiresome English Parliament which always blocked the patriarchal administration of the Protector. Nevertheless, Leighton persevered, and in 1657, by another personal visit, obtained "after Mr. Gillespie's example, some £200 sterling to the college out of some Church-lands; which in my mind," adds Baillie sourly, "will be as soon obtained as the flim-flams of Mr. Gillespie's gifts."[27]

Apart from endowments Cromwell made gifts to Glasgow University for its building programme. In 1633 Charles I had promised, but not paid, £200. Cromwell paid it.[28] Monck and the English officers in the north also subscribed to the building funds of Aberdeen. With this support, the new principals of both universities set to work. John Row

26. Hugh Binning, like Patrick Gillespie, began as a Remonstrant. He died young, in 1653, and some of his works were afterwards edited by Gillespie, who praised him for freeing religion from "the superfluity of vain and fruitless perplexing questions wherewith later times have corrupted it" (Epistle prefixed to Binning's *The Common Principles of the Christian Religion*, 1659). For Leighton, see especially W. L. Mathieson, *Politics and Religon*, II, 218 ff. For Andrew Gray (whose sermons in "the new guise," like those of Leighton and Binning, continued to be printed) and Richard Robertson, see Baillie, *Letters and Journals*, III, 223–24, 239–40, 258.

27. Firth and Rait, *Acts and Ordinances*, III, p. cxii; *Thurloe State Papers*, IV, 566. Leighton's application is printed in *Cal. S.P. Dom. 1657–58*, p. 77; for its success see Baillie, *Letters and Journals*, III, 366.

28. Baillie afterwards disingenuously concealed this fact, partly no doubt in order not to give credit to the usurper, and sought to get the money paid over again, doubled, and with interest, by Charles II (*Letters and Journals*, III, 413, etc.).

at Aberdeen built "Cromwell's Tower"; at Glasgow even Baillie had to admire the "gallant buildings" which the hated principal raised "as good as alone" with "very great care, industry and dexterity"—though of course he grumbled at the daily din of masons, wrights, carters and smiths, questioned Gillespie's "strange ways of getting money for it," and afterwards worked himself into tantrums at the "vanity and prodigality" of those "vainglorious buildings." At Edinburgh, Cromwell went further: in 1656 he issued a patent setting up a College of Physicians with wide powers: a real contribution to lay studies. Like so many of Cromwell's reforms, it had abortive precedents: James VI and Charles I had projected such a college, but done nothing practical; and like all Cromwell's constructive work, it foundered at his death; but like Durham University and the Royal Society, the Edinburgh Medical School owes something to the attempts of Oliver Cromwell.[29]

The Cromwellian reform of the universities was incidentally a reform of education, but it was primarily a means of evangelizing the country. Once the basis had been established, the work went ahead. Loud and many were the complaints of Baillie as he watched the working out of "Gillespie's charter." Gillespie, he complained, had seized the purse; no minister could get any stipend unless he satisfied the new Independent triers: when a handful of Remonstrants or Independents called a man "he gets a kirk and a stipend; but whom the Presbytery and well near the whole congregation calls and admits, he must preach in the fields, or in a barn, without stipend. So a sectary is planted in Kilbride, another in Lenzie . . ."[30]

But it was not only in Kilbride and Lenzie that the Cromwellian government hoped to "plant" ministers. Ultimately the wild Highlands, beyond the settled organization of the Kirk, must be evangelized. The need was there. The whole Highlands and Islands, the government was told, "are all atheists, but their inclination is to popery." From Orkney and Shetland came complaints of vacant livings and school-endowments swallowed up by the gentry. The power of the Kirk, so formidable and so exclusive in the Lowlands, did not reach to those waste lands. "I have not yet met with any grandees of the Presbytery," a royalist agent wrote from Thurso; "they keep in the warmer and fatter pastures, sending out their colonies of the younger fry to the leaner

29. Sir Alexander Grant, *Edinburgh University*, I, 221–22.
30. Baillie, *Letters and Journals*, p. 244; cf. 248.

and more remote quarters." But the opportunity was there too. "A very precious people who seek the face of God" was reported from Sutherland and "divers other parts beyond Inverness," and another evangelist wrote that some of the Highlanders, though often "as brutish as heathens," listened to the new gospel "with great attention and groanings, and seeming affection for it." "To get the Highlands planted with ministers," one of the English commissioners declared, was "the only way to bring them to civility." At present, however, the Highlands were hardly attainable: the source of disorderly royalist risings, they were held in awe only by Cromwell's forts; and as in Wales, it was unorthodox missionaries who accepted the challenge. In 1657 George Fox crossed into Scotland, and saw the same opportunities which the Anabaptist preachers had previously seen in Wales: "as soon as ever my horse set his foot on Scottish ground, the infinite sparks of life sparkled about me, and . . . I saw the seed of the seedsman Christ." [31]

Destruction of "feudal" power and introduction of English law, reformed and simplified as in England; vigorous local administration of poor law and poor relief; destruction of clerical tyranny and liberalization of the established Church by the infusion of lay influence in and alongside it; reform of education, endowment of universities, competent maintenance for the new, liberal ministers, and evangelization of the neglected parts of the country—such was the Puritan ideal for the Scotland which had been "incorporated" in the new Commonwealth. But how was such a programme to be applied? Where, in Scotland, was a party to be found which would carry through such a work? The Scots had failed to carry out their social revolution in England because, in spite of solemn covenants and identical names, there was, in the social structure of England, no basis for a "Presbyterian" party in their sense of the word. Would the English, having conquered Scotland, find in that very different society, not merely individuals like Lockhart, Swinton or Gillespie, but a party prepared to realize their ideal? By definition it must be an anti-aristocratic, anti-clerical party, and its basis should be found, as in England, in the independent laity, and particularly among their leaders, the educated gentry.

31. *Thurloe State Papers*, IV, 401, 646; Terry, *The Cromwellian Union*, p. 124; Firth, *Scotland and the Protectorate*, p. 122; *Scotland and the Commonwealth*, pp. 31, 363–64; Swarthmore MSS. II, 121, quoted by G. B. Burnet, *The History of Quakerism in Scotland, 1650–1850* (1952), p. 35. Cf. George Fox, *Journal* (Everyman), p. 163.

At first it seemed possible. The Scottish gentry might have disappointed Charles I by supporting the Covenant, but they had soon resented the tyranny of the Church. In 1644 it was among the mutinous laity that Montrose, that former Covenanter who cared not for presbyters and present royalist who cared not for bishops, had found his followers. In 1648 it was the laity in the Scottish Parliament who had insisted, against the General Assembly, on fulfilling the "Engagement" and going to the rescue of an uncovenanted king. In both those adventures they had failed. After Preston, as after Philiphaugh, the clerical tyranny had been sharpened; but so had the resentment of the laity; and when the zealots were finally crushed at Dunbar, there were some Scotsmen who were disillusioned and others who had long sighed for release.

Foremost among those who had sighed for release were the old royalists; and indeed, once their own hopes were dashed at Worcester, they were the first to accept, even to welcome, English rule. It was "those gentlemen whom they call malignants" who, in 1651, were found to be "most free to serve the English interest." "I find the old royalists generally throughout the country tendering their *devoir*," wrote an English agent in 1652, and he added that the "fiery kirkists cannot digest a thought of the loss of their infinite power and prerogative." Already, before the union was settled, the royalists were said to have done "more real and visible services than the whole generation of Presbyterians" would ever do. Cromwell, with his eagerness to restore the old alliance of 1640, welcomed this ex-royalist support, which he found from some of the most distinguished of Scottish laymen. Apart from Sir William Lockhart, he drew towards him Sir Thomas Urquhart, the translator of Rabelais; Sir John Scot of Scotstarvet, the publisher (with Cromwell's aid) of the first maps of Scotland; and Sir Alexander Irvine of Drum, who was delighted to be able to defy the local presbytery, and the dreadful Andrew Cant himself, by appealing to the English commander. In vain the presbytery thundered excommunications; in vain it declared that any appeal from spiritual to secular tribunals was "Erastianism," "contrary to our Covenant and liberties of this Kirk." "I altogether decline their judicature," declared the unabashed knight, "as not being established by the Commonwealth of England," and having secured the support of General Monck against "the fury of a superstitious clergy," he wrote genially to his persecutors begging them not to trouble him with any "more such papers, that are but undigested rhapsodies of confused nonsense." Both Irvine and Urquhart explicitly declared—indeed, it was one of the charges against Irvine—what so many Englishmen had already shown, that there was more natural sympathy between a royalist and an Independent than between either and a Scotch presbyter.[32]

Royalist support might be welcome to Cromwell, in Scotland as in England; but it could hardly be the basis of republican policy. For that he looked elsewhere, and since the Presbyterian laity were inarticulate, he had to look to the parties in the Kirk. There the majority party, the party of the General Resolutioners, was hostile on all counts: both in religion, since it was the party of the General Assembly which Cromwell dissolved, and in politics, since it was the party of Charles II, whom he had beaten. Their rivals, the Remonstrants, might be the extremists of the Kirk, but their primitive Presbyterian purity was at least counter-balanced by their hatred of Charles II. It was the Remonstrants, in their previous incarnation as the whiggamore zealots, whom Cromwell had, in effect, put into power after the defeat of the Engagers in 1648, and it was in their broken ranks, after Dunbar, that he discovered his first converts, including Gillespie, Menzies and their companion in London, John Livingstone. Unfortunately, these converted Remonstrants were a minority of a minority; the majority of their party listened to the last-ditch, anti-Stuart, anti-Independent fanaticism of Johnston of Wariston and the hysterical trumpet-blasts of James Guthrie: men whom the Cromwellian rulers of Scotland regarded as "Fifth-Monarchy Presbyterians," the irreconcilable foes of all government. It soon became clear that a wider basis must be found if Cromwell's policy in Scotland was to rest on a Scottish party.

Moreover, it also became clear that Cromwell's personal allies in Scotland, estimable though they might be in themselves, were not a reliable bloc. In the summer of 1653 Lockhart, Swinton, Hope and Jaffray had all come south to sit in the Barebones Parliament. The Barebones Parliament did not concern itself much with Scottish affairs; but the Scottish members played a decisive part in the crisis which caused its dissolution. In the last division of that Parliament, when the radicals, to Cromwell's indignation, obtained a majority of two votes for the abolition of tithes, it was noted that "the English in this vote were equal, and

---

32. For royalist support of English rule, see Terry, *The Cromwellian Union*, p. 7; Firth, *Scotland and the Commonwealth*, pp. xxvi, 29–30, 339, 348–50. For Cromwell's help to Scot of Scotstarvet, see *Cal. S.P. Dom. 1654*, p. 158; Firth, *Scotland and the Protectorate*, p. 45.

the Scots did cast it." For although Lockhart voted with the "conservatives," Hope, Swinton and Jaffray all voted with the "radicals." What their motives were, whether English or Scottish, we do not know; but Cromwell evidently distinguished between Swinton and Jaffray, whom he continued to trust, and Hope whom, like the radical leaders, he never forgave. Next year Hope was dropped from the commission for the administration of justice and never again employed. The reason afterwards given was that he "had not so well conducted himself to His Highness at the dissolution of the Little Parliament" and his post was offered to Jaffray (who refused). In future, Cromwell did not rely much on parliaments: he relied on administrators. It became the task of his president of the Council in Scotland to create there a party through which the Protector could realize his ideals: a party which must rest on a wider basis than a few royalists who used the republic against the Kirk, the minority of a radical minority within the Kirk, and a few officials who went dangerously wrong in Parliament.[33]

Fortunately, by 1655, the president was fit for the task. In that year Cromwell sent to Edinburgh his ablest political adviser, another ex-royalist, the man who would nearly save the English Revolution by making the Protector king: Lord Broghill. In his new post, Broghill used all his political skill and personal charm to make the Cromwellian settlement work. Beginning on the narrow basis of Gillespie and his friends, he sought to win over to them the most reasonable of the Resolutioners. But he soon gave this up as "hopeless." The spirit of party, he wrote, dominated the clergy, and any sign of reconciliation between "the honestest sort of public resolutioners and remonstrators" only caused such men to be disowned by their followers, who were determined to "have that thread of distinction run through all their work." Finally, he decided to shift his basis altogether. Since it was impossible to gain either of the two parties as a whole, he proposed to woo the Resolutioners, who at least were the larger and more united party, and then, having purged those of them whose laxity might be "scandalous to

33. See Jaffray, *Diary*, pp. 51–52; Hope, *Diary 1646–54*, pp. 163–67; *Thurloe State Papers*, IV, 268–69; Firth, *Scotland and the Protectorate*, pp. 214, 385. Since Swinton and Jaffray both afterwards became Quakers, it is probable that the opposition of both was on religious grounds and respected by Cromwell as such. But the incident reveals, once again, Cromwell's inability to create a party in Parliament. (Cf. my essay "Oliver Cromwell and His Parliaments," above, pp. 317–58.) Since the Scottish members were generally regarded as mere government dummies, it is particularly ironical that, in this instance, they should have caused a significant government defeat.

conscientious Christians," to join to them "Mr. Gillespie, Mr. Livingstone and their friends." Thus a party would be gained of "the most sober, most honest and most godly of this nation"; the Stuarts would lose the support of the Scotch ministers, "whose power over the people has been such that hardly has ever anything been done without them, and all that has been done has been with or by them"; and Scotland might enjoy the same kind of moderate Presbyterianism as England might have accepted in 1647 and might still accept in 1657. For when the Scots had failed to unite the two countries under a rigid clericalism, and the English had failed to unite them under a godly Independency, might not a "lame erastian Presbytery," in the end, prove to be the form which would divide them least?[34]

Broghill obtained Cromwell's sanction; he wooed the Resolutioners; he ended Gillespie's monopoly over appointments by securing an amendment to his "charter": from now on, it was agreed, any minister could be appointed, and enjoy his stipend, if he undertook to live peaceably under the present government. Broghill even persuaded the ministers, by private treaty with the leading Resolutioners—"by his courtesies more than his threats," as Baillie wrote—to cease praying publicly for Charles II. Before long, he forecast, the Stuarts would be forgotten; every minister in Scotland would have obliged himself, "under his own hand, freely," to own the government, "and being engaged themselves, they will in interest, if for nothing else, engage the people." On that Erastian basis the social revolution could go forward. "If we manage these things well," Broghill wrote, "the two parties in Scotland, viz. Remonstrants and Public Resolutioners, shall both court us, as too long we have courted them." And indeed, this is exactly what happened. Alarmed by Broghill's favour to the Resolutioners, the Remonstrants sent emissaries up to London to lobby the Protector; but their rivals had an emissary too, who appeared with a letter of personal recommendation from Broghill, and was briefed, as Baillie wrote, "to mar the Protesters' designs and further ours." This emissary of the Resolutioners was Baillie's friend—his candidate for the principalship of Glasgow University if Gillespie should die—"that very worthy, pious, wise and diligent young man, Mr. Sharp."[35]

34. For Broghill's policy, see *Thurloe State Papers*, v, 127, 222, 268, 460, 479, 557, 597, 700.

35. *Thurloe State Papers*, v, 301, 323, 655; Baillie, *Letters and Journals*, iii, 321, 344, 352, 356–57.

The Union of Britain, 1641

If ever there was a chance of saving the revolution, in Scotland as in England, Broghill was the man who might have saved it. A "lame, erastian Presbytery" in both countries, with a large measure of toleration, under a reconstructed parliamentary monarchy of the house of Cromwell—such, it seems, was his ideal. And he was hastening towards it. On going to Scotland, he had stipulated that he should not stay there more than a year. In that year he secured notable results. "If men of my Lord Broghill's parts and temper be long among us," wrote Baillie, "they will make the present government more beloved than some men wish." Then Broghill passed over to Ireland and organized his patronage there so well that at the next Parliament he had a solid Anglo-Irish party ready to support his plans for Cromwell's kingship. And yet, as we know, all foundered. Shortness of time and the opposition of the Army frustrated him in England. In Scotland there was also another fatal flaw. Just as the Scottish party in England, which seemed so strong in 1646, was found in fact to have no real basis, so the English party in Scotland, which Broghill nursed into being in 1656, lacked real solidity. In spite of everything, the only solid organization in Scotland remained that of the Kirk: the Kirk which, widely hated though it was, nevertheless, in the universal defeat, remained the one reuniting focus of national feeling.[36]

We can see this at many levels. In the Church half the Scottish triers refused to act. They declared that Gillespie's charter was an encroachment by the state on the jurisdiction of the Church courts, and ministers had to be intruded by the English soldiers. In the law there was the same reluctance. The Scottish commissioners resisted the legal reforms and the Council, who at first had wanted Scotch judges, since they alone understood their system, ended by recommending English judges, who alone were reliable. Scottish justices of the peace also refused office as "a manifest encroachment on the liberties of the Kirk," contrary to the Solemn League and Covenant, and incompatible with Malachi ii. 10. On the other hand the Kirk parties grew confident. Broghill thought that he was using the Resolutioners to laicize Scotland, but the Resolutioners assumed that, through this favour, they would reassert the old clericalism in England. As usual, Baillie is the perfect barometer. As soon as Broghill turned from the Remonstrants to the Resolutioners, Baillie was back at his old trade, lecturing his English brethren and re-

36. For evidence of the continuing hatred of the Kirk in the late 1650s, see Baillie, *Letters and Journals*, III, 448; *Wariston's Diary*, III, 27, 180–81.

400 THE CRISIS OF THE SEVENTEENTH CENTURY

buking them for the timidity of their ambitions. Why, he asked, had they only "a show of a Presbytery and Synod"? "Why want you a General Assembly? Why have ye no power at all to execute ecclesiastic jurisdiction?" He was not going to be content with a "lame, erastian Presbytery," even in England, let alone in Scotland. It was with some reason that Monck, unlike Broghill, continued to believe—until he too was disillusioned—that, for Cromwell's purposes, the Remonstrants were "better to be trusted than . . . the General Resolution men."[37]

So Broghill's policy quickly crumbled against the social facts of Scottish life. Cromwellian policy depended on the existence of a self-conscious, independent laity with gentry leadership. It was this class which had broken the Scottish attempt to impose Presbyterianism on England; it was the absence of such a class that rendered futile the English attempt to laicize Scotland. For where is the Scottish laity, the equivalent of that vocal, powerful estate of the realm which, in England, was transforming politics, religion, education? We read the private diaries which should reveal it, and what do we find? Here is Sir Thomas Hope of Craighall, that great lawyer, constantly making vows to the Lord and recording his superstitious dreams. Here is Sir Archibald Johnston of Wariston exuding page after page of rhapsodical bigotry. Here is Alexander Brodie of Brodie recording the remarkable providences of the Lord towards him, lamenting, occasionally, his own sins, such as impure thoughts in church and a "sinful affection" (very rare in Scotland) for planting trees, and, more regularly, the sins of others, the "gross inbreaking of idolatry, blasphemy, superstition, heresy and all manner of wickedness," denouncing Quakers and Jews, transcribing the scandalous activities of witches, and deploring "the corrupt and dangerous principle of toleration and liberty." Here is Andrew Hay of Craignethan, regularly recording, along with the weather, his freedom (or not) from temptation, calculating the days to the last Trump, nosing out witches, prying into cases of fornication, and reading, with unctuous relish, the dismal ends of heretics, whoremongers, apostates, atheists, witches and Quakers.[38] Here are John Lamont of Newton, gloating over the fate of Montrose and a long list of "witches, adulterers, buggers, incestuous persons and such as had lain with beasts," and John Nicoll, who, to an equal curiosity and zeal in

37. Firth, *Scotland and the Protectorate*, pp. 211, 345; *Thurloe State Papers*, IV, 324, 480; Baillie, *Letters and Journals*, III, 303.

38. See, for instance, his record of "a tolerable day," 22 Jan. 1660.

these interesting matters, and a particular hatred of Lockhart, Swinton and Gillespie, adds a devout conviction that a great storm in the neighbourhood was caused by the wrath of God at a new tax of a halfpenny per pint of beer in Edinburgh.[39]

All these were educated men. They read Greek, Hebrew, Latin, Italian; some of them had studied abroad; but they had no independent lay attitude, and reading their diaries we see why neither the ruling elders nor the Parliament of Scotland had any laicizing influence on the Church. Nor were the Scottish merchants any better than the gentry. Monck regarded the burghs as "generally the most faithful people to us of any people in this nation." They were, he said, "the very first that owned us and have ever since lived peaceably under us, and whose interest is most agreeable to ours, by reason of their trade and traffic." For that reason he urged that their taxes should be kept down and their privileges kept up. But there is a difference between peaceable life and positive support, and it is clear that if the burghs gave the English no trouble, being "impoverished through want of trade and the late troubles," they equally gave no constructive help. In fact, Monck's defence of the burghs was elicited by Cromwell's proposal to interfere with their liberties in order to gain some support by putting the Remonstrant minority in power in Glasgow—clear evidence that the Resolutioners who actually represented them, and who persecuted Principal Gillespie, were unsatisfactory. Scottish trade was too slight and static to sustain a dynamic policy, and the royal burghs which controlled it were timid oligarchies. A glance at the eight or nine members whom they returned to Cromwell's parliaments sufficiently shows their lack of independence. Most of those members are English officers or officials: the burghs would accept anyone who would pay his own expenses. In 1656 only one of the burgh members was a known Scottish merchant, Sir Alexander Wedderburn of Dundee; and he had been a royalist.[40]

But perhaps the most striking evidence of the contrast between the

39. See *The Diary of Sir Thomas Hope of Craighall* (Edinburgh, Bannatyne Club, 1843); *The Diary of Andrew Hay of Craignethan, 1659–60* (ibid. 1901). The other diaries have already been cited.

40. For Monck's support of the burghs, see Firth, *Scotland and the Protectorate*, p. 195; *Thurloe State Papers*, VI, 529. For the list of burgh M.P.s, see Terry, *The Cromwellian Union*, pp. lvi–lvii, lxiii–lxiv. For the conditions of their appointment, see *Thurloe State Papers*, VII, 555, 616–17, etc.

social claims of England and Scotland is provided by the petitions of their counties. All through the civil war the English counties sent up petitions to Parliament. Sometimes these petitions were organized by gentry in grand juries or other meetings, sometimes by radical propagandists; but whatever particular interest may colour them, they represented local forces, and their positive demands were, in one form or another, for that decentralization and laicization summarized as "reformation of law and clergy." In Scotland there was no such initiative in petitioning;[41] but in 1652 the English government invited the shires and burghs to assent to the proposed union and express their particular desires. And what was the result?[42] Meetings dominated by "fiery kirkists" protested against the "vast and boundless toleration" of all sorts of errors and heresies whose extirpation was a duty imposed by the Solemn League and Covenant; they repudiated the Erastian subjection of the Church to the magistrate; then, after the natural demands for freedom from cess or confiscation, reduction of the army of occupation and release of prisoners of war, a few positive requests were made: "that those who enjoy heritable privileges . . . may be protected and established in them"; "that gentlemen's houses be exempted from quartering and that their gardens, parks or orchards and other policies may be protected from destruction"; and, above all, "that the people of this land may be governed by our own law, though the power of administration be derived from the parliament of the Commonwealth of England." From the outer fringes of the country, where the Kirk was not yet firmly planted, a faint voice might seem to welcome the union for the social change it might chance to bring;[43] from the lower classes in the cities an even fainter voice might have been enlisted;[44] but from the men of substance in settled, historic Scotland the answer was firm: no reformation of law or clergy.

41. Cf. *Thurloe State Papers*, VII, 593.

42. All the replies of the counties and burghs are printed in Terry, *The Cromwellian Union*.

43. I refer to the "Assent and Desires of Orkney and Shetland," Terry, *The Cromwellian Union*, pp. 122–26.

44. In 1659 Gillespie's party in Glasgow sought to use the craftsmen as a means of capturing control of the town council (Baillie, *Letters and Journals*, III, 433), and two hundred "well-affected persons in and about Edinburgh" petitioned in favour of toleration (Nicoll, *Diary*, p. 245; *Wariston's Diary*, III, 126, 128). But I know no other or

So the necessary basis for Cromwell's policy in Scotland was lacking. As an independent estate the laity simply did not exist. In that poor and backward country the organized Calvinist Church was the only institution which could rise, and raise others, out of ignorance and squalor. As such, it claimed a monopoly of salvation. It also claimed the right to crush down all those deviationists who, by individual effort or foreign example, sought to rise or to raise men higher. And in that society, aided by the fact of defeat and the destruction of national organs, it made good its claim. Monck himself, in a moment of despair, recognized its success when he declared, in 1657, that the only hope of Scottish support was in a drastic reduction of taxes, "and then, in case they be not quiet, I think it were just reason to plant it with English" — in other words, to treat it like Ireland where also, in the ruin of all other organs, the Church had become the engine of nationality. The clergy might no longer pray openly for the king, but it was vain to hope, said Monck, that they would observe the day of thanksgiving for the Protector's narrow escape from assassination. "This people generally," he wrote, a few months before Cromwell's death, "are in as fit a temper for rising as ever I knew since I came into Scotland."[45]

Scotland did not rise. Whatever its temper, it was physically apathetic, and all knew it. Its force was spent, and it simply waited on events. But as soon as the events had happened, and Monck, marching out of Scotland, had restored the Stuarts, all the Cromwellian reforms in that country were swept away. In this at least Scotland was not like Ireland. The hereditary jurisdictions returned. Cromwellian justice was denounced, even by those who had lately extolled it, as "iniquity and oppression over a poor, distracted land." The Independent preachers and professors disappeared from Kirk and college. Robert Baillie himself replaced Gillespie at Glasgow, and being nominated by the king, forgot his former zeal for the rights of electors. Even if Presbytery did not recover its monopoly, at least the infamous doctrine of toleration was no more heard. And to signalize the victory of religion and justice, Kirk and Parliament were happily united in the greatest of all Scottish witch-hunts. As a Scottish historian writes, the number of victims can be explained only on the assumption that nine years of En-

---

earlier evidence of participation by the classes which, in England, played so prominent a part in the democratic movement.

45. *Thurloe State Papers*, vi, 330, 664, 762.

glish mildness had left a heavy backlog of candidates to be despatched. The holocaust of 1661 was the reply of Scottish society to the English attempt at "laicization."[46]

Meanwhile what of the Scottish Cromwellians? They had rejected the established Kirk parties and sought, by serving the usurper, to import a new form of society for which Scotland itself supplied no base. Now they were scattered. Some, indeed, though not the best of them, navigated the change. John Menzies was one of them. It was "dangerous to slip a buckle," said this timorous Independent, and put his neck back, in good time, into the old Presbyterian harness. Others sought niches, comfortable or uncomfortable, to the Left or Right of the new Establishment. Gillespie and Livingstone, the old Remonstrants, went Left: the restored Presbyterians rejected the first and were rejected by the second. On the other hand the Cromwellian Resolutioners went Right. Robert Leighton[47] accepted episcopacy and became Archbishop of Glasgow. And as for Baillie's worthy, pious, wise and diligent friend, James Sharp, he was able to prove yet again the infallible knack of the Glasgow professor for getting everything exactly wrong.

For in 1660 Baillie was confident once again that the glorious day of pure Presbyterianism had dawned, not only for Scotland, but for England too; and he intended to play his part. He had no intention of accepting the advice "so oft inculcate from London" that the Scots should mind their own business. "What is the Scots of this," he asked, "but that we shall sit dumb and never open our mouth, neither to the King nor Parliament nor our brethren the ministers of England to request them to adhere to their Covenant and Petition against Books and Bishops? I fear we cannot answer for our miserable slackness herein already." So Baillie once again threw his weight about. Did someone mention "moderate episcopacy"? The good Scotsman choked at the thought: one might as well speak of "moderate Papacy"! The forces of the Covenant must be mobilized to end this mismanagement in London. Offices in Church and State must be redistributed. Lord Chancellor Hyde must be dismissed. Church patronage must be properly disposed. It was all perfectly simple. "A few hours' treaty" would do it

46. Nicoll, *Diary*, p. 304; Mathieson, *Politics and Religion*, ii, 171–72. It is interesting to note that in Lorraine, freed at the same time from civilizing French rule, there was a similar atavistic outbreak of witch-burning.

47. Leighton was not, strictly speaking, a Resolutioner, but as he accepted membership of the General Assembly just before its dissolution, he can be counted as such.

. . . And who should be Baillie's agent in all these matters but his reverend and beloved brother James Sharp? Sharp was to see Cromwell's protégé, "that ass Lockyer," kicked out of the provostship of Eton and a learned friend put in; Sharp was to commission a team of English "Presbyterians" to publish a manifesto "for the crushing of that high, proud, malicious and now very active and dangerous party," the English episcopalians. But, alas, brother Sharp had other fish to fry. He was not wasting his time seeking to put back the shattered Humpty-Dumpty of Presbyterianism in England. As agent of the Kirk in London he was quietly selling out his employers as fast as he could and securing for himself, as his reward, an archbishop's mitre—and, afterwards, a somewhat dubious martyr's crown.[48]

These were the Cromwellian clergy. The Cromwellian laity faced the same choice. Lockhart, predictably, went Right, and found his way back from the protectoral to the royal Court. So did James Dalrymple, whom Cromwell had made a judge of the reformed Court of Session and who was to show himself, in the next forty years, the greatest, most liberal of Scottish judges. The three "radical" members of the Barebones Parliament, as predictably, went Left. Sir James Hope, "laid aside" by a disgusted Protector, was, by 1659, known as a republican.[49] Death in 1661 saved him from defining his position in the new reign.[50] Swinton and Jaffray, like so many other genuine ex-Cromwellian laymen, became Quakers. Perhaps it was no accident that the strongest centre of early Scottish Quakerism was in Aberdeen, the area where the Covenant had always been weakest, where there was an old tradition of lay life and where Cromwell had found most local support.[51] In Scot-

---

48. Baillie, *Letters and Journals*, III, 400–401, 408, 444–45.

49. Firth, *Scotland and the Protectorate*, p. 385.

50. I suspect he would have gone Left. His long verse-epitaph in Cramond church-yard dwells on his mineral interests and judicial virtues, but of his political ideals merely states that he pursued "public peace and wealth." The first editor of his diary, Sir J. B. Paul, dismisses Hope as "wobbly" and "pusillanimous," but all the evidence of his views seems to me compatible with a consistent policy: the material improvement of Scotland on a national basis.

51. Cromwell also bequeathed a more utilitarian legacy to Aberdeen. There, according to Boswell, "Mr. Johnson laughed to hear that Cromwell's soldiers taught the Aberdeen people to make shoes and stockings and brought in cabbages" (*Boswell's Journal of a Tour to the Hebrides with Samuel Johnson LL.D.*, ed. Frederick A. Pottle and Charles H. Bennett, 1936, p. 59).

land as in England, Quakerism was the ghost of deceased Independency sitting hatless in the seat thereof.

Leighton, Lockhart, Dalrymple, Swinton, Jaffray—these are among the most enlightened, most attractive spirits of mid-seventeenth-century Scotland. In Scotland, as in England, Cromwell showed his genius for eliciting that latent talent which the Stuarts never failed to stifle or repel, and though the attempt ended in disaster, the men whom he discovered deserve to be remembered as distant precursors of the Enlightenment which would dawn in Scotland a century later. For although England and Scotland were separated again in 1660, the union of crowns was as uncomfortable after as before the Great Rebellion. In 1707 a more cautious union of the two kingdoms was carried through. This time there was no assimilation of Church or Law; but there was equal freedom of trade in a large part of the world. Thanks to these mercantile opportunities, Scotland, in the next generation— it took a full generation—gradually acquired, in a new independent laity, the social basis for those changes which Cromwell had too hastily sought to impose on it. In 1727 the last witch was burnt in Scotland. From 1733 a series of secessions relieved the Kirk of its fanatics. Thereafter lay ideas transformed the Erastian Scottish clergy, whose liberal members, the champions of the lay Enlightenment, would be accused of the same heresies as Patrick Gillespie and Robert Leighton. From 1745 the Highlands were opened up and kirks were "planted" to civilize them as the Cromwellian commissioners had wished. In 1748 the hereditary jurisdictions were finally abolished, and the Scottish landlords, as the Cromwellians had prophesied, exchanged old, barbarous power for new agricultural wealth.[52] By the end of the eighteenth century, when English aristocrats sent their sons to study agriculture in East Lothian, or politics in the universities of Edinburgh or Glasgow, and used Scottish architects to rebuild their country houses, the old difference between the two countries, which had made their contact in the previous century so explosive, had indeed changed.

52. See H. G. Graham, *The Social Life of Scotland in the 18th century* (1901), pp. 209–10, 494–97. In 1883 some of the greatest British fortunes from land were enjoyed by the old Scottish aristocracy, whose poverty had been a byword in the seventeenth century (see John Bateman, *Great Landowners*, 1883, quoted in G.E.C., *Complete Peerage*, vi, App. H, p. 713).

9 | The Union of Britain in the Seventeenth Century

The seventeenth century was the age of revolution in western Europe. It was also the age of national unification. The facts are not entirely unrelated. The rulers of the new centralized monarchies, threatened by internal opposition in their different States, sought naturally to deepen their power by bringing all those different States under their control; and the classes which resisted those rulers sought, no less naturally, to strengthen their resistance by finding allies among their fellow-subjects in other States. In the Iberian Peninsula Olivares sought to unite the separate kingdoms and States of the Peninsula into a unitary kingdom of Spain. In England both Crown and Parliament sought to create a unitary kingdom or commonwealth of Great Britain. Like the Spaniards, the English failed in the seventeenth century, but succeeded in the eighteenth, though with an important difference: in Spain it was the monarchy which united the kingdoms, in England the Parliament.

The attempted unification of the two countries has certain obvious parallels. In both Spain and Britain the century began with a complete union of crowns. In both one kingdom—here England, there Castile—bore the main cost of government. In both there were degrees of independence under the crown: Portugal and Scotland had an independence denied to Aragon and Ireland. There were also important social differences between the several kingdoms of each monarchy which rendered a uniform policy impossible: in Scotland, as in Aragon (to which James I likened it), the nobility had tiresome, archaic powers which they could no longer exercise in England or Castile. For this reason, England and Castile supplied the models for kings, Scotland and Aragon for dissident magnates. There were racial differences too. The unassimilable Moriscos in the kingdom of Granada, alien in race, uncertain in religion, and different in social organization, constituted a problem which was similar to that of the Celtic and Catholic "Old Irish" in Ireland and was solved no less drastically. But these parallels between the two countries (which did not escape contemporary observers) were also accompanied by great differences. The economic and cultural predominance of England over Scotland and Ireland was more absolute than any which Castile could claim over Aragon or Portugal. Castile had no institution comparable in strength with the English Parliament. Above all, there was in Britain the added complexity of internal religious difference. In Portugal and Catalonia the Crown of Castile provoked the opposition of social classes and gave a new content to old traditions. But neither in Portugal nor in Catalonia did religion sharpen that opposition. In Scotland and Ireland, on the other hand, English aggression provoked the opposition of national Churches and ended by creating new obstacles to union. The Catholic Church and the Presbyterian Kirk became the organs of Scottish and Irish nationalism. Thus the religious identity of Britain, which was at first universally assumed, was ultimately found to be unattainable.

These foreign parallels help to illustrate the problem which faced the rulers of England from 1603 to 1707; but the working out of that problem depended, of course, on local conditions and circumstances. To these local conditions and circumstances we shall now turn. We will seek to show how dynastic opportunity and political necessity combined to make a perfect union of the three kingdoms both necessary and natural; but how social tensions and local loyalties aggravated the problem, showing, once again, that there are no short-cuts in politics. The course which seemed necessary and natural to the forward-looking Jacobean politicians would lead their successors over sunken reefs and through dangerous currents. But before examining those concealed dangers we must consider the smooth superficial prospect which tempted the English statesmen of 1603 when they looked at Ireland and Scotland, now for the first time all governed from London.

First Ireland. Originally Ireland had been a separate lordship under the English Crown. In 1540 it had been declared a kingdom. Thereafter the Tudors had gradually brought it to order. They had recovered its administration from the great Irish (generally Anglo-Irish) families; the last revolt by the old Gaelic chiefs—the revolt of the O'Neills and the O'Donnells—had been crushed; and society had been gradually subjected to English law and to the State-controlled Protestant episcopal Church. The triumph of Protestantism in Ireland had been remarkably easy—indeed too easy. The established Roman Catholic Church had been abolished without resistance. Consequently the new Protestant Church had hardly felt the need of missionary activity. The danger of that easy triumph was not yet obvious. What was obvious was the need to establish effective English control over the whole island. This need had been emphasized by the last episode of the Anglo-Spanish war: the Spanish attempt to exploit tribal rebellion and establish a bridgehead against England at Kinsale. In 1604, the Spanish war being over, it seemed prudent to settle Ireland before such a danger should recur. The final defeat of the Ulster rebellion seemed also to make such settlement possible.

In Scotland the order of events had been different, but their character was similar. There too foreign influence had been excluded, royal power extended, a State Church established. As in Ireland, the Catholic Church had collapsed with hardly a struggle. The foreign influence—the old alliance with France—had not lasted much longer. By the revolution of 1567 the Protestant Church had been secured, and with it a new dependence on England. But the Protestant Church of Scotland had been different from those of England and Ireland. For whereas they had been imposed by the Crown, it was imposed upon the Crown by the nobility. While they were essentially monarchical, it was in some respects disagreeably republican. However, it had been imposed with the assistance of the English Crown, and in its first generation it was far more compatible with the English system than later writers, looking at it through the struggles of the next century, have supposed. In particular, it was compatible with the English system by 1604; for by then the fanaticism of the Calvinist clergy had overreached itself and James VI, with the support of the aristocracy and gentry, had asserted lay control over the Scottish just as Queen Elizabeth had done over the English Church. Since the English Church was then closer to Calvinism than it would afterwards become, the differences in organization were easier to overlook: and they often were overlooked. "It is immaterial," a Scotsman wrote in 1605, "that the two nations differ in the forms of public worship . . . for in the essentials of doctrine a solid foundation of uniformity exists"; and on the English side Bacon declared that "for matter of religion, the union is perfect in points of doctrine," imperfect only in matter of discipline and government.[1] Meanwhile, in 1603, the parallel with Ireland had been completed by the union of crowns and the recovery of political power by the king from the great Scottish families. In London James VI was free from the physical dangers and humiliations which his predecessors (and he himself in his youth) had suffered at the hands of the Scottish nobility; and with the added patronage of England he was able to build up the royal authority over his turbulent northern kingdom. Finally, settlement of Scotland was no less important to the security of England than settlement of Ireland. As late as 1616 the famous Spanish ambassador Gondomar would assure Philip III that England could be conquered from a bridge-head, this time, in Scotland.[2]

Such were the resemblances between the positions in Ireland and in Scotland: resemblances which suggested that the time was now ripe for a fuller union. But there were also differences. Two differences were important in the matter of union. One was social, the difference caused by the presence of the new English "planters" in Ireland. The other was political, the difference in the character of the political links binding the two countries to England.

Both Scotland and Ireland contained two societies, an original Celtic society and an "Anglo-Norman" society which had occupied and settled part of the country in the Middle Ages. In Scotland these two societies were described as Highlanders and Lowlanders respectively, in Ireland as "Old Irish" and "New Irish" or (as they came to be known in the seventeenth century) "Old Irish" and "Old English." Between these two societies relations were, in general, stabilized. The Lowlanders provided the basis of royal government in Scotland, and the "Old English," though many of them had adopted Irish ways and remained Catholic in religion, had done the same in Ireland. But in the second half of the sixteenth century the relative stability of the two societies in Ireland received a rude shock. A second English invasion imposed upon

---

1. Sir Thomas Craig, *de Unione Regnorum Britanniae Tractatus* (1605), ed. C. S. Terry (Scottish History Society, 1909), pp. 286–87; cf. 464. *The Letters and Life of Francis Bacon*, ed. James Spedding, III (1868), 223.

2. Gondomar to Secretary Ciriza, 1616, printed in Pascual de Gayangos, *Cinco cartas político-literarias de D. Diego Sarmiento de Acuña conde de Gondomar* (Madrid, Soc. de Bibliófilos, IV, 1869), letter no. 3.

them a third society, which could not be so easily assimilated. This was the invasion of the "planters," who established themselves on the lands, mainly, of the "Old Irish," whom they dispossessed. This third force in Ireland, which had no parallel in Scotland, was of the greatest significance. It created a problem of land and, because the planters were Protestant, exasperated a social struggle by a religious difference. In Scotland in the early seventeenth century the Highlanders, though nominally Catholic, were barely touched by the Counter-Reformation. English observers described them impartially as atheist or Papist. But in Ireland the situation was very different. There the "Old English"— a landed conservative class—might have remained largely indifferent: "state Catholics" like the loyal recusants in England. But the dispossessed and resentful "Old Irish" went another way. Neglected by the unevangelical established Church of Ireland, they were won over by the missionaries of the new Rome. It seems incontestable that it was the pressure of the English planters which gave these recruits to the forces of the Counter-Reformation.[3]

The political link between Ireland and England was also very different from that between Scotland and England. The difference lay at the parliamentary level. Both the Irish and the Scottish parliaments were rudimentary bodies compared with that of England; but whereas the Scottish Parliament was at least free from English influence, the Irish Parliament was not. By the so-called "Poyning's Act" of 1495, the initiative in legislation for Ireland had been transferred, not indeed to the English Parliament, but to the English Council. It thus followed that no one who had not the support of the English Council could control the Irish Parliament. This was a fact which Irish parliaments sometimes found useful and Irish viceroys disconcerting. It was to become very important when the king and Parliament of England were struggling for control of the English Council.

These differences between Scotland and Ireland were significant, but they were not fundamental. They affected the means whereby the three kingdoms might be united, but they did not prevent a uniform policy. Such a policy was clearly necessary: the security of the three kingdoms required it. The constitutional struggles in the course of the century made it doubly necessary: neither king nor Parliament could feel safe if the other kingdoms of the Crown could be mobilized against

3. See H. F. Kearney, "Ecclesiastical Politics and the Counter-Reformation in Ireland, 1618–1648," *Journal of Ecclesiastical History*, 1960.

them. In the course of those struggles from 1600 to 1660 no less than three versions of union were successively attempted, and each version was different from the others. The differences lay not only in the circumstances in which each version was advanced, but also in the social basis on which it was built. In this essay I shall deal with these three versions: the royal version of James I; the aristocratic version of the Long Parliament; and the revolutionary version of Oliver Cromwell.

James I of England, the first king of all three countries, was eager to be king not merely of England and Scotland, but of "Great Britain." He indeed is the author of the name which later Scots have forced Englishmen to impose on their country. For reasons of security, government and power he aimed at "a perfect union of laws and persons," "one worship of God, one kingdom entirely governed, one uniformity of law." He did not want a union of parliaments. At first he thought that he did, but experience soon dissuaded him.[4] From its central position the Crown would obviously be at an advantage in dealing with three separate parliaments, and there was no point in bringing the tame parliaments of Scotland and Ireland to learn bad habits from the more formidable Parliament of England. But a uniform law would be enforced by judges appointed by the Crown, and a uniform Church would be ruled by bishops appointed by the Crown. English law and the English Church had already been extended to Ireland. There seemed no reason why they should not equally be extended, with merely minor differences, to Scotland. We have seen that the established Protestant Churches of England and Scotland were judged to be easily assimilable, one to the other. James' Scottish lawyers also assured him that English and Scottish law were only superficially different and could be reconciled in essentials by being brought back to their common "feudal" principles.[5] These were the presuppositions which lay behind the proposed union of 1604-7.

James I's proposed union by legislation was not achieved. It failed

4. James originally thought of a union of parliaments, but this was before his experience of the English Parliament. When the commissioners for the union met, the union of parliaments was not discussed. On the other hand the English parliamentary opposition took up the proposal and by insisting on a full parliamentary union or nothing, wrecked the whole project.

5. Craig, *de Unione*, p. 90. Craig's analysis of the law rests on his own *Jus Feudale* (1603).

through the jealousy of the English Parliament, which feared an invasion of fat English pastures by lean Scottish kine. But throughout his reign the king pursued the same policy: he sought to build up, in all three countries, the necessary basis of union. To him, that basis was not a common parliament nor a uniform economy, but a single Court, a loyal Protestant nobility, a centralized system of justice, an established episcopal Church. It was a unity of royal government, held together by royal patronage, and it was to be strengthened by the creation of a strong, educated class of court noblemen, officers and episcopal clergy.

In Scotland this policy was largely successful. The Scottish nobility was won over, partly by English patronage. At the same time the greatest abuse of their power—the hereditary jurisdictions which they exercised—was undermined by the establishment of justices of the peace on the English model. Episcopacy was reimposed through royal power, and maintained by royal patronage. This was done very discreetly, without a direct affront to the Calvinist Church or a threat to the new owners of Church lands and tithes. Finally, by an ingenious constitutional device—the "Lords of the Articles"—the king ensured that his Scottish ministers could control the Scottish Parliament: a body which, having little character of its own, would otherwise be at the mercy of noble faction. At the end of his reign James I could boast, smugly but truly, that he governed by his pen a country which his ancestors had never been able to govern by the sword.

In Ireland the policy was similar. With the collapse of the last revolt of the Gaelic chiefs, efforts were made to reform local government on the English model. As in Scotland, the Anglican structure was advanced without too direct an affront to the religion of the "Anglo-Norman" landlords, who were powerful in society and parliament. Ultimately, it was hoped, these "Old English" landlords would quietly conform. Meanwhile, to create a favourable balance in the Irish Parliament, new, Protestant boroughs were enfranchised; and the establishment of an Irish Court of Wards in 1617 supplied not merely a new fiscal engine, but also a means of educating the "Old English" nobility in the religion of state. Much has been written about the fiscal activities of the Court of Wards in England, but its importance as a means of patronage was just as great. It was a Scottish nobleman, anglicized at the court of James I, who urged the King not to abolish the court for any financial compensation; and he convinced him by pointing to the immense significance of its patronage. "No King in Christendom," he said, "had such a tie on his subjects"—no doubt reflecting on the lack of such a tie in Scotland.[6] At all events, the Irish Court of Wards at once scored one notable success. One of its first converts was the 12th Earl of Ormond, who would become the leader of Irish Protestant royalism in the years of revolution.

It can be objected that the proposed royal union of James I did not rest firmly on any solid economic basis. It depended on the uniform and unifying class of "officers." That class was an educated class, lay, even tolerant, in its outlook, and held together by the bonds of patronage. Tolerance sprang from its education and was imposed by practical necessity. Even the established clergy, being officers of a state institution, shared, within their limits, this lay outlook, and did not seek to coerce either the Catholicism of Ireland or the Calvinism of Scotland. James I's three primates, Archbishop Abbott in England, Archbishop Ussher in Ireland, Archbishop Spottiswood in Scotland, were all men of the same cast. It was patronage that was to solve all problems. By patronage the Irish nobility and Parliament were to be protestantized; by patronage the Scottish nobility and Parliament were to be controlled; by patronage—the "Undertakers" of 1614—even the English Parliament was to be managed. And by patronage the Protestant episcopal Church was to establish itself in all three societies and be yet another, a social bond of union. Such patronage, it can be said, may supply a means of government, but it is no substitute for an economic basis of unity.

To this objection there is an adequate answer. Economics do not necessarily precede politics. The royal union, once effected, might well have created its own economic basis. An educated court aristocracy, the patron of liberal ideas, can give the impulse to economic development, and such development can lead to the formation of an independent laity which may in turn become the support of the political system under which it has risen. The ablest of the Jacobean politicians looked forward to such a development. In Ireland Robert Cecil sought, first, to restrain the new "planters," who too easily exploited the rebellions which they had often provoked, then to hold the balance between them and the Catholic "Old English," and finally to allow a gradual improvement of the economy through internal peace. Francis Bacon urged a property-qualification for planters: they should bring wealth to

6. G. Goodman, *The Court of King James I*, ed. J. S. Brewer (1839), I, 36–42. In the discussions concerning King James' projected union, the English Parliament feared that the Scots might exploit the machinery of the English Court of Wards (J. Bruce, *Report on . . . the Union of the Kingdoms of England and Scotland*, 1799, II, cxxxiii, cxl).

the country, and invest it there, instead of acquiring it there by spoliation. "His Majesty rejoiceth not," he wrote, "in the shedding of blood, nor the displanting of ancient generations"; time was on the English side if only there was a good English example; and the example would be strengthened by English institutions.[7] In Scotland Sir Thomas Craig saw the pull of the English Court as an incentive to Scottish industry: a native cloth-trade, he wrote, must be established in order to supply that liquid wealth which was necessary to finance the attendance of the Scottish nobility on their distant king. The alliance of the English Court with the City of London, which existed throughout the reign of James I, would also help to build up local industry in a united Great Britain. On the other hand such a policy could not be hastened. It required time and peace. James I possessed the necessary virtues. He had both patience and love of peace. Unfortunately, they were personal virtues, which were not inherited. When Charles I came to the throne, it soon became clear that he had neither.

It is sometimes said of Charles I that he only sought to maintain the rights of the Crown, not to increase them. He said it himself. But (as his subjects found) it is not wise to believe his words. His actions—if we can see past the multiple forms in which he simultaneously pursued every aim—clearly show that he looked forward to a definite ideal, which he intended to achieve in his own reign. He envisaged an absolute monarchy, financially self-supporting, dispensed from the necessity of political discussion with his subjects. With the deceptive mildness of his character he combined an obstinate, uncompromising authoritarianism which showed itself at the beginning of his reign. At the age of twenty-five, while still clinging to the worthless Buckingham in England, and seeming to pursue there a Puritan foreign policy, the absentee King of Scotland coolly dismissed the greatest minister of his father's successful policy, the Earl of Melrose. Melrose's last advice to King James had been not to go so fast; Charles I intended to go faster.

Charles I's policy in the three kingdoms, like that of his father, was all of one piece; but the emphasis was very different. James I had sought to bring Ireland and Scotland, slowly, into line with England; Charles I used the more rudimentary societies of Ireland and Scotland as models for a new course which he hoped to introduce, without delay, in England. By his Act of Revocation in Scotland he sought to enhance the status and income of the established Church several years before Arch-

7. *The Letters and the Life of Francis Bacon*, III, 46–51; IV, 116–26; V, 378–80.

bishop Laud sought to do the same in England, and by his ecclesiastical measures he sought to transform that Church from a Presbyterian into a royal and episcopal Church. In Ireland Strafford and Bishop Bramhall would do the same, recovering from "Old English" and new planter alike "concealed lands" for the established Church. At the same time the public revenues of both countries were raised. In Scotland taxation was increased and made more regular. In Ireland Strafford so improved the revenue that the country began to supply instead of to drain the royal Exchequer. Finally, "feudal" taxes outside parliamentary control were enforced in Ireland as in England. The new Irish Court of Wards became, like its English pattern, a fiscal engine and its jurisdiction was extended to new victims.[8] By 1637 it was clear that fiscalism and clericalism were designed to create, in all three kingdoms, not merely a united government and society, but a united absolutism.

Unfortunately for their prospect of success, these policies were carried out, in all three kingdoms, at the expense of the very means whereby James I had pursued his ends: the patronage of the nobility. James I had shown himself indifferent to the gentry, who had to support the burden of his Court, but at least, by his lavish patronage, he had kept the nobility of all three countries in place. Charles I, with his impatience of political management, drove them into opposition. The Scottish Act of Revocation was a direct blow to the "Lords of Erection," the great nobles who had secured the Church lands and tithes of Scotland. Strafford's ruthless fiscalism struck impartially at the old Catholic and the new Protestant nobility of Ireland. And these blows at the nobility (in spite of what he himself said about Scotland and what Strafford's biographers have written about Ireland[9]) were not accompanied by any benefits to the gentry. The event proved it. In Scotland, to the dismay of the king, the gentry formed, for a time, the strength of the Covenanters; in Ireland, Catholic and Protestant alike, they pressed for the death of Strafford. In all three kingdoms the naked fiscalism, the

8. See Kearney, *Strafford in Ireland* (Manchester, 1959), pp. 74–81.

9. Charles I argued that by his "harmless Revocation" he had rescued the Scottish clergy from dependence on the nobility, and that the gentry had expressed their gratitude to him ([W. Balcanquhall] *His Majesties Large Declaration*, 1639, pp. 7–9); but he had to admit, as is confirmed by other sources, that it was the gentry who, as ruling elders, formed the strength of the Covenant. Mr. Terence Ranger, in his study of the Earl of Cork (D.Phil. thesis, Oxon., 1958), has shown that Strafford's policy weighed as heavily on the gentry as on the magnates of Ireland.

impatient clericalism of Charles I, did not break the bonds of patronage: they solidified them—against the Crown. They also convinced the nobility and gentry of all three kingdoms that a union was necessary not merely in the person of the king, but at a lower level: a union of parliamentary opposition. Such a union was what the enemies of Charles I sought to achieve, not by institutional change but by political skill, in the years 1637–41.

To achieve it was a delicate and difficult matter. The three parliaments were very unequal in strength. The Scottish Parliament had little initiative and was effectively controlled by the Lords of the Articles. The Irish Parliament still, in 1640, had a Catholic majority and, anyway, by Poyning's Law was subject to the English Council. Naturally, therefore, the managers of English opposition dealt mainly with individuals, not institutions. But even this was dangerous, especially in Scotland: for the Scots were by now in open rebellion, and for Englishmen to practise with them was treason. For this reason the evidence of such practices was carefully hidden and we know little about the details. However, the fact is clear enough. In Scotland John Pym and his friends kept an agent, "a gentleman of quality in England who was afterwards a great parliament man," [10] in order to concert measures with the Scottish leaders, and the similarity of measures adopted and demands made tells its own story. In Ireland they worked through their friends and kinsmen among the "New English" planters, several of whom, through aristocratic patronage, or thanks to English lands, were returned to the English Parliament.[11] But they also fostered a party among the Catholic Members of the Irish Parliament, which sent a committee to London to work with the English Parliament. This Puritan-Catholic alliance did not in fact survive its original objective, the ruin of Strafford, but it was not necessarily foredoomed to failure. The established planter-gentry needed peace in Ireland and the basis of peace was, as Bacon had seen, agreement, even fusion, with the "Old English" of the Pale. If the political position could have been consolidated in 1641, this might have been secured. It would have been an aristocratic solution, secured by

10. Gilbert Burnet, *The Memoirs . . . of James and William, Dukes of Hamilton* (Oxford, 1852), Preface, p. xvi.

11. E.g., Sir John Clotworthy; Richard Lord Dungarvan; Arthur Jones (Lord Ranelagh); and William Jephson. Clotworthy's presence in the English Parliament was regarded as vital by the opposition, and he was returned for two seats, one controlled by the Earl of Pembroke, the other by the Earl of Warwick.

aristocratic patronage: the patronage of the earls of Bedford, Warwick and Pembroke in England, the Earl of Argyll in Scotland, the Earl of Cork in Ireland.

In the autumn of 1641 it was widely supposed that the position had been consolidated in all three countries. A parliamentary nominee had succeeded Strafford as viceroy of Ireland. The Earl of Cork's success was so complete that he declared himself unwilling to change fortunes with any man in the three kingdoms. All the demands of the Scottish Parliament were confirmed, and the Earl of Argyll was the uncrowned king of the country. On 7 September the church bells rang throughout England to celebrate the general settlement and the agreement with Scotland by which it had been secured. At the same time there was published a tract, *The Great Happiness of England and Scotland by being reunited into one Great Britain*. It was in fact a new version of two tracts which an English bishop had published in 1604–5 in favour of King James' proposed union: a union which had now been achieved at a different level, not to amplify but to contain the union of crowns.[12]

The success was short-lived. Defeated, as he supposed, by the mobilization of his other kingdoms, which he had used as models for the government of England, Charles I struck back in the same field. First he tried to recover Scotland. In September 1641 he went in person to Scotland in the hope of finding a party there. The hope was not fulfilled. Then an opportunity presented itself in Ireland. The Irish revolution demanded executive action, and whatever else he had yielded, the king had not yielded control of the English Council, the legal executive in both England and Ireland. Thus the revolution in Ireland transferred the struggle to this last citadel of royal power and the aristocratic solution of 1641 foundered in civil war.

By the time that it re-emerged, at the close of the first civil war in 1646, circumstances had changed and tempers risen. Aristocratic patronage had been whittled away, new interests had been created, and, above all, nationalist feeling had been aroused and consecrated by religious forms. These changes had led to a polarization of forces. In 1641, both in Ireland and in Scotland, the king had appealed to the old royalist classes, the secular, tolerant "official" aristocracy and gentry on whose support his father's union would have rested. In Ireland he had

12. The original work, *The Joyful and Blessed Reuniting of the Two Mighty and Famous Kingdoms of England and Scotland*, by John Thornborough, then Bishop of Bristol, had been published in 1605.

relied on the Protestant leader of the "Old English" landlords, the Earl of Ormond, who sought to unite both religions in the old policy. In Scotland he had relied on the Earl of Montrose, who showed his religious indifference by renouncing the Covenant which he had accepted, but denying any interest in episcopacy, for which he fought. But as these parties proved insufficient, the king had fallen back, in both countries, on the Celtic fringe. In Ireland the royalist cause had been committed to the "Old Irish," rising in mutiny against the English planters who had despoiled them; and in Scotland it was entrusted to the Highlanders, descending to plunder the settled Lowlands. Thus in both countries, the king, in his necessity, was undoing the work of his predecessors, the champions of Saxon "civility" against Celtic "barbarism." The result was fatal: he alienated his Protestant supporters and exasperated his enemies. Montrose was never forgiven for using Highland barbarians against settled cities, and Ormond, when he had to surrender Dublin, would choose to surrender it to the English Parliament rather than to his "Old Irish" allies. On the other hand the English Parliament had equally been driven into dependence on its Scottish and Irish allies. As the price of renewed military assistance, it had submitted to Scottish terms and undertaken, what it had refused to do in 1641, to establish a Presbyterian Church system in England. In Ireland it had jettisoned finally any idea of working with the "Old English" Catholics, who, since 1641, had been excluded from the Irish Parliament. Indeed, in order to finance the war in Ireland, the Parliament had committed itself to a new "plantation" at the expense, this time, of "Old English" as well as "Old Irish." The indirect result of these tensions was to exasperate national feeling between the three countries which had seemed united in 1641.

Nevertheless, in spite of all changes of circumstance, the aim of the English Parliament, between 1640 and 1648, remained basically constant. Ideally, in order to secure the future, a united Parliament should face a united Crown; but that would be a revolutionary demand, and the Parliament was not revolutionary: its leaders still sought to consolidate the position so nearly won in 1641. If settlement had been achieved in the years 1646–47, there can be no doubt that it would still have been, basically, an aristocratic settlement. The aristocracy would have recovered its patronage, but the patronage of the Crown, including the right to make new peers, would have been under parliamentary control. The Scottish gains of 1641 would have been confirmed, the English completed by control of the Council. Through that control, the English

Parliament would indirectly, by means of Poyning's Law, control reconquered Ireland. The nexus with Ireland, at a parliamentary level, would remain essentially one of patronage: Irish planters would sit in the English Parliament, either through aristocratic control of borough elections or because they were themselves landlords in both countries. The nexus with Scotland would remain one of diplomacy, which would again depend on aristocratic contacts. Only English magnates could deal with Scottish magnates like Hamilton or Argyll.

The only difference between the settlement envisaged in 1641 and that envisaged in 1646–47 lay in religion. In 1641 the Church in England and Ireland would have been episcopal; in Scotland it would have been Presbyterian. In 1646–47 Presbyterianism would have been established in all three countries. But even this difference is more apparent than real. It is inconceivable that the Presbyterian system of Scotland would ever have been established in England, and so, if it had been prevented from going forward into Independency, the Church of England (and Ireland) would probably have slid back into episcopacy. This was what the king intended when he proposed a probationary period of three years for Presbyterianism, and the English "Presbyterians," who were prepared to settle for such a period, were evidently content that it should be so. For practical purposes, therefore, the proposed general settlement of 1646–47 does not differ from that of 1641.

Short of revolution this "aristocratic" union was the only settlement which the English Parliament devised. Having failed in 1641 and 1647, it was revived in 1648, and even Oliver Cromwell, in the last month before he decided to overthrow the monarchy, clutched at the same mirage.[13] But once the revolution had taken place, and the monarchy had been destroyed, it vanished. For essentially it depended on the monarchy which, unsatisfactory though it was when Charles I was the monarch, was the only institutional link between the three countries. That gone, a new and more satisfactory link had to be created at a new level. Otherwise the three countries would fall apart.

Such disintegration was not inconceivable. It had advocates in all

13. In the autumn of 1648, when Cromwell was in Scotland, in touch with Argyll and away from the revolutionary Council of Officers, he evidently envisaged a "Presbyterian" settlement. This is shown by his letter of 6 Nov. 1648 to Hammond (W. C. Abbott, *The Writings and Speeches of Oliver Cromwell*, Cambridge, Mass., 1937, II, 676–78) and also by his conversation with the Edinburgh ministers reported in William Row, *The Life of Mr. Robert Blair* . . . (Edinburgh, Wodrow Society, 1848), p. 210.

three countries. In Ireland, before 1649, the constitutionalists of the Catholic party had aimed at complete legislative independence under the Crown.[14] Now, with the end of the monarchy, the Catholic Confederacy which directed Irish resistance reverted to what Henry VIII's viceroy had called the "foolish opinion that the Bishop of Rome is King of Ireland." In Scotland, where Charles II had been proclaimed king, there were also advocates of complete independence. Such was Sir James Hope of Hopetoun, the son of Charles I's greatest lawyer. Hope advised Charles II to recognize the fact of the English republic and content himself with his ancestral crown. For this he was accused of mere cowardice; but his view was perhaps a national expression of the interest of his class. He was an able lawyer and an active mining entrepreneur. Neither Scotch law nor Scotch industry gained from union with England: the natural links of both were with Holland. Scotch lawyers for two centuries studied at Utrecht; Hope marketed his minerals at Amsterdam; and the ideal of Scottish government was supplied by the Netherlands, where a hereditary prince was limited by a Calvinist republic. In fact, Scottish commerce in general stood to gain little — as yet — from union with England, and this may have been one reason for the lack of enthusiasm among the Scottish *bourgeoisie* for King James' project.[15] At all events, by 1649 it had tasted the expensive ambitions of both king and Kirk, and being too weak to resist, sought to contract those ambitions within narrower limits and concentrate on economic improvement.

Moreover, these centrifugal tendencies found an echo in England. The most consistent, most secular-minded of the Independents, including John Selden and Henry Marten, urged complete toleration of all religions, including Catholicism. This could only have led to the independence of the Irish Parliament. The Levellers wrote vigorously against the conquest of Ireland: the Irish, they said, were entitled to their freedom, their natural rights and their religious convictions. The

14. See Thomas L. Coonan, *The Irish Catholic Confederacy and the Puritan Revolution* (1954).

15. King James himself did not condescend to explain any economic advantage to Scotland. If the Scots disliked the union, he said, "he would compel their assents having a stronger party there than the opposite party of the mutineers" (J. Bruce, *Report on the . . . Union of the Kingdoms of England and Scotland*, ii, xxii). Cf. S. G. E. Lythe, "The Union of the Crowns in 1603 and the Debate on Economic Integration," in *Scottish Journal of Political Economy*, v, 219-28.

Levellers indeed were the first "Little Englanders," preferring social reform at home to imperial opportunities or responsibilities. And there were many in England who opposed Cromwell's aggressive war against Scotland. Indeed, Cromwell's own commanding general, Fairfax, resigned his command rather than conduct it.

All these arguments, however, failed in the face of political necessity. Revolutions must protect themselves, and Scotland and Ireland, unless brought into line, could be as fatal to the English republic as they had been to the English monarchy. So the republic set out to reduce them both and, having reduced them, to find a new unitary and unifying institution in place of Crown and aristocracy alike. In the circumstances of the time that institution could only be a single House of Commons dominated by the English members. Such a parliamentary union was duly imposed by the republic; but by the time it was implemented, the unitary Parliament itself was subordinate to a new executive: Oliver Cromwell, conqueror and "Protector" of all three kingdoms. The new union therefore took the social character of this new institution.

The Protectorate of Oliver Cromwell represented a fusion of two social groups. On one hand there were the men who had made the revolution. These were, essentially, the lesser gentry and freeholders supported by some local merchants: men who demanded decentralization and were opposed to aristocratic patronage and the centralized economy of the City of London. These classes formed the solid core of the Independents, and dominated the Army. On the other hand there were also members of the original "aristocratic" opposition of 1640 who, though they had been driven into political radicalism, would have been happy with the settlements of 1641 or 1647. These men had generally stood aside from the revolutionary acts of 1649–53, but rallied to Cromwell as a "saviour of society" when he became Protector. At first the Protectorate was dominated by the former of these social groups, and it was their policy which was represented in all three countries: a policy of decentralization and destruction of traditional patronage, carried through— of necessity—by their instrument, the Army.

In England the original constitution of the Protectorate declared this policy. The old borough-franchise, which had been the means of aristocratic patronage in Parliament, was drastically cut down and the county-franchise, the means of direct gentry representation, greatly increased. The franchise was also extended to the clothing towns of

northern England. In Scotland the feudal rights and hereditary jurisdictions of the nobility were swept away and the disciplinary power
of the clergy—the other element in the Covenanting revolution—was
undermined. Against the magnates and the Kirk the Cromwellian government supported the Scottish gentry, even the royalist gentry, and
the hitherto inarticulate Scottish burghs "whose interest is most agreeable with ours." [16] Ireland, to Cromwell, was "a clean paper" on which
he might imprint an ideal society, "a good precedent even to England
itself"; and his followers saw themselves as social crusaders, "framing
or forming a commonwealth out of a corrupt, rude mass," as well as—
like other crusaders—"dividing the country amongst the servants of
the Lord." This Irish "commonwealth" was to be a commonwealth of
new, Protestant "planter-gentry," and they protested against the formation of any new aristocracy: there were men, one of them added
darkly, "possessed with high conceits" that the spoils of Ireland were
not enough for their reward, and that the republic had "cut off the heads
of dukes and earls to have them placed on their shoulders." [17] Thus in
all three countries the old aristocratic patronage was destroyed. The
gentry and boroughs of England, the lairds and burghs of Scotland, the
English planters in Ireland, these were the social forces represented in
the Protectorate of Oliver Cromwell.

Unfortunately they were also, by definition, a centrifugal class.
Neither decentralization nor toleration, as a policy, holds men together,
and the presence of a revolutionary foreign army was more exasperating to those who did not depend on it than the pretensions of their own
aristocracy or their own Church. By his efforts to sustain the minority
of "New English" planters in Ireland and the slender "godly party"
in Scotland, Cromwell created Irish and Scottish nationalism and, by
his brief factual union (which was never a real union, since the Scotch
and Irish members of parliament were largely nominees), he finally destroyed the prospect, which had seemed so near in 1604, of religious
uniformity in the three kingdoms.

By the beginning of 1656 these facts were clear. By this time the old
"aristocratic" opponents of Charles I were returning to politics and,
while they accepted the fact of Cromwellian rule, were demanding not,
as their enemies said, that the revolution be "betrayed," but that it re-

16. The phrase is General Monck's (*Thurloe State Papers*, 1742, vi, 529).

17. Ludlow, *Memoirs*, i, 246–47; Jones correspondence (National Library of
Wales MS. 11440-D).

turn to its original basis: in other words, that "liberty and property" be secured, on the basis of the reforms of 1641. These men were prepared to accept the overthrow of the Stuarts and the parliamentary union of the three kingdoms as final; they would also have accepted some of the social changes of the revolution; but otherwise they wished to return to a civilian basis for government and a civil and religious bond of union between the three countries. Their leader was one of the ablest of Cromwell's servants and one who had a large interest in securing the permanence of his achievement, at least in Ireland. He was Roger Boyle, Lord Broghill, one of the sons of the greatest of English planters in Ireland, the Earl of Cork.

Like Charles I, Broghill used Scotland and Ireland as a means towards change in England. He began in Ireland, which he had helped Cromwell to reconquer, and where his family had soon recovered their influence and patronage. When Colonel John Jones wrote of men who sought to replace the old pre-revolutionary "dukes and earls" in Ireland, there is no doubt that he was referring to Broghill, whom he regarded as ambitious of power, indifferent in religion, and "more than ordinarily willing to submit to a royal or lordly interest." Having secured his position in Ireland, Broghill accepted—but for one year only—the office of President of the Scottish Council in Edinburgh. There he promptly reversed the existing policy. Hitherto Cromwell, regarding the General Assembly of the Kirk as the enemy of the English republic, had sustained in Scotland an alliance of its enemies. Broghill persuaded him to transfer his support to the party of the General Assembly, and in a very short time won over the majority of the clergy and persuaded them to cease praying publicly for the Stuarts. His aim was clear. The Scots had failed to impose Presbyterianism on England, because they had insisted on a rigid clericalism which the English laity would not tolerate. But if a lax, Erastian Presbyterianism could be established in Scotland, through the majority party in the native Church, a return to uniformity with England was possible. The next step was to bring the government of England back to the same state. To do this, Broghill exerted all the patronage at his disposal, in both Scotland and Ireland, and it was his nominees in the united Parliament of 1656–57 who carried through the programme of making Cromwell king of a united kingdom, with a House of Lords and an established Church "for the settlement of the nation, and of liberty, and of property"—the old watchwords of 1640.

In Scotland as in Ireland Broghill had been opposed by the military party. Ireton had feared and distrusted him in Ireland, Monck in Scotland. Rather than support his policy in Scotland, Monck even, at one time, proposed to unite the country by the same means which had been used in Ireland—"to plant it with English." In England, naturally, the Army leaders brought all their pressure to bear against Broghill's programme. Here they succeeded. The parliamentary monarchy of the house of Cromwell, approved by Parliament, was wrecked by the private pressure of the Army—or rather, of the classes represented in the Army. With it there crumbled the last attempt to save something from the failure of the revolution and to create an effective union between the three countries.

The Cromwellian revolution in England was not a complete failure. It prevented—at a heavy cost—the absolutism of Charles I. The memory of it discouraged his successors, at least for a time—although it must be added that it also discouraged their opponents. But its positive programme ended in disaster. After 1660 England reverted to its position before Cromwell's Army had intervened in politics, and the restored Stuarts were able, retrospectively, to justify all the evasions and obstinacies of Charles I: he had obtained better terms for the monarchy, by waiting for the revolution to fail, than he could have obtained by any settlement after 1641, or perhaps even then. Cromwell even discredited the parliamentary union by turning the Scotch and Irish members into nominees of the executive. So after 1660 there was little hope that this experiment, tainted by its republican origin, would be preserved. Only in Ireland the Cromwellian conquest was permanent; but even that conquest had been planned before Cromwell: it was the continuation of the policy of a generation, made fierce and certain by the Irish revolt of 1641.

So the relationship of the three countries returned to its old form, with only one difference: the factual exclusion of the Irish Catholics from the Irish Parliament. But the problem remained; and because it remained, and was a real problem, the whole history was played over again. Charles II, like James I, used official patronage to set up a secular, relatively tolerant Anglican system in Scotland and Ireland and groped after a union with Scotland. James II, like Charles I, sought to use the more rudimentary societies of Scotland and Ireland as models for despotism in England and, failing, turned gradually aside from the Anglo-Irish laity, Anglican and Catholic alike, the party of Ormond, and the Scottish Lowland laity, episcopalian and Presbyterian alike, the party of Lauderdale, to the Celtic fringe. William III, like Cromwell, completed his capture of power in England by the conquest of Ireland and Scotland and began the process, which would be concluded under his successor, of still further subjecting the Irish, and uniting the Scottish, to the English Parliament. The union of 1707 was the revised version of the Cromwellian union of 1652.

But whatever the resemblances between the earlier and the later unions, there was one great and permanent difference. The legal and religious identity which Cromwell had imposed could not now be secured. Legal unity was indeed an aspiration in 1707. "Those great men who conceived and framed the plan of the union," wrote Lord Hardwicke half a century later, ". . . wished to attain it, but found it impracticable in the outset." [18] It has been impracticable ever since. But religious unity was recognized from the start to be unattainable. That dream, which had seemed so near to fulfilment in the early seventeenth century, had been shattered for ever in the 1640s and 1650s. The three kingdoms, after their violent encounters with each other, clung more tenaciously each to its own national Church. England, having been forced to yield to Scotch Presbyterianism in the 1640s, embraced its old episcopacy with a new zeal in the 1660s. The rigour of the Clarendon code, the intransigence of the non-jurors, are to be explained, in part, by the experience of those years when England so nearly had a constitution forced on it by the Presbyterian Scots and a king by the Catholic French. Scotland, having once been subjected to Cromwellian Independents, would cling to its national Kirk through "the Killing Times" and preserve it, intact, under the Union of 1707. As the Anglicanism of England and the Presbyterianism of Scotland were more rigid than ever after 1660, so was the Catholicism of Ireland. Before 1640 the gradual protestantization of Ireland had seemed a possibility. After the Cromwellian conquest it never was. Like the Scottish Union of 1707, the Irish Union of 1800 would not be extended to the Church. It would assume — though it would take a generation for the assumption to be applied — that Ireland was now an irredeemably Catholic country.

18. Hardwicke to Lord Kames, 17 Oct. 1754, cited in A. F. Tytler of Woodhouselee, *Memoirs of the Honourable Henry Home of Kames* (Edinburgh, 1807), I, 294 ff.

INDEX

427

Janson, the typeface used in this book, was designed not by the Dutch-born, Leipzig-based type founder Anton Janson (1620–87) whose name it bears, but by Miklos Kis (1650–1702), a Hungarian type designer working in Amsterdam. The typeface was cut sometime around 1690.

This book is printed on paper that is acid-free and meets the requirements of the American National Standard for Permanence of Paper for Printed Library Materials, Z39.48-1992. ♾

Book design by Martin Lubin Graphic Design,
   Jackson Heights, New York

Typography by Tseng Information Systems, Inc.,
   Durham, North Carolina

Printed and bound by Color House Graphics,
   Grand Rapids, Michigan